Handbook On Teaching

Social Issues

NCSS BULLETIN 93

edited by

Ronald W. Evans and David Warren Saxe

National Council for the Social Studies

Founded 1921

Editorial staff on this publication: *Michael Simpson, Paul Degnan, Beth Hatch, Melissa Spead*
Editorial services provided by *Carol Bloom*, Bloom Ink Publishing Professionals, West Lafayette, IN
Production Manager: *Gene Cowan*
Design and Layout: *Paul Wolski*

Library of Congress Catalog Card Number: 96-071673
ISBN 0-87986-071-5

Contents

Foreword

Shirley H. Engle

The great philosopher-educator Alfred North Whitehead (1929) posed a rationale for issues-centered curriculum some sixty years ago that still holds validity today:

In training a child to activity of thought, above all things we must beware of what I shall call " inert ideas"—that is to say, ideas that are merely received into the mind without being utilized, or tested, or thrown into fresh combinations. In the history of education, the most striking phenomena is that schools of learning, which in one epoch are alive with ferment of genius, in a succeeding generation exhibit merely pedantry and routine. The reason is that they are overladen with inert ideas. Education with inert ideas is not only useless: It is above all things harmful(1).

The statement continues to be a remarkably accurate assessment of education, particularly citizenship education, in the United States today. Citizenship education is largely reduced to a process of memorizing isolated facts or bits of information without verifying their truth or using them to either assess the meaning of past events or suggest answers to our own newly emerging questions. As focused as it is on instilling recallable knowledge of the past, schooling has become in Whitehead's words mere "pedantry and routine," utterly detached from real and present questions.

John Goodlad (1983), who conducted one of the most thorough observational studies of recent American social studies, recalls:

[Students] rarely planned or initiated anything, read or wrote anything of some length, or created their own products. And they scarcely ever speculated on meaning, discussed alternative interpretations, or engaged in projects calling for collaborative effort. The topics of the curriculum, it appears to me, were something to be acquired, not something to be explored, reckoned with, and converted into personal meaning and development.

One would expect the teaching of social studies and science in schools to provide ample opportunities for the development of reasoning: deriving concepts from related events, testing in a new situation hypotheses derived from examining other circumstances, drawing conclusions from an array of data, and so on. Teachers listed those skills and more as intended learnings. We observed little of the activities that their lists implied, and teachers' tests reflected quite different priorities—mainly the recall of information. The topics that come to mind as representing the natural and social sciences appear to be of great human interest. But on the way to the classroom they are apparently transformed and homogenized into something of limited appeal. (Alfred North Whitehead's words on the uselessness of inert knowledge come to mind.) The fact that students rated the social studies to be of relatively low interest among the subject fields (at the bottom of the list for those in the upper elementary grades) must give us pause. Why this curricular sterility? (468).

Goodlad's picture of education in the United States is a static one, very similar to the view given us by Whitehead. America has engaged in educational reforms for decades, only to produce a remarkably unchanged situation. The realities facing our young are full of upheavals and new challenges. Perhaps the greatest challenge of all is the rate of change itself. Cultural stability has given way to an ongoing state of dynamic change in which decisions must be made even as the questions themselves undergo revision.

When more things are changing than are staying fixed, necessity demands an issues-centered curriculum. Past lessons can no longer be depended upon to be copied. As humankind develops new social and political ways of life, it must also develop an ethic toward those ways of life. What in the past could prepare us for such a challenge? Even the problems that arise from such an issue are not fully understood. Historians and philosophers confidently say that we have experienced more change in the present century than in all of previous time. On the plus side, we have revolutionized the way people make a living and have multiplied many times over the variety and availability of material goods. On the negative side, we are consuming the earth's natural resources at a rate that threatens to make the earth ultimately uninhabitable. We threaten to overpopulate the world to such a point that massive poverty and starvation ensue, potentially leading to human extinction. Hundreds of such problems confront us today concerning how humans can continue to survive as a species. We have reached a time in citizenship education when history can only play a minor role in our preparation for citizenship.

Facts are often talked about as though they were exclusive claims to truth upon which knowledgeable people agree and against which no evidence can be cited to refute. In the real world, there are few claims to factuality that can meet these criteria, and those that do are usually so narrow in scope as to be practically useless in thinking about any question. The exact time when an event takes place may be of only limited use in addressing real issues. When one extends facts to interpret or explain an event, the factuality becomes more difficult to establish beyond doubt. Most so-called facts are not facts beyond question, but interpretations of the truth. Although such facts upon which we base decisions every day are immensely useful, they are useful only to the extent that their limitations are recognized. These limitations and uncertainties

likewise apply to claims of factuality pertaining to the distant past. Facts about the past are rightly being questioned every day. New questions are being asked about past events, and new information is being uncovered. Historians change their views of history, and new text books are written to reflect these changes. A new set of facts replaces the old. An example of this shift in historical perspective is the difference in portrayals of Christopher Columbus. The Columbus story was rewritten once new questions had been asked and new possibilities explored. Such revision should continue as the past is studied and new meaning is derived.

The educational situation is greatly complicated when fixed ideas about reality are continually substituted for real issues. Students are required to memorize answers without questioning the truth of these answers. One example of society imposing fixed ideas on students is the popular notion of the ideal American family. The stereotypical family often referred to involves two parents living together for life in a single household with the father working and the mother remaining at home to nurture the development of the children. This once ideal family structure dates back about 50 years and can no longer be held as the American norm. More common today are situations where both parents work and the upbringing of children is more heavily influenced by television than by parents, church, or school. Families are frequently torn apart by divorce and may include children from different marriages. Children have a great deal of independence from their parents and siblings and too often must learn to deal with the threat of drugs, crime, and idleness on their own. Thus, studying and upholding the typical family structure of former times as the norm for today's society can hardly confront the issues related to family living in modern America. Students must reevaluate the popular definition of family to reflect modern norms.

Similar issues reflecting change in our society and global community can be addressed in schools today. By the most widely held appraisal of our affairs, we are in deep, deep trouble as a country and, in fact, as a world. Overpopulation presses the earth with far more people than can possibly be sustained. Nevertheless, large numbers of people oppose population control because of their deeply held religious beliefs or long-standing cultural ways of behaving. Over a third of the earth's population lives today in abject poverty, and the situation is growing worse. Most schools hardly touch upon this issue. Egged on by industrialization, we continue to trash our soil, forests, water, air, oceans, and magnificent landscapes at a rate that scientists say will reduce the earth to penury in less than a hundred years. Resistance, especially among many multinational business entrepreneurs, continues against quite reasonable controls over the consumption of resources. One common defense against such environmental restrictions is that money can't be made if the use of natural resources is curtailed, and if the generation of profit is restricted, so, too, will be that of jobs. Despite tremendous increases in industrial productivity, however, the poor continue to increase as a proportion of the population while the rich grow richer. We are at odds to deal with a myriad of issues, from crime and drugs in the streets to equitable education, from prayer in schools to abortion, from the rights of labor to strike and be secure in their jobs to the control of television and gun sales. Such issues cannot be avoided in developing responsible citizens and should therefore be a part of formal education.

Even our most precious beliefs about the right to live freely and pursue happiness have become controversial. Whose rights shall take precedence? Is the right to work more important than the right to a safe and stable environment? Where does one person's license to use the earth's resources interfere with another's right to enjoy clean air and water? The Supreme Court cannot be the sole arbiter of all these many issues. We and our children must take them on, working through the many problems that confront us.

It is often said, especially by historians, that since the present is such a challenge, we should look to the past for insight. This assertion is perhaps valid only when we remember that even the past is issue-laden and problematic. When we explore more penetrating questions of history, a new and changing history emerges. Savages become native Americans credited with being the first true conservationists. Black Americans are at last recognized for the tremendous contribution they have made to our culture. Christopher Columbus is recognized for being the mercenary he was. As we continually ask new questions about the reality of past events, we come up with different answers. In the end, it is this questioning and challenging that allows the past to become useful as a point of departure for the study of the present and the future.

Educators of the social studies are not so much involved with the establishment of immutable truths as they are with the charting of an improved state of affairs. The sooner people understand this conception of what the social studies is about, the closer they will come to dealing with large-scale problems. Citizenship education needs to involve a continued conversation between students and their mentors while they search together for better ways of doing things.

Looked at in this light, the issues-centered curriculum is not a curriculum to be added on to an otherwise conventional education devoted to memorizing the insignificant minutia of science and history. It is not a remedial curriculum to rectify the errors of fact and process of the conventional curriculum. It is not a belated effort to acknowledge the usefulness of focusing some part of education on the study of real problems, past and present, which confront our society and the world. Rather, it is a substitute for the non-thinking, memory-bound process which constitutes so much of the educational curriculum today. It is the way all education should be approached to produce informed citizens who are involved in working out better solutions to our problems.

The following example of issues-centered education provides a clear contrast to the conventional curriculum: The author enrolled in a class on the history of the West at the University of Wisconsin in the summer of 1936. The class was taught by Professor Frederick Paxson, visiting professor of history from the University of California at Berkeley. Paxson was widely recognized as the leading authority on the history of the American West. When he spoke on the West, the whole scholarly establishment stopped to listen. Notwithstanding his acknowledged reputation as the leading authority in Western history, Paxon devoted the entire summer to talking with his students about the problems he had interpreting Western history. He questioned the explanations given by historians for the events at Wounded Knee. Were the contributing factors of the battle the real causes? Were the purported consequences the real consequences? Paxson turned every question in the entire course into a further exploration of that very question. Paxson was not so much interested that we memorize the claims that passed for truth in textbooks and lectures as he was in enlisting his students in the real pursuit of truth, a pursuit in which he himself was genuinely enlisted and in which he worked diligently to recruit his students.

To Paxson, as with all issues-centered curricularists, the search for knowledge is always an open-ended process. It takes place always on the edge of claims to knowledge and is never finalized. It is characterized by both penetrating questions and the expectation of change. It cannot be pursued with a series of factually-oriented questions to which only one correct answer exists; rather, the open-ended search for knowledge embodies a continuous search for more authentic knowledge.

Paxson directed the study of history toward the uncertain and the controversial; that is, he directed study toward those "facts" and questions of meaning that were both in doubt and hotly debated among professional historians. He sought not so much to perpetuate an accepted version of history as to open it up for further scrutiny. Memorizing the most widely held interpretations of history was thus subjugated to the exploration and possible revision or expansion of these interpretations, and therein lies the quintessential nature of issues-centered education.

We often speak of the explosion of knowledge as a fundamental reality of our age which inevitably renders much of our old knowledge obsolete. The issues-centered curricularists rest their case on the proposition that in our rapidly changing world, the cutting edge of education must be at the emergence of new knowledge rather than at the persistence of old and frequently obsolete knowledge.

The essays which follow explore the potential and means for extending an issues-centered curriculum to all of education.

Indiana University 1993

References

Goodlad, J. I. "Study of Schooling: Some Findings and Hypotheses." *Phi Delta Kappan*, 64, 7:465-470, 1983.

Paxson, F. Lecture notes, "History of the West." University of Wisconsin, Madison, 1936 Summer.

Whitehead, A. N. *The Aims of Education and Other Essays*. New York: The Free Press, 1929.

Part One: Definition and Rationale

Introduction by Anna S. Ochoa-Becker

Part 1 of the *Handbook* provides the strongest possible justification for an issues-centered curriculum. Unlike conventional or traditional social studies curricula, the issues-centered curriculum does not measure success by the degree to which students can regurgitate the so-called facts presented in textbooks and teacher lectures. Rather, it measures success by the degree to which student performance reflects an intellectual capacity to address public issues. Rather than stressing the recall of information, the issues-centered curriculum encourages students to actively participate in the improvement of society.

By definition, public issues are controversial. They involve multiple points of view, with ideas and insights from many fields of study, including the humanities as well as the social sciences. In dealing with public issues, citizens must analyze, create, and appraise evidence and, most importantly, make decisions. Consequently, an issues-centered curriculum emphasizes not only content, but also the development of advanced intellectual abilities. Instead of memorizing textbook facts, students define problems, actively search for and evaluate evidence, make defensible decisions, and engage in projects that impact persistent and pervasive real world issues. An issues-centered curriculum offers the greatest promise for improving citizen participation and the quality of democratic life in this society.

Specifically, the chapters of this handbook seek to provide insight into such questions as the following:
- Why teach about public issues?
- What are the historical underpinnings for an issues-centered curriculum?
- What support does research provide for an issues-centered curriculum?

The authors selected to address these matters are scholars and teachers who have devoted their careers to exploring issues-centered curriculums in both their teaching and their research. The dedication and expertise with which they have pursued the development of issues-centered curriculums are seldom matched.

In the first chapter, Ron Evans, Fred Newmann and David Saxe describe the basic principles of issues-centered education, and its implications for curriculum, teaching practice and assessment. My subsequent chapter on rationale draws heavily on my work with the late Shirley H. Engle, who devoted his career to promoting a curriculum focused on social issues and decision making.

Jack Nelson emphasizes the intellectual and historical foundations of different aspects of social studies education.

Carole Hahn has engaged in extensive research on controversial issues and is probably as knowledgeable as anyone in this country about teaching controversial issues. Her chapter presents a comprehensive view of the research efforts supporting an issued-centered curriculum.

A note to the reader: If you are already familiar with the literature regarding social issues, you may wish to read this section first. If not, reading it at the end may serve to tie the ideas presented together for you. In any case, I wish you reflective, stimulating, and provocative reading.

DEFINING ISSUES-CENTERED EDUCATION

by Ronald W. Evans, Fred M. Newmann, and David Warren Saxe

Issues-centered education focuses on problematic questions that need to be addressed and answered, at least provisionally. Problematic questions are those on which intelligent, well-informed people may disagree. Such disagreement, in many cases, leads to controversy and discussion marked by expression of opposing views. The questions may address problems of the past, present or future. They may involve disagreement over facts, definitions, values and beliefs. Answers may be rooted in a person's cultural background, in formal knowledge accumulated in disciplines, and in "common sense" experience. Examples of such problematic questions on the topic of governmental powers include:

- What is a legitimate government and where does its power originate?
- When should governmental authority be ignored or rejected?
- Should student newspapers have the same right to freedom of the press as other newspapers?
- Should I write a letter to the principal to protest censorship?
- Should the colonists have protested British actions with violent demonstrations? (Giese and Glade 1988)

To say that questions are problematic means there are no conclusive, finally "right" answers. But some answers, however tentative or provisional and subject to change in the future, are clearly better or more valid than others. The purpose of issues-centered education is not just to raise the questions and expose students to them, but to teach students to offer defensible and intellectually well-grounded answers to these questions. Judgements about the validity of some answers may depend upon the context in which the judge-

ment is offered. But issues-centered education should not be construed as people expressing biases and values that cannot be reconciled. The point of issues-centered education is just the opposite: to develop well-reasoned responses based on disciplined inquiry, on thoughtful, in-depth study, and to move beyond relativistic notions of truth.

Ultimately, an issues-centered approach to social studies aims at empowering the learner. As Alquist suggests, social studies should help us solve everyday problems in our lives, help us develop an ethical foundation for personal and social relationships. "This is not critical thinking for the sake of debate, argument or logical reasoning, but for constructive change, for the transformation of society" (Alquist 1990). For many, but not all advocates of issues-centered approaches, the approach also includes developing a critical consciousness, or "conscientization" (Freire 1970). This means developing skills in perspective consciousness, the ability to recognize, examine, evaluate and appreciate multiple perspectives on a particular issue or concern (Hanvey 1975), including perspectives critical of mainstream institutions and social practice.

This definition of issues-centered education leaves many problems yet to answer. Other chapters in the Handbook will offer the justification and rationale for why an issues-centered approach should be pursued, and they will address various aspects of implementation. As part of the definitional task in this chapter, we will foreshadow some especially important implications for curriculum, pedagogy, and assessment.

Curriculum Implications

Important social issues may arise in the study of a variety of disciplines and human affairs, and there is no inherent curricular logic or sequence in which they should be studied. It must be left up to teachers and curriculum developers to arrange and organize topics and to select the most fundamental content. These arrangements might follow a variety of structures (chronological, thematic, discipline-based, concepts, problem-topics, etc.). Regardless of the structure chosen, the study of social issues is often most productively pursued through interdisciplinary and extradisciplinary inquiry (Wraga 1993). However, there are at least four important principles upon which all issues-centered curricula should be built.

First, depth of understanding is more important than coverage and superficial exposure. This means that topics must be studied in sustained ways that introduce students to important complexities and details. For example, in a unit on the American revolution, students might explore the issues listed in the previous section. However, to make the study of these issues most meaningful, the students will need to develop an understanding of the context in which colonial protests occurred. They will need to study specific instances in which governmental power was challenged in sufficient depth and with enough detail to appreciate the multiple perspectives they will discuss, and to provide sufficient evidence for quality decision making. The same is true for studying the protest of a censorship policy. Students will need in-depth detail and contextual understanding in order to develop a well reasoned position and intellectually well-grounded arguments.

Second, topics and issues need to be connected through some kind of thematic, disciplinary, interdisciplinary, or historical structure. Simply studying one issue after another will fail to give students the intellectual structures they need to organize and think about relationships among various issues and how their resolution might add to social justice. Where feasible, these structures need to be developed both within individual classes and across classes and grade levels so that they flow logically and build on previous learning.

At least three curricular structures are possible. First is a discipline-based structure in which courses are organized according to familiar disciplinary formats (e.g., history is presented through chronological narrative, government is conceptualized as a set of structures-of-control) and issues are infused to illustrate and extend the meaning of traditional content. For example, the study of governmental authority and protest of unjust authority might be undertaken in a United States history course during a unit on the American Revolution. A second possibility is development of conceptual units, spiraling through the grades, but retaining discipline based courses. For example, in a course on World History, units could be organized around categories such as power and authority, revolution, race and ethnicity, social class, etc. Another possible structure, for a secondary social studies curriculum, might be to create an introductory course focused exclusively on problems and issues, followed by in-depth topical courses which would focus on particular concepts connected to certain sets of issues, followed by a concluding course on philosophy and life (see Evans and Brodkey's article in this book, pp. 254-64).

Third, as indicated in the definition, the study of issues must be substantively grounded in challenging content. A simple sharing of opinions is not sufficient. This will require teaching students forms of reasoning, interrogation and presentation of evidence, and also the mastery of concepts and theories that bring expert knowledge to bear in understanding persistent social issues. Intellectually challenging content includes critical perspectives and consideration of alternatives not commonly included in the curriculum: multicultural perspectives, diverse voices on issues related to race, class, and gender and other domains of discourse commonly devalued by traditional curricula and textbooks. The study of issues, if it is to lead to development of in-depth understanding, must also include content from historical cases, literature, art and music. For example, a unit on immigration issues cannot generate depth of understanding simply by raising a current policy issue. Study of the issue should include data and cases from the historical record that can be used to form conclusions about the results of immigration policy during different time periods. First person accounts of immigrants' lives could be examined, and media and scholarly sources as well as school curricular materials and community resources could be tapped. Specific content would depend upon student and teacher interest as well as the curricular framework within which learning occurs (see the article by Massialas, pp. 44-50).

Fourth, students must experience influence and control in the inquiry process. A delicate, judicious balance should be struck between teacher guidance in selection of issues and materials to be studied and student choices in their own education. Content selection in a productive issues-centered curriculum is responsive to students' interest, their prior knowledge, and the local school and community context.

Issues-centered teaching has long been associated with liberal-progressive social ideas, but the approach to teaching issues in this book does not prevent teachers from applying traditional methods of teaching such as lectures, objective testing, memory reliance, or repetition to complement the many issues-centered techniques that will be found in this book. Issues-centered teaching does not necessarily promote liberal-progressive ideas for social policy. Teachers and students can use issues-centered teaching to explore and extend conservative ideas about social life just as well as liberal-progressive ones.

In applying an issues-centered program, a strong measure of reliance must be placed upon students' learning (or at least being exposed to) a common core of knowledge, skills, and dispositions (see Hirsch 1996). Issues-centered teaching should lead students to accept democratic principles as the basis of competent American citizenship. That is, issues-centered teaching should lead students to acknowledge the differences we find in our communities, regions, and nation, but more importantly to identify those similarities and principles that bind us together as citizens.

Implications for Teaching Practice

There are no particular techniques or practices that "work" all of the time. Effective pedagogy is responsive to special conditions of the teachers, courses and students. However, teaching will be most effective if guided by principles such as the following:

First, issues must take the form of truly problematic questions, even for the teacher. Although the teacher will have more knowledge about the issues than students, the teacher must be involved in continual learning, in part by considering the students' own solutions. Students must be convinced that they are constructing answers to make sense for themselves, and are not simply trying to follow some script for learning that has been predetermined by the teacher.

Second, in working out well-reasoned positions on issues, students will need access to a variety of resources and tools that extend beyond the teacher and the classic textbooks—books, articles,

newspapers, computers, the opportunity to interview other adults in the community, interaction with peers in their class and in other classes. The study of issues is often enhanced through use of multiple resources drawn from several disciplines and by taking a historical perspective.

Third, students need continuous practice in using extended oral and written language. Students can't learn how to offer sound responses to issues by speaking in three word phrases. They have to learn to weave thoughts and evidence together in sentences, to construct reasoned and well grounded arguments. This use of language can be assisted and complemented through symbolic art and graphics and physical models, but ultimately should be expressed in the form of students' oral and written text.

Fourth, a major pedagogical challenge for teachers is to learn how to help students feel comfortable with the cognitive ambiguity that issues-centered education introduces. Not being able to find the "right," conclusive answer is often troubling for both youth and adults. Teachers will need to help students see how they make intellectual progress by expanding their understanding, even though they may not achieve complete certainty. This aspect of issues-centered education is significant, and requires the development of skills in "perspectives consciousness" (Hanvey 1975). This can be supported by consideration of alternative cultural and ideological perspectives often omitted from the standard curriculum. It is also crucial for the teacher to offer a psychologically safe environment for students to express doubt, to change their minds, and to adopt playful attitudes toward uncertainty. The intellectual work of issues-centered curriculum demands tolerance, respect for diversity of ideas, and open-mindedness. These qualities can be nurtured only in classrooms that convey a commitment to critical studies and a solid knowledge base.

Implications for Assessment

New forms of assessment will have to be developed to see how well students understand issues, can resolve them, and offer defensible positions. There are occasions when testing for factual and conceptual accuracy through traditional methods is warranted and helpful. But new forms of assessment that focus on the arguments that students construct orally and in writing must be developed (see the article by Harris in this book, pp. 289-97). As part of the effort to develop new forms of assessment, it will be important to introduce students to "models" of proficient performance in dealing with issues. These could come from journalistic and editorial writing, from televised debates, talk shows and speeches, from court opinions and policy briefs, and from many other sources. Teachers and researchers will need to explore ways to evaluate these, and develop standards to expect from students. Students will need to be convinced of the importance of these standards to their effectiveness as citizens.

Conclusion

We have tried to offer a definition of issues-centered education broad and inclusive enough to be useful to a diverse group of educational professionals and concerned citizens, but also focused enough to show its distinctive features. We hope that a number of diverse but related approaches may find enough common ground in this definition to advance issues-centered education itself as a field of practice and research. As seen in the chapters that follow, the primary intent of issues-centered education is to assist teachers in developing curricular practices that are intensely reflective, focused on problematic questions. We believe that this approach, if meaningfully implemented, can help to improve the intellectual quality of discourse in social studies classrooms. The approach is built upon a tradition of social studies theory and curricular practice centered around the teaching of social issues, an approach developed and refined by the work of Dewey (1910), Rugg (1939), Griffin (1942), Hunt and Metcalf (1955 and 1968), Oliver and Shaver (1966), Massialas and Cox (1966), Newmann and Oliver (1970), Gross and Muessig (1971), Newmann (1975), and Engle and Ochoa (1988) among many others.

References

Alquist, Alberta. "Critical Pedagogy for Social Studies Teachers." *Social Studies Review* 29 (1990): 53-57.

Dewey, John. *How We Think.* Boston: D. C. Heath and Company, 1910.

Engle, Shirley H. and Anna S. Ochoa. *Educating Citizens for Democracy: Decision Making in Social Studies.* New York: Teachers College Press, 1988.

Freire, Paulo. *Pedagogy of the Oppressed.* New York: Continuum, 1970.

Giese, James R. and Mary E. Glade. *Public Issues Series: American Revolution, Crisis of Law and Change.* Boulder, CO: Social Science Education Consortium, 1988.

Griffin, Alan. *The Subject Matter Preparation of Teachers of History.* Ed.D. diss., Ohio State University, 1942.

Gross, Richard E. and Robert H. Muessig, eds. *Problem-Centered Social Studies Instruction: Approaches to Reflective Thinking.* Curriculum Series no. 14. Washington, DC: National Council for the Social Studies, 1971.

Hanvey, R. G. *An Attainable Global Perspective.* New York: Center for War/Peace Studies, 1975.

Hirsch, E. D., Jr. *The Schools We Need.* New York: Doubleday, 1996.

Hunt, Maurice P. and Lawrence E. Metcalf. *Teaching High School Social Studies: Problems in Reflective Thinking and Social Understanding.* New York: Harper and Row, 1955 and 1968.

Massialas, Byron and Benjamin Cox. *Inquiry in Social Studies.* New York: McGraw-Hill, 1966.

Newmann, Fred M. *Education for Citizen Action: Challenge for Secondary Curriculum.* Berkeley, CA: McCutchan, 1975.

Newmann, Fred M. and Donald W. Oliver. *Clarifying Public Controversy: An Approach to Social Studies.* Boston: Little, Brown and Co, 1970.

Oliver, Donald W. and James P. Shaver. *Teaching Public Issues in the High School.* Boston: Houghton Mifflin, 1966.

Rugg, Harold O. "Curriculum Design in the Social Sciences: What I Believe." In *The Future of the Social Studies,* edited by James A. Michener. Curriculum Series, no.1. Washington, DC: National Council for the Social Studies, 1939.

Wraga, William G. "The Interdisciplinary Imperative for Citizenship Education." *Theory and Research in Social Education* 21 (1993): 201-231.

BUILDING A RATIONALE FOR ISSUES-CENTERED EDUCATION

by Anna S. Ochoa-Becker

Despite the diversity of definitions and contrasting views in the social studies field, most social studies educators agree that preparation for citizenship is our most important goal. However, we do not agree on how to define citizenship nor how to reach such a goal. While some define citizenship as loyalty to the nation, others promote issues-centered education, which hopes to prepare citizens who, consistent with democratic principles, are informed but skeptical and will become critical decision makers in public life. The author is among those who strongly support issues-centered education.

Issues-centered education is a curriculum that uses public issues to emphasize controversial questions as the content for social studies. It is an approach toward teaching and learning that does not intend to provide right answers, but underscores the need for students to learn how to examine significant questions and become more thoughtful decision makers about public life. An issues-centered approach highlights the critical examination of social practices through the direct study of persistent and compelling social issues. It requires analysis and evaluation of evidence, values, and decision making.

The purpose of this chapter is to provide a set of concepts for educators to employ at all levels when developing a rationale for an issues-centered curriculum. Since issues-centered education represents an educational thrust that deviates from conventional social studies, which emphasizes history, geography, textbooks, questions at the ends of chapters, and the lecture method (Shaver, Davis, and Helburn 1979), it behooves its proponents to advance a rationale statement that justifies this curriculum as an alternative to current social studies practice.

The Need for a Rationale

Rationales for such subjects as math and reading are virtually self-explanatory; they only state the obvious—these skill areas are essential for literacy. If people can't read or write, they can hardly be expected to be effective citizens. Social studies curriculum, by contrast, carries competing claims regarding its goals, methods, and content. Consequently, educators—like those promoting issues-centered education—who pursue one set of views over others must make their reasons for such claims explicit and public. As Shaver (1977) stated:

> A rationale necessarily includes the salient values and beliefs that are of particular importance to its author(s). In the case of promoting critical and informed citizenship for productive citizen action in a democracy, one must ask what are these salient values.

The salient values the author advances within an issues-centered curriculum emphasize *democratic* citizenship and necessarily test the principle of self-government. Can the people govern themselves? *Can educators prepare young people for democratic citizenship?* Of course they can, claims the issues-centered educator. But if democracy is to achieve its full potential, issues-centered educators believe we must strengthen the current social studies curriculum, leading it away from its linear study of the separate social science disciplines and its methods of covering textbook chapters and depending on rote memory as a measure of learning. Rather, the needed curriculum emphasizes the issues that citizens persistently face—from those concerning the environment to issues of pluralism and distribution of wealth—using the social science disciplines, where appropriate, to substantially deepen student understanding.

Another salient value, derived from the belief that democracy is preferred over other political systems, holds that democratic citizens must rise above pure self-interest and be sensitive to the needs of others and the common good. Addressing this tension between self-centeredness and the public welfare is fundamental to cohesion in a free society. The tension is evident in such questions as: **1.** Should I support the building of an incinerator in my community despite its impact on the environment? **2.** Should the community build a new library even if it means higher taxes for me? **3.** Should the United States change its health-care systems to cover all Americans even if it means that I will not be able to choose my own doctor? Issues-centered education would bring selected issues (see the chapter by Byron G. Massialas in this handbook) to the forefront, guiding citizens to think of the public welfare, not confining themselves to their own self-interest. Without explicit attention to the importance of the common good, democracy will flounder.

Examining other salient democratic values reveals tensions between freedom and equality or freedom and security. Maximizing justice, human dignity, equity, and the importance of due process are values that are also centrally embedded in democratic thought.

Professional educators, parents, community persons, and school board members should collaborate when developing a rationale statement for issues-centered education. They must view their work as a starting point that represents initial thinking about the purposes and reasons for a particular curriculum. They must also understand that complete agreement among these groups is not possible. The rationale is a carefully constructed statement of goals—well developed, clearly defined, and reconsidered regularly. Such statements, which will vary from community to community, from district to district, and from school to school, must be revisited and revised on a continuing basis so they respond to the realities of implementation and to local, societal, and global changes. Shaver (1992) reminded us that mindless issues-centered education is no more justifiable than mindless rote education.

While it is one thing to say that conventional programs have not resulted in competent and critical citizens, advocates of issues-centered education must assume that the burden of proof is theirs. They must explain why issues-centered education will accomplish what the conventional history-bound curriculum cannot. The need for competent and critical citizens has never been greater. Polls, surveys and assessment results constantly remind us that many citizens lack the knowledge and/or the commitment needed to take advantage fully of democratic principles in today's complex world. Proponents of issues-centered education believe that conventional social studies practices have not and will not help us achieve this important goal.

To arrive at a set of concepts that may serve as a guide in developing issues-centered education rationale statements, I compared several existing rationales—Evans (1989 a and b), Shaver (1977 b), and Engle and Ochoa (1988). This comparison, however preliminary, of their prominent features, identified several domains that any rationale should seriously consider. These concepts are:

- Key democratic values (such as freedom, equality, due process, justice, etc.).
- The nature of knowledge (interdisciplinary focus on issues with supporting content from the social science disciplines and the humanities).
- The nature of teachers and teaching (focusing on the shift from authoritarian to facilitative, probing, and interactive teaching).
- The nature of learners and learning (intellectual development and cultural background of students).
- The nature of society, domestic and global, including all aspects of diversity.

This author found much common ground across these three rationales.

Three Existing Rationales

The three rationales presented here were selected for specific reasons. No prioritization of their worth against that of others is intended. Obviously, Engle and Ochoa were selected because the author knows that work best. No one has given more thought to or has more vigorously called for thoughtful rationale-building in social studies education than James P. Shaver. And Ron Evans represents a new generation of young scholars whose own work has demonstrated commitment to the benefits of issues-centered education. Even though Evans does not regard himself as a theorist, his publications and professional efforts demonstrate that he has given serious thought to the principles underlying issues-centered education. Other theorists whose works deserve consideration but are not included here are Hunt and Metcalf (1968), Massialas and Cox (1966), Stanley and Nelson (1986), and Hartoonian (1985), to name a few.

To understand a rationale more thoroughly, it is worth examining what it implies about the nature of knowledge, learning and learners, teaching and teachers, and society. The table on page 13 presents summarizing assumptions about the Evans and Shaver rationales with inferences made by this author about significant aspects of their curricula, along with Engle and Ochoa's position on the same aspects.

These three theorists reveal ideas that are certainly compatible with each other. Their similarities mask any minor differences between them. Unfortunately, diversity of all kinds (disability, gender, race, ethnicity, religion, social class) is not given explicit attention by any of them. In the future, theorists cannot and should not ignore diversity as a penetrating dimension of both this society and the global community.

1. The Evans Rationale

It seems clear to me that Evans (1989) sees social studies curriculum as an effort in learning to become a democratic citizen and not one of promoting knowledge for its own sake. One does not study history just to know that Andrew Jackson vetoed the proposal for the national bank in 1828. Rather, issues-centered educators would use this knowledge as it relates to banking issues and the role of the federal government.

Evans asks a major and most appropriate question, "What are the organizing principles of the course (U.S. History)?" He states that teachers have typically used the textbook to build course structure rather than structuring the course around the ideas they consider important. He urges teachers to identify issues that link the past to the present, although generally they have not explored societal issues.

Social studies as it is currently taught and practiced, he argues, is dysfunctional. A significant indicator of the failure of conventional social studies is the low percentage of people voting. Today's social studies does not teach young people to make full use of the knowledge they learn to aid them in making critical decisions. Not surprisingly, students find social studies boring, a point Fred Newmann (1986) addressed. Students also find history courses meaningless, and Evans

emphasizes that history courses must be organized to apply history to contemporary issues and to the lives of students. Evans thoughtfully provides his own example of an issue-centered approach involving the study of issues related to government and the economy.

The Evans rationale cries out for deeper development in one area. In fact, this criticism applies to most of us who have tried to build a rationale for issues-centered education. As do Engle and Ochoa, Evans advances the notion of identifying problems that are of interest to learners, but he really does not talk about how that might be done in classrooms. He ignores, as others do, the conditions that are needed to create an issues-centered learning environment in both the classroom and the school. (This need for attention to school and classroom climate and the hidden curriculum is affirmed in Carole Hahn's research chapter on pages 25-41 of this book.) However, the importance of the Evans rationale is in its explicit relationship between social studies and developing critical citizens for a democracy (see chapter 28 by Evans and Brodkey, below, pp. 254-64.)

2. The Shaver Rationale

No one has done as much to heighten the awareness level of the profession to the importance of developing rationales for the social studies than James P. Shaver. His writings on the subject are legion, and those developing such rationales are well advised to consult them. His own rationale for issues-centered education (Shaver 1960 1977a, 1977b) emphasizes issues that are drawn from the personal experiences of students, the social science disciplines, and/or significant concerns of society. Necessarily, these issues can be described as value-laden, having both ethical implications and competing truth claims. Teachers must create a context where social issues engage learners, relating the issue to the personal concerns of students wherever possible. Shaver has further emphasized that issues-centered education must be interdisciplinary in nature, including not only the social sciences, but literature and the arts as well as an awareness of current and relevant research.

3. The Engle-Ochoa Rationale

The rationale put forward by Engle and Ochoa (1988) places strong emphasis on the relationship between an issues-centered social studies curriculum and the distinctive role of the citizen, particularly the citizen in a democracy. Democracy, in their view, is the preferred form of government because of its potential to afford dignity to each individual by way of its significant values such as freedom, equality, and justice. Recognizing that this democratic society has a long way to go to realize its full potential, Engle and Ochoa criticize current practices in the social studies that emphasize textbooks, lectures, and memorization and discourage students from thinking for themselves. Such practices might fit citizenship education in nations with autocratic forms of government; but they clearly contradict democratic beliefs and practices. Instead, Engle and Ochoa advance an issues-centered curriculum tied to intellectual processes that contribute to reflective decision-making abilities in citizens—citizens who will understand and hold reasoned value commitments to democratic principles and practices so that this democracy is preserved, nourished, and expanded. Most indicators (voter apathy, dependence on images created by the media, etc.) reveal that the public at large does not demonstrate the democratic values and practices that sustain and expand democracy. Learning must center on the use of facts and values in making decisions—a complex intellectual process.

An important aspect of the Engle and Ochoa rationale resides in the concepts of socialization and countersocialization and the relationship between them. Socialization is an inescapable process in all cultures as a means to preserving cultural values and traditions in the next generation. Here, parents, teachers, peers, and the media teach very young children to fit in and conform to the existing social order. At these ages, socialization is highly conforming and neither reflective nor analytical; that is, very young children often absorb cultural values quite mindlessly. However, as youth mature into would-be citizens for a democracy, they must become skeptical, questioning, and critical. Democratic citizens must be proactive—knowledgeable and challenging regarding the issues that manifest themselves in their public lives. The aim of countersocialization is to foster independent thought and social criticism that is so crucial for democratic citizens. Countersocialization calls for a consciously reflective process where students learn to ask challenging questions and probe for thoughtful and responsible answers. The following questions are representative:

- How do we know that a particular statement is true? (Validating truth claims; evaluating evidence)
- What must be done to improve specific social conditions such as crime, homelessness, foreign policy, inequalities, etc.?
- How can I justify my decisions? (What values? What evidence? What logic?)

In the Engle-Ochoa framework, knowledge is seen as tentative in nature and is always open to further investigation. Their vision places equivalent emphasis on content (knowledge) and intellectual process, which are inextricably intertwined. Content takes the form of social issues that citizens face. The social science disciplines can and do strengthen the understanding of social issues. Knowledge, or truth, claims in those disciplines can also serve as the basis of student investigation. Salient statements in textbooks can be used as hypotheses to be tested for their truth value in the classroom. For example:

1. How did the Japanese perceive their first encounter with Admiral Perry? How does this view, as presented in Japanese textbooks, differ from the view in U.S. textbooks?
2. Lincoln freed the slaves, but was he a reluctant emancipator?
3. The oldest U.S. public building is not on the East Coast where the colonists landed but in New Mexico. Is this statement true? How can we find out? What is its meaning?

Such statements and questions confront students with controversy and the opportunity to validate truth claims over others. They may learn that, in many if not most cases, we are not able to reach the truth with complete certainty.

Engle and Ochoa believe that skepticism on any matter is the basis upon which issues-centered education is built. Any serious scholar working in the social science disciplines is more concerned with the unanswered questions in the discipline than with mimicking the so-called facts. Are facts really the facts? How do the facts reveal the bias and ideology of those reflecting? Social studies educators must guide citizens to ask: What are the facts? Are they facts or opinions? What meaning do these so-called facts have? Because the range of doubt is so vast, so is the range of matters issues-centered education can present. There is no shortage of issues to consider and all knowledge must be related to issues.

The Engle-Ochoa rationale describes teaching as highly interactive: the teacher and students are both learners and teachers concurrently. The teacher facilitates, probes, and learns. Students investigate, probe their fellow learners and the teacher, and are engaged in the rigorous study of social issues, involving intellectual analysis, decision making, and social action.

The inherent curiosity of learners can be tapped to enhance learning. Problematic scenarios are likely to capture their interest more effectively than the mere coverage of linear topics can do. Engle and Ochoa recommend socializing the very young to democratic values by way of biographies of a widely diverse set of heroes and heroines who represent the cultural mix of our population and speak to democratic values through real-life scenarios. This process of countersocialization can result in a reappraisal of beliefs and ideas acquired through the conventional socialization process.

> Citizens who have engaged in a thoughtful and critical analysis of their beliefs and who recognize the complexity of public issues and public opinion are more likely to contribute effectively to the negotiated consensus required for meaningful and active democratic life. (Engle and Ochoa 1988, 51)

Preparing for Criticisms of Issues-Centered Education

Critics of issues-centered education come from many sources and raise various arguments. Those educators who are advancing issues-centered education must be mindful of some arguments critics may raise when presenting a rationale for issues-centered education.

Loyalty to Nation through the Study of History Argument

Some critics feel that issues-centered education sublimates or diminishes the role of history or other social sciences to one of subordination. Critics argue that issues-centered education erodes attachment to nation because it characterizes history, and especially written history, as problematic and conflictive and not focused on the nation's heroes, heritage, and positive accomplishments. The American Federation of Teachers (Gagnon 1989), as well as other groups, also emphasize the goal of loyalty to the nation.

Contrary to the charges of some critics, issues-centered education values history and other disciplines that shed light on contemporary citizen dilemmas. History and the social sciences and issues-centered education are not mutually exclusive. These disciplines provide perspectives, research, and scholarship that strengthen the citizen's hand in addressing social issues. However, while these disciplines provide knowledge that is somewhat dependable, this knowledge is always open to intellectual challenges, and, furthermore, the social sciences do not supply all of the wisdom needed to make sound public decisions based on democratic values.

In fact, some critics may argue that if issues-centered education becomes the order of the day, entire sets of important events such as the War of 1812, westward migration, and even the world wars may be omitted and ignored in the curriculum and that diminished attention to these events will reduce loyalty to the United States as a whole. This point overstates the case. No curriculum can teach everything; selection is always required. Further, selection is always guided by values, either implicitly or explicitly. No curriculum is value-free. Conventional social studies practices also reflect a value base. This author believes that issues-centered educators come closer to the realities of democratic citizenship than the conventional social studies curriculum through their emphasis on social issues and developing the capacity for critical thinking skills. Young people need guidance when it comes to values and value decisions. Periodically, the school is likely to challenge the values of the home. Neither the school nor the classroom teacher can reflect all the differences in family values that exist in a particular class of students. Despite conflicting community views, students must gain experience in addressing controversial issues and value dilemmas as they influence public decisions.

The Great Books Argument

Mortimer Adler (1982) and others who support education via "great" books and "great" literature feel that individuals can only receive a complete education through reading these materials. Issues-centered education could undoubtedly identify many penetrating public issues in the great books identified by the Great Books Foundation. However, the intellectual process of problem solving and public decision making needs explicit attention in the implementation of an issues-centered education for democratic citizens. It is also interesting to note that the Great Books Foundation is currently identifying contemporary as well as classical works, seemingly to attract the current generation of learners.

The Changing Teaching Model Argument

Educating teachers so they can engage their students in both the content and intellectual processes of issues-centered education is an extremely difficult task because it involves not only a change in the ways we teach more interactively but also involves a substantial change in the role of teachers from an authoritative stance to one more facilitative and supportive, yet probing.

This concern has some merit. However, just because something is difficult to do doesn't mean it cannot or should not be done. Given the need to heighten the education of citizens, a deeper and more thoughtful teacher education program at both the in-service and preservice levels is clearly in order for professionals who will implement social studies in our schools. Universities as well as schools have some rationale building and curriculum work to do.

The Essential Knowledge Argument

Occasionally, some critics—especially essentialists—will complain that issues-centered education is too amorphous, too vague about its content and not specific enough about its intellectual process. Essentialism is that school of thought that claims that essential knowledge or content that is necessary for all students can and should be identified. Such vagueness, according to these critics, prevents setting explicit standards and undermines accountability.

It is true that issues-centered education specifies content in categorical rather than specific ways (e.g., if social studies centers on social issues, clarifying which issues students address is left to local schools and teachers). Learning is believed to be most effective and knowledge most useful when it is related to an issue that applies to student-related concerns as well as to extant issues in the larger society. Unfortunately, the content of the social studies curriculum is often defined by textbooks produced for a national market, a condition that nourishes standardization of the curriculum, standardized tests, and in too many cases, mindless teaching.

A last note of caution: Documents, such as the American Federation of Teachers (1987) publication, can be seductive because they provide a rationale that issues-centered education can accept. However, their conclusion that history is the major discipline seems to be a complete non-sequitur. History is far from being the only source of knowledge and wisdom, and other social sciences, literature (*All the Kings Men, The Last Hurrah,* etc.) and the arts can provide great insights into persistent social issues.

Building the Rationale

This chapter has emphasized ideas central to building a rationale for an issues-centered curriculum. Involving a broad base of professional and community participants in the rationale-building process at the local level is critical. While educators must acknowledge the contributions of theorists and curriculum specialists in rationale building, those most responsible for implementing the issues-centered approaches must play key roles in the planning process. Broad participation in the early stages is essential to the success of both a sound rationale as well as fostering the necessary local support for implementation of an issues-centered curriculum.

The rationale itself must address the relationship of issues-centered education to a democracy and to democratic values, which must be defined. In a democratic society, issues-centered education is critical because a democracy has distinctive features that demand much stronger participation from its citizens than other political systems. Education for informed and thoughtful citizenship in a democracy must reflect those essential characteristics of skepticism, independence, and decision making.

We must also be mindful of engaging the learner and demonstrate sensitivity to the climate of the classroom and the school. A sound rationale must address the critical factors that influence all curriculum building, i.e., the nature of knowledge; the nature of learners or learning; the nature of teachers and teaching; and the nature of global and domestic society with all aspects of diversity. Examining assumptions in regard to these concepts can result in a more comprehensive and thoughtful rationale as well as a more meaningful social studies curriculum.

In presenting some of the arguments advanced by critics of issues-centered education, the author advises those building rationales to prepare for local resistance and initially respond within their statements.

The comparative process used in examining three issues-centered rationales resulted in the identification of commonalities, differences, and omissions. This process, expanded and deepened, could be applied to rationales that have been created since the writings of John Dewey (1933, 1961) and could also be applied to rationale statements yet to be developed in local settings. Since the rationales reviewed all supported issues-centered education, it is not surprising that a high degree of similarity was found. More detailed analysis could identify finer distinctions. Future efforts could promote a basis for more substantial dialogue and scholarship regarding issues-centered education.

In addition to this chapter, educators developing rationale statements can look to other resources for assistance. Research related to issues-centered education (see Carole Hahn's article on research in this Handbook) provides significant touchstones for rationale development as well. Since issues-centered education gives rise to a distinctive model of teaching and learning—one differentiated from conventional social studies practice—it may also be instructive to review Joyce and Weil's (1986) models of teaching, categorized in terms of syntax, principles of reaction, social systems, and support systems.

Acknowledgment

Parts of this manuscript were written by Shirley H. Engle prior to his death.

References

Adler, M. J. *The Paideia Proposal: An Educational Manifesto.* New York, Macmillan, 1982.

American Federation of Teachers. *Education for Democracy: A Statement of Principles.* Washington, D.C.: American Federation of Teachers, 1987.

Curtis, C.K., and J. P. Shaver. "Slow Learners and the Study of Contemporary Problems." *Social Education* 44 (1980): 302-8.

Dewey, J. *How We Think: A Restatement of the Relation of Reflective Thinking to the Educative Process.* Boston: D. C. Heath, 1933.

Dewey, J. *Democracy and Education: An Introduction to the Philosophy of Education.* New York: Macmillan, 1961

Engle, S. H. "Decision Making: The Heart of Social Studies Instruction." *Social Education* 24 (1960): 301-4, 306.

Engle, S. H., and A. S. Ochoa. *Education for Democratic Citizenship: Decision Making in the Social Studies.* New York: Teacher College Press, 1988.

Evans, R. W. "A Dream Unrealized: A Brief Look at the History of Issue-Centered Approaches." *The Social Studies* 80 (1989a): 178-84.

Evans, R. W. "A Societal-Problems Approach and the Teaching of History." *Social Education* 80 (January 1989b): 50-52, 69.

Gagnon P. *Democracy's Half-Told Story. Education for Democracy Project.* Washington, D.C.: American Federation of Teachers, 1989.

Hartoonian, H. M. "The Social Studies: Foundations for Citizenship Education in Our Democratic Republic," *The Social Studies* 76 (1985): 5-8.

Hunt, Maurice P., and Lawrence E. Metcalf. *Teaching High School Social Studies: Problems in Reflective Thinking and Social Understanding.* 2d ed. New York: Harper and Row, 1968.

Joyce, B., and M. Weilz. *Models of Teaching.* 3rd ed. Englewood Cliffs, N.J.: Prentice-Hall, 1986.

Massialas, B. G., and C. B. Cox. *Inquiry in the Social Studies.* New York: McGraw-Hill Book Company, 1966.

Newmann, Fred. "Priorities for the Future: Toward a Common Agenda." *Social Education* 50 (April/May 1986): 240-50.

Oliver, D., and J. P. Shaver. *Teaching Public Issues in the High School.* Boston: Houghton Mifflin, 1966.

Shaver, J. P. "Lessons from the Past: The Future of an Issues-Centered Social Studies Curriculum." *The Social Studies* 80 (September/October 1989): 192-96.

Shaver, J. P. "Needed: A Deweyan Rationale for Social Studies." *The High School Journal* 60 (1977a): 345-52.

Shaver, J. P. "Implication from Research: What Should Be Taught in Social Studies?" In *Educators' Handbook: A Research Perspective,* edited by V. Richardson-Koehler, 112-38. New York: Longman, 1987.

Shaver, J. P., ed. *Building Rationales for Citizenship Education.* Bulletin 52. Washington, D.C.: National Council for the Social Studies, 1977b.

Shaver, J. P. "Rationales for Issues-Centered Social Studies Education." *The Social Studies* 83 (May/June 1992): 95-99.

Shaver, J. P., O. L. Davis Jr., and S. Helburn. "The Status of Social Studies Education: Impressions from the Three NSF Studies." *Social Education* 43 (1979): 150-53.

Stanley, W. and J. Nelson. "Social Education for Social Transformation." *Social Education* 50 (1986): 528-30, 532-40.

Three Rationales for Issues-Centered Education

CONCEPT	EVANS	SHAVER	ENGLE AND OCHOA
nature of knowledge	Knowledge is tentative, not absolute, and is always in need of verification. The thoughtful citizen is always skeptical of truth claims. There is little, if any knowledge that can be defined as absolutely essential, yet knowledge is critically important to the complete understanding of social issues.	Knowledge is seen as both tentative and testable. It is relevant when it provides insight into social dilemmas. Knowledge that concerns citizens provides the basis for testing truth claims whether they are found in the disciplines, in social issues, or in the interests and experiences of the learner. This view of knowledge is interdisciplinary.	Since knowledge is tentative in nature, all claims to knowledge may raise questions and foster skepticism. Content (knowledge) and intellectual processes are inextricably intertwined. The social science disciplines strengthen the understanding of social issues. Students investigate truth claims from textbooks, lectures, video, and/or newspapers. This view of knowledge is interdisciplinary.
nature of teachers and teaching	Teaching is a facilitative process that helps students define issues and resolve problems. It is not merely a matter of direct teaching, lecturing or textbook reading.	The jurisprudential model of teaching helps the learners learn how to resolve public issues (Oliver and Shaver 1966). Based on Socratic dialogue, it seeks to challenge students' thinking about their choices and decisions, as well as the values involved in such choices. Teachers are more than facilitators; they pose areas of conflict in values, focus students on the need to justify their position on issues, and consistently probe students for the strongest evidence justification possible.	Teaching is highly interactive: teacher and students are both learners and teachers concurrently. The teacher facilitates, probes, and learns. Students investigate, probe their fellow learners as well as the teacher, and are engaged in the rigorous study of social issues, which involves intellectual analysis, decision making, and social action.
nature of learners and learning	Learning is an active and reflective process engaged in by learners who are more likely to be energized by examining contemporary and controversial issues than by chronological treatments of history.	Learners must be viewed as citizens who, if properly motivated, can be energized to be concerned about social issues, both public and private. Learning is an active and reflective intellectual process that is intricately tied to the content and processes needed to address public issues. To build effective citizens for a democracy, learners must confront these matters in intellectually thoughtful ways.	Learners are curious and this curiosity can be tapped to enhance learning. Socialize the young to democratic values by way of biographies of heroes and heroines. Countersocialize youth to foster independent thought and social criticism that is crucial to political freedom.
nature of society	Whether conceived at domestic or global levels, society is problematic, conflictive, and constantly changing. These public issues impact our lives, whether we give deliberate thought to them or not. It is the thoughtful analysis of social issues and how they impact the lives of citizens and people everywhere that must form the basis of the social studies curriculum in a democracy.	Society, especially a democratic one, is plagued by value dilemmas (conflict) that need thoughtful and critical attention by its citizens if conflictual issues are to be alleviated or resolved. Conflict characterizes democratic public life.	Society, both global and domestic, is persistently problematic, conflictual, and pluralistic. It is constantly changing. In recent years there has been fairly widespread recognition that many issues facing citizens in this democracy have not only implied domestic obligations but also manifest a global reality. Such issues may be addressed in many parts of the school curriculum.
diversity	Not explicitly addressed	Not explicitly addressed	Not explicitly addressed

3 THE HISTORICAL IMPERATIVE FOR ISSUES-CENTERED EDUCATION

by Jack L. Nelson

The historical imperative for organizing social studies around social issues is conceptual, or intellectual. The power of issues-centered education lies in the context of its social and intellectual traditions, providing the main conceptual fabric of this chapter:

- The roots of social studies education lie in human issues and in efforts to develop and test knowledge.
- Knowledge derives from issues that permeate the earliest to the latest developments in human thought.
- Humans construct forms of knowledge in a time and place; these forms are likely to change and deserve skeptical examination.
- Restrictive or rigid forms of knowledge are inconsistent with the nature of human knowledge and the complexity of human issues.
- It is time to return to an issues focus and reliberate schools and students from rigid formalism.

Issues and Social Studies Teaching

Pervasive human issues remain at the center of the human condition and at the core of knowledge. The legitimate study of society, human knowledge, and competing views, therefore, requires a focus on issues. This imperative—historic and contemporary—should be the hallmark of social studies teaching.

Good teachers find that fulfilling this obligation is difficult but necessary. Charles Beard, the progressive historian and leading figure in social studies education in the 1920s and 1930s, addressed the idea of social studies and its complex expectations for teachers:

Amid all the fuss and feathers, there is substance, there is reality, in social studies. ... it will be said that the growth of social studies places on teachers an impossible burden, it compels them to deal with controversial questions. ... They are in a different position from that of a teacher of Latin or mathematics. They cannot master their subject reasonably well and settle back to a ripe old age early in life. The subject matter of their instruction is infinitely difficult and it is continually changing. If American democracy is to fulfill its high mission, those who train its youth must be among the wisest, most fearless, and most highly trained men and women this broad land can furnish. (1929, 372)

The social studies foundation most consistent with Beard's statement is the study of issues.

Finding the Roots of Social Studies

David Saxe (1992a) criticized authors of standard histories of social studies (Wesley 1937; Johnson 1940) for assuming that the field began with the traditional teaching of history in schools. That literature traces origins of the field back only to a 1916 National Education Association Committee on the Social Studies or to late nineteenth- and early twentieth-century American Historical Association committees. Saxe challenged the limited and limiting view that the field's orientation was traditional history teaching, showing that social studies actually had its beginnings in issues—in the social welfare and humanitarian literature earlier in the nineteenth century. Contemporary social studies in the United States owes at least as much allegiance to social issues for its founding and orientation as it does to the discipline of history.

The basic concept of social studies instruction—to develop competent civic participants—has roots far deeper and more widespread than a recent century or a single nation. Social studies can be traced back far beyond the first use of the term. The elemental roots of social studies rest in human issues that inform the human condition and organize human knowledge through the need to find resolutions. Social studies follows from the earliest of human experiences. It is this history, not a set of formal dates, that positions the imperative for issues study at the core.

Increasing Complexity of Human Issues

Life in any society at any time is complex. Sadly, even at the end of the twentieth century, pure survival is still the prime concern for some, but many confront problems of life and society beyond those of essential existence. Improvements in life quality, civilization, and knowledge have themselves produced more complicated lives and more complex human issues. Medical knowledge has increased life expectancy and improved public health but created other problems related to aging, the political economy of health care, and ethical questions about dying and equality of treatment. Advances in communication and transportation contribute to increased human issues around privacy, pollution, and national sovereignty. Technological development has increased the pace and the horizons of human existence—but with a collateral increase in life's complexity. Individual and social choices have become and will continue to be more complex.

Among civilization's improvements is the global expansion of democracy. Political and economic life for predemocratic common people was comparatively simple, though humanly debasing. With democratic ideas, people were offered more complicated responsibility coupled with increasing freedoms. Democracy expects decision making after consideration of diverse evidence and perspectives so mass education, became a necessary condition for democracy and a primary component of improved quality of life and civilization. Such educational expansion contributed to a more complex life. Education can create frustrations because it increases expectations and confusion concerning the indeterminate quality of truth and incisive criticism of contemporary society. Few would argue that increased democracy and improved education are not worth the increased complications, but the result is that more issues need to be confronted.

Global democratization in societies and schools offers less separation between the world of affairs and the world of scholars than was the case in older western civilizations. America represented a break from the classical tradition, which made scholarship a leisure class activity unrelated to the world of action or human issues. Classically, scholars were expected to contemplate great thoughts and avoid contact with the practical issues of life. Ancient class distinctions separated those presumed to be naturally suited to the life of the mind from those suited to action, whereas modern democratic education assumes that students of all classes engage in consideration of issues.

Criticism and the Development of Knowledge

For thousands of years, humans were essentially predatory and nomadic, but, as one economic historian noted, "in the course of time, particular skills and techniques were invented and developed, the cutting of stones, the making of special weapons, the building of transport vehicles" (Cipolla 1964, 18). Prehistoric data suggest that humans discovered many of their most important adaptations to the environment and social life in the millions of years before recorded history. Increasing sophistication in trying and testing ideas and practice is a mark of human life. Paleoanthropologist Richard Leakey said, "The urge to know is a defining feature of humanity" (1992 [with Lewin], 23).

Social studies, including ideas about the nature and purpose of knowledge, emerged as humans tried to understand and cope with human problems. Animism, witchcraft, astrology, myth, science, humanities, and social science developed as ways to explain the human condition. Although schemes of absolute truth or dogma have emerged in every time period, our understanding of knowledge carries the expectation of criticism and of disagreement with ideas and actions. That approach challenges dogmatic answers to human problems. Criticism has been a part of social life throughout human history, but as Bottomore (1968, 4) noted:

It is only in societies which have become literate, possess economic reserves, have developed an urban life and in some measure a professional intellectual class, that any sustained criticism of the working of society is possible.

Dissenters challenged early versions of science and humanities. Sometimes critics suffered heinous punishments for their dissent, but critics served to test ideas and patterns of thought. Superstition, alchemy, and moral trial by fire are pre-scientific and pre-humanities efforts to organize knowledge for understanding and for coping with human issues. The working of the mind on problems and solutions is a topic of social study, a very large body of philosophic, religious, and psychological literature going back through recorded history.

Scientific and intellectual inquiry flourished in early India, China, and Africa. In the millennium preceding the birth of Christ, ethical teachings involving the relation of nature to human destiny were a feature of early Indian Veda (hymns related to knowledge). Upanishads writings of that time, as well as Buddhism, point out that reality is beyond time and space. Mayer (1960, 32) claims that western cultures have difficulty understanding these ideas because we are so "intensely conscious of historical events," and do not do as well in grasping reality as a whole as those who share Indian concepts.

Dogmatism Interrupts Development

Western cultures consider the medieval period as intellectually dark, one of conformity and uniformity. In actuality, there was significant dissent. Even though the main thread was orthodoxy in knowledge, consistent with religious doctrine, there were deviations based on increasing secularization and more flexible ideas of knowledge. The dominant view, however, incorporated strictures that religion imposed and the authoritarian nature and formal categories of knowledge that scholasticism stressed.

During the Middle Ages, knowledge was codified into the Trivium (grammar, rhetoric, and logic) and the Quadrivium (arithmetic, geometry, astronomy, and music), solidifying what was then conceived to be the ultimate structure of knowledge for the leisure classes—the seven liberal arts. Not liberal in the sense of liberating humans through education, the form of education was "bookish," reading from and reciting memorized material from books (Butts 1955). By this time the formal codification of knowledge in the West superseded human issues and had become a set of prescribed and static ideas linked to religion and social class. That codification, as we know, did not adequately explain or enlighten humankind, and its static quality limited intellectual activity and consideration of human issues.

The original seven liberal arts from the monasteries are not what we now call liberal arts. As Butts (1955, 177) indicated, "In the realm of intellectual affairs, the center of gravity began to shift from the religious to human experience." It also marked a return to human issues as social study. The Renaissance emerged as a challenge to religious domination and to established authorities, even as it embraced the classical tradition of knowledge.

Such evidence of traditional codifications of knowledge, including dogma from classical periods and formal religion, is readily found in the American colonies. An early colonial example of the intellectual limitations often placed upon schools is in the Massachusetts School Law of 1647 (The Deluder Satan Act), which ordered every township of fifty households to teach children to read the Scriptures and foil Satan. Social education of this time was often religious indoctrination, not the examination of issues, and the dogmatic approach to religion exempted legitimate issues analysis.

At various times in history, the static dogma of established subjects, the absolutism of religions, and excessive nationalism have restricted knowledge and education. Copernicus rediscovered and recast ideas from ancient Greek astronomers like Aristarchus of Samos, whose work had been defamed by stoic philosophers as outside existing ideas of knowledge. Galileo, in proving Copernicus right, suffered attack from religious zealots. Traditional scholars and religious leaders ridiculed Charles Darwin's work when first presented (Russell 1959). Scholarly paradigms organize the structure of knowledge, and religion assists in understanding the human condition, but their rigidity can also restrict thinking and nontraditional scholarly inquiry in the human quest for knowledge (Kuhn 1970b; Skybreak 1984; Nencel and Pels 1991).

Scholastic and static forms of knowledge were challenged after the Renaissance. Francis Bacon (1606), despite his undemocratic premise that social status should determine the level of education available, argued that theory be tested by experience, that social progress depended upon applying knowledge to problems of daily life (Cressy 1980). In more recent times, Merle Curti (1956) documented the evolution of tension between scholastic intellectuals and real human issues in the United States, showing that U.S. democracy assisted in closing that gap, even though tensions still remained at the middle of the twentieth century.

Nationalistic pride also constructs static and false boundaries for knowledge, limiting examination of human issues. Traditional school-level history and civics often incorporate myths that brook no scholarly challenge or skepticism. Studies of nationalistic history and civics taught in schools show that nations manipulate their own histories, creating and sustaining myths, to inspire and perpetuate national chauvinism through schooling (Merriam 1934; Key 1961; Nelson 1971, 1976). The United States is among those nations most actively perpetuating nationalistic myths through history teaching (Pierce 1933; Beale 1936; Gellerman 1938; Billington 1966; Nelson and Weltman 1990). History professor Nancy Shoemaker (1993, A48) commented, *'I wasn't sure I wanted to teach it [a course on the American West] again. The myth of the West was just too powerful. The mythological baggage that students brought to the course continually surprised me.'* Her students had completed the standard school curriculum of U.S. history with myths taught as truths from the discipline rather than as human issues subject to skepticism and criticism. By the middle of the nineteenth century, the center of social studies in common schools had shifted from dogmatic religion to nearly-as-dogmatic uncritical nationalism. Nationalistic interest following the War of 1812 led to significantly increased teaching of U.S. history and related citizenship training. The new religion of the secular schools was nationalism, a dogma that was not issues-centered. Rather, the goal was inculcating patriotic loyalty, not debating. Formalized nationalistic history and civics were the main means of this instruction.

Religious dogma is no longer a core of social studies education, but nationalistic influence remains significant. It represents traditional uncritical citizenship training similar to previous inflexible codifications of knowledge. While absolute answers make some feel secure, intellectual challenges to this limitation of knowledge and of pedagogy continue to arise.

Rigid scholastic, dogmatic religious, and uncritical nationalistic education notwithstanding, conceptions of knowledge change. In one sense traditional non-issues approaches to schooling have been temporary interruptions in the long-term development of knowledge. Despite efforts to codify and rigidify learnings, the core purpose of knowledge remains: to provide insights into potential answers for human issues.

Current philosophic writing raises the question that we may be in a new period of scholasticism, emphasizing technical, mechanical, and materialistic distinctions between categories of knowing. That literature recognizes that "the lifeblood of philosophy is argument and counter-argument," a continuing philosophic revolution and challenge to old beliefs about knowledge (Hamblyn 1987, 333). This debate is also about social studies content as an intellectual issue.

Myth and Theory as Constructs for Knowledge

Joseph Campbell (1990) examined the process of comprehending and responding to human issues, using myths from differing cultures to show their transformation over time in explaining the human condition. An American Navaho Indian myth follows the evolving maturity of young people through a series of human issues, none of which would be resolved by formal study of a current single subject field. Asian, African, and other myths have similar themes— human problems and knowledge development— as a focus for understanding and overcoming. The Greek myth has Prometheus stealing the secret of fire for humans to provide them the means to reason, understanding, and the civilizing arts—the bases for knowledge. Homer's *Iliad* and *Odyssey* are examples of interpretations of human issues. While the stories are inconsistent, they try to record old events as they provide a world view, a myth or interpretation of life. Greek, Indian, Egyptian, and other myths attempted also to explain life after death (Russell 1957). Myths, mingled with observable evidence, attempt to explain human and superhuman life.

Many myths, of course, are detrimental to human progress and knowledge, keeping humans in the shackles of ignorance and under the oppression of superstition. But myths not only predate and surround our ideas of knowledge, they also permeate those ideas and the categories of knowledge we construct and use. Commonly defined as false stories, myths are also properly defined as traditional stories intended to explain phenomena or customs (which is actually the preferred definition in standard English dictionaries). The result of scholarly work that explains the phenomena described in these traditional stories is an improvement of existing knowledge. The topic of knowledge is itself a proper social studies subject—another human issue worthy of study and consistent with the historic and future development of civilization. The process of argument and counterargument to improve knowledge is used in issues-centered education in social studies. Students deserve the intellectual opportunity and academic freedom necessary to engage in such arguments; issues-centered education offers that potential.

Myth can be applied, at least metaphorically, to theoretical constructs in separate disciplines. Philosopher of history Peter Heehs (1994) noted the "interpenetration" of history and myth; they are not distinct and separate. History is not truth, but interpretation as a form of myth, a point also made almost a century ago by historian Sydney Fisher (1913).

The idea of myth does not denigrate scholarly theory, nor does it suggest that theories are false. It does suggest that they are theories, not truth, and should be subject to skepticism even as they are tentatively accepted as ways to help us to explain phenomena. Many earlier theories of physical and mental phenomena have been shown to be false as knowledge has become more sophisticated. Presumably, this knowledge revolution will continue for as long as we can foresee. A major premise of knowledge, and thus, of social studies is therefore that things change.

The Copernican Revolution, revising existing ideas that the earth was flat and the center of the universe, occurred because of the possibility and power of skepticism about existing theories (Kuhn 1970a). Similarly, Darwin's theories replaced existing theory on the origin of living things in the mid-nineteenth century, over the strong objections of scholars and theologians whose beliefs or reputations rested on previous views. Does that mean that current conceptions of Copernican and Darwinian theories are irrefutable truth? No, they are just more contemporary and sophisticated theories, acceptable to mainstream scholars and supported so far by available evidence. There is still dispute. Some orthodox religions oppose Darwinism and other people question the social application of

Darwinism. And Russell suggested, although facetiously, that the flat-earth society may have been right despite Copernicus (Russell 1928).

Issues and the Weakness of Single-Subject Approaches

Not only do the separate disciplines have the potential for rigid scholasticism, but no individual subject is adequate to deal with the complexity of human issues. By imposing serious limitations, and squeezing, any of the humanities or social sciences could frame an issue solely within its own narrow borders, but that does not account for the intellectual loss created by such limits and compression. Examining only historian-approved documents on a human issue such as poverty or war may be exhaustive for the student, but is not exhaustive as an intellectual enterprise. It would leave out current or historian-ignored philosophic, economic, political, sociological, psychological, literary, scientific, ethnic, legal, religious, or other dimensions. Issues range beyond the arbitrary limits of traditional subjects. Time is larger than conventional history; space is larger than conventional geography; and humans are more than the sum of separate studies in sociology, economics, political science, religion, law, education, women's studies, ethnic studies, anthropology, psychology or other traditional or emerging social sciences.

Regarding the narrowness of social science disciplines, sociologist Robert Lynd (1939, 16) wrote:

So, despite our (social scientists) protestations that everything is interdependent, preoccupation with our specializations tends to put blinkers on us social scientists and to make us state our problems as if they concerned, in fact, isolated economic, or political, or sociological problems.

Pervasive human issues do not come neatly packaged and formally organized along the lines of formal subjects. Such issues as crime, war, and hunger are not simple and are not simply examined only through the lenses of historians or economists or other social scientists. Information and interpretations from history are valuable in understanding and coping with contemporary life; information and interpretations from social sciences, literature, philosophy, other humanities, and the sciences are also valuable in comprehending and dealing with human issues. Poverty and discrimination, for example, can be examined using history, political science, geography, economics, and psychology. Sociology, anthropology, law, religion, education, literature, philosophy, and the arts and sciences provide other important knowledge about their causes and effects. The whole topic, however, is more than the sum of these parts. A separatist curriculum that requires students to study national history, economics, political science, sociology, psychology, law, and geography in compartmentalized segments as though each had no relation to the other is unlikely to provide students with sufficient opportunity to examine and understand those human issues as holistic concerns.

Early twentieth-century social studies educators recognized the need to shift from static history teaching to issues. Prior to the establishment of the National Council for the Social Studies, teachers recognized that issue study was more important than standard history (Stockton 1919). Harold Rugg (1921) suggested that social studies diminish the grip of professional associations of historians on the school curriculum, eliminate nonessential military and political details, and focus on crucial issues.

Good teachers have long recognized serious limits in standard disciplinary history instruction. Tyler Kepner, a 1930s high school social studies chair and the only member of the College Board Commission on History who refused to sign its final report endorsing increased traditional history instruction, wrote in the first issue of *Social Education*:

> One cannot long discuss the curriculum in the social studies without frankly acknowledging the strained relations between the proponents of history and the advocates of the other social studies. ... the fact remains that the historians still like to assign to history the role of the city cousin who looks with disdain upon her naive country cousin—the other social studies. ... it may be that a fundamental difference in aims and purposes exists in the teaching of the social subjects at the school and college levels. (1937, 82–83)

Social studies, then, is itself an issue, and exploring issues requires evidence and interpretations from a variety of conventional and unconventional fields of study.

Issues and Integration in Social Education

Questions coming from human issues are more significant than the possible answers produced by any single subject. Issues develop questions of personal and social importance to students and scholars, the basis of knowledge. Single disciplines provide useful approaches to information, answers, and perspectives to consider specific parts of the questions. For social education, however, the focus should be on the whole of knowledge, skeptical examination of ideas, and the search for knowledge. Social studies incorporates the broad study of society, to include human prehistory and the future as well as the forms and types of human knowledge. It explores questions such as: What is it to be human? To be social? To know? To engage in civic life? To make decisions? To be ethical? To be competent? These questions elicit different answers in different settings and different time periods. Wraga (1993, 202) noted it well:

> Because societal problems are complex and they transcend conventional subject divisions, civic competence depends upon integrating knowledge from a variety of subjects. ... the ability and inclination to integrate and apply knowledge constitute an essential civic competence.

The intellectual rationale for issues-centered social education involves more than a single subject. Biologist and ethnologist Gregory Bateson (1979, 8), criticizing the form of separatist subject-field education found in western culture, wrote, "Break the pattern which connects the items of learning and you necessarily destroy all quality." He noted that science is based on presuppositions that deserve critical examination in schools rather than teaching as truth: "Science probes, it does not prove" (32). In literature, writer Doris Lessing (1993) expressed a similar concern with the pattern of connections. She sees a parallel between intellectual defects resulting from compartmentalized thinking and the illogical separations of categories of knowledge in schools and libraries. Political theorist Harold Laski (1929, 567) hoped that: "The student learns that knowledge is, after all, a seamless web and that our categories are, at bottom, merely ways of arranging conveniently the facts we have acquired." Whitehead (1929, 23) also recognized that "you may not divide the seamless coat of learning." And Dewey (1897) remarked on the natural involvement of individuals in human issues, pointing out that education develops from the individual's involvement in the social consciousness.

Charles Beard (1929, 369) presented a similar rationale for the centrality of human issues in social studies:

> Human beings live not by election statistics and battle alone, but also by industry, by homekeeping, by co-operation with their fellows, by all the arts of love, joy, and admiration—as Ruskin put it. In a democracy the schools simply cannot ignore the demands of life, keep aloof from its pressing problems of choice and conduct. ... Those who have put aside their professional pride [historians and social scientists] and fixed their minds on their pupils and the world of struggle, sacrifice, and perplexities in which pupils must live have come to [recognize] one object, namely, to throw light on the way of life in which boys and girls must walk.

Good teachers, those transformative intellectuals whom Henry Giroux (1985) advocated, would agree. Both knowledge and teaching are complex and dynamic, more than can be encompassed in a single, conventional subject. Issues offer a framework that stresses interrelationships—that seamless web—within knowledge, and relies on human interest in the development of civilization. Issues have a historic and pervasive role in framing, interpreting, and challenging that social consciousness.

Issues and School Knowledge

Human issues occur in the earliest human societies and continue through the latest. That comment seems obvious, but the essentiality of it is lost in the conventional history-based and static social studies curriculum. Dewey (1938, 18, 19) pointed to this problem in traditional education:

> Since the subject-matter as well as standards of proper conduct are handed down from the past, the attitude of pupils must, upon the whole, be one of docility, receptivity, and obedience. ... The traditional scheme is, in essence, one of imposition from above and from outside. It imposes adult standards,

subject-matter, and methods upon those who are only growing slowly toward maturity. The gap is so great that the required subject-matter, the methods of learning and of behaving are foreign to the existing capacities of the young ... that which is taught is thought of as essentially static. It is taught as a finished product, with little regard either to the ways in which it was originally built up or to changes that will surely occur in the future.

Progressive, reconstructionist, and critical educators have been discontent with traditional formalistic approaches that hide, sterilize, or ignore social problems (Cremin 1961; Giroux 1988; Stanley 1992). Although they differ significantly on many issues, they express a vision of a democratic society that requires the examination of social problems as a focus of school study. The strong intellectual and democratic premises that underlie this view are at odds with static forms of knowledge which have permeated schools. Dewey (1961, 8, 9), discussing the necessity in a democracy of relating human issues to school knowledge, identified the problem in compelling language:

> There is the standing danger that the material of formal instruction will be merely the subject matter of the schools, isolated from the subject matter of life-experience. The permanent social interests are likely to be lost from view. ... As formal teaching and training grow in extent, there is the danger of creating an undesirable split between the experience gained in more direct associations and what is acquired in school.

A 1993 report by editors of *Science* noted that traditional mainstream paradigms in the social sciences are undergoing serious rethinking based on renewed interest in human problems rather than through discipline-enhancement. *Science* (1993, 1796) further reported:

> All these new questions are being raised in the context of a disciplinary structure that is no longer very well suited to them. ... Trouble is, traditional disciplinary boundaries are nowadays being blurred and bent almost out of recognition to accommodate new torrents of new knowledge, to respond

to the demands for socially relevant research … and to reflect the fact that the problems of greatest moment today have to be tackled by multiple approaches.

The essence of the purposes of knowledge—to provide understanding of and potential solutions for human problems—is not what traditional social studies instruction provides. Rather, traditional social studies aims to teach formal disciplinary information and perspectives to students in learning settings where criticism is discouraged. For example, the curriculum proposed by the National Commission on Social Studies in the Schools (1989), a commission established by the American Historical Association with the support of some leaders of the National Council for the Social Studies, postponed student engagement in social issues until after they have been subjected to about eleven years of traditional history and geography lessons. These lessons appear to be a return to a codification of static history from the early twentieth century (Nelson and Weltman 1991). Presumably, this proposal rests upon the idea that long-term formal study of traditional history and geography is necessary before one can comprehend a social issue. That presumption denies the complex and dynamic nature of issues, knowledge, and human motivations. It also denies the historical imperative for human issues as the center of social education.

Issues provide a more suitable and natural framework for organizing social studies instruction than is provided by the conventional, socially constructed, and intellectually limited categories of knowledge such as history, the separate social sciences, or other common disciplinary structures.

Issues-Centered Education and Current Conservative Reforms

The basic idea that human issues are the real focus of human interests and should be the focus of social studies schooling is not an extraordinary position; indeed, it appears self-evident. But traditional schools emphasize formal and sterile structures of knowledge, i.e., separate subjects taught as static factual information. And traditional schools diminish the study of human issues, often because issues are perceived as too fluid and too current to be academically respectable.

It is ironic that traditional schools and disciplines dominate social studies instruction, while human issues dominate the lives of students and teachers. Thoughtful teachers and students find the disparity between the imperative for the social study of issues and the traditional issue-free approach of schools perplexing. This point is not new. Dewey (1910) considered subject-matter instruction "worse than useless" when it did not connect with problems existing in the student's experience, and Alfred North Whitehead (1929, 13) pleaded against the proliferation in schools of "inert ideas … ideas received into the mind without being utilized, or tested."

The idea that problems and issues should be central to the enterprise of education, however, must be reconstructed during each cycle of conservative school reform. The study of human and controversial issues that expect students to engage in critical thinking is an early victim of such school reforms. Traditional and progressive educators disagree over the relative value and best approach to discipline-based or issues-centered knowledge structures. Another debate is over the extent to which students are capable of critical thought.

Much conservative educational reform advocates static organization of knowledge with an overemphasis on testable information, technocratic and deskilling limits on teaching, and scholasticism (Apple 1970; Aronowitz and Giroux 1983; Presseisen 1985; Purpel 1989; Perrone 1991). The conformist compartmentalization of knowledge of today's typical schools appears unrelated to human issues. This traditionalist approach has not been strikingly successful in producing critical thinking or an informed populace. Instead, it appears successful only in separating societal interests from schooling and in boring students with static details of history.

Issues-centered education challenges the traditional and common subject-centered form of social studies instruction in schools. Conservative school reform assumes that basic education is student learning of and testing on traditional formal structures of subjects. Issues-centered education assumes that issues are basic and that subjects are valuable in providing information and ideas, but are not adequate social education in themselves. Issues appear messier and less controllable than neat chronological outlines of standard nationalistic history or highly structured lessons on skills and information from geography or other social sciences. Human issues usually have no clear-cut and obviously true answers. They would not be issues if the answer was obvious. Many teachers find comfort and ease in traditional social studies teaching of factual information on nationalistic history, physical geography, economic chart reading, or definitions of terms in sociology or political science. That kind of teaching can be done to all classes of students over several years of practice in a career. The material is easily testable, and can quickly be made into seatwork and memorization tasks.

Issues, however, are more complex, more dynamic, and more engaging than traditional social studies teaching. Progressive teachers and students realize the sound pedagogy behind using the vitality of important issues to energize instruction and stimulate interest. They also intuitively or intellectually recognize that high quality social studies instruction must focus on human issues. In addition to the contemporary reasons for issues-centered education, there are historic groundings for recognizing issues as central to social studies instruction.

The Mandate for Issues-Centered Education

Throughout human existence and across cultures and regions, issues have been at the core of the human quest for knowledge. Issues provide motivation, challenge ideas, inform scholars and students, and set criteria for judging progress in civilization. They represent the cauldron within which myth, theory, fact, value, and perspective mix with multiple realities. Over the course of human development, social education has been a major focus of social and intellectual life. That education requires engagement in human issues and consideration and modification of social knowledge.

Existing paradigms, theories, and identified principles of the disciplines that undergird the separate subjects are similar to myths; they attempt to explain phenomena and they are often stories considered plausible or valuable to the initiated. For a society interested in civilizational and intellectual progress, we must require a level of skepticism and criticism and a willingness to consider thoughtful alternative views. That position states an essential purpose of education, and particularly of social education—developing critical inquiry about human issues.

Although absolutistic answers to human problems have been presented in various historic times and geographic settings, these have been accepted only by true believers of that time and place. They interrupt the development of knowledge. Even in highly restricted communities of mandated religious conformity, dissenters and disbelievers exist. Leakey (1992 [with Lewin], 23), reflecting on his years of study of the origins of humankind, stated: "Absolute truth is like a mirage; it disappears as you approach it." At any time a very small number of absolute disciples of a particular ideology believe they have truth and suffer no indecision; but, in common existence over time and place, human lives are entwined with personal and social issues, issues unbound by the strictures of a particular subject.

Bertrand Russell (1959, 313), summarizing the history of western philosophy, stated: "It is recognized quite freely ... that the sum total of what man knows is vanishingly small. What seems in the end more important is that one should pursue knowledge." That pursuit, says Russell, is "linked with freedom," and requires no avenue to be "closed by artificial strictures" (313). Artificial strictures include disciplinary dogma and boundaries that limit thinking and discourage skepticism.

People live in diverse situations and conditions; difficult choices and perplexing problems vex all societies. Although each generation meets and tries to cope with its own set of problems, fundamental human issues remain for people in modern and postmodern times (Stanley 1992). The future will not hold less complexity or fewer human issues. That change occurs is not disputed. At issue is the nature of change, regress or progress, and humankind's attempts to influence the direction of change.

The challenge for education is to provide appropriate means for comprehending and coping with personal and social issues. Schools should be locations for identifying and critically examining significant human issues and for thoughtful consideration of potential answers and consequences. The social studies bear special responsibility for this examination of issues and responses. This requires exploration of diverse evidence and interpretations, and it requires practice in thoughtful decision making. Legitimate social studies instruction necessarily incorporates human issues and knowledge development as the oldest and most pervasive of human educational activities. The study of human issues provides opportunity for the pursuit of knowledge in a setting of freedom. This is the historical imperative for the centrality of the study of issues—an intellectual and democratic mandate.

References

Apple, M. *Ideology and Curriculum.* London: Routledge, 1970.

Aronowitz S., and H. Giroux. *Education under Siege: Conservative, Liberal and Radical Debate over Schooling.* Granby, Mass.: Bergin and Garvey, 1983.

Bacon, F. *The Advancement of Learning.* Book I. 1606. London: Macmillan, 1892.

Bateson, G. *Mind and Nature.* New York: Bantam, 1979.

Beale, H. *Are American Teachers Free?* New York: Charles Scribner's Sons, 1936.

Beard, C. "The Trend in Social Studies."*Historical Outlook* 20 (1929): 369–72.

Billington, R.A. *The Historian's Contribution to Anglo-American Misunderstanding.* New York: Hobbs, Dorman, 1966.

Bottomore, T. B. *Critics of Society.* New York: Pantheon Books, 1968.

Butts, R. F. *A Cultural History of Western Education.* New York: McGraw-Hill, 1955.

Campbell, J. *Transformation of Myth through Time.* New York: Harper and Row, 1990.

Cipolla. C. M. *The Economic History of World Population.* Baltimore, Md.: Penguin Books, 1964.

Cremin, L. *The Transformation of the School.* New York: Random House, 1961.

Cressy, D. *Literacy and the Social Order.* Cambridge, England: Cambridge University Press, 1980.

Curti, M. *American Paradox: The Conflict of Thought and Action.* New Brunswick, N.J,: Rutgers University Press, 1956.

Dewey, J. *Democracy and Education.* New York: Macmillan, 1961.

Dewey, J. "My Pedagogic Creed." In *John Dewey: The Early Works, 1882–1898.* Vol. 5. 1897. Carbondale, Ill: Southern Illinois University Press, 1972.

Dewey, J. *How We Think.* Boston: Heath, 1910.

Dewey, J. *Experience and Education.* 1938. West Lafayette, Ind.: Kappa Delta Pi, 1963.

Fisher, S. "The Legendary and Myth-Making Process in Histories of the American Revolution." *The History Teacher's Magazine* 4, no. 3 (1913): 63–71.

Gellerman, W. *The American Legion as Educator.* New York: Teachers College Press, 1938.

Giroux, H. "Teachers as Transformative Intellectuals." *Social Education* 49 (May 1985): 376-79.

Giroux, H. *Schooling and the Struggle for Public Life.* Minneapolis: University of Minnesota Press, 1988.

Hamblyn, D. W. *A History of Western Philosophy.* New York: Viking/Penguin, 1987.

Heehs, P. "Myth, History, and Theory." *History and Theory* 33 (1994): 1–19.

Johnson, H. *The Teaching of History in Elementary and Secondary Schools.* New York: Macmillan, 1940.

Kepner, T. "The Dilemma of the Secondary-School Social Studies Teacher." *Social Education* 1 (1937): 81–87.

Key, V. O. *Public Opinion and American Democracy.* New York: Knopf, 1961.

Kuhn, T. *The Copernican Revolution.* Cambridge Mass.: Harvard University Press, 1970a.

Kuhn, T. *The Structure of Scientific Revolutions.* 2d ed. Chicago: University of Chicago Press, 1970b.

Laski, H. "Teacher and Student." *The Century Magazine* 117 (March 1929): 566–77.

Leakey, R., and R. Lewin. *Origins Reconsidered.* New York: Doubleday, 1992.

Lessing, D. Presentation given at the Rutgers University Colloquium, New Brunswick, New Jersey, 7 October 1993.

Lum, P. *The Growth of Civilization in East Asia.* New York: S. G. Phillips Books, 1969.

Mayer, F. *A History of Educational Thought.* Columbus, Ohio: Merrill, 1960.

Merriam, C. *Civic Education in the United States.* New York: Charles Scribner's Sons, 1934.

National Commission on Social Studies in the Schools. *Charting a Course: Social Studies for the 21st Century.* Washington, DC: National Council for the Social Studies, 1989.

Nelson, J. "Nationalistic Education and the Free Man." In *Humanistic Frontiers in Education,* edited by R. P. Fairfield. Englewood Cliffs, N.J.: Prentice-Hall, 1971.

Nelson, J. "Nationalistic vs. Global Education." *Theory and Research in Social Education* 1 (1976): 33–50.

Nelson, J., and B. Weltman. "Ideologies in Civic Values." Paper presented at the International Society for Political Psychology Annual Scientific Meeting, Washington, DC, May 1990.

Nelson, J. "Charting a Course Backward." *Social Education* 55 (1990): 412.

Nencel, L., and P. Pels, ed. *Constructing Knowledge: Authority and Critiques in Social Sciences.* London: Sage, 1991.

Perrone, V. *A Letter to Teachers.* San Francisco, Calif.: Jossey-Bass, 1991.

Pierce, B. *Citizens' Organizations and the Civic Training of Youth.* New York: Charles Scribner's Sons, 1933.

Presseisen, B. *Unlearned Lessons.* Philadelphia, Pa.: Falmer, 1985.

Purpel, D. *The Moral and Spiritual Crisis in Education.* Granby, Mass.: Bergin and Garvey, 1989.

Rugg, H. "How Shall We Reconstruct the Social Studies Curriculum?" *The Historical Outlook* 12 (1921): 184–89.

Russell, B. *Skeptical Essays.* New York: W. W. Norton, 1928.

Russell, B. *Understanding History.* New York: Philosophical Library, 1957

Russell, B. *Wisdom of the West.* London: Rathbone Books, 1959.

Saxe, D. W. "Framing a Theory for Social Studies Foundations." *Review of Educational Research* 62 (1992a): 259–77.

Saxe, D. W. "An Introduction to the Seminal Social Welfare and Efficiency Prototype: The Founders of 1916 Social Studies." *Theory and Research in Social Education* 20 (1992b):156–78.

Science editors. "New Life Ahead for Social Sciences." *Science* 261 (September 24, 1993): 1796–98.

Shoemaker, N. "Teaching the Truth about the History of the American West." *The Chronicle of Higher Education* 40 (October 27, 1993): A48.

Skybreak, A. *Of Primeval Steps and Future Leaps.* Chicago: Banner Press, 1984.

Stanley, W. B. *Curriculum for Utopia.* Albany, N.Y.: State University of New York Press, 1992.

Stockton, J. "Teaching Current Events." *The Historical Outlook* 9 (1919): 13–15.

Wesley, E. B. *Teaching the Social Studies.* New York: Heath, 1937.

Wraga, W. G. "The Interdisciplinary Imperative for Citizenship Education." *Theory and Research in Social Education* 21 (1993): 201-31.

4 RESEARCH ON ISSUES-CENTERED SOCIAL STUDIES

by Carole L. Hahn

For many years social studies educators have advocated the use of issues-centered instruction on philosophic grounds, similar to those put forth in the first chapters of this handbook. But skeptics and believers alike have wondered whether empirical evidence exists to warrant its use. This chapter addresses the question: Is there evidence that issues-centered social studies yields benefits? The answer must first be qualified in that studies conducted in particular contexts in the past cannot prove or predict what will happen in a future setting, and available research tends to be correlational, not causal. That is, researchers studying particular classrooms found that issues-centered instruction was associated with various phenomena; they did not establish cause-and-effect relationships as one might in a laboratory. Examining the available research can, however, be insightful to those considering the implementation of issues-centered teaching because there is reason to believe that when this approach is used under certain conditions, students may like social studies, and may develop higher-order thinking skills, participatory political attitudes, and an awareness and concern about global or other important societal issues. But before examining the research base for such possibilities, a few cautions are in order.

First, despite numerous calls for issues-centered social studies instruction over the years, the few schools that offered such programs have not reported their effectiveness. Consequently, no evidence exists from long-term participation. Nevertheless, researchers pursuing diverse lines of inquiry have identified a number of positive outcomes—and some obstacles—when students experience issues-centered social studies instruction for short periods in their schooling. All of the studies reported here are focused on samples of middle and high school students. That is not to say that issues-centered teaching cannot occur at the elementary school level; indeed, many elementary teachers design interdisciplinary units around issues (Angell and Avery 1992). At this time, however, there is not a cumulative research base for that age level.

Additional cautions relate to the definition and nature of issues-centered instruction. The editors of this handbook define issues-centered instruction as a teaching approach that uses social issues to emphasize reflective and often controversial questions in contemporary and historic contexts as the heart of social studies. The approach encourages students to become more thoughtful about the way they view social life, rather than seeking right answers to unproblematic questions, while it engages them in the challenges and dilemmas citizens confront. In earlier decades, issues-centered instruction had slightly different emphases and went by different names. For example, in the 1940s and 1950s social studies authors (Quillen and Hanna 1948) wrote of a "problems approach" that applied John Dewey's ideas to the tasks of preparing young citizens. This approach was most commonly used in U.S. history and "Problems of American Democracy" courses. Students were encouraged to select problems for investigation that interested them and concerned society. In the 1950s and 1960s Hunt and Metcalf (1955, 1968) extended the tradition with "reflective inquiry" into the "closed areas" of society. They proposed a systematic model for analyzing problems that integrated value, semantic, and empirical analyses. Their work was followed by two differing streams—one that emphasized "inquiry" into intellectual issues with a disciplinary focus and one that recommended a "jurisprudential" approach to analyzing enduring dilemmas in which core social values were in conflict. (Massialas 1963, Oliver and Shaver 1966)

Previous chapters in this handbook have more thoroughly explicated the distinctions within an issues-centered tradition. This chapter notes that researchers working from differing perspectives, using differing methodologies and emphases, focused on different features within the approach with the result that from one decade to the next, researchers shed light on a classroom scene from different angles. Some researchers included verbatim notes of selected classroom dialogues; others described a particular set of issues-centered materials. Yet, others assumed that a particular approach was used, and/or asked students if they felt comfortable expressing their opinions on issues. In truth, the research base for issues-centered instruction relies on studies of an amorphous dynamic "independent variable" because no two days of issues-centered instruction were/are the same. What the teachers and many of the researchers shared was a belief that students ought to be actively engaged in discovering knowledge useful to them in reflecting upon issues that face citizens across time and social contexts.

Throughout this chapter are references to three components of issues-centered teaching—content, pedagogy, and climate. Various researchers focus on differing parts of that triad, and their findings overlap with different emphases. Nevertheless, it is clear that the three separate parts of that equation alone are not sufficient. Combined, however, they can make a difference in achieving the goals of social studies. That is, if students **1.** study issues-centered content, **2.** are in classes where discussions, research projects, debates, simulations, or writing assignments encourage them to consider differing views or interpretations of issues, and **3.** they perceive the classroom climate as sufficiently supportive so they are comfortable expressing their own views and considering those of others, then achieving social studies goals in the knowledge, skill, and attitude domains is likely.

Dominant Patterns of Social Studies Instruction and Student Attitudes

Despite many calls in the past for issues-centered teaching, rarely do teachers promote systematic inquiry into contemporary and historic social problems, encourage students to weigh arguments and express their opinions on value conflicts in the society, and create a classroom atmosphere that is accepting and supportive of diverse viewpoints. Indeed, in a study of Michigan high school social studies teachers, only 26 out of 150 randomly selected teachers said they held discussions of social issues on a regular basis (Massialas, Sprague, and Hurst 1975). Most who research "typical" social studies classes conclude that classes tend to be textbook based, dominated by teacher talk with some student recitation, and devoid of controversial issues (Goodlad 1984; McNeil 1986; Shaver, Davis, and Helburn 1979). Given those general trends, it is not surprising that researchers found that many students do not like social studies and say it is boring and unrelated to the real world (Schug, Todd, and Berry 1984; Shaughnessy and Haladyna 1985; Shaver et al. 1979). Furthermore, researchers found that, although social studies classes can be effective in increasing knowledge about specific topics, instruction has a negligible influence on student attitudes and behaviors (Ehman 1980a; Grossman 1975/1976; Langton and Jennings 1968; Litt 1963; Miller 1985). Remarkably, the research reviewed in this chapter stands in stark contrast to this negative litany. It demonstrates that under particular conditions social studies instruction can have positive effects on students. Moreover, it reveals that issues-centered social studies instruction, in particular, holds much promise.

Several researchers, for example, found that students would like to experience issues discussions more than they do (Long and Long 1975; Remy 1972). In studying the classes of 17 Michigan teachers who said they regularly held discussions of social issues, Sugrue (cited in Massialas et al. 1975) found that, on the whole, students in those classes tended to like their teacher and class.[1] Examining more closely the differences between classes where inquiry methods provided a structure for issues discussion and "opining" classes where students merely aired their views, Massialas et al. (1975) found that students liked inquiry teachers and classes better than opining teachers and classes. Students in the inquiry classes felt their discussions had an order and purpose and that teachers were sensitive to their ideas.

In an Illinois study, social studies students who experienced controversial issues discussions had positive feelings toward their social studies courses, textbooks, and teachers—in contrast to students without such exposure. The correlations between reported issues discussions and students saying they liked social studies were substantial—.70 for junior high school students and .65 for senior high school students (Long and Long 1975). At a time when many educators and the public are concerned with making schools more humane communities for young citizens, such findings are important. But just what is issues-centered teaching and learning? What does it look like inside real classrooms?

Characteristics of Issues-Centered Classes and Teachers

In recent years researchers studying teachers and classrooms have gained insights into the roles of teachers and students in classes that might be called issues-centered. Although not using the term issues-centered in her study of four teachers' social studies classes, Bickmore (1991, 1993) revealed the dimensions of two components of issues-centered instruction—content and pedagogy. Central to her analysis of the use of conflict or controversy in social studies classes were two concepts she called *conflictual content* and *conflictual pedagogy*.

Conflictual content includes the use of controversial material or the stimulation of criticism by including perspectives from different cultures, different ideologies, and divergent sources of information. In Bickmore's study, Tom, a U.S. history teacher, organized each unit around central concepts or problems, and presented multiple viewpoints about those ideas. For example, he made the westward expansion unit problematic by attending to Native American viewpoints. Additionally, Tom showed that historians often interpret historical information differently by, for example, presenting differing views on why the United States entered World War I. To present conflictual content, Tom supplemented the textbook with many examples of differing viewpoints, and he frequently brought in current events as analogies and perspectives to illuminate historical concepts. Ruth, a world studies teacher, also approached content as problems or conflicts the students would analyze to better understand. Central to her curriculum were differences and conflicts between cultures, countries, ideologies, and ethnic or economic groups. Her goal was for students to acquire information and become tolerant of differences. She tried to present ideas that her students might build upon in future classes or out-of-school experiences. Thus, she used conflictual content but not pedagogy.

Conflictual pedagogy is the process whereby a teacher encourages students to confront conflicts that either occur spontaneously in the classroom or are teacher initiated. By frequently inviting divergent student opinions, Sarah, a world studies teacher, used conflictual pedagogy; however, she did not employ conflictual content. Tom used conflictual pedagogy as well as content. Ken, the fourth teacher, used neither conflictual content nor pedagogy in his teaching of U.S. history.[2]

Bickmore concluded that conflictual curricular content was "necessary but not sufficient" to teach for democratic citizenship. For the most part, students who were exposed to conflicts in Ruth's world studies content but did not engage in confrontation with the issues, were passive learners. An exception occurred when the class was physically organized on sides of the Palestinian-Israeli conflict and directed to express any and all opinions to each other. During that session, more students participated—more frequently and more extensively in terms of number, length, and quality of responses than in any other lessons. Students gave detailed reasons for their opinions, and, in responding to objections from the other side, they clarified and elaborated their arguments. Conflictual content was reinforced by the use of conflictual pedagogy.

Tom's class exemplified the many ways that a teacher can prepare students for participatory citizenship by using issues-centered content and pedagogy (Bickmore 1991). It also revealed some of the difficulties that can arise. His history curriculum was complex and challenging—for the teacher to prepare and for students to learn. Not every class period focused on controversy, but at some time in every week and in every unit, students engaged actively in decision making or problem solving about historic or contemporary issues. Moreover, not every student was engaged every day. Sometimes there was confusion or frustration, and sometimes the gaps in participation and achievement seemed to increase during controversial issues discussions. Sometimes confrontation of conflict stimulated student interest and brought previously nonparticipating students into the dialogue; other times it seemed to have no effect.

Rossi (1995) observed in-depth study in an issues-centered social studies classroom. He concluded that in-depth issues instruction is not a panacea because of dilemmas it creates for the teachers and the demands it places on students.

Other recent research on teachers, while not focusing on issues-centered teaching per se, further illuminates that topic. Several researchers associated with Lee Shulman at Stanford University obtained useful insights concerning the diverse ways teachers center instruction on issues. Gudmundsdottir (1988) found that two "expert" history teachers used conflict and controversy to achieve their goals of developing students' capacity for independent and critical thought and reducing their indifference. One teacher, David, used controversies and their interpretation as connecting links in his classes, emphasizing that doing history means interpreting and comparing differing perspectives on issues and events. Additionally, he frequently drew analogies between historical controversies and current events or student realities. The other teacher, Harry, viewed himself as a conflict historian and frequently presented contrasting opinions about historical events to his classes. Unlike David, Harry focused on texts, making only occasional references to current events and student realities. He used readings to supplement the students' textbook and to highlight controversies and simulations to stage conflictual situations.

Wineburg and Wilson (1988) interviewed and observed expert teachers as they taught the Revolutionary War period. One teacher highlighted a controversial historic issue by having her students read differing primary and secondary accounts in preparation for a role-played debate about the legitimacy of British taxation in the North American colonies. The teacher's goal was for students to understand that "there were two points of view, that there was legitimacy to both sides" (18). She further wanted students to participate actively in conflict by taking different positions and inventing solutions to problems.

Mason (1990) interviewed and observed expert world history teachers in Georgia. She, too, found that expert teachers used historic issues, historical debates, and contemporary analogies regularly in their teaching. These studies are important in revealing that excellent or "expert" teachers share a willingness to encourage students to explore contentious issues, using both content and pedagogy to give students practice in decision making about issues that citizens face. This stands out in contrast to the studies of large numbers of teachers and classrooms, where "average" or "typical" teachers de-emphasize or avoid controversial material in order to maintain classroom control and cover large amounts of material (Goodlad 1984; McNeil 1986; Shaver et al. 1979).

Summary. These qualitative studies of social studies teachers' beliefs and of naturally occurring classroom interaction reveal a sense of what occurs in issues-centered classes. Potential benefits of issues-centered teaching are opportunities to model democratic discourse in a pluralistic society, stimulate student interest and tolerance of diverse views, and convey the conflictual nature of scholarly discourse and community life. But the question remains: What difference does issues-centered instruction make to student learning? Is there research to indicate that student knowledge, skills, and values may be affected by such an approach?

Student Outcomes and Issues-Centered Instruction

Since the earliest debates over the form that social studies should take, the advocates of what educators now call issues-centered instruction have argued that in a democracy the appropriate preparation for citizenship is to give students practice in exploring problematic issues facing society. They advocated that, through such practice, students would not only acquire the knowledge they would need as adult citizens, but, more importantly, they would develop the necessary abilities to critically analyze public issues and to participate in a democracy. Over the years special projects demonstrated that such outcomes were associated with the use of problems-or issues-centered practices.

Critical or Higher-Order Thinking

One of the earliest studies to measure the effects of issues-centered instruction was conducted in the 1940s by the staff of the Stanford Social Education Project (Quillen and Hanna 1948). Teachers volunteered to teach an eleventh-grade U.S. history course or a twelfth-grade Problems of Democracy course using one of three approaches—problems, topical, or chronological. A problems approach was defined as an approach that applied Dewey's method of reflective inquiry to areas of public concern that could be resolved by finding a solution to the problem from among several alternatives. At the beginning and end of a school year, the Stanford researchers measured the students' critical thinking abilities as well as their knowledge and commitment to a number of social attitudes.

The evaluators concluded that seniors exposed to a problems approach as compared to matched students in classes that used a topical approach made significant growth in the following areas: critical thinking, study skills, the use of library and research skills, and social studies knowledge.[3] Students in the problems group also made more progress toward consistency and certainty in their views than did the topical group. For the juniors the differences between the problems and chronological groups were not as clear cut. Neither group significantly improved in critical thinking. The chronological group students showed more growth on the tests of social studies knowledge, but the problems group students seemed to become more consistent and certain of their views on the measure of social attitudes.[4]

In the 1960s four researchers at Indiana University similarly examined the relationship between students' critical thinking abilities and the use of a "reflective inquiry" approach to social studies instruction. In the Indiana Experiments in Inquiry (Massialas 1963), teachers of experimental group classes presented "springboards" that contained discrepant or other puzzling information and encouraged students to try to resolve the problematic situation through a process similar to the one used by teachers of the problems approach in the Stanford investigation. When using the inquiry approach, rather than asking questions for the purpose of obtaining a correct answer, the teacher probed to elicit explanatory hypotheses about human behavior, which students then tested with evidence.[5]

The four studies revealed some evidence, although not conclusive, that the use of an inquiry approach could facilitate students' higher-order thinking (Cousins 1963, Cox 1963, Elsmere 1963, Massialas 1963). In one study Cousins concluded that a class of eighth-grade students studying U.S. history using an inquiry approach made statistically significant mean score gains on the Watson-Glaser Critical Thinking Appraisal and on a teacher-constructed test of reflective thinking. The students also made significant gains on a standardized test of social studies knowledge.[6] In another of the studies, Elsmere concluded that high school students

who regularly used a problem-solving approach in their U.S. history class scored significantly higher on two researcher-designed tests measuring ability to use the problem-solving steps and knowledge of U.S. history than did comparison group students; they also did better on delayed posttests than did the comparison group.[7]

However, neither Massialas, who studied four world history classes, nor Cox, who studied four U.S. history classes, identified statistically significant differences between students in reflective inquiry or comparison classes on standardized tests of critical thinking and knowledge.[8] Nevertheless, the teacher-researchers' daily anecdotal diaries and tape recordings of several classes led both Massialas and Cox to conclude that students in the inquiry group excelled over students in the comparison group in their ability to engage in critical or reflective thinking, despite the test results.

One of the most extensive research projects on issues-centered curriculum and student thinking was the evaluation of the Harvard Social Studies Project (Levin, Newmann, and Oliver 1969; Oliver and Shaver 1966). Project students were taught to analyze controversial public policy issues using a "jurisprudential" approach, which relates a contemporary public issue to cases and raises ethical, legal, factual, and definitional questions. Unlike the emphasis on deductive reasoning characteristic of much critical thinking research, the project directors' approach emphasized the clarification of two or more legitimately held points of view as they bear on public policy issues and emphasized dialogue between teacher and students and among students—incorporating both issues content and pedagogy. Researchers examined the effects on students of using the curriculum for three years in a senior high school and for four years in a junior high school in middle-class Boston suburbs. The junior high materials promoted an analytic approach to value issues in geography, U.S. history, and current events. Comparing the experimental group students to a comparison group on a variety of measures, the evaluators concluded that the issues-centered junior high students were better able to analyze argumentative dialogues. Furthermore, the time spent in the analysis of issues did not reduce the amount of traditional content the students learned.

The senior high school units in the Harvard

Project focused on controversies arising from enduring problem areas such as equality, morality, and responsibility. Historical and fictional cases were used to stimulate discussion about conflicting values. The project students performed better than the comparison group of similar ability on a concept application test and on a structured dialogue analysis test called the Social Issues Analysis Test (SIAT).[9] As for acquiring traditional content, the average-ability project students did as well on a standardized content test as comparison group students of similar ability on a Problems of Democracy test; however, they did less well on a U.S. history test.

After almost a 15-year hiatus of research on issues-centered curriculum and the development of higher-order thinking skills, researchers working with the Channel One news programs recently tested the effects of conducting structured public issues discussions about issues raised in some broadcasts (Johnston, Anderman, Milne, Klenk, and Harris 1994). During "You Decide" segments, students heard conflicting views on an enduring public issue that had surfaced in a current news event. Eight teachers were trained in the use of public issues discussion strategies similar to the Harvard Project's jurisprudential approach. The teachers used the strategies when their students discussed the You Decide segments over a three-month period. The comparison group was made up of students in the same school enrolled in the same subject; they viewed the programs, but their teachers had no particular training to lead discussions. Students in both groups participated in a constructed dialogue session before and after the treatment. Additionally, they completed a Public Issues Analysis Test that was adapted from the SIAT to assess their ability to critically analyze a public issues discussion. The experimental group students scored significantly higher than the control group students on the written measure, but their oral performance was not noticeably better. Experimental group students also did better on a test of current events knowledge than did those in the comparison group.[10] Moreover, the researchers claimed that lower-ability students seemed to benefit the most when the structured public issues discussions were combined with news viewing (22).

An objection that is sometimes voiced by critics of issues-centered teaching is that it is fine for average and above-average students, but is too difficult for low-ability students. That criticism was challenged in a study of slow learners in British Columbia (Curtis and Shaver 1980). Experimental group students examined newspaper articles and booklets on housing problems and conducted a community survey of attitudes toward the local housing situation. At the conclusion of the unit, experimental group students demonstrated increased scores on a test of critical thinking as compared to comparison group students. They also showed decreased levels of dogmatism and increased levels of self-esteem.[11] Additionally, in responding to open-ended questions, experimental group students were more likely than comparison group students to express beliefs that citizens could make a difference in improving housing conditions—indicating an increase in political efficacy.

Summary. One of the most important yet most difficult goals to achieve in social studies is the development of critical analytic abilities that will enable citizens to make informed decisions about public policy issues. Issues-centered teaching is a promising approach for the development of such higher-level cognitive thinking. Successfully implementing that approach, however, is not easy. Most projects described here used a complex instructional model for the systematic analysis of public issues with carefully structured instructional materials and trained teachers. Underlying the projects was a belief that young people can learn to investigate controversial social issues and come to a more sophisticated understanding of human behavior by considering alternative views. The next section reveals why the classroom climate in which those discussions and investigations occur is of paramount importance.

Participatory Political Attitudes and Behaviors

A line of inquiry often cited for supporting an issues-centered approach to social studies is one derived from studies of youth political socialization. In particular, political socialization researchers find that students who perceive that they are encouraged to investigate and discuss controversial issues and to express their opinions develop political attitudes that support participatory citizenship. On the other hand, students who recall few opportunities to express their opinions about controversial public policy issues possess less positive attitudes toward participation, including low levels of political interest and political efficacy—the belief that citizens can influence government decisions.

Research by Ehman was particularly important in identifying a connection between adolescent political attitudes and a "classroom climate" in which democratic discourse is modeled. To operationalize the concept of classroom climate, Ehman developed a Classroom Climate Scale, which contained items to measure the extent to which students perceived that their social studies teachers dealt with social problems, discussed both sides of issues, and took neutral positions on issues (Ehman 1969). One item on the scale also asked whether students felt free to express their opinions in their social studies classes.

In the first study in a series, Ehman found that students in a Detroit high school who had higher scores on the Classroom Climate Scale reported higher degrees of controversial issues exposure in their classes, had taken more social studies classes, and had higher scores on the scale measuring political efficacy than other students. Additionally, students in open-climate classrooms also reported higher levels of political participation and a sense of citizen duty and lower levels of cynicism, although the magnitude of the relationships were "quite low indeed" with the highest correlation coefficient being .25 for climate and participation (Ehman 1969).

Within the sample Ehman (1969) compared African-American and European-American students in open and closed classroom climates and found that a closed climate was associated with negative outcomes for both black and white students. In closed climates, both groups reported low levels of political efficacy, participation, and citizen duty. Further, white students in the closed-climate group additionally expressed relatively high levels of political cynicism.[12] Clearly, the mere presence of controversial issues in the curriculum is not sufficient to bring about positive student attitudes; when issues are presented in a closed climate, there can be negative consequences.

On the other hand, Ehman and subsequent researchers found that an open classroom climate is often associated with positive student political attitudes. For both the black and white Detroit students who experienced an open climate, there was a positive correlation between issues exposure and sense of citizen duty. Additionally, for the African-American students, there were positive correlations between reported issues exposure in an open climate and a sense of political efficacy and participation and a negative correlation with cynicism.[13] In this study, however, there was virtually no relationship between open climate and those variables for white students (Ehman 1969). In later studies of adolescents, in which findings were not broken down by race, researchers found positive correlations between an open classroom climate and political efficacy and interest (Baughman 1975; Blankenship 1990; Ehman 1980b; Hahn 1991; Hahn and Tocci 1990; Harwood 1991). Most recently in a study I conducted in England, Germany, Denmark, the Netherlands, and the United States, I found similar positive correlations between an open climate and adolescents' reported levels of political interest and efficacy (Hahn, forthcoming).

By supplementing questionnaire data with classroom observations in the Detroit classrooms, Ehman (1970) discovered clues to what teachers can do to facilitate issues-centered discussions. Defining a "normative mode" as when the teacher or students made value-laden statements or asked value-oriented questions characterized by words such as *should, ought, good,* or *bad,* Ehman related the amount of time each social studies teacher's class spent in the normative mode to the political attitude change scores of students exposed to particular teachers. An important finding was that very few value discussions occurred, which is consistent with later observational studies of social studies classes (McNeil 1986; Shaver et al. 1979). Nevertheless, Ehman did find that students who were exposed to the few teachers who raised value issues experienced a very slight increase in political efficacy over two years, but he emphasized that the relationship was too small to be considered meaningful. Unfortunately, subsequent researchers have not explored this question to determine whether effects would be greater when more discussion of value issues occurs.

Additionally, Ehman found that students in more normative classrooms appeared to become more politically cynical, or less trusting of government officials, as indicated by their responses to political trust items. In later studies, researchers similarly found an inverse relationship between open climate and students' level of political trust (Baughman 1975; Long and Long 1975; Zevin 1983). On the other hand, I did not find in my recent cross-national study that climate and trust were negatively correlated (Hahn, forthcoming). This may mean that if teachers and students regularly make evaluative comments in issues-centered classes, high school students may sometimes move away from the idealistic trusting view of government officials that is often found among young children to a more realistic and somewhat skeptical view of politicians and governmental decision makers.

With a sample of students in nine midwestern high schools, Ehman (1980b) found that students who recalled that a wider range of views was explored in social studies classes, as compared to students who recalled only one perspective being presented, had higher levels of both school and society-wide political interest and confidence. Also, they were more trusting of other students and school adults, more trusting in society, and more socially integrated than their peers. Finally, in this study as in the earlier one, students' perceived freedom to express their opinions during issues discussions was the strongest predictor of positive attitudinal outcomes with regard to both school and society.

Adding to the work on attitudes, other researchers identified political behaviors associated with an open classroom climate that might be found in an issues-centered class. For example, Long and Long (1975) examined the connection between student reports of their political behaviors outside the class and their perceptions of their social studies classroom climate. To assess student political behaviors, the researchers asked students how frequently they discussed political matters with friends and family, how frequently they followed current events in the media, and the extent of their participation in student activities, such as student government, clubs, and sports. An open classroom climate that was characterized by discussion of controversial issues correlated positively with responses on the political behavior index.[14]

Summary. Although for the most part researchers used samples of convenience and the correlations they found between climate and political attitudes were quite modest—usually ranging between .20 and .40—the consistency of findings across studies is impressive. Discussions in issues-centered social studies classes characterized by a climate of openness and acceptance of diverse viewpoints and student opinions may be associated with positive civic outcomes. Students in such

classes, as compared to students without that experience, are more likely to develop **1.** an interest in the political world, **2.** a sense that they and citizens like themselves can have some influence on political decisions in a democracy, and **3.** a belief that citizens have a duty to be actively engaged in politics. Further, they are likely to report feeling integrated into—rather than alienated from—the school culture and the wider society.

Political socialization studies also caution a few concerns. First, when issues are presented in a closed climate, students may acquire negative attitudes toward political participation. Second, when students regularly examine issues and hear diverse views, they may become skeptical of politicians. Although some would call that a healthy skepticism, others may be troubled by such an outcome.

Tolerance of Dissent and Support for Civil Liberties

Closely associated with the political socialization literature on students' political attitudes and behaviors are four studies that focus on toleration of dissent and support for civil liberties. Philosophic rationales for issues-centered discussion emphasize that in a democracy students should consider differing views so that they develop skills and attitudes for evaluating competing claims in the "free marketplace of ideas." It is hoped that they will then come to value dissent, pluralism, and civil liberties that protect diversity and democracy.

Importantly, several studies seem to confirm the realization of that goal. For example, Grossman (1975/1976) found that for a sample of California high school students, the number of controversial issues courses they had taken was related to the students' toleration of dissent and their participation in dissent activities, such as protests.[15] Further, Baughman (1975) found that students who perceived their ninth-grade civics classes to have open, or what he called "participatory" climates, showed higher levels of support for rights guaranteed by the Bill of Rights than did their peers in closed-climate, low-participatory classes. Evaluations of several curriculum projects have reinforced the finding in these studies that controversial issues discussions in social studies classes were associated, however slightly, with student support for free expression and tolerance of dissent. Further, those evaluations provide descriptions of both the content and processes of some issues-centered instruction.

For example, Goldenson (1978) examined the effects of an issues-centered unit of instruction about civil liberties. During a three-week curriculum unit, students in a working-class high school near Minneapolis were exposed to a series of issues that involved the application of abstract constitutional principles to concrete situations. Group research projects on topics such as search and seizure, freedom of religion, freedom of expression, and due process of law were the focus of the unit. Students spoke with community members, including police, lawyers, and representatives of the American Civil Liberties Union to hear varied and often conflicting perspectives on their topics. Twenty percent more of the students who participated in the experimental issues-centered program than of the comparison group students reported attitude changes in support of civil liberties, and experimental group students showed an increased level of concern for the issues presented in the case studies. Interestingly, Goldenson speculated that the methods, which encouraged students to research an issue about which people disagreed, affected students more than the particular materials.

Recently, the evaluators of another issues-centered curriculum project found similarly positive effects in terms of increasing students' scores on a scale measuring civic tolerance, a willingness to extend rights to all groups (Avery, Bird, Johnstone, Sullivan, and Thalhammer 1992). *Tolerance for Diversity of Belief* (Avery, Sullivan, and others, 1993) is a four-week curriculum unit in which junior high school students explore issues associated with freedom of expression and belief. The authors incorporated a variety of activities into the program, including role-playing, analysis of case studies, and mock interviews. The purpose of the project was to facilitate student understanding of the psychological, sociological, and historical dimensions of intolerance and tolerance. Toward that end, students were confronted with concrete scenarios and asked to decide for themselves what limits, if any, should be placed on freedom of expression in a democratic society. Experimental group students, as compared to the control group students, significantly increased their scores on a Political Tolerance Scale over the treatment period. Most experimental group students moved from mild intolerance to mild tolerance. Moreover, four

weeks following the conclusion of the treatment, the differences persisted.[16]

In another recent study, Broudy (1994, 8) measured the effects of a civics program on student attitudes supportive of civil liberties. The experimental program, *We the People*, was described by researchers as one in which students were encouraged to give their opinion about constitutional issues.

The researchers concluded that students who were exposed to the experimental program were more supportive than comparison group students of the rights of free speech, freedom of assembly, and due process for diverse groups. Furthermore, the experimental group students reported higher levels of political efficacy and political interest than did comparison group students.[17] The students who were the most willing to extend civil liberties to diverse groups were those who had participated in competitions where they had to "explain and defend their points of view and listen carefully to the viewpoints of others" (27).

Summary. Issues-centered instruction on civil liberties and tolerance can be effective in increasing students' knowledge of the subject matter as well as improving their attitudes toward dissent and the rights of all to express their ideas. Knowledge and attitudinal outcomes occur when the classroom or extracurricular activity models democratic discourse in which all ideas, no matter how controversial, can be explored. Although the evaluators of curriculum projects did not measure classroom climate, it is possible that because the teachers volunteered to teach curricula focusing on free expression issues and inquiry into value conflicts, they had themselves internalized those principles and reflected them in their teaching practices.

Global Knowledge and Attitudes

In recent years, global education has itself become an issue in social studies. In another review, Leming (1992) concluded that, for the most part, global education curricula had not been effective. Indeed, in studies where researchers were unable to document the ways in which global issues materials were implemented, few if any differences were found between students exposed to global issues and those who were not (Armstrong 1979; McAlvin 1989; Smith 1977; Soley 1982).[18] However, in those cases where students were encouraged to discuss controversial global issues in an open classroom climate, positive changes (in attitudes toward global issues) occurred.

In one study that yielded positive outcomes, Kehoe (1980) compared different approaches to teaching about the Universal Declaration of Human Rights—a common topic in global education. He examined the effects of two days of lessons about human rights issues on eighth-grade students in one middle-class urban school. In one experimental group, the teacher led discussions of cases whereby situations in various countries contravened articles in the Declaration, such as examples of slavery in the world today. During the discussion, the teacher-researcher asked questions to stimulate consideration of cultural differences and universal ethical principles. He encouraged students to consider the consistency and underlying value premises of their positions. In the second experimental group, or "investigation" group, the students briefly discussed in small groups their understanding of the articles in the Universal Declaration, then they individually read news articles and wrote their position on contraventions of human rights principles. The third group—a comparison group—viewed a filmstrip on the United Nations. Students in both treatment groups that explored human rights issues in the context of large group discussions and individual investigation were more likely than comparison group students to say that a practice condoned in a given culture was wrong if it contradicted the provisions of the Universal Declaration of Human Rights.[19]

By making classroom observations and by administering a classroom climate scale to students, Blankenship (1990) determined that an issues-centered global education program used in conjunction with classroom discussion in an open climate was associated with the development of worldmindedness and an interest in global issues. He investigated the relationship between classroom climate and global attitudes and knowledge in high school international relations and world affairs courses where students used the issues-centered materials, *Great Decisions*. Blankenship reported that the program developers encouraged the use of a variety of instructional methods including value analysis and decision making "to enable students to examine controversial public policy issues." Blankenship found a positive correlation between climate and global attitudes.[20] Although this particular study had important limitations (a self-selected sample of students in

an elective course, no comparison group, and many students did not complete both the pretest and posttests), this line of inquiry is worth pursuing in the future. Additionally, this is one of the few studies related to issues-centered instruction in which the researcher analyzed the data by race and gender. Female students perceived the classes to be more open than did male students and African-American students perceived them to be more open than did European-American students. Hopefully, future studies will explore further the relationships among race, gender, class, issues-centered teaching, and student outcomes.

A second global education study that attended to content, method, and climate, conducted in eight Bay Area California high schools, was the evaluation of part of the Stanford and the Schools Study called the American Schools and the World project (Duggan, Grossman, and Thorpe 1986; Torney-Purta and Lansdale 1986). The evaluators found that teaching strategies, rather than issues content, yielded differences in student understanding and appreciation of international material. The most effective teaching strategies included using divergent questioning styles, giving students conflicting sources of information to investigate, and encouraging tolerance for democratic dissent. Moreover, students reporting that they felt free to express opinions different from the teacher's was a significant predictor of both global knowledge and concern for global issues (Torney-Purta and Lansdale 1986).[21]

Similarly, in a study of four Michigan high schools, Yocum (1989) found that global education courses were a significant predictor of global attitudes if—and only if—students perceived that their class discussed issues and that they felt comfortable expressing their views. Yocum separated the 618 sample students into those who took a course with a global emphasis and those who did not. He then compared their pretest and posttest scores on a scale measuring globalmindedness. He also examined scores on the discussion index of the Classroom Environment scale, which contained items similar to those on the Classroom Climate scale used by other researchers. Controlling for pretest scores, he found that the courses did not have an effect on globalmindedness, except when level of classroom discussion—or climate—was taken into account. However, Yocum cautioned, even then the differences were substantively minimal; to bring about substantial change may demand more intense and lengthy interventions.

Summary. When attention to the triple variables of content, pedagogy, and climate results in presenting content from multiple perspectives, using interactive pedagogical strategies, and maintaining an open classroom climate, then essential ingredients for effective issues-centered instruction in global education, as well as in other social studies content areas, appear to be present. In particular, there is some evidence that students may increase in their knowledge of global issues and in attitudes of globalmindedness and concern for global issues. When they have the opportunity to actively engage in decision making about global issues, they may develop a more complex understanding of the international arena and of global issues; they may also experience a reduction in stereotyping about other peoples and cultures. Given the recent interest in global education, it is hoped that there will soon be more research to add depth to understanding the ways in which global issues-centered instruction can be most effective.

Discussion and Questioning in Issues-Centered Teaching

Because the controversial nature of any issue can be confronted or avoided by the questions that a teacher asks and how a teacher responds to student comments and questions, research on questioning patterns and discussion is important to examine. The British educational philosopher David Bridges (1979) argued that primary attributes of a discussion are that understanding and judgment of the issue under consideration are developed, more than one point of view is offered, and participants are open to differing points of view. Bridges believed that discussion is an essential component of democracy because it reflects democratic values and processes including rationality, decision making, commitment to fairness, and respect for others' opinions, feelings, and interests.

Such discussion is particularly appropriate to issues-centered classes, whereas the more frequently found recitations will not achieve the goals Bridges identified. Numerous researchers have identified the predominance of recitation in social studies classes—and unfortunately, many well-intended teachers believe they are leading a discussion of an issue when they ask students questions about a reading, video, or current event

when in reality they are leading a recitation (Larsen and Parker 1994). During recitation the teacher seeks a known or correct answer. In their review of research on discourse and interaction in social studies classes, Wilen and White (1991) limited their use of the term discussion to discourse that does not include recitation. Citing Gage's 1969 definition, they highlighted features whereby a teacher engages "two or more learners in a cooperative examination and comparison of views in order to illuminate an issue and contribute to the learners' understanding" (Wilen and White 1991, 489). Wilen and White concluded from their synthesis of research that in true discussions, the pace slows, both student and teacher remarks are longer than in recitations, the tone drops to a quieter, more intimate one, and there are pauses. The sequence of speakers changes from teacher-student-teacher to more student-to-student interaction between teacher interventions.

To enhance the breadth and depth of student participation in issues-centered discussions, teachers can incorporate practices supported by research on questioning. Redirecting can be useful in increasing the number of students who participate in a classroom discussion—an important goal if one's rationale for issues-centered teaching is to prepare students for dialogue in a participatory democracy. For example, in a discussion of an issue, a teacher may, without first commenting on a student response, redirect a question to several students with such questions as, "Does anyone else have an idea or opinion about that?" "What do you think about that?" Also, teachers can use such nonverbal cues as eye contact to encourage additional students to enter a discussion. Probing—the use of either verbal or nonverbal cues to encourage students to elaborate—may also enhance issues-centered discussions.

Another point about questioning is troubling. Several researchers found that students from low socioeconomic status homes and those of low ability are less likely than their high ability and high socioeconomic peers to be asked high level, divergent, and evaluative questions—for which there is not a single right answer (Wilen and White 1991). Such a pattern is not only unjust but unwarranted because there is no evidence that low ability and low socioeconomic students are any less able than their peers to work effectively with issues-centered approaches. Indeed, such an approach may be particularly motivating for them and bring more students into discussions if teachers offer opportunities for all to reflect upon challenging and personally meaningful questions (Bickmore 1991, 1993; Curtis and Shaver 1980).

Finally, researchers distinguish discussions from "bull sessions" in which opinions are merely exchanged.[22] Roby (1988, 171, cited in Wilen and White 1991) claimed that when participants merely argue about the "rightness" of their ideas rather than thoughtfully "entertain[ing] the validity of more than one idea," they are not engaged in a discussion. A discussion, then, often requires a teacher to skillfully lead students to evaluate one another's comments with attention to evidence, logic, and consideration of consequences and values.

Effective discussions can occur in small groups—or "on-line" with computers as Torney-Purta (1990) observed—as well as in whole class sessions. Several chapters in this handbook present varied formats for effective discussion.

New Research Directions in Issues-Centered Instruction

Researchers are currently pursuing several additional lines of inquiry that are yielding insights relevant to issues-centered instruction. For example, because issues-centered instruction requires students to thoughtfully analyze complex issues without a single correct answer, recent research on dialectical thinking, problem solving, and thoughtfulness is relevant.

Parker and colleagues have applied the principle of scaffolding to help middle and high school students reason about public issues (Parker, Mueller, and Wendling 1989; Parker, McDaniel, and Valencia 1991). They have been successful in teaching students a process of dialectical thinking in which they interrogate a number of positions and supporting arguments including their own, and reflect upon the cognitive and affective processes they used in constructing their arguments and counterarguments. Thus, students develop critical thinking and metacognitive abilities that are needed to reason well about social, political, and economic issues. Additionally, Voss has conducted research on problem solving by experts and novices when they tackle social, economic, and political problems. Recently, Carretero and Voss (1994) have begun to direct their work toward learning and teaching in social studies. [23]

If one purpose for using an issues-centered approach is to develop students' higher-order thinking abilities in social studies, then the characteristics of classes and schools that are successful in promoting thoughtfulness will be instructive. In particular, educators who want to implement issues-centered instruction will gain insights from the work of Newmann (1991, 426) and his colleagues on social studies classrooms, departments, and schools that promote thoughtfulness (see *Theory and Research in Social Education* 19, no. 4 Fall, 1991). Further, in planning evaluations of their programs, they should take heed of Newmann's point that "success in meeting higher order challenges in a specific content area demands in-depth knowledge in the area, not simply general skills and dispositions." Perhaps future researchers investigating issues-centered instruction will be able to demonstrate greater effects on student thinking than did the early studies at Stanford, Indiana, Michigan, and Harvard if content-specific assessment instruments are used to measure high-level thinking and the treatment includes issues content, conflictual pedagogy, and a supportive classroom climate for the open, careful examination of controversial issues.

Another area that warrants further attention is one identified by Bickmore (1991) in her case studies of four classes. She noted than in classes with issues content and pedagogy as well as in the other classes, the vast majority of students most of the time did not speak up, initiate discussion, or participate in collective evaluation of ideas. She noticed that across all classes from one third to one half of the class "had learned a trick of invisibility." When students did speak in class, it was often in a drill format, filling in short answers to a teacher's convergent questions. Further studies are needed to determine whether issues-centered classes can be created that engage all students in the exploration of social issues. Bickmore's case studies also illustrate that diverse students in the same classroom experience issues-centered instruction differently and that even the most masterful issues-centered teachers face difficult challenges. Bickmore deliberately selected teachers in schools with mixed ethnic, economic, and ability levels so that she could attend to differential effects of the use of conflict on differing students. She noted, however, that she could only infer from her observations about the effects of the different teaching styles on particular students. Future researchers might shift the focus from classroom interaction to student information processing by analyzing student interviews. Thus, they could assess the different meanings diverse students make from issues-centered instruction.

Issues-centered educators, like all educators, can benefit from new research on the instructional implications of gender, race, ethnicity, and class. There is some indication that females and males have differing interests in and ways of thinking about public issues (Hahn 1996). Political socialization researchers have identified differing effects of race, class, and ethnicity on attitudes toward democratic participation. Researchers studying culturally sensitive pedagogy (Irvine 1990; Hollins, King, and Haymen 1994) point out that by making changes in content, pedagogy, and climate, educators can better help so-called minority youth perceive social studies as more personally meaningful. Researchers studying the outcomes and processes of issues-centered teaching in the future should pay much more attention to variables of gender, race, class, and ethnicity than they have done in the past.

Finally, with attention to the ways different students are affected by issues-centered instruction, researchers should investigate such instruction at the elementary school level and the long-term effects of issues-centered teaching over the school years. The ultimate question is whether individuals and a democratic society benefit when youth experience an issues-centered civic education. In the end, do they become reflective, participating adult citizens? The answer to that question remains the yet unfulfilled challenge of social studies teachers, curriculum developers, teacher educators, and researchers.

Conclusions

Despite the limited research evidence that is available, social studies educators who make a commitment to issues-centered instruction are likely to find that their students become more interested in the political arena, develop a greater sense of political efficacy and confidence, and become more interested in the issues that they have studied as well as knowledgeable about them. Moreover, when issues content, conflictual pedagogy, and an open classroom climate are combined, more students may participate in class discussions, and express more reflective thinking and in-depth understanding than they would otherwise. Furthermore, students are likely to enjoy social studies more and to perceive that

social studies instruction is useful for understanding the world around them. As readers build cases for the use of issues-centered curriculum, pedagogy, and climate in social studies classes, they should realize that insights gained from research in other settings can be helpful. With more issues-centered schools to study in the future, researchers can determine the long-term effects of such programs with diverse students in diverse settings. The benefits for students and society will be many, and teachers who use an issues-centered approach will find their work a stimulating and continuing challenge.

Acknowledgment

Thanks to Ann Angell, Patricia Avery, Beverly Armento, Lee Ehman, Anna Ochoa, Ronald VanSickle, and the four anonymous reviewers who read earlier drafts of this chapter and made helpful suggestions.

References

Angell, A. V., and P. G. Avery. "Examining Global Issues in the Elementary Classroom." *The Social Studies* 83 (May/June 1992): 113-17.

Armstrong, P. M. "The Effect of Global Studies Instructional Materials on Dimensions of the Global Attitudes of Middle School Students." Ph.D. diss., Indiana University, 1979. Abstract in *Dissertation Abstracts International* 40 (1979): 3731A.

Avery, P. G., K. Bird, S. Johnstone, J. L. Sullivan, and K. Thalhammer. "Exploring Political Tolerance with Adolescents." *Theory and Research in Social Education* 20 (1992): 386-420.

Avery, P. G., Sullivan, J. L., and others. *Tolerance for Diversity of Belief.* Boulder, CO: Social Science Education Consortium, 1993.

Baughman, J. E. "An Investigation of the Impact of Civics on Political Attitudes of Adolescents. Ph.D., diss., University of Maryland, 1975. Abstract in *Dissertation Abstracts International* 36 (1975): 3974A-75A.

Bickmore, K. "Practicing Conflict: Citizenship Education in High School Social Studies." Ph.D. diss., Stanford University, 1991. Abstract in *Dissertation Abstracts International* 52-09A (1991): 3239A.

Bickmore, K. "Learning Inclusion/Inclusion in Learning: Citizenship Education for a Pluralistic Society." *Theory and Research in Social Education* 21 (1993): 341-84.

Blankenship, G. "Classroom Climate, Global Knowledge, Global Attitudes, Political Attitudes." *Theory and*

Research in Social Education 18 (1990): 363-84.

Bridges, D. *Education, Democracy, and Discussion.* Oxford, England: NFER Publishing Company Ltd., 1979.

Broudy, R. A. "Secondary Education and Political Attitudes: Examining the Effects on Political Tolerance of the We the People Curriculum." Paper presented at the meeting of the Comparative and International Education Society, San Diego, March 1994.

Carretero, M., and J. F. Voss, ed. *Cognitive and Instructional Processes in History and the Social Sciences.* Hillsdale: Erlbaum, 1994.

Cousins, J. E. "The Development of Reflective Thinking in an Eighth Grade Social Studies Class." *Bulletin of the School of Education, Indiana University* 39, no. 3, (1963): 36-73.

Cox, C. B., "Description and Appraisal of a Reflective Method of Teaching United States History." *Bulletin of the School of Education, Indiana University* 39, no. 3, (1963): 74-112.

Curtis, C. K., and J. P. Shaver. "Slow Learners and the Study of Contemporary Problems." *Social Education* 44 (1980): 302–9.

Duggan, S., D. Grossman, and S. Thorpe. "Curriculum Content, Instructional Strategies, and Classroom Climate: Classroom Observations of Global Education." Paper presented at the annual meeting of the American Educational Research Association, San Francisco, April 1986.

Ehman, L. H. "An Analysis of the Relationships of Selected Educational Variables with the Political Socialization of High School Students." *American Educational Research Journal* 6 (1969): 559–80.

Ehman, L. H. "Normative Discourse and Attitude Change in the Social Studies Classroom." *The High School Journal* 54 (1970): 76–83.

Ehman, L. H. "The American School in the Political Socialization Process." *Review of Educational Research* 50 (1980a): 99–119.

Ehman, L. H. "Change in High School Students' Political Attitudes as a Function of Social Studies Classroom Climate." *American Educational Research Journal* 17 (1980b): 253–65.

Elsmere, R. T. "An Experimental Study Utilizing the Problem-Solving Approach in Teaching United States History." *Bulletin of the School of Education Indiana University* 39, no. 3 (1963): 114-139.

Gage, N. L. "Teaching Methods." In *Encyclopedia of Educational Research,* edited by R. L. Ebel, 1446-1458. London: Macmillan.

Goldenson, A. R. "An Alternative View about the Role of the Secondary School in Political Socialization: A Field Experimental Study of the Development of Civil Liberties Attitudes." *Theory and Research in*

Social Education 6, (1978): 44–72.

Goodlad, J. I. *A Place Called School: Prospects for the Future.* New York: McGraw Hill, 1984.

Grossman, D. L. "Educational Climates and Attitudes toward Dissent: A Study of Political Socialization of Conflict Norms in Adolescents." Ph.D. diss., Stanford University, 1975. Abstract in *Dissertation Abstracts International* 36 (1975/1976): 7980.

Gudmundsdottir, S. "Knowledge Use among Experienced Teachers." Ph.D. diss., Stanford University, 1988. *Dissertation Abstracts International* 49-12A (1988): 3688.

Hahn, C. L. *Comparative Perspectives on Citizenship Education.* Albany, NY: SUNY Press, forthcoming.

Hahn, C. L. "Gender and Political Learning." *Theory and Research in Social Education* 24 (1996): 8-35.

Hahn, C. L. "Classroom Climate: The Complementary Roles of Quantitative and Qualitative Data." Paper presented at the annual meeting of the National Council for the Social Studies, Washington, D. C., November 1991.

Hahn, C. L., and C. Tocci. "Classroom Climate and Controversial Issues Discussions: A Five Nation Study." *Theory and Research in Social Education* 18 (1990): 344–62.

Harwood, A. M. "Social Studies Classroom Climates and Students' Political Attitudes: Views from Three High School Civics Classes." Ph.D. diss., Emory University, 1991. Abstract in *Dissertation Abstracts International* 52-09A (1991): 3240.

Hollins, E. R., J. E. King, and W. C. Haymen, ed. *Teaching Diverse Populations.* Albany, N.Y.: State University of New York Press, 1994.

Hunt, M. P. and Metcalf, L. E. *Teaching High School Social Studies.* New York: Harper & Row.

Irvine, J. J. *Black Students and School Failure.* New York: Greenwood Press, 1990.

Johnston, J., E. Anderman, L. Milne, L. Klenk, and D. Harris. *Improving Civic Discourse in the Classroom: Taking the Measure of Channel One.* Research Report 4. Ann Arbor, Mich.: Institute for Social Research, University of Michigan, 1994.

Kehoe, J. "An Examination of Alternative Approaches to Teaching the Universal Declaration of Human Rights." *International Journal of Political Education* 3 (1980): 193–204.

Langton, K. P., and M. K. Jennings. "Political Socialization and the High School Civics Curriculum in the United States." *American Political Science Review* 62 (1968): 852–69.

Larsen, B., and W. Parker. "Teachers Conceptions of Discussion." Paper presented at the annual meeting of the American Educational Research Association,

New Orleans, April 1994.

Leming, J. S. "The Influence of Contemporary Issues Curricula on School Aged Youth." *Review of Research in Education* 18 (1992): 112–62.

Levin, M., F. M. Newmann, and D. W. Oliver. *A Law and Social Science Curriculum Based on the Analysis of Public Issues*. Final report project no. HS 058. Grant no. OE 310142. Washington, D.C.: U.S. Department of Health, Education, and Welfare, Office of Education, 1969.

Litt, E. "Civic Education, Community Norms, and Political Indoctrination." *American Sociological Review* 28 (1963): 69–75.

Long, S., and R. Long. "Controversy in the Classroom: Student Viewpoint and Educational Outcome." *Teaching Political Science* 2 (1975): 275–99.

Massialas, B. G., "Developing a Method of Inquiry in Teaching World History." *Bulletin of the School of Education, Indiana University* 39, no. 3 (1963): 1-35.

Massialas, B. G., N. F. Sprague, and J. B. Hurst. *Social Issues through Inquiry*. Englewood Cliffs, N.J.: Prentice Hall, 1975.

Mason, M. "Pedagogical Content Knowledge: Case Studies of Expert World History Teachers." Diploma in Advanced Studies in Teaching thesis, Emory University, 1990.

McAlvin, D. W. "The Effect of Alternative Contents and Instructional Strategies on the Global Knowledge and Attitudes of Sixth and Ninth Grade Students." Ph.D. diss., Georgia State University, 1989. Abstract in *Dissertation Abstracts International* 51 (1989): 130A.

McNeil, L. M. *Contradictions of Control: School Structure and School Knowledge*. New York: Routledge, and Kegan Paul, 1986.

Miller, J. "The Influence of High School Social Studies Courses on Young Adult Political Participation." Paper presented at the annual meeting of the American Educational Research Association, Chicago, April 1985.

Newmann, F. "Classroom Thoughtfulness and Students' Higher Order Thinking: Common Indicators and Diverse Social Studies Courses." *Theory and Research in Social Education* 19 (1991): 410–33.

Oliver, D. W., and J. P. Shaver. *Teaching Public Issues in the High School*. Boston: Houghton-Mifflin Co., 1966.

Parker, W. C., M. Mueller, and L. Wendling. "Critical Reasoning on Civic Issues." *Theory and Research in Social Education* 17 (1989): 7–32.

Parker, W. C., J. E. Mc Daniel, and S. W. Valencia. "Helping Students Think about Public Issues." *Social Education* 55 (1991): 41–44, 67.

Quillen, I. J., and L. A. Hanna. *Education for Social Competence*. New York: Scott Foresman and Company, 1948.

Remy, R. C. "High School Seniors' Attitudes toward Their Civics and Government Instruction." *Social Education* 36 (1972): 590–97, 622.

Roby, T. W. "Models of Discussion." In *Questioning and Discussion: A Multidisciplinary Study*, edited by J. T. Dillon, 163-191. Norwood, NJ: Ablex, 1988.

Rossi, J. A. "In-Depth Study in an Issues-Oriented Social Studies Classroom." *Theory and Research in Social Education* 23 (1995): 88-120.

Schug, M. C., R. J. Todd, and R. Berry. "Why Kids Don't Like Social Studies." *Social Education* 48 (1984): 382–87.

Shaughnessy, J. M., and T. M. Haladyna. "Research on Student Attitude toward Social Studies." *Social Education* 49 (1985): 692–95.

Shaver, J. P., O. L. Davis Jr., and S. W. Helburn. "The Status of Social Studies Education: Impressions from Three NSF Studies." *Social Education* 43 (1979): 150–53.

Smith, V. A. "The Effects of a Global Studies Course on the International Attitudes of Junior High Students." Ph.D. diss., Indiana University, 1977. Abstract in *Dissertation Abstracts International* 38 (1977): 5388A.

Soley, M. "The Effects of Global Studies Curriculum on the Perspective Consciousness Development of Middle School Students." Ph.D. diss., Indiana University, 1982. Abstract in *Dissertation Abstracts International* 43 (1982): 2626A.

Torney-Purta, J. "Political Socialization." In *Citizenship for the 21st Century*, edited by W. T. Callahan Jr. and R. A. Banaszak, 171–98. Bloomington, Ind.: ERIC Clearinghouse for Social Studies/Social Science Education, 1990.

Torney-Purta, J., and D. Lansdale. "Classroom Climate and Process in International Studies: Qualitative and Quantitative Evidence from the American Schools and the World Project, Stanford and the Schools Study." Paper presented at the annual meeting of the American Educational Research Association, San Francisco, April 1986.

Wilen, W. W., and J. White. "Interaction and Discourse in Social Studies Classrooms." In *Handbook of Research on Social Studies Teaching and Learning*, edited by J. P. Shaver, 483–95. New York: Macmillan, 1991.

Wineburg, S., and S. M. Wilson. "Models of Wisdom in the Teaching of History." *Phi Delta Kappan* (1988): 50-58.

Yocum, M. J. "An Investigation of the Effects of a Global Education on the Attitudes of High School Students." Ph.D. diss., Michigan State University,

1989. Abstract in *Dissertation Abstracts International* 50, no. 3 (1989): 620A.

Zevin, J. "Future Citizens: Children and Politics. *Teaching Political Science* 10 (1983): 119–26.

[1] Students who believed that students had a right to express their opinions in class liked their class, and some felt their teacher was one of the best they ever had. However, those who gave little credence to student expression and who did not like to participate in class discussions were more negative in their evaluations.

[2] Examining the perspectives of teachers such as Ken may help us to understand why the majority of teachers do not use an issues-centered approach. Ken wanted all students to be successful, and he did not want to embarrass slow students, so he was careful not to give students tasks that would be too difficult for them. For that reason, on most days Ken had students work independently reading or doing worksheets, and once a week they heard a speaker or viewed a film. Social studies knowledge was presented as "unchanging fragments of neutral data" (Bickmore 1991, 95).

[3] The sample for this study consisted of 465 students in five schools with predominantly white populations in western states. Instruments developed by the staff of the Eight Year Study of Progressive Education were used to measure critical thinking and social attitudes, whereas standardized tests of U.S. history and contemporary issues information were used to measure knowledge. The criteria set for "significant growth" was the gain in mean score for a treatment group on the posttest over the pretest mean, which, if divided by the standard error of that difference, would yield a critical ratio of three or more, indicating that the difference was too great to be due to chance (Quillen and Hanna 1948, 156). Students in treatment groups were matched by intelligence, age, reading ability, and socioeconomic background.

[4] Interestingly, the researchers said they thought that the competence of the teacher was more important to the use of the problems approach than was the subject matter or the age of the students (178–79). Having rated all teachers on a checklist of teaching behaviors, they noted that the U. S. history teachers were not as strong in their teaching ability as were those who taught the seniors, and it was the authors' judgment that the problems approach requires superior teaching. The report of the Stanford Research project did not include specific descriptions of the eight classes that were studied so it is not possible to determine whether the three treatment groups varied in the controversial nature of content that was presented, in the number of positions or perspectives considered on an issue, or the extent to which students were encouraged to

express their opinions. Those features of issues-centered instruction may have been more difficult to implement in a problems approach where the content was history than in a course designed to focus on social problems.

[5] Subjects in three of the Indiana studies were students in the university laboratory school; those in the fourth study attended another high school in the state. The four researchers administered pretests in September and posttests in December or January; one further administered a delayed posttest 12 weeks after the conclusion of the treatment.

[6] The t-test differences between pretest and posttest scores were 5.18 ($p < .01$) on the Watson-Glaser test, 4.90 ($p < .01$) on the teacher-designed test, and 5.18 ($p < .01$) on the standardized knowledge test. No comparison group was used.

[7] The t-test differences between experimental and comparison groups on the posttests were 10.09 ($p < .001$) on the problem-solving measure and 2.37 ($p. < .05$) on the knowledge test. On the delayed posttests, the t-test differences were 11.42 ($p < .001$) on the problem-solving test and 3.49 ($p < .01$) on the knowledge test.

[8] Differences between groups on the test of critical thinking were $t = 1.40$, $F(1.40)$ for the world history classes and $t = .37$, $F(1.27)$ for the U.S. history classes. Differences between groups on the knowledge tests were $t = .77$, $F(1.53)$ for the world history classes and $t = .29$, $F(1.34)$ for the U.S. history classes. Massialas speculated that it was possible that the researchers serving as the teacher for both treatments, and possibly inadvertently using the same approach with both groups, could have accounted for the finding of no difference on the standardized instruments.

[9] On the open-ended SIAT, the project group performed substantially higher than the comparison group (experimental group mean 48.6, s. d. 13.6 compared to a mean of 34.8 for the comparison group).

[10] The differences between the groups were: for the written analysis of an issue, Beta .28, $p. < .001$ and on the current events knowledge measure, Beta .21, $p < .001$.

[11] On the critical thinking test, adjusted posttest means for the experimental and comparison groups, respectively, were 27.12, and 22.96, Eta .03, $p < .01$. Means for dogmatism were 132.67 and 148.48, Eta .09, $p < .01$. Means for self-esteem were 132.67, 148.48, Eta .09, $p < .01$.

[12] In the closed-climate condition correlations for black and white students, respectively, were: for political efficacy, -.20 and -.32; for participation -.30 and -.66; for citizen duty, -.39, -52; and for political cynicism -.05, and .45.

[13] In the open-climate condition, the correlations between climate and citizen duty were .13 for blacks and .24 for whites. Additionally, for blacks, the correlations between open climate and political efficacy, participation,

and cynicism, respectively, were .29, .43, and -.28.

[14] The correlations between open climate and political behaviors were .60 for junior high media use and .40 for senior high discussions with friends and family; all other correlations were .10 to.31. Contrary to other studies, however, Long and Long found a negative correlation between issues discussion and political efficacy (-.24 for junior high and -.27 for senior high school students). That they did not ask whether teachers maintained a neutral position regarding issues nor whether students felt comfortable expressing opinions may hold the key to the apparently contradictory findings.

[15] The correlation between toleration of dissent and participation in dissent activities was .11. However, students' perceptions of freedom to express their views in class had only a negligible positive correlation with toleration of dissent (.07).

[16] To measure the effects of the curriculum on ninth-grade students, the researchers administered pretests, posttests, and delayed posttests to experimental and comparison groups in two rural schools with predominantly white populations and one urban school where the population was 44 percent people of color. The difference between the experimental and comparison groups' change scores on the Political Tolerance Scale was p=.002, effect size .15. On the delayed posttests, the mean tolerance scores of the experimental group students remained higher than their mean pretest scores (p= .000, effect size .63), but neither their dislike of their least-liked group nor their threat perception changed significantly (p=.755, effect size .04). That is, although they still did not like a group and believed they were dangerous, they were willing to extend rights to the group.

[17] The experimental group consisted of 861 students in 30 classes that used the text *With Liberty and Justice for All*, produced by the staff of the *We the People* project. Comparison group students (n=490) were in U.S. history or government classes taught by members of the National Council for the Social Studies who were not using the same text. The differences between groups for support of free speech, assembly, and due process, respectively, were t= 6.85, 5.38, and 2.56. The differences for political efficacy and political interest, respectively were t=6.32 and t=8.51.

[18] Armstrong (1979) and Smith (1977) found no effects on student attitudes, comparing students exposed to two or more units in the Global Studies Project developed at Indiana University. Soley (1982), on the other hand, did find that middle school students who completed six units of the Global Studies in Geography Project (also based at Indiana University) exhibited reduced levels of ethnocentrism and increased ability to recognize that others in various cultures have perspectives different from

their own. McAlvin (1989) compared students exposed to *The Developing World* program developed by staff of the World Bank to students exposed to a more traditional area studies approach to geography. She concluded that neither content, strategies, nor grade level significantly affected posttest attitude scores (148). The data with regard to knowledge gains were inconclusive, varying depending on grade level, ability group, methods, and content used. Because the researchers did not report observational data on how the various curricula were actually implemented, it is not possible to determine whether or not issues-centered content was taught in such a manner that students confronted issues, weighed alternatives, and expressed their opinions in an open climate.

[19] The differences between the two treatment groups and the comparison group saying that contraventions were wrong were t=2.20, p<.03 and t=2.59, p<.01. Students in the investigation group scored significantly higher on knowledge of the law than did students in either the discussion or control group (t=3.95, p<.01, t=4.65, p<.01). Students in the discussion group were more accepting of customs that were not contraventions of the Universal Declaration than were students in the control group (t=2.53, p<.01).

[20] At the conclusion of a semester-long course in one southeastern metropolitan area, students completed questionnaires measuring their global knowledge and global attitudes. Additionally, Blankenship analyzed teachers' daily logs and observers' checklists. Two observations were made in each class to assess climate and how the issues-centered program was taught. The correlation between climate and attitudes, as measured by the questionnaires, was .32. The mean score on the classroom climate scale was 4.6 on a 6-point Likert scale, leading one to believe that students perceived the climate to be relatively open. However, observers noted that, when they were present, most class time was spent in lecture and recitation rather than in open discussion.

[21] For knowledge: Betas .22, p<.001, .13, p<.001; and for attitudes: Betas .16, p<.01, .09, p<.01.

[22] The research conducted by Massialas and his colleagues at the University of Michigan distinguished between opining and inquiry classes for that reason (Massialas et al. 1975).

[23] Other research on learning theory is applicable to issues-centered instruction as well as to other approaches to social studies. The chapter on issues-centered economics instruction by Armento, Rushing, and Cook in this handbook demonstrates the use of learning principles related to motivation, prior knowledge, and restructuring of existing schema.

Part Two: Reflective Teaching Strategies

Introduction by Byron G. Massialas

This section deals with teaching methods and attendant curriculum concerns in reflectively analyzing social issues in the classroom. Each of the contributors offers an instructional model or a curricular paradigm which has over the years withstood the test of time.

In presenting their respective instructional models, the contributors share a number of common characteristics. First of all, they believe that the classroom should be a microsociety where democratic concepts and methods prevail. Instruction is connected to learning in an environment which emphasizes student direct participation in discussion and related activities. Social issues form the focus of instruction and learning. These issues stem from inconsistencies in our culture, inconsistencies in which our classroom participants have a personal stake. All contributors emphasize the method of reflection, i. e., the method which one employs in order to subject the issue at hand to critical analysis. This analysis includes the application of such skills as defining key concepts, probing the evidential base of assertions and knowledge claims, identifying and articulating positions, clarifying values which underlie positions, and tracing the consequences of acting on these positions, etc. Finally, the contributors agree that the organized disciplines of knowledge, e. g. anthropology, history, political science, geography, sociology, economics, psychology, play an important role in the process of examining values.

The section opens with a chapter on criteria for selecting issue-based content. It is followed by chapters dealing with reflective teaching methodologies and related activities. The chapter on content selection by Byron Massialas clearly makes the case that social issues should form the center of classroom learning and instruction.

Recent changes in the social structure of the school and the influence of the hidden curriculum more or less compel teachers to deal with issues directly and systematically. Content is thus considered to be emerging as various cultural inconsistencies or social issues envelop the students and their teachers into emotional confrontations. The values school actors bring to the classroom form the springboard of a curriculum which is based on experience as its core. In this context, selection of content is predicated on the application of five key criteria—relevance, reflection, action, practicality, and depth of understanding. The end result of instruction based on this type of curriculum is reasoned social action.

The chapter by Rodney Allen on the Engle-Ochoa model exemplifies a decision-making classroom procedure for resolving social problems, contemporary or historic. Probing questions on the part of all classroom participants form the heart of the reflective process of decision making—questions seeking definition, evidence, speculation or policy recommendations. One of the results of this reflective process is to arrive at a reasoned solution of the initial problem to be followed, to the extent possible, with political action, i.e., "to exercise political influence toward implementing justifiable decisions..."

The jurisprudential or public issues approach conceptualized by Oliver and Shaver (chapter by Laurel Singleton and James Giese) presents another model for classroom instruction on social issues. The model is centered on policy issues which are controversial, i.e., conflicting values underlie the various positions. The goal is to systematically analyze the policies and the related values. A type of Socratic exchange is normally implemented in the classroom to clarify meaning and identify authoritative sources of evidence to justify participants' positions on public concerns. All this exchange takes place in a democratically organized classroom environment. In this environment students learn to respect each other and to carefully reason out the controversial issues at hand.

The social inquiry model conceptualized by Massialas and Cox (as rendered by Jo Ann Sweeney and Stuart Foster) draws from John Dewey's complete act of thought in dealing with issues or indeterminancies in one's culture. Springboards generated by all classroom participants create the problematic situation—a situation which fosters the application of such inquiry processes as hypothesizing, defining, exploring, evidencing, and generalizing. Validation of hypotheses or confirmation of a solution to a problem is the end-in-view of classroom deliberations. The ultimate goal of this deliberation classroom process is, as quoted by the authors, for students "to outline steps to be taken, roads to be traveled, utilizing both analytic and creative processes and skills." The lesson on the issue of allowing a student to have a "pony tail" in school is an example of how the process of social inquiry can be implemented in the classroom.

The chapter on critical pedagogy and social education by Cleo Cherryholmes further elaborates and makes salient the critical skills needed by individuals to understand and meet the challenges of their environment. It is argued that students need to probe deeply into assertions which make knowledge-claims, whether these are offered by teachers, a textbook author, a curriculum guideline, courses of study, or tests. By clarifying the language used in daily classroom communications and by critically analyzing the implicit values in these exchanges, students and their teachers begin to control their political and social environment rather than being controlled by it.

The chapter by Joseph Onosko and Lee Swenson on designing issue-based units offers suggestions on how to gather materials and related activities so that issues can be systematically and reflectively examined in class. The lesson should begin with a good central issue, an issue which would meet such criteria as whether or not the issue is important, debatable, manageable, reasearchable, memorable and interesting. A well thought out springboard (a unit grabber) should motivate students to engage in higher order thinking. The important idea that teachers con-structing an issues-centered unit need to remember is to avoid delivery of a "fragmented" lesson.

The chapter on discussion methods by Ron Evans and Jeff Passe seeks to synthesize ideas on how to apply various discussion-generating techniques in the classroom. The authors offer concrete examples on how classroom participants can engage in fruitful exchanges on social issues.

5 CRITERIA FOR ISSUES-CENTERED CONTENT SELECTION

by Byron G. Massialas

As I have argued elsewhere (Massialas 1989), individual and social problems have recently penetrated the walls of schools willy-nilly. In the past, schools were children's sanctuaries where they were protected from the ills and conflicts of the larger society. The school presented a Pollyanna view of life, and traditional textbook-based content was an effective tool in separating school from real life. Teachers taught social studies—especially world and U.S. history and geography—either as a chronology of events or as a list of places on a map that students committed to memory for future use.

In this traditional environment, youth's daily pressing issues—drugs, possession and use of weapons in schools, teenage pregnancies, transmission of venereal diseases and other sexually transmitted diseases, including AIDS, to name a few—were, and continue to be, ignored. Social problems have now become part of school life. Yet as surveys indicate, educators are reluctant to accept the fact that the school as a sanctuary has been violated. They are reluctant to propose changes in the curriculum to address the burning issues that the students bring to school from the larger social environment. (Hahn 1991)

I believe that the systematic study of social issues should be the core of the school program, and selecting the content for such a curriculum is critical. The traditional disciplines must only provide a resource for the reflective analysis of social and personal issues. Reflective emphasis on issues would give students rational and democratically based models to cope with the inevitable conflict and controversy in their lives.

The Individual, Social Issues, and the Hidden Curriculum

In 1955, Hunt and Metcalf proposed that schools develop curricula based on a catalog of "cultural inconsistencies," namely, deeply seated beliefs held by groups in a society that are different from each other, especially in the "closed areas" of subjects that are considered taboo in the classroom (sexuality, etc.). Educators thought this an unrealistic proposal. Today, more than forty years later, their proposal makes more sense than ever. First of all, we know that very little or no learning takes place unless the individual is involved personally in the topic of presentation or discussion. It is very difficult to imagine how a presentation of the Hundred Years War or the Napoleonic Wars, by itself, will aid students in resolving problems they bring to class that day. Very rarely will the teacher connect a description of the European wars with a contemporary problem.

Another reason for focusing on social issues or cultural inconsistencies is that students, teachers, and other school personnel are inescapably involved with them. As numerous studies have indicated, the "hidden curriculum" significantly influences school learning. Factors connected with race, ethnicity, gender, socioeconomic status, and linguistic background—the basic staples of the hidden curriculum—as well as classroom psychological milieu, make an important difference in what is learned, how it is learned, and for what purposes. For example, students learn to be apathetic, dependent on authority, accepting of the structural inequity of the American economic system, and passive in adopting second-class citizenship roles in society (Goodlad 1984; Bowles and Gintis 1976; Anyon 1988; Apple 1988; Giroux and Penna 1979; Dreeben 1968). Because passivity and dependence is forced onto them, minorities are usually negatively affected by the hidden curriculum. Memory work is typically emphasized with minority students. On the other hand, the hidden curriculum usually supports students of the mainstream, as they learn, through it, the values of leadership and independence. Critical thinking is typically emphasized with mainstream students. Obviously, the content of the hidden curriculum is tantamount to the content of the social issues curriculum.

The hidden curriculum reflects the social cleavages, the cultural inconsistencies, and the social controversies of society. If students were to systematically study the social structure of their school instead of the structure of knowledge of each subject, they would be involved directly in social issues instruction. In this sense, the school does not need to fabricate individual or social problems. The problems are part of the school's natural setting. These are real problems in the Deweyan sense, since all students are experiencing difficulties that must be overcome. Isn't it appropriate that these problems and issues, largely stemming from the hidden curriculum, be subjected to systematic study and critical analysis resulting in reasoned action? The springboards and the data of reflection are there, but are school people willing to use them as the prime content of instruction?

Selecting Issues Content

The traditional way educators select social studies content for instruction in today's classrooms is dysfunctional. Traditional curriculum building is based on the disciplines of knowledge—history and the various social sciences. The content of these disciplines is, for the most part, devoid of issues or problems that are of utmost importance to individual students and their communities.

Hunt and Metcalf (1955, 214) drew a significant distinction between content based on the scholarly disciplines of the social sciences and reflective content:

the content of reflection—in contrast to the content of history, political science, geography, and so on—includes every relevant aspect of the mental and physical environment in which a given act of thought occurs, everything a thinker brings to bear on a problem.

In *How We Think,* John Dewey (1933) reasoned that an act of thought begins when an individual experiences a felt need. He or she then moves on to explore alternative solutions to the difficulty, projecting and testing implications and logical consequences. During the process of thinking, the individual draws upon relevant resources, including previous personal experiences as well as information contained in the traditional social sciences. In this process, "content assumes an *emergent* character. From the standpoint of a learner, it comes into existence as it is needed; it does not have a life independent of its own" (Hunt and Metcalf 1955, 215).

When educators prepare to select social issues content, they will discover a significant distinction between content in the traditional discipline-based mode and emergent content. The content in state- or district-approved textbooks best represents the traditional mode. How much of this content is pertinent to solving the problems that occur in students' daily lives? The relevance of the textbook's content to students' felt difficulties apparently varies, depending on the subject. For example, sociological content might be more relevant than historical content. In all cases, however, prepackaged material— presented as if it were the product of scholarly research in the field but "simplified for pedagogical purposes"—does not, by itself, fulfill the individual's need to solve immediate problems. These problems might be thought of as personal, but, as Hunt and Metcalf (1955, 220) point out, they are usually results "of problem-generating features of the culture." For example, an unemployed person may struggle with his or her personal finances, but unemployment stems from a larger societal problem as well as regional or local employment and production policies. Traditional texts and other prepackaged materials rarely address these personal and societal needs.

The emergent content mode focuses on societal and personal problems. Because content is not static, it emerges from the social context where individuals interact with each other. Content comes not only from the curriculum and the textbooks, but from the experience of students and teachers interacting through classroom discussion.

Proposed Criteria for Content Selection

I suggest five key criteria for content selection: relevance, reflection, action, practicality, and depth of understanding.

1 THE CRITERION OF RELEVANCE.

Educators responsible for content selection must ask these key questions to determine relevance: How does the curriculum relate to the students and the social context in which they find themselves? In other words, is the content of daily classroom lessons, textbooks, videos, teacher presentations, student assignments and reports, or computer-generated programs related to the concerns of students as they go about making decisions in their lives, in and out of school? How does the curriculum of the classroom address an increasing number of students' concerns about safety in the schools? How does the curriculum relate to the concerns of minority students (especially, racial, ethnic, and linguistic minorities) who, *a priori*, are routinely considered the culprits in any order-disruption incidents? How does the curriculum relate to the career aspirations of young men and young women who are forced, primarily through the hidden curriculum, to avoid entering fields dominated by the opposite sex? How does the curriculum relate to problems encountered by children of single-parent families?

Questions on critical issues and problems of children and youth are numerous. The answer, in most cases, is that the curriculum as it presently exists has very little or no relevance to the burning issues of the students, issues many of which stem from larger societal issues. (Shaver 1989). Such issues and problems are extensions of current societal issues—gun control, schooling for minorities, employment opportunities for men and women, aid to dependent children, sex education in the schools, sexual harassment, etc.

Curriculum relevance could be achieved if such a criterion is applied. Traditional subject content would be used in class simply to provide the data and the arguments that relate to the issue at hand. In the issues-centered environment proposed here, prior experience of students would be part of the core material explored systematically.

2 THE CRITERION OF REFLECTION.

Educators responsible for content selection must ask these key questions to determine reflection: Does the content trigger thinking? Does the content engage the students in taking positions that can be explicitly grounded? Does the content (including the experiences of students) provide opportunities for all sides of the issue to be presented and critically analyzed? Are the materials that support different positions on the issue reliable? Are the student experiences generalizable?

Reflective content must open and not close discussion and rational thought. If it leads to indoctrination, as was the case of some courses such as "Americanism versus Communism," "Problems of American Democracy," or "Citizenship," then the opportunity for critical or reflective thinking is stifled. If reflection is limited to just some classroom participants, including the teacher, then the curriculum or the content item should be excluded from consideration altogether. The role of the teacher, of course, is pivotal in this type of classroom. The teacher must foster a climate that provides for an exchange of views on issues based on established rules of logic and evidence. In this environment, students begin to internalize the value that ideas and positions on issues are as good as the grounds that support them when presented in open forum. (Massialas, Sprague, Hurst 1975) Content and methods of learning and instruction are inseparable components of the process of reflective thinking.

3 THE CRITERION OF ACTION.

Educators responsible for content selection must ask these key questions to determine action: Will the inclusion of the curriculum item or springboard (whether from traditional sources, the emerging experiences of students in a social context, or both) be likely to result in some plan of action? In other words, will the critical and systematic analysis of the curriculum items at hand produce action? Or will the ringing of the bell terminate discussion and deliberation? For example, will a reflective discussion of safety in the schools lead to a class proposal to the school authorities for a schoolwide policy change on the matter? Will this proposal lend itself to a follow-up and actual student participation on matters concerning school safety including safety on school buses? Could this also be connected with issues of safety in the students' neighborhood?

While the content may lead to critical thinking, it is also necessary, if social conditions are to be changed in a desirable way, to lead to some social action. Social action that takes place as a result of reasoned deliberation is consistent with the principles of democracy that emphasize citizen participation and involvement in all matters of individual and public concern. Given the conflicts and cultural inconsistencies of our times, the social-issues curriculum can no longer be viewed as a source for purely academic debate without consideration for student and teacher involvement in the process of social change.

4 THE CRITERION OF PRACTICALITY.
Educators responsible for content selection must ask these key questions to determine practicality: Is the emerging curriculum or program of studies usable? Given the state of affairs in schools, where the traditional is emphasized and bureaucratically sustained, will change, as proposed here, be feasible? If administrators, teachers, and parents are not ready for a drastic change, should there be some accommodation or compromise? Are there some paradigms that provide students with the opportunity to focus on social issues within the confines of the traditional curriculum, subject by subject? Are appropriate resources—human and material—available to support the effort?

Even a meticulous construction of a curriculum based on a catalogue of "cultural inconsistencies" or social issues (Hunt and Metcalf 1955) would not ensure, by itself, its use in the classroom. The teacher must feel at ease with the issues before finding appropriate ways to include them in instruction, possibly within the context of traditional materials. Examples of ways to integrate social issues instruction with traditional subject-based content are available in the literature (Engle 1989; Hunt and Metcalf 1955; Massialas and Cox 1966; Oliver and Shaver 1966;1974). The realities of educational decision-making, as indicated by Shaver (1989), make the inclusion of this selection criterion important. The outcome of the movement to replace the traditional program with the New Social Studies is a glaring example of failure to consider practicality in curriculum planning (Massialas 1992).

5 DEPTH OF UNDERSTANDING. Educators responsible for selection must ask these key questions to determine depth of understanding: Does the curriculum promote or hinder reflection on perennial or persistent problems of humankind? Do the curriculum, and the teachers applying it, allow the classroom participants to connect the issue or problem at hand with relevant sources, sources that relate to similar occurrences experienced by people in different historical periods, cultures, or regions?

For example, issues related to immigration unavoidably concern a great number of students attending schools in the United States as well as in other parts of the world. In the United States, the recent influx of Haitians and Cubans into Florida brought the issue of immigration to the forefront and became a national concern. Both legal and illegal immigration affect the lives of children and youth in many parts of the country. Many students are either immigrants or are directly involved with children of immigrants and such issues and policies. Immigrants' housing, employment, education, and health, are all of vital concern to them. But other students have a key interest on the topic because immigration directly affects them as well. How will the new immigrants be absorbed by the local community? Will there be enough jobs for them, or will they displace others? Where will the new immigrants live? Where will the children of the new immigrants go to school? How will the new immigrants maintain their health? Will the new immigration create additional cleavages and conflicts in society? Should a policy of assimilation or multiculturalism be implemented?

The relevance of the topic to the lives of students makes it almost obligatory for its systematic treatment in the social studies classroom. At this point, in addition to current reports extracted from newspapers, magazines, radio and television broadcasts, and reports of personal experiences and observations, teachers may suggest that immigration, being a persistent occurrence worldwide, may be understood better by studying relevant historical events. For example, students may research historical sources including textbooks dealing with the new arrivals to the United States during the period 1880 to 1920. Where did the immigrants come from? What were their cultural backgrounds? Were their value systems, customs, mores, habits, and languages, in conflict or in harmony with those of the old residents of the new world? What were the consequences of this massive immigration for the new immigrants and for the old residents? What were the effects of the policy of assimilation on the new immigrants? Do we agree or disagree with such a policy and on what grounds? Should the same policy prevail today? What are some personal and social implications if the same policy prevails? What action can we personally or collectively take to change an immigration policy which we consider to be unfair? If we have taken action, what strategies have we employed? Were these strategies successful or unsuccessful? Explain.

As shown in the example above, it is obvious that linking a perennial problem of humankind, a problem that relates to a current personal and societal concern, to sources in history and the social sciences contributes to depth of understanding. The approach is also practical (meeting another criterion) because teachers unavoidably use commercial textbooks and other technology-generated materials in the classroom. These materials can provide a source of information to address what Engle and Ochoa (1988) refer to as definitional and evidential questions. The point to be made, however, is that classroom deliberation is a necessary but not sufficient condition to bring about social change. Action should always follow reflection and debate of the social issue at hand.

Curricular Frameworks

A curricular framework that selects content carefully, reflective of the criteria recommended here, is the Public Issues Series developed by the Harvard Social Studies Project (Oliver and Shaver 1966; 1974). The Harvard Project's curriculum focused on the analysis of public controversy and used inquiry-type approaches to probe into recurring policy issues in U.S. history. Materials were prepared in the form of curriculum units with case studies relating to a particular topic and period in U.S. history. For example, a unit on the rise of organized labor (American Education Publications [AEP] 1967) raised questions about employer-employee relations in the context of the public interest and traces these relations from the beginning of U.S. industry to the 1966 airlines strike. Basic questions include: "How free should an employee be to conduct his business as he sees fit? How far do workers' personal rights extend?" (AEP 1967, back cover) Each case study or springboard that the booklet presents is accompanied by a section on "Persisting Questions of History." These questions ask students to take a position on various management-labor issues in the context of U.S. history. For example, "Is it fair to organize a slowdown of workers at the time the company is working on a major order?" (35) Thus while students bring to the forefront their personal values, they also consider various precedents in U.S. society and cul-

ture. U.S. constitutional principles, especially those focusing on individual freedom and human dignity, provide a methodological framework for analyzing the public issues at hand. The Harvard group's approach may be thought of as a "curriculum infusion approach" where the traditional content of the social studies, best represented by the adopted textbooks, is infused with motivating springboards that raise significant value questions, the answers to which have important personal and societal implications. The study in-depth of history or government centers around the study of significant public issues.

Another curriculum framework that systematically develops a program of studies focusing on social issues is that of Hunt and Metcalf (1955; 1968). These authors envisage that selection of content in the social studies should be based on

1. the problematic or controversial areas of the culture (the closed areas);
2. the individual beliefs, values, and knowledge of students; and
3. related data from the social sciences. (1968, 288)

Drawing from all of these sources, a "core" curriculum can be formed that is "problem centered, and organized on the basis of a series of apparent contradictions in belief in problematic areas of the culture which we might expect to be shared by most students." (Hunt and Metcalf 1968, 291) In 1968, the authors identified seven broad problematic areas of culture, acknowledging that there could be more. These areas were: power and the law; economics; nationalism, patriotism, and foreign affairs; social class; religion and morality; race and minority-group relations; sex, courtship, and marriage. Each problematic area would be organized in sequence and would constitute blocks of time in the social studies program. Two or three of these specialized core areas would be studied each year. From the practical standpoint, selection of a given problematic area of culture by the teacher should be based on several criteria including whether or not the topic is too controversial or "too touchy" for the local community and whether the teacher has competence in dealing with the subject. Naturally, the authors assume that the method of reflection would be applied in the classroom as the participants deliberate in suggesting possible solutions to the cultural problems at hand.

My own position for a defensible social issues curriculum framework is similar to that of Hunt and Metcalf with two possible exceptions. Certainly, we must attend systematically to the problematic areas of our culture delivered as a core social studies curriculum. But, as I argued earlier, since the school is no longer society's sanctuary but society's exact replica, we must select the content based on the critical issues pertinent to each school and its surrounding community. The issues-centered curriculum should begin with these issues since they are directly relevant to students' lives. Their treatment in the classroom should be expanded, however, to in-depth investigations of the larger societal problems. Is it a perennial problem of humankind? How is the problem treated in societies elsewhere, and how was it treated in the past? What were the conflicting points of view represented in the controversy and how were they rationalized? These questions would inescapably encourage classroom participants to look at sources from history and the social sciences in addition to their own experiences. How can the problem at hand be resolved? What are the alternatives and what are the consequences for actions on these alternatives? Against which standards should the choice of alternatives be measured? It is obvious that these types of questions would promote students' reflective thinking. The critical examination of these school-based issues in a larger societal context would increase students' decision-making competence as well as enhance the student's self concept and sense of social and political efficacy. Research in this area supports this conclusion (Hahn 1991).

The second point of departure from the Hunt and Metcalf curriculum model is the degree to which the program of studies encourages social action. As discussed in connection with the third criterion for the selection of content, reflection on issues, by itself, may not produce involvement and action. For example, why do minority students have proportionately more school suspensions than mainstream students? Is the practice just? Is it fair? What can be done about it? What action are we taking to change this condition? Has our action been successful? These are some of the questions that must be raised in order to prompt students, teachers, parents, administrators, and community leaders to act. Ongoing, responsible social action, then, is the ultimate goal of all social issues instruction. The curriculum should have a built-in mechanism whereby such action is encouraged and implemented. Naturally, the school-related issues, which as proposed here, form the basis of the core curriculum, are more prone to action than larger societal issues such as the issue related to a disproportionate number of minorities being dismissed in private businesses compared to members of the majority. The relative proximity of the social issue to all the actors involved in it, makes the school-generated, issues-centered curriculum a most appropriate instrument promoting in-depth analysis of a personal/social issue, reflection and commensurate social action.

The proposal for a school-derived, social issues curriculum stems from the assumption that the proper role of the teacher in the classroom is that of defensible partisanship, which Massialas and Cox (1966, 175) described:

> Defensible partisanship assumes that the teacher inevitably makes preferential choices among competing ethical alternatives and creates the conditions in the classroom for choices based on the most rational criteria. The teacher takes the position that methods of value analysis and discussion which are consistent with our democratic ideals produce the most defensible conclusions. Thus the teacher is partisan for selecting the method of inquiry as the most appropriate means to adjudicate values and for taking a stand on a social issue based on the process of inquiry.

Such a teacher is partisan in issues selection, but this partisanship, as in the actual treatment of issues, is always open to criticism and questioning. Since by definition issues are student-based, the teacher is mainly responsible in prioritizing and defending the sequence. If teachers accept the defensible partisan role, they would have to reject such traditional teacher roles as the uncritical perpetuator of the status quo, the indoctrinator, the teacher as impartial coordinator, or the role of functioning under conditions of ethical neutrality.

Given the rationale above, I have offered five key criteria for selecting content. This proposal assumes that content is not static, but rather emerges from the social context where individuals interact with each other. Relevance, reflection, action, practicality, and depth of understanding

Table 1: Criteria in Selecting Issues-Centered Content

Relevance
- Does the content relate to the students and the social context in which they find themselves?
- Is the content related to the concerns of students as they go about making decisions in their lives, both in and out of school?

Reflection
- Does the content trigger thinking?
- Does the content engage the students in taking positions that can be explicitly grounded?

Action
- Will the critical and systematic analysis of the content produce action?

Practicality
- Is the emerging content or program of studies usable?

Depth of Understanding
- Does the content promote or hinder reflection on perennial or persistent problems of humankind?

are critical criteria in developing a defensible issues-centered curriculum.

We are at a critical juncture in our educational development. There is consensus that school restructuring is necessary. Will this restructuring entail the restructuring of the curriculum to attend to the needs of children and youth confronted with an increasing number of conflicting cultural alternatives? Is the profession ready to assume leadership in this regard or will it be content to proceed on the mode of business as usual?

References

American Education Publications. *The Rise of Organized Labor.* Middletown, Conn.: American Education Publications, Public Issues Series/Harvard Social Studies Project, 1967.

Anyon, J. "Social Class and the Hidden Curriculum of Women." In *Curriculum: An Introduction to the Field,* edited by J.R. Gress, 366–89. Berkeley, Calif.: McCutchan, 1988.

Apple, M. W. "The Culture and Commerce of the Textbook." In *Curriculum: An Introduction to the Field,* edited by J. R. Gress, 390–407. Berkeley, Calif.: McCutchan, 1988.

Bowles, S., and H. Gintis. *Schooling in Capitalist America: Educational Reform and the Contradictions of Economic Life.* New York, N.Y.: Basic Books, 1976.

Dewey, J. *How We Think.* New York, N.Y.: D. C. Heath and Company, 1933.

Dreeben, R. *On What Is Learned in School.* Reading, Mass.: Addison-Wesley, 1968.

Engle, S. H. "Proposals for a Typical Issues-Centered Curriculum." *The Social Studies,* 80 (1989): 187–91.

Engle, S. H. and A. S. Ochoa. *Education for Democratic Citizenship: Decision Making in the Social Studies.* New York: Teachers College, Columbia University, 1988.

Giroux, H., and A. Penna. "Social Education in the Classroom: The Dynamics of the Hidden Curriculum." *Theory and Research in Social Education* 7(1979): 21–42.

Goodlad, J. I. *A Place Called School.* New York, N.Y.: McGraw-Hill, 1984.

Hahn, C. L. "Controversial Issues in Social Studies." In *Handbook of Research on Social Studies Teaching and Learning,* edited by J. P. Shaver, 470–80. New York, N.Y.: Macmillan Publishing Company, 1991.

Hunt, M. P., and L.E. Metcalf. *Teaching High School Social Studies: Problems in Reflective Thinking and Social Understanding.* New York, N.Y.: Harper and Brothers, 1955.

Hunt, M. P., and L.E. Metcalf. *Teaching High School Social Studies: Problems in Reflective Thinking and Social Understanding.* 2d. ed. New York, N.Y.: Harper and Brothers, 1968.

Massialas, B. G. "The Inevitability of Issues-Centered Discourse in the Classroom." *The Social Studies* 80 (1989): 173–75.

Massialas, B. G., and C. B. Cox. *Inquiry in Social Studies.* New York, N.Y.: McGraw-Hill, 1966.

Massialas, B. G. "The `New Social Studies'— Retrospect and Prospect." *The Social Studies* 83 (1992): 120–24.

Massialas, B. G., N. F. Sprague, and J. B. Hurst. *Social Issues through Inquiry: Coping in an Age of Crises.* Englewood Cliffs, N.J.: Prentice-Hall, 1975.

Oliver, D. W., and J. P. Shaver. *Teaching Public Issues in the High School.* 1966. Logan, Utah: Utah State University Press, 1974.

Shaver, J. P. "Lessons from the Past: The Future of an Issues-Centered Social Studies Curriculum." *The Social Studies* 80 (1989): 192–96.

Spener, D. "Traditional Bilingual Education and the Socialization of Immigrants". *Harvard Educational Review* 58 (1988): 133–53.

6 THE ENGLE-OCHOA DECISION MAKING MODEL FOR CITIZENSHIP EDUCATION

by Rodney F. Allen

SCENARIO

Mrs. Diaz's high school United States history class is beginning to study the agrarian movement that began after the Civil War and culminated in the Populist Party, influencing national elections in 1892 and 1896. The students elected to focus upon the movement in the Great Plains. Dividing into groups, student teams use different textbooks and references to gather information on the state of the agrarian economy on the Plains during this era. Their texts inform them about climate and weather patterns (drought), overexpansion of agricultural production on marginal farmland spawned by speculation and railroad development, decline in real farm income, and the resultant consequences for the quality of life. The students learned that the Depression of 1893, capping a decade of decline, brought wide spread economic distress and bitter feelings. Between 1889 and 1894, 11,000 Kansas farm families lost their lands through bank foreclosure; nine out of ten farms in Kansas and Nebraska changed hands, many lay abandoned for a decade. Many farm families were left homeless, while the number of tenant farmers, working others' land, doubled to more than two million.

Working with Mrs. Diaz, the students develop a bulletin board display of photocopied pictures showing life on the Great Plains in the 1880s and 1890s.. Adding to the pathos of this display, one group discovers the transcript of a letter written to Kansas Governor Lewelling on June 29, 1894, by a farmer's wife living in Mendota, Kansas (Kansas State Historical Society, Topeka):

Dear Governor
I take my Pen In hand to let you know that we are Starving to death. It is Pretty hard to do without any thing to Eat hear in this God for saken country[.] [[W]e would of had Plenty to Eat if the hail hadent cut our rye down and ruined our corn and Potatoes[.] I had the Prettiest Garden that you Ever seen and the hail ruined It and I have nothing to look at[.] My Husband went a way to find work and came home last night and told me that we would have to Starve[.] He has bin in ten countys and did not Get no work[.] It is Pretty hard for a woman to do with out any thing to Eat when She doesent no what minute She will be confined to bed[.] If I was In Iowa I would be all right[.] I was born there and raised there[.] I havent had nothing to Eat to day and It is three o clock[.] well I will close rite Soon From Mrs. Susan Orcutt

Mrs. Diaz is pleased with the students' response to the letter. They focus upon Mrs. Orcutt's desperation about the loss of control over her life and about her family's wellbeing. The quandaries of poor, debtor farmers on marginal Western land are made vivid by Mrs. Orcutt's words. One group tells Mrs. Diaz that they want to investigate Mrs. Orcutt's sense of isolation as a stranger in Kansas from Iowa. Why would she feel more secure in Iowa? What were the social support networks available to her there —and by implication to others in their native states in the 1890s? Was Robert Frost (1914) in "The Death of the Hired Man" right when he wrote that home "is the place where, when you have to go there, they have to take you in?" Mrs. Diaz knows that later, after students examine

Mrs. Orcutt's Kansas and Iowa, she can broaden their reflective inquiry to ask about familial and community obligations to "take in" their delinquent children, their elderly, their homeless, and others in despair.

A second group wants to examine Mrs. Orcutt's political acumen in writing to Governor Lewelling. What did she expect the governor to do in response to her plight? What did the laws of Kansas allow? What private resources might the governor muster? Why did Mrs. Orcutt write, in the 1890s, to the state governor rather than to her elected officials in the nation's capital city? Mrs. Diaz was especially pleased with this group's interest, because she was planning to turn to greater questions of the obligation of government to manage the economy and to take responsibility for the hardships and disasters which befall citizens, both economic and natural.

A third group declares its intention to focus upon agrarian protest through political organization. From their earlier studies, students inferred that agrarians would join together to seek relief by influencing, or even controlling, government. Students are interested in emerging political leadership and farmers' mastery of political participation skills. Again, Mrs. Diaz is pleased with her students' choice. As they examine this history, she will engage their attention in questions of legitimate and inappropriate protest and rebellion within a democratic credo. Under what conditions may people protest or rebel and with which appropriate strategies and force?

For this history class at Washington Park High School, cooperative inquiry initiates three groups' in-depth examinations of historic social problems, with contemporary analogues, where decisions must be made. Mrs. Diaz's students will use personal experience and knowledge from history, social sciences and the humanities to reflect upon the nature of the problems, the policy options open to decision makers and the consequences of the option chosen and justified in dialogue with one another.

Shirley H. Engle and Anna S. Ochoa (1988) created their decision-making model to help students and their teachers link social studies teaching and learning to democratic ideals. They realize that democratic societies are beset with grievous problems and disharmonies, but the systematic, in-depth examination of these problems and reflection upon social conflicts are the best preparation for mature participation in any democracy. Conflicts, problems, and issues are not only the test of democratic government, they are the whetstone of democratic citizenship education. The Engle-Ochoa decision-making model requires students to identify and carefully define socio-civic problems, to use multiple sources of information, to reflect upon value assumptions and diverse perspectives, to lay out alternative solutions or courses of action, and to make choices and justify those choices with reference to their grasp of democratic values.

Philosophical Orientation

The most basic value of democracy, according to Engle and Ochoa (1988), is respect for the dignity of the individual. With this declaration, Engle and Ochoa begin to reveal their conception of democracy in the Western liberal tradition, grounded in limited government, individual liberty, and active participation. In this tradition, representative government requires a citizenry capable of knowing and doing the public good; the people must have the civic intelligence necessary to maintain a democratic society. When individuals know and do the public good, they are not performing individual acts, but engaging in shared public practices. Citizens learn and relearn public virtues and civic values in social contexts by interacting in a community with others. The learning of civic values and patterns of curbing self-interest for a common good are wrought through interactions with fellow citizens who feel a common political kinship, or what Wilson Cary McWilliams (1973) calls the idea of fraternity. In this tradition, citizens are committed to acting in ways which preserve *community*, local to national to global, an expanding sense of others, bound over to one's self in a common life, where self-interest is curbed out of regard for others. The individual is known to exist, function, and thrive, only in a democratic social context.

Citizenship education for Engle and Ochoa is decidedly political education. They expect teachers and schools to model democratic values and behavior in their treatment of students, in the open exploration of issues, and in their organization of students for learning. The classroom and the school should be a *community* where learners democratically engage in the study of conflict and the active rational discussion of problems, where persons may disagree and debate different points of view.

Schools and social studies programs are perceived as sterile, inane, and oppressive (Engle, 1977) and as failing to deal rigorously with current social problems (Engle, 1960, 1985). Traditional social studies curricula are no longer relevant to helping students cope as informed and active citizens in a changing society. Social education focused upon single disciplines, rather than social concerns, is perceived as unconscionable (Engle and Longstreet, 1972). Social studies should address the solving of social problems, and not impose political bias on students or engage them in the slavish mastery of information.

In another paper, Engle (1986b) suggested that social studies educators have rejected issues-oriented teaching because teachers are comfortable teaching as they were taught (including what they were taught). This leaves them incompetent to deal democratically with controversy and uncertainty. Teachers and school leaders can avoid conflict by textbook teaching, remote from the life experience of learners and their parents. Textbook publishers thrive on the expository method, while exposition and textbooks are fixed in the constellations of conventional thinking among parents and elected officials who influence curriculum (see Apple, 1993). Engle (1986a) observed: "Ancient beliefs hold that education means that elders instruct the young, not that they work out problems together."

Seeing education as the process of enculturation, Engle and Ochoa (1988) argue for a political education within the social studies curriculum which provides socialization into the ideas of democratic culture and a *counter-socialization* which builds critical capacity, political skills, and a profound skepticism into the civic dispositions of learners. Problem solving, reflective inquiry and critical thinking are both instructional activities and instructional goals in schools which take their civic education duties seriously. Henry Giroux (1988) used the concept "emancipatory rationality" to capture the essence of Engle and Ochoa's intensive regard for schooling which liberates through reflective inquiry on social problems while building commitment to the core values which hold democratic communities together.

Ever more threatening to the *status quo* in schooling, Engle and Ochoa (1988) want a reflective inquiry which does not simply lead to further inquiry. Their proposal expects an issues-centered inquiry which engages learners in policy recommendations, and grants them free choice in avenues for learning. They want schools to be launching grounds not only for learning and the development of democratic commitments: they anticipate students participating in community life, including politics (Engle, 1972). To expect action is not to determine what the action should be. Their conception of citizenship education, which rejects conventional school textbook and curriculum impositions, does not impose specific participation or actions as educational outcomes.

The origins of the Engle-Ochoa conception of citizenship education are to be found in the Deweyan notion of reflective inquiry (Dewey, 1933; Griffin, 1992). Dewey urged educators to open sensitive areas of social life to responsible examination and to educate, not by exposition, but with an interactive teacher-student dialogue, wherein facts, inferences, generalizations, and conclusions would be questioned by students as well as their teachers. Dewey advocated the study of real social problems reflectively so as to be inclusive of the students' concerns and experiences. Recognizing that so much of school learning was disconnected from students' experience, Dewey urged the study of social problems to better insure connectedness to students' experience, to help learners make connections, and to provide future insights and applications—a generative knowledge with rich ramifications in the civic lives of learners.

Some Curriculum Implications of The Model

Given the perceived irrelevancy of the current social studies curriculum and its numbing effect on teaching, Engle and Ochoa (1988) suggest two complementary reforms. First, they would celebrate the route taken above by Mrs. Diaz of Washington Park High School when she regularly included the in-depth study of social problems with contemporary significance in her U. S. history course. In this shift, teachers would abandon the expository mode to teach in a hypothetical mode centered on questions and the quest for answers, rather than the mastery of others' knowledge. "Questions and criticism would need to be encouraged over ready answers," and, according to Engle and Ochoa (1988) "The whole process should be directed to opening minds to new possibilities rather than closing them" (p. 116).

Second, the other option described by Engle and Ochoa (1988) requires a most fundamental transformation in how history and social sciences are taught. The discipline-focused courses would give way to courses which integrated the social sciences and focused them upon the examination of social problems. Geography, for example, might be taught with economics and focused upon world environmental and development problems. Sociology and anthropology might center on understanding the problems of human culture, tribalism, and conflict. Psychology might combine with law studies for an intensive mini-course on crime and corrections across cultures.

Most important is the emphasis upon important social problems and active student learning which regularly rises above the roar of problems, alternatives, and hypotheses on specific issues, to address what might be called *mega-queries* about values and value conflicts in democratic credos. For example, students might reflect upon such questions as:

- Under what conditions should individuals disobey legally constituted authority?
- Do all citizens have a right to participation in the institutions by which they are governed? Is increased political participation by citizens desirable? What advantages and disadvantages might come from greater participation?
- Must liberal democratic theory be revised in light of changing circumstances? How do we account in our theory for greater interdependence, greater complexity, and the rapid impact of national and global media networks?
- Is the toleration of divergent views and practices a rational, democratic policy? What are the limits of toleration?
- In a democratic society human dignity is a fundamental value and persons are respected as persons, but is there a concomitant obligation that we respect or approve of a person's or a group's behavior or lifestyle? What are the connections between freedom of expression, for example, and liberty in behavior?

Based upon their philosophical orientation, Engle and Ochoa (1988, 128-129) encapsulate their curriculum views into seven principles:

1 The curriculum should be highly selective of a relatively small number of topics or episodes, each of which will be studied in great depth. The effort to cover superficially a large number of topics would be abandoned.

2 The topics of episodes to be selected should be those with the greatest potential for encouraging thinking, or even controversy, about matters of fact, or about matters of historical interpretation of events in the past, or about alternative resolutions to social problems in the present. Topics or episodes that cannot be conceived as problematical would be omitted from the curriculum.

3 Students should continually be asked to make judgments about such matters as what really are the facts, how facts should be interpreted, what should be done about a problem or, if the problem is historical, what should have been done differently. Students should continually be asked to make value judgments as to whether the decisions made or about to be made, past or present, are good or bad. The study of such problems needs to be open-ended, in the hypothetical mode, and without pressure for closure for a correct answer.

4 Geography, history, and the other social science disciplines will be treated not as an end product or summary of supposed knowledge to be accepted as true and then memorized but rather as alternative sources of information to be utilized in resolving questions such as those suggested above.

5 Since questions of what is good and what is bad are involved in most or all of these kinds of questions and since models for thinking about questions of good and bad are more likely to be found in the humanities than in the social sciences, selections from literature, art, music, religion, philosophy, and journalism would be utilized alongside and on a par with selections from the social sciences and history in the thoughtful study of any topic, episode, or problem. For instance, historians have much that is important to say about the institution of slavery, but so do authors like Harriet Beecher Stowe, William Lloyd Garrison, and Stephen Crane.

6 The curriculum should utilize relatively large quantities of data (much more than could possibly be held in memory) from a variety of sources (more than could possibly be encompassed in a single textbook) to study in depth a relatively small number of topics.

7 The firsthand experience of students and teachers would be respected as one of the important sources of information bearing on any question or problem.

The Instructional Model

Like John Dewey's conception of constructive thought in *How We Think* (1933), the Engle and Ochoa (1988) process model of a problem-oriented instructional encounter should not be conceived as a lock-step, sequential formula to be followed by teachers and students. The model is dynamic. While the phases in their model are "numbered," Engle and Ochoa are not advocating simplistic linear thinking. Study groups can redefine their problem, add alternatives for examination, recast value assumptions as they listen to other voices in the community, and revise their decisions when justifications turn out to be less than satisfying.

The use of the Engle-Ochoa model assumes that the teacher continues to create an open and informed classroom environment where the free exchange of ideas is not only possible but celebrated. The only restrictions on dialogue are those imposed by available evidence, reason, and democratic values. The model also assumes an informed teacher who has collected reasonable amounts of resources for students' continuing engagement in the study of a social problem.

PHASE 1:
Orientation to a Problem Area

The teacher uses questions and high-interest springboards to engage students in reflection. These materials will suggest conflicts and controversy surrounding a contemporary or historic social problem. The exploratory discussion of these materials should identify the conflicts and controversy, some of the values and feelings involved by the parties to the controversy, and the emergent blockage in the cultural, social or political systems which causes or sustains the problem.

The teacher's use of a springboard in Phase One is to raise incongruities—to create what reading teachers call the "disruption of expectation." For example, the teacher presents evidence of the current cost of health care for the poor without universal health plans. Students who have been arguing about the additional cost of national health insurance are taken back, given pause, by this unexpected, incongruent information. Engle

and Ochoa (1988, 88) discuss this use of cognitive dissonance and its effect on initial student motivation to explore a problem area. Mrs. Diaz's unexpected discovery and use of the Susan Orcutt letter (see Scenario) instantly personalized historic information, giving it a face, a pathos which breathed life into the social problem.

PHASE 2:
Identify and Define One Problem

Students continue to manipulate information, adding to the materials and ideas under discussion. As an outcome of these discussions, the students select and define one issue or problem for investigation and decision making. The teacher and class will decide whether the entire class shall address a common problem or, as in the case of Mrs. Diaz's class, groups of students elect to examine different issues. Whatever the decision, it is important that students carefully state their problem clearly, agreeing upon the meanings of concepts used in that definition, and achieve consensus upon its worth as a problem for collective in-depth study.

PHASE 3: Engage Students by the Use of Probing Questions

The teacher has been using probing questions in Phases One and Two, and continues to do so, engaging students in posing definitional, evidential, speculative, value and policy questions. The teacher serves as a model of reflective inquiry—of thoughtfulness—getting students to follow the example. **Definition questions** request the contextual meaning of the use of a concept—*"What does hate crime mean as you are using it today?"* **Evidential questions** request factual support for a claim and challenge the basis for accepting a "fact" or a claim purporting to be true—*"How do you know that his motivation was racial hatred?" "Upon whose property was the cross burned?"* **Speculative questions** are imaginative and often address predicted consequences—*"If he had not screamed an ethnic slur, what might the charges be in this courtroom today?" "If you tack on additional penalties for crimes involving racial, ethnic, gender or religious hate, what do you think will be the effect in our communities?"* **Value questions** ask about inherent value assumptions by discussing priorities—*"Which is more important to you today, protecting the dignity of particular groups of persons or* *preserving rights to free expression?"* **Policy questions** ask about positions on issues or solutions to problems—*"Should affected interested groups use the suggested human relations policy to remove books from the library which they perceive as offensive?"*

PHASE 4:
Identify Value Assumptions

Which are the values to be enhanced or favored in deciding upon any solutions to the social problem under examination? Why favor these values over others? Students must reflect upon their own frames of reference and the values and interests inherent in their perspectives, and in the perspectives of their sources of information when they study this problem. Students should seek out informants with differing points-of-view and value orientations, in order to broaden their own perspectives. But the main task in Phase Four is to initially determine the values to be used to make and to justify a decision in Phase Six.

PHASE 5: Identify Alternatives
and Predict Consequences

Decision making involves choices among alternative courses of action and these choices are selected based upon the projected consequences of each feasible alternative available. Often a decision on a social problem will involve an action plan or strategy which is multifaceted and pursues several complementary courses of action. In Phase Five it is necessary that students and their teacher perceive the alternatives available and then determine their feasibility and imagine the likely consequences flowing from each possibility. "Can you do X, that is, do we have the resources or can we get them?" "If we do X, then what will happen? How many needy will get basic health care?" Student research and the teacher's use of "If..., then... ." questioning are vital to this phase and the persistence in the reflective study of an issue. It should not be surprising for students to go back and redefine the problem during these dialogues.

PHASE 6:
Reach and Justify a Decision

The students rank order their alternatives (with the consequences) given the values that they wish to enhance or favor in their decision. Given the uncertainty of predicting conse-

quences, students may select several alternatives to function together in an action plan. This action plan would be justified with the strongest reasons, arguments, and evidence available to the decision makers, while they also give reasons for rejecting other courses of action. Student decisions are open to the same skeptical queries which they used on others' information and ideas. Bias, foggy evidence and polemics are to be identified and questions brought to bear.

PHASE 7: Proclaim the Results
and Reflect upon the Process.

This phase is implied by the Engle-Ochoa model, but not overtly stated. At the culmination of their study, students should have the experience of proclaiming their findings to a significant audience—the school board, newspaper editors, congressional delegation, a state legislative staff meeting, or a community assembly. Something should happen to engage others in responding to the students' investigations, showing that their concerns and endeavor are reflected in their broader community of citizens. These outcomes might include volunteer action or political action.

Also, students should have the time to reexamine the process of their investigation. Which skills were developed further? Which turns were wasted? Which errors of judgment were fruitful errors, leading to insights? And, how might students enhance their procedures on the next occasion for problem study?

Conclusion

In 1894 Mrs. Susan Orcutt took her pen in hand to petition her government to solve a problem she faced along with her family and neighbors. Using this letter as a remnant of Mrs. Orcutt's nineteenth century civic education, Mrs. Diaz's students at Washington Park High School studied the problems and the inherent sociopolitical issues faced by Mrs. Orcutt in order to further their comprehension of American history and to further their own political education. The conceptual model provided by the lifework of Professors Shirley H. Engle and Anna S. Ochoa served Mrs. Diaz's students well. The issues identified and examined were as engaging as they were profound. In Mrs. Diaz's American history course, students could periodically examine public issues in depth and connect past problems with current realities. Problems and

Syntax of the Engle-Ochoa Model

PHASE 1:
Orientation to a Problem Area

■ The teacher uses questions and high-interest springboards (e.g., video, newspaper clippings, art photographs, literature, and other texts) to establish a backdrop and engage students in reflection.

PHASE 2:
Identify and Define One Problem

■ Students manipulate information, values and feelings to identify an issue or problem worthy of in-depth study.

■ Students carefully state that problem or issue clearly, with agreed-upon meanings of concepts, and achieve consensus upon its worth as a problem for in-depth study.

PHASE 3: Engage Students by the Use of Probing Questions.

■ Teachers and students pose and search for answers to definitional, evidential, speculative, value questions, and policy questions, increasing the level of intellectual exchange in the classroom.

■ Students draw upon print, electronic, and other community resources in their quest to develop thoughtful responses to the probing questions.

PHASE 4: Identify Value Assumptions

■ Students will reflect upon their own frames of reference which shape their view of the problem and its explanation and resolution.

■ Students might gather other perspectives, with implicit values, on the issue under examination to broaden their perspectives.

■ Students will decide upon the values which they will use to decide what should be done to solve a problem or to resolve an issue.

PHASE 5: Identify Alternatives and Predict Consequences

■ Through research and discussion, students will lay out the alternative policies (courses of action) and predict the consequences which might resolve the issue or solve the problem under examination.

■ The teacher probes students' ideas with "What if..." and "If..., then..." style questions to sustain a reflective classroom climate.

■ Students and the teacher will consider alternatives suggested in light of the values established earlier. Which alternatives are most consistent with our goals?

PHASE 6: Reach and Justify a Decision

■ Students will rank their alternatives (and the predicted consequences of each).

■ Students will select the better alternative policies or courses of action and justify them with the strongest reasons, arguments, and evidence; students must give reasons for rejecting other alternatives.

PHASE 7: (Implied by Engle and Ochoa) Proclaim the Results and Reflect upon the Process

■ As a culmination of study, students will share their positions and justifications with others in class and in the larger community of citizens.

■ Teachers and students reflect upon the process of issue-oriented study—what it meant and how they might enhance the reflective procedures.

---

contexts may change, but fundamental mega-issues endure and return in new forms and contexts for civic reflection and action. Mrs. Diaz sensed Engle and Ochoa's zest for the study of civic issues within groups, wherein students may develop their group investigation skills and cooperative learning skills. The cooperative learning and group dynamics research of Thelen (1954, 1967), Slavin (1983), and Sharan (1990) are especially appropriate to complement the Engle-Ochoa decision making model for civic education. It was not by chance that Mrs. Diaz's students divided into groups and did their investigations and deliberations cooperatively.

References

Apple, Michael W. *Official Knowledge: Democratic Education in a Conservative Age.* New York: Routledge, 1993.

Dewey, John. *How We Think.* Boston: D. C. Heath, 1933.

Engle, Shirley H. "Decision-Making: The Heart of Social Studies Instruction." *Social Education* 24:6 (October 1960), 301-304.

Engle, Shirley H. "Needed: A Democratizing of the Schools?" Unpublished mss. ED 073020 11pp., 1972.

Engle, Shirley H. "The Search for a More Adequate Definition of Citizenship Education." Unpublished mss. ED148720. 12pp., 1977.

Engle, Shirley H. "A Social Studies Imperative." *Social Education,* 49:4 (April 1985), 264-265.

Engle, Shirley H. 1986a. "Decision-Making: The Heart

Theme: Hate Crime

Area of Discussion:

Attempts in democratic communities to foster civility and freedom of expression while addressing the perceived problem of hate crime.

Teacher Preparation: The teacher has collected newspaper clippings, magazine articles, and court decisions on hate crime. She has identified sources of information, speakers, and contact persons for student inquiries.

PHASE 1: *Orientation*

The teacher provides copies of data charts which reveal crimes against persons who are in various racial, ethnic, gender, religious, and sexual preference categories within the United States. Students examine these data and conduct an open discussion wherein views are shared. As the discussion proceeds, the teacher provides a newspaper clipping and shares a story of hate crime in their school, without using the concept "hate crime."

PHASE 2: *Identify and Define a Problem*

The teacher provides more clippings on current happenings and asks students to look for commonalities in the data, and then to label these commonalities. The discussion at times focuses upon one news article on cross burning or another on telephone harassment. Students develop the label "hate crime" and discuss the meaning and parameters of this problem. The teacher provides the Anti-Defamation League definition and the students watch an ADL video on this topic:

Hate crimes are unlawful actions to frighten or harm an individual because of his or her race, religion, ethnicity, or sexual orientation. They can range from verbal intimidation and harassment to damage and desecration of property, to physical violence and murder.

The students learn that almost every state has a hate crimes statute. Most states collect hate crimes data and issue annual reports.

PHASE 3: *Probing Questions*

Using articles from the teacher, students begin to discern types of hate crimes, motivations/causes for hate crimes, and the extent of hate crime in their area. They arrange for speakers and do telephone interviews. Through e-mail, students gather information and hate crime stories from other schools and regions.

PHASE 4: *Identify Value Assumptions*

Students interview judges, legislators, and attorneys, to gather stories on hate crime and to discern the values in conflict. Is hate crime new? If so, why now? How do commitments to pluralism and diversity conflict with traditional and emerging understandings of freedom of expression. Should we separate actions from motives, behavior from expressions? How might respect for dignity of all persons chill freedom of expression in a democracy?

PHASE 5: *Identify Alternatives and Predict Consequences*

Students sort through their information collection, and turn to court decisions as well as law enforcement and legal system informants. Students examine Supreme Court decisions in Dawson v. Delaware (1992), Texas v. Johnson (1989), and R.A.V. v. St. Paul, MN (1992), and then, turn to Wisconsin v. Mitchell (1993).

What are the situations which arise surrounding hate crimes? What are the points of disagreement in society and its law? What are the alternatives open within the body of law society might create? What are possible consequences from each alternative? Are legal system remedies adequate to the task? What are the non-legal system alternatives and their consequences?

PHASE 6: *Reach and Justify a Decision*

Students develop an action plan, selecting alternative courses of action while rejecting others and providing an argument to support those decisions.

PHASE 7: *Proclaim and Reflect*

Students proclaim the results of their deliberation with school officials and offer an action plan for the school dealing with hate crimes and hate crime prevention. Later, selected students report to the local bar association and a debate is arranged for a forthcoming school assembly. Meanwhile, study groups meet to review their examination of hate crimes and note needed improvements for future social problem investigations.

of Social Studies Instruction." *Contemporary Education*, 58:1 (Fall 1986), 13-17.

Engle, Shirley H. "Late Night Thoughts about the New Social Studies." *Social Education*, 50:1 (January 1986b), 20-22.

Engle, Shirley H., and Wilma S. Longstreet. *A Design for Social Education in the Open Curriculum.* New York: Harper & Row, 1972.

Engle, Shirley H., and Anna S. Ochoa. *Education for Democratic Citizenship: Decision-making in the Social Studies.* New York: Teachers College Press, 1988.

Giroux, Henry A. *Teachers as Intellectuals: Toward a Critical Pedagogy of Learning.* Granby, MA: Bergin and Garvey, 1989.

Griffin, Alan F. *A Philosophical Approach to the Subject-Matter Preparation of Teachers of History.* Dubuque, IA: Kendall-Hunt for the National Council for the Social Studies, 1992.

McWilliams, Wilson Carey. *The Idea of Fraternity in America.* Berkeley: University of California Press, 1973.

Sharan, Shlomo, Editor. *Cooperative Learning: Theory and Research.* New York: Praeger, 1990.

Slavin, Robert. *Cooperative Learning.* New York: Longman, 1983.

Thelen, Herbert. *Dynamics of Groups at Work.* Chicago: University of Chicago Press, 1954.

Thelen, Herbert. *Classroom Grouping for Teachability.* New York: Wiley, 1967.

7 PREPARING CITIZENS TO PARTICIPATE IN DEMOCRATIC DISCOURSE: The Public Issues Model

by Laurel R. Singleton and James R. Giese

Introduction

"At the heart of strong democracy is talk."
Benjamin Barber (1984)

"Let us begin with a simple proposition: What democracy requires is public debate, not information ... We do not know what we need to know until we ask the right questions, and we can identify the right questions only by subjecting our own ideas about the world to the test of public controversy."
Christopher Lasch (1990)

These statements [by Barber and Lasch] reflect beliefs at the heart of the jurisprudential inquiry model for teaching public issues. This model, developed by the Harvard Social Studies project during the 1960s and 1970s, rests on the idea that citizens in a democracy differ in their views and priorities and that democratic values often conflict when applied in specific cases. The resolution of complex public issues within democratic society requires citizens to negotiate their differences through careful analysis and public discussion. Helping students develop their abilities to take part in this conversation is thus a critical, if not the foundational, aspect of social studies education.

The public issues model posits that U.S. citizens must possess several characteristics. First, the citizen must be familiar with the values of American civic culture as embodied in the Constitution, Bill of Rights, and Declaration of Independence. Second, the citizen must have skills for clarifying and resolving various kinds of (e.g., political, social, and economic) issues. These skills include being able to gather and weigh evidence, to analyze the legal and ethical issues involved, to evaluate arguments on various

sides of a case, and then to synthesize facts, issues, and arguments in making the best possible decision. Third, the citizen must be a passionate, committed participant who is motivated to use her skills and knowledge in concert with other citizens to arrive at new understandings and the best possible decisions.

The Legal/Ethical Values Framework

In the United States, resolution of public issues occurs, at least in part, through discourse based on shared civic commitments. According to Oliver and Shaver, two of the developers of the public issues model:

> In dealing with problems of public conflict and controversy, the American nation has both inherited and developed a tradition that government and law should be the outgrowth of public debate. Important to this tradition is the value placed on the dignity and worth of each individual and, as a corollary, the value placed on reason and persuasion in resolving disputes among people with different definitions of human dignity and the conditions that promote it. From our point of view, a major goal of the society is to develop a public awareness that these basic values should be respected and applied as standards for making public policy (Oliver and Shaver 1966, pp. 81-82).

The public issues model assumes several general legal/ethical values upon which American constitutional democracy rests. Some of these ideals are procedural and guide the manner in which democratic government operates. Procedural ideals include the rule of law, consent of the governed, due process, equal protection of the law, federalism, and limited government. Other ideals are more substantive and deal with specific ends of legitimate governmental action—justice, liberty, public safety and security, the general welfare, and the like.

These ideals of American civic culture should help guide us in developing public policies of all kinds. Often, however, controversy arises when two (or more) general democratic values or principles are in conflict with one another. When these situations occur, the public issues model assumes that the best policy stance involves a rational balancing among fundamental values. That is, citizens and their representatives must make compromises between or among conflicting values, but these compromises should violate each contending value to the least extent possible.

For example, Oliver and Shaver (1966) suggest that if we view freedom of speech as an absolute ideal—a value to be protected at all costs and in all situations—it is virtually impossible to deal with situations in which it might be desirable to limit the right to free speech when it conflicts with the value of public safety. Should a sidewalk speaker be prevented from continuing a speech to a hostile crowd that is about to violently remove him from his platform? Should the American Nazi Party be allowed to conduct a parade through a predominantly Jewish community if violent confrontations between the two groups are likely? Viewing the values of American civic culture on a continuum allows us to consider possible policy alternatives.

The public issues model first focuses students' attention on case studies dealing with limited factual situations rather than on sweeping sets of events. While the situations are limited in scope, they are powerful because they may be linked conceptually to enduring dilemmas faced by people living at widely varying times and in diverse places. Examples of these include:
- Should citizens in northern states before the Civil War have defied the Fugitive Slave Law?
- Who was responsible for assisting the urban poor at the turn of the century—voluntary organizations or government?
- Should the publication of scientific research in nuclear physics in the 1930s have been banned to prevent the information from being available to Nazi scientists?

Each of these issues, although grounded in a particular time period, embodies persistent value dilemmas faced by democratic societies. One can think of numerous instances in which citizens, or

officials acting in their stead, have faced issues regarding when government authority should be challenged, the issue underlying the first example above. The second issue revolves around questions of how we define and balance public and private interests; these questions have played themselves out in many different arenas and time periods. The final issue centers on yet another recurring question: What reasons (if any) justify keeping new knowledge secret?

How should particular events, episodes, or issues be selected for inclusion in the curriculum? There is no single answer appropriate for all classes. Two major criteria, however, should be kept in mind: **1.** the overall importance of the issues to the society and body politic in which we all live and **2.** the possible personal significance the stories and issues might have for ourselves and the particular students we are teaching.

The availability of materials on a topic may also be a factor influencing the choice of specific cases. Among the sources that can be used are stories and vignettes, research data, primary sources, journalistic narratives, textbook accounts, and interpretive essays. In addition, students' experiences and concerns may provide possible case material.

Because of the complexity of the discussion process, the initial cases probably should be relatively simple. We would also argue that "less is more" in that any single case should be treated in depth over a fairly lengthy period of time. Relatively short, one-time debates about complex public issues should be avoided.

Clarifying and Resolving Public Issues through Discussion

The ability to discuss issues rationally and civilly does not develop without experience and reflection. The public issues model provides a vehicle for helping students develop not only the ability to ask the right questions and seek relevant information, but to pursue their questions in a way that advances democratic values.

Any given situation or case can stimulate controversy and disagreement in a number of directions. For example, consider the following situation related to the issue of immigration:

In 1988, a Hmong man living in Denver practiced his culture's traditional way of finding a wife—"marriage by capture." Lee Fong took his teenaged bride from her home and paid her family a $3,000 dowry. They were married for three months. Then the girl went to the Denver police, charging Fong with kidnapping, sexual assault, and menacing (Glade and Giese 1989).

This case might provoke disagreement and raise questions on several levels. The discussion of Lee Fong's case might first turn to questions of fact or explanation. For example, was the bride taken against her will, or did she, in fact, consent to the marriage and then later change her mind? Did Lee Fong realize that the Hmong custom of "marriage by capture" violated U.S. laws and customs? How widespread is this practice among Hmong people in the United States?

A second area of possible disagreement involves the meaning of words or phrases. In the case above, for example, opinions on whether the legal system should be tolerant of offenses that result from different cultural traditions might hinge on what is meant by *tolerant* or what behaviors are included as offenses.

The third area of possible dispute involves judgments about what should or ought to be done—judgments concerned with the legitimacy and rightness or wrongness of actions and policy. Such ethical or value issues might be expressed as follows: Should immigrants give up cultural traditions that are in conflict with customs and laws in the United States? Should the legal system be more lenient on offenders whose actions were based on cultural traditions at variance with the dominant culture? Should immigration policy be based on similarity between American culture and that of the immigrant's native land?

Although the various types of issues are often intertwined in discussion, distinguishing among them makes clear that there are various avenues of inquiry available in the classroom. Furthermore, recognizing the various types of issues allows students to apply appropriate strategies in advancing discussion.

FACT-EXPLANATION ISSUES. Factual issues are disagreements about the descriptions or explanations of events. There are many kinds of factual claims, some involving little generalization and some involving a great deal. "The Fong family immigrated last month" is a claim about a specific event that occurred recently. "Immigration increased rapidly in the late 1800s and early 1900s" summarizes a large amount of data

and infers a trend over several years. "The United States will develop more restrictive immigration policies over the next 40 years" is a prediction involving several future events. "Koreans emigrate from their country because they do not support the actions of the Korean government" summarizes a large number of events and includes an explanation of why these events have occurred.

The various types of claims may be based on wide-ranging types of evidence. For example, the initial claim above may be based on personal observation or firsthand accounts. In contrast, the third claim, which makes a prediction about future events, may be inferred from interviews with public officials, public opinion polls, and historians' accounts of other time periods in which immigration was restricted.

Some disagreements over factual claims occur because relevant evidence is not available. Other disagreements, which tend to be more difficult to resolve, occur because the evidence available is interpreted differently by different people. To assess the accuracy of conflicting claims, a discussant would need to know on what kind of evidence the claims are based and the line of reasoning that each individual used in developing the positions being promulgated.

In discussion, factual claims may be supported in a number of ways:

- **Appealing to "common knowledge" or "common sense."** "Common knowledge" or "common sense" is a relatively weak source of evidence, since it suggests no additional process by which to resolve the disagreement.

- **Citing personal observations.** Personal observation is of somewhat limited use in the study of public issues, since few of us have the opportunity to actually witness the events. For this reason, we rely heavily on the reports of others, in hopes that they can provide reliable information.

- **Reference to an authoritative source.** When referring to an authoritative source, however, we also must inquire into the quality of the authority. Is the authority really an expert? Is there information about the authority indicating that he/she has a personal bias on the topic? Do different authorities make contradictory claims, or do authorities support each other? If there are differences, where do they lie?

At times, factual claims can be tested by gathering more evidence. At other times, finding the information needed may be difficult if not impossible. If students cannot take time out to gather more evidence or if the evidence needed simply does not exist (as is the case in many policy contexts), they can use one of the following strategies to continue discussion: **1.** the group may agree to stipulate that the discussion will proceed on the basis of one set of facts or factual claims, or **2.** the members of the group may agree to bypass or temporarily ignore the issue, using other arguments to make their cases.

DEFINITIONAL ISSUES. Definitional issues revolve around how people use words or phrases in discussion. For example, two people might disagree on whether a group was oppressed. One person might say *oppressed* means having no political freedoms, while the other person holds that *oppressed* means being in a degrading situation due to someone else's actions (e.g., without a job because of governmental policies).

Some definitional disputes are only labeling problems. There is no disagreement on the nature of the thing begin labeled, but over the appropriate label. For example, in different parts of the country, flavored carbonated water may be called "tonic," "soda," or "pop." Two strategies can move discussion along by helping reach agreement on definitional issues that are primarily labeling problems:

- **Stipulation.** People can agree to use a word consistently in a specific way. ("Whenever we use the term *responsible*, we mean consciously causing an event to occur.")
- **Use of an authoritative source.** Discussants can use a dictionary or other authoritative source to find support for the particular use of a word or phrase.

More common and more difficult to resolve are definitional disputes in which people disagree over the nature or quality of an action being named. For example, a key question in discussing immigration issues may be the meaning of *American.* One of the major problems in the process of definition is the need to arrive at enough precise criteria—standards—to identify the term under discussion. Thus, resolving definitional disputes involves two steps: **1.** selecting general criteria for a definition and **2.** deciding which examples fit the criteria.

ETHICAL OR VALUE ISSUES. Ethical or value statements suggest that some object, person, or conduct is good or bad and that this quality is based on an important general principle, such as peace and stability, security from physical harm, or equal treatment before the law. Value conflicts are at the core of most controversies regarding public policy decisions. For example, consider the following:

Controversial Policy Question:
VALUE CONFLICTS

? Should rap or heavy metal music be censored? Freedom of speech versus morals of the majority

? Should the federal government fund universal health care for all Americans? Individual well-being and human dignity versus business autonomy and individual choice

? Should the United States intervene in Rwanda? Human rights versus national self-determination

---

A public policy concerning any of these issues cannot be decided upon without violating a value held by some people. The challenge in discussing these issues is finding the policy alternatives that least violate important democratic values.

Discussants who recognize value statements can use several strategies to challenge or support such statements:

- **Use of a respected or venerable source.** Value statements may be justified by showing that they are supported by a source that most people consider sacred, respected, or venerable. For example, the statement *"Rap music should not be censored"* might be supported by reference to the First Amendment or the words of Thomas Jefferson.
- **Prediction of a valued consequence.** Policy positions and value judgments are often used together to show that support of a particular policy will lead to a desirable end or will avoid undesirable consequences.
- **Analogy.** One of the most powerful techniques for clarifying our thinking on ethical-value issues is to suggest that an issue might be resolved differently in one or more related cases.

To illustrate, consider the following conversation, in which two students are discussing the case of Mrs. Webster, who operates a small rooming house in her own home. The city had recently expanded its fair housing ordinance to forbid discrimination against homosexuals. Nevertheless, Mrs. Webster evicted Mr. Smith and Mr. Jones because she believed they were gay and her religion teaches that homosexuality is wrong.

Sam: The government should not tell Mrs. Webster how to run her business.

Rayna: Suppose Mrs. Webster ran a restaurant. In order to save money, she served leftover food the next day. Occasionally the food spoiled and customers got sick, but since most of the customers were transient, moving through town, they never really complained. Do you think the government should force Mrs. Webster to abide by certain health standards?

Sam: Yes, of course.

Rayna: Well, that's government control. I thought you were opposed to government interference with a person's business.

Sam: Well, a restaurant is different from a rooming house. It affects a person's health.

Rayna: Having a place to live also affects your health. If Mr. Smith and Mr. Jones cannot find a place to stay and have to sleep out in the cold, Mrs. Webster is hurting them—maybe even more than a person who just has a stomachache from old food.

Sam: But this is her own home. She shouldn't be forced to open her home to people who make her feel uncomfortable or who would cause other renters to move out (Singleton 1989).

The analogy may force discussants to make distinctions and qualifications that strengthen and clarify their positions on important value conflicts. Sam can no longer say that he is always against government control of business; he is obviously for some government control under certain conditions, which serves to qualify and strengthen his position.

The use of analogies also allows teachers and students to make connections across time and place. For example, the decision faced by American colonists when they chose to defy the established authority of the British government in order to protest unjust laws may be compared to similar decisions made by civil rights activists in the 1960s and contemporary anti-abortion protesters. Furthermore, powerful analogies may (and should) be drawn from the students' and the teacher's own personal experiences.

The Discussion/Conversation Process

In the classroom, the point of discussing public issues is to use the power of both critical and caring relationships to educate individuals and the group. In applying the public issues model, the teacher becomes a facilitator, helping students to make productive conversations with each other. To prepare students for such discussions, teachers must focus considerable attention on creating a climate supportive of authentic discourse and developing students' discussion skills.

CLASSROOM CULTURE AND DISCUSSION. A major challenge in discussing controversial issues is to achieve sufficient unity and harmony within the group so that conversation leads to productive problem solving. People with opposing views do not have to adopt a combative or avoidance posture in conversations. Instead, the discussion process helps them press toward mutual clarification and exploration, to see discussion as a process of inquiry, and to value the whole group for its unique ability to provide a setting in which this can happen.

Significant conversation about public issues is in some ways like a team sport. When we are caught up in a soccer or basketball game, the essence of the situation is not a separate ego doing something but rather a set of relationships among the various players. Each requires the use of personal disciplined techniques but also the letting go that happens when a team is playing well together. An exciting conversation cannot be constructed by an individual; it requires the wholehearted involvement of a group. There is a kind of alternative pulse between the letting go to express one's most significant and authentic feelings and ideas and the skilled personal and group reflection that gives direction to these moments of letting go. If trust is not sufficient to permit letting go, the game will never be played—no significant conversation will happen. Likewise, if no disciplined critique of the conversation occurs, the quality of the discussion may hardly merit participation.

To achieve a discussion that can truly educate individuals and the group, all members of the group must be involved, and all must hear and understand, as best they can, the feelings and ideas of members of the group. In classroom discussions, student talk is most often channeled through the teacher, but it is important for the teacher to encourage students to talk directly to and try to understand each other. In addition, the teacher is encouraged to model certain attitudes toward the discussion of public issues—careful listening, respect, and the willingness to change one's mind.

DISCUSSION SKILLS. To take part in productive discussions of public issues, students need a variety of skills, many of which require breaking unproductive habits they employ in casual conversation; that is, they must learn techniques of disciplined discussion. Among these techniques are **1.** sensitivity to what others are saying, **2.** stating the issue over which discussants disagree, **3.** setting an agenda and pursuing it with some degree of continuity, **4.** making explicit the changes or transitions in the conversation, **5.** dealing with potential roadblocks, and **6.** reflecting on the discussion process.

1 Sensitivity. Conversations often seem to go around in circles because the participants don't seem to be talking about the same issue, even though they are on the same general topic or problem. They do not respond to one another's statements. When this happens, people are not being sensitive to one another. Being sensitive usually involves making a conscious effort to connect the speakers with the issues being expressed. Some tips that can be helpful to students include the following:
• Put yourself in the other person's place to understand what that person is saying and how he or she feels.
• Show understanding and acceptance through such nonverbal behaviors as gestures, eye contact, posture, and facial expression.
• When a person has finished speaking, try restating the person's most important thought or feeling.
• If there seems to be confusion about the issue under discussion, clarify by summarizing the statements of several of the people who have spoken.

2 Stating the Issue. Discussion often begins by concentrating on one aspect of a situation. In a complicated situation, many different opinions

are soon thrown into the discussion. One of the first challenges of disciplined discussion is to sort out how many different things are being said about different issues or topics. Another immediate need is to identify points of agreement and disagreement. These steps allow the participants to focus on a limited number of issues and pursue them systematically.

To state issues clearly, it is useful to translate the main positions, or opinions that people have, into questions. Stating the issue in question form focuses the discussion on a specific topic that requires reasoning and justification.

Sometimes it is necessary to stop and summarize the nature of the issue over which you are disagreeing. One advantage of this skill is that it provides focus and direction for the discussion. A second major advantage of stating issues explicitly is that it tends to broaden the discussion and show how a number of similar situations can be related, compared, and contrasted.

3 Setting an Agenda. An agenda is a list of issues that a group agrees to consider in the course of a discussion. When a group begins discussing a complicated situation, different people see different issues. Each usually talks about the issue he or she thinks is most important and is insensitive to the issues that others see. One way of dealing with this problem is to list all the issues that seem important. The discussants then decide which issues they wish to discuss and in what order.

Having made this decision, members of the group can remind one another of what points are relevant and what points are not. If someone jumps to the third issue when the group is still entangled in the first, he or she can be reminded that this contribution is not relevant at this point.

Pursuing issues with continuity is important. Changing issues too quickly tends to disrupt attempts to clarify or resolve basic disagreements. The systematic pursuit of an issue means sticking with it long enough to deal with its problems thoroughly.

4 Making Clear Transitions. There are points in discussion where it is useful to leave one issue and move on to another. An argument between two discussants may become so deadlocked that no agreement is likely. They may then agree to disagree and to take up another issue related to the general topic. Another member of a group may see that there is a prior issue that must be settled before the issue under discussion can productively be explored.

When someone chooses to change the issue under consideration, he or she should make this known with an explicit transitional statement, explaining why a change of issue at that point would move the discussion forward. When making a transition, it may be helpful to summarize the differences between the two discussants before moving on to the next issue.

5Potential Roadblocks. For discussion to be productive, students also need to recognize roadblocks and develop strategies for dealing with them. Such roadblocks may include failure to listen and pursue issues systematically, monopolizing the conversation, proof by repetition, personal attack, and worry about winning the argument. Two potentially difficult roadblocks result when participants have little or no interest in the controversial situation and therefore feel unmotivated to participate in the conversation or, conversely, have such deep interests and convictions that it is difficult for them to be reasonable about the topic. These two problems speak to the necessity to select issues carefully.

6Reflecting on the Disucssion. Involving students in reflecting on the quality of the discussion may be one of the most direct paths to productive discussion. During a discussion, a group can pause and ask "What's happening now?" The general questions below can be used to determine if the discussion is moving along productively or "going in circles":
- What issues have been discussed?
- What positions were taken, and by whom?
- Was agreement reached on any issue? Which ones?
- What things helped move the discussion along?
- What things bogged the discussion down or made it unproductive?
- What things should be discussed next? Why?

While the answers to these kinds of questions will help students reflect on and improve their discussion skills, they are not the ultimate determinant of whether a discussion has been productive. In order to better measure the quality of discussion, we would advocate the following benchmark: When positions are more complex (in the sense of including distinctions, qualifications, stipulations, etc.) than when the discussion

began, then the discussion has been productive.

Final Thoughts

Open-ended issues that involve emotion-laden value commitments present both a risk and a challenge to teacher and students. The risk lies in a person's sense of frustration when confronted with ambiguity, the lack of clear answers, or the difficulty of arriving at logical justifications for "gut-level" feelings. The challenge lies in achieving the sense of satisfaction and intellectual accomplishment that a productive discussion of such an issue generates. The teacher's goal should not be to have students master tidy bits of information, but to have students understand the complexity of a problem and be able to make their positions reflect that complexity. Consensus may not be reached, and doubts may remain, but this is a more authentic outcome than leaving students submerged in isolated, decontextualized, and meaningless bits of information.

References

Barber, Benjamin. *Strong Democracy: Participatory Politics for a New Age.* Berkeley, CA: University of California Press, 1984.

Glade, Mary Elizabeth, and James R. Giese. *Immigration: Pluralism and National Identity,* The Public Issues Series. Boulder, CO: Social Science Education Consortium, 1989.

Lasch, Christopher. "Journalism, Publicity, and the Lost Art of Argument." *Gannett Center Journal* (Spring 1990).

Newmann, Fred M. *Clarifying Public Controversy: An Approach to Teaching Social Studies.* Boston: Little, Brown, 1970.

Oliver, Donald W., and James P. Shaver. *Teaching Public Issues in the High School.* Boston: Houghton Mifflin; reprinted by Logan, UT: Utah State University Press, 1966.

Public Issues Series (Boulder, CO: Social Science Education Consortium, 1988-1993).

Singleton, Laurel. *The Civil War: Teacher's Guide, Public Issues Series.* Boulder, CO: Social Science Education Consortium, 1989.

Acknowledgement

The authors are deeply indebted to Donald W. Oliver and Fred M. Newmann, who have provided leadership in the SSEC's work republishing the *Public Issues Series,* which they originally conceived and developed at Harvard. For more information on the approach described in this chapter, we would refer you to Oliver and Shaver (1966) and Newmann (1970).

8 TEACHING CONTROVERSIAL ISSUES THROUGH MASSIALAS AND COX INQUIRY

by JoAnn Cutler Sweeney and Stuart Foster

In 1966 Massialas and Cox[1] explained to social studies teachers the process of inquiry and reflective thinking as a methodology for addressing some of modern society's most critical questions. They asserted that, because it was not possible to define a distinguishable, homogeneous, and stable modern culture in the United States, the conventional role of education as a means of preparing children for citizenship within a dominant culture should be in question. Because of the rapid pace of change, the pluralistic nature of society, and the complexities of the modern era, it was no longer the role of education to transmit the values of a single dominant culture. Rather, because of existing tensions, Massialas and Cox (1966, 3) saw modern society as a "culture in crisis." They declared that education, through critical inquiry, should ultimately perform the function of harmonizing society's divergent elements and controversies. By confronting the major conflicts and tensions within society, Massialas and Cox envisioned schools as agents for change and classrooms as environments in which students solved the problems of the modern era, ultimately improving society. The authors recommended that schools accept their role as the "'progressive reconstruction' of the culture. There the school is deliberately critical and creative in its selection and examination of the values of the society" (22). Based on this assertion, the goal of education, therefore, would be "the reflective examination of values and issues of current import" (12).

The U.S. social fabric during the 1960s included the ideological struggles of the cold war, social conflicts over racial equality, the catastrophic effects of the Vietnam War, and cultural fragmentation evidenced by student radicalism and a chasm between traditional and emergent values. Massialas and Cox described this period of rapid change in which youth felt "a loss of identity" amidst a tide of "disruptive racial, religious, ethnic, social prestige, and other cleavages." They believed schools had a responsibility to engage students in the study of these crises. Educators should seek to "prepare citizens who are capable of dealing with this crisis in rational and creative ways" (21).

Massialas and Cox's proposition is as relevant for today's social studies instruction as it was in the 1960s. Although issues such as the Cold War and Vietnam no longer dominate society, many of the other social "crises" have persisted. Arguably, racial conflict, crime and delinquency, the breakdown of the family, inner-city tensions, and global inequalities describe today's society much as they did the United States in 1966. The belief that schools must deal critically and actively with social issues is still pertinent.

The Function of Social Studies Teaching

The position of social studies in the curriculum is central to the inquiry-based approach. Social studies, according to Massialas and Cox, should not ask students to absorb a static culture, but rather to engage in examining the society's changing norms and values. "The social studies curriculum should be comprised of a series of encounters with ideas about mankind" that stimulate the learner to "discover new knowledge of and new solutions to social problems" (24). Social studies should, therefore, be directed toward certain goals:

1. It should furnish the forum for the analysis and evaluation of normative propositions or value judgments about man and society.

2. It should operate within the requisites of inquiry that relate the development of hypotheses and ideas about social relationships to supporting evidence.

3. The end results of inquiry should be the production of a body of tested principles and generalizations about human relations and societies. The social studies classroom should afford the student the avenue for the creative venture. (24)

The pervasive notion that the social studies classroom is a theater for examining controversial issues is central to the process of inquiry. According to Massialas and Cox, "controversial issues have social, emotional and cognitive dimensions" (52). Such issues provide a framework for rich and meaningful thought and discussion, and by wrestling with the problems of modern society through a scheme of investigation, the outcomes can be "conducive to the achievement of our prime goal, the decision making citizen" (54). Consequently, the teacher has to make a conscious decision to examine values in a systematic manner. "Once this decision is made, the classroom becomes the forum of inquiry into social values" (174).

Characteristics of the Inquiry Classroom

To critically examine social issues, Massialas and Cox asserted that students would engage in the "constant agony" of reflection and reflective thinking, defined as "a process of identifying problems of fact and value, assessing them in view of the assumptions in which they are grounded, and subjecting them to proof in terms of certain criteria" (90). By evaluating the process in the classroom and by drawing on several studies of reflective thinking, Massialas and Cox concluded that the process of inquiry and reflection progressed through identifiable phases. The authors explained, however, that the social studies classroom must take on three main characteristics before inquiry can begin:

1. The classroom should engender "an open climate for discussion." All comments and points of view are valued, and all ideas merit critical examination.
2. In the reflective classroom, hypotheses become the focus of discussion. The understanding of a certain issue should be elicited through the continual evaluation of hypotheses through discussion and negotiation.
3. "The functional application of facts to support hypotheses." The class should

explore hypotheses by examining the validity and reliability of the evidence supporting them. Clarifying and validating evidence are of paramount importance to the inquiry's outcome.

Massialas and Cox were careful to point out that "facts" are not sacrosanct and absolute but human judgments about reality. In the reflective classroom, students should deliberate upon and continually question such judgments. They must appreciate that nowhere in the social studies does an objective, verifiable reality exist, and that as citizens, it is not possible to make factual decisions simply based on objective analyses of data. Rather, they may make decisions only after considerable reflection and as a result of judgments grounded in the best available evidence.

The teacher's role in an inquiry-based classroom is significant. For Massialas and Cox, the teacher is not an authority figure directing the class toward predetermined conclusions but a "manager or co-ordinator of inquiry" (62). The teacher participates in the process of inquiry and injects his or her views in a sensitive and democratic way, thereby validating his or her own position. The authors termed this activity *defensible partisanship*.

The student's role in the process of inquiry is central. For successful inquiry the student must be actively involved, taking the position of *participant* and *discoverer*. The process directs the student toward making effective choices regarding crucial social issues. Massialas and Cox asserted, "It is important that young people know how to discriminate critically among choices and to avoid unreflective acceptance of 'time-honored prescriptions'" (155).

Ultimately, Massialas and Cox argued that, by following certain phases of investigation, students would arrive at *dependable generalizations*. Generalizations are not solutions nor final answers, but choices that represent "the most tenable solution to the problem based on all available evidence" (119). Generalizations, therefore, must always be tentative and considered an approximation of reality. Thus, the process of discovering these generalizations is as meaningful as the outcome. Massialas and Cox continually returned to this essential goal:

It should be remembered that the purpose of the social studies enterprise is not only

The Social Studies Inquiry Model

There are six proposed phases in the Social Studies Inquiry Model. These phases, Massialas and Cox argued, are central to the effective analysis of controversial issues and form the basis of exemplary teaching materials. Often the phases are interrelated and overlap, not always following a sequential order. Even though the phases, described below, outline how the process of inquiry may operate, the teacher must keep in mind the fluid and dynamic nature of inquiry.

Orientation Phase

The teacher essentially presents to students a perplexing or controversial issue over which there is genuine conflict. The aim is to engage students in inquiry and help them define and clarify a given problem.

Hypothesis Phase

The students and teacher develop one or more hypotheses for the purposes of investigating and exploring the problem. The teacher focuses discussion on the hypotheses, guiding students in formulating ideas about the nature of the problem and its possible resolution.

Definition Phase

The students clarify the meaning of the terms of each hypothesis to facilitate effective communication. Clarity of meaning is essential for a class to achieve a focused discussion. The teacher must keep the "definition" principle in place throughout all phases of the model.

Exploration Phase

During the exploration phase, dimensions of the

hypotheses as search models are developed and extended, and multiple hypotheses may exist simultaneously. The students critically examine, evaluate, and reevaluate the meanings, implications, and logic of each hypothesis. Because the nature of the exploration is diverse and chaotic, the inquiry process may often lack formal coherence. The "chaos," however, has a purpose because students are actively engaging in inquiry and exploration.

Evidencing Phase

In this phase, the inquirers gather evidence and data to support or reject each hypothesis as defined. Insufficient data may limit the inquiry at this phase, or suggest that further investigation is unwarranted. The evidencing process may also reveal opinions, belief systems, or philosophical issues. As a consequence, students must deal with issues that involve more than tangible facts, e.g., feelings, values, attitudes, and standards.

Generalization Phase

In this final phase, students express the solution to the problem, but, according to Massialas and Cox, the generalization phase "is never taken to represent a final truth. Its tentative nature is recognized" (119). Consequently, although the group may have carefully followed the inquiry phases and arrived at "a solution," this can never be any more than the best possible statement under the circumstances. Other hypotheses and "solutions" may also be acceptable. In addition, students should appreciate that there is no obligation to arrive at a definitive conclusion because the process of inquiry—not the generalizations reached—is the essence of the Social Studies Inquiry Model.

to identify dependable generalizations, but to be able to outline steps to be taken, roads to be traveled, utilizing both analytic and creative processes and skills. All these are indispensable elements and constitute inseparable components of the new social studies. (138)

Applying the Inquiry Model in the Social Studies Curriculum

In the social studies, students regularly encounter topics in which the lives of individual people are affected by the decisions of others. Human experience necessitates conflict, controversy, consensus, and cooperation. For discipline-

specific examples and the sample lesson plan described below—and in many other instances—the Social Studies Inquiry Model may be used effectively in the social studies classroom.

Discipline-Specific Issues

World and U.S. history is an area of study with numerous examples of human conflict and issues of personal and national freedom. Issues such as the rights of indigenous peoples are manifest throughout the world and have historical and contemporary significance. For example, the claims of Palestinians, Native Americans, the Irish, or the peoples of the former Yugoslavia all have deep roots in historical experience and are relevant to our understanding today's world.

In addressing such issues, students will gain valuable insights into how past experience shapes the modern world and how today's global tensions and problems are difficult to resolve.

In world geography, students might explore issues such as the population explosion and whether national governments have the right to control population growth. Because environmental issues are central to the subject, students can be encouraged to weigh a society's need for factories, houses, roads, and tourists against the desire to preserve the natural environment.

In economics, students might analyze the role of national government in the management of a country's economy and evaluate, for example, the efficacy of increased taxation and increased government interference in business. Students might also inquire into the costs and benefits of schooling, health insurance, and defense, all in an effort to appreciate the economic forces shaping their lives.

In civics and U.S. government, students might wrestle with issues such as freedom of speech, abortion, smoking in public places, and gun control in order to understand the nature of society, institutional power, and human freedom. By confronting important social questions, students learn to appreciate that many issues are not easily resolved.

The "Pony Tail" Lesson

This sample lesson deals with a student's freedom and a Texas school board's institutional power. The lesson walks through the phases in the Social Studies Inquiry Model.

Orientation Phase. In the first phase students learn about a perplexing or controversial issue, which centers around the conflict over hair length between an eight-year-old boy (supported by his parents) and a local Texas school board. The students, in adopting the role of the school board, will address and resolve the issue, if possible. However, before students learn any specifics, the teacher asks the class to establish a dress/appearance code for an elementary school in Texas. Students should have no prior knowledge of the actual problems faced by the particular Texas school board.

The teacher implements the lesson using the following guidelines:

1. **Divide** the class into groups of approximately five students each.
2. **Inform** the class that each group, acting as a school board, will draft a set of rules governing aspects of personal appearance for a school in a small semirural community that is generally conservative and traditional in outlook, composed of citizens who are strong supporters of the local schools.
3. **Guide** the groups in formulating a code of appearance appropriate for a school in such an area. The code may be in the form of a general statement, or it may be a specific, itemized list of what is acceptable and what is not. Students may wish to draw up a more specific code first, then formulate a more general policy statement later.
4. **Facilitate** each group in sharing its code with the class in a general discussion. Ask each group to write down the key elements of their code on an overhead transparency to help focus discussion.
5. **Encourage** other class members to comment upon and critique each proposed dress code. Encourage students to defend their adopted positions. For example, if groups suggest different codes for girls and boys, or different codes for different ages, or that the school should have no dress code, then students should discuss the consequences of such decisions.
6. **Ask** each group to meet again to discuss the feedback and refine its code. When the students are satisfied that they have arrived at the best code for their school, the teacher should distribute the newspaper article describing an actual Texas school dress code.
7. After the students have read the article, **Ask** each group to discuss the issue and identify the key problem the school board in the district must address. Each group should write a short statement that explains what the problem is. For example, "The school board's problem is a lawsuit by the student's parents on the basis of sex discrimination. The parents argue that the length-of-hair rule applies to boys only and is, therefore, discriminatory."
8. **State** that each group represents members of the Texas school board. They must confront the issue and contemplate the problem.

Hypothesis Phase. This phase of the Social Studies Inquiry Model asks students to form a hypothesis about the dress code issue. In this context students are concerned with analyzing and reflecting on: What is a desirable code of personal appearance in school? How will the

The situation described in the given example concerns *Toungate v. Bastrop Independent School District*, 842 S.W. 2d 823 (Texas App.1992)

School's policy makes boy with ponytail a loner

By Christy Hoppe
Dallas Morning News

BASTROP, Texas — For six weeks, Zach Toungate has jumped off the bus in the scattered morning light and said goodbye to his elementary school classmates.

He heads, alone, to his dreary 10- by 13-foot classroom, its windows covered with butcher paper, and sits in one of the six chairs. He eats there because he's not allowed in the lunchroom.

During recess he goes to the blacktop, but plays by himself, bouncing a basketball his mother gave him. He cannot attend the art and choir classes he liked.

What separates 8-year-old Zachariah from his classmates is a wispy 7 inches of hair.

Zach has a ponytail. Not much of one, because the thin strand falls from the base of his hairline. Otherwise, he wears a burr.

But the tail is enough to violate a Bastrop Independent School District dress code adopted this year that prohibits a boy's hair from touching his shirt collar.

September and Stanley Toungate have refused to force their son to cut the tail that he loves. The school board has refused to make an exception to the rule and since Oct. 5 has relegated Zach to an "alternative education setting," reserved primarily for disciplinary problems.

The battle of wills is now being fought in court while Zach sits alone each day, taught by a procession of substitute teachers.

In his isolation, Zach is learning mostly about principle and how much it can cost, even a third-grader.

He says he misses his schoolmates, the choir class he barely got to attend and his regular teacher. He also has awakened at night, moaning and scared.

"I've had bad nightmares," Zach said at home in Bastrop, 30 miles east of Austin. "I dreamed I was in that room and I couldn't get out and it kept getting smaller and it crushed me. It was bad."

But, with all the logic of his age, he argues for his ponytail.

"I just want it. I like the way my hair looks."

September Toungate said she has listened to arguments from the Mina Elementary School principal and school board members, but "they didn't give me any reasonable answer, other than that they want all little boys to look exactly alike."

Appearance, she said, is for the parents to decide. Her son's hair is well-groomed, and he has the right to wear it as he likes.

"I'm not going to make him cut his hair," said the mother, who at 29 is too young to have been part of the rebellious 1960s.

With both children in school, she is studying to be a nurse.

"I'm trying real hard to raise my children to not judge someone by appearance, not by skin color, not by sex, not by hair length, not by anything but what's inside of them," she said.

Bastrop School Superintendent Paul Fleming admits that the ponytail flap—now at six weeks and with no end in sight—has "gone a lot further than it should have gone."

He has rejected compromises offered by the family of pinning up the offending tail, tucking it under a shirt collar or allowing Zach to wear a wig.

Fleming said there is only one solution, and it is easy: Cut the tail.

"It would be a simple matter to cut the child's hair and fight the rule," he said. "If the board were to change its mind or the court were to rule we could not set hair-length rules, then the kid could grow it back."

The Toungates have sued the school district for discrimination, alleging that the hair-length rules are gender-based and unfairly apply solely to boys.

Fleming said the courts long have upheld the right of school boards to establish and enforce dress codes.

establishment of such a code affect the school board's dilemma?

Hypotheses may be rich and varied, and such diversity should be encouraged. Some students may hypothesize about the amount of control any organization should have over individuals, while others may hypothesize that a clearly defined code is essential to the smooth functioning of any organization.

Definition Phase. A pervasive feature of the Social Studies Inquiry Model is the need to define words and expressions. Through this lesson, such terms as "sensible," "appropriate," "offensive," "liberal," "conservative," and "objectionable" may be expressed and must be defined. Students should be aware that terminology may be misleading, confusing, or vary in meaning depending on the context. Such considerations are central in the discussion of controversial issues where language often is value-laden. For example, what is considered "shocking" to one individual may be considered "liberal" by another, and what is considered "suitable attire" differs from individual to individual.

9. **Seek** definitions from each group based on the language of each dress code. Clarify the meaning of each. Reach consensus for understanding.

Exploration Phase. During this phase the students develop and extend the drafted codes. The aim of exploration is to "locate internal inconsistencies, develop a coherent theory, and extend the search toward needed evidence" (332). A part of such critical reflection is challenging and reevaluating the original statements and positions. The teacher should emphasize that modifying, reconsidering, or possibly abandoning earlier positions is a sign of careful analysis and critical thinking.

10. **Ask** each group to reexamine its draft and, where appropriate, alter its code in the light of classroom discussion. The group should spend time considering how the boy's situation relates to the proposed code. Each group should discuss the issue and how each group member would react if they were actually on the school board.

11. **Guide** each group in preparing a statement describing how they would resolve the issue.

12. **Encourage** each group to share its decision with the class as a whole.

13. **Summarize** the position of each group on the blackboard, and lead a discussion on the differences between groups. One group may decide that the boy should be allowed in school because he does not violate their dress code, whereas another group would not allow the boy into the school because he does. Encourage discussion also about the criteria used in making their final decision.

Evidencing Phase. The purpose of the evidencing phase is to allow students to test their hypotheses through the use of available evidence and resources. This may require students to use newspapers and magazines as a resource and to research in libraries, places of work, and areas of special interest. They may use legal precedents, state regulations, the opinions of public figures, and codes of practice, which are examples that form part of a culture and its norms and will help students understand a wider decision framework. Students must engage actively in the process of social inquiry and not learn exclusively from materials provided by the teacher.

14. **Encourage** students to find evidence that will help them more clearly evaluate the problem. In this instance, students would be expected to locate and examine their own school dress/appearance code; to investigate other workplace codes; to identify state regulations; to discuss such issues with peers, parents, and other community members; to research the issue by investigating any scholarly research on the issue (e.g., studies on the relationship of appearance and dress to student achievement); or to uncover previous examples of such controversies and consider how they were resolved in court cases and rulings.

15. **Allocate** discussion time for students to share and discuss their evidence both in their original group and with the class as a whole.

Generalization Phase. The final phase of the Social Studies Inquiry Model requires the students to try to resolve the problem. If they were the school board, what would they do? What would be the implications of such actions? How does their position relate to their hypotheses regarding, for example, the nature of institutional power? The students should realize that this controversial issue is difficult to resolve and that a resolution may not be possible.

The actual dress code at the time the ponytail controversy began.

Students are expected to come to school well-groomed and appropriately dressed every day. Hair will be clean and properly combed, and clothing will be neat and clean. Boys' hair must meet the following guidelines: The rear length must be no longer than to the bottom of a regular shirt collar. On the sides, the bottom of the earlobe must be visible. In the front, the length cannot be longer than the top of the eyebrows. Afro style is limited to a maximum of 3 inches in length.

Special rules about dress include:
1. All students may wear shorts.
2. T-Shirts with writings or drawings on them are not to be vulgar or in poor taste. Fish net shirts and tank tops are not acceptable.
3. Shirts must be hemmed and cover the shoulders and stomach.
4. Boys are not allowed to wear earrings or studs.
5. Thongs are unacceptable footwear.
6. Headgear will not be permitted inside buildings (i.e., hats, caps, etc.) during the regular school day.

Parents can help the children participate in the physical education program by dressing them appropriately. The P.E. teacher recommends tennis shoes—boots and sandals are not safe. Girls may wear pants or shorts under dresses. The teacher further recommends pullover tops and pants so children can move freely on the floor without the discomfort of buttons and zippers. When purchasing school clothes, please keep in mind these guidelines.

16. Encourage the students to arrive at a best possible outcome based on their hypotheses, codes of appearance, deliberations, and the evidence supporting or rejecting their positions. Their final proposal should not be described as a "conclusion" but a "generalization," which is tentative in nature and may be changed in light of new evidence, further reflection and continued inquiry.

17. Require each student, if you wish, to prepare a final class paper that outlines the process his or her group used to arrive at the final "generalization."

18. Distribute copies of Document 1 and Document 2, which are the 1990 and 1993-94 codes of appearance in the actual Texas court case, *Toungate v. Bastrop Independent School District*. Ask students to compare the two codes and comment upon their differences. Pose to students whether the new code will likely prevent future controversies over dress and appearance from arising. The teacher may ask through the process:

- In drawing up your code of personal appearance, did you all agree? Over which issues was there disagreement? What happened when you disagreed?
- Did any one individual dominate the group? Why do you think this was? Did some members of the group contribute less than the others? If so, why was this?
- Did your group change its mind or reexamine its position at any phase? Why did this occur? Did any particular individual or argument change your point of view?
- Did any particular evidence strongly influence you? Which evidence? Why?

The Inquiry Process. Central to this inquiry model, and even more important than the final outcome, is the process the students utilized. As a consequence, the teacher must spend time discussing, analyzing and evaluating the process of inquiry as it evolves.

19. Conduct a final discussion that focuses on the whole issue of dress codes and student rights. Revolve it around questions such as:

- What rights do students have at school?
- What authority do schools have over students?
- How important do you think appearance is in society?
- Do you think that "giving in" to parents would be better than causing a great deal of tension and controversy?
- Are there some principles that should be upheld by institutions?
- What are the most important principles and rules that should govern student

1993-94 codes as set out in the Parent/Student Handbook.

Generally, a strong relationship exists between a student's appearance and his or her conduct. Good grooming and appropriate dress are encouraged and expected of the students enrolled in the district. A student's grooming, dress, and conduct not only relate to the student, but reflect on the student's family, school, and community. The following shall apply:

Administrative Guidelines

1. The principal will be the authority in all decisions regarding the grooming and dress code. Any provision not covered in the code, or any interpretation of the code, or any exception to the code will be the administration's responsibility.
2. Upon recommendations from the principal, the Superintendent has the authority to add to the dress code prohibition of any identifying marks, hairstyles, clothing, etc. associated with gangs or gang activities.
3. The grooming and dress code applies to all students enrolled in the Bastrop Independent School District while at the school, or while participating in a school sponsored or school-related activity.
4. Compliance with the grooming and dress code will be checked each day.

General

1. Cleanliness will be expected at all times.
2. Students shall come to school looking clean and neat and wearing clothing and exhibiting grooming that will not be a health or safety hazard to the student or others. The district prohibits pictures, emblems, or writings on clothing that are lewd, offensive, vulgar, or obscene, or that advertise or depict tobacco products, alcoholic beverages, drugs or any other substance prohibited under policy FNCF(L) and prohibits any clothing or grooming that in the principal's judgement may reasonably be expected to cause disruption of or interference with normal school operations.
3. See-through attire will not be permitted.
4. The midriff must be covered in a normal standing, sitting, or moving position.
5. Clothes are to be worn only as originally designed by the manufacturer.
6. Appropriate undergarments must be worn but not visible.
7. Shoes must be worn.
8. Metal or hard taps on shoes will not be permitted.
9. Sunglasses may not be worn inside building unless prescribed by a doctor for inside use.
10. Jewelry that in the principal's judgement would interfere with instruction or disrupt the regular educational program will not be permitted.
11. Headbands, neckbands, legbands, or armbands will not be permitted.
12. Hats and caps may not be worn inside the building.
13. Visible tattoos that, in the principal's judgment would interfere with instruction or disrupt the regular educational program, will not be permitted.
14. Shirts and blouses must be kept properly zipped or buttoned, and no low-neck or low-back garments will be permitted.
15. Tank tops will not be worn.
16. Clothes that have holes or that are cut up will not be permitted.
17. Cut-offs, biker shorts, and wind shorts, or warm-ups are not to be worn to school. (Warm-ups that resemble slacks are permitted.)
18. Walking shorts are permitted, and must be to the bottom of the fingertips when standing straight and arms are held down.

Specific Guidelines for Boys' Grooming

1. Faces must be completely clean shaven (no beards or mustaches of any style).
2. Hair must be neat and clean. The rear length must be no longer than to the bottom of a regular shirt collar. On the sides, the bottom of the earlobe must be visible. In the front, the length cannot be longer than the top of the eyebrows. Afro style is limited to a maximum of 3 inches in length.
3. Wearing of earrings or studs is not allowed.

Specific Guidelines for Girls' Grooming

1. Split skirts for girls may be worn if they meet the dress requirements for length.
2. Girls' skirt lengths must be no shorter than 3 inches above the knee.
3. Dresses with spaghetti straps or exposed backs are not permitted.

behavior in schools?
- Should parents have more power in deciding the nature of their child's education?
- Should children of different sexes be treated differently in school? Why? Why not?
- What, if any, human rights do you think are denied to students in schools?

Such a discussion provides an important entry point into fundamental political, social, philosophical, and historical issues centered on subjects such as civil disobedience, the need for control for organizational efficiency, the nature of authority, human rights, the stability of institutions, totalitarianism, and individual freedom.

After following the Social Studies Inquiry model and reflecting on the outcomes and processes involved, the student will have actively participated in the intellectual process of critical inquiry, and the classroom will have in effect become a laboratory for actively reflecting and resolving social issues.

Reference

[1]Massialas, Byron G., and C. Benjamin Cox. *Inquiry in Social Studies.* New York: McGraw-Hill Books, Inc., 1966.

Table 1: Lesson Overview

Orientation

- Establish groups
- Groups decide on a code for student appearance in school
- Present codes for class discussion
- Formulate or modify codes in groups after discussion
- Introduce newspaper article
- Identify the problems posed by the social issue covered in the newspaper article
- Groups become the school board and address the problem

Hypothesis

- Students create hypotheses in groups

Exploration

- Students relate their codes and hypotheses to the problem faced by the school board
- Discuss the problem in groups in order to arrive at a position on the issue
- A representative from each group shares the group's position with the class
- Discuss and evaluate the groups' positions in class discussion

Evidencing

- Students seek evidence on the issue
- Students share the evidence they accumulate in group and class discussion

Generalizations

- Form generalizations
- Discuss generalizations in group discussion
- Groups justify their decisions to the class (with decisions being grounded in the best evidence available)
- Assess the process of inquiry
- Discuss the entire problem in relation to wider social issues

CRITICAL PEDAGOGY AND SOCIAL EDUCATION

by Cleo H. Cherryholmes

CONSENSUS AND CONFLICT

Critical pedagogy is a vague and ambiguous term. It gained currency in England in the late 1960s in reference to teaching practices related to the "new sociology of education." Beginning in the 1970s and extending to the present in the United States, critical pedagogy has referred, more or less, to the teaching complement of curriculum theory's "reconceptualist" movement (Pinar 1975). This movement has never been unified and continues to defy easy description. In the United States it is historically related to such "reconstructionist" educators of the pre-World War II period as John Dewey and Charles Rugg. It also exhibits influences from various western European intellectual developments that range from phenomenology to critical theory to poststructural and postmodern thought. Recently, critical pedagogy in the United States has incorporated ideas from literary criticism and theory, various strands of feminist thought and practice, and pragmatism. Even though critical pedagogy has been written about from time to time by, among others, Henry Giroux (1983), Kenneth Kickbusch (1985), Nancy Lesko (1988), Walter Parker (1986), Thomas Popkewitz (1980), Bill Stanley (1992), Tony Whitson (1991), and the author (Cherryholmes 1991), it has never been a major theme in social education.

Why should this be the case? Why should social educators show little interest in these approaches to thinking about society and its problems? Here is one answer. When they think about society, many social educators, along with social scientists and historians, implicitly, if not explicitly, distinguish between social consensus and social conflict. Social conflict in its various forms always poses a threat to whatever civil peace and stability we are fortunate enough to have. By demarcating consensus from conflict, we are encouraged to emphasize the consensual and agreeable aspects of social order, thereby turning our attention away from its darker side. Our collective fears of social distrust, civil unrest, and the potential for societal disintegration, this answer goes, is so threatening that it is tempting simply to ignore them.

A consensus-conflict distinction, however, is artificial and quickly deconstructs. Social consensus always presumes and cannot exist without social conflict. Social consensus, whenever we find it, exists because previous conflicts have been resolved or put aside, at least for the time being. But, unless we happen to be living in a utopia at the end of history, we are likely, I believe, to experience renewed social disagreements and conflicts that, in turn, will be superseded by social agreements. The link between this argument and critical pedagogy is that the latter assumes that **1.** criticism is important and integral to a responsible study of society and to a healthy social order, and **2.** criticism itself raises the specter of social unrest and conflict that brings related fears and anxieties from the background into the foreground.

Critical pedagogy is complex and marked by numerous disagreements and contradictions. In this chapter I have chosen to highlight only a few of its themes—those that draw from linguistic philosophy, critical theory, and pragmatism. My central focus is on criticism because social education, as we know it, has always assumed the importance of social criticism even though social educators historically have given it little attention.

Language, Speech, and Criticism

Language and speech are almost never discussed, analyzed, or criticized—and are rarely mentioned—as a part of social education. This is surprising because our social life, our knowledge of it, and our teaching about it cannot exist without language and speech. Social educators use language to describe, explain, cajole, or praise, but neither language nor speech are subjects of study. It is important to distinguish between language and speech in developing this line of argument. Language is constituted by words and the rules by which they are put together. A seemingly infinite number of things can be spoken or written. Speech, however, refers to what is spoken and written. Social education makes up only a tiny fraction of what can be said. A critical social educator is interested, among other things, in this question: Why do we choose to say the things we do and not something else?

One assumption about language that seems to animate social education is that language is a value-neutral medium that educators necessarily use but is not itself profitable to study. This is sometimes called a descriptivist view of language because it conceptualizes language in a descriptive way to make statements that are true or false or meaningless. In this view language is passive—it can be used to say things but not do things. This view of language, which has had and retains widespread intuitive appeal, has been discredited, however, for forty years. Why it is flawed provides some insight into the reasons many critical educators are trying to reconceptualize important aspects of curriculum and teaching.

J. L. Austin (1968) in *How To Do Things with Words* pointed out that many statements are neither true nor false nor meaningless. Statements like "I bet you that Bill Clinton will be reelected president in 1996" are actions. They are not simply true or false, and certainly they are not meaningless. This line of investigation leads to the conclusion that all statements are actions. Here is the reasoning. The word *statement* is structurally ambiguous. A statement means, in one sense, "what is stated"; this is speech as description. A statement means, in another sense, "the act of stating"; this is speech as action. Every statement is an action, and some statements can be true or false.

What, one is entitled to ask, does this have to do with social education? One implication is that values always precede speech, and a second is that values always precede facts. The effect is to deconstruct the fact-value distinction that has been an article of faith for decades among social educators. Here is the argument:

1. Statements are actions.
2. Actions cannot be taken without reference to criteria, standards, or values.
3. Therefore, values always precede speech.

Whenever one makes a statement, it is because one believes it is worth making; it is worth making more than another statement; it is the kind of statement one is entitled to make; and so on.

Factual statements, because they are statements, are also actions that are products of value judgments. Factual statements, such as "for comparable work women tend to be paid less than men," or "for the last twenty years, an increasing percentage of children have been living below the poverty line," embody value judgments.

Teachers and students can expose and critically inquire into the values, beliefs, ideologies, and points of view represented in the factual claims of their textbooks, curriculum guidelines, tests, and courses of study.

Social studies textbooks often purport to provide simply a "factual" account of, say, U.S. history, world geographic regions, or world history. Textbooks describe and sometimes attempt to explain political developments, military victories and losses, and cultural differences, for example. Because values always precede speech, social studies textbooks may be factually correct but *they are not value-free.* Textbooks result from choices about who and what to include, who and what to exclude, what to praise, what to condemn, and so on. Notwithstanding the fact that they are the products of many decisions, textbooks usually present themselves (are presented by publishers and authors) as providing a "natural" account of their subject—"this is just the way things are," "this is just the way things happened." But historical events can be described, as can any event or object, in an indefinitely large number of ways. Each description and each textbook presents a point of view—one among many. When reading textbooks, social educators should occasionally think of themselves and their students as social critics instead of simply viewing textbooks as authoritative sources of information. Critical educators would like to see social education come into the intellectual latter half of the twentieth century by discarding the outdated descriptivist view of language and the fact-value distinction.

Clarity and Criticism

To say the obvious, communication is as important to social education as language. It also is often overlooked. Whether communication takes the form of textbooks, classroom interactions, computer exercises or simulations, or otherwise, it is easily taken for granted. But clarity and cooperation are important both for the effective communication of ideas and information and for their criticism. H. P. Grice, a noted British analytic philosopher, believes that much of our communication is a cooperative effort with a common purpose. His observations about effective communication, which he summarizes in what is called Grice's Cooperative Principle, are useful in thinking critically about social education. Grice's (1975, 48-52) Cooperative Principle has four parts:

1. Quantity (provide as much information as needed and no more);
2. Quality (avoid saying something that you believe is false or for which you have no evidence);
3. Relation (make it relevant); and
4. Manner (be orderly, brief, clear, and avoid ambiguity and obscurity).

As odd as it might seem, perhaps one of the most productive uses of criticism occurs in the context of cooperation. An important effect of cooperation in communication is to produce clarity. At its simplest, clarity in communication will lead to agreement or disagreement, either of which lays the basis for future intellectual development and understanding. Grice's principle is useful in avoiding disagreements brought about by foggy, fuzzy, ambiguous, or obscure communication that might otherwise pose as criticism.

Teachers should promote clarity in classroom interactions in order to enhance critical insights or, at least, indicate when clarity is not desirable.

Sometimes, to be sure, we desire to be playful, obscure, and poetic in what we say in order to explore ideas and their consequences. But as we wend our way through the mazes of our thoughts and arguments, it is useful to distinguish between disagreements that arise from our inability to express ourselves clearly and disagreements about ideas themselves. Clarity is important in advancing criticism and understanding.

Power and Criticism

It would be an excessively narrow and idealistic view of criticism if it were to be restricted to the observation that facts are not value-free. Where do our values come from? The values and preferences of teachers and students come from somewhere; they do not appear out of nowhere. The knots of power in which all of us find ourselves are the source of many of our values and preferences. By power I mean asymmetrical social, political, and material relationships among people that lead some to be rewarded and others to be deprived. These inequalities, in turn, are based on differences among people in possessions or characteristics, and power is determined by the relationships that emanate from these differences. In this way power becomes embedded and crystallized in social institutions and cultural habits because such inequalities often are perpetuated from one generation to the next (Cherryholmes 1988).

Social education is one social institution and collection of habits that can either contribute to these inequalities and our beliefs about them or can expose them to open deliberation and criticism. Because social education purports to educate about what we know and understand about society, it necessarily includes education in the virtues that support existing power structures. These virtues and power arrangements make our society what it is. Critical educators believe that it is important to open up this aspect of social education and make it an explicit part of the curriculum instead of letting it remain hidden.

Teachers and students can critically inquire into the exercise and effects of power in society as well as how power operates to constitute social studies education (textbooks, curriculum guides, tests, scopes and sequences, etc.).

One effect of discussing and criticizing the effects and exercise of power in social studies education is to promote social self-understanding. Here is the line of reasoning. For an individual to be socialized into a society—to be a member of society as it were—she must first learn and then explicitly accept its social norms and values. But we are rarely reminded—or rarely choose to remind ourselves—that our society is the outcome of a series of choices in addition to happenstance. Our societies give the appearance of being "natural"—that this is just the way they are and could not be otherwise. But things *could* be otherwise. For example, freedom of expression and congregation, which are in the First Amendment, could have been excluded from the Bill of Rights. Had this happened, our current conceptions of political protest, legitimate scope of the mass media, and definitions of pornography, for example, would likely be different. By critically inquiring into the exercise and effects of power that structure society, teachers and students can understand more fully who they are as members of society, how things got that way, and become increasingly aware of the existence of alternatives. Values precede facts, and power precedes speech.

Criticism and the Classroom

Social educators are sometimes seduced into believing that their classroom is not part of those aspects of society that are proper subject matter for their curriculum. The temptation is to believe that what they should be studying is "outside" and not "inside" the classroom. This is based, however, on a false distinction between those "subjects" who study society and the "objects" of their study. This is one form of the subject-object distinction that characterizes much of modern thinking about the nature of the social sciences; it would be surprising if it were not shared by many social educators. That people widely believe and act upon a distinction between subject and object perpetuates an ideology of control. The problem with the distinction is that it is not possible to draw a firm and clear distinction between what is "inside" and what is "outside" the classroom. Teachers and students are products of the same historical and social trends and processes that mark the larger social world. Classrooms are distinguished by differences in authority, expertise, gender, ethnicity, age, and ability—as is the larger world.

Jurgen Habermas, an important contemporary German philosopher and critic, has outlined a theory of communicative competence that suggests a number of avenues that social educators can take if they should choose to investigate how they and their students interact. He argues that normal communicative interaction proceeds smoothly as long as four criteria are satisfied.
1. What is said is understandable.
2. The speaker is sincere.
3. What is said is truthful.

4. The speaker and hearer agree on the values and norms of what is said. (Habermas 1979, 65)

The first and second criteria, for the most part, are minimum requirements if social education is to occur at all. If classroom communications are not understandable or if someone's sincerity is questioned, normal interaction is interrupted. These interruptions, Habermas contends, can be rectified by further communication. If words are used that are new or complicated, one offers explanations and elaborations until an acceptable level of understanding is achieved. If one's sincerity is doubted, the problem is solved likewise; communication continues until the question of intention is resolved.

IV. **Teachers and students can monitor and criticize their classroom interactions in terms of the biases, values, prejudices, and points of view, including those expressing the perspectives of class, gender, ethnicity, age, etc.**

When the third and fourth criteria for normal interaction become problematic—truthfulness and normative agreement—it becomes much more difficult to bring about resolution. Habermas's arguments along these lines, however, suggest what social educators can try in their classrooms. He has yet to deal with normative disagreement in detail, but in the case of truthfulness, he proposes that we should proceed to what he calls critical discourse. He acknowledges that speech is shaped and formed by values, power, ideology, ignorance, and bias. Given this, how does one move the communication to agreeing about what is truthful and not distorted or biased? What is required is an ideal speech situation. He poses: If we could describe a speech situation (classroom interaction) that is not distorted, what would it look like? Here is his answer:
1. The discourse should be non-dominated and symmetrical where every participant, teacher and students, is accorded equal status and power.
2. Each participant may make any comment, challenge any statement, question any theoretical or ethical orientation.
3. All interests must be represented.
4. The discourse cannot be allowed to turn into a contest. Voting, debating, and other strategic behaviors and outcomes are prohibited.
5. The goal is to follow the best argument until consensus is achieved. (Habermas 1979)

Critical discourse is demanding. Social educators should attempt critical discourse only on irregular and, perhaps, rather rare occasions. But critical discourse is well suited for teaching social issues because the latter invite the controversy and disagreement for which critical discourse is designed. On those occasions when the norms of critical discourse are invoked, the power and interests of the society and classroom become quickly illuminated.

Pragmatism, Aesthetics, and Criticism

American pragmatists, beginning with Charles Sanders Peirce and William James at the turn of the century and continuing through John Dewey and into the present to Richard Rorty, Donald Davidson, and Cornel West, have brought criticism into the public arena in a number of creative ways. Here is Peirce's 1905 version of the pragmatic maxim:

> The method prescribed in the [pragmatic] maxim is to trace out in the imagination the conceivable practical consequences—that is, the consequences for deliberate, self-controlled conduct—of the affirmation or denial of the concept; and the assertion of the maxim is that herein lies the whole of the purport of the word, the *entire* concept. (Thayer 1984, 493)

Many implications of Peirce's maxim for criticism in social education are quite straightforward. For example, if one is interested in determining the meaning of a policy proposal or court decision or administrative ruling or an interpretation of an historical event, one proceeds by estimating its consequences. By focusing on the practical consequences of an idea or proposal, pragmatists contend, many needless disagreements can be avoided.

V. Teachers and students should pragmatically appraise the meaning of social phenomena and the aesthetics of ordinary experience, considering what kind of society they wish to live in and what kind of lives they wish to live.

If criticism is pursued pragmatically, a number of implications follow. Here is an abbreviated list:

1. Pragmatists do not make sharp distinctions between the text of a concept or idea and its context. In order to understand what an idea means, pragmatically speaking, is to put it into the context of its application.

2. Pragmatists think holistically. They try to avoid fragmenting tasks, routines, and responses because to do so is to ignore some consequences and, as a result, may become less pragmatic.

3. Pragmatists do not make sharp distinctions between fact and value or theory and practice. This is because the consequences of any set of factual statements have evaluative implications and each value position leads to some facts instead of to others.

4. Pragmatists are fallibilists. They assume that whatever they think they know and believe could be in error. They expect that whatever strategies they pursue will at some time be found wanting.

5. Pragmatists believe in democracy. This is related to the earlier discussion of Habermas's critical discourse. If some people and their critical perspectives are excluded from our conversations, then we are more likely to overlook possibly some consequences that may turn out to be important in achieving our purposes.

6. Pragmatists are guided by the aesthetics of ordinary experience. The consequences they seek are pleasurable, joyful, satisfying, productive, beautiful, ethical, efficacious, and fit together.

7. Therefore, criticism from a pragmatic perspective is a continuing conversation and experiment, a discourse on the consequences of thinking, if you will, about what is beautiful, what our ideas mean, what democracy means, and how we wish to live our lives.

The pragmatists address, I believe, the question that animates social education as well as critical pedagogy: Why do we do what we do? Their answer: In order to lead beautiful, satisfying, productive, and pleasurable lives. It is remarkable how far removed most of the time we are from pragmatism and its aesthetic impulses. Evidence for this last observation is provided by the fact that we rarely pose questions of aesthetic consequence either to ourselves or to others. Perhaps pragmatism, aesthetics, and the criticism they require are too demanding to be seriously included in social education. If that is the case, all of us, I believe, will be the lesser for it.

References

Austin, J. L. *How To Do Things with Words.* New York: Oxford University Press, 1968.

Cherryholmes, Cleo H. *Power and Criticism: Poststructural Investigations in Education.* New York: Teachers College Press, 1988.

Cherryholmes, Cleo H. "Critical Research and Social Studies Education." In *Handbook of Research on Social Studies Teaching and Learning.* edited by James Shaver, 41–55. New York: Macmillan Publishing Co., 1991.

Giroux, Henry. (1983). *Theory and Resistance in Education: A Pedagogy for the Opposition.* Boston, MA: Bergin and Garvey, Publishers, Inc.

Grice. H. P. "Logic and Conversation." In Vol. 3. of *Syntax and Semantics,* edited by Peter Cole and Jerry Morgan, 41–58. New York: Academic Press, 1975.

Habermas, Jurgen. *Communication and the Evolution of Society.* Boston: Beacon Press, 1979.

James, William. *Pragmatism.* 1907. Indianapolis, Ind.: Hackett Publishing Co., 1981.

Kickbusch, Kenneth. "Ideological Innocence and Dialogue: A Critical Perspective on Discourse in the Social Studies," *Theory and Research in Social Education* 13, no. 3 (1985): 45-56.

Lesko, Nancy. *Symbolizing Society: Stories, Rights and Structure in a Catholic High School.* London: Falmer Press, 1988.

Parker, Walter. "Justice, Social Studies and the Subjectivity/Structure Problem," in *Theory and Research in Social Education* 14, no. 4 (1986): 277-295.

Pinar, William. *Curriculum Theorizing: The Reconceptualists.* Berkeley, Calif.: McCutchan Publishing, Co., 1975.

Popkewitz, Thomas. "Global Education as a Slogan System," in *Curriculum Inquiry* 10, no. 3 (1980): 303-316.

Stanley, William. *Curriculum for Utopia: Social Reconstructionism and Critical Pedagogy in the Postmodern Era.* Albany, NY: State University of New York Press, 1992.

Whitson, Tony. *Constitution and Curriculum.* London: Falmer Press, 1991.

10 DISCUSSION METHODS IN AN ISSUES-CENTERED CURRICULUM

by Jeff Passe and Ronald W. Evans

Classroom discussion is an essential element of an issues-centered curriculum. Wilen and White (1991) define discussion as "an educative and structured group conversation between teacher and students about subject matter at the higher cognitive levels." Discussion provides opportunities for students to reach several educational goals, including a depth of knowledge, rationality, commitment to fairness, development of critical thinking skills, a strengthening of oral expression and listening comprehension, development of insight into the values of oneself and others, and practice in the democratic process (Bridges 1979). Without discussion, an issues-centered curriculum is unlikely to progress past a cursory review of the topic and with shallow reflection.

Classroom discourse has long been present in schools, but not always in a manner that promotes the goals of an issues-centered curriculum (Wilen and White 1991). Teachers who choose to emphasize the study of issues must consider the following factors:

- Teacher impartiality
- Creating an atmosphere conducive to discussion
- Choice of topics
- Background knowledge
- The role of the teacher
- Teacher questioning
- Discussion management
- Discussion format
- Concluding the discussion

If handled properly, classroom discussion can be instrumental in student growth and, ultimately, in the development of democratic citizens. Poor implementation, however, can promote cynicism, intolerance, shallowness, and docility.

In other words, it can negate the very curricular goals it was designed to strengthen.

Teacher Impartiality

A longstanding belief by many educators is that teachers must maintain strict neutrality in all controversial discussions. In an issues-centered curriculum, which is built upon controversy, the teacher's role would be considerably restricted if implemented in such an environment. Kelly (1986) takes issue with this approach, citing several impediments, the most practical of which is the difficulty inherent in maintaining a neutral posture. Can teachers conduct a discussion on an issue that is near and dear to their hearts, such as abortion rights, racial discrimination, or teacher salaries, without tipping off their feelings through body language, voice inflection, or words? Most adults would agree that they could not do so. Besides, why would they want to?

One popular reason for maintaining neutrality is the threat of indoctrination of the students by the teachers. Teacher influence over student opinions, however, may be overrated. Research on the development of political socialization has yet to show convincing evidence that schools, negatively or positively, affect students' attitudes toward political issues (Nelson 1991). The role of the family, however, is certainly a powerful one, especially in the early years (Sunal 1991); the influence of mass media (Splaine 1991), peers (Cusick 1991), and the church must also be considered. Without more definitive research findings, it must be concluded that political socialization is a complex process with multiple factors. One teacher among the dozens that children encounter throughout their lives is unlikely to indoctrinate children to a significant degree.

Of greater concern than undue influence by

teachers is the development of democratic models. Kelly (1986) argues that students need to learn how to present an argument in a responsible manner, and that teachers can demonstrate how to do so with integrity. Addressing the concern that students' opinions will be unfairly swayed by teacher power, Kelly urges teachers to exercise impartiality rather than neutrality. Being neutral is refusing to take a side, which adds nothing to a debate and often frustrates students who are willing to risk sharing their own opinions. Impartiality, on the other hand, has teachers sharing their opinions but also encouraging dissenting opinions and discouraging parroting. Teachers exercising impartiality appear to have the best chance of developing students' skills in classroom discourse, which is a goal that is of greater import than having students agree with the teacher. The key is remaining true to the goals of the curriculum.

Creating an Atmosphere Conducive to Discussion

One aspect of impartiality is creating a classroom climate in which all student opinions receive respect. If students believe that their opinions will subject them to ridicule, emotional outbursts, or discrimination, they will refuse to participate. To avoid the specter of a discussion in which no opinions are expressed—one of the great teacher nightmares—ground rules must be set and enforced. While many of these guidelines appear to be mere common sense or basic classroom management, they are often ignored, promoting student dissatisfaction with classroom discussion.

The primary rule for any group discussion is that only one person speaks at a time; basic etiquette insures that the speaker's opinions will be heard by everyone, thus avoiding the inefficiency of debaters repeating one another's points or criticizing arguments that were never expressed. It also precludes the possibility of students interrupting one another when a disagreeable statement is made. While calling on raised hands may limit the spontaneity of a conversation, it is the standard for any large meeting.

A second key rule is that discussion be moderated. When students engage in one-to-one debates without moderation, they quickly digress into shouting matches with little intellectual quality. A system of rules, such as Robert's Rules of Order, while cumbersome, can help maintain

an impartial climate while students practice the system. Teachers should usually serve as discussion leaders because they can also interject questions, provide background knowledge, and serve other pedagogical functions in addition to being moderator. At certain points, however, allowing students to serve as moderators aids development of their own leadership skills and allows the teacher to take on other roles.

A third rule, which is more difficult to enforce, is the prohibition of eye rolling, groans, and other disrespectful behavior. For many students, those gestures appear to be ingrained in their personalities, but teachers must outlaw them anyway. The best strategy for achieving this may be a simple appeal to the students' sense of fair play, with a discussion of the negative consequences on individuals' self-esteem, classroom climate, and the quality of the discussion. If teachers can state this rule firmly and enforce it by banishing violators from the discussion, students will be more willing to appreciate the rule and abide by it. Ultimately, the sense of comfort that results from a positive classroom climate will reinforce students' observance of the rules.

Choice of Topics

Successful discussions seldom arise spontaneously. They are more likely to be the result of teacher planning. Choosing the right topic for discussion is a primary responsibility for teachers in an issues-centered curriculum. Presumably, any discussion will be based on topics for which the students have already indicated an interest. Even so, there are other considerations that will insure maximum discourse.

Discussions must be based on an issue that students seek to explore. Without some sort of intellectual curiosity, the discussion will never evolve. Piaget's concept of disequilibration may be helpful for teachers who wish to choose effective discussion starters. When people are confronted with a situation that does not match their expectations, they become intent on resolving the discrepancy—or, equalizing the disequilibration. In a discussion, disequilibration is relieved through the exchange of views.

It is not difficult to achieve disequilibration in an issues-centered curriculum because there are so many issues that are difficult to resolve: Why do people—be they criminals, assassins, philanthropists, political leaders, or teachers—behave the way they do? What should be done to solve the problem of pollution or war, hunger, homelessness, or poor school lunches? What will be the effect of a new health care policy or deficit reduction or in-school suspension?

One key to successful discussion is controversy. When students disagree, they may be exposed to viewpoints that they never have heard, resulting in further disequilibration. Dialogue between disagreeing parties promotes the self-reflection and analysis that is part of the critical thinking model (Beyer 1985). This goal can also be achieved without controversy, such as when students agree on something but for different reasons. In planning discussion topics, teachers should anticipate the range of responses students will offer, to insure that sufficient disequilibration takes place.

Certain topics lend themselves to us as what Roby (1988) calls "perennial puzzlers." These are the questions that have appeared in scholarly discussions since the earliest days of academia. Some are open-ended, focused on defining justice, truth, or the nature of humankind; others are more dialectic, such as the nature versus nurture debate. Value conflicts, such as those studied by Kohlberg (1984) and Gilligan (1982), almost always make good perennial puzzlers: Is stealing permissible to save a life? Is it ever okay to lie? Schuncke and Krogh (1983) have developed a series of decision stories that create value conflicts that are particularly vexing for children in the lower elementary grades.

Most topics in an issues-centered curriculum lend themselves to value discussions because they involve decisions. Any decision requires a consideration of conflicting values. Schools, for example, are constantly choosing between rules that promote efficiency but possibly violate freedom. Communities must sometimes choose between property rights and equality. Individuals must decide whether to sacrifice short-term benefits for long-term goals. Teachers can promote high-level discussions if they look for the value conflicts inherent in issues.

Background Knowledge

Before students can operate at a high level concerning a particular issue, they need background knowledge (Passe 1988). Children cannot offer solutions for the problems in the Middle East without an overview of the history, geography, politics, and culture of that region. They cannot delve into the beliefs of slaveholders without

learning about conditions in the nineteenth century. If teachers are disappointed with the quality of student discourse, they would be wise to examine how prepared their students are to discuss topics at high levels. While much learning can take place during a discussion, sometimes direct instruction is necessary beforehand.

The Role of the Teacher

The greatest stress on the teacher in an issues-centered curriculum is promoting an honest and fair discussion of the issues. The literature on classroom discourse identifies several possible teacher roles, including moderator, mediator, proponent, and devil's advocate, some of which may be played simultaneously. Most teachers take on several roles during the same discussion (Roby 1988).

Teachers must monitor themselves to determine the best role to play at certain times. Without careful self-reflection, teachers may neglect a role that could be helpful in achieving a goal, or worse, may subvert it. As a case in point, suppose a student makes a remark that provokes a strong reaction from several perspectives, such as blaming the poor for their poverty. When students are eagerly waving their hands to react to the comment, the teacher may be tempted to strictly serve as a moderator, passively insuring that each student is called upon in turn. In a best-case scenario, the teacher would have already prepared the students for the expected flood of opinions, by attempting to identify the range of viewpoints. These perspectives could then be reviewed at the conclusion of the debate. The key for the teacher is anticipating the course of the discussion by noticing cues.

Another temptation may be to raise the level of tension by egging on students. While adding liveliness to the discussion, this strategy could be harmful because it may promote an unhealthy environment for rational discussion. Teachers who are vigilant at monitoring the situation will promote the goals of the lesson and avoid letting themselves or the students be drawn into a debate that challenges the opinion but also poisons the atmosphere.

Teacher Questioning

During a discussion, the teacher's strategy of questioning can be effective in promoting curricular goals. Two key determinants of an effective issues-centered discussion are ownership of the answer and leadership of the discussion. If the teacher has the answer and the leadership, the classroom discourse is more like a quiz show, with no real discussion taking place. If the teacher has neither the leadership nor the answer, the discourse is more of a free-for-all, with only a slight chance of achieving depth and focus (Roby 1988). Ideally, the teacher should maintain discussion leadership with no one person owning the answer. That permits the teacher to guide students toward higher-level thinking.

During the course of discussion, questions should be geared toward higher-level thinking. An open-ended question—such as What should be done about?—avoids either/or choices and encourages creative problem solving. Affective questions, such as those addressing the values behind a decision or the feelings of individuals or groups—which can only be inferred and are, therefore, not owned by anyone—promote self-reflection and insight into the belief systems of others (Taba 1967).

"Wait time" (Rowe 1978) is essential in promoting the kind of thoughtful, meaningful discourse that characterizes a strong discussion. Increasing the length of pauses after a question is asked and before the teacher responds to the answer has been shown to significantly increase student achievement. In an issues-centered discussion, the need for thoughtfulness is paramount. Poorly thought-out comments distract students from the central issues and often provoke animosity. Thoughtfulness is also crucial in maximizing the degree of participation, as hesitant students have additional time to prepare their comments.

Discussion Management

Because questions are so efficient during recitation, teachers sometimes overuse them in discussion (Dillon 1983). A teacher who asks a question usually has the answer, so students tend to avoid the creative thought, critical thinking, or careful listening to classmates that discussion entails. A discussion may develop the more natural tone of a conversation if teachers use wait time or statements instead of questions in response to student comments.

Klinzing and Klinzing-Eurich (1988) recommend that teachers not always respond to student answers and instead let other students react. Providing a response to every student comment tends to move the discussion back to the front of the room, placing considerable power in the hands of the teacher. This results in a type of inquisition, instead of a free-flowing exchange of ideas between students. The atmosphere for genuine conversation becomes perverted when teachers talk too much. Besides, the ultimate goal is student empowerment that will lead to personal and societal benefits. Those who can listen to one another without the constant intervention of a moderator may be best suited to the demands of both the interpersonal and political arenas.

This is not to argue that teachers should never interject comments. To skirt the line between a discussion and a free-for-all, teachers should look for opportunities to raise the level of discourse. At certain points, a probing question or the contrasting of student utterances can move the discussion in a positive direction (Klinzing and Klinzing-Eurich 1988). Probing questions, which encourage students to clarify or expand on their ideas, have been correlated with general student achievement (Brophy and Good 1986). Such questions are particularly valuable in an issues-centered discussion. Unclear statements are common in public discourse, especially among those with little experience at it, such as children. A probing question can avoid misunderstanding and promote communication.

One type of probing question that is often overlooked is the kind that asks for evidence to support a particular point. Teachers can help students strengthen their arguments by asking for supporting data (Russell 1988). Of course, students can eventually learn to ask for such evidence themselves, thus removing the teacher from the role of arbiter. Either way, the result of this strategy should be higher-level arguments.

Teacher comments can serve other purposes besides higher-level thought. At times, a humorous comment may be needed to reduce tension. A lengthy or convoluted discussion may require periodic summaries. Certainly, if the teacher becomes aware of the need for additional background information, an interjection is essential (Passe 1984). In general, however, less teacher talk and more student talk is the goal (Flanders 1970).

Discussion Format

Many teachers find it helpful to employ a variety of formats for structuring different portions of a discussion. In this section we will describe formats that we believe teachers will find helpful in conducting discussions in both small- and large-group settings.

Small-group discussion may take a variety of forms, including groupwork and cooperative learning. Small-group discussion may be used for brief periods. Dyads or triads, for example, can be formed to get students talking for a few minutes prior to a full-group discussion or other activity. Groupwork can be employed for portions of a class period, fifteen to forty minutes or more, depending on the question being discussed and the time necessary for completion. Cooperative learning groups can continue over the course of a unit, a semester, or even longer.

Like any discussion, groupwork will be more effective if a few simple guidelines are followed. As Cohen (1986) writes, small-group discussion works best when groups are limited to four or five members, students are placed in heterogeneous groups (based on gender, ethnicity, and academic skills), students are held accountable for the work of the group and for their individual contributions, and students have an interesting decision to make or problem to resolve.

Large-group discussion can include a variety of formats and activities ranging from panel discussions and debates to mock trials and simulations. Large-group discussion formats vary depending on whether roles are assigned, on whether the full class participates at all times, and on the type of structure guiding the discussion. The discussion can focus on various kinds of problematic questions related to issues of the past, present, or future. Several styles of formats—Socratic, council, and Quaker—allow for full participation of all class members during the entire activity, but also provide strict guidelines for participation. In every format, the structured discussion of the full group is followed by comment and question.

Format Styles

Socratic. Students sit in a horseshoe pattern (if feasible), with the teacher at the opening of the horseshoe or moving about inside. The teacher directs questions about a thought-provoking selection of text (not a textbook) to individual students, asking them to explain the meaning of a particular passage, define the issue posed, take a stand on the author's viewpoint, react to the opinion of another student, or provide evidence to support a contention, etc. (Adler 1984).

Council. Students sit in one large circle. A talking stick is passed from student to student.

Each person has the opportunity to speak, only when he or she has the stick. The guidelines are to talk honestly, be brief (one minute), and speak from the heart.

Quaker. Students sit in a large circle. Individual students may stand and move into the center of the circle—one person at a time—when moved to speak. Individuals may speak until they have completed all they want to say. Other than the individual speaking, students sit in silence throughout the activity; no questions or comments are allowed. Objects related to the topic may be used as props for student commentary; for example, on gender issues a Barbie doll or a baseball could be used.

Fishbowl. Students work in small groups discussing an issue or problem and send a representative from their group to sit inside the fishbowl—an inner circle of concentric circles. Student representatives inside the fishbowl discuss the issue or problem and attempt to reach a consensus. Students outside the fishbowl may communicate with their representatives by passing notes (Grambs and Carr 1991).

Panel Discussion. A small group of students, seated in front of the class, hold a discussion on a topic, issue, or problem. Discussion is led by a moderator, usually the teacher. What will emerge is an informal conversation that is not as formally structured as a debate.

Debate. Two teams of students debate a resolution, pro versus con, in front of a class audience. The teams are given time to prepare arguments and counter-arguments. An opening statement from a member of the pro team is followed by a rebuttal statement from the con team, and then each member of the team is allowed a statement in turn, followed by rebuttal from the opposition. Following open debate and questions from the floor, team members may be asked to drop or reverse their roles.

Role Playing Debate. This is debate enhanced with specific biographical or situational roles. A debate on a zoning ruling, for example, might include an industrialist, a labor leader, and an unemployed worker.

Role Playing for Social Values. A small group of students prepares for and acts out a skit portraying a difficult, value-laden issue. Following the first enactment, the class discusses alternative choices, and members of the class are asked to act out their choices and the consequences they think will follow (Shaftel and Shaftel 1967).

Variations on Format Styles

There are many other variations on these formats, including the town meeting, congressional debate, presidential cabinet discussion, and personal decision making. Teachers should keep in mind the following aspects of conducting large-group discussion activities, especially when conducting one of the more complex ones:

- Set a context for the activity, providing sufficient background for the students so that they know the key facts and are clear about the key issue and its importance.
- Make sure the central question or resolution is simple, direct, and clear. The positions to be assumed by participants (pro, con, various roles, etc.) must also be clearly specified.
- Clarify procedures for students in advance and set behavior guidelines.

- Allow students time to prepare for the activity by studying their roles, ask questions, etc. If only a select number of students is involved in an activity, appoint "understudies" for key roles in case of absence.
- Write brief role descriptions for students, building in argument and evidence. A preferred option, when feasible, is to have students research their roles or positions.
- Ask students to think like the people in the roles they will play, and to argue from that viewpoint.
- Serve as moderator for the activity. After the class has gained experience with the exercise, appoint a student as moderator.
- After the activity, have a debriefing and connect the issue studied and the method to future lessons: What have we learned about this topic? What do we believe now? Why? What have we learned about participating in this type of discussion activity?

Mock Trial. Students assume the roles of judge (or a panel of judges), lawyers, witnesses, bailiff, jury, etc. After being given role descriptions, students conduct a mock trial and jury deliberation.

Simulation. This is an activity in which students re-create an environment simulating some social situation of the past or present. This activity involves individual and group decision making.

Concluding the Discussion

Most public forums use discussion as a method of resolving differences. Political leaders are expected to vote on a course of action and implement it. Most classroom discussions do not have that expectation. The major emphasis of schools, and of the issues-centered curriculum in particular, is on process. Therefore, there is no harm in students merely agreeing to disagree, but this is often overlooked. Many classroom discussions end when the bell rings. That usually signifies an enthusiastic class session in which so many hands were raised and so many ideas abounded that teachers and students lost track of the time. Having a discussion end because time runs out will happen occasionally, but it should be the exception rather than the rule. Teachers have a responsibility to end discussions in a man-

ner that maximizes learning.

If a discussion involves a variety of opinions, students need an opportunity to tie the different viewpoints together. Most children are not adept at looking at the gestalt of the discussion, and are more likely to focus on particular arguments or incidents. Teachers can help students look for common or disparate themes by asking them to analyze the discussion. Students can also be asked to create a summary of what was said.

It is essential that students perform this function, rather than the teacher. Students need to practice the skill and will not do so if the teacher does it for them. Of course, younger children will need help in this process, but teachers should still avoid putting words into their mouths. Often, when students are asked to analyze or summarize, their perceptions are quite different from the teacher's. This is a perfect opportunity for formative evaluation.

Summaries and analyses do not have to take place in full-class sessions. All too often, it is the brightest or most verbal students who offer summaries and analysis while the rest of the class does not attempt to do so. Arranging students in pairs or small groups will allow the same processes to take place, but with more participation. Having students write a summary or analysis in their notebooks maximizes the level of participation and also improves the quality of the students' notes. After all, most students do not take notes during discussions unless the teacher reminds them to do so at certain points (although the knowledge that comes from the discussions may be even more valuable than notes based on direct instruction).

Journal writing is an excellent strategy for processing a discussion. This time for contemplation of the different viewpoints and reflection upon the student's own role in the discussion may make for a better understanding of the topic and of the self. A major body of research has identified student writing as a powerful learning tool (Gilstrap 1991).

In addition to summarizing, analyzing, and processing discussions, students may also focus on subsequent courses of action. Should the discussion be continued? Should some sort of resolution be proposed? Is social or political action viable? In other words, what do students want to do about the issue that has been discussed? This question, of course, may lead to an entirely new discussion, but it is a worthy one because it emphasizes that discussion does not have to be just for discussion's sake.

All of these approaches to concluding a discussion require time. When there are insufficient minutes during a class period to end a discussion properly, plans should be made to do so at the beginning of the next session—otherwise, students may not grasp the key ideas of the discussion, see their implications, or evaluate the experience. Teachers who are aware of the time will be more likely to manage the discussion to promote maximum learning.

References

Adler, Mortimer. *The Paideia Program: An Educational Syllabus.* New York: Macmillan, 1984.

Beyer, B. K. "Critical Thinking: What Is It?" *Social Education* 49 (1985): 270-76.

Bridges, David. *Education, Democracy, and Discussion.* Windsor, England: National Foundation for Educational Research, 1979.

Brophy, J. E., and T. L. Good. "Teacher Behavior and Student Achievement." In *Handbook of Research on Teaching,* 3rd edition, edited by M. C. Wittrock. New York: Macmillan, 1986.

Cohen, Elizabeth. *Designing Groupwork.* New York: Teachers College Press, 1986.

Cusick, P. A. "Student Groups and School Structure." In *Handbook of Research on Social Studies Teaching and Learning,* edited by J. P. Shaver. New York: Macmillan, 1991.

Dillon, J. T. *Teaching and the Art of Questioning.* Bloomington, IN: Phi Delta Kappa, 1983.

Flanders, N. E. *Analyzing Teaching Behavior.* Reading, Mass.: Addison-Wesley, 1970.

Gilligan, C. *In a Different Voice: Psychological Theory and Women's Development.* Cambridge, Mass.: Harvard University Press, 1982.

Gilstrap, R. L. "Writing for the Social Studies." In *Handbook of Research on Social Studies Teaching and Learning,* edited by J. P. Shaver. New York: Macmillan, 1991.

Grambs, Jean D., and John C. Carr. *Modern Methods in Secondary Education.* Fort Worth: Holt, Rinehart and Winston, 1991.

Kelly, T. E. "Discussing Controversial Issues: Four Perspectives on the Teacher's Role." *Theory and Research in Social Education,* 14 (1986):113-38.

Klinzing, H. G. and G. Klinzing-Eurich. "Questions, Responses, and Reactions." In *Questioning and Discussion: A Multidisciplinary Study,* edited by J. T. Dillon. Norwood, N. J.: Ablex, 1988.

Kohlberg. L. Essays on Moral Development, Vol. 2, *The Psychology of Moral Development.* New York: Harper and Row, 1984.

Nelson, J. L. "Communities, Local to National, as Influence on Social Studies Education." In *Handbook of Research on Social Studies Teaching and Learning,* edited by J. P. Shaver. New York: Macmillan, 1991.

Passe, J. "Developing Current Events Awareness in Children." *Social Education* 52 (1988): 531-33.

---. "Phil Donahue: An Excellent Model for Leading a Discussion." *Journal of Teacher Education* 35 (1984): 43-8.

Roby, T. W. "Models of Discussion". In *Questioning and Discussion: A Multidisciplinary Study,* edited by J. T. Dillon. Norwood, N. J.: Ablex, 1988.

Rowe, M. B. *Teaching Science as Continuous Inquiry.* 2nd edition. New York: McGraw-Hill, 1978.

Russell, T. L. "Questions and Arguments." In *Questioning and Discussion: A Multidisciplinary Study,* edited by J. T. Dillon. Norwood, N. J.: Ablex, 1988.

Schuncke, G. M, and S. L. Krogh. *Helping Children Choose.* Glenview, Ill.: Scott-Foresman, 1983.

Shaftel, Fannie R., and George Shaftel. *Role Playing for Social Values: Decision Making in the Social Studies.* Englewood Cliffs, N. J.: Prentice Hall, 1967.

Splaine, J. E. "The Mass Media as an Influence on Social Studies." In *Handbook of Research on Social Studies Teaching and Learning,* edited by J. P. Shaver.

New York: Macmillan, 1991.

Sunal, C. S. "The Influence of the Home on Social Studies." In *Handbook of Research on Social Studies Teaching and Learning,* edited by J. P. Shaver. New York: Macmillan, 1991.

Taba, H. *Teacher's Handbook for Elementary Social Studies.* Reading, Mass.: Addison-Wesley, 1967.

Wilen, W. W. and J. J. White. "Interaction and Discourse in Social Studies Classrooms." In *Handbook of Research on Social Studies Teaching and Learning,* edited by J. P. Shaver. New York: Macmillan, 1991.

11 DESIGNING ISSUE-BASED UNIT PLANS

by Joseph J. Onosko
Lee Swenson

I. INTRODUCTION

"How to" discussions of planning too often focus on the daily lesson rather than on the unit's overall design, whether it be among social studies teachers in schools or in practitioner journals and even in some instructional methods books. The unit becomes nothing more than the sum total of daily lessons addressing various facets of a topic, event or period of time. When this orientation to planning is combined with a bloated curriculum and didactic instruction, is it any surprise that student learning is fragmented[1], superficial[2], and passive[3]? While we readily acknowledge that numerous other barriers in and out of school contribute to this kind of student learning (Gross, 1989; Onosko & Newmann, 1994; Shaver, Davis & Helburn, 1979), we believe that ill-conceived unit design plays an important role.

In this chapter we provide a 5-part framework for issue-based unit planning that enables daily lessons to become more than the sum of their parts, and that promotes active, cohesive, in-depth student learning. The five main features of the framework are:
1. a central unit issue
2. an introductory "grabber"
3. lessons that link to the central issue
4. richly detailed source material; and,
5. one or more culminating projects.

A sample unit plan is also provided to illustrate this design model.

II. A Central Unit Issue
Rationale

Too many social studies units are designed around a list of facts, names, concepts, events and/or topics. This often leads to fragmented teaching and learning, broad and superficial content coverage, and lower-order cognitive tasks. Units designed around a central issue, however, provide a distinct shape or "backbone" that link daily lessons into a cohesive whole.[4] A central issue also ensures that students will be faced with an intellectual challenge, for without a challenging task there is little motivation or need to think. In addition, the exploration of an issue serves to check content coverage, thereby reducing the likelihood of fragmented, superficial treatment of subject matter. A reduction in coverage is necessary if students are to develop dispositions and skills associated with higher-order thinking (Newmann, 1988; Onosko, 1991; Wiggins, 1989). Finally, teachers become facilitators of student inquiry and knowledge construction (rather than dispensers of ready made understandings) when units possess a central issue.

Consider the potential for fragmentation and superficial understanding in a unit designed around the topic, The Revolutionary Period. As stated, the topic provides very little direction for teachers and students. All social, political, religious, geographic, and economic aspects of the period are appropriate for study. (History textbooks usually reflect this encompassing approach.) When a unit lacks focus, too often the teacher's content selection is diverse, lengthy and fragmented. Worse yet, no selection at all occurs as the teacher indiscriminately attempts to cover everything. Bewildered students during and after such an experience typically ask: "How does everything fit together?", "I'm confused—what does this have to do with what we did the other day?", or, "It seems that all we do is memorize all these events from the past." Even many teachers have difficulty explaining how their daily lessons link together into a coherent whole. Students are reduced to consumers of fragmented bits of information and ideas rather than challenged to become productive thinkers and problem solvers.

Compare the above topical approach to an issue-based approach framed around the following question, *"Were the Colonists Justified in Revolting from England?"* Knowing they must work throughout the unit to answer this challenging question, students are engaged from the start.[5] Students must learn about the contentious relations between England and the colonies, assume the perspectives of both sides, consider the legitimacy of civil disobedience in this and possibly other contexts, and then decide whether they could support the actions of the revolutionaries. The central issue enables the teacher and students to identify (and therefore narrow) what content is needed for study (i.e., British and American actions that generated tension and the underlying rationales for these actions), and provides a purposeful and challenging reason for studying the period (i.e., to take a position on the central issue).[6]

Not only is it more difficult to control content when units are structured around a topic rather than an issue, there is a greater chance that controversy will be minimized or avoided altogether. For example, the Vietnam War could be taught as a matter-of-fact, "and-then-this-happened" serialization of events, or students could be asked to summarize the views of the Johnson Administration, Ho Chi Minh and the Vietcong, the student war protesters, WWII veterans, etc., without having students themselves think about their own views or consider the validity of the perspectives they have summarized. However, when an issue structures a unit of study (e.g., *Was U.S. Intervention in Vietnam Justified?*), controversy assumes a prominent place in classroom activities. In short, social studies topics become opportunities for inquiry only when specific unresolved issues are raised.

Finally, a central unit issue helps teachers control the urge to address too many issues during a unit of study—particularly ancillary or tangential issues. For example, instead of focusing analysis on whether or not colonists were justified in revolting from England, some teachers might add the following marginally related issues: What enabled the colonial militia to defeat the better equipped and trained British forces? Should John Adams have defended the

British soldiers implicated in the Boston Massacre? Was France justified in providing aid to the colonists during the Revolution? Could the War have been won without the military leadership of George Washington? How should Loyalists have been treated during the war? and, Was it in the best interest of Native Americans to fight on either side during the War? While each of the above issues can provide an opportunity for serious inquiry, the sheer number and diversity of issues precludes its occurance—unless, of course, a semester is devoted to the American Revolution! The result is fragmented and superficial treatment of complex issues. Typically it is coverage pressure that compels teachers toward overinclusion during unit design.[7] Structuring a unit around a central issue can check this tendency and ensure directed, sustained, and challenging inquiry.

Table 1 on the next page offers examples of how topics can be transformed into central issues.

Creating A Good Central Issue

Issues in the social studies can be classified in a variety of ways. Some issues are grounded in the past (e.g., What alternative, if any, would you recommend to Jackson's "Indian" removal policy?), others involve the present (e.g., How should nuclear waste be disposed?), while others project into the future (e.g., What would happen if abortions were outlawed?). Many issues can be classified as disciplinary as they emerge from or are linked to scholarly work in particular disciplines (e.g., from economics—Is raising the prime lending rate the best way to control inflation? or from anthropology—Were neanderthals absorbed into the Cro-Magnon population or killed off?). Other issues are interdisciplinary and require the appropriation of information and ideas from two or more fields of study; for example, Should all-girl math classes be created to improve girls' math achievement? (education, law, psychology, sociology, political science). Policy issues (e.g., Should the U.S. accept gays in the military? Should Town X build a new pool?) and perennial issues (e.g., When does public safety override the rights of the individual? When is civil disobedience justified?) have also been identified and recommended for study. Issues can also be classified as primarily factual (e.g., Would an embargo have Iraq to withdraw from Kuwait?), definitional (e.g., What is a U.S. vital interest?), ethical (e.g., To what extent

Table 1: Transforming a Unit Topic into a Unit Issue

TRADITIONAL UNIT	ISSUE-BASED UNIT
The Women's Movement ⟶	Has the Women's Movement of the last three decades helped or hurt American society?
Exploration in the New World ⟶	Are the New World explorers to be praised or condemned for their efforts?
The First Amendment and Free Speech ▶	When, if ever, should free speech be limited?
Immigration ⟶	Immigration: Who should get in and Why?
Global Pollution ⟶	What should the U.S. do about global pollution?
The Legislative Branch ⟶	Does Congress have too much power?
The Cradles of Civilization ⟶	What makes a culture a "Civilization"?

should the state help the unemployed?), legal (e.g., Were Bakke's constitutional rights to equal protection violated?), or aesthetic (e.g., What makes a work of art a masterpiece?). Presumably, social studies teachers will explore many of the above types of issues with their students.[8]

Four criteria to keep in mind when creating an issue are suggested below.

1. Is it Controversial? Because issues are debatable (by definition), this criterion may seem quite unnecessary. However, it is sometimes unclear if a question selected for study constitutes an issue. Assess whether or not multiple perspectives exist; that is, can reasonable arguments be constructed which reflect opposing viewpoints on the question. If opposing perspectives cannot be identified, is it due to an inherent lack of controversy in the question or the teacher's (or students') lack of current understanding? As an example, the question, "Did the New Deal End the Great Depression?" is not an issue because most historians agree that WWII was the decisive catalyst of economic recovery. A much more debatable question (and therefore issue) is the following: "Was the New Deal a failed social experiment?" Here students must weigh the benefits and costs of a variety of federal programs, consider philosophical issues regarding the appropriate size and role of government, and so on. Checking the "debatableness" of a question (or proposition) in the early planning stages of a unit will reward teachers and students with more lively, engaging discourse later on.

2. Is the Issue Important? Defining what is an "important" issue is beyond the scope of this chapter, however, the Handbook's introductory chapter attempts to address this difficult matter. In light of the immense size and contentious nature of the social studies field it is unlikely that consensus will ever be reached on what counts as an important issue. We defer to the judgement of social studies teachers in the selection of issues for study, acknowledging that (a) reasonable people will disagree on what counts as an important issue, and that (b) even if consensus could be reached, the set of agreed upon issues would probably exceed what could be thoughtfully explored. Nonetheless, we encourage teachers to consider the following questions when identifying issues for study:

Is it an issue that has been debated in the past and continues to be debated? In other words, is it a persistent, enduring issue? Examples include the following: What resources should be publicly owned and how should their use be regulated? When is the state justified in limiting the free expression of its citizens?

Is it a matter of public concern that requires civic judgement or decision making? For example, civic judgement and action are necessary when disagreement arises over the placement of a new town dump, a state roadway initiative, a Congressional bill, and so on.

Do scholars in a discipline or across disciplines tend to agree that the issue is important? Issues that capture the attention of most scholars in or across disciplines are probably worthy candidates for study. As an example, consider the following:

Will continued depletion of the ozone layer lead to catastrophic global warming? or, To what extent does television violence contribute to violence in society?

Is an understanding of the issue likely to promote students' development? A wide range of issues have the potential to help students become more mature and socially responsible. Issues that might serve this purpose include: What responsibilities do you have to yourself and society? For the most part, is peer pressure a good or bad thing? Are some moral beliefs better than others or are they all just opinions?

3. Is the Issue Interesting? If the number of important social studies issues exceeds what can be thoughtfully explored with students, then select a subset of important issues that students are also likely to find interesting—and that the teacher already finds interesting (especially since teacher enthusiasm can significantly influence student learning). Having identified an issue of importance and interest, further enhance student interest (and motivation) by constructing a provocative phrasing. Compare, for example, the following two questions involving similar analyses: *"What Caused the American Revolution?"* and *"Did the Founding Fathers Revolt Because of Greed?"* Student interest is more likely to be perked by the irreverent suggestion that greed motivated the founding fathers compared to a rather bland and all too common query about causation.

Interest can also be enhanced by phrasing the issue in a memorable way. Take, for example, the following issue on homelessness stated as a proposition which is provocative but not memorable: "There are actually very few economic, political, social, or religious efforts that our government can attempt to help solve the problem of homelessness in the United States today." More memorable ways to state this issue include the following: *"Government's efforts to help the homeless are futile.";* *"What policies do you recommend to help the homeless?";* or, *"How would you combat homelessness if you were the President?"*

Finally, consider weaving an ethical dimension into central issues as students cannot resist invitations to make assessments of right v. wrong, good v. bad, proper v. improper, and so on. For example, most students would prefer to grapple with the ethically-charged question, *"Would you have supported or protested the Vietnam War*

Effort?" than the factual question, "What primarily led Americans to either support or protest the War?" Both queries contain issues; however, the latter is a factual issue focusing on the reasons for American support or opposition to the war, whereas the former requires both an understanding of these reasons and an ethical judgement of the appropriateness of U.S. involvement.

4. Can the Issue be Researched Effectively? Even the most important and interesting issues are rendered useless if resource materials cannot be acquired or are written at a level inappropriate for students. Successful issue analysis requires materials that reflect the perspectives and underlying rationales of the competing "camps", not just the viewpoint of one side or a very select few. These materials help trigger student interest and must promote student expertise. Presumably, important facts and ideas related to the issue will be revealed and contested areas explored. These materials might include lively readings, such as eye-witness accounts and other primary source materials, or images and pictures that provide a "visual text" for students. Some "digging" by the teacher prior to actual study can help determine if sufficient materials are available. Note that most textbooks fail as resources for issues analysis because they typically contain inadequate detail, are rarely framed around issues, and do not present competing perspectives when they do address issues (Kahane, 1984; Loewen, 1995).

III. An Introductory "Grabber"

An introductory grabber is an activity at the very beginning of a unit that draws students into the material and introduces the unit's central issue. The grabber might involve a film clip, primary document, short story, slide show, set of data, song and lyrics, brainstorming session with students, simulation, poem, quote, political cartoon, writing activity, field trip, or guest speaker. Whether brief (10 minutes) or long (1 or 2 class sessions) and whatever the format, an effective grabber triggers student interest in and reveals the teacher's enthusiasm for the upcoming unit. Introductory grabbers may include a brief look at some of the perspectives or positions one might adopt on the central issue. Students themselves may be asked to take a preliminary stand orally or in writing, knowing, of course, that it is preliminary and that viewpoints are subject to change as the investigation details perspectives and reveals new information.

The opening lessons of a unit are most critical for unit success. Failing to capture student interest and imagination may result in students "checking out" or remaining marginally engaged for the remainder of the unit. Too many teachers expend their greatest effort at the end of a unit during "mop up", "salvage the unit" review sessions rather than at the beginning when the crucial task of engaging minds must take place. The assumption behind the need for a grabber is that poor student performance in social studies is due primarily to some combination of student disinterest and low motivation, not deficiencies in students' cognitive capacities, abilities, or prior knowledge (Dweck, 1986; Keating, 1994).

A Classroom "Grabber"

For a variety of innovative and effective practical ideas on how to increase student engagement throughout a unit of study, see Bower, Lobdell & Swenson's (1994), *History Alive*. An example of a unit grabber is provided below:

Begin class by showing students 6-10 slides depicting life during the Industrial Era. Some slides convey a very positive image of the era (e.g., robust, clean, engaged workers forging steel, or ships and trains busily hauling cargo), while others reflect appalling working and living conditions (e.g., children standing at an assembly line, crowded tenements). Following an analysis of each slide, pose the unit's central issue: *Was the Industrial Revolution Good for the United States?* Drawing upon information culled from the slides and prior knowledge, students brainstorm possible "pro" and "con" responses. End class by informing students they will eventually be asked to take a position on the issue. Briefly summarize for students some of the interesting primary and secondary source materials they will study during the unit to help them in their analysis (e.g., diary accounts of life during the period, film excerpts). Ask students to think about the kinds of additional information they will need to better inform their decision making (e.g., infant mortality rates, average worker salaries, and other quality of life indicators before and during the Industrial Revolution).

IV. Connecting Lessons to the Unit's Central Issue

Structuring a unit around an issue increases the likelihood but does not guarantee that individual lessons will add up to more than the sum of their parts. To assume a purpose beyond their own internal coherence, lessons need to be sequenced in ways that advance students' understanding of and ability to answer the central issue. There is no one correct way to sequence lessons to achieve this purpose, primarily because there is no one correct way to think about an issue. However, we provide a few general curriculum and instructional suggestions on how to connect lessons to the central unit issue.

Curriculum Suggestions

Identify competing arguments and perspectives advanced by opposing sides to an issue. These perspectives can serve to guide the design of daily lessons. For example, students in a psychology class might address the question, "Why do we dream?" Two or more lessons could be devoted to Freud's theory that dreams represent repressed ideas and experiences that the ego attempts to keep submerged in the unconscious. Next, students might spend two or more days exploring Jung's view that dreams are symbolic expressions (not repressions) that provide important opportunities for self-discovery, individuation, and wholeness. Other perspectives might include Adler's view that dreams provide insight into impending decisions (rather than reflect unresolved conflicts from the past), or Crick's dismissal of dreams as a series of meaningless images resulting from REM and other brain processing activities. Following exposure to a handful of theorists, students would begin to formulate their own position on the nature and purpose of dreams.

A second way to link lessons is to identify key concepts, events, persons, and other terms that students need to effectively address the central issue. These key elements then serve to structure daily lessons. They should not be taught as ends in themselves, but rather explored in the context of students' growing understanding of the issue. For example, in a unit exploring the question, "Were the Colonists Justified in Revolting from England?", students must consider a series of British and American actions and reactions (e.g., Sugar Act, Stamp Act, Townshend Acts, Boston Tea Party, Boston Massacre) and also come to understand important concepts (e.g., virtual v. direct representation, social contract, civil disobedience) in order to answer the central issue.

A third approach that is probably least familiar to teachers but may be the most important is to identify the various sub-questions and sub-issues that need to be analyzed in order to effectively address the central issue. As noted earlier, Newmann & Oliver (1970) have provided a very helpful conceptual model that distinguishes between five types of issues; policy, ethical, definitional, factual, and legal. For example, to address the policy issue of whether or not State X should adopt the death penalty, a number of related sub-issues emerge: Will the death penalty reduce a state's homocide rate? (factual issue); When, if ever, is a state justified in taking a human life? (ethical issue); By what legal means can an execution be stayed? (legal issue); and, What is the difference between 1st and 2nd degree murder? (definitional/legal).

Regardless of the method used to coherently link lessons, the teacher (and eventually the students) must identify and understand the competing perspectives, important sub-questions, and key concepts and terms related to the central issue if honest, authentic inquiry is to occur. The teacher must also ensure that students are exposed to "best case" presentations of the various perspectives, though the order in which they are explored can vary.

Instructional Suggestions
* Prominently display the central issue somewhere in the room for easy and frequent reference.
* Remind students of the overall unit goal at the beginning of each lesson (i.e., to answer the unit's central question).
* Explain to students or have them explain how today's lesson relates to the central unit issue (whether it be the exploration of a sub-issue, particular perspective on the issue, or key event, concept, or person).
* At the end of a lesson show students or have

students explain how today's activity contributed to their growing knowledge of the central issue.
* Briefly explain to students (or have them determine) the next day's activity and how it will relate to the central issue.
* Scaffold reading and other homework assignments by explaining how the activity contributes to the mission of answering the central issue.

V. Richly Detailed Source Material
What is richly detailed source material? One way to describe these materials is in relation to the dominant social studies resource—the textbook! Textbooks typically exhibit a paucity of detail and are rarely framed around questions or issues. The presentation of material often lacks coherence or meaningful organization within and across chapters. Textbooks tend to make claims and offer conclusions with little empirical or logical support and, therefore, are of little help in promoting students' critical thinking (Kahane, 1984). Concepts are presented but go undefined, or concepts are defined but examples are not given. The writing is typically banal and devoid of controversy (Fitzgerald, 1979; Tyson-Bernstein, 1988), and on rare occasions when issues are mentioned, competing perspectives are not summarized. Too often the cumulative effect is fragmented and superficial learning by disengaged students.

Richly detailed source material ("rich detail"), on the other hand, triggers student interest and promotes students' subject matter expertise. Students learn about competing viewpoints and their underlying rationales. Important facts are stated and contested factual claims explored. Concepts receive elaboration, including the presentation of examples, counterexamples, and analogies. Rich detail also facilitates students' empathic entry into issues that might otherwise have remained personally remote and overly intellectual. Rich detail includes lively readings, such as eye-witness accounts and other primary source materials, or images and pictures that provide a "visual text." In short, rich detail helps students become and remain interested in exploring and developing a perspective on the unit's central issue.

Examples of rich detail from the sample unit on cults (see Appendix A) and from other illustrative issues mentioned in this chapter, include:

- videotape of Federal agents storming the Branch Davidian compound;
- movie excerpt of the Jonestown Massacre;
- an excerpt on the meaning of dreams from Jung's (1964) *Man and His Symbols* and,
- statistics on homicide rates before and after the implementation of capital punishment.

VI. Culminating Projects

Culminating projects ensure active student learning and greatly increase the likelihood of students gaining both in-depth and cohesive understanding of an issue. These activities give students opportunities to share the fruits of their labor; that is, to explain or share their understanding of and perspective on the central issue. They are not traditional pen and paper tests, though one format could be a well-crafted essay or position paper that is shared with others. Culminating projects often encourage group interaction and creativity, and appeal to multiple learning styles. Examples include a speech, skit or play, a radio broadcast, "live" or videotaped television newscast, a whole class or small group debate, poster display, newspaper publication, metaphorical representation of an idea, person or event, or a small group presentation. Regardless of format, culminating projects ask students to share their own perspectives on the unit's central question, not the teacher's or some other authority's perspective (though at some point the teacher may want to share his/her perspective). Units may contain more than one culminating activity. For example, a class might spend a day or two discussing or formally debating the proposition, *"Hate speech should be regulated."* A day or two later student small groups might present poster board representations of the kinds of hate speech and expression, if any, they believe should be regulated.

Culminating projects are motivating as students realize the end result is not just a written test privately graded and returned by the teacher, but rather an opportunity to demonstrate their understanding and intellectual prowess to peers. These activities are also motivating because students prefer working on collaborative projects with their peers (Goodlad, 1984). To capitalize on their motivating power, we recommend that students are introduced to project options and requirements at the beginning of a unit.

Culminating projects are a powerful means to develop students' thinking, and not only because the central unit issue must be addressed. Many students are very insecure about their ideas. Culminating projects, due to their public nature, provide students access to the ideas of others and serve to confirm the validity (or at least reasonableness) of their own thinking—both when working collaboratively in a team and when observing the presentations of other individuals and groups.

Three culminating activities can be found in the sample unit on cults in Appendix A (see Lessons 10-12). First, students address the central unit issue in a roundtable discussion. The discussion is scored by the teacher to encourage all students to participate and to enhance the quality of dialogue (see Chapter 31 by D. Harris for details on scored discussions). Second, students are to create a one-half hour videotaped or live, in-class "special report" that addresses the central issue. For instance, students might include in their presentation actual or mock interviews with current or former members of cults to discover how these cult and ex-cult members answer the central issue. Students might discuss with legal experts the ramifications of kidnapping and deprogramming or attempting to limit cult members' right to free speech. Third, students are to write a position paper articulating their position on the central issue. Outstanding papers will be read in class. All papers will be made available for peers to read.

VII. Final Thoughts

To further increase curriculum integration, issue-based unit design can be applied at the course level. Course-level issues to consider throughout a year's study of U.S. history might include: *Is the Historical Record of the U.S. One of Progress or Simply Change? Does Our History Justify the Claim that the U.S. Was and Still is a "Land of Opportunity?"* or, *Overall, Does the History of the U.S. Make You Proud to be an American?* In a world cultures course students might continually return to the question, *Are the World's Cultures Essentially Similar or Different?* In a Civics/Government class students might continually revisit the question, *What Responsibilities, If Any, Do You Have as a Citizen in a Democracy?* World history students might be asked to construct a year-end culminating project that addresses the following question: *What Lessons from History Can Help Us Create a Better World Today?*

Unit Issue: "What, if anything, should we do about cults?"

Lesson 1: DAY ONE
INTRODUCTORY GRABBER

Students watch a videotape (5 minutes) of the Branch Davidian compound in Waco, Texas turn into a fiery inferno when raided by Federal agents, and watch excerpts of a made-for-T.V. movie on the Jonestown Massacre (10 minutes). Students then share their understanding of the events leading up to the two disasters. The teacher provides supporting information. Next, the teacher poses the following questions for student response: Might the Jonestown Massacre have been avoided? Could the Branch Davidian firestorm have been avoided? Both questions are addressed. Indirectly, students have already begun to consider the unit's central question: What, if anything, should we do about cults? Students are introduced to the central question. The class agrees that more needs to be known about cults—their beliefs, activities, etc. The class then brainstorms a list of images and ideas about cults drawn from their personal knowledge.

INTRODUCE CULMINATING ACTIVITIES

Near the end of class students are informed that a round table scored discussion of the central issue will occur at the end of the unit and that 4-5 person teams will produce half-hour video-taped "special reports" or in-class presentations that explain what they believe should be done about cults.

Lesson 2: DAY TWO
FOCUS SUB-QUESTION:

What exactly is a cult?

As a class they read a newspaper article describing the history of the Jonestown cult and its leader, Jim Jones. Then in their 4-5 person teams, students attempt to construct a working definition of cults based upon yesterday's work and today's reading. The class reconvenes, each group reports the fundamental characteristics or attributes of cults they have identified, and the whole class then develops a working definition of cults. At the end of the lesson students are given two articles to read and a writing task for homework (see Lesson 3 for details).

Lesson 3: DAYS THREE & FOUR
FOCUS SUB-QUESTION:

Are the two organizations we read about last night cults?

Students come to class prepared to state whether or not they think the two organizations (the Mormons and the Nazi Party) they read about for homework are cults. The purpose of the lesson is to further develop a working definition of cults and to show students that one must think of cults on a "more or less" continuum rather than in discrete "yes or no" terms. The teacher leads a whole class discussion in which students share their analyses. Teacher questions include the fol-lowing: Do either of these organizations have similarities with the Jonestown group or the Branch Davidians? Does either organization reflect your working definition of a cult? For homework students are given an article by an expert on cults who attempts to identify essential features of cults. Students are asked to determine if their working definition of cults should be modified in light of this article.

Lesson 4: DAY FIVE
FOCUS SUB-QUESTION:

Does our definition of a cult match that of the expert?

In a whole class discussion students summarize the expert's definition and compare it to their working definition. Students then determine if they want to modify their working definition. (The definition that emerges typically includes the following characteristics: charismatic leader, physical and psychological isolation, apocalyptic vision of the future, controllers of the new order following the apocalypse, manipulation and mind control, and so on). For homework they read about two more organizations (a drug rehab center called Marathon House and a notorious cult of the late 1970's/early 80's called Synanon) and decide whether or not they are cults.

We hope the above framework for designing issue-based social studies units contributes to your teaching success with students. Though the intellectual and time demands this framework places on teachers and students exceed those of traditional textbook-driven units of study, the rewards for everyone make it all worthwhile.

References

Bower, B., Lobdell, J. & Swenson, L. *History Alive.* San Francisco: Addison-Wesley, 1994.

Dweck, C. "Motivational processes affecting learning." *American Psychologist* 41, no.10 (1986): 1040-1048.

Fitzgerald, F. *America Revised.* NY: Vintage Books, 1979.

Goodlad, J. *A Place Called School: Prospects for the Future.* New York: McGraw-Hill, 1984.

Gross, R. "Reasons for the Limited Acceptance of the Problems Approach." *The Social Studies* (September/October, 1989): 185-186.

Jung, C. *Man and his Symbols.* New York: Dell, 1964.

Kahane, H. *Logic and Contemporary Rhetoric.* Belmont, CA: Wadsworth, 1984.

Keating, D. "Critical Periods for Critical Thinking: The Adolescent in School." In *Schooling & Society,* edited by F. Miller. Albany, NY: SUNY Press, 1994.

Loewen, J.W. *Lies My Teacher Told Me: Everything Your American History Textbook Got Wrong.* New York: The New Press. 1995

Newmann F. "Can Depth Replace Coverage in the High School Curriculum?" *Phi Delta Kappan* 68, no.5 (1988): 345-348.

Newmann, F. & Oliver, D. *Clarifying Public Controversy.* Boston: Little, Brown, & Co., 1970.

Onosko, J. "Comparing Teachers' Thinking about Promoting Students' Thinking." *Theory and Research*

Lesson 5: DAYS SIX & SEVEN
FOCUS SUB-QUESTION:

Does our working definition help us identify cults?

Over two days students discuss whether or not the two organizations described in the homework readings are cults and whether or not their working definition helped them in their assessments. Through discussion students discover that their definition has discriminating power and that they now possess a clear enough understanding of cults to return to the central issue.

Lesson 6: DAY EIGHT
FOCUS SUB-QUESTION:

What can be done to stop cults?

In today's whole class teacher-directed discussion, students brainstorm and discuss possible actions to stop cults, regardless of whether or not they personally think such actions should be used. A variety of ideas are generated. Typically, at least five kinds of interventions are suggested (see Lesson 7 for details).

Lesson 7: DAYS NINE & TEN
LIBRARY RESEARCH:

Students search for information and arguments to determine whether or not the following approaches to stop cults should be advocated: (a) kidnap and deprogram; (b) limit a cult's right to free speech and expression; (c) identify in advance the kind of person likely to join a cult and intervene before it happens; (d) shut down the cult (using physical means if necessary); or, (e) nothing. Questions that are typically pursued with respect to the above five approaches are: Is it legal to kidnap a cult member? Does deprogramming work? Is it a good idea to curb the speech of some members of society? Is it constitutional to do so? Are there effective ways to identify personality types likely to join cults? Should the government step in and shut them down, including the use of force if necessary? Why is doing nothing the best course of action?

Lesson 8: DAYS ELEVEN & TWELVE
FOCUS SUB-QUESTION:

How does our research inform our perspectives?

For two days in large and small group formats the class discusses and continues to research the questions listed in Lesson 7 above. Students share important information and ideas and take notes. For homework, students continue to review their research materials in preparation for tomorrow's team meetings.

Lesson 9: DAY THIRTEEN
PREPARING FOR THE SCORED DISCUSSION:

Teams meet to formulate an agreed upon response to the central issue in preparation for the scored discussion activity on Day 14.

Lesson 10: DAY FOURTEEN
CULMINATING ACTIVITY:

Students engage in a roundtable discussion of the central unit issue: What, if anything, should we do about cults? The teacher will score the discussion (see Harris, Chapter 31).

Lesson 11: DAYS FIFTEEN & SIXTEEN
CULMINATING ACTIVITY:

Videotaped "special reports" are shown or live presentations are given by each team that reveals their response to the central issue. If time remains, students individually begin to organize and write a position paper that addresses the central unit issue.

Lesson 12: DAY SEVENTEEN
CULMINATING ACTIVITY:

Students are given one class period to outline and begin to write their position paper. The essay is due in two days. Students will be given an opportunity to rewrite their essay. Outstanding essays will be read aloud next week in class and all essays will be displayed for classmates to read.

in Social Education, 17 no.3 (1989), 174-195.

Onosko, J. "Barriers to the Promotion of Higher-Order Thinking." *Theory and Research in Social Education* 19, no.4 (1991): 341-366

Onosko, J. & Newmann, F. "Creating More Thoughtful Learning Environments in Secondary Classrooms and Schools." In *Advanced Educational Psychology: Creating Effective Schools and Powerful Thinkers,* edited by J. Mangieri & C. Collins Block. New York: Harcourt Brace & Jovanovich, 1994.

Shaver, J., Davis, O., & Helburn, S. "The Status of Social Studies Education: Impressions from Three NSF Studies." *Social Education* 43 (February, 1979): 150-153.

Tyson-Bernstein, H. *A Conspiracy of Good Intentions: America's Textbook Fiasco.* Washington, D.C.: Council for Basic Education, 1988.

Wiggins, G. (1989). "The Futility of Trying to Teach Everything of Importance." *Educational Leadership,* 47 (1989), 44-48.

[1] Fragmented learning refers to the unsystematic, unorganized way in which students are exposed to information and ideas. Fragmented learning is revealed when students are unable to connect information and ideas within and across lessons and units, even though these connections may be readily apparent to the teacher. Various facts, ideas, events, generalizations and so on may be acquired, but these learnings seem to occupy separate, isolated compartments in students' minds. Teachers can check for content fragmentation in their own units in the following ways. List 10-15 facts, events, ideas, and/or people that were addressed in class over the past week or that appeared on a recent exam. Ask students if these items can be connected in some meaningful way. Similarly, ask students to generate 10-15 facts, events, ideas, and/or people from a recent unit and then have them create an outline or diagram that connects these items in a meaningful way.

2 Superficial learning refers to students' limited exposure to most everything they study in social studies. Rarely are students asked or allowed to explore material in-depth. This situation prevents students from acquiring rich, complex, nuanced, and personally constructed understanding of ideas, events, and issues, and ensures that lower- rather than higher-order thinking dominates their cognitive activity. Note that superficial learning is different from fragmented learning, though the two barriers often occur together. One can imagine students gaining a cohesive (non-fragmented) understanding of the events and underlying causes that led to United States entry into World War I, yet their understanding is superficial as they cannot explain any event or cause in more than a few sentences. Conversely, one can imagine students gaining in-depth (non-superficial) understanding of various New Deal programs, yet their understanding is fragmented as they cannot make connections between the various programs or see the relationship between these programs and the underlying philosophy of the New Deal.

3 Passive learning refers to students receiving the textbook's and/or teacher's repackaged declarative statements about knowledge constructed by experts and other authorities. Didactic teaching and other transmission forms of instruction shove students from the playing field to the sidelines, reducing their participation in knowledge construction to that of an inactive, disengaged spectator. Instead of developing the intellectual abilities (and dispositions) needed to construct knowledge, student-spectators simply comprehend and recall the performances (or constructions) of others.

4 A fundamental assumption of this model is that students are capable of analyzing an issue at the same time they are developing knowledge of it. Stated another way, students need not spend days or weeks on content acquisition before they are allowed to wrestle with an issue. A related assumption is that students are less able to learn and remember information and ideas without the organizing and motivating power of an issue (or some other question or problem).

5 Issue-based curriculum design need not be exclusively teacher driven. Central issues can be identified by the teacher, students, or both—either before the analysis begins or during the early stages of study. A potential problem with this approach is that teachers may have little time to determine if resource materials are available to adequately address the issue selected by students. On the other hand, with greater ownership of the curriculum, students are more likely to experience the activity as authentic and intrinsically valuable.

6 If there is a desire or need to study other aspects of the period (e.g., various religious issues of the time, the colonists' contentious relations with Native Americans), additional issue-based units, brief or long, could follow or precede the present unit. An alternative approach is to embed these tangential topics (maybe a day or two of lessons) into the current unit of study. This, of course, has a fragmenting effect on student thinking and learning.

7 The source of this coverage pressure is often teachers' substantial subject matter knowledge which leads to over-inclusion of topics and issues. This has led one outstanding social studies teacher to observe: "The more a teacher knows, the more important it is that the teacher have an effective pedagogy to hold the information in restraint" (Onosko, 1989). A central unit issue serves to keep teachers' knowledge in check.

8 Systems or methods of classifying issues overlap; that is, many issues can be labelled as more than one type. Consider, for example, a few of the issues just mentioned: How should nuclear waste be disposed? (present, policy); What would happen if abortions were outlawed? (future, factual); Were neanderthals absorbed into the Cro-Magnon population or killed off? (past, factual, disciplinary). See Newmann & Oliver (1970) for a more detailed discussion of the types of issues one might encounter when exploring issues of public controversy.

Part Three: Cultural Diversity

Introduction by Jesus Garcia

This section of the *Handbook,* dealing with issues-centered education and cultural diversity, focuses on the relevancy of issues-centered education for exploring the concept of cultural diversity and the status of minorities and other marginalized groups in social studies instruction. The selected authors promote a definition of social studies that is committed to helping young children develop the ability to make informed and reasoned decisions for the public good as citizens of a culturally diverse, democratic society in an interdependent world. They view issues-centered education as an approach to the teaching of social studies that addresses many of the criticisms teachers, students, parents, and representatives of pressure groups have directed at social studies education.

The authors are: Sharon L. Pugh, a faculty member in the School of Education and Director of the Learning Skills Center at Indiana University, who specializes in issues related to language and literacy; Gloria Ladson-Billings, who writes in the area of curriculum and social studies and minority education and is a member of the Department of Curriculum and Instruction at the University of Wisconsin-Madison; Hilda Hernandez, who researches and teaches in the areas of bilingual education and language acquisition; and Devon Metzger, who focuses on issues relating to social studies and teacher education. Professors Hernandez and Metzger are faculty members in the Department of Education at California State University, Chico. Jesus Garcia is Director of Social Studies Education at the University of Illinois at Urbana-Champaign, and is involved in teacher education. Jesus teaches courses in social studies and multicultural education.

Ladson-Billings begins by drawing a distinc-

tion between multiculturalism and multicultural education in "Multicultural Issues in the Classroom: Race, Class, and Gender." She argues for support of Banks' definition of multicultural education: "to restructure curricula and educational institutions so that students from diverse social-class, racial and ethnic groups—as well as both gender groups—will experience equal educational opportunities." She contends that in many social studies classrooms, teachers fall short of seriously addressing this goal because "the dominant theories or paradigms that shape the way information, curriculum, and pedagogy are presented in schools prohibits this type of integration (race, class and gender) of thought." However, her experiences in teacher education lead her to believe that students are interested in social studies issues and problems and enjoy examining them from multiple perspectives. She concludes by offering teachers ways of inserting race, class, and gender into the social studies curriculum and re-constructing instruction into an issues-centered approach.

Hernandez and Metzger focus on language-minority students to argue for issues-centered education. The authors begin by briefly describing the fears and concerns language minority students bring to the classroom and argue that "teaching for democracy" brings about the sharing of power, giving teachers the opportunity to provide students with "voice" when making curricular decisions. Issues-centered education in classrooms with language-minority students provides teachers the opportunity to focus on student strengths while addressing their academic, personal, and social needs. Hernandez and Metzger believe that issues-centered education allows teachers to develop social studies programs that address the issues and problems that are relevant and important to students while introducing them to main ideas in social studies. The authors believe that issues-centered education is a valuable approach with language-minority students because of the interaction of ethnicity, social class, religion, education, and language. And as the authors conclude, "it involves students in social action projects that bridge home, school and community, and promote language and critical literacy development." Certainly the new paradigm the authors are suggesting is issues-centered social studies.

In "Challenges and Realities: Issues-Centered Education in Multicultural Environments," Pugh and Garcia describe the status of social studies in public education and the conservative forces influencing education The authors, employing a definition of multicultural education with a global perspective, argue for a curriculum that includes student perspectives and addresses conceptual learning in the social studies. They conclude by lobbying for an issues-centered social studies in which instruction is based on dialogical reasoning.

12 MULTICULTURAL ISSUES IN THE CLASSROOM: RACE, CLASS, AND GENDER

by Gloria Ladson-Billings

INTRODUCTION

Over the past few years there has been a growing controversy over the issues of multiculturalism and multicultural education. Scholars and activists from a variety of perspectives have argued the relative merits or shortcomings of these issues (Asante 1991; Banks 1993a; Graff 1992; Leo 1990; Schlesinger 1991). This chapter addresses the specific issues of race, class, and gender, what is happening in classrooms around these issues, and what possibilities exist for improving classroom experiences involving them.

The terms "multiculturalism" and "multicultural education" have become commonplace in U. S. society, but their meanings are not standardized. For the purpose of this chapter, I use the term "multiculturalism" to refer to the political and/or ideological position that groups that are diverse in race, ethnicity, gender, linguistics, ability, or sexual orientation can co-exist, appreciate, understand, respect, and learn from each other. This does not necessarily imply formal educational structures. For example, it is impossible to turn on a television in the United States without seeing a variety of representations of people (no matter how stereotyped or distorted), particularly in commercial advertising. This inclusion of "differences" is not the direct result of multicultural education, but rather of the political and social changes demanded by various groups of people. It reflects the society's increasing multiculturalism.

The term "multicultural education," according to Banks, is "an educational reform movement whose major goal is to restructure curricula and educational institutions so that students from diverse social-class, racial, and ethnic groups—as well as both gender groups—will experience equal educational opportunities" (Banks 1993a, 102). Many scholars have worked on creating conceptual and theoretical schema, as well as a consensus, from which to discuss the goals, meanings, and scope of this emergent field (see for example, Banks 1989; Gay 1992; Gibson 1976; Sleeter and Grant 1987). The scholarly literature, although widely varied, does provide some common themes about what is meant by multicultural education. For the purpose of this chapter, I use Banks' definition when referring to multicultural education.

Although volumes can be (and have been) written about the issues of race, class, and gender, this chapter will focus on selected aspects of that literature that are either directly related to or have some bearing on schooling and classrooms. It will conclude with a survey of strategies for considering these issues in classrooms, and provide examples of these strategies at work in various schools and school-related organizations.

Considering Race in the Classroom

Issues of race are avoided in U. S. classrooms for the same reasons that they are avoided in everyday life. We have not found ways to talk about them without feelings of rancor and guilt. Lee (1993) informs us that "[Q]uestions of race have been included in all US population censuses since the first one in 1790" (86). But Omi and Winant (1993a) argue, "[T]heories of race—of its meaning, its transformations, the significance of racial events—have never been a top priority in social science" (9). They argue also that popular notions of race as either an ideological construct or as an objective condition both have shortcomings (Omi and Winant 1993b). Thinking of race strictly as an ideological concept denies the reality of a racialized society and its impact on people in their everyday lives. On the other hand, thinking of race solely as an objective condition denies the problematic issues of racial categorization. How do we determine who fits into which racial categories? To which race do the offspring of racially different parents belong?

So complex is the notion of race (and its use in U. S. society) that even when it fails to "make sense" we continue to employ it. According to Nobel laureate Toni Morrison (1992),

Race has become metaphorical—a way of referring to and disguising forces, events, classes and expressions of social decay and economic division far more threatening to the body politic than biological "race" ever was. Expensively kept, economically unsound, a spurious and useless political asset in election campaigns, racism is as healthy today as it was during the Enlightenment. It seems to have a utility far beyond economy, beyond the sequestering of classes from one another, and has assumed a metaphorical life so completely embedded in daily discourse that it is perhaps more necessary and more on display than ever before. (63)

Studies of the role and impact of race in education have a long history. In the 1950s Clark and Clark's (1940) study of doll color preference was used as legal evidence to combat segregated schooling in the United States. In a comprehensive review of the literature on racial and ethnic attitudes, Banks (1993b) documents that children are aware of their race and ethnicity at an early age and "can be helped to develop more positive racial attitudes if realistic images of ethnic and racial groups are included in teaching materials in a consistent, natural, and integrated fashion" (241). However, Banks (1993c, 24) also suggests that "curriculum changes linked with issues related to race evoke primordial feelings and reflect the racial crisis in American society." Scholars and social commentators such as Cornel West (1992) and Studs Terkel (1991), respectively, have argued that (public) talk about race continues to confound Americans.

No matter what position one takes on the salience of race in U.S. society, there is no denying its import vis-a-vis social, political, economic, and educational inequality. The comparison between black and white children is striking. Irvine (1990) cites statistics from the Children's Defense Fund, the College Board, and the Carnegie Quarterly that demonstrate this sharp contrast. For example, compared to white children, black children are two to four times as likely to

• die before adulthood because of inadequate prenatal or postnatal health care conditions, abuse, or murder;
• live in a single-parent household because of parental death, separation, divorce, or no marriage;
• live in foster care or custody of a child welfare agency;
• be poor, and live in substandard housing with an unemployed teenage mother. (xiii-xvi)

The contrast continues at school:
• Black students, particularly black male students, are three times as likely to be in a class for the educable mentally retarded as are white students, but only one-half as likely to be in a class for the gifted or talented.
• Black students are more likely than white students to be enrolled in general and vocational tracks and take fewer academically rigorous courses.
• Blacks continue to score significantly lower than whites on the Scholastic Aptitude Test (SAT). (Ibid.)
• High school drop-out rates for urban blacks are close to 50 percent.

What opportunities for studying race as a critical issue exist in our schools? Unfortunately, typical course offerings and textbooks avoid substantive discussions of race and ethnicity. In general, race is confined to discussions of slavery and/or the civil rights movement. These curriculum patterns hold even though students are surrounded by racial and ethnic realities in their communities, the media, and their schools. Rather than rely on bland textbook descriptions, teachers can seize upon these pervasive racial messages to engage students in serious considerations of race.

Teachers serious about confronting issues of race and racism can begin by having students examine the racial dynamics in their own school. Students can participate in action research to learn about race and racism. They may choose some of the following topics: How many students of various races and ethnicities attend a particular school? Why? How many students of color are enrolled in honors and advanced placement classes and in vocational and general classes? How many students of color have been suspended or expelled? How many students of color are in special education classes? What is the drop-out rate for students of color? What is the participation of students of color in extra-curricular activities, such as student government, band, orchestra, or sports? A systematic examination of this kind of demographic information should provoke questions about the school's role in reproducing inequality. Each time students uncover a pattern of participation (or enrollment), they should be encouraged to ask, "Why?"

In addition to an examination of the school's demographic information, students should be encouraged to look at perceived and actual acts of racism, prejudice, and discrimination. Once again, surveys can be employed to capture students' perceptions and documentation of discrimination. Grant (1984) has shown that black girls, for instance, are on the margins of both the teacher's "sphere of influence" and that of numerous peer groups. To examine the accuracy of Grant's assertion, students could interview groups of students to determine dating and peergroup patterns or student-teacher relations.

Students need accurate information about issues of race and racism both in their local environment and throughout the larger society. The way to get that information is through a combination of primary and secondary sources. Thus, while conducting their own research, students should be reading the first-person accounts of people of color throughout history. Readings by James Baldwin, Richard Wright, Toni Morrison, Alice Walker, Maxine Hong Kingston, Carlos Bulosan, Mary Crow Dog, and others can provide students with opportunities to understand how others see the world, as well as help them question their own assumptions. In addition to reading, students need the chance to view films and videos from other than the dominant perspectives. Films such as *El Norte, Daughters of the Dust, Dim Sum*, and *The Lemon Grove Incident* demonstrate that realities are socially and culturally constructed and that students must work to understand multiple perspectives.

The Failure to Include Class in the Classroom

Sociologist William Julius Wilson argued in *The Declining Significance of Race* (1978) that class, and not race, was the determining factor in the deplorable life circumstances of inner-city Chicago residents. Lauded by conservatives and a leery liberal constituency, Wilson's thesis places us in the somewhat untenable position of acknowledging class in a society that has long discounted it or denied its existence.

Despite the very real presence of class stratification, the United States has been a nation that prides itself in muting its class distinctions. Thus, the folk wisdom has insisted that individual strivings and hard work in our "meritocratic" society afford people the opportunity to transcend class lines and barriers. Students in U. S. classrooms study rigid caste distinctions in India and in feudal Europe. However, the lens of class stratification rarely, if ever, turns on our society. As a culture, we talk about class in an almost metaphysical way. Election-year sloganeering plays on popular fears about a "shrinking middle class" because of the almost total identification with the middle class by our citizens.

Our failure to teach effectively about class is tied to our lack of understanding about how class operates in our society and a fear that substantive discussions about class are "un-American." The fear that class discussions border on the un-American is linked to our understanding of class as a central unit of analysis for Marxist theorists. Thus, talking about class is seen as a way of emphasizing social divisions and challenging cultural unity. Consider, for example, that during the infamous 1992 Los Angeles riots (or rebellion) after the acquittal of police officers in the Rodney King beating case, several media commentators noted that the destruction of South Central Los Angeles was partially "class warfare," as evidenced by the participation of Latinos, African Americans, and whites. However, soon after the fires of Los Angeles died down, this class warfare was converted to a "race war."

Our failure to acknowledge class does not diminish its impact upon our lives. Wilson (1978) reports that the "long-term poor"—those who are poor for eight or more years—constitute 60 percent of those in poverty at any one time. This group, often referred to as the "underclass" is composed of, according to Gorder (1988)

• a substantial number of female-headed

households (83 percent)
- people who are employed but unable to make it on their salaries (43 percent)
- children under the age of five (60 percent)
- families with an average of two children
- parents whose average age is twenty-nine (68)

One of the places that class issues manifest themselves is in the unequal distribution of income. According to the U.S. Bureau of the Census (1988), the top 20 percent of the population earned 43.7 percent of the total income, while the bottom 20 percent earned 4.6 percent of the total income. The 5 percent of the population who received the highest income earned 17 percent of the total income. These huge income disparities serve to exacerbate issues of inequality and class tensions.

Class issues also manifest themselves in schools and classrooms. Teacher expectations (Winfield 1986), curriculum and instructional decisions, assessment, and organizational policies are regularly informed by class. Indeed, much has been written about the school performance of poor children (under the rubric of a "cultural deficit," or being "culturally deprived," or "culturally disadvantaged"), but scholarly issues of class largely have been absent from K-12 classrooms.

Research and intellectual paradigms of the past that suggested that the poor were responsible for their own low school performance continue to hold sway in the minds of educators. An example of this framework is Bloom et al. (1965), who argued that:

> ... the roots of [poor children's] problem may in large part be traced to their experiences in homes which do not transmit the cultural patterns necessary for the types of learning characteristic of the larger society (4).

What can teachers do to critically engage students in issues of class? At a basic level, a serious study of the labor movement will provide students with an opportunity to examine how the working class was formed in a nation that boasted an egalitarian philosophy and disdain for royal hierarchy. Studies of economic trends in various communities may help students to understand fluctuations in the homeless population, crime statistics, and job opportunities.

Teacher Paul Sylvester (1994) reported that his third graders were capable of creating a class-room economy that replicated their surrounding low-income community. Sylvester developed a system of "paying" his students for their classroom jobs, one of which was cleaning the gerbil cage. After one weekend, the students discovered that the gerbil cage was missing. Sylvester, who had moved the cage to another classroom, explained that the gerbil cleaning job—one of the "highest paying" in the class—had moved to the "suburbs." The students had to figure out how they could continue to do that job or replace it with a comparable job. Sylvester's reason for moving the gerbil cage was to simulate the fact that 60,000 jobs had left the city within the preceding few years.

In my ethnographic research with successful teachers of African American students (Ladson-Billings 1994) one of the teachers had a keen interest in helping to rekindle the "work ethic" among her class of African American sixth graders. Because of the lure of easy money through the illegal drug trade, students seemed increasingly alienated from the prospect of working in traditional school-age job opportunities such as those offered by fast food restaurants, newspaper delivery, and employment as store clerks. The teacher called upon working-class people—the school custodian, a bus driver, and blue collar parents—to come into the classroom to explain their work and to offer 2-3 day "internships" to her students. By understanding the nature of work, its ability to support individual dignity and self-worth, the students would be able to make more intelligent decisions about their lives. The teacher purposely shied away from traditional middle-class African American "role models"—doctors, lawyers, and bankers—because of the "social distance" they represented.

Another place that we see the pernicious effect of social class is in school tracking practices. Jeannie Oakes (1985) argues that the combination of race and class is a determining factor in which students end up in which academic tracks. Working-class students of color are more likely to be placed in the lowest, non-college preparatory tracks. Even when schools have attempted to desegregate on the basis of race, Lomotey and Staley (1990) found that so called "magnet schools," designed to draw diverse groups of students to a school through special course and program offerings, often re-segregated students once they were assigned to courses and programs. The "double mantle" of race and class positions students as eligible only for the lower tracks, where they may receive less instruction and less interaction with the teacher, and reproduce the expected low performances (Rist 1970).

Even when "uncoupled" from race (and gender), class still can have a powerful effect on school performance and life chances. Weiss (1993) points out that:

> Until recently, the white male working class was relatively privileged in the economy in relation to African American men and women, and white women. While certainly not privileged in comparison with middle-class white men, many working-class men have been enabled by labor union struggles to command good steady jobs with benefits. (238)

This separation of working-class members along a racial divide was explored by W.E.B. DuBois (1977/1935), who asserted that the problem was not that the white working class was manipulated into racism, but that it came to think of itself and its interests as white:

> They were given public deference... because they were white. They were admitted freely, with all classes of white people to public functions [and] public parks... The police were drawn from their ranks and the courts, dependent on their votes, treated them with leniency. ... Their votes selected public officials and while this had small effect upon the economic situation, it had great effect upon their personal treatment.(700-701)

Thus, issues of class and race are sometimes conflated and other times at odds. Because students of color are also among the working class they may find themselves in a struggle against white working-class students, over racial and ethnic issues rather than class issues. Teachers must help students uncouple these issues and see them as both separate and shared, depending upon circumstances and historical moments.

Gender and Schooling

A third issue of multicultural education is that of gender. Called the "intimately oppressed" by historian Howard Zinn (1980), women represent a numerical majority in the society while continuing to be a sociopolitical and economic minority. Despite efforts at gender equity, women continue to earn less money than men, are over-represented among the poor, are confronted with a glass ceiling in jobs, and are more likely the victims of sexual and domestic abuse (Gollnick and Chinn 1990; Joseph and Lewis 1981). School is one of the places where this gender inequity is reinforced.

According to Myra and David Sadker, "sitting in the same classroom, reading the same textbook, listening to the same teacher, boys and girls receive very different educations" (Golden 1994, 57). In a synthesis of research on girls and schooling, the American Association of University Women reports that "[girls and boys] enter school roughly equal in measured ability. Twelve years later, [however], girls have fallen behind their male classmates in key areas such as higher-level mathematics and measures of self-esteem" (AAUW 1992, 1). Consequently, in subjects such as mathematics and science, girls score substantially lower than boys on standardized tests and find themselves discouraged from pursuing higher levels of math and science.

Sadker and Sadker (1986) found that "male students are given more time to talk in classrooms" (512) even though teachers often are unaware that they are directing more of their attention toward boys. Teachers may, in fact, have neither the resources nor the reward structure for changing inequitable school and classroom dynamics. Although many teachers are women, they "are actors and agents in complex social sites where social forces powerfully shape the limits of what is possible" (Weiler 1988, 148).

However, there are things that teachers can do in classrooms to make students more aware of gender inequities and work toward change. Since social studies classes generally are not sex segregated, teachers have an opportunity to observe student interactions between the genders. They can also become more aware of participation structures along gender lines. Which students volunteer answers in class and which do not? How often are women and women's issues the subject of study? What is the classroom/school climate like for girls? Are females, their bodily functions, or their body parts the object of ridicule? Are females subjected to unwanted sexual comments and advances? Do all students understand what constitutes sexual harassment? Do all students understand that sexual harassment is illegal?

Sadker and Sadker's (1991) comprehensive look at gender in elementary and secondary education indicates that although there has been a "significant body of research on gender equity in education" (314) over the past twenty years, "its influence on teacher preparation and educational reform remains marginal" (314). Thus, other disciplines and popular culture become the major carriers of research and scholarship about gender, while teachers and teacher education remain relatively insulated from knowledge about the damaging effects of gender inequity.

Organizing Social Studies Classrooms to Deal with Race, Class, and Gender

Despite knowing demographic information that points to the racial, class, and gender inequities in our society, teachers often are overwhelmed at the thought of integrating these issues into an already demanding curriculum. Even at the college level, this kind of integration has been difficult (Rothenberg 1988). I suggest that one of the reasons for the difficulty of teaching in this way is "paradigmatic," i.e. the dominant theories or paradigms that shape the way information, curriculum, and pedagogy are presented in schools prohibits this type of integration of thought. Much of schooling (as well as educational research) is shaped by a rationalist-positivist paradigm. Students are encouraged to accept "objective," linear, simplistic thinking in which only the observable and measurable represents the truth.

Teachers who want to encourage multicultural aspects of social studies within this paradigm often are limited to superficial representations of material culture. Thus, a multicultural, ethnic, or international festival where students "study" a specific culture, dress in "native" costumes, eat "ethnic" foods, and perform "cultural" dances, becomes the totality of their experience. Or students engage in an essentialized study of "groups" by inserting them in the existing curriculum; for example, in U.S. History students study a chronological, military, political history that adds different "others" into the master script (Schwartz 1992). Students might study various Indian tribes, bands, and federations as they study the "westward expansion" but they would not engage in a debate that challenges east-to-west perceptions of American development. Or, they might learn of the role of particular women

in U.S. History, but they will not study why women's voices are silent or muted throughout much of history.

Students may also experience the interpretivist paradigm. Here students would have the chance to examine cultures within their own contexts. Thus, some ethnic studies (e.g. Native American studies, African American history) or cultural studies courses (e.g. Far East studies) attempt to have students explore cultures from an emic, or insider perspective. However, students' own limited understandings of their own culture and the way it affects their way of thinking and being in the world may force them to make invidious comparisons between the cultures they are studying and themselves. Consequently, students may come to see other cultures as "weird," "exotic," or "strange."

A far less likely scholarly paradigm for precollegiate students is a critical one. Here, point of view or perspective, as well as the issue of whose interests are being served, become essential aspects of scholarship. One of the best examples of this paradigm at work is that of Central Park East Secondary School (CPESS)(Wood 1992). CPESS serves low income and minority students in grades 7-12 and helps them to develop into high-achieving, articulate, critical students by encouraging some very specific "habits of mind" that require students to be able to respond to the following questions in every area they study (ibid.):
- How do we know what we know?
- What's the evidence?
- What's the viewpoint?
- How else may it be considered?
- What difference does it make? (Ibid., 48-49)

In a CPESS course that seventh and eighth graders take entitled, "Contemporary Political Issues with an Emphasis on United States History," the students use the following essential questions to drive their inquiry:
1. What is political power?
2. Who has it?
3. How did they get it?
4. How does power change hands?
5. What gives laws their power?
6. How do people respond to being deprived of power? (Ibid., 180)

Both sets of questions illustrate a very different orientation toward learning and suggest that this school and its teachers want to help students challenge the rationalist-positivist paradigm with its Eurocentric, masculinist perspective. Unfortunately, most teachers do not have the luxury of a school design and administration that supports the kind of thinking that is encouraged, indeed required, at Central Park East. However, there are things that teachers can do to interrupt students' narrow perceptions of knowledge grounded in social issues.

Here are some suggestions for ways that teachers might rethink the way that they teach about issues of race, class, and gender:

1 **Have students grapple with the complexity of the construct of race.** Although much of our language and discourse is racially coded, students rarely examine race as a social construct with powerful social, political, and economic consequences. Perhaps in conjunction with a biology teacher or geneticist, teachers can expose students to the scientific constructions of race. Here students can identify examples of how race frames social issues—e.g., crime, welfare, school desegregation, the judicial system.

2 **Have students juxtapose race and ethnicity.** Challenge students to consider what they see as the difference between race and ethnicity? Why is it that some groups in the U.S. are referred to in racial terms while others are seen in terms of ethnicity? How do students identify themselves?

3 **Have students observe and discuss how race, class, and gender affect them on a personal level.** One of the persis-

tent complaints students have about school is its lack of relevance to their everyday lives. Teachers can ask students to generate a list of how they think their racial, class, and gender identity either help or hinder their lives. What privileges or disadvantages do they believe they experience as a result of their racial, class, or gender categories?

4 **Study the multiple effects of race, class, and gender through biography and fiction.** The complexity of race, class, and gender forces scholars and teachers to attempt to isolate them for analytical and pedagogical purposes. However, by studying biographies and/or fiction students can begin to understand how these multiple social categories affect individuals and groups. Biographies of women such as Fannie Lou Hamer, Ida B. Wells, Maxine Hong Kingston, Mary Crow Dog and Sojourner Truth are all good sources for studying the intersections of race, class, and gender. Literature by writers such as Toni Morrison, Richard Wright, Leslie Marmon Silko, Louise Erdrich, Gabriel Garcia Marquez and Sandra Cisneros provide exquisite contexts for understanding how culture can be revealed through literature.

5 **Work deliberately to unlearn racism, sexism, and classism.** Most Americans vehemently deny that they are racist, sexist, or elitist (classist). Yet, the ways that inequity is institutionalized and ingrained in our everyday lives means that we have to work proactively toward unlearning it. Work done by McIntosh (1990) demonstrates that many taken for granted experiences that people enjoy daily are not shared by others because of their race, class,

Examples of Multicultural Education at Work

Perhaps the most difficult task that teachers face is that of turning theory into practice. While scholars may do a good job of explicating the theoretical and conceptual rubrics under which change can occur, they may fall short of helping teachers put theory into practice. Indeed, it may not be the job of theorists to implement programs, but teachers do need assistance in translating theoretical notions into practical everyday teaching/learning experiences.

One of the ways that teachers can be helped

to implement the conceptual understandings of multicultural education is through exemplar. Below is a less than comprehensive list of teaching and learning examples of different forms of multicultural education in action.

CENTRAL PARK EAST SECONDARY SCHOOL (New York City). As described above, CPESS is an outstanding example of Banks' (1993c) notion of "knowledge construction." Here students are challenged to critically examine what they learn and raise questions about its value. *continued*

HARRIET TUBMAN ELEMENTARY SCHOOL (Newark, NJ) – In the heart of Newark, Harriet Tubman Elementary School is a model of an empowering school culture (Banks 1993c). Here the administrator, teachers, parents, community members, and students all take responsibility for student learning and achievement. In them, students have as models of teaching excellence people of various races and backgrounds. By implementing an "informal curriculum," the janitor, crossing guard, and other community members have the opportunity to act as "teachers" of such varied subjects as cooking, bowling, and basketball.

MARTIN LUTHER KING AND MALCOLM X ACADEMY (Milwaukee, WI) Milwaukee has instituted two experimental schools—one elementary, one middle—to test out "African-centered" education. Despite the attempt to "demonize" African-centered approaches to education (see for example, Schlesinger, 1990, Ravitch, 1990) teachers in urban centers that serve segregated school populations are finding that this new approach to education may begin to raise the achievement level of students while simultaneously raising their social consciousness. At this time, however, it is too early to determine the merit of these (and similar) programs.

LA ESCUELA FRATNEY (Milwaukee, WI). Along with its African-centered program, Milwaukee has also developed one of the most successful bilingual programs in the nation. As a two-way bilingual school, i.e., both English and Spanish speaking students will become bilingual, Fratney School has attempted to develop a "multicultural, gender equal" program. In its first year, Fratney School was organized around six themes: Roots in the School and the Community, the Native American Experience, the African American Experience, the Hispanic Experience, the Asian American/Pacific American Experience, and We Are a Multicultural Nation.

THE FOXFIRE EXPERIENCE (Rabun Gap, GA). Students in Rabun Gap, GA have published the quarterly *Foxfire* for the past 25 years. Their work came as a result of having the opportunity to develop curricula rooted in their own lives and experiences. By interviewing community elders, students are able to understand how working-class and poor people contribute to the vitality of the community culture:

For [the] students, all of the southern Appalachian region is their classroom. The premise of Foxfire is that students are on a mission to collect, record, and preserve the history and heritage of their area. To do this, students seek out what are known as "community contacts," senior members of the community who are willing to share their skills, insights, and wisdom with students. (Wood 1992, 62)

While Foxfire was not created as a representative of multicultural education, it exemplifies some of its best elements—content integration, knowledge construction, and equity pedagogy (Banks 1993c). Its focus on class and cultural issues makes it unique among educational programs.

RE-THINKING SCHOOLS, (Milwaukee, WI) Beyond classrooms, there exist institutions and organizations designed to help teachers as professionals reconsider the ways in which teachers and teaching can work toward social justice and equity. One such institution is Re-thinking Schools, a organization of committed teachers who publish a newspaper (also entitled, Re-thinking Schools) designed to critically examine schooling and the professional lives of teachers.

Among the issues addressed in Re-thinking Schools are racism, sexism, sexual harassment, homophobia, and ablism as well as contemporary issues of national standards, Goals 2000, choice of schools, and school funding. The newspaper has become a forum for teachers interested in social justice and inequity by providing editorial and background articles, examples of teacher-written lessons and activities, and student work. The existence of this teacher-led publication is a testimony to the ability and willingness of teachers to think deeply and carefully about how issues of race, class, and gender (among other issues) can be included in school curricula.

SOUTHERN POVERTY LAW CENTER (Atlanta, GA). Although organized as a non-profit organization to fight racism via legal channels, the SPLC also has an educational arm that produces the journal *Teaching Tolerance*. By combining biographical profiles, lesson suggestions, and student work, the journal provides teachers with a handy reference for including issues of race and racism in the class.

and/or gender. Students need to understand that their own privileges are connected to disadvantages suffered by others.

Concluding Thoughts

There are multiple strategies for confronting race, class, and gender in the classroom. This does not imply, however, that these are the only issues that fall under the rubric of multicultural education. Issues of language, ability, and sexual orientation also enter into the multicultural debate. Even in the consideration of race, class, and gender, there exist additional complexities of intragroup variability and overlapping categories (e.g. race/class versus race/gender).

Race, class, and gender affect students' schooling experiences despite our reluctance to deal forthrightly with them in the classroom. As social studies educators, issues of race, class, and gender are an integral part of our subject area. History, civics, economics, sociology, anthropology, psychology, and geography all have links to issues of race, class, and gender. Teachers who are serious about helping students develop into responsible citizens must develop these links and help students examine their own lives through the critical lenses of race, class, and gender.

The power of issues-oriented social studies lies in the willingness of teachers to confront multicultural issues of the past and present with an eye toward the future. Our increasing diversity, changing economic picture, and rapid progression into the "information age" all underscore the imperative for students and teachers alike to develop critical perspectives toward social inequities and injustice.

References

American Association of University Women. *How Schools Shortchange Girls: A Study of Major Findings on Girls and Education.* Washington, DC: AAUW Educational Foundation and National Education Association, 1992.

Asante, M. K. "The Afrocentric Idea in Education." *Journal of Negro Education,* 60 (1991): 170-80.

Banks, J. A. (1989). "Multicultural Education: Characteristics and Goals." In *Multicultural Education: Issues and Perspectives,* edited by J. A. Banks and C.M. Banks. Boston: Allyn and Bacon, 1989.

_____. *An Introduction to Multicultural Education.* Boston: Allyn and Bacon, 1993a.

_____ "Multicultural Education for Young Children: Racial and Ethnic Attitudes and their Modification." In *Handbook of Research on the Education of Young Children,* edited by B. Spodek. New York: Macmillan, 1993b.

_____. (1993c). "Multicultural Education: Development, Dimensions, and Challenges." *Phi Delta Kappan,* 75 (1993c): 22-28.

Bloom, B. S., A. Davis and R. Hess. *Compensatory Education for Cultural Deprivation.* New York: Holt, 1965.

Clark, K. B. and Clark, M. P. "Skin Color as a Factor in Racial Identification and Preference in Negro Children." *The Journal of Negro Education* 19 (1940): 341-58.

DuBois, W. E. B. *Black Reconstruction in the United States, 1860–1880.* New York: [1935] 1977.

Gay, G. (1992). "The State of Multicultural Education in the United States." In *Education in Plural Societies: International Perspectives,* edited by K. Adam-Moodley,. Calgary, Alberta, Canada: Detselig, 1992.

Gibson, M. A. "Approaches to Multicultural Education in the United States: Some Concepts and Assumptions." *Anthropology and Education Quarterly* 7 (1976): 7-18.

Golden, K. "What do Girls See?" *Ms.* (May/June 1994): 53-61.

Gollnick, D. and P. Chinn. *Multicultural Education in a Pluralistic Society* (3rd ed.). Columbus, OH: Merrill, 1990.

Gorder, C. *Homeless!: Without Addresses in America: The Social Crisis of the Decade.* Tempe, AZ: Blue Bird, 1988.

Graff, G. *Beyond the Culture Wars.* New York: W. W. Norton, 1992.

Grant, L. "Black Females' 'Place' in Desegregated Classrooms." *Sociology of Education* 57 (1984): 98-111.

Irvine, J. *Black Students and School Failure.* Westport CT: Greenwood Press, 1990.

Joseph, G. and L. Lewis. *Common Differences: Conflicts in Black and White Feminist Perspectives.* Boston: South End Press, 1981.

Ladson-Billings, G. *The Dreamkeepers: Successful Teachers for African American Students.* San Francisco: Jossey Bass, 1994.

Lee, S. "Racial Classifications in the US Census: 1890-1990." *Ethnic and Racial Studies* 16 (1993): 75-94.

Leo, J. "A Fringe History of the World." *US News and World Report* (November 12, 1990): 25-26.

Lomotey, K. and J. Staley. "The Education of African Americans in the Buffalo Public Schools: An Exploratory Study." Paper presented at the Annual Meeting of the American Educational Research Association, Boston, MA, April 1990.

McIntosh, P. "White Privilege: Unpacking the Invisible Knapsack." *Independent School* (Winter 1990): 31-36.

Morrison, T. *Playing in the Dark: Whiteness and the Literary Imagination.* Cambridge, MA: Harvard University Press, 1992.

Oakes, J. *Keeping Track. How Schools Structure Inequality.* New Haven: Yale University Press, 1985.

Omi, M. and H. Winant, H. *Racial Formation in the United States.* New York: Routledge, 1993a.

_____. "On the Theoretical Concept of Race." In *Race, Identity and Representation in Education,* edited by C. McCarthy and W.Crichlow. New York: Routledge, 1993b.

Ravitch, D. "Multiculturalism: E Pluribus Plures." *The American Scholar* (Summer 1990): 337-54.

Rist, R. "Student Social Class and Teacher Expectations: The Self-fulfilling Prophecy in Ghetto Education." *Harvard Educational Review* (1970): 40, 411-51.

Rothenberg, P. "Integrating the Study of Race, Gender, and Class: Some Preliminary Observations." *Feminist Teacher* 3 (1988): 37-42.

Sadker, M. and D. Sadker. "Sexism in the Classroom: From Grade School to Graduate School." *Phi Delta Kappan* 67 (1986): 512-15.

_____. "The Issue of Gender in Elementary and Secondary Education." In *Review of Research in Education* 17 (1991): 269-334.

Schlesinger, A. *The Disuniting of America.* Knoxville, TN: Whittle Direct Books, 1991.

Schwartz, E. "Emancipatory Narratives: Rewriting the Master Script in the School Curriculum." *The Journal of Negro Education,* 61 (1988): 341-55.

Sleeter, C. E. and Grant, C.A. "An Analysis of Multicultural Education in the United States." *Harvard Educational Review:* 57 (1987): 421-44.

Sylvester, P. S. "Elementary School Curricula and Urban Transformation." *Harvard Educational Review* 64 (1994): 309-31.

Terkel, S. *Race: How Blacks and Whites Think and Feel About the American Obsession.* New York: The New Press, 1991.

United States Bureau of the Census. *Statistical Abstract of the United States,* 1988. Washington, DC: Government Printing Office, 1988.

Weiler, K. *Women Teaching for Change: Gender, Class, and Power.* New York: Bergin and Garvey, 1988.

Weiss, L. "White Male Working-Class Youth: An Exploration of Relative Privilege and Loss." In *Beyond Silenced Voices: Class, Race, and Gender in United States Schools,* edited by L. Weiss and M. Fine. Albany, NY: State University of New York Press, 1993.

West, C. *Race Matters.* New York: Basic Books, 1992.

Wilson, William Julius. *The Declining Significance of Race: Blacks and Changing American Institutions.* Chicago: University of Chicago Press, 1978.

Winfield, L. "Teacher Beliefs Toward At-Risk Students in Inner-Urban Schools." *The Urban Review,* 18 (1986): 253-67.

Wood, G.H. *Schools That Work.* New York: Dutton, 1992.

Zinn, H. *A People's History of the United States* New York: Harper and Row, 1980.

13 ISSUES-CENTERED EDUCATION FOR LANGUAGE-MINORITY STUDENTS

by Hilda Hernández and Devon Metzger

In some form or another, issues-centered education has always been a part of social studies. Whenever social studies teachers, either by design or through informal chats with students, become involved in discussions that relate to students' lives, they are involving students in issues-centered education. Teachers who adopt issues-centered education generally give equal weight to process and content when addressing the specific needs and interests of the students. Issues-centered education places student issues, concerns, and topics of interest at the center of the curriculum.

Connecting the curriculum to the student is of utmost importance, equal only to using both the experience of the learner and the learning process as tools for student empowerment. Teachers who embrace issues-centered education are as concerned with the social and political context of what is learned, as with the learning process itself. Although what the authors propose is directed toward assisting teachers in meeting the needs of language-minority students, it should not go unnoticed that these instructional practices are beneficial to *all* students.

Initially, some teachers may be concerned that issues-centered education is not compatible with, or is "an addition to" the various mandated state or district curriculum frameworks. However, issues are embedded within all frameworks. While some frameworks specifically call for contemporary or controversial issues to be included in the mandated curriculum (e.g., California Department of Education [1987]), all designated content naturally includes unresolved and/or value-laden issues that have both a historical context and relevance to contemporary events. Teachers who accept the usefulness and importance of issues-centered education quickly become adept at integrating issues-centered education into the curriculum.

Essential to the success of issues-centered education is determining how teachers view students and to what extent students are involved in their own learning. Teachers who are attracted to issues-centered education tend to view students as practicing young citizens—capable and actively involved citizens who make decisions and value judgments directed toward improving their lives and those of others. Issues-centered classrooms are characterized by authentic student participation in the teaching/learning process. Students experience democratic environments rather than just reading or talking about democracy. In its simplest form, democracy involves the sharing of power among groups of people in order to establish a rule of order and authority (Gutmann 1987). As Metzger and Marker (1992, 72–73) stated:

> If, in teaching for democracy, we do not provide for the sharing of power between teachers and students, we run the risk of leaving the rule of order and authority solely to the teacher. To do so makes students voiceless, and to make students voiceless is to make students powerless. Without sharing power in the classroom with students, it is impossible, no matter what we say or do, to teach for democracy.

Sharing power is especially critical for language-minority students who are English-language learners—children and young adults whose primary language is not English. Many are native-born, members of nondominant ethnolinguistic groups; others are immigrants and refugees. Describing the demographic metamorphosis taking place in many of our schools, Richard-Amato and Snow (1992, 1) observed that "as our society becomes more and more pluralistic, so do our classrooms." This, they argued, presents a multitude of challenges to content-area teachers. One of the most critical is empowerment. As Cummins (1989, 57) asserted:

> For real change to occur, educational interventions must be oriented toward empowerment—toward allowing children to feel a sense of efficacy and control over what they are committed to doing in the classroom and in their lives outside the school. In other words, real change must challenge the power structure … that disables minority children.

Herein lies social studies educators' challenge and the critical opportunity to make a commitment to *all* young citizens living and learning in a pluralistic, democratic, and multicultural society. For students in general and language-minority students in particular, an issues-centered approach to social studies education has the potential to involve students in selecting content, making decisions about the process of learning, and determining potential courses of action. The teacher is an integral part of the learning community, facilitating access to knowledge, providing a classroom and learning structure, offering guidance, asking questions, and serving as a content and process resource. Through questioning and probing, the teacher plays an active role in defining social issues, avoiding the problem of trivial and superficial content selection (Barr, Barth, and Shermis 1977; Stanley and Whitson 1992).

Social studies educators who elect to develop an issues-centered classroom have the opportunity to play an important role in the empowerment of all students. Unquestionably, social studies teachers can and do make a positive difference. However, to make an even greater difference, particularly in the lives of language-minority students, the challenge is to adopt a new paradigm that encourages exploration of learner-centered social issues, involves students in social action projects that bridge home, school, and community, and promotes language and critical literacy development. The authors believe that to benefit most from issues-centered instruction, teachers must focus on the learner as well as the content.

Focus on the Learner

Social studies teachers often ask, "What should I teach?" and "How should I teach?" The response is the same to both questions. Begin by listening to and involving your language-minority students. When appropriate and with students' permission, place them on center stage with their peers. Placing language-minority students on center stage means using or creating learning activities that encourage and invite language-minority students to openly share their experience and voice their views. On center stage language-minority students have an opportunity to explore their cultural identity, engage in more cooperative interaction with others, enhance their self-esteem, and accept greater responsibility for their own learning.

An issues-centered approach incorporates students' experiences in ways that promote exploration of cultural identities: it "is automatically 'culture-fair' in that all students are actively involved in expressing, sharing, and amplifying their experiences within the classroom" (Cummins 1989, 65). Ahlquist (1990, 56) recommended that teachers "ask *students* what *they* think are the most important issues and concerns in life and how they might be addressed." Banks (1993, 8) reminded us, however, that while it is very important to use the personal and cultural knowledge of students, "an important goal of education is to free students from their cultural and ethnic boundaries and enable them to cross cultural borders freely."

The ultimate purpose is to have language-minority students take ownership of the learning process. The teacher's primary role is to help students empower themselves: "Teachers do not empower or disempower anyone, nor do schools. They merely create the conditions under which people can *empower themselves,* or not" (Ruiz 1991, 223). Listening to students' perspectives and experiences is critical to teachers' willingness to be involved in the learning process. Freire (1985) refers to the student ownership process as dialogical education. Students create new knowledge by voicing, sharing, and reflecting on life experiences: "As a teacher I help students locate their experiences socially; I involve students in probing the social factors that make and limit who they are and I try to help them reflect on who they *could* be" (Bigelow 1990, 437). Ultimately, the critical thinking skills that students develop will transform society, as students learn "to grab hold of real life problems and construct solutions to them" (Ahlquist 1990, 54).

When inviting language-minority students to take charge of their own learning, it is equally important to develop a positive classroom community. Cooperation is favored over competition. Rather than fostering alienation by making children work independently and in competition with one another, "schools should establish a 'society of intimates'—a collective identity and collective responsibility" (Kornfeld 1993, 77). Kagan's (1995) research on cooperative learning and minority students strongly endorsed the importance of cooperative learning:

> Minority students may lack motivation to learn, but only when they are placed in traditional, competitive/individualistic classroom structures. As demonstrated so clearly by the [research], in a relatively short time what appears to be a long-term minority student deficiency in basic language skills can be overcome by transforming the social organization of the classroom. Thus, the gap in achievement between majority and minority students is best not attributed to personal deficiencies of minority students, but rather to the relatively exclusive reliance in public schools on competitive and individualistic classroom structures (Kagan 1995, 246-247).

Developing self-esteem is also an important component of issues-centered education because it is so closely related to student achievement. It is especially critical for academically underachieving students from minority groups. While some critics question self-esteem as a useful and worthy goal (Kohn 1994, 272-283), self-esteem is inextricably related to the overarching goal of learning about one's own culture and its societal context:

> We may argue that instilling self-esteem is no business of the schools, but we are deluding ourselves if we think there isn't a link between self-esteem and achievement. … If students have confidence in their ability, then success or failure in school and in life is largely a function of effort. Whether children achieve is contingent on whether they possess self-esteem and confidence in their ability—and on whether their teachers share that confidence in them (Price 1992, 211–12).

Self-esteem is perhaps the key to the success of language-minority students in the issues-centered classroom. With a positive identity, the language-minority student will become willingly and genuinely involved in the learning process.

Cortes (1990, 14) spoke directly to those who teach language-minority students when he wrote of his vision for multiculturation—"the mutual acculturation of people, cultures and institutions." The vision is a quest to build a nation of the contributions of one and all, based on the positive commonalities that unite us, respecting, maintaining, and nourishing the constructive uniqueness that marks our diversity. To this end, he called for several kinds of acculturation, among these acculturation that empowers and sensitizes. Acculturation that *empowers* helps all students to:

> develop socially unifying knowledge, understanding, beliefs, values and loyalties … [and] effective English, advanced knowledge and empowering skills that will provide them with a reasonable chance of taking advantage of opportunities for reaching the fabled American dream. (Cortés 1990, 14)

Acculturation that *sensitizes* will help all Americans:

> to develop better intercultural understanding and become more dedicated to living with concern and sensitivity in a multiethnic society where racial, ethnic and cultural differences co-exist with national and human commonalties (14).

Multiculturation is for all students.

Focus on Content

Let's imagine an issues-centered classroom that maximizes the academic, personal, and social development of all students. What would it look like? What would be the salient features, those most critical for language-minority students? Several dimensions would certainly stand out. For example, the classroom would be a place to explore learner-centered social issues, foster connections between home, school, and community, and provide opportunities for social action.

It would also be a learning environment that promotes language and literacy development as well as critical thinking. The outcome of what students do would empower them as learners. This section will help social studies educators better understand how to approach and teach social issues to language-minority students by examining each of these dimensions in greater detail.

Explore Learner-Centered Social Issues

Given the immediacy of certain concerns in the lives of language-minority students (e.g., family, language, culture, school climate), some social issues will be more relevant than others. This is why it is imperative that instruction be learner-centered. Meaningful themes should be drawn from the experiences and concerns of the students themselves. These will vary from one context to another. Once identified, the themes can serve as the basis for school-wide and local community action projects.

Themes are everywhere, and students' voices offer an essential guide in making decisions about selecting social issues. Just listening to what immigrant students have to say about their experiences in *Crossing the Schoolhouse Border* (Olsen 1988, 35, 30) will suggest possibilities. Note how issues such as immigration, discrimination, and ethnic identity emerge:

> *The Americans tell us to go back to our own country. I say we don't have a country to go back to. I wish I was born here and nobody would fight me and beat me up. They don't understand. I want to tell them if they had tried to cross the river and were afraid of being caught and killed and lost their sisters, they might feel like me, they might look like me, and they, too, might find themselves in a new country.*
>
> —10th grade Cambodian boy,
> immigrated at age 12

> *I'm glad to be American. I think you can be a lot more open here and we have a lot of fun. But I don't think it's right that some kids try so hard to not be Latin. They won't speak Spanish, and some of them don't even know how anymore. To me that is sad. My children will be born here, and they will be fully American, but I want them to know our language. I want them to be able to speak to my grandmother, and to go back to Mexico and*

> *feel it is also their home. Without a connection to where you come from, without your family and your past, you are just lost.*
>
> —10th grade Mexican girl,
> immigrated at age 14

Perspective is a critical element in teaching social issues in any classroom. It affects how teachers present and students respond to social issues. Because of the divergent cultural and linguistic backgrounds that language-minority students bring to the classroom, teachers should anticipate that their own perspectives on some issues in relation to gender, religion, social class, ethnic group, or nationality, for instance, will differ from that of their students. Due to the interaction of ethnicity, social class, religion, and education, students from language-minority groups, for example, may have alternative, i.e., nonmainstream U.S., views on women's issues. Definitions of role, family, interpersonal relationships, expectations, and aspirations may also vary.

Adopting frames of reference different from those traditionally used in the social studies is critical. For example, geocultural and global perspectives are educationally and conceptually valid alternatives to ethnocentric points of view that distort views of U.S. society and the rest of the world (Hernández 1989). Cortés (1976, 1981; Cortés and Fleming 1986b) has repeatedly made the point that established ethnic-language groups have traditionally been ignored, described as obstacles to progress, or characterized as problems in society. He has long recommended use of a multidirectional frame of reference that is geocultural—subsuming the cultures and experiences of the nation as a whole by recognizing "the northwesterly flow of civilization from Africa to America, the northerly flow of Hispanic and Mexican civilization into what is today the U.S. Southwest, and the easterly flow of civilization and cultures from Asia" (Cortés 1981, 15). This, he argued, enables educators to deal with multiple group perspectives (e.g., ethnic, racial, cultural, gender, religious) as integral elements in teaching the American experience.

Along similar lines, Cortés also advocated a multifaceted global perspective for presenting information on areas outside the United States. Failure to adopt such a framework encourages students to "view the world with knowledge drawn almost entirely from Western and middle-class traditions. But the majority of Earth's people are not white; although they may be influenced by the West, their cultures are neither Western nor dominated by a middle class."

It is inevitable that issues-centered instruction will not be limited by national boundaries. If students are to attain an accurate understanding of people in other countries in the process, then outsider perspectives will not suffice. Students must be taught about different cultures and societies in ways that recognize and value perspectives from within. Geocultural and global perspectives provide the divergent interpretations of reality that will help students appreciate the insight captured in the words of Ortega y Gasset: "The sole false perspective is that which claims to be the only one there is."

Promote Language Development

In the issues-centered classroom envisioned here, language and literacy development would be a priority. Aronowitz and Giroux (1985) wrote that "if students are to be empowered by school experiences, one of the key elements of their education must be that they acquire mastery of language as well as the capacity to think conceptually and critically (p. 158 in original Aronowitz and Giroux)" (Sleeter and Grant, 1988, p. 190). To achieve academically, language-minority students must attain high levels of academic language proficiency, and issues-centered instruction provides an ideal forum for enhancing English-language and literacy skills. Moreover, given the nature of issues-centered activities, there are also ample opportunities for incorporation of the primary language.

Research by Edelsky and Hudelson (1980) reviewed by Fillmore and Valadez (1986) indicated that encouraging students to use their primary language in school is not enough to ensure that they will actually do so. In a setting such as a school, speakers of languages other than the dominant language in the community often find it difficult or awkward to use their native language to talk with each other. Even when second-language learners interact with classmates who are bilingual, the speakers will almost invariably shift into English.

Social studies teachers working with second-language learners—even teachers who are not bilingual—must convey the message to students that the primary language is accepted and valued. Cummins (1989, 60) hypothesized that:

Educators who see their role as adding a second language and cultural affiliation to students' repertoire are likely to empower students more than those who see their role as replacing or subtracting students' primary language and culture in the process of assimilating them to the dominant culture.

This acceptance can best be achieved by creating opportunities for incorporating the primary language into classroom activities. From an academic, linguistic and affective standpoint, this is sound practice conducive to the study of social issues.

Díaz, Moll, and Mehan (1986) illustrated one strategy that effectively integrates the study of social issues within the classroom and community with the development of literacy and thinking skills in both languages. This strategy was implemented successfully in an English-as-a-second-language classroom at a secondary school in which there was no support provided for literacy development in the primary language. In directing students through their examination of campus and community attitudes toward language, the teacher used surveys and questionnaires as a technique for soliciting people's opinions toward English and their primary language. To promote literacy development, information collected from the Spanish-speaking community was reported using essays written in English.

On the first day, the teacher framed the assignment by requiring that all of the students ask these three questions (Díaz et al. 1986, 214):

1. What language do you speak best?
2. What language do you read and write best?
3. Do any members of your family who live with you speak another language besides English?

Two other questions were made optional:
• Would you be willing to take classes to become bilingual?
• What career do you foresee in your future in which you would benefit by being bilingual?

For the survey, each student was required to interview other people—two adults not working on campus, two adults who work on campus, three students whose first language is English, and three students whose first language is not English.

As homework, students developed three additional questions related to the issue they were exploring, which were discussed the next day, generating ten additional questions for possible use in the student questionnaires (Diaz et al. 1986, 215):

1. Would you prefer to live around bilingual people in a bilingual community?
2. Are your closest friends bilingual?
3. Would you like to go to the university? Do you know that the best university requires four years of second-language training?
4. Which language do you like the best of the ones you don't speak?
5. What language do you speak with your friends? Why?
6. How many teachers do you have that speak some Spanish?
7. Do you think you would like to return to live where you learned your first language?
8. Which language does your closest friend speak with you?
9. Do you think speaking another language is important?
10. Is it comparatively hard for you to learn another language?

The teacher guided the process from the initial interviewing through essay writing and reporting. In writing their essays, students followed a model structure of formula paragraphs. The following are two *unedited* student essays:

Student A:

The people in my cummunity think that being bilingual is very important for several good reasons. Firts, I felt very proud doing the Survey. the people in our community feel very proud at them self that they speak Spanish and Eanglish because they can talk with there friends in any of those two lenguages. Secondly, the people I ask Some were bilingual students and adults 60 percent were bilingual people and 40 percent weren't bilingual people. Also, I ask a teacher and a student if they would be willing to work as a bilingual person and they said no and than I ask a Student this qiestion Do you think Speaking Another lenguage is important and he said no that amazed me because I never herd one person that thinks that speaking another lenguage ain't important. finally, I ask a teacher that What career was he interested in that would require a second language and he said no common and he told this I don't know What lauguage I'm interestes that would require a 2nd lenguage because I don't know it and I ask two Students this question what career are yo interested in that would require a 2nd lenguage and 50 percent said Fransh 10 percent said Germen 10 percent said Italian and 20 percent said no coman as you can see I was having fun. (Díaz et al. 1986, 217).

Student B:

I found that people in our community feel good about belingualism for several good reasons. They think it it very important because they can communicate with other people. The people I ask are 60 percent students, 40 percent adults, 70 percent are Spanish speakers, 20 percent were English speakers, 70 percent can write and read English, 20 percent can write and read Spanish well. Most of the people told me that in there house can speak English and Spanish. The people I ask the questions, answers me very polite and they said the questions were very interesting. Some person said that these project was very good for me and interesting for him. When he said that I feel very good about the work I was doing. The most interesting thing that I found wat that the people like the project. Most of the people said that they were willing to take classes to become totally belingual because it could help them right now and in the future. The students I ask said that they have only friends that speak only Spanish and English not othey language. They adults I ask said that been belingual is very important for them because they can communicate with more people and they can have more opportunitis for some jobs that othey people do I fee very good about the way people answer me. (Diaz et al. 1986, 217–18)

By assigning this task, teachers can draw upon skills that students have developed in their first language and use them in support of academic goals in the second language. In doing so, instruction is also responsive to community dynamics. In working within this particular community, the researchers found that writing, schooling, and social issues were complex, related phenomena. Establishing connections between the community and classroom were critical to student success. Díaz et al. (1986) emphasized that this activity is also consistent with Vygotsky's (1978) notion of creating zones of proximal development, as students move from teacher guidance to self direction, from social to individual experience.

Promote Critical Literacy Development and Social Action

It is not enough, however, to develop language and literacy skills. If students are to be empowered by what they learn, pedagogy must take them one step further. McLeod (1986, 37) articulated this view:

> Being literate … means having the power to use language—writing and reading, speaking and listening—for our own purposes, as well as those that the institutions of our society require of us. The classroom processes by which that power is achieved include the first exercise of that power.

Ada (1986) could have had social studies educators in mind when she drew on Freire's work to develop her "model" for critical literacy. It is a powerful tool for all social issues classrooms. As described by Cummins (1989), her approach integrates critical thinking skills with curriculum content that involves reading. The first of Ada's (1988) four phases in this creative reading process is the *descriptive phase*. At the outset, children are asked to deal with information from a written text. To check for understanding, the teacher poses: "Where, when, how, did it happen? Who did it? Why?" (Ada 1988, 104).

After the student has provided input, the process moves into the *personal interpretative phase*. The teacher invites the students to relate what they have read to their own feelings and experiences: Have you ever seen (felt, thought, experienced) something similar? How does this information make you feel? How would you react in these circumstances? (Ada 1988; Ada and Zubizarreta). Ada emphasized that children's self-esteem is enhanced as members of the classroom community validate their feelings and experiences. She also contended that "true learning occurs only when the information received is analyzed in light of one's own experiences and emotions" (Ada, 1988, 104).

At the next level, the *critical phase*, students are involved in the critical analysis of issues and problems. Questions now focus on making inferences and formulating generalizations based on what they have read: *Is it fair? Is it right? Does it benefit everyone alike? Are there any alternatives to this situation? What would the consequences of each alternative be? Would people of different cultures (classes, genders) have acted differently? How? Why?"* (Ada, 1988; Ada and Zubizarreta, 1989, 13). According to Ada and Zubizarreta (1989), these questions serve to enhance critical thinking skills and promote the realization that situations often present alternative courses of action. In turn, students become more cognizant of their ability to influence their own reality.

Finally, students enter the *creative phase* in which ideas become actions. Students confront issues and explore alternatives for resolving the problems identified. They engage in activities that can make a difference in their lives. For example, teachers might ask: *What can you do to … ? How would you change (improve, alter, transform) … ? What are you going to do when … ? How would you prevent … ?"* (Ada and Zubizarreta 1989, 13).

Cummins (1989) gave the example of students engaged in research on environmental pollution problems. After investigating newspapers, periodicals and other sources of information, the students would critically analyze causes, propose solutions, and pursue a course of action. They might then make other students aware of the problems. For example, students can pursue issues in a class or school newsletter, circulate a petition around their school or neighborhood, or contact people involved in local, state, or national government. Cummins (1989, 74–75) compared this process with the one developed by Taba (1965). While similar in many ways, one important difference exists between the two processes:

> As pointed out by Wallerstein (1983, 17), however, Freire and Taba differ primarily in the final step of the process where Taba asks for summations and applications to other situations whereas Freire (and Ada) calls for action to promote alternatives to current

problematic or negative situations.

For educators working from an interactive/experiential pedagogical orientation, critical thinking is more than a skill to be transmitted (Cummins 1989, 75):

> Critical/creative thinking is manifested through active use of oral and written language for collaborative exploration of issues and resolution of the *real* problems that form the curriculum. In other words, the primary focus is on *process* rather than transmission of content.

Combining critical literacy development and social action offers teachers and students exciting possibilities. In one second-grade, bilingual classroom (Hernandez 1992), for example, issues related to animal rights took on an international perspective. Concern regarding the care and treatment of pets in the children's neighborhood generated interest in reading *Ferdinand the Bull.* The children asked: "Why did bullfighting persist? Does everyone in Spain like bullfighting?" They wanted answers, and ideas became actions. The children wrote letters to the mayor of Tossa, a small village in Spain that was the first to ban bullfighting. The children used real and imaginary images to describe what the bulls might do if they were no longer doomed to enter the bullring. The mayor of Tossa wrote back, appreciative of their interest in a movement that he regards as inevitable. He also forwarded their names to the spokesperson for the local animal defense league, who has continued the correspondence, keeping the students informed of activities throughout the European community.

When children in Hernandez's classroom explored smoking and its related health issues, they traced the history of smoking around the world. The more the children learned, the more they wanted to do something. The children decided to create antismoking posters. When they realized that children in other parts of the world made similar posters, the pupils organized a poster exchange. They sent their posters to Spain in exchange for posters drawn by third, fourth and fifth graders in Barcelona. Posters were in three languages: Catalan, English, and Spanish. In both countries the posters were displayed in classrooms. One group of children also decided to send posters carrying their message

for exhibition in the state capitol.

Foster Student Empowerment

In the final analysis, issues-centered instruction should empower all students. As Cummins (1989, 63) observed: "Instruction that empowers ... will aim to liberate students from dependence on instruction in the sense of encouraging them to become active generators of their own knowledge." This is particularly critical for language-minority students.

Educators have developed a vision of the type of instruction that empowers language-minority students. As described by Cummins (1989, 64), this interactive/experiential model is predicated upon strategies consistent with basic principles of language acquisition and literacy development that promote reciprocal inter-action between teachers and students. Among the strategies that characterize instruction that empowers language-minority students, Cummins included the following:

- **Discourse**—genuine oral and written discourse between teacher and students;
- **Teacher role**—greater emphasis on teachers in the role of guides and facilitators rather than as imparters of knowledge and controllers of learning;
- **Context**—creation of a collaborative learning context in which peers are encouraged to interact;
- **Language**—greater emphasis on the use of language that is meaningful and less emphasis on correctness of form;
- **Integration**—strong integration of language development and subject matter content;
- **Thinking skills**—emphasis on the development of higher-level cognitive skills; and
- **Motivation**—focus on engaging students in tasks that foster intrinsic motivation.

Adhering to the tenets of the model, teachers can help students to "assume greater control over setting their own learning goals and to collaborate actively with each other in achieving these goals" (Cummins 1989, 64).

A Time for Change in Social Studies Education

What role do social studies educators play in this very serious debate about culture, diversity, and power? How do social studies educators define and, hence, teach the goal of democratic citizenship education? Garcia and Pugh (1992, 218) offered the ideal by stating, "Because multiculturalism is our national reality, we are best served by an education system that preserves democratic ideals while it helps us move toward a more complete realization of these ideals for all people." They warned that, "Changing national demographics, if not timeless democratic ideals, suggest that complacency now will sow the seeds of an immense educational failure later" (219).

The realities of our multicultural society, as increasingly reflected in our culturally diverse population, may serve to motivate and demand change in the social studies classroom. More and more social studies teachers are looking over their classrooms and seeing a larger number of students who are different from the traditional mainstream students. Students and parents from nonmainstream cultures are becoming less forgiving of instructional practices that are inequitable, and less tolerant of distortions of reality in social studies content and materials (especially when these distortions sanction racial and ethnic stereotypes).

Are social studies educators open to the challenge? In her NCSS presidential address, Charlotte C. Anderson (1993, 160) spoke to this need for change:

> We must discard familiar and therefore comfortable images of reality and embrace unfamiliar and disorienting ones. These new images, although they may be threatening and disconcerting to those of us firmly rooted in the mid-twentieth century, are nonetheless congruent with emerging realities of the world our children will experience. If what I say is true, we social studies educators face a task that may shake the very foundation on which most of us have built our personal and professional lives.

References

Ada, A. F. "Creative Education for Bilingual Teachers." *Harvard Educational Review* 56 (1986, no. 4): 386–94.

Ada, A. F. (1988). "Creative Reading: A Relevant Methodology for Language Minority Children." In L. M. Malave (Ed.) *NABE '87. Theory, Research, and Application: Selected Papers.* Buffalo: State University of New York.

Ada, A. F., and R. Zubizarreta. *Language Arts through Children's Literature.* Emeryville, Calif.: Children's Book Press, 1989.

Ahlquist, A. "Critical Pedagogy for Social Studies Teachers." *Social Studies Review* 29, no. 3 (1990): 53–57.

Anderson, C. "The Context of Civic Competence and Education Five Hundred Years after Columbus." *Social Education* 57, no. 4 (1993) , 160–63.

Aronowitz, S. and Giroux, H. A. (1985). *Education Under Siege.* South Hadley, MA: Bergin and Garvey.

Banks, J. A. "The Canon Debate, Knowledge Construction, and Multicultural Education." *Educational Researcher* 22, no. 5 (1993): 4–14.

Barr, R. D. , J. L. Barth, and S. S. Shermis. *Defining the Social Studies.* NCSS Bulletin 51. Arlington, Va.: National Council for the Social Studies, 1977.

Bigelow, W. "Inside the Classroom: Social Vision and Critical Pedagogy." *Teachers College Record* 91, no. 3 (1990): 437–47.

California State Department of Education. *History-Social Science Framework.* Sacramento: California State Department of Education, 1987.

Cortés, C.E. "Need for a Geo-Cultural Perspective in the Bicentennial." *Educational Leadership* 33, no. 4 (1976): 290–92.

Cortés, C.E. (1981) "Dealing with the Density of Diversity: Groupness and Individuality in the California History/Social Science Framework." *Social Studies Review*, 21(1), 12-18.

Cortés, C.E. "E Pluribus Unum: Out of Many One." In Vol. 1 of *California Perspectives: An Anthology from the Immigrant Students Project*, 13–16. San Francisco: California Tomorrow, 1990.

Cortés, C.E., and D. B. Fleming. "Global Education and Textbooks." *Social Education* 50 (1986a, no. 5): 340–44.

Cortés, C.E., and D. B. Fleming. "Changing Global Perspectives in Textbooks." *Social Education* 50 (1986b, no. 5): 376–84.

Cummins, J. *Empowering Minority Students.* Sacramento : California Association for Bilingual Education, 1989.

Díaz, S., L. C. Moll, and H. Mehan. "Sociocultural Resources in Instruction: A Context-Specific Approach." In *Beyond Language: Social and Cultural Factors in Schooling Minority Students.* Los Angeles: Evaluation, Dissemination and Assessment Center, School of Education, California State University, Los Angeles, 1986.

Edelsky, C., and Hudelson, S. (1980). "Acquiring a Second Language When You're Not the Underdog." In R. Scarcella and S. Krashen (Eds.), *Research in Second Language Acquisition.* Rowley, MA: Newbury House.

Fillmore, L. W., and C. Valadez. "Teaching Bilingual

Learners." In *Handbook of Research on Teaching*, 3rd ed., edited by M. C. Wittrock, 648–85. New York: Macmillan, 1986.

Freire, P. *The Politics of Education*. Granby, Mass.: Bergin and Garvey, 1985.

García, J., and S. L. Pugh. "Multicultural Education in Teacher Preparation Programs: A Political or an Educational Concept?" *Phi Delta Kappan* 74, no. 3 (1992): 214–19.

Gutmann, A. *Democratic Education*. Princeton, N. J. : Princeton University Press, 1987.

Hernández, F. "California History and Its Multicultural Heritage for Elementary School Instruction." Paper presented at the annual conference of the California Historical Society, September 1992.

Hernández, H. *Multicultural Education: A Teacher's Guide to Content and Process*. Columbus, Ohio: Merrill Publishing, 1989.

Kagan, S. (1995). "Cooperative Learning and Sociocultural Factors in Schooling" (pp. 231-298). In *Beyond Language: Social and Cultural Factors in Schooling Language Minority Students*. Los Angeles: Evaluation, Dissemination and Assessment Center, School of Education, California State University, Los Angeles.

Kohn, A. "The Truth About Self-Esteem." *Phi Delta Kappan* 76, no. 4 (1994): 272-283.

Kornfeld, J. H. "Teaching for Democracy in the Social Studies Classroom." *Theory and Research in Social Education* 21, no. 1 (1993): 75-83.

McLeod, A. "Critical Literacy: Taking Control of Our Own Lives." *Language Arts* 63, no. 1 (1986): 37–50.

Metzger, D. J., and P. M. Marker. "Teaching for Democracy: An Agenda for Social Studies Teacher Education in the Twenty-First Century." *The International Journal of Social Education* 7, no. 2 (1992): 67–75.

NCSS Ad Hoc Committee on Social Studies Curriculum Guidelines, "Revision of the NCSS Social Studies Guidelines," National Council for the Social Studies, 1979.

Olsen, L. *Crossing the Schoolhouse Border*. A California Tomorrow Policy Research Report. San Francisco: California Tomorrow, 1988.

Price, H. B. "Multiculturalism: Myths and Realities." *Phi Delta Kappan* 74, no. 3 (1992): 208–13.

Richard-Amato, P. A., and M. A. Snow, ed. *The Multicultural Classroom: Readings for Content-Area Teachers*. White Plains, N.Y.; Longman, 1992.

Ruiz, R. "Empowerment of Language-Minority Students." In *Empowerment through Multicultural Education*, edited by C. E. Sleeter, 217–27. Albany, N.Y.: State University of New York Press, 1991.

Sleeter, C.E., and C. A. Grant. *Making Choices for Multicultural Education*. Columbus, Ohio: Merrill Publishing, 1988.

Smith, G.R., and G. Otero. *Teaching about Cultural Awareness*. Denver, Colo.: University of Denver, Center for Teaching International Relations, 1982.

Stanley, W. B., and J. A. Whitson. "Citizenship as Practical Competence: A Response to the New Reform Movement in Social Studies Education." *The International Journal of Social Education* 7, no. 2 (1992): 57–66.

Taba, H. (1965). "The Teaching of Thinking." *Elementary English*, 42, 534-542.

Vygotsky, L. S. (1978). *Mind in Society: The Development of Higher Psychological Process*. Cambridge, MA: Harvard University Press.

Wallerstein, N. (1983). "The Teaching Approach of Paulo Freire." In J. W. Oller, Jr., and P. A. Richard-Amato (Eds.) *Methods That Work: A Smorgasbord of Ideas for Language Teachers*. Rowley, MA: Newbury House.

14 ISSUES-CENTERED EDUCATION IN MULTICULTURAL ENVIRONMENTS

by Sharon L. Pugh and Jesus Garcia

Mandates that focus on what and how much students should learn in social studies typically ignore how they learn. Most educators would agree that there is nothing inherently wrong with enriching history and geography learning (Bradley Commission 1985; Gagnon 1989; National Commission on Social Studies in the Schools 1989) and insisting on a high standard of student knowledge in these areas (Beatty, 1994, Rothman 1990). Yet increasing the content of the social studies curriculum is not likely to improve students' dismal attitudes toward the subject. Indeed, student voices are strikingly absent from the ongoing discussion of how social studies can become a vital force in their education and lives.

The irony of this situation is that voice is the essence of democratic participation, so that learning to exercise this voice in thoughtful and effective ways would seem to be a primary objective of education for citizenship. Students, moreover, are not just individuals but also members of communities, the many communities that reflect the cultural diversity of the United States. This diversity is nowhere as apparent as in public schools, especially those in metropolitan areas but also those in suburbs, once considered white enclaves. Cultural diversity is especially dramatic in communities in California and Texas, where, within the predictable future, non-Caucasian populations will constitute the majority. From Anchorage to Miami, cultural diversity is nearly everyone's reality.

Social studies education models that neglect to address the complexities of the teaching-learning process legitimately raise concerns. Today, surrounded by an information explosion of largely alarming news, students need basic knowledge along with the thinking and language tools necessary to enter into an adult lifetime of negotiation and problem solving. It is not enough to teach them about their past, vital as this dimension is; they must develop depth perception by relating the past to their present and future. Acknowledging that both tradition and change should be examined together, we promote in this chapter a model of issues-centered social studies education that meets the needs of students preparing for citizenship in the twenty-first century.

Issues-Centered Social Studies Education

Issues-centered social studies education, as the phrase implies, focuses on matters of actual concern to society. It also recognizes and, indeed, makes pedagogical use of the complexity of issues in a democratic system. In addition to relating history and geography knowledge to contemporary issues, this approach incorporates the key elements of **1.** multiculturalism in a global context, **2.** multiple perspectives, and **3.** strong-sense (dialogical) critical reasoning. Thus, students are not only exposed to information but develop experience in processes that employ such information in problem-solving situations.

Our information-age culture presents the rationale for this kind of curriculum. Satellite television, on-line electronic mail and news services, fax machines, high-tech library networks, and sophisticated computer software have changed the nature of basic literacy. The educational challenge for students in the late 1990s is not only to acquire and retain a given body of knowledge but also to master the tools for using knowledge.

Such acquisition of information and the

mastery of obtaining information blends easily into the context of problem solving. Our students, who have known only this information culture, will sense the relevance of such an approach to social studies learning, and what many now experience as a dreary and routine subject may become the most vital and stimulating in their school experience. In the following discussion, we explore the possibilities of issues-centered social studies education in terms of its three key elements

Global Multiculturalism

We have previously defined multiculturalism with a global perspective as:

> a layered concept that includes not only the experiences of particular individuals and groups but also their shared interests and relationships, which in turn are embedded in the interconnectedness of all peoples of the world. In its full complexity, then, *multiculturalism* implies the cultivation of a global view of human affairs. Paradoxically, perhaps, this expanded view of multiculturalism places primary emphasis on the individual and on the importance of individual decisions regarding all issues concerning the welfare of humankind. (Garcia and Pugh 1992, 218)

Although politicians and the general public may not agree on a definition of "the new world order" or on what is the U.S. role as the world's solitary superpower, the momentous changes of the late eighties and early nineties have made us acutely aware that today's pace goes at roller-coaster speed when compared to earlier times. To cite just two events—the dismantling of the real wall in Berlin and the symbolic wall of apartheid in South Africa—we have witnessed breathtaking liberation along with the consequent confusion that often follows the toppling of an oppressive structure. The electronic network that keeps all nations of the world in touch with and under the scrutiny of all others is a metaphor for the actual interconnectedness of the whole human race.

Environmental concerns make global thinking an urgent necessity. The destruction of rain forests in South America and Southeast Asia, for example, affects medical research and even breathing in the United States, just as the pollu-

tion generated by our affluent lifestyles is damaging the ozone that protects these regions. Poverty and overpopulation in developing countries call for moral and economic responsibilities in rich countries, who, in turn, become recipients of increased numbers of immigrants and refugees.

Indeed, the "international global village," prophesied by Marshall McLuhan (1968) and documented twenty-five years later (Iyer 1993) is defined by an international youth culture driven by an international economy. Despite youth's notorious ignorance of geography, an international outlook is as natural to young people as playing with computers. We must now accept that an individual without a computer or international awareness is deprived of knowledge necessary for successful functioning in today's world.

The metaphor that might best describe today's global perspective is the holograph, which presents all dimensions simultaneously to create an image-in-the-round, vastly different from the sequential presentation of "expanding horizons," the popular social studies curriculum model that "begins with the immediate environment—family, home, school, neighborhood and community—and moves outward to state, regional, national, and international environments" (Michaelis 1992, 14). In an issues-centered approach, instruction emphasizes the students' belonging simultaneously to all levels of the social environment. Issues may be immediate, but their implications are far-reaching. Diversity itself is such an issue. In both school and community, issues arise naturally concerning the degree and nature of diversity, and the analysis of these issues will link the school and local environment to the state, national, and global environment.

Many school and societal issues are available for critical examination within an issues-centered approach. For example, the school issue of tracking would open to the larger issue of how school differentiates students and treats them accordingly, often appearing to follow class and race lines, and with particular implications for newly arrived Americans. When students look at how group membership can affect one's treatment and experience in school, they consider attitudes toward societies defined as more distant than others as well as the role of wealth in both power and opportunity. Another school issue is segregation, integration, and separatism, recently parodied in a Doonesbury series featuring a liberal college president facing the opposition of the

"Multiracial, Bi-Gender Student Alliance" over the issue of social desegregation on a college campus (he wants it, they don't). The entire history of our nation can be contextualized in that issue, with particular emphasis on events before, during, and after the Civil War. Studying this major dimension of our own cultural history helps students consider racial and ethnic conflicts and reforms in other parts of the world and such international movements as the rise of the "skinhead" culture and the globalization of virtually all aspects of African American popular culture.

Other issues that can be explored simultaneously from school to planet include environmental issues from school recycling to the Earth Summit, residential patterns from neighborhoods to international immigration trends, and employment patterns from the local factory to NAFTA. Virtually any major issue leads to the necessity of taking a global and multicultural perspective in order to begin to address the rights—and perhaps to some extent the welfare—of all groups on a planet that is shrinking in more ways than one.

Multiple Perspectives

The New York State Social Studies Review and Development Committee (1991) identified four pillars of social studies instruction: shared values for nation-building, appreciation of cultural diversity, inclusiveness of all cultures, and, as the culminating point, the development of reasoning from multiple perspectives. Committee members, such as Edmund Gordon of Yale University, Nathan Glazer of the Harvard School of Education, Arthur Schlesinger, Jr., of the City University of New York, Asa Hilliard III of Georgia State University, and Francis Roberts of New York's Cold Spring Harbor Schools, identified seven basic concepts to guide social studies curriculum reform: democratic ideals, diversity, economic and social justice, globalism, ecological balance, ethics and values, and individual participation in society. These educators' concern with developing the capacity to view issues and reason from multiple perspectives is explained in the following passage (italics ours):

Not only the world, but also our nation and the peoples who inhabit it, are changing. The nature of our knowledge and the criteria for being judged an educated person are changing, as are our conceptions of effective teaching and learning. Especially in the humanities and the social sciences, we are beginning to realize that understanding and the ability to appreciate things from more than one perspective may be as important as is factual knowledge, among the goals of education. One result of this changing perception is the Committee's assertion that the social studies should be concerned, not so much with "whose culture" (vii) and "whose history" are to be taught and learned, as with the *development of intellectual competence in learners, with intellectual competence viewed as having as one of its major components the capacity to view the world and understand it from multiple perspectives.* Thus the report takes the position that a few fundamental concepts should be the focus of teaching and learning in the social studies, with applications, contexts, and examples drawn from multiple cultural sources, differing perspectives, and diverse groups. *Multicultural knowledge in this conception of the social studies becomes a vehicle and not the goal. Multicultural content and experience become instruments by which we enable students to develop their intelligence and to function as human and humane persons* (519).

Schlesinger, it should be noted, expressed strong misgivings with the emphasis of the report on pluralism and the value of different cultures and heritages instead of participation in a common culture. In addition, he criticized the report for diminishing the importance of European civilization, which he asserted was the "unique" source of American institutions and values. He also took issue with what he called the "politicization" of the curriculum, citing such statements as "students must be taught social criticism," that "[they should] see themselves as active makers and changers of culture and society," and "that [they should prepare to] bring about change in their communities, the nation, and the world." The publication of both the majority report and the dissenting opinion in the New York State Social Studies Review and Development Committee report is an excellent illustration of what is fundamental to discussion in a democratic society—dialogical/dialectical reasoning.

Dialogical Reasoning

Richard Paul (1985) defines "strong-sense" critical thinking as dialectical; that is, integrating different viewpoints. He characterizes such subjects as history, psychology, sociology, anthropology, and economics as based on debate and controversy rather than on unanimously agreed-upon premises, a view that can probably be extended to the sciences and mathematics—and certainly to the humanities. An extended excerpt from his explanation of "dialectical reasoning" is appropriate to explain the concept here:

> Generate a question within them [the fields mentioned above], and you typically generate a field of possible conflicting lines of reasoning and answers. Raise questions about their application to everyday life problems, and the debate often intensifies. The issues are properly understood as dialectical, as calling for dialogical reasoning, for thinking critically and reciprocally within opposing points of view. This ability to move up and back between contradictory lines of reasoning, using each to critically cross-examine the other, is not characteristic of the technical mind. Technical knowledge is typically developed by restriction to one frame of reference, to one standpoint. Knowledge arrived at dialectically, in contrast, is like the verdict, with supporting reasoning, of a jury. There are at least two points of view to entertain. It is not, as problem-solving theorists tend to characterize all problems, a movement from an initial state through a series of transformations (or operations) to a final (answering) state (156).

In class, particularly in small groups, students should discuss and debate, practicing the arts of thoughtful listening and clear expression. The ultimate purpose of exploring different viewpoints is to reach the best possible understanding of an issue in order to take action. As the major tool of social science inquiry, dialogical reasoning is also the basis for developing strong critical thinking skills.

It is here, in its emphasis on critical thinking and problem solving, that the issues-centered approach stands out from other models that may claim to address "issues" as topics or content. The issues-centered approach fuses process and content, so that they are always mutually reinforcing. Critical thinking entails the ability to comprehend and evaluate arguments. An argument is a basic form of reasoning utilized in problem solving and the development of knowledge in all fields. A hypothesis is the foundation of an argument, a premise, and a claim. The evidence that supports or negates the hypothesis represents the next part of the argument, and the outcome is the conclusion one reaches on the basis of the evidence. This basic structure of reasoning is used in any writing that takes a point of view that might be challenged or compared to another point of view, whether it is an essay, an editorial, a speech, a scholarly article, or a legal document. The Declaration of Independence is a prime example of an argument. It begins with an issue, which is the question of whether a nation is justified in separating from an unjust government, takes a position, which is an affirmative answer to that question, and then lists all the evidence to support that action. The outcome is the independent nation we are today. This analysis has been encapsulated in a heuristic we call IPSO (Issues, Position, Support, Outcome), developed for a course on critical reasoning for new college students, a course necessitated by students' general lack of experience with critical reading and thinking in high school. The IPSO tool for argument analysis is outlined in the Table on the next page.

The term "obligated" in the issue statement is not explained or qualified, so that one might ask in what ways obligation is intended—legal, moral, military, etc. Both arguments in their given form are cast as opinions. The arguments may seem simplistic for a graduating senior, yet they are typical of the work of many students at the end of their high school career, demonstrating their lack of experience with both argument and analysis. Begun much earlier, IPSO could launch students into critical reading and comparison of viewpoints throughout high school, preparing them both for college and for adult decision making.

IPSO does not cover all aspects of argumentation, so teachers may wish to supplement with discussion of what makes a topic an issue, what premises lie behind the formulation of an issue, and what assumptions underlie any part of an argument. Such refinement of critical reading and thinking skills builds on IPSO's basic structure.

Because the process of dialogical reasoning actively involves students in developing their own positions and attending to the perspectives and arguments of others, they experience a dynamic

IPSO: A Guide for Analyzing Argument Structures

Issue: What is the argument's problem or question?

Position: What is the major position (thesis) asserted in this argument?

Support: What evidence, reasoning, or other persuasive means support the position?

Outcome: What is likely to happen if the argument is accepted?

PSO, a heuristic and not a technical model, uses ordinary language to identify basic elements of most arguments. The structure represents a commonsense way of presenting and supporting a thesis on an issue. Students can use it in both reading and writing, and it is especially useful for comparing arguments, as illustrated in the following presentation of opposing viewpoints by a high school senior in a 1993 college skills course:

ISSUE: Is the United States obligated to intervene in Bosnia?

Position I:

No, the United States does not have a responsibility to intervene.

Support:

1. We have nothing to do with their problems.
2. We have our own economic and political problems.
3. Conflicts with other nations might ensue.
4. Thousands of American troops could be killed.

Outcome: Bosnia and the rest of the world would learn to stand on their own feet.

Position II:

Yes, the United States does have a responsibility to intervene.

Support:

1. United Nations treaty is being violated.
2. United Nations troops are being attacked.
3. We should help Bosnia as we have helped other countries.
4. Thousands of innocent people are being killed.

Outcome: The war would stop and we would have a more peaceful world.

---

relationship with social studies content. They acquire content in context, leading to a meaning orientation (Ramsden 1988), and the habit of constructive knowing (Baxter-Magolda 1992). In other words, they expect information to be complex, never entirely complete, subject to critical evaluation, and, above all, useful in forming views and making decisions. In short, school-acquired information now becomes as relevant and necessary as information acquired in other important settings. With repeated experiences with challenging peer interactions, students come to expect more and more of themselves and others.

The Issues-Centered Classroom

The issues-centered classroom has a number of key elements. One of these is the use of appropriate classroom methods. Among the most useful means of teaching issues in the classroom are simulations and case studies. These and other methods should be employed in a way that keeps sight of the powerful general concepts that are an

important part of social studies learning. Secondly, an issues-centered approach must focus on offering students strategies for organizing knowledge; these strategies do not necessarily conflict (as it is sometimes argued) with "core knowledge" approaches that advocate significant similarity of curriculum content among American schools. Finally, it is important that the assessment of student achievement be consistent with issues-centered education.

Case Studies

The essence of the issues-centered approach is its problematizing function. As the "I" in IPSO suggests, information is related to the real and controversial questions of civic life. Historical as well as contemporary topics can be cast in problem formats. Oliver, Newmann, and Singleton (1992), for example, suggest revisiting the turning points in U.S. history by reconsidering the momentous questions of these times: Should the United States have declared its independence? What measures should have been taken, and by whom, to assist the urban poor at the turn of the twentieth century? Should the United States have entered the Second World War sooner than it did?

Involving students in the complexities and ambiguities surrounding historical issues helps them understand that history evolves as a series of negotiations, decisions, and consequences. Cases and simulations drive this point home. For example, by projecting themselves into the position of an ordinary citizen in Indiana just prior to the Civil War, they can pursue the question of whether they would have supported or rejected the Fugitive Slave Law, the Underground Railroad, or the mobilization of northern troops against the southern states for seceding from the union. Because these are not yes/no issues, students must understand the position of Indiana as a "border" state in which certain kinds of pre-Civil War activity and dilemmas were prominent. A case set in this locale and time could present the different viewpoints of citizens in a primarily rural state and in a nation not yet a century old. Playing out the implications of such a case will help students understand the historical implications of this episode in our nation's story more deeply and more memorably than other forms of presentation, whether textbook descriptions, a time line, or a video drama of the phenomenon. The difference is in the emphasis. Students' attention is focused on concrete situations rather than sweeping events, providing the foundation for building the conceptual understanding of history and human affairs that is the point of social studies learning.

Cases may combine real and imagined components, such as presenting fictional characters in authentic history or contemporary situations. Oliver et al (1992) identify four kinds of issues that can provide the basis for cases: **1.** *general issues*, such as whether the government should require the use of basic protective devices like seat belts for automobile passengers or crash helmets for motorcyclists; **2.** *ethical/moral issues*, such as the right of individual choice versus the greater good for all; **3.** *definitional issues*, such as what should be included in the category of "basic protective devices," for example, air bags; and **4.** *fact-explanation issues*, such as the research supporting or refuting the effectiveness of using protective devices.

The selection of issues or incidents to devel-op into cases can be based on overall social or historical importance, significance to a particular community or group, or both (Oliver et al 1992). Students can also compose their own case studies by identifying issues or questions, researching different perspectives on such questions, and creating scenarios that illustrate the conflicts of interest involved and the basis for dialogical reasoning and negotiations that emerges. By composing their own cases and responding to one another's, students experience the actual identification and definition of salient issues, reinforcing the often neglected aspect of problem solving—problem finding.

One pitfall to be avoided in the case approach, or the issues-centered approach in general, is losing sight of the general concepts and broad perspectives that are an important part of social studies learning. Cases and issues are not ends in themselves. The teacher should regularly assess both teacher-generated and student-generated cases for their relevance to the conceptual content of the curriculum. Roth (1994) warns against thematic approaches that dilute the powerful concepts of any subject or discipline, arguing that "we best develop our students' understanding of the world and its connectedness by giving them access to a variety of powerful lenses through which to view it." (48)

The Core Knowledge Question

Another consideration important to an argument for an issues-centered approach is whether it subverts the idea of core knowledge in the social studies, and, if so, whether that is a problem. Perhaps the place to begin is with the question of whether there is a conflict. According to Hirsch (1993), foremost proponent of the core knowledge philosophy, about 50 percent of the curriculum in any subject area should comprise content that is common among all American schools at that grade level. Such a provision, he argues, would bring national standards into focus and ensure comparability of education across all regions and communities. In response to critics who disapprove of the content emphasis of the concept of core knowledge, he contends that *"a coherent approach to specific content enhances students' critical thinking and higher-order thinking skills.* [emphasis his]" (144). One line of reasoning with which Hirsch supports this position is that thoughtful selection and sequencing of content facilitates the constructive process of building new knowledge upon the foundation of existing knowledge.

Apart from whether we agree with the core knowledge concept or Hirsch's claims for it, it is our position that it is not necessarily incompatible with an issues-centered approach. Frazee (1993), who has worked with a number of "Core Knowledge" schools, refutes the belief that the theory leads to mechanical accumulation of information. Rather, teachers who are successfully implementing it "organize content into thematic units of their choosing; they can also select strategies and resources conducive to in-depth learning. Assessment of progress can be accomplished through student writing, bulletin boards, projects, performances, portfolios, and much more" (149). An issues-centered approach does not imply either the inclusion or the exclusion of any specific content, but rather a set of strategies for organizing content and the experiences that students have with it.

Assessment in the Issues-centered Curriculum

Like the core knowledge issue, assessment and standards may be viewed as compromised by an issues-centered approach, but again we contend such a view is basically misconceived.

During the past decade of school reforms and since the publication of *A Nation at Risk* (1993), McKenna (1994) points out that crossnational assessments still show that American students are achieving far below the levels of students from other countries with national standards. In response to the frustration experienced by educators, employers, and the public at large, the government enacted Goals 2000 legislation (1991), which created a National Education and Standards Improvement Council to develop content-based standards and assessments and a National Skills Standards Board to develop occupational standards. Federal dollars for education are tied to states' voluntary compliance with these standards.

The negative specter of national assessment, taking the form of reductionist discrete testing for particular facts and microskills, fortunately has been countered by reforms in the assessment field itself. Despite the challenges of achieving high levels of reliability, educators and policy makers now favor portfolios and other forms of qualitative assessment that highlight students' abilities to apply higher order literacy and math

skills, to solve problems, and to continue learning on the job or in lifelong education. Such competency standards place emphasis on an integrated range of abilities that cannot be developed through passive learning of content but require the engagement of students in that content in ways wholly compatible with an issues-centered approach. For example, describing Oregon's Proficiency-Based Admissions Standards System, McKenna (1994, 5) points out that in order to gain admission to public colleges, high school graduates will have to demonstrate proficiency in "reading, writing, oral expression, critical/analytical thinking, problem solving, technology as a learning tool, systems/integrative thinking, teamwork and quality work," assessed in the context of the content areas. If, as indicated on many fronts, Oregon's approach to standards is indicative of the nation as a whole, issues-centered teaching in the social studies may be the only way to prepare students adequately for assessment.

Issues-centered Teacher Preparation

One aspect of criticism against public education during the past decade has been dissatisfaction with teacher education itself, most frequently on grounds of inadequate content preparation and an insufficient grounding in sound learning theory and teaching strategies. Teachers are accused of teaching as they were taught, an accusation that frequently implies authoritarian delivery of content to passive learners, the infamous "lecture format" of university teaching.

Another problem is the insufficiency of preparation for teaching in multicultural schools (Pugh and Garcia, 1994). Currently, most teacher education programs provide some exposure to multicultural education, more isolated than pervasive. Instruction may focus on similarities or "common culture," particularly as a legacy of the eighties when "common culture" was used as a rationale for dismantling civil rights gains. At the same time, students in teacher education programs often have sporadic exposure to critical reading and critical thinking. Collaborative and cooperative learning strategies, now popular in many areas of education, are likely to be part of the program, though not necessarily well integrated.

In order to successfully manage an issues-centered approach, teachers must themselves experience learning in such an environment. Hence, we recommend that an issues-centered approach be implemented in the teacher education curriculum itself in both content and methods courses. Prospective teachers should be involved in both responding to and constructing cases centering on educational problems and issues, along with practicing dialogical/dialectical reasoning and negotiation of solutions in pluralistic contexts. Teacher education students should experience collaborative and cooperative approaches to learning with such a framework of issues-centered education and critical thinking. In social studies, such training should orient prospective teachers to actively participate in the governance of their professional and social environments. Ideally, we would train not just for teaching but for educational leadership, with implications for social leadership, as well.

An important dimension of active teacher preparation is an emphasis on a global concept of multiculturalism throughout the teacher education curriculum. As Cottrol (1990, 28) noted, the real challenge is teaching

> the very complicated story of American history to students—complicated because it includes so much that is terrible and so much that is remarkable. It is a history of contradiction and dilemmas. ... In judging a particular multicultural education effort, we should ask whether it tells the story of how American culture was shaped and transformed by a multicultural population. And we should ask whether it helps our students come to grips with the contradictions at the core of our history.

For as long as our nation retains its particular democratic ideals, which honor the uniqueness of the individual, the rights of all groups, and the principle of diversity within unity, tensions between pluralism and the common culture will provide our basic dynamic. As a people, we will assert and defend particular interests within a framework of argument, negotiation, and compromise. In this configuration, "common" culture is not the same as "mainstream" culture. The latter may be identified primarily with the majority—white, middle class population—but the common culture is not the property of any single group. It will ever be in a state of evolution, a process that prevents its becoming a "melting

Global Multiculturalism

Multicultural contexts for issues provide realistic dimensionality and emphasize experiences and contributions of different groups. A global perspective supports wide-ranging discussion of issues at several levels.

▼

Multiple Perspectives

An appreciation of complexity is required for strong-sense critical thinking, which, in turn, provides reasoning operations and attitudes for considering issues and events fairly from multiple perspectives.

▼

Dialogical Reasoning

Reasoning within alternative frameworks supports the suspension of egocentric and ethnocentric thinking. Dialogical reasoning provides a combined social and cognitive framework for examining presuppositions, stereotypes, and prejudices as well as for considering complex issues from multiple perspectives.

▼

Problem-Based Assessment

Assessment based on productive reasoning and literacy competencies will reinforce values placed on higher order thinking, problem solving, and new learning abilities in society and the workplace today. In this way, an issues-centered approach to assessment, with its effect on the curriculum, helps address the quandaries of educational standards and excellence in the United States.

pot"—a metaphor challenged by many others, including "salad bowl," "mosaic," and "bouillabaisse." It is, in sum, an issues-centered culture, which is the bottom-line support for implementing an issues-centered approach in the social studies and incorporating this approach in the preparation of social studies (and all) teachers.

Key Elements and Outcomes

Key elements of issues-centered social studies education include global multiculturalism, multiple perspectives on complex issues, dialogical/dialectical reasoning, and problem-based assessment. Working in mutual reinforcement, these elements will support the development of a complex and expandable information base along with the cognitive abilities and critical skills for complex problem solving. Participating in an issues-centered curriculum will empower students for participation in vital social processes. Perhaps most importantly, it will lay the foundation for students to develop the moral imagination and vision to work toward a just and equitable world society.

References

America 2000: An Education Strategy. Washington, DC: U.S. Department of Education, 1991.

Baxter-Magolda, Marcia. *Knowing and Reasoning in College: Gender Related Patterns in Students' Intellectual Development.* San Francisco: Jossey-Bass, 1992.

Beatty, Alexandra S., et al. *NAEP 1994 U.S. History Report Card: Findings from the National Assessment of Educational Progress.* Washington, DC: U.S. Department of Education, 1996.

Bradley Commission on History in Schools. *Building a History Curriculum: Guidelines for Teaching History in Schools.* Washington, DC: Educational Excellence Network, 1988.

Cottrol, Robert. "America The Multicultural." *American Educator* 14(Winter 1990): 18–21.

Gagnon, Paul, ed. *Historical Literacy: The Case for History in American Education.* Boston: Houghton Mifflin Co., 1989.

Garcia, Jesus, and Sharon L. Pugh. "Multicultural Education in Teacher Education Programs: A Political or Educational Concept?" *Phi Delta Kappan* 74(November 1992): 214–19.

Iyer, Pico. "The Global Village Finally Arrives." *Time* 142(Fall 1993): 86–87.

McKenna, Barbara. "What Is This Thing Called Standards, and Why Should We Care?" *On Campus* 13(1994): 4–5+.

McLuhan, Marshall and Quentin Fiore. *War and Peace in the Global Village.* New York: McGraw-Hill, 1968.

Michaelis, John U. *Social Studies for Children: A Guide to Basic Instruction.* Boston: Allyn and Bacon, 1992.

A Nation at Risk: The Imperative for Educational Reform. Washington, DC: National Commission on Excellence in Education, U.S. Department of Education, 1983.

National Commission on Social Studies in the Schools. *Charting a Course: Social Studies for the 21st Century.* Washington, DC: National Commission on Social Studies in the Schools, 1989.

New York State Social Studies Review and Development Committee. *One Nation, Many Peoples: A Declaration of Cultural Interdependence.* Albany, N.Y.: New York State Education Department, 1991. Reprinted in *Face to Face: Readings on Confrontation and Accommodation in America,* edited by Joseph

Zaitchik, William Roberts, and Holly Zaitchik. Boston: Houghton Mifflin Co., 1994.

Oliver, Donald W., Fred M. Newmann, and Laurel R. Singleton. "Teaching Public Issues in the Secondary School Classroom." *The Social Studies* 83 (May/June 1992): 100–103.

Paul, Richard. "Dialectical Reasoning." In *Developing Minds: A Resource Book for Teaching Thinking,* edited by Arthur L. Costa. Alexandria, Va.: Association for Supervision and Curriculum Development, 1985.

Pugh, Sharon L., and Jesus Garcia. "Multicultural Education: Who Will Teach the Teachers?" Unpublished paper. Indiana University at Bloomington, 1994.

Ramsden, Paul. *Improving Learning: New Perspectives.* New York: Nichols Publishing Co., 1988.

Roth, Kathleen. "Second Thoughts about Interdisciplinary Studies." *American Educator* 18(Spring 1994): 44–48.

Rothman, Robert. "History and Civics Tests Reveal Knowledge Gaps." *Education Week* 9 (April 11, 1990): 5+.

Part Four: Historical Topics and Themes

Introduction by David Warren Saxe

THE USES OF HISTORY: INTRODUCTION TO ISSUES-CENTERED HISTORY

When social studies was in its infancy, a new history was proclaimed by James Harvey Robinson and Charles Beard. This new history added social and economic perspectives to the old history of kings, battles, and great events. As a result, it broadened the curricular depth of what teachers could offer students.

The new history was also well suited to social studies as a means to cultivate an active, competent citizenship. Robinson, serving on the seminal 1916 Committee on the Social Studies, was clearly influential in forging strong ties between social studies and the new history. The report of the Committee on Social Studies, as part of a larger reorganization of secondary schools, signaled a formal introduction of social studies (and with it the new history) for school administrators, textbook companies, and teachers.

While the new history thrived within social studies, the old history supported by the American Historical Association did not die. Today a new, new history has moved into universities, public schools, and textbooks. This new, new history of the dispossessed, marginalized, and oppressed presented a story unlike the old history or the new history. It is a history of victimization, deconstruction, and politics. It was the cultivation and popularization of this new, new history that spawned and now supports multiculturalism, the new orthodoxy of education.

While the old history and new history were different, the commonalities between the two were strong. Both the old and new relied upon methodologies, evidence, and thorough research and critique. The old and new histories highlighted the salient events of the past (albeit from different perspectives). Moreover, the old and new histories could be revised in light of new evidence or powerful analysis of earlier works. In sum, the old and new histories, while different in focus, at least were not incompatible in school settings.

In contrast, the new, new history disregards salient (major) events that are described as classist, racist, and largely Eurocentric in vision and practice. The real stories of history are seen as being about common people left out of the discourse. It is the history of the oppressed that merits attention. The old and new histories are dead and irrelevant.

When the old history and the new history are juxtaposed with the new, new history, it is clear that something has to give. The study of Columbus cannot be simply an examination of historical records and notation of turning points in history. For the new, new history, Columbus is all about racism, vile colonialism, white hegemony, and genocide. There is no weighing of evidence required, no sifting through conflicting historical data on Mezzo-American Indian life, or critique of the pronouncement of Columbian guilt. The old and new history of social studies have no place here.

It is this author's view that issues-centered teaching is vital for all. Moreover, that issues-centered social studies goes beyond efforts to politicize social studies. Issues-centered teaching is essentially liberal (in the classical sense of opening the mind) and democratic (in the grass roots sense of the willingness to explore any problem, controversial or not). In the chapters that follow are three interpretations of issues-centered history for your consideration. Patrick Ferguson provides a detailed examination of issue use within any history context. Richard Gross explores the use of issues in world history. Ron Evans attends to critical approaches to history, and I offer a challenge of how issues-centered themes can be applied in American history courses.

As this introduction was prepared, the Enola Gay controversy at the Smithsonian Institution came to a uneasy resolution. The exhibit of the airplane that carried the Atomic Bomb to Hiroshima to commemorate the 50th anniversary of the end of World War II and the dawn of the atomic age would not contain a revisionist (new, new history) account on the dropping of the bomb. A great public outcry had taken place against casting American leaders and soldiers as aggressors and Japanese as victims. Another example of new, new history and cultural relativism in support of multiculturalism was the publishing of the National History Standards. After an outcry at the application of new, new history thinking to American and world history, the standards needed to be revised. Such examples point to the need for issues-centered studies. The exploration of how we should think about World War II or what sort of history is most appropriate for our children *invites* differences of opinion. It is precisely at such times that issues study is most relevant and appropriate.

Hopefully, after reading through these chapters, you will agree that teachers and students can bring life to past events. Issues-centered teaching can provide opportunities for sharpening students' skills in dealing with historical events, and making sense of their present life.

15 TEACHING ISSUES-CENTERED HISTORY

by Patrick Ferguson

This chapter addresses teachers in search of innovative ways to advance their students' comprehension of contemporary issues through the investigative study of history (Fisher 1970; Griffin 1942; Kennedy 1993). It is assumed that the teacher is in agreement with Forrest McDonald's belief that expertise in history is not judged by how many facts, dates, and events one can recall, but whether one can demonstrate skill in classifying, probing, and formulating solutions (McDonald 1994).

In this chapter, a strategy for teaching issues-centered history is introduced and illustrated by examples of its application in world and U.S. history courses. This is followed by a discussion of recommended activities and resources. The chapter then closes with suggestions for shifting from traditional to issues-centered history.

A Strategy for Teaching Issues-Centered History

The strategy suggested here for teaching issues-centered history is based on a model of analogical reasoning, involving students in the comparison of past and present events. It fuses a general problem-solving paradigm—defining and clarifying a problem, exploring possible strategies, implementing the strategies, and evaluating the outcomes—with the modes of inquiry distinctive to the study of history—documentary analysis, logical inquiry, and literary critique. The resultant strategy calls for students to select and define a social issue of contemporary significance, identify historically analogous circumstances, use primary and secondary sources to investigate these occurrences, list their findings in the form of generalizations, compare and contrast the historical findings with the issue in the contemporary setting, propose historically tenable solutions, and

take action to resolve the problem.[1]

Selecting and Defining the Issue

Cultivating student interest is a critical first step. Research demonstrates that success in analogical thinking is optimized when students are motivated to inquire into the problem at hand (Armour-Thomas and Allen 1990; Holyoak 1984). If the issue is to be defined by the students, they can peruse television reports, newspapers, and library resources to identify an issue of interest. Sometimes, an issue emerges during the discussion of a historical event. For example, a discussion of Hammurabi's Code, with its harsh penalties for criminal misconduct, held at the time of the news of the switching punishment of an American teenager for defacing property in Singapore, might evince interest in the relationship between the incidence of criminal behavior and the enforcement of laws entailing stern penalties. If intrinsic interest in the issue is not apparent, the teacher will have to devise an activity or approach to elicit motivation.

Once interest has been cultivated, students are assigned to teams of three or four to draft a one-page statement of the issue in response to the following questions:

? What is the controversy in question?
? Who are the contending parties in the controversy?
? What are the specific points of contention?
? What social values are in conflict?
? What makes this dispute a matter of public importance?
? What are the key problems that require solution?

After completion of the teams' statements, the teacher conducts a discussion for the purpose of synthesizing them into a class-defined statement of the issue.

Identifying Relevant Historical Occurrences

Working again in their teams, students consult their textbook and other references to generate a list of ten to twenty analogous historical circumstances. The events chosen need not precisely mirror the circumstances of the modern issue, but students should be cautioned that the more widely disparate the historical circumstances, the greater the risk that they will formulate false analogies (Fisher 1970). The teams' lists are then pooled and narrowed to a short list of perhaps five to seven events, depending on the size of the class. The students are then instructed to do in-depth studies of the events. An optional approach would be for each team to select its own short list and assign one event to each team member for investigation.

Defining the Research Procedure; Locating and Analyzing Sources

Let us assume that each team is responsible for researching a single event. Teams are informed that their goal will be twofold: first, to arrive at a list of five to ten findings for their historical circumstance; second, to produce a list of five to ten statements comparing various aspects of the issue then and now. Teams are instructed that whenever feasible, they are to write their findings in the form of social-science-type generalizations.[2] The teacher should provide examples.

Four cautionary rules need to be introduced and posted to guide team investigations:

1. The issues explored in historical context are to be viewed in the light of the standards, values, and attitudes of their time rather than those of the present.

2. Issues and events are the product of multiple causations, not simple, one-to-one, cause-and-effect relationships.

3. The record of past issues is necessarily fragmented, selective, and biased.

4. History is more likely to suggest possible rather than probable solutions to contemporary issues (Muessig and Rogers 1965).

Each team is instructed to draw a time line for its investigation, including a list of the tasks assigned to each team member.

Students should next be instructed to complete a teacher-provided form for each source of information they decide to use. The form calls for a summary of the information obtained and information about its significance, accuracy, consistency, evidence of bias, emotionality, values and beliefs, unstated assumptions, reasoning, and evidenced-based conclusions (National Archives 1989). Teams should meet regularly with the teacher to discuss their progress and receive advice on additional sources and avenues of investigation.

Formulating Findings and Conclusions

This phase of the exercise involves three steps. First, with the four cautionary rules in mind, each team produces a list of findings for their historical circumstance. Second, using the original statement of the issue formulated by the class, the team generates a list of statements comparing and contrasting their historical findings with the issue in the contemporary setting. These statements should be carefully monitored for their evidentiary basis, logical consistency, and soundness of analogical thought (Fisher 1970). Third, the teams present their findings and comparative statements to the class. The class then examines the accumulated evidence to decide whether any "lessons from history" can be applied to the issue in the contemporary setting.

Proposing Solutions and Taking Action

In this last step, students make projections about future developments and theorize about possible solutions. When feasible, they take action on their proposed solutions.

The Strategy in Action

Selecting and Defining the Issue

The conflict that has persisted over history concerning the appropriate balance between governmental authority and personal liberty will be used to illustrate the strategy here. The events following the collapse of the Soviet Union serve as the immediate catalyst for interest in this issue.

Creating Interest in the Issue. To generate interest in the issue, the teacher begins by asking students to consider the following question: When is a government justified in regulating the freedom of its citizens? A list of governmental functions could be listed on the chalkboard under the heading "The government is justified in":

collecting taxes, issuing licenses, requiring school prayer, compelling military service, enforcing school attendance, regulating the production of food and drugs, establishing curfews for young people, regulating radio and television airways, and appropriating property to build roads and highways. After discussing the legitimacy of these governmental functions, the focus shifts to the current problem of defining the authority of the newly emergent government in Russia. To heighten interest, the students are asked to consider the implications of this issue for young people in Russia as they conduct their investigation into the problem.

Defining the Issue in its Present Context. Students begin their inquiry by collecting information on events that have transpired in Russia since the breakup of the Soviet Union. The teacher provides selected articles from recent news sources and excerpts from some of the excellent recently published materials on this issue. These include short articles from *The Breakup of the Soviet Union* (Greenhaven 1994) and the *End of the Soviet Union* (Southern Center for International Studies 1994). From these sources, teams compose statements describing the dispute in question, identify the contending parties, list the main points of disagreement, delineate the values that appear to be in conflict, indicate why the controversy in Russia is a matter of national and international importance, and list key problems that must be resolved. Students might be asked to explain why they think a Russian citizen would make this statement: "The Russian people want order and a strong state; democracy is a luxury Russia cannot yet afford" (Watson 1995).

Identifying Relevant Historical Occurrences. Using their textbook, historical encyclopedias, books on Russian history, and Hedrick Smith's *The New Russians* (1990), the teams compile a list of between ten and twenty relevant circumstances in Russian history that are in some way related to the theme of government authority and personal liberty. The lists might include the breakdown of the czar's power during the "time of troubles," the use of governmental authority to enact reforms by Peter and Catherine the Great, the Decembrist Revolt, Alexander II's freeing of the serfs and plan to establish local forms of self-government, the anarchists' revolt, uprisings against the monarchical authority of Alexander III, the 1917 revolution, the declaration of the 1936 "Stalin Constitution," and the introduction

of *"perestroika"* and *"glasnost"* reforms under Gorbachev. The entire class discusses each team's list and narrows them down to six items. Each team is then assigned one of the six historical circumstances for further investigation. As the example here, we will choose the exercise of authority under Peter the Great.

Defining the Research Procedure/ Locating and Analyzing Sources

The team first turns to the textbook and finds a brief and laudatory account of Peter the Great's success in improving scientific, cultural, military, and economic conditions in Russia. They infer that an authoritative approach to government may be justified when there is a strong need to advance the economic and political status of a "backward" nation. The teacher has them note that this same argument is used by those who support strong authoritative governments in developing nations in Africa, Asia, and Latin America, and, of course, in present-day Russia.

Turning to other sources, students find somewhat contrasting pictures to the one in their textbook. They learn that in his zeal to modernize Russia, Peter heavily taxed an already impoverished citizenry, forbade citizens to garb themselves in western dress, and repressed the traditional religion of the people. Indeed, the great majority of Russians continued to exist in extreme poverty and ignorance during and following Peter's reign (Oliva 1969; Massie 1980; Summer 1962). This new information appears to support the views of those who caution against the establishment of overly authoritative approaches to government in contemporary Russia. Specific comparisons are also noted, for example, between Peter's ruthless use of the military to quickly quell rebellious factions and the use of military force by the current government in the Chechnyan crisis. If feasible, team members extend their investigation to surrounding libraries, search for material using computers and other media sources, and interview historians who are specialists in Russian history.

Formulating Findings and Conclusions

The team concludes that Peter's absolutist approach greatly facilitated the modernization of a backward nation, but at the expense of the quality of life of the Russian people. The team also constructs statements comparing and contrasting the actions of government in coping with political, economic, and social conditions in Peter's time with those of the present Russian government. After each team has reported its conclusions to the class, the teacher reintroduces the original issue to synthesize the teams' results. The overall general conclusion of the class might be that the beneficial or detrimental effects of the actions of authoritative governments are largely determined by two factors: the conditions of the times, and the personalities, beliefs, and perceptions of those who are in control.

Proposing Solutions and Taking Action

To conclude the experience, the teacher has the students read "How Should the U.S. Respond to the Break-Up of the Soviet Union?" (Greenhaven 1994) and debate the role to be taken by the United States. They decide to communicate their views to their congressperson, write a letter to the editor of the local newspaper, and correspond with students at a Russian school about the issue. The teacher urges students to reexamine their conclusions regarding the legitimate exercise of governmental authority as contemporary and historical events dictate during the course of the year.

Using the Strategy in American history

The debate over the legitimate role of government may be seen as the key to understanding the evolution and current function of the American political system. The approach in an American history course would closely follow the world history illustration. Following the interest-generating exercise on the legitimate functions of government, the teacher could introduce students to the present controversy over the constitutionality of the motor voter law, which requires the states, at considerable expense, to provide voter registration information and materials at offices where drivers' licenses are issued. The governors of several states are challenging the legitimate authority of the federal government to enforce this measure. After reading to the class the limited powers clause of the Tenth Amendment, the teacher could ask whether the federal government is exceeding its constitutional authority and infringing on the right of their state to allocate its resources pursuant to its own priorities. The class could then compose a statement of the issue using the guideline questions as in the world history example.

Next, student teams develop their lists of relevant historical events—the Whiskey Rebellion, the passage and enforcement of the Alien and Sedition Acts, the refusal of President Jackson to enforce the Supreme Court decision against the state of Georgia regarding the usurpation of Cherokee land, Calhoun's doctrine of nullification maintaining that a state can interpose its sovereignty between its citizens and the central government, the Civil War, the Pullman strike, and Roosevelt's exercise of authority under the New Deal. From this point forward, the instructional procedure, with appropriate adaptations, would replicate that in the Russian example.

The Role of the Teacher

Ideally, the teacher's role is primarily that of facilitator—posing issues for consideration, prompting team investigations, suggesting and providing sources of information, interposing questions, and encouraging and challenging students to support their findings with logic and evidence. A growing body of evidence, however, reveals that teachers view such idealized characterizations as either impractical or much too drastic a departure from their usual style of teaching (Nelson and Drake 1994; White 1994). Moreover, the wisdom of practice research suggests that effective history teaching may occur in both highly structured and relatively unstructured classrooms (Wineburg and Wilson 1988).

The strategy here is meant to be adaptable. Using a more structured approach, the teacher might open the lesson with the governmental functions motivational exercise, show a short video describing the crisis in governmental authority in present-day Russia, model the application of the four cautionary rules through a comparison of the contemporary issue with one or two historical examples, engage the students in a guided exercise in which the students practice applying the four-rule template to one or two additional historical circumstances, and conclude the lesson with a discussion of the implications. The entire practice lesson could be conducted within a single class period. The issue under discussion would be revisited as it became germane at subsequent points in the course.

It is important to recognize that there are limitations to the structured approach. First, research suggests that students' interest, efficacy, and understanding of controversial issues are decreased when the classroom environment is

135

closed and overly directive (Harwood 1990). Second, engaging students in the process of analogical thinking necessarily entails higher-order thinking in which the instructional procedures cannot be specified to the same degree as in "lower-order" learning tasks (Rosenshine 1993). The example in the previous paragraph is consistent with Rosenshine's adaptation of direct instruction to the mastery of higher-order cognitive strategies in which the teacher models the appropriate cognitive strategies and then engages students in practicing the strategies with new material. To help students bridge the gap between their current abilities and the goal of getting them to think independently, the teacher might assume a structured modeling posture at the beginning of the course and gradually move toward a more facilitative approach as the course progresses.

Other factors that affect how open or structured the approach should be are the teacher's intentions regarding how far the students are to proceed along the continuum from rudimentary awareness to in-depth insight on any particular issue, the age and ability levels of the students (see note 1), the availability of materials and resources, and concern for student achievement on standardized or advanced placement tests.

Selecting Issues

While virtually any issue of contemporary significance may be profitably examined from a historical perspective, a two-pronged test may help to ascertain its suitability: **1.** What central concepts in history are embodied in the issue? **2.** Is the issue the extension of some historically persistent debate over fundamental values?

Our example of defining the legitimacy of governmental authority meets this test. It involves students in the study of key concepts: absolutism, despotism, revolution, dictatorship, autocracy, the divine right of kings, democracy, representative government, and anarchism. It also involves debate concerning fundamental values: justice, liberty, tyranny, and civic responsibility. Examples of other issues that meet the two-pronged test are those identified by the historian Paul Kennedy (1993): population growth, man's use of the environment, human rights, food production, conflict among nations, the role of the nation-state, industrial growth, economic development, and science and technology. Another key to selecting issues is that virtually any debate

involving a question of elemental political, social, economic, or technological change is likely to be appropriate. These tests are bi-directional—that is, if an issue were to emerge within the context of a particular historical event, the concepts, values, and change tests would help determine whether the issue has contemporary relevance.

All of this may suggest that issues are to be viewed primarily from a global or national frame of reference. This is not necessarily the case. To accentuate interest and relevance, issues may also be approached from a local perspective. A proposal to construct a nuclear power plant in the community, a proposed change in land use ordinances, complaints over the enforcement of air and water pollution regulations, a movement to restrict access to certain materials in the local library, or a debate over adding a school holiday for Martin Luther King Jr.'s birthday are all examples of possible springboards into local history. Once students have examined the historical and contemporary aspects of the problem in its community setting, discussion can be extended to the issue in its larger national or international context.

An Area Studies Approach

Examining issues one at a time provides focus and facilitates manageability, but it also limits the students' opportunity to see the complex interrelationships among issues. One way to provide a more integrative approach is through an area studies approach. Africa will be used as an example.

To set the stage and create interest, students might read and discuss Christopher Hitchen's (1994) portrayal of contemporary Africa in his travelogue "African Gothic." Hitchens writes of witnessing the sober gatherings of Kenyan intellectuals, the stark contrasts between the goodwill and sanity in newborn nations such as Eritrea and the degraded regimes of Mobutu's Zaire and Banda's Malawi, the struggles in the emerging democratic states, widespread environmental deterioration, the rampant spread of HIV, extensive poverty, and bloody tribal rivalries. Students might then be assigned roles as historians in the twenty-first century charged with the task of ver sovereignty bet portrayal of the African continent in the year 1994.

Consulting world almanacs, learning materials available from the Africa Outreach Program (Brown 1994), and other sources, students might work in teams to find answers to questions. An example would be: of the twenty most impoverished nations in the world, how many are in Africa? Eighteen. What has happened to per capita GNP growth in Africa since 1980? It has steadily declined to about 2 percent a year. What has happened to Africa's share of the world's trade since 1970? It has declined to less than 2 percent. What proportion of the world's people who have been diagnosed with HIV reside in Africa? Two-thirds. What is the economic status of the nations in the sub-Saharan area? The national debt level is currently 110 percent of total GNP. A statement comparing their findings on political, economic, and social conditions and the extent to which they support or refute the accuracy of Hitchens' report would be given by the teams.

Students might then be assigned to "era" teams: early civilizations; the introduction of Christianity and Islam; the west, central, and southern kingdoms; and the beginnings of European control, colonial rule, and the movement toward independence. Using sources on African history (Masrui 1986; Davidson 1991), team members would inquire into the standards of living, literacy, food supply, ethnic conflict, systems of political governance, war, and living conditions for their period. As in the Russian example, teams would formulate the historical findings and comparison statements for their era and then combine them into generalizations about the African continent. Returning to their original statement of the issues, the class would then discuss future developments, reflect on the possible roles of the United States and various international organizations, propose solutions, and take action toward the amelioration of these problems.

As an alternative to the era approach, student teams might be assigned to investigate groups of African nations according to a common attribute: current political or economic status or perhaps by geographical location. Historical findings and comparison statements would be made for these groupings. The activity could culminate with a mock meeting of the Organization of African Unity, the West African Economic Community, or the United Nations, convened to address the issues.

Teaching Methods and Resources

Any of the plethora of methods on teaching history as a problem-solving endeavor—that is, those that engage students in thinking and behaving in the manner of historians—are readily adaptable to issues-centered history. It is not within the purview of this chapter to delineate these methods. Nevertheless, several methods particularly useful for issues-centered teaching will be discussed: documentary analysis, biographies and case studies, argumentation-based activities, and team investigation methods.

Documentary analysis

Teaching with Documents (National Archives 1989) is an inexpensive and practical guide to involving students in the analysis of issues-related primary sources. The archive also publishes inexpensive teaching units containing letters, diary accounts, charts, photographs, political cartoons, and other primary source materials with an issues orientation. One example is the Holocaust unit that involves students in a documentary analysis of the "revisionist" historians' contention that no conclusive evidence exists that the Holocaust ever occurred. Other units cover the right to vote, the Bill of Rights, presidential impeachment, the framing of the Constitution, propaganda, and women in history. A catalogue of these materials as well as information on courses and workshops for teachers locating and using archival materials in the classroom is available from the National Archives (1-800-24-8861). Other accessible sources of issues-relevant documents are the "Jackdaws" kits advertised in *Social Education,* CD-ROM compilations of documents for world and American history, and issues-based documentary histories, such as the Great Issues volumes edited by Richard and Beatrice Hofstadter (1982).

Students can get a first-hand feel for issues through the analysis of historical and contemporary speeches such as Alfred Beveridge's "March of the Flag" defending the expansive policies of the United States at the turn of the century, Martin Luther King Jr.'s inspirational "I Have a Dream," or the most recent State of the Union presidential address (Ferguson 1972).

Biographies and Case Studies

Students may also view issues through the eyes of people who had to make critical personal decisions in previous times. Examples might include Truman's agonizing dilemma over whether to use the atomic bomb to end World

War II, Gandhi's decision to pursue a life of nonviolent protest, or Dietrich Bonhoffer's predicament over whether to join in the conspiracy to kill Hitler. Brook Kroeger's recently published biography of Nellie Bly (Kroeger 1994) provides an excellent illustration for taking a biographical approach. The acknowledged progenitor of full-scale investigative journalism and with an impressive list of other accomplishments, Bly devoted herself to alleviating suffering in her time, most notably taking on the plight of unwed indigent mothers and their offspring. Students might compare Bly's original employment of investigative journalism with the tactics used by investigative reporters today. Students might find it interesting to inquire into the issues that were the subject of Bly's inquiries earlier in this century. Turning a critical eye toward the field of history itself, students could respond to Kroeger's concern that despite Bly's acknowledged role as one of the most notable figures of her time, no historian had had sufficient interest in her life to conduct a documented investigation of it prior to hers.

Collections of American history case studies, such as those published by Gardner (1976), are available in most libraries. A particularly useful source of historical case studies on persistent religious, political, social, and economic issues is the Public Issues Series available through the Social Science Education Consortium (Oliver and Newmann 1991).

Argumentative Methods

Of course, any method involving students in a debate over two or more sides of an issue is tailor-made for issues-centered history. These include mock trials, debates, point-counterpoint reenactments, mock legislative and organizational meetings, and historical reenactments of events such as the First Constitutional Convention or the Congress of Vienna. An excellent example is provided in Wineburg and Wilson's 1988 analysis of a classroom in which students are engaged in research and debate concerning the legitimate authority of the British government to tax the American colonists.

Other Techniques and Sources

Simulations are useful for issues-centered history. Examples of these are "Mahopa," a simulation of the history, culture, and problems faced by North American Indians over the last four

centuries that culminates in an analysis of the problems that American Indians face today; "Pacific Rim," a simulation of the Ku, political, and social issues faced by Asian emigrants and immigrants over the past several decades; "Statehood," where students trace the development of their own state's history and use this knowledge as the foundation for understanding the state's current problems; and "Explosion," which calls on students to analyze the history and future of the world population problem.

Other methods involve the use of fiction (Nadeau 1994), posters and broadsides (Allen 1994), modeling historical essay and document-based questions from the Advanced Placement examinations (Alpern 1976), oral history (which is particularly useful for the historical study of local issues) (Sitton, Mehaffey, and Davis 1983), newspapers (Wesley and McLendon 1949), and political cartoons (Singer 1994).

Several journals are good sources of articles on teaching issues-centered history. *The History Teacher*, the Organization of American Historians' *Magazine of History*, *Social Education*, and *The Social Studies* have all published articles useful for teaching issues-related history. For example, articles on teaching about nuclear development (Holi and Convis 1991), the Vietnam conflict (Shaughnessy 1991), and labor history (DeChenne 1993) have appeared in *The History Teacher*. *Social Education* has recently published articles on teaching the history of science (Hvolbeck 1993) and a special edition about teaching the history of women in wartime (Haas 1994).

Team Investigation Methods

The issues strategy introduced in this chapter recommends the use of student investigation teams. Three cooperative learning techniques are particularly useful for this purpose: group investigation, jigsaw, and structured controversy.

Group Investigation. Thelen's group investigation model as refined by Sharan and Hertz-Lazarowitz (1980) is the teaming model used as the basis for the issues strategy in this chapter. Students are grouped into teams and begin by identifying an issue of common interest. The team plans its historical investigation and assigns specific responsibilities to each member. The group meets to synthesize its findings and produce a report stating its conclusions and recommendations for action. Although the method may be adapted to provide more structure for the students, Sharan (1990) believes that the main advantage of this technique lies in its open-endedness and freedom of inquiry.

Jigsaw. In this more structured method, students work in teams of three to six members to accomplish a group-assigned task (Aronson 1978). Ferguson (1988) provides an example of its application involving conflict between traditionalists and modernists during the era of seeping social and economic change in late-nineteenth-century Japan. The lesson opens with the teacher introducing the issue and defining the terms "traditionalist" and "modernist." The class is arranged into teams of four, and each team member is given a different biographical sketch of four nineteenth-century Japanese citizens representing diverse views on the modernization of Meiji Japan: two espouse traditionalist views and two advocate modernization. The teams are told their goal is to resolve the conflicting viewpoints and compose a consensus essay on the pros and cons of westernization. Students then move out of their jigsaw teams to form four expert groups, one for each personality. The objective for each group is to define the viewpoint of their personage and decide how they will advocate that viewpoint once back in their jigsaw groups. The jigsaw groups are then reconvened, viewpoints are exchanged and debated, and the group produces its consensus essay. The exercise culminates with a discussion of the issue as it exists in contemporary Japan and in other settings where traditionalist and modernist views are in conflict. The jigsaw method is useful whenever the teacher wants students to work independently on different aspects of an issue or on different historical events and then synthesize their findings (Aronson 1978, Ferguson 1983; 1988).

Structured Controversy. Constructive (or structured) controversy (Johnson and Johnson 1979, 1985, 1988) is another useful method. Students are assigned to groups of four, each composed of two two-person advocacy teams. One advocacy team is assigned a position on an issue—perhaps the conservative view on the legitimate role of government—while the other team is assigned the opposing liberal view. Both teams work on constructing a presentation using their historical findings to support their assigned positions. The teams present their positions to each other, rebut the opposing viewpoint, and then switch sides to argue from the opposing perspec-

tive. To culminate the activity, the four group members synthesize the best evidence and reasoning from both sides to reach a consensus about the issue in its contemporary setting. Other suggestions for cooperative learning methods having application to issues-centered history appear in the recently published handbook on cooperative learning for social studies teachers (Stahl 1994).

Two Caveats

Involving students in issues-centered history can be a rewarding experience. Two caveats must, however, be mentioned. One relates to the inclination toward reductionist thinking. Developmental research indicates that young people tend to hold idealistic world views that prompt them to view issues from a black-and-white perspective. The teacher can counteract this inclination by cautioning students to resist the tendency to reduce the number of positions to two and then choose one side or the other. This is particularly important when using the argumentation-based methods of mock trials, debates, and point-counterpoint activities. The tendency toward black-and-white thinking can also be curtailed through constant reminders that issues are the product of multiple causations and that issues must be examined in the light of the particular standards, values, and attitudes of their time (Muessig and Rogers 1965).

The second pitfall is the danger that students may acquire an overly pessimistic view of the future. Continual exposure to critical issues that have eluded resolution in the past—the population explosion, deterioration of the natural environment, poverty, illiteracy, human rights violations, the world agricultural crisis, the nuclear threat, the decline of the family structure, and expanding conflict among nations—can unintentionally have a demoralizing effect on students. Promoting awareness of the various groups and organizations that are actively working to resolve these problems and encouraging students to take some immediate action on the issue can help balance the seriousness of these issues with a sense of hope for the future.

In closing, teachers need not view the prospect of infusing the study of issues into their history courses as daunting. One can begin by gradually infusing issues into daily lessons and then expanding the approach as interest and experience dictate. The main requirement is simply that the teacher hold some affinity for the notion that learning history ought to be a problem-solving endeavor and that its main purpose is to advance students' insight into contemporary issues.

References

Allen, R. "Posters as Historical Documents: A Resource for Teaching Twentieth-Century History." *Social Studies* 85 (1994): 52-61.

Alpern, M. "Develop Your Own Tests in World History." *Social Education* 40 (1976): 517-523.

Armour-Thomas, E., and B. A. Allen. "Componential Analysis of Analogical-Reasoning Performance of High and Low Achievers." *Psychology in the Schools* 27 (1990): 269-275.

Aronson, E. *The Jigsaw Classroom.* Beverly Hills, Calif: Sage Publications, 1978.

Brophy, J., B. Van Sledright and N. Breding. "What Do Entering Fifth-Graders Know About History?" *Journal of Social Studies Research* 16/17 (1993): 2-16.

Brown, B. B. "Africa: Myth and Reality." *Social Education* 58 (1994): 374-375.

Davidson, B. *Discovering Africa's Past.* New York: Macmillan, 1991.

Ferguson, P. "A Technique for Evaluating a Public Speech." *Social Education* 36 (1972): 289-292.

—. "Aronson's Jigsaw: A Research Method and Teaching Technique." *Social Studies Teacher* 4 (1983): 5.

—. "Modernization in Meiji Japan: A Jigsaw Lesson." *Social Education* 52 (1988): 392-393.

—, and L. C. Smith. "Treatment of the Sexes in Instructional Materials." In *Teaching about Women in the Social Studies,* edited by Jean D. Grambs. Washington, D.C.: National Council for the Social Studies, 1976.

Fisher, D. H. *Historian's Fallacies: Toward a Logic of Historical Thought.* New York: Harper and Row, 1970.

Gardner, W. *Selected Case Studies in American History.* Boston: Allyn and Bacon, 1976.

Greene, S. "The Problems of Learning to Think Like a Historian: Writing History in the Culture of the Classroom." *Educational Psychologist* 29 (1994): 89-96.

Greenhaven Press. *The Breakup of the Soviet Union,* San Diego, Calif.: Greenhaven Press, 1994.

Griffin, A. F. *A Philosophical Approach to the Subject-Matter Preparation of Teachers of History.* Ph.D. Diss., The Ohio State University, 1942.

Haas, M. E., ed. "Homefront to Front Lines: Women in Wartime." Special section in *Social Education* 58 (1994): 65-103.

Hallam, R. N. "Piaget and Thinking in History." In *New Movements in the Teaching of History,* edited by M. Ballard. London: Temple Smith, 1970.

Hitchens, C. "African Gothic." *Vanity Fair* 57 (1994): 92-117.

Hofstadter, R., and B. Hofstadter, eds. *Great Issues in American History.* 3 Volumes. New York: Vintage Books, 1982.

Holi, J. and S. Convis. "Teaching Nuclear History." *History Teacher* 24 (1991): 175-190.

Holyoak, K. J. "Analogical Thinking and Human Intelligence." In *Advances in the Psychology of Human Intelligence,* edited by R. J. Sternberg. Hillsdale, N.J.: Erlbaum, 1984.

Hunt, M. P., and L. E. Metcalf. *Teaching High School Social Studies: Problems in Reflective Thinking and Social Understanding.* New York: Harper and Row, 1968.

Hvolbeck, R. H. "Teaching the History of Science." *Social Education* 57 (1993): 384-387.

Johnson, D. W., and R. Johnson. "Conflict in the Classroom: Controversy and Learning." *Review of Educational Research* 49 (1979): 51-61.

—. "Classroom Conflict: Controversy Versus Debate in Learning Groups." *American Educational Research Journal* 22 (1985): 237-256.

—. "Critical Thinking through Structured Controversy." *Educational Leadership* 45 (1988): 58-65.

Karras, R. W. "Teaching History Through Argumentation." *History Teacher* 26 (1993): 419-438.

Kennedy, P. *Preparing for the Twenty-first Century.* New York: Random House, 1993.

Kroeger, B. *Nellie Bly: Daredevil, Reporter, Feminist.* New York: Random House, 1994.

Leinhart, G. "Weaving Instructional Explanations in History." *British Journal of Educational Psychology* 63 (1993): 46-74.

Lerner, G. *Teaching Women's History.* Washington D.C.: American Historical Association, 1981.

Lewis, J. "When We Generalize and Compare, Can We Always Rely on the Absence of Evidence: A Sociologist Looks at Historical Methodology." *History Teacher* 24 (1991): 455-469.

Masrui, A. A. *The Africans: A Triple Heritage.* Boston: Little, Brown, 1986.

Massie, R. K. *Peter the Great: His Life and World.* New York: Ballentine Books, 1980.

McDonald, F. Interview on "Booknotes," C-SPAN Network, October 23, 1994.

Muessig, R. H. and V. R. Rogers. "Suggested Methods for Teachers." In *The Nature and Study of History,* edited by H. Commager. New York: Merrill Publishing, 1965.

Nadeau, F. "Fiction as a Springboard into U.S. History Projects." *Social Studies* 85 (1994): 17-25.

National Archives. *Teaching with Documents.* Washington,

D.C.: National Archives Publications, 1989.

Nelson, L. R. and R. D. Drake. "Secondary Teachers' Reactions to the New Social Studies." *Theory and Research in Social Education* 22 (1994): 44-73.

Oliva, L. J. *Russia in the Era of Peter the Great.* Englewood Cliffs, N.J.: Prentice-Hall, 1969.

Oliver, D., and F. Newmann. Public Issues Series. Boulder, Colo.: Social Science Education Consortium, 1991.

Rosenshine, B. "Is Direct Instruction Different from Expert Scaffolding?" Paper presented at the Annual Meeting of the American Educational Research Association, Atlanta, Georgia, April 1993.

Sharan, S. "Cooperative Learning: A Perspective on Research and Practice." In *Cooperative Learning: Theory and Research,* edited by S. Sharan. New York: Praeger, 1990.

— and R. A. Hertz-Lazarowitz. "Group Investigation Method of Cooperative Learning in the Classroom." In *Cooperation in Education,* edited by S. Sharan et. al. Provo, Utah: Brigham Young University Press, 1980.

Shaughnessy, C. "The Vietnam Conflict. America's Best Discussed War." *History Teacher* 24 (1991): 135-147.

Singer, A. "The Impact of Industrialization on American Society: Alternative Assessments." *Social Education* 58 (1994): 171-172.

Sitton, T., G. L. Mehaffey and O. L. Davis. *Oral History: A Guide for Teachers.* Austin: University of Texas Press, 1983.

Smith, H. *The New Russians.* New York: Random House, 1990.

Spoehr, K. T. & Spoehr, L. W. "Learning to Think Historically." *Educational Psychologist* 29 (1994): 71-78.

Stahl, R. J. *Cooperative Learning in Social Studies: A Handbook for Teachers.* New York: Addison-Wesley, 1994.

Summer, B. H. *Peter the Great and the Emergence of Russia.* New York: Collier Books, 1962.

Swartz, A. "What Does a Historian Do: Middle School Students Present Their Views." *Social Studies* 85 (1994): 114-116.

Watson, R. "Yeltsin Rules." *Newsweek,* January 23, 1995, pp. 32-34.

Wesley, F. W., and J. C. McLendon. "Organizing World History around Current World Affairs." In *Improving the Teaching of World History,* edited by Edith West. Washington, D.C.: National Council for the Social Studies, 1949.

White, R. M. "An Alternative Approach to Teaching History." *OAH Magazine of History* 8 (1994): 58-60.

Wilson, J. C. "History: Signpost or Lamppost?" *Social Education* 57 (1994): 122-126.

Wineburg, S., and S. Wilson. "Models of Wisdom in the Teaching of History." *Phi Delta Kappan* 70 (1988): 50-58.

---

[1] Students must be capable of comprehending the investigative nature of history. In light of this condition the strategy is not likely to be effective with students below the fifth grade (Brophy, Van Sledright, & Breding 1993; Greene 1994; Hallam 1970; Spoehr and Spoehr 1994; Swartz 1994).

[2] Chapter 5 "Teaching Generalizations" and Chapter 6 "Teaching History Reflectively" in Lawrence Metcalf's book *Teaching High School Social Studies* (Metcalf 1968), are highly recommended reading for the teacher who is seriously considering an issues-centered approach to history. Also see Leinhart's (1994) article on weaving generalizations into the teaching of history.

16 USING ISSUES IN THE TEACHING OF AMERICAN HISTORY

by David Warren Saxe

For the past one hundred years American history[1] has been a subject to which nearly all citizens who have attended public schools have been exposed in some form. American history is remembered by older citizens as the course with thick and heavy textbooks, extended lectures, and countless worksheets. American history is also the course that declared to these young citizens that the past of the United States, which happened a long time ago, had little to do with them. For better or worse, American history has been the centerpiece of social studies education for nearly eighty years. Moreover, the public perception of American history is sometimes linked regrettably to boring teaching. Despite this, most citizens agree that American history is essential to citizenship education, and that our children should know something about how the nation was formed, including the issues, themes, great men, great women, great stories, and the great reasons for the United States.

It would seem natural for a teaching handbook that includes a chapter on U. S. history to detail lesson plans, highlight films, good books, and other handy ideas, but there are no tricks or gimmicks here, no clever anecdotes or vignettes, no 101 ways to do American history. I offer no advice on how one can do justice to hundreds of years of history in 180 days or less. While I enter neither into the discussion of what 5,000 dates, events, or personalities should be taught, nor of "whose history" should garner our attention, I make a single assumption in this chapter—that teachers already know what to teach regarding American history and how to teach it, and, in the absence of such knowledge and skills, novices can turn to the teaching helps that are commonly available in such places as teachers' editions of the history textbooks or other accounts (see Center for Civic Education 1994; Engle and Ochoa 1986; National Center for History in the Schools 1994; and National Council for the Social Studies 1994). These aids include not merely what should be taught, but also pre-planned units, written objectives, targeted lesson plans, lists of suggested activities, teaching strategies, testing materials, supplemental maps, charts, workbooks and more. While I have reservations about teacher-proof materials for liberal democratic schooling as well as so-called national history standards, I do invite readers to investigate, assess, explore, and experiment with the use of such aids as necessary. This chapter, however, has a different focus: the conscious and deliberate introduction and use of issues into American history courses.

While all teachers should exercise discretion and common sense in the use of issues in schools, young children, for the most part, are not at the stage where they are capable of rational, liberal scholarship. It is not so much that the under-twelve set are not mature enough, it is more a matter that these young citizens have not yet acquired the necessary dispositions, skills, and knowledge needed for issues study. Nonetheless, all teachers at all levels should help prepare children to work with issues, and they should teach about and provide practice for liberal democratic dispositions, skills, and knowledge (see Saxe 1994). Although teachers can find any number of issues in current newspaper articles to apply in class, teachers and students can also find issues throughout history. Issues can be found in the lives and actions of people present and past. Students can also identify issues in definitions, policies, perceived problems, textbook readings, films, and other media. The number of issues for class study is limitless.

The introduction of issues into American history courses does not necessarily change standard, traditional offerings; the content certainly can remain essentially the same if the teacher so chooses. Additionally, the methods of lecture-recitation-worksheets also can remain intact. What is different about the conscious and deliberate introduction of issues is that importance is attached to learning American history for the purpose of liberal democratic citizenship. The terms *liberal* and *democratic* require definition here. *Liberal* underscores the notion of open-mindedness—that through liberal scholarship students become more interested in building a warranted point of view rather than simply expressing what is on their minds or thinking that all positions should be viewed in culturally relative terms. To be liberal in a scholarly sense is to adapt the notion of suspending judgment, of thoroughly investigating subjects, of making claims that are supported by verified evidence, of using reason and logic, and, then, proposing tentative conclusions (for it is necessary to acknowledge that positions or findings are not necessarily final or absolute). Liberal in a scholarly sense is not necessarily the equivalent of being liberal in the political sense found in many Democratic Party policies (e.g. believing that government is the best solution for social problems).[2]

"Democratic" means the acceptance of majority rule, of the people having a voice in the public affairs of their country, and of the idea that citizens vote for and against such things as candidates, issues, and policies. Moreover, being democratic also means that citizens willingly acknowledge and abide by the laws, institutions, and systems created by our democracy. For citizens, being democratic also means taking responsibility for knowing and adhering to the principles upon which such founding documents as the Declaration of Independence, the Federalist Papers, the U. S. Constitution, and the Bill of Rights are based.

The full sense of American citizenship is revealed in the juxtaposition of liberal and democratic, where we find the open-mindedness of liberalism necessary for a vibrant democracy. Scholarly liberalism is what prevents democracy from becoming a tyranny. The opened, unfettered conditions of scholarly liberalism erect barriers to the formation of despotic rule through the establishment of the necessary language, processes, and structures that specifically inhibit tyranny. This is not to say that tyranny cannot rear its ugly head in liberal democratic nations. However, it is to say that liberal democratic citizens can use or create mechanisms to reduce the intrusions of tyranny: citizens can simply and painlessly vote the rascals out! If citizens are not happy with or not accepting of something, the ballot—not bullets—can effectively be used to redirect national laws, policies, and programs through the election of representatives they think are more in touch with the will of the majority (of voters).[3]

What is confusing to many in the mid-1990s is that people such as the Republican leader Newt Gingrich may be conservative politically, but his take on American values is clearly liberal democratic. On the other hand, people such as President Bill Clinton may be liberal politically, but his principles, much like Gingrich's, are also rooted in liberal democracy. Although they stand on opposite sides politically, each seemingly agrees that the people are entitled to vote, that the majority rules, and that laws must be obeyed—all of which are democratic characteristics. Also, both Gingrich and Clinton presumably agree that arguments must be supported, held to scrutiny, and subjected to criticism—all of which are liberal characteristics. The point is that for the United States to work, citizens need to accept, as a fundamental principle, that liberal democratic characteristics are necessary ingredients for competent American citizenship.

Given the acceptance of liberal democracy, in this chapter I seek to illustrate that American history taught in the context of liberal democratic tenets is a vital dimension in the education of young citizens. In part, issues study is one way to accomplish the goal of educating young citizens whose developing views and politics may reflect such contrasts as Newt Gingrich and Bill Clinton or Clarence Thomas and Lani Guinier or Rush Limbaugh and Larry King or William J. Bennett and Sheldon Hackney—or even citizens whose views are reflective of Walter Williams and Stanley Fish or Diane Ravitch and Leonard Jefferies or Christina Sommers and Betty Friedan or Pat Robertson and Carl Sagan. As such controversial books as *The Bell Curve*, by Richard J. Herrnstein and Charles Murray (1994), *The Lucifer Principle*, by Howard Bloom (1995), and *Race and Culture*, by Thomas Sowell (1994) demonstrate, we need to understand more, not less, about human commonalties and differences. Regardless of one's politics, agendas, or personal views, the point is that American history teachers contribute to the essential commonality of American citizenship by accepting the notion that every American citizen should come to know and practice the founding principles of liberal democracy. This commonality is the glue the supports the freedom and hope of all Americans.

While issues can be employed in any course, at any time, when issues are introduced in American history courses, two preconditions must be addressed. First, if knowledge of American history is a necessary condition for competent citizenship, it follows that students must come to some fundamental understanding of the history of the United States (see Hirsch 1996). Second, if American history is acknowledged as critical for competent citizenship, then students must come to some fundamental understanding of the nature of history. This fundamental notion of the nature of history is called historical perspective. Thus, we can separate citizenship education overall into three discrete but intersecting elements: the study and acquisition of historical perspective; the study and understanding of American history; and, given the historical antecedents of liberal democracy, the introduction, study, and practice of competent citizenship. Clearly, citizens can display a semblance of competent citizenship without historical perspective or without knowledge of American history, and/or without even practicing or experiencing citizenship education in schools. But to paraphrase Jefferson, ignorant citizens do not, nor ever will, make a great free nation. The challenge, to sustain our liberal democratic heritage over time, is for teachers to educate young citizens for civic competence.

Unlike other chapters of the Handbook where issues-centered models are suggested, I assume the prime audience to be history teachers who deal with American history in chronological or topical fashion, in either broad, sweeping strokes or in great depth. I assume the tenets of this chapter may be useful in classes where textbooks, worksheets, and lectures are standard, where facts and generalizations are key, and where precision and knowing are expected. In addition, I assume this chapter's ideas will be used in classes where simple and straightforward assessments of essay, multiple-choice, fill-in-the-blank, and matching are commonplace. These observations are not meant as a criticism of such teaching; these statements are merely an acknowledgment that didactic, chronologically based American history is a fact of life in many quarters.

Given these norms, as you contemplate the standard American history course, you might also gauge the impact of infusing issues-centered ideas into your teaching. The good news is that issues study is ideally suited to the furtherance of liberal democracy. However, issues-centered teaching has a number of nagging considerations that must be met head on. First, issues-centered teaching is labor-intensive, and the techniques used often take considerably more time to plan, prepare, execute, and assess. Second, issues-centered teaching is less precise than didactic teaching; you cannot rely on particular results, nor can you often measure the results you do get. Third, issues-centered activities have a tendency to get students "off track"—that is, whether because of the loose nature of issues-centered teaching or because issues-centered teaching is a change from the routine, students may have fun with it and question why you do not do such teaching more often, or, conversely, why you are doing it at all. Fourth, issues-centered lessons do not, as a rule, cover much ground. A single issue, such as the treatment of prisoners of war at Andersonville and Elmira or a dissection of Lincoln's Emancipation Proclamation, might take several days, whereas a competent history-centered teacher could cover the American Civil War from the events leading up to Fort Sumter, to Gettysburg, or to Appomattox Court House in seven days or less. Finally, what might be the most problematic aspect of issues-centered teaching in American history courses is that issues raised may detract from students' gaining a practical sense of historical perspective—namely, an understanding of the nature of chronology, the concepts of time, the past, continuity, and change (Saxe 1994).

Like it or not, no educational plan for acquiring historical perspective has been able to improve upon the age-old methods of intense historical readings and investigations, informative and interesting lectures, and carefully designed and assessed writing assignments. I do not mean to suggest that history study should abandon traditional, time-tested methods for teaching historical perspective. I do, however, argue that, for the development of competent citizens, the knowledge of historical perspective and/or the learning of discrete facts from American history are not enough. The problem is that there is nothing to suggest that the acquisition of historical perspective alone—though necessary for understanding history itself—is connected to the development of citizenship. Moreover, there is nothing to suggest that the acquisition of facts about American history alone, which may lead to historical perspective, is connected to the development of citizenship. Finally, there is nothing to suggest that the practice of citizenship skills without historical context is directly connected to the development of competent American citizenship.

The key to competent citizenship education is that all three elements above must be present: first, students need to acquire historical perspective in order to make better sense of history; second, citizens need a strong understanding of American history in order to make sense of the rights and responsibilities of citizenship; and, third, developing citizens need to practice the skills associated with liberal democratic citizenship. Therefore, it is not the teaching of any one of these activities alone—the acquisition of historical perspective, the learning of American history, or the development of citizenship skills—but the deliberate teaching of all three that offers the greatest opportunity for competent, liberal democratic citizenship.

As for potential reservations about issues-centered teaching—that is, where time, results, and staying on track are important factors for teachers—it is useful to remember that history-centered teachers face similar considerations in dealing with the question of coverage, i.e., scope and sequence. Herein lies a dilemma. On one hand, it is important that students have in-depth exposure to American history, but is depth of knowledge as important as gaining some sense of the major events and people found in the past of our nation, albeit through a quick survey? If only a week or so of time is available, is it better that students grasp at least a superficial knowledge of life during the aftermath of World War I, and on through the start of the Great Depression, than to take the week and explore all the ins and outs of the Tea-Pot Dome scandal? Maybe yes, maybe no.

Answers to questions of depth versus breadth will remain in those schools that cast American history in one-year courses, typically in the fifth, eighth, and eleventh grades. Conditions at these grade levels dictate that superficial treatments will persist. To do anything that requires depth, something of breadth must be sacrificed, rather than continue to cram huge amounts of content into curricular spaces of about 180 days or less. Despite new models to deliver social studies, we find that American history curricula, regardless of orientation, are already filled to the brim, and new curricular possibilities continue to press for space. From notable current events, to revisions of older views, to suggestions from untested and unproven multicultural perspectives, to state-mandated programs, American history teachers are under a virtual curricular siege. Whether such changes are warranted, the influx of new programs, materials, and models has caused some teachers to close their curricular borders. Many teachers already believe that they are teaching as much as they can and literally cannot add anything more to their curricula. Where, for example, are teachers going to place new material on the fall of the Soviet-bloc nations and its implications for American foreign policy? What will be cut? What needs to be revised? Clearly, from the history-centered perspective, if you are going to do anything different, including issues-centered teaching, something in the curriculum has to be pushed out, rearranged, or condensed. The question is what?

Consensus might be reached that issues-centered teaching affords good opportunities for students to explore and digest American history. Also, it might be agreed that depth-of-field knowledge is something that we would like our students not only to appreciate, but hopefully to obtain. The issue of depth versus breadth often places teachers and their curricular efforts in conflict. If a teacher can proceed with the assumption that, despite course constraints often dictating a broad approach, he or she should be working toward improving a student's depth of knowledge, then the teacher becomes better able to include issues-centered ideas within history-centered programs.

To many history-centered advocates, history—particularly American history—is the lens through which all social studies subject areas can be viewed. In the sense of acquiring knowledge and skills, history serves as the umbrella course in which elements of geography, sociology, anthropology, economics, political science, and philosophy can be studied. From the perspective of promoting citizenship education, or the acquisition of civic competence, American history includes blending aspects from social studies subject areas for the purpose of activating a student's full participation in civic affairs. In either case—and I am sensitive to the fact that many teachers do not distinguish between academic and civic competencies for American history—issues-centered education can become an effective tool in advancing acquisitions of discipline-centered knowledge and skills as well as civically competent dispositions. Arguably, the richest and most easily accessible context for issues-centered study can be found in American history and its connection to the present lives of students.

Three general patterns have emerged for exploring issues in American history. They are useful singularly or in any combination:

- Issues are raised with students: Teachers tell the students that something is an issue.
- Issues emerge from lectures, presentations, readings, discussions, projects, or activities: Students identify an issue.
- Issues are used to relate past to present or present to past: An issue is raised by either teachers or students.

In the first context, because teachers are better read and possess greater experience in the study and teaching of American history, they will be able to identify any number of issues that are appropriate for introduction, study, and discussion. Predetermined teacher-selected issues offer teachers several advantages: they can plan the lesson in advance of instruction, select readings, prepare stimulating questions, anticipate different opinions, and develop and consider appropriate alternatives. In addition, teachers can gear discussion for particular groups of students, consider a variety of approaches to teaching the lesson, outline key terms and phrases, and prepare assessment and evaluation instruments.

One thing to keep in mind about issues-centered education is that topics are not issues. For example, for a lesson on the coming of the Civil War, topics such as state's rights versus federal rights, slavery, King Cotton, Manifest Destiny, the abolitionist movement, Bleeding Kansas, and sectionalism may be loaded with issues, but in and of themselves they are simply topics. The issue part of the topic or history occurs when a question is raised, some doubt is suggested, or something contradictory is noticed. In short,

issues are raised from a text, a story, a lecture, a film, or other presentation by the student when something does not quite seem right. *Gone with the Wind* has been hailed as one of the greatest films ever made, and I am not prepared to critically challenge that. It has been argued, however, that the film did not accurately depict southern life, particularly that of slaves. If someone says Big Sam (the former slave who came to Miss Scarlett's rescue following the war) is a fictional stereotype, an issue is raised. If someone questions Rhett Butler's role in the Civil War, an issue is raised. If someone questions Sherman's march on Atlanta, another issue is raised.

If someone says, during a lesson on American presidents, "Why haven't any females been elected president?" an issue is raised. If someone questions J. P. Morgan's financial interests in England prior to America's entry into World War I (he supported going to war to protect England) an issue is raised. If someone looks at the Warren Commission Report and begins to ask questions about the actions of the FBI, an issue is being raised. In this, our second context, once an issue is raised, the student, class, and teacher can explore and examine it in the hopes of seeking greater understanding, if not resolution, of the initial interest or inquiry.

As you have read elsewhere in this book, although I understand the importance of chronology and of moving forward, using issues-centered techniques does involve slowing the curriculum in order to help students comprehend the importance of an event. In slowing the pace, students will hopefully gain the time necessary to grasp the connective nature between various and often isolated events or bits of history and themselves. John Dewey described experience as having two parts: an active, doing part and a passive, undergoing part.[4] In the doing part, students have or are given an experience about which they actively explore information, ask questions, and formulate ideas. In the undergoing part that follows, students make a connection between the experience and themselves. This undergoing is reflective; it is the instructive part of learning. The undergoing highlights the changes a student makes or has as a result of the active doing. In addition to being the essential learning part of the experience, undergoing is also the part that makes the learning meaningful for the student. As Dewey put it, "doing" is "trying" things out to see what they mean, and "undergoing" is "instruction."[5]

In learning history, simply reading or hearing about selected topics in American history is not enough. Teachers must do what they can to help students understand what it is they are reading or hearing about. Our interest is not merely to do things in a clinical sense—to help students become better reciters of facts or readers or spellers or even writers—but to help students become more thoughtful and reflective about the lesson at hand. To succeed in this goal, providing students with experiences is only half the task. We cannot simply assume that students learn merely by having an experience—learn by doing. Teachers must also consider the next step students make—undergoing an experience. By undergoing an experience, the student takes stock of what the experience meant to him or her. For example, in what ways were students changed as a result of learning how history was rewritten for the Smithsonian's Enola Gay Exhibit in 1995? What was the lesson's point? What were the important features of this issue? If a student can create in his or her own mind the relationship of this lesson to other lessons—that is, build bridges to other ideas—we may conclude that learning has occurred. It may also be said that we have succeeded in our teaching if our students can come to the point of not only explaining the lesson (and not repeating or parroting the readings or lecture) but of truly demonstrating their learning to us and themselves by identifying the issues embedded in the lesson.

By accepting the responsibility to facilitate as many experiences as possible, to guide students as they undergo experiences, or to make sense of issues discovered or used, a teacher is acknowledging that learning will occur. In addition, when students begin to identify issues found in readings, lectures, discussions, or other activities, either orally or in writing, it may be argued that a student is making the critical transition toward undergoing the experience. That is, when students begin recognizing issues on their own, they are signaling the beginning of understanding history. In the context of the third use of issues, teachers can select experiences in which particular issues are used to confirm the success of a lesson taught and, perhaps more importantly, demonstrate the student's own understanding of the lesson.

Given our discussion thus far, we might now identify four treatments of issues in the classroom:

- The teacher presents an issue: doing or having an experience.
- Students recognize the issue imbedded in a lesson: signaling a transition to undergoing.
- Students successfully explain the issue: undergoing or demonstrating learning.
- Students test their new learning against or in different contexts, under different or similar conditions: confirming or challenging the new learning.

In using issues-study as a model, teachers are not bound to approach issues in a linear fashion. In presenting a lesson, teachers do not need to begin with an issue. Students may identify issues at any time. However, teachers need to become aware of a student's recognition of an issue. For example, if a teacher presents a lecture on the dropping of atomic bombs on Hiroshima and Nagasaki, students might raise the issue of how President Truman came to that seemingly inhumane decision: If we (Allied forces) were winning the war, why did we need to kill tens of thousands of innocent people? Where is the justice in this decision? The teacher may answer that the decision was based upon strictly military, not humanitarian conditions, replying that the United States needed to end the war as quickly as possible, and the atomic bomb increased the probability of Japan's immediate surrender. In this case, if the teacher's intention had been to lead the students to "discover" this issue, the teacher's strategy would be the equivalent of presenting the issue. On the other hand, while presenting the lesson, if the teacher had not intended to point to the issue of military objectives versus humanitarian actions in time of war, the student's ability to raise the issue signals a high level of maturity and understanding of extracting issues from content. In either case, once the issue is brought onto the floor, it is open to debate and discussion (if the teacher permits).

At this point, the teacher has at least two decisions to make: proceed with the next lesson on the development of the Marshall Plan and the Nuremberg Trials, or take a step back to deal with the atomic bomb issue. If the teacher has anticipated a discussion on issues related to the dropping of the first atomic bombs, then the next few days should have already been marked out for discussion and activities. However, if students raised the issue independently, then the teacher needs to decide whether it is worth the time to explore the issue. In proceeding with the student-generated atomic issue, lessons and follow-ups need to be prepared for the next few days. However, if the teacher decides to press ahead with the Marshall Plan, it is with the knowledge that some students have recognized a critical issue that the instructor has decided is not worth class time to pursue.

Whatever decision you make, your actions carry important implications for student learning. Through your accumulated teaching experience or through good guessing, it is an advantage if you can anticipate what issues will emerge in class and prepare lessons accordingly. Failing predicted student participation, you can proceed by highlighting the target issue yourself and remain hopeful that students will be able to find collateral issues embedded in the lesson. You can then select other confirming issues that will prove student learning—where students will show that they have connected the lesson to prior learning, as well as demonstrated the potential to connect the lesson to future lessons. However, if you ignore, and continue to ignore, students who raise issues—preferring to present only your issues—eventually students may become detached from the lesson and, unfortunately, further removed from history study. At best, students may glean a few scattered thoughts from the lesson that may or may not be applied in the future, and, at worst, students will leave the lesson with little in hand or head, perhaps only remembering that history is boring, of little value, and thus, has nothing to do with them.

In this argument for highlighting issues in American history, we have now come full circle. In brief review, issues are a central component of history study. Issues help to frame content into meaningful elements that can be used by students to construct learning. In addition to using issues to help teachers and students relate to content, issues can be employed as springboards to other experiences and learning. Notwithstanding the positive aspects of issues, as mentioned earlier, the use of issues takes time, often has uneven results, takes turns off the traditional curricular road, and, finally, is prone to slow the curricular train. Despite these potential drawbacks, issues offer any number of opportunities for students to become engaged in their own learning. Finally, the most important aspect of issues-centered education in American history is its connection to the teaching and learning of historical per-spective, the teaching and learning of discrete facts of American history, and practical experience with liberal democratic principles grounded in historical contexts.

In schools, the movement of issues-centered American history into the curricula will require a certain integrity and scholarship for both teachers and students. At this point, we arrive at the crucial test of issues-centered teaching: Is the teacher willing to set aside preconceived views for the sake of hearing out and sifting through differing perspectives and conflicting data? The issue of being eager to air other views and standing ready to modify your position in light of compelling evidence is central to issues-centered teaching. Issues-centered teaching is not preaching, nor is it persuading. Issues-centered teaching is about getting as close as humanly possible to unvarnished truth or, at the least, to being able to recognize the inconsistency or incongruent nature of a position. In addition, issues-centered teaching helps students recognize the difference between opinion and fact and between bias and objectivity.

To proceed with any presentation of issues, we must come to grips with the reality that issues, by nature, involve values and emotions. As such, values and emotions must often be suspended in order to make sense of the small pieces of the past that are recoverable. More directly, to teach issues-centered American history, teachers must often suspend not only values and emotions, but also political views, personal convictions, and religious beliefs for the sake of seeking truth. Underlying the suspension of values, emotions, and other convictions are morals. As individuals, our sense of morality directs our personal values, convictions, and beliefs, and is manifest in our behaviors—what we determine as right or wrong. When society seeks to apply laws that engage our moral sensibilities, we ask (among other questions), On whose authority is this action taken? How does this benefit society as a whole? and What evidence does the state have to support the action?

As teachers, intellectual leaders of the class, we must be prepared to examine claims of individuals as well as states (collective groups of individuals). As teachers of history, we need to examine the thoughts and actions of past individuals or states to root out explanations and understandings. This action often requires the suspension of moralistic judgment in the interest of disinterested scholarship. Other than as an attention-getter or pedagogical device used to focus students on a particular topic, issues-centered teachers should not begin the study of something like Columbus and the Age of Exploration with the claim that Columbus was a murderer. Adults may have acquired this questionable view, but young citizens have not had the chance to fully study the historical significance of Columbus. As it is against standard practice for the judge to hang the accused before trial, teachers should allow students to hear the historical facts prior to passing judgment.

This attitude of inquiry and skepticism strikes at the core of both issues-centeredness and the establishment of historical perspective—the central features of which highlight a willingness to raise and/or attend to issues openly, to explore the many sides of each issue, to seek out data, to make judgments from data, and to hold up our judgments, supporting data, and methods of critical examination. As an issues-centered teacher you must look for problems, inconsistencies, and contradictions in your own interpretations and values, as well as those interpretations and values found in others. You must also become sensitive to uncomfortable feelings, that a certain statement or piece of information simply does not seem right. You need to keep looking under whatever stones there are to keep your judgments tentative until you have gathered sufficient data to support your suppositions. As with your own conduct as a teacher, you must also seek to instill these goals in your students. As outlined by John Stuart Mill (1982), presumed facts are inherently problematic when not open to full critique and subject to the production of supporting data.

It is worth mentioning, even briefly, that the roots of issues-centered education are found in the Enlightenment and, for American history in particular, in the founding of the United States. More than two centuries have passed since the cornerstones of our nation were laid by the founders, framers, and common citizens. Colonial America of 1776 was not a homogeneous monocultural society. The American Revolution and subsequent new nationhood was, of course, an experiment that united people of very real differences—in ethnicity, region, occupation, income, religion, political conviction, property, status, and any number of personally held beliefs. From Locke to Jefferson to Madison, we find the foundations for issues-centered teaching in principle. First, Locke leveled the absolute nature of the divine rights of kings and, thus, raised the prospect of free (protected) speech for citizens. Jefferson actualized the validity of a people's revolution against a tyranny of a few on the basis of securing life, liberty, and the pursuit of happiness.[6] Finally, Madison, master architect of the U. S. Constitution, explained the difference between a narrowly defined Lockean material and earthly view of property, and Jefferson's broadly defined property rights that highlighted a citizen's right to opinion, religious conviction and other personally held beliefs.

It is these latter property rights—to access, examine, hold, and proclaim ideas—that give form to issues-centered education and make possible the formal study of ideas and issues. Certainly during the revolution, as now, things were not socially, politically, or economically perfect. On issues of race and gender, for example, there was much to be desired in eighteenth-century life when judged by late-twentieth-century standards. While taking issue with inconsistencies noted in the past—raised by values of our time versus values that predominated in the eighteenth-century—teachers should be careful to teach about history within the context of the period. Despite differing interpretations of the past, the period of the American Revolution did plant the seeds of human freedom, not only in the United States, but for many other nations as well. Within time, as the effects of the American experience unfolded, the sons and daughters of former slaves, Polish peasants, Japanese workers, Irish farmers, Chinese laborers—as well as hosts of other ethnic, political, and religious groups—would become beneficiaries of American democracy.

Of course there are serious challenges to liberal democracy. Aside from the very real natural challenges of living out liberal democratic principles, two human phenomena simultaneously undermine the successful establishment and maintenance of liberal democracy. First, it must be recognized that multigroup societies that attempt to actualize liberal democratic principles are inherently unstable. Second, liberal democracy is not genetically inherited. Together, the notion of multiple-group perspectives and the challenge of (re)inventing liberal democracy with each generation (child-by-child) not only create conditions that pull communities into any number of directions, but also pose a direct threat by undermining liberal democratic institutions, values, and actions. Our successes have often been limited, for just when we think we have created and brought forth something special from our differences, a new generation challenges our compromises. Few can deny the struggles, failures, mistakes, injustices, and tragedies that are salient features of humanity. Yet, when the principles of liberal democratic living are applied—where life, liberty, and the pursuit of happiness are constitutionally guaranteed—we become enabled to transcend human frailties to reveal the delicate beauty of democracy.

Conclusion

In a very real sense, teachers are stewards in the search for truth. By using issues study as a tool to reveal truths that either confirm or alter positions (or call into account the need for more study), we need to be careful not to apply or dictate for students unwarranted, predetermined pedagogical decisions, or perspectives, about the past. By taking responsibility as the intellectual leader of a liberal democratic classroom, the teacher should work to direct student attention toward issues and problems that facilitate meaningful reflective study and appropriate action. The purpose of the teacher's work is not so much to impart answers that students should know, but to assist students in taking responsibility for their own deliberations, decision making, and actions. Finally, to achieve the goal of facilitating competent citizenship, American history teachers should guide students toward acquiring the necessary historical knowledge, to demonstrate the necessary liberal democratic dispositions, and, more importantly, to practice the necessary skills of liberal democratic citizenship.[7]

While this chapter makes a case for issues-centered history teaching, the next move is yours. By considering this chapter and others found in this *Handbook* against your own experiences and knowledge, you have already taken the first reflective step toward engaging issues-centered American history. If you are willing to experiment with the ideas contained in this chapter, the next step is to bring issues study to your students.

References

Bloom, Allan. *The Closing of the American Mind.* New York: Simon and Schuster, 1987.

Bloom, Howard. *The Lucifer Principle.* New York: Atlantic Monthly Press, 1995.

Center for Civic Education. *National Standards for Civics and Government.* Calabasas, Calif: Center for Civic Education, 1994.

Dewey, John. "Democracy and Education, [1916]." In *The Middle Works of John Dewey, 1899-1924,* edited by JoAnn Boydston. Carbondale, Ill.: Southern Illinois Press, 1980.

Engle, Shirley, and Anna Ochoa. *Education for Democracy.* New York: Teachers College Press, 1986.

Fonte, John. "Ill Liberalism", *National Review,* February 1995, 48-54.

Herrnstein, Richard J. and Charles Murray. *The Bell Curve.* New York: Free Press, 1994.

Hirsch, Jr. E. D. *The Schools We Need.* New York: Doubleday, 1996.

Mill, John Stuart. *On Liberty.* New York: Penguin Books, 1982 (originally published in 1859).

National Center for History in the Schools. *National Standards History for Grades K-4, National Standards for United States History,* and *National Standards for World History.* Los Angeles: National Center for History in the Schools, 1994.

National Council for the Social Studies. *Curriculum Standards for Social Studies: Expectations of Excellence.* Washington, D. C.: The National Council for the Social Studies, 1994.

Saxe, David Warren. *Social Studies for Elementary Teachers.* Boston: Allyn-Bacon, 1994.

Sowell, Thomas. *Race and Culture.* New York: Basic Books, 1994.

Weaver, Richard M. *Ideas Have Consequences.* Chicago: University of Chicago Press, 1948.

---

[1] "U.S. history" is often confused with the term "American history". American history is the history of the whole of the Americas. The history of the United States is meant to focus on the history of the United States since 1776. Although U. S. history often includes historical antecedents to the founding of Jamestown in 1607—including European and pre-Columbian forms—to 1776, most states require the teaching of U. S. history, not the teaching of a comprehensive history of the North, South, and Central Americas. For this chapter (for reasons of style), I will adopt the less cumbersome and more inclusive "American history"; however, readers should be alert to distinguish between the two terms.

[2] Few books have captured the essence of liberal education better than Richard Weaver's classic, *Ideas Have Consequences* (1948). For a more contemporary

view of Weaver's thesis, consult Bloom's *Closing of the American Mind* (1987).

[3] John Fonte presents a first-rate discussion of the differences between liberal democracy and what he calls "cultural democracy." Fonte argues that cultural democracy—of which multiculturalism and cultural relativity are a part—is potentially a greater threat to the United States than was the Soviet Union. See *National Review* (1995, 48-54).

[4] Deweyan thought raises a number of issues in and of itself. First, arguing in pragmatic terms, Dewey makes a case that ideas are made true through experience. That is, we take an idea and give it a sense of trueness by testing it in reality. By nature, ideas, then, are not absolute or above or outside of the experience of individuals. While the "absolute" ideas of things like justice, freedom, and beauty can be made real through experience, they are not true independent of our actions. This shift from absolutes to relative thinking has created conflict in education. The suggestion here of using Dewey's doing and undergoing theory for experience is not necessarily an endorsement of pragmatic theory. Rather, the suggestion indicates that issues can be made known through doing and undergoing. The fact that an issue is or is not absolute or does or does not have absolute properties is not necessarily promoted here.

[5] Ibid., 139.

[6] The idea that principles of life, liberty, and the pursuit of happiness exist and stand applicable to every citizen raises the notion of absolutes (discussed in note 4). As issues-centered teaching is applied, we thus acknowledge an acceptance of absolutes in the form of democratic principles. But we also (paradoxically) highlight the existence of relative facts or unproved truths. It is argued here that, through issues study, ideas are made true by experience—doing and undergoing. However, some ideas appear to us as steady and absolute, and thus require no formal testing, although it is satisfying to be reminded that these absolutes (democratic principles) survive the test of time.

[7] In the most important educational book of the 1990s, Hirsch (1996) argues the case for core knowledge, skills, and dispositions. Issues-centered teaching follows from this premise. There is no genuine issues-centered teaching without a strong content base. Ignorance of issue background information or acknowledged skills or necessary scholarly dispositions renders issues-centered discussions mere bull sessions where, at best, unwarranted opinions rule or, at worse, where teachers use the power of pedagogy and a captive audience to preach social activism or some personal pet interest. This isn't issues-centered teaching.

17 A CRITICAL APPROACH TO TEACHING UNITED STATES HISTORY

by Ronald W. Evans

I believe that the central purpose of social studies instruction in schools is to inspire critical reflection on society, and by so doing, to contribute to the improvement and eventual transformation of society toward a vision of a more just society, a society that is "worthy, lovely, and harmonious" (Dewey, 1899). Thus, in teaching United States History, I believe that our central aim should be to inspire critical reflection on our past, present and future. This aim might best be accomplished by emphasizing critical perspectives, by exploring crucial issues, and by including alternative views and knowledge that are traditionally omitted from courses in United States History, and from the social studies curriculum as a whole. This is a biased perspective. I believe that the stories of common people in their struggle to improve their lot should receive more time and in-depth attention than the stories of the elite, businessmen and politicians, who have held dominant positions in the American power structure. This does not mean that the "heroes" still getting most of the space in our history books would be left out. It means that our emphasis would shift to asking critical questions, analyzing assumptions, and devoting a good deal of our time to studying the ways of empowerment, the ways that oppressed people challenged the society in which they were living and generated social progress. Thus, the approach I am suggesting is built on the American dream of equity and hopefulness.

With the recent revival of history in schools, the dominance of history in the social studies is reaching a new high (Gagnon, 1989). Thus, for the time being, if critical and issues oriented approaches to social studies instruction are to find a place in the social studies curriculum, it is in history courses, and especially U. S. History (the most common course required by law) that these approaches will have the best chance of being applied. We have substantial evidence to illustrate the general lack of reflection in history and social studies courses (Shaver, Davis and Helburn, 1979; Goodlad, 1984). An important commonality among these reports is the finding that a central underlying goal of courses in U. S. History is to transmit selected factual knowledge and positive feelings about our society and the American way of life.

While the casual reader might assume that my aim would be just the opposite, to inspire negative feelings about our society, that would be an unfair characterization, and a misunderstanding of a critical approach. Instead, we should develop in our students an appreciation of the complexity of our society and the world, and an understanding of the critical issues that have, and that continue to determine the shape of our lives. We should aim to inspire deep dreams of justice and fair play, dreams of a truly democratic society, utopian dreams tempered by the reality of the fray, by the ambiguity of the issues and the ironies of life.

Unfortunately, much of what is currently taught as U. S. History in schools does little to further this goal. In some classrooms, history is trivialized into a game in which students answer quiz and test questions for points, with little understanding of the significance or consequences of history for people's lives, even their own. In such classrooms, history instruction may be counterproductive, or even dangerous for democracy. In others, it becomes an occasionally interesting story, imparted by teachers, textbooks and supplementary materials. In some, a few rare classrooms, history becomes a source of reflection on the choices we have made in the past and the decisions we will make in the future. This is the kind of teaching this volume seeks to advance.

How might teachers best approach the aim of developing in students an understanding of crucial issues, facilitating critical reflection on society, and inspiring deep dreams of justice? I believe that this goal might best be accomplished through a critical, issues-centered approach to teaching, an approach which emphasizes the struggles of common Americans against oppression, an approach which takes a critical stance toward dominant interests of our past and present and leads students to ask and to reflect on difficult and controversial questions.

Ways of Implementing a Critical Approach

This approach raises several important questions regarding pedagogy, teacher and student roles, curricular content, and course organization. Let me suggest several ways of implementing a critical, issues-centered approach in the teaching of U. S. History, each of which may be appropriate for different teachers depending on their readiness, philosophical orientation, skill and experience as discussion leader, and student reading and inquiry skills.

First, infusing issues and critical perspectives may be most appropriate for a majority of teachers. Certainly, this approach is most easily accomplished without changing the basic format and structure of most chronologically sequenced textbooks and courses. The issues, knowledge, and perspectives detailed below would enhance any social studies course, and will no doubt be useful for all teachers and students to consider.

A second approach would be to retain a broad chronological structure, studying particular topics in depth within the stream of chronology, but develop critical issues and perspectives as themes to be developed and explored by teacher and students within each unit and topic studied. This approach implies a more consistent application of a critical understanding and a more thorough revision of course goals and format. Thematic issues could be introduced in the form of persistent questions at the start of the course, developed in each unit of study, and returned to at the end of the year for culminating discussion of the implications of the historical data studied. For many teachers, given current student and parent expectations and the format of most textbooks,

this may seem a reasonable and thoughtful alternative because it can be readily applied within a traditional chronological course structure.

A third approach would be to develop topical units in which major critical issues are studied in depth, breaking the broad chronological organizational scheme. Because I favor this approach, especially for high school courses, I will frame later portions of the chapter around this idea. An obvious advantage of this organizing scheme is that it emphasizes the in-depth, interdisciplinary study of persistent issues, yet allows development of chronological strands by topic. An even more radical approach would imply dismantling current course offerings and creating courses organized by critical issues, but we will save discussion of that intriguing possibility for another chapter.

Guidelines for Critical Teaching

Regardless which of these approaches is deemed most appropriate, the following general guidelines would apply for teachers and students:

A critical approach to teaching U. S. History would seek to stimulate a critical dialogue, with emphasis on student to student communication and student led inquiry. While the teacher would openly discuss her or his biases and frame of reference, teachers would carefully consider the timing and potential impact of their views on student beliefs. As a general rule, the teacher's perspective will be shared as one of many, to be opened to critical examination and discussion (Evans, 1993).

A critical approach would foster deep reflection on critical questions and issues about our society, about our past and future. The questions and issues to be studied would be those holding the greatest potential for increasing our understanding of dominant institutions and interests in our society, and in the world. In the classroom, openness and the freedom to hold contrary beliefs would be prized.

Course content would emphasize alternative voices, seeking out the voices of the oppressed, of those who have offered critical perspectives on social institutions, historical events, and decisions of the past and present. It would necessarily draw heavily on revisionist interpretations of history as fuel for thinking critically about mainstream sources and interpretations found in the typical textbooks. While the balance of course content would draw from non-traditional sources, teacher and students would take great pains to include traditional sources and mainstream voices and perspectives as well.

This approach requires a rethinking of the dictum that historians, teachers, and students must carry on disinterested, neutral, scientific, and objective scholarship. As Howard Zinn suggests, neutrality is impossible. Instead, historians, teachers, and students of history can follow these guidelines:

1. We can intensify, expand, sharpen our perception of how bad things are, for the victims of the world.
2. We can expose the pretensions of government to either neutrality or beneficence.
3. We can expose the ideology that pervades our culture—using "ideology" in Mannheim's sense: rationale for the going order.
4. We can recapture those few moments in the past which show the possibility of a better way of life than that which has dominated the earth thus far (Zinn, 1970, 36-47).

While the course would be based in the discipline of history, teacher and students would consciously seek relevant information and perspectives from divergent fields of study, including literature and the arts. The study of problems and issues must be interdisciplinary and extradisciplinary for the course to realize its full potential. Thus, a critical approach would challenge the traditional admonition to "stick to your discipline" (Zinn, 1970, 11).

Teacher and students would seek full inclusion of social realities of present and past. No issues, questions, or content would be deemed too controversial. In fact, controversy would be prized partly for the motivating emotional charge it can give to any inquiry. This would challenge the traditional scholarly edict to "avoid emotionalism" (Zinn, 1970, 12). A critical approach would emphasize a meaningful reason for studying historical sources, events, and trends for the wisdom we may gain in thinking about our society, our world, and our collective lives together.

Teachers and students would still seek balance, would search out competing and divergent voices, and would strive to be scrupulously careful in reporting evidence, but would abandon the naive attempt to remain "neutral" and "disinterested". Selection of meaningful and important topics, issues, and questions which can shed light on the struggles of common people to gain power

will mean that students and teachers have a biased interest in the study. Again, Howard Zinn writes:

> History is not inevitably useful. It can bind us or free us. It can destroy compassion by showing us the world through the eyes of the comfortable ("the slaves are happy, just listen to them"—leading to "the poor are content, just look at them"). It can oppress any resolve to act by mountains of trivia, by diverting us into intellectual games, by pretentious "interpretations" which spur contemplation rather than action, by limiting our vision to an endless story of disaster and thus promoting cynical withdrawal, by befogging us with the encyclopedic eclecticism of the standard textbook.

> But history can untie our minds, our bodies, our disposition to move—to engage life rather than contemplating it as an outsider. It can do this by widening our view to include the silent voices of the past, so that we look behind the silence of the present (Zinn, 1970, 54).

These insights are not exclusive to the new left historians of the 1960s, nor are they uncommon. In fact, historians as a group have shifted in emphasis from telling a traditional story undergirding national pride, with the concomitant emphasis on detachment and objectivity, to a focus on social history and on human responses to structures of power (Kammen, 1980). In fact, by 1980, Michael Kammen wrote that the discipline as a whole had witnessed a "stunning inversion with respect to these two traditional values" (22). National chauvinism has given way to national self-criticism in historical writing, to a challenge to liberalism and the liberal tradition. Increasingly, motives of national leaders are discussed cynically, and makers of foreign policy are chastised on the basis of revisionist historical interpretations. In the 1960s and 1970s, university teachers were sometimes forced by students to abandon academic impartiality and to declare their allegiances, and even to admit their emotions. This led to a shift concerning the desirability of historians making moral judgements, a shift from the thinking of Commager, "the historian is not God," to a search for truth "consciously suffused by a commitment to some deeply held humane values" (Kammen, 1980, 22-24).

Truth is dependent upon perspective. Historiography necessarily involves interpretation, making judgements on the importance of evidence and the implications of one event for another. Thus, a critical approach to teaching and learning U. S. History would mean questioning of assumptions and values. It would mean discussion of frame of reference whenever we consider a source or interpretation, even our own. The all pervasive importance and inescapability of frame of reference was eloquently summed up by Charles Beard more than half a century ago when he wrote:

> Any written history involves the selection of a topic and arbitrary delimitation of its borders cutting off connections with the universal. Within the borders arbitrarily established, there is a selection and organization of facts by the processes of thought. This selection and organization—a single act—will be controlled by the historian's frame of reference composed of things deemed necessary and of things deemed desirable. The frame may be a narrow class, sectional, national, or group conception of history, clear and frank or confused and half conscious, or it may be a large, generous conception, clarified by association with the great spirits of all ages. Whatever its nature, the frame is inexorably there, in the mind... (1934, 29).

Finally, and most importantly, a critical approach will mean reflection on student's lives, discussion of the significance of the topics studied for the lives of students and for society. The growing literature on critical theory in education, notably Cherryholmes (1991; chapter 9 of this volume), Stanley (1992), Freire (1970), Giroux (1992), Apple (1979), and Bigelow (1987), instructs social studies educators to lead our students to look to history, to examine the effects and exercise of power, and to search for distorted beliefs and communications in trying to understand the world. Texts cannot be perceived as authoritative and foundational, but must instead be interrogated and critiqued by student and teacher, with student's lives viewed as a text or source to analyze. Reader-response theory posits readers' lives as texts to be explored, examined, and critiqued. Like written texts, students' lives are a

construction, developed in the context of power relationships. Thus, students' lived experiences will be a central focus (Cherryholmes, 1991).

Problematics: The Big Issues

The following issues and problem-topics may serve as a starting point for teachers and students who wish to apply a critical, issues-centered approach to United States History courses. For each topic I have listed key critical issues, perspectives and voices that might be included, and a few books and sources that should prove helpful. Readers may also wish to consult previously developed models for applying issues-centered approaches which would also be useful in teaching United States History. Among these are Hunt and Metcalf (1955; 1968) and Oliver and Shaver (1966).

The problematic topic areas are listed in an order that may be helpful, though experimentation could help a teacher find an order that makes sense, assuming that teacher chooses option three, issues-centered units. It seems eminently true that some of our most troubling and persistent problem areas, race, class, and gender, might be a good place to start. It also seems true that a study of power and knowledge might lead naturally into a culminating unit on ideology and reform, leading as a point of transition into a discussion of personal responsibility and social action.

I have created nine topic areas. In a one-year course, these could become units of about four weeks each, though length may vary by topic, and by teacher and student interest. Each unit would begin with the present, with continuing questions and issues and exploration of relevant data. Within each unit students would spend the bulk of time with the historical strand of development and chronology, cases from the past that may have special relevance over time, inquiry into historians' questions, and reflection on important decisions. Each unit would conclude with development of meaning, that is, with students developing implications from the historical topics and additional evidence studied for present belief and social policy on the topic. A few helpful sources are listed for each topic.

Race and Ethnicity: The American Obsession

Because of the confluence of issues that impact this topic, and because of its persistence throughout our history, race and ethnicity deserve top billing. At present, schools seem to be promoting the idea that we have achieved racial equality of opportunity in a nation in which the ratio of White to Black net worth is 12:1. Something is obviously amiss. I believe that this impression of growing equity and the knowledge that undergirds it are dangerous. Instead, we need direct attention to the following questions:

> **?** What impact do race and ethnicity have on our lives?
> **?** Are quotas and affirmative action good ideas?
> **?** Are we responsible for the sins of the past?
> **?** What is the socioeconomic status of different ethnic groups in American life?
> **?** How may we best explain differences in status?

What should we do about differences in social and economic status that coincide with a history of racial oppression?

How have historical developments in American society influenced race and ethnicity and impacted the pursuit of equity? How have these issues and institutions changed over time?

After exploring some of these questions, teachers may want to lead students to study the historical development of race and ethnicity in American life. This could be handled chronologically, with in-depth study of one or two groups, and a focus on particular cases that are especially illuminating. Teacher and students may find the following works helpful:

Bennett, Lerone. (1969). *Before the Mayflower.*

Brown, Dee. (1971). *Bury My Heart at Wounded Knee.*

Daniels & Kitano. (1970). *American Racism.*

Daniels, Roger. (1990). *Coming to America.*

Genovese, Eugene. (1974). *Roll, Jordan, Roll.*

Hacker, Andrew. (1992). *Two Nations: Black and White, Separate, Hostile, and Unequal.*

Konig, Hans. (1993). *The Conquest of America.*

Malcolm X. (1965). *The Autobiography of Malcolm X.*

Meltzer, M. (1982). *The Hispanic Americans.*

Sowell, Thomas. (1984). *Ethnic America.*

Takaki, Ronald. (1989). *Strangers From a Different Shore.*

Takaki, Ronald. (1993) *A Different Mirror: A History of Multicultural America.*

Terkel, Studs. (1992). *Race: How Blacks and Whites Think and Feel About the American Obsession.*

Woodward, C. Vann. (1955). *The Strange Career of Jim Crow.*

Zinn, Howard. (1980). *A People's History of the United States.*

Textbook coverage of topics related to race and ethnicity should also prove helpful, especially if used as a resource to be critiqued. Following extensive study, teachers and students will want to re-visit several of the key questions posed at the start of the unit, drawing on their study of race and ethnicity in framing perspectives that are still tentative, yet better informed. In this and subsequent units, teachers may want to use panel discussions, debates, simulations, and a full range of large and small group discussion activities to facilitate student communication, reflection and critique.

Social Class in America

Most textbooks on U. S. History hardly mention social class, and tend to emphasize the stories of elites, of those who were at the top of the ladder. Permeating textbook treatment of social class is the myth of social mobility in America, that the poorest person, with hard work and diligence, and maybe a little luck, can achieve the height of success. This is the Horatio Alger myth, and it is dangerous as well because it ignores the overwhelming evidence on the entrenchment of social class in America and the impact of socioeconomic status and ethnicity on individual chances for success in American life. Continuing questions on social class include:

> **?** What attitude and policy positions should government take on social class issues? What role should government play in caring for the general welfare of citizens?
> **?** What impact does social class play on American lives, on opportunity for social and economic success?
> **?** How are wealth and income distributed in the United States? What determines this pattern?
> **?** What are the origins of social stratification in America?
> **?** How much mobility do American citizens actually have?

After exploring some of these questions at the start of the unit, teacher and students may want to study the history of social class in the United States, perhaps focusing on different regions and different time periods, and exploring changes in the social class structure over time, as well as changing government policy and role on social welfare. Many of the following works may be helpful:

Harrington, Michael. (1960). *The Other America.*

Harrington, Michael. (1984). *The New American Poverty.*

Lundberg, F. (1968). *The Rich and the Super Rich.*

Phillips, Kevin. (1992). *The Politics of Rich and Poor in America.*

Piven and Cloward. (1977). *Poor People's Movements.*

Rose, Stephen. (1992). *Social Stratification in the United States.*

Ryan, William. (1971). *Blaming the Victim.*

Terkel, Studs. (1970). *Hard Times: An Oral History of the Great Depression in America.*

Wasserman, Harvey. (1989). *Harvey Wasserman's History of the United States.*

Gender and Sexuality in American Life

Sex is still the great taboo in schools. Despite the increased mentioning of women at different points in the chronological story of America, we seldom study gender, sexuality, or human relationships in depth. We need to. Another of the dangerous myths promoted in schools is that with the women's rights movement of the 1960s and beyond, we have achieved gender equity. In a unit on gender and sexuality, teacher and students may want to explore some of the following questions:

> **?** To what extent have we achieved gender equity?
>
> **?** How can we assure gender equity? What specific policies should we pursue? Should our nation and schools promote feminism?
>
> **?** What role has sexuality played in American life? What role should sexuality play in our lives?
>
> **?** How should we address heterosexism and homophobia in school and society?
>
> **?** What are the origins of gender inequality in the United States?
>
> **?** How has the role of gender in our lives changed over time? How might we best explain the changing roles of women and men?

After examining some of these questions, you will probably want to study several in depth over time, especially the changing role of women in American society. Several of the following sources may prove helpful:

Faludi, Susan. (1991). *Backlash: The Undeclared War Against American Women.*

Flexner, Eleanor. (1975). *A Century of Struggle.*

Friedan, Betty. (1963). *The Feminine Mystique.*

Gilligan, Carol. (1982). *In a Different Voice.*

Millett, Kate. (1969). *Sexual Politics.*

Nelson, Jack. (1972). *Teens and Sexuality.*

Sadker and Sadker. (1994). *Failing at Fairness: How American Schools Cheat Girls.*

Zinn, Howard. (1981). *A People's History of the United States.*

Labor and Business

The history of America is the history of business; therefore, the critical history of America is the history of labor, the study of the efforts of common people to gain dignity and rights in a society which has valued dollars over people. Perhaps the central myth in capitalist America, one which undergirds a continuing reverence for largely unchecked economic power, is the notion that "what's good for business is good for America." The corollary to this myth is that labor organizers are viewed as "agitators," frequently as mobsters or crooks, and sometimes as un-American advocates of an "alien" ideology, socialism, communism, or anarchism. Much of the history of labor is underexposed in the typical U. S. History course. Dramatic events such as the Ludlow Massacre and the Seattle General Strike receive little or no attention. Some of the central questions that teachers and students could be investigating may include:

> **?** What are the rights of labor? How have these rights evolved over time?
>
> **?** What role should government play in protecting and advocating the rights of labor?
>
> **?** What is the proper role of government in regulating business?
>
> **?** How and why has the role of government in the economy changed over time?

Several of the following sources may be helpful in exploring the history of these issues in American life.

Bigelow, W. and S. Diamond. (1988). *The Power in Our Hands: A Curriculum on Workers in the U. S.*

Foner, Phillip. (1947-1964). *A History of the Labor Movements in the United States.*

Greene, Laura. (1992). *Child Labor Then and Now.*

Public Issues Series. *The New Deal.*

Public Issues Series. *The Progressive Era.*

Public Issues Series. *The Railroad Era.*

Public Issues Series. *The Rise of Organized Labor.*

Josephson, Matthew. (1962). *The Robber Barons.*

Thompson, E. P. (1963). *The Making of the English Working Class.*

Sinclair, Upton. (1906). *The Jungle.*

Wasserman, Harvey. (1989). *Harvey Wasserman's History of the United States.*

Yellen, Samuel. (1974). *American Labor Struggles.*

Zinn, Howard. (1980). *A People's History of the United States.*

Industry, Technology, and Human Survival

More than at any previous time in human history, we are witnessing the combined effects of technology and human greed on the planet, on species of life, on the very air we breathe. Our current ecological crisis is a direct and undesirable consequence of the forces of progress, technology, and industrialization. Continuing issues include:

> **?** What actions, policies and lifestyles should we choose in order to protect the environment?
>
> **?** What role should government play in regulating and directing technological development and growth?
>
> **?** What are the origins of our post-industrial economy?

The following sources may be helpful in exploring the history and current status of this topic:

Brown, Lester. (Annual). *State of the World.*

Public Issues Series. *Science and Technology.*

Toffler, Alvin. (1980). *The Third Wave.*

Mumford, Lewis. (1961). *The City in History.*

Landes, David. (1969). *The Unbound Prometheus.*

Thompson, E. P. (1963). *The Making of the English Working Class.*

Wasserman, Harvey. (1989). *Harvey Wasserman's History of the United States.*

Empire and American Life

We are living in the heart of the American empire. While many Americans may refuse to recognize this fact, due to the ideology of spreading democracy and freedom, our nation is at present, the dominant imperial power on earth, culturally, economically, and militarily.

In studying this topic, the entire history of American diplomacy would be relevant. However, it may be most helpful to focus on one

> **?** How should we define the term empire? Is the U. S. an imperial power?
>
> **?** What role should the U. S. play in the world?
>
> **?** How has the role of the United States in the world changed over time?
>
> **?** What are the origins of American globalism? Empire?

or two interpretations and to examine a few cases in depth while giving some attention to the span of time. The Spanish American war and Vietnam may be especially important because of their impact on a changing U. S. role in the world. The following sources would be especially helpful:

American Friends Service Committee. (1991) *The Sun Never Sets: Confronting the Network of Foreign U. S. Military Bases.*

Remarque, E. (1929). *All Quiet on the Western Front.*

Foreign Policy Association. (Annual). *Great Decisions.*

Keen, Sam. (1988). Faces of the Enemy: Reflections on the Hostile Imagination.

Schell, Jonathan. (1982). *The Fate of the Earth.*

Williams, W. A. (1959). *The Tragedy of American Diplomacy.*

Williams, W. A. (1980). *Empire as a Way of Life.*

Power in America

Americans are alternately suspicious of the power elite, and skeptical of the ideological orientation of anyone who raises the notion of some groups having more power than others. Pluralists argue that interest groups strike bargains to determine decisions in the general interest. This argument perpetuates the myth of a democratic power structure in which constituents are represented fairly in decision-making. The myth ignores the silencing of entire groups of people too tired or otherwise disenfranchised to impact decisions or even vote. Case studies of groups who have challenged the power structure and of times in which governmental authority has been challenged would be meaningful.

Some of the key continuing questions include:

> **?** Who rules America? Is there a power elite? Is a hierarchical power structure inevitable?
>
> **?** How, and to what extent, is power shared?
>
> **?** How should we alter or reform the power structure in the United States?

> **?** Who ruled America in the earliest years? How and why has this changed over time?
>
> **?** When, under what conditions, should citizens challenge legally constituted authority? By what means?

Some of the following readings will be helpful:

Alinsky, Saul. (1946). *Reveille for Radicals.*

Beard, Charles. (1921). *An Economic Interpretation of the Constitution of the United States.*

Domhoff, G. William. (1983). *Who Rules America Now?*

Issac, Katherine. (1992). *Civics for Democracy: A Journey for Teachers and Students.*

Machiavelli. (1897). *The Prince.* (translation).

Markovits, A. (1988). *The Politics of Scandal.*

Mills, C. Wright. (1956). *The Power Elite.*

Parenti, Michael. (1974). *Democracy for the Few.*

Piven and Cloward. (1988). *Why Americans Don't Vote.*

Public Issues Series. *American Revolution.*

Public Issues Series. *The Civil War.*

Power and Knowledge

The study of power and knowledge might begin with the media or with schools. A good place to start may be the U. S. History textbook which is already present in the classroom. The central myth to be explored is the pervasive notion that knowledge, and schools, are neutral. Nothing could be further from the truth. Knowledge has historically been used to manipulate opinion and voting, through propaganda and political campaigning and through schooling, in both the hidden and overt curriculum. Sometimes, knowledge has served dangerous purposes, such as the categorization of people into mental groupings, or the girding of myth in American life that supports little or no social change. Some of the continuing questions which might be posed:

> **?** Who controls the knowledge we gain through the media? In schools?
>
> **?** Who benefits? In whose interest does the knowledge structure operate?
>
> **?** What determines the content of school curricula and textbooks?
>
> **?** How has the role of knowledge changed over time?
>
> **?** What are the political and social implications of the technological revolutions which have transformed the use of knowledge?

The following sources may be helpful:

Harris, J. A. (1930). *The Measurement of Man.*

Fitzgerald, Francis. (1979). *America Revised.*

Foucault, Michel. (1980). *Power/Knowledge.*

Kozol, Jonathan. (1991). *Savage Inequalities.*

Lee, Maritn and Solomon, Norman. (1991). *Unreliable Sources: A Guide to Detecting Bias in News Media.*

Noble, William. (1990). *Bookbanning in America.*

Oakes, Jeannie. (1985). *Keeping Track: How Schools Structure Inequality.*

Parenti, Michael. (1986). *Inventing Reality: The Politics of the Mass Media.*

Ideology, Social Theory, and Reform

A culminating unit of study for all courses in history might focus on the reflective examination of competing ideologies and social theories by in-depth examination of current ideological possibilities, ranging from extreme left to extreme right, and a similar in-depth study of reform movements in American history. Socialism, Populism, and Progressivism might serve as a good starting point. Perhaps the most debilitating myth is that of the American Ideology, the myth of freedom. The corollary to that myth is the notion that certain "other" ideologies are un-American and must be suppressed, or at best, grudgingly tolerated. Religious freedom poses similar issues.

The study of ideology, social theory, and reform might include exploration of some of the following questions:

> **?** What is the American ideology?
>
> **?** Are there ideologies that should be labeled unAmerican?
>
> **?** What are the ideological orientations salient to American life?
>
> **?** What is the proper relationship between religion and government?
>
> **?** What impact have reform movements had in American history?
>
> **?** What can we learn from the history of reform?
>
> **?** What reforms should we support?
>
> **?** When, if ever, is violence justified in pursuing a cause?

The following sources may be helpful:

Bellamy, Edward. (1988). *Looking Backward.*

Birnbaum, Norman. (1988). *The Radical Renewal.*

Dolbeare, Kenneth and Patricia. (1976). *American Ideologies*

Ginger, Ray. (1949). *The Bending Cross: A Biography of Eugene V. Debs.*

Gitlin, Todd. (1987). *The Sixties: Years of Hope, Days of Rage.*

Goodwyn. (1978). *The Populist Moment.*

Harrington, Michael. (1968). *Socialism.*

Marx and Engels. (1848). *The Communist Manifesto.*

Public Issues Series. *The Progressive Era.*

Zinn, Howard. (1980). *A People's History of the United States.*

Education for Social Action

A social action/service learning component is a profound need, and one that is receiving increased endorsement from mainstream educators (Boyer, 1981; Newmann, 1975). One of our great failings is not to imbue students with a sense of community needs, a reality of which I have become painfully aware while collecting signatures on a petition for health care reform. Americans tend to be concerned about their individual situations, and to vote and act accordingly. This tendency is natural, but it is also an indication that civic education is failing to awaken people to the interests of the community over the interest of self. Service learning might take place in a separate course, or, better yet, it might begin early on and become a part of all educational endeavors.

In conclusion, a critical approach to the teaching of history deserves consideration by all teachers because of the potential it offers for enlivening the curriculum, because of its potential for inspiring dreams of social justice, and because of the attitude toward learning which it promotes, a critical and inquiring stance in which assumptions are questioned and points-of-view are challenged. As I have illustrated, a critical approach may take a variety of pedagogical forms, depending on teacher and student preference, readiness, or institutional context. Regardless of course organization or teacher ideology, I believe that most teachers will find infusion of critical perspectives challenging and beneficial in promoting student interest, critical analysis, and thoughtful citizenship.

References

Apple, M. W. *Ideology and Curriculum.* London: Routledge and Kegan Paul, 1979.

Beard, C. A. "Written History as an Act of Faith." *American Historical Review* 39 (1934): 219-229.

Boyer, Ernest R. *Higher Learning in the Nation's Service.* Washington, DC: Carnegie Foundation for the Advancement of Teaching, 1981.

Cherryholmes, C. "Critical Research and Social Studies Education." In Shaver, James P., ed. *Handbook of Research on Social Studies Teaching and Learning.* New York: Macmillan, 1991.

Dewey, John. *The Schools and Society.* Chicago: University of Chicago Press, 1899.

Evans, Ronald W. "Utopian Visions and Mainstream Practice: A Review Essay on *Curriculum for Utopia: Social Reconstructionism and Critical Pedagogy in the Postmodern Era*, by William B. Stanley." *Theory and Research in Social Education,* 21 (1993):161-173.

Freire, Paulo. *Pedagogy of the Oppressed.* New York: Continuum, 1970.

Gagnon, Paul. *Historical Literacy: The Case for History in American Education.* New York: Macmillan, 1989.

Giroux, Henry. *Border Crossings.* London: Routledge,1992.

Goodlad, John. *A Place Called School: Prospects for the Future.* New York: McGraw-Hill, 1984.

Hunt, Maurice P. and Metcalf, Lawrence E. *Teaching High School Social Studies: Problems in Reflective Thinking and Social Understanding.* New York: Harper & Row, 1955 & 1968.

Kammen, Michael. "The Historian's Vocation and the State of the Discipline in the United States." In Kammen, Michael, ed. *The Past Before Us.* Ithaca, NY: Cornell University Press, 1980.

Newmann, Fred M. *Education for Citizen Action: Challenge for Secondary Curriculum.* Berkeley, CA: McCutchan, 1975.

Oliver, Donald and Shaver, James P. *Teaching Public Issues in the High School.* Boston: Houghton Mifflin, 1966.

Shaver, J. P., Davis, O. L., and Helburn, S. W. "The Status of Social Studies Education: Impressions From Three NSF Studies." *Social Education* 43 (1979): 150-153.

Stanley, William B. *Curriculum for Utopia: Social Reconstructionism and Critical Pedagogy in the Postmodern Era.* Albany, NY: State University of New York Press, 1993.

Zinn, Howard. *The Politics of History.* Boston: Beacon Press, 1970.

18 WORLD HISTORY AND ISSUES-CENTERED INSTRUCTION

by Richard E. Gross

Elements of World History are commonly taught in grades six and seven and in grades nine and ten. The most frequent placement of a single year offering is in the tenth year of high school. Numerous surveys and studies have revealed this offering characterized by pupils as the least interesting of all of their curricular experiences in social studies and history classes. In spite of this longtime complaint, few school districts have moved to the one most logical change, making World History a two-year course. This reluctance is understandable for such an extension of the subject would require controversial adjustments in a school program and social studies curricula already overcrowded with competing subjects, all claiming their import as a necessity in the general education of future citizens.

Nevertheless teachers and schools have experimented with a number of variations to try and satisfy students as well as instructors who are unhappy with the futile expectations of adequately treating World History in a single year survey course.

One of these approaches, as suggested above, is to organize a two-year integrated offering which includes key elements of World Geography and/or World Cultural Regions with history. Such a course, however, may not materially increase conventional history content; indeed, it may reduce it. But such an arrangement, whether treated in a basic regional organization or a chronological one, can reduce the mass of superficial historical names, dates, and events which typically bore students and are claimed by them to be unimportant. Shallow reviews can be avoided in two-year offerings that integrate the subject matter into selected longer or deeper exposures that provide for the inclusion of more motivation-

al, human, and learnable blocks of content. Indeed, by this blending of depth and breadth, such courses come closer to representing the true principle of the social studies.

Nevertheless, in our present age of international intercommunications and contacts with their multi-cultural emphases, a truly global World History course becomes more impossible than ever. In the past, in attempting to meet the problem of too much content, so-called World History courses have frequently featured Western Civilization with, for example, limited coverage of the Asiatic peoples and minimal attention to much of Africa and Latin America. Today, however, curriculum planners and teachers must meet an increased challenge to western myopia. The growing demand for increased attention to overlooked portions of the human experience must be met. There follow with brief explanations and examples a number of attempts at redesigning conventional World History offerings that have been and are being tried in schools throughout the nation.

Probably the most frequent variation is a course of selected studies in depth. Sometimes called postholing, this organization is based on thorough examinations of key eras such as: "The Greco-Roman Age," "The Renaissance," and "Nineteenth-Century Issues." A variation of this patchwork approach selects certain nations or periods of their development for extended study such as "India's Struggle for Democracy," "The Emergence of Germany," or "Modern Japan."

Treating particular areas or cultures is another approach of selectivity. Often these courses may be designated as World Regions and are centered on a geographical organization. Also known as World Studies courses, these offerings are characterized by enrichment from other disciplines in the social sciences as well as from the arts and the sciences. The geographically oriented area studies courses may be labeled "Latin America," "The Middle East Since 1914," "China" or "Western Europe." Similar titles may be found for the balanced emphases in the culturally highlighted courses which may treat a variety of subportions, including attention to economics, government, family life, and religion. The approach to these classes may employ a flashback organization. The teacher begins a unit with initial study of the current conditions characterizing an area or a group of people. Questions are raised as to how and why these conditions exist. In attempting to help students find the answers the teacher then moves back to an appropriate beginning point or event in the past and then progresses chronologically toward the present.

For some teachers, a preferred adjustment is to merely treat the modern time-periods of World History. Typically such organization begins with a study of events occurring since the Renaissance or the 1500s with a few looks backward if necessary in explaining some development. This avoidance of the ancient and early history of countries still leaves large gaps to be treated if the course is a truly global one. Courses may be labeled as those identified above for key era depth studies: "1588 and Future History," "The Revolutions of 1776 and 1789," "The Impact of Paper and the Printing Press," or "The Steam Engine, the Automobile, and the Airplane." In the minds of numerous, more traditional instructors, such segmental and somewhat limited courses are unsatisfactory.

Other educators prefer a topical or thematic organization for World History. Again such arrangements reflect necessary selectivity. The subjects are usually treated chronologically. Conventional examples of such offerings may be entitled: "War and Peace," "How We Have Governed," "Living Religions," or "International Connections and Cooperation." Somewhat more unconventional themes or topics may be entitled: "The World of the Family," "Cities Through Time," "The Artistic Imagination," or "Inventions That Changed the World." Teachers preferring these and other variations of the usual chronological survey find the lack of related textbooks a basic deterrent to course implementation. In recent years, however, following the paperback revolution, publishers have produced numerous specialized booklets, soft bound, and relatively short, that can take the place of the usual large, inclusive, hardbound texts which students frequently refuse to carry out of their lockers or home. The growing variety of these minitexts provides satisfactory references for basic information that teachers of these courses want their students to share in common.

Several further alternatives in World History have been suggested, but these have been employed by but a few mentors of a creative or experimental nature. Included are offerings with a biographical emphasis that treat seminal ideas and great personalities in history. Such a human emphasis can be very intriguing and valuable for students but with such organization even with the help of timelines, supplemental reading, and visual media, large portions of history fall by the wayside. Titles may include: "Charlemagne and His Times," "Mohammed and His Heritage," "Pioneers of the Industrial Revolution," or "Marx and Lenin."

A further World History variation is based upon studying the evolution of prime concepts and generalizations that characterize the human experience. The following "universals," some being similar to topical units, have been suggested as important across most societies: "Power," "Revolution," "Families," "Freedom," "Justice," and "Survival." Concepts, of course, can be featured in numerous other units that are entitled: "The Rise of Christianity," "Prime Architectural Innovations," or "Popular Culture versus High Culture." It is recognized that good teaching depends upon concept building, no matter what the form of course organization is. Where possible, at the conclusion of a study unit students need to be encouraged to draw generalizations from the concepts they have been learning and dealing with.

Case studies have been suggested as a means of increased involvement of students in the content of history and as a means for the sharpening of analytical skills. Such studies can be inserted or used from time to time in World History classes that are organized in other ways and some teachers have gone as far as developing an entire course built upon case studies. Few materials are available commercially in this area and most mentors have had to develop representative cases by themselves, sometimes working in teams. Case studies often tend to emphasize anthropological, social, psychological, and economic aspects of history. Typical titles include: "The

Reformation in Great Britain," "Communism in the USSR," "A Village in India," or "The Evolution of the Nigerian State."

A prime suggestion for meeting the aims and content of World History rests in a focus on a Problem of Humanity, Moral Dilemmas, or Continuing Issues Organization. Two major variations of this inquiry approach exist. One is built upon the advanced selection of longtime human problems, such as: "Education for All," "Struggles for Independence," or "Attaining Individual Rights." Ideally such topics are stated in a question format so as to emphasize the problem-resolution elements of a unit. Representative titles include: "How and to What Extent Has Slavery Been Ended?," "Why Do People and Nations Fight?," "How Have the Roles of Women Changed Since 1900?" or "Why Do Some Nations Try to Restrict Population Growth and Others Promote It?" The more radical form of such organization includes teacher/pupil selection and planning of the study of such problems, many of which are of vital contemporary significance. Samples of this category include: "Can Divided Ireland Be Unified," "What Are the Essentials of a Lasting Palestinian-Israeli Agreement," or "How Can International Drug Traffic Be Controlled?" Naturally, in such studies the extensive historical backgrounds and interrelationships of the problem are explored in depth.

Viewing history as inquiry into the foregoing issues helps materially to avoid the storytelling, purely narrative approach that so commonly characterizes World History classes. It can also result in the valuable understanding for learners that any one explanation or conclusion about an historical event is open to question and usually cannot be accepted as the full and accurate truth. The two major reasons for historical study are **1.** to develop knowledge of why we are, where we are, as we are on this planet, and **2.** to introduce and employ the historical method of research as a means to reach understanding of the foregoing elements and aspects of the current human condition. With these aims the course will include necessary instruction in the methods used by historians in arriving at answers, past as well as present. History never repeats itself but accurate understanding of former developments in studies such as "What Caused the Cold War?" or "International Factors in Creating the Great Depression" can clearly link past to present issues. The historian's concern about the reliability and validity of primary as well as secondary sources and accounts remains at the heart of his search for truth as best it can be ascertained. Thus the students' involvement in historical examination promotes the development of critical thinking skills, now frequently cited as a major need to be addressed in social education. Growth in these competencies is naturally at the center of inquiry into issues, past and present.

This writer recognizes the numerous conditions that tend to prevent any of the foregoing variations in designing World History courses in the schools. However, much is lost if any one of these options is selected in name only and is presented in merely a traditional expository manner. Much of the motivation and encouragement of pupil involvement and resulting learning does not occur in this long discredited manner of instruction.

The problems approach is highly dependent upon the review of source documents, and the consideration of opposing views held in different groups or societies by, for example, citizens, politicians, religious leaders, or business people. The analyses of conflicting positions held by authors, economists, labor unions, land owners, media personnel, and historians provide the critical content of problem-centered World History classes. In probing these elements, pupil introduction to and continuing experience with the steps and phases of problem resolution as described in other sections of this volume are essential.

Additionally, there is much value in a problems approach for history, in that it utilizes all of the social sciences and related disciplines in bringing more complete knowledge to learners. Indeed, it is one of the best means of attaining true social studies in the schools. What should also be understood is that an issue-oriented approach can be employed with or within any of the curricular options discussed previously for the presentation of World History. It is a key to the attainment of learning goals in topical, area, and depth studies, as well as in chronologically arranged courses. Any of these approaches is enriched or motivated through the inquiry, analyses, and concluding activities that mark the issue-oriented approach. I repeat, the true goals of the social education of young citizens are well attained in the application of the qualities of critical thinking in decision making in any organization for World History. The truism holds; the means determine the attainment of our ends.

Part Five: Geography, Global Studies and the Environment

Introduction by Josiah Tlou

What is issues-centered social studies education? How should it be taught? Ronald Evans' (1992) discussion of issues-centered social studies programs involves interdisciplinary and discipline-based education. It uses reflective teaching and probing inquiry to utilize relevant evidence. It evaluates a variety of competing options and values for the best possible answers. In dealing with issues-centered perspectives, one should consider flexible approaches to knowledge, concepts, and attitudes and use inquiry as a method of instruction and discussion. Issues-centered approaches have a practical application to human social problems, for implicit in the issues-centered education is the idea of self-improvement in the quality of human lives through social problem-solving techniques. The issues-centered approach to teaching social studies is still an evolving strategy that has not enjoyed the consensus approval in the social studies education field (Evans 1992).

Issues-centered social studies education is consistent with democratic values and ideals. It provides open discourse and careful examination of the issues under discussion, thereby providing new views on problems, encouraging divergent thinking, and valuing different perspectives (Pang & Park 1992: 108). Hence, issues-centered approaches to problem-solving encourage students to have open-minded views in seeking solutions to human problems. It could be said that issues-centered education has a crosscultural base to it. As the values of society change from one generation to another, the issues-centered approach allows students to question the actions and practices of previous generations. An issues-centered curriculum does not have a preset solution to problems. Rather, it allows students to develop analytical skills in articulating the issues and raising pertinent questions in problem-posing and problem-solving. In a multicultural and pluralistic society, it is very important to provide the young with the skills and attitudes necessary for communicating with each another. Issues-centered approaches to social studies programs should include experiences that provide for the study of people, places, and environments (NCSS 1994).

This section of the handbook deals with issues-centered approaches to teaching geography, the environment, and global issues. The common theme that ties together the three subject areas is the global linkage that transcends all national boundaries.

In their article "Issues-Centered Approaches to Teaching Geography Courses," David Hill and Salvatore J. Natoli offer insightful suggestions for how the classroom teacher should handle geography. They suggest that teachers should view and analyze an issue according to its spatial context; that events and issues occur at different places on the earth's surface, and that physical and cultural characteristics of these spaces or places add significant dimensions to the issues and events. The many issues affecting the planet likewise have a tremendous impact on people's daily lives. Many of these issues and events are caused by humans, and others are caused by natural phenomena. In dealing with some of these issues, the authors suggest raising important questions with students on how to solve environmental problems such as pollution, global conflicts, conservation, waste management, deforestation, hazards, infant and child mortality, drought and famine, poverty, race relations, and human rights.

Hill and Natoli point out that students must learn to respect other people and other lands as well as environmental unity and natural diversity. Both teachers and materials should avoid the use of sexist and racist language and challenge stereotypes, as well as discourage ethnocentricity and attempts to find simple solutions. Geographic skills help people make rational political decisions on issues pertaining to problems of air, water and land pollution. Local problems affecting residential areas and places where industries and schools are located also require skillful use of geographic information. Whether the issues involve the evaluation of foreign affairs and international foreign policy or local zoning and land use, geographic skills enable us to collect and analyze information, come to an informed conclusion, and make rational decisions for a course of action (Geography Standards 1994).

In the chapter on environmental issues, Stephen C. Fleury and Adam Sheldon portray issues-centered social studies as a solid affirmation of the environmentalist belief that humans are shaped by their environment. In *Dynamic Sociology* (1993), Lester Ward introduces the concept that humans can bring about a better society by shaping their environment. Teaching students about environmental concerns in a way that will liberate rather than crystallize their thinking is therefore crucial.

Like geography, the environmental problems created by human beings extend beyond national boundaries and cut across disciplines. In order to deal with environmental problems more effectively, we need to consider two different questions that always concern environmental policy: "What will be the societal result of this policy?" and "Why are some policies acted on and others are not?" In working with students, it is necessary to understand the problem of the environment as it relates to and affects policy. Find out who is attempting to influence policy and what specific environmental conditions would be affected by the proposed policy. Have students come up with their own ways of approaching the proposed policy. Using newspapers and publications from environmental groups like the Sierra Club may prove helpful.

Teachers might stress the idea of sustainable development and the necessity to better manage environmental resources in order to preserve our current quality of life. Accordingly, "placing environmental concerns within the political and moral framework of the U.S. makes every environmental problem the concern of all citizens." Using an issues-centered approach to teaching environmental problems provides for active discussion about environmentalism and conservation. Students can discuss environmentalism as it pertains to the growth of natural rights, the expansion of ethics, the uses and misuses of scientific knowledge, the economic basis of social policies, and the practice of social issue analysis.

In their chapter on issues-centered global education, M. Merryfield and C. White provide a framework for dealing with global issues in a social studies curriculum. Collaboration with other globally-oriented teachers is encouraged, as well as input from the students to select global critical issues that fit into a holistic framework for global education. The issues identified should challenge and concern citizens of today and tomorrow as well as affect the lives of people in many parts of the world.

Merryfield and White stress the nature of both the interdisciplinary and discipline-based content of issues-centered global education. The realities of global interdependence require understanding the increasingly important and diverse global connections among world societies (NCSS 1994). Instructional strategies utilizing inquiry, reflection, and simulation provide important insight into handling the materials on global issues-centered education. Issues-centered global education is as much a way of teaching as it is a focus on certain issues (Merryfield and White 1995). The teacher is a facilitator of inquiry who questions, challenges, probes, creates opportunity for extensive student research, and develops methods for authentic assessment and evaluation of student learning (Shapiro and Merryfield 1995).

The issues-centered global approach to education is pragmatic as it reflects the reality in the classroom. Students are inspired and motivated to learn when the teacher connects social studies content to students' interests and needs. The flexibility of the issues-centered global perspective approach to education furthermore allows for frequent updating, so that the content may remain recent, fresh, stimulating, and exciting, thereby appealing to a variety of different students.

The Curriculum Standards for Social Studies and the *National Geography Standards* speak directly to the issue of global connection and interdependence in both cultural and economic relationships. A financial crisis in Mexico greatly impacted the United States, Brazil, Germany, Malaysia, Canada, and other parts of the world.

An earthquake in Kobe had significant ramifications for financial markets in the United States, Britain, and Singapore. We are not insulated from the vagaries of global changes. We should therefore train our students not to view the issues and problems of the world in isolation, but to see instead that what is done in one part of the world affects everyone's environment and economy. World issues become our issues.

References

Coplin, W. D. and M. K. O'Leary. *Basic Policy Studies Skills*, Crotonon-Hudson: Policy Associates, 1981.

Evans, Ronald. "What Do We Mean by IssueCentered Social Studies Education," *The Social Student*, May/June 1992, pp. 93-94.

Geography Education Standards Project. *Geography for Life: National Geography Standards*, Washington, D.C., 1994.

Klein, P. "Expressions of Interest in Environmental Issues by U.S. Secondary Geography Students," *International Research in Geographical and Environment Education* 2, no. 2 (1993) 108-12.

National Council for the Social Studies. *Expectations of Excellence: Curriculum Standards for Social Studies*, Washington, D.C., 1994.

Pang, Valerie O. and Cynthia Park. "Issue Centered Approaches to Multicultural Education in the Middle Grades," *The Social Studies*, May/June 1992, p. 108.

Shapiro, Steve and Merry Merryfield. "A Case Study of Unit Planning in the Context of School Reform," *Teaching About International Conflict and Peace*, edited by Merry Merryfield and Richard Remy. Albany, NY: SUNY Press, 1995.

19

ISSUES-CENTERED APPROACHES TO TEACHING GEOGRAPHY COURSES

by A. David Hill and Salvatore J. Natoli

Different scientists study the same events for entirely different purposes. A sociologist may regard an environmental issue as an event or experience that will affect, change, or seriously modify the nature and structure of social institutions. A physicist might pose a question on whether a given energy source is sufficient to sustain a population or the industrial and service infrastructure of a community. Environmental issues seem to concern many scientists, but each seems only to have a particular knowledge or point of view about any given issue. For example, if the issue is water pollution, political scientists will ponder the nature of the political processes and institutions best able to cope with the problem. At the same time, biologists will examine organisms affected by the pollutants, attempt to trace the sources of the pollutants, and examine the changes these may bring about in the ecosystem.

Geography and Issues-Oriented Education

Geographers view and analyze issues according to spatial contexts. Such issues, and the events that trigger them, occur at specific places on the Earth's surface. The physical and cultural characteristics of these spaces or places add a significant dimension to the issue or the event. In examining the spatial characteristics of water pollution, the geographer begins the analysis by studying the pollution's locational characteristics and their implications. The geographer then formulates a series of questions about the spread of the pollutants from point or diffuse sources, their distribution over space and time, and the relative severity of their effects on various areas. Issues to geographers are problems that have both direct and indirect relationships to places

and that affect people in these and other places.

Because most modern geographical research has become the study of the spatial aspects of issues, geographers have rich resource materials upon which they can draw to develop and organize curricula and courses related to significant social, economic, and political issues. Consider, for example, the issues involved in the titles of some recent doctoral dissertations in geography, chosen randomly from the *Guide to Departments of Geography/AAG Handbook* and the *Directory of Geographers, 1994-1995:* "China's Potential for International Industrial Growth," "The Role of Fourth World Nations and Synchronous Geopolitical Factors in the Breakdown of States," "Ties to People, Bonds to Place: The Urban Geography of Low-Income Women's Survival Strategies," "A Geographical Analysis of Poverty in the United States, 1980-1990," "Race, Class, and Health: Health Behavior and Hypertension in Black and White Americans," "The Terms of Trade: The Restructuring of Canadian Society under the Canada-United States Free Trade Agreement," "Peer Educators' Geographic Range Effect: An Analysis of an AIDS Intervention Program in the Dominican Republic," "The Emergence and Dynamics of Citizen Participation in Wyoming Energy Conflicts in the 1970's," "An Examination of Factors Influencing Citizen's Actions in Response to Superfund Site Cleaning Decisions in the State of Texas," and "Understanding the Effects of Small Hospital Closures on Rural Communities."

Master's-level research has become even more practical, or applied, than doctoral-level work in geography. [1] At the elementary, middle, and high school levels, developing geography programs around the study of issues is a path toward engaging students' interest in the learning of geography.

According to the *Guidelines for Geographic Education: Elementary and Secondary Schools* (Joint Committee 1984) and the *National Geography Standards, 1994: Geography for Life* (1994), their rationales for applying geographic knowledge constitute a clear mandate for learning geography today and in the future. The *Guidelines for Geographic Education* state

> Every day we make important decisions about our well-being and every day we use geographic knowledge or encounter important geographical influences in our lives. We interpret complicated geographic factors to determine the places where we choose to live—physical factors... [and] cultural factors... all have a bearing on our quality of life. ...Geographic knowledge is crucial in dealing with issues such as nuclear armament buildups, siting nuclear power plants, safe disposal of radioactive and toxic chemicals, segregation, race, age, or economic status, discrimination against women and minorities, and inequitable distribution of economic resources in and among developed and developing countries. Careful geographic scrutiny can benefit the analysis of problems of environmental degradation, rational use of ocean resources, the resettlement of refugees from war-torn nations, and political repression and terrorism. (p.1)

Two imperatives drove the creation of the National Geography Standards: "First, geographic understanding must be set into a process of lifelong learning, thus requiring a connection between school and adult life" (1994, 26). An inseparable and seamless bond connects formal educational contexts—preschool, K through 12, and college—and adult life. "Second, geographic understanding must be set into life contexts: school, family, society, and occupation" (ibid., 26). Educated citizens must make thoughtful decisions about their world while living among so-called patterns of normalcy made significant only by their regular anomalies. Rather than attempt to develop a theoretical system for explaining an issues-centered geography, we might develop this discussion by highlighting four contemporary projects in geographic education that embody such systems.

The High School Geography Project (HSGP)

In the 1960's, the High School Geography Project pioneered issues-centered (problem-solving) instruction in geography using inquiry learning techniques (Table 1). Although not planned as an issues-oriented project, its teaching and learning strategies as well as the media, procedures, skill development, desired attitudes, and related optional assignments allowed experienced geography teachers to translate and transform the program's activities into issue-oriented lessons or modules (Patton et al. 1970). The basic conservatism of U. S. education and the difficulties in introducing educational innovations in the schools, especially in the form of non-text materials, constrained the HSGP and similar projects in the new social studies (see the section below on GIGI and the politics of textbook adoption).

Geography in an Urban Age (High School Geography Project 1970) reflected the major social, cultural, and economic issues of the 1960's, including the following: the persistent and continuing problems of urbanization and the growth and spread of cities, with their attendant social and economic consequences; patterns and issues of manufacturing (planned versus marketing economies) and agriculture (planning, risk taking, mechanization, and decision making); cultural diffusion and cultural influences influencing land use (the implied loss of national and cultural distinctiveness and identities); issues in political geography (boundary disputes, gerrymandering, regional politics and governance); and habitat and resources (natural hazards, resources management, and waste management). There was also a regional unit on Japan concerning problems associated with the tension between retaining traditional values in the midst of rapid modernization.

One of the High School Geography Project activities, "School Districts for Millersburg," asks students to read background material on Millersburg's growth that includes the racial and ethnic background of the population and describes some of the physical characteristics of this hypothetical city. The teacher then asks students to design school districts for six new high schools, each which will serve an equal number of students—about 2,000. Class members must infer the student population from population density maps and their general knowledge about where families with teen-age children

Table 1: HSGP Activities by Unit

UNIT	INTEGRAL ACTIVITIES	RELATED OPTIONAL ACTIVITES
1 **geography of cities**	1. City Location and Growth 2. New Orleans 3. City Shape and Structure 4. Portsville 5. Sizes and Spacing of Cities 6. Cities with Special Functions	A Tale of Three Cities Bruges Time-Distance Migrants to the City Megalopolis Local Community Study Local Shopping Survey
2 **manufacturing and agriculture**	1. Geographic Patterns of Manufacturing 2. The Importance of Manufacturing 3. Location of the Metfab Company 4. Graphic Examples of Industrial Location 5. Hunger 6. The Agricultural Realm 7. Interviews with Farmers 8. The Game of Farming 9. Enough Food for the World	Locating Metfab in the U.S.S.R. Two Case Studies
3 **cultural geography**	1. Different Ideas about Cattle 2. A Lesson from Sports 3. Expansion of Islam 4. Canada: A Regional Question 5. Cultural Change: A Trend Toward Uniformity	Games Illustrating the Spread of Ideas Supplementary Reading The Long Road
4 **political geography**	1. Section 2. One Man, One Vote 3. School Districts for Millersburg 4. London 5. Point Roberts	
5 **habitat**	1. Habitat and Man 2. Two Rivers 3. Wachung 4. Rutile and the Beach 5. Flood Hazards 6. Water Balance 7. Waste Management	
6 **Japan**	1. Introduction to Japan 2. Traditional Japan 3. Japan Today 4. The Modernization of Japan	

Source: High School Geography Project, *Geography in an Urban Age* (New York: Macmillan, 1970). The 1976 revised edition included several changes in activities and strategies to reflect new attitudes toward the environment and resources. Other information was also updated where available.

Table 2: Global Geography—Examples of Issues for Study

South Asia: *Why Are Forests Disappearing?*

Features population growth and shrinking forests. In a family in Nepal, deforestation forces a father and son to travel far in search of firewood. The deforestation has caused soil erosion and flooding. Other examples from Kenya, West Germany, and Canada also show causes and remedies.

Southeast Asia: *How Does Change Occur?*

Focuses on modern techniques that help farmers produce food for a growing population. A change agent and village headman urge a Filipino farmer to try new ways of growing rice. Provides examples of how agents in India, Guatemala, and the United States also help farmers adopt new ideas.

Japan: *Why Does Trade Occur?*

Discusses Japan's import needs, especially for energy, and their effects on an urban Japanese family. Examines how Japan imports natural resources to manufacture goods for export. Other examples include how West Germany, Kenya, and the United States also depend on trade.

Soviet Union: *Why Does Planning Occur?*

Visits with two Siberian families show how the government owns and manages vast resources, dividing the country into different economic planning regions with ties between them for sharing goods. Cities' different planning strategies in the Netherlands, the United States, and North Africa are presented.

East Asia: *Why Do People Live Where They Do?*

A view of population distribution in China introduces a family on a cooperative farm in Beijing, where soils are fertile, water plentiful, and the growing season adequate for the crops they grow. In contrast, western China is presented, which has poor soil, scarce water, and fewer people. Population distribution in Egypt, Japan, and Canada are also discussed.

Australia/New Zealand: *Why Is The World Shrinking?*

An Australian wholesale florist and his children receive a telephone order from the United States for flowers, and they are able to get them to the United States the next day. Examples from Mexico, Canada, and the United States show that places move together or apart as the time-distance between them changes.

North Africa/Southwest Asia: *What Are The Consequences Of Change?*

Background on desert, dams, and irrigation canals shows how the life of a three-generation Tunisian family has changed, as a newly drilled well replaces the yearly flooding needed for irrigation. Technology has also brought new costs and problems. Comparisons include Australia and the United States.

Africa—South of the Sahara: *How Do People Use Their Environment?*

A brief historical overview introduces a family—today and 15 years ago—on Mt. Marsabit, Kenya, and how they have used scarce water resources in four distinct ways over many years. The ideas are presented of groups in Japan, France, and the United States about how to use the environment.

Central and South America: *Why Do People Move?*

This overview of population movement introduces a Central American family that settles in the city to escape the hardships of their former rural life and to provide schooling and medical care for their children. The program also highlights reasons for moving in Malaysia, the Netherlands, and the United States.

Europe: *How Do People Deal With Natural Hazards?*

A map of the population distribution of Europe introduces a family living in the southwestern part of the Netherlands. The mother recalls a devastating flood that occurred when she was young. One focus is on Dutch engineers and how they control flooding with dikes, dunes, and dams. How people in Bangladesh, Japan, and Canada deal with water-related natural hazards is also presented.

Table 3: BGGS-GIGI: Module Inquiry Focus and Case Study Locations

PRIMARY CASE STUDY REGION	MODULE, FOCUS, AND LOCATIONS	
South Asia	**POPULATION AND RESOURCES** How does world population growth affect resource availability? **Bangladesh, Haiti**	**RELIGIOUS CONFLICT** Where do religious differences contribute to conflict? **Kashmir, Northern Ireland, United States**
Southeast Asia	**SUSTAINABLE AGRICULTURE** How can the world achieve sustainable agriculture? **Malaysia, Cameroon, Western United States**	**HUMAN RIGHTS** How is freedom of movement a basic human right? **Cambodia, Cuba, United States**
Japan	**NATURAL HAZARDS** How do the effects of natural hazards vary from place to place? **Japan, Bangladesh, United States**	**GLOBAL ECONOMY** How does the global economy affect people and places? **Japan, Colombia, United States**
Former Soviet Union	**ENVIRONMENTAL POLLUTION** What are the effects of severe environmental area pollution? **Aral Sea, Madagascar, United States**	**DIVERSITY AND NATIONALISM** How do nations cope with cultural diversity? **Commonwealth of Independent States, Brazil, United States, Canada**
East Asia	**POLITICAL CHANGE** How does political change affect people and places? **Hong Kong, South Korea, Taiwan, Singapore, China, Canada**	**POPULATION GROWTH** How is population growth to be managed? **China, United States**
Australia New Zealand Pacific	**GLOBAL CLIMATE CHANGE** What happens as global warming occurs? **Australia, New Zealand, Developing Countries, United States, Gulf Coast**	**INTERDEPENDENCE** What are the causes and effects of global interdependence? **Australia, Falkland Islands, United States**
North Africa Southwest Asia	**HUNGER** Why are people hungry? **Sudan, India, Canada**	**OIL AND SOCIETY** How have oil riches changed nations? **Saudi Arabia, Venezuela, United States (Alaska)**
Africa–South of the Sahara	**INFANT AND CHILD MORTALITY** Why do so many children suffer from poor health? **Central Africa, United States**	**BUILDING NEW NATIONS** How are nation-states built? **Nigeria, South Africa, Kurdish**
Latin America	**DEVELOPMENT** How does development affect people and places? **Amazonia, Eastern Europe, United States (Tennessee Valley)**	**URBAN GROWTH** What are the causes and effects of rapid urbanization and urban growth? **Mexico, United States**
Europe	**WASTE MANAGEMENT** Why is waste management both a local and global concern? **Western Europe, Japan, United States**	**REGIONAL INTEGRATION** What are the advantages and barriers to regional integration? **Europe, United States, Mexico, Canada**

Source: *Britannica Global Geography System* (Chicago: Britannica/Encyclopedia Britannica Educational Corporation, 1994).

live. The number of students in Millersburg is but one consideration in the problem of districting. The materials also include a series of maps containing information on family income, population density, the ethnic composition of the population, industrial and commercial zones, transportation facilities, and the locations of elementary schools. Students will grapple with such issues as integration, the potential for segregation, busing, and future growth. The key question is, What sorts of information should you think about before you start to draw the district boundaries on your map? Students can work individually or in groups and must be able to defend their boundaries based on the data they have accumulated and analyzed, and to communicate their arguments via prose, statistical tables, graphics, recordings, transparencies, or film strips.

Global Geography

The Agency for Instructional Technology (AIT), in cooperation with geography and social studies consultants, developed a video series, Global Geography, that brought the study of world problems into the classrooms and hometowns of middle-level students. Each of the self-contained programs examines an issue or problem in a different region of the world and analyzes each according to fundamental themes in geography. Each of the ten case studies features one region of the world (Europe, for example), and dramatizes an issue (e.g., how people deal with natural hazards), and its importance to a topic (e.g., population distribution and flood hazards as well as their relationship to the presence or absence of flood mitigation measures such as dikes, dunes, and dams).

Students and teachers examine the problem according to a variety of geographical concepts and ideas derived from the five fundamental themes of geography (Joint Committee 1984), such as human-environmental interactions, the movement of waters, patterns of population distribution, and the social and economic effects of flooding. Students also study and examine examples from other parts of the world experiencing similar hazards, such as Bangladesh, Japan, and Canada. Among the other issues highlighted in this project (in addition to floods in southwestern Netherlands) are deforestation in Nepal, Kenya, West Germany, and Canada; modern agricultural techniques in producing food for growing populations in Southeast Asia

(the Philippines), India, Guatemala, and the United States; import needs in Japan, West Germany, Kenya, and the United States; government ownership and management of resources in the former Soviet Union, the Netherlands, the United States, and North Africa; population distribution and problems in China, Egypt, Japan, and Canada; the shrinking world with examples from Australia, New Zealand, the United States, Mexico, and Canada; the consequences of technological changes in agriculture in North Africa, Southwest Asia, Australia, and the United States; water resource scarcity in Africa South of the Sahara, Kenya, Japan, France, and the United States; and rural-to-urban migration in Central America, Malaysia, the Netherlands, and the United States. Each of the case studies includes not only comparison-contrasts with different regions of the world but also makes reference to the United States and how studying global issues in a local context can provide students with a global perspective.

The Influence of the Geography Education Standards Project[2]

The emerging geography standards escalated expectations for strong instructional materials. *The National Geography Standards, 1994: Geography for Life* are rigorous because by mandate they are to be internationally competitive in that they identify what the United States needs and wants from a systematic program in geography, namely what geography students should know and be able to do in order to be active and responsible citizens in an internationally competitive environment. The study of geography has the added practical value of viewing life situations through a spatial prism. For our purposes, we can define "life situations" as "issues."

The Basis for the Development of Issue-Based Materials

Three elements are necessary for developing strong, issue-based geography materials and all emphasize the role of the teacher: teacher training in the use of good materials, the widespread adoption of these materials, and their use by well-trained teachers. Issues-based education faces some formidable barriers because of the present heavy reliance of teachers on textbooks for content in geography, which is fact-oriented, rather than process oriented (see the earlier section of the High School Geography Project).

Textbook adoption processes are dominated by hidebound procedures and by form and content prescriptions that discourage innovation; school budgets traditionally favor textbook purchase over supplementary materials (Association of American Geographers and American Sociological Association 1974). Since colleges and universities have been untangling themselves from the stranglehold of textbooks as a result of electronic technology and print-to-order course packets (Cox 1993), perhaps the school market will follow.

The GIGI Project

The Geographic Inquiry into Global Issues (GIGI) Project was funded by a grant from the National Science Foundation and directed by A. David Hill. Since 1990, the project has engaged Hill and a large group of writers, editors, and consultants in developing materials designed to help meet the goals of responsible citizenship, modern geographic knowledge, and critical and reflective thinking. The project has created challenging, useful, and relevant issues-oriented materials for motivating students to acquire geographic knowledge, skills, and perspectives.

GIGI Components

GIGI developed two issues-based modules for each of ten world regions (Table 3).[3] Each module is free-standing and independent. Teachers can use all twenty modules (in any desired order), a small subset, or a single module. Each module requires ten to fifteen class periods to complete. Modules typically begin with a broad introduction to a global issue, after which a primary case study, lasting three to four lessons, examines the issue in a selected part of the world. Next, usually in a single lesson, students explore a comparative case in a different region—much like the Agency for Instructional Technology series—which gives a variant of the issue and a sense of its global nature. Because North America is not one of the world regions in the modules, these variant issues bring the issue close to home wherever possible. Each study contains a print module—a teacher's guide that includes overhead transparencies, handouts, activities masters, student databooks, laminated mini-atlas maps plus multimedia packages that include videodiscs, a CD-ROM and user's manual, and barcode guides. The student databooks contain questions and data in a variety of textual and graphic forms. Students will not understand the databook by itself, and so will derive meaning from the text only with the teacher's guidance. The teacher's guide serves two purposes: to suggest teaching procedures and to help the teacher with content and process.

All of GIGI's modules ask students to interpret data critically in order to find supporting evidence for generalizations. For example, the religious conflict module, Lesson 3 ("What is the nature of religious conflict in Kashmir?") has a section entitled "What events and conditions contributed to religious conflicts in Kashmir?" The teacher's guide suggests that the class be divided into three cooperative learning groups to examine data on Kashmir's colonial history, its resources, and religious discrimination. Each of these three parts contains associated questions for the students. Three tables on religious discrimination present data on Kashmir's population, religious groups, and the state and central governments' employment of religious groups. Students are asked whether these data support the Kashmiri Muslims' claims of religious discrimination and how the data might be related to Kashmiri Muslims' desires for independence from India. In addition, students are asked to speculate about what other information they would need to test the discrimination claims of Kashmiri Muslims. The teacher's guide emphasizes the importance of critically examining a wide range of data as well as the scientific postulate that although scientific generalizations may be supported, they are usually difficult to prove absolutely.

The Role of Questions

GIGI is based on Frances Slater's inquiry planning model (1993), which is designed to merge the inquiry process with the conclusions the users draw. Directly linking questions and answers helps achieve an intellectually satisfying understanding of a problem. According to Slater (1993)

> the progression from questions to generalizations is crucial as a structure for developing meaning and understanding. Meaning and understanding define the process of tying little factual knots of information into bigger knots so that geography begins to make sense, not as a heap of isolated facts but as a network of ideas and procedures. (p. 60)

When we ask students to learn conclusions without learning how to draw them, we perpetuate the tradition of an education centered upon getting answers and bereft of higher thinking.

GIGI strives for a balance between convergent and divergent questions. Too much convergent thinking inhibits critical thinking and leads to little else than rote memorization, whereas too much divergent questioning may discourage learning about facts and substance. We think teachers should supplement the questions in GIGI by asking students additional convergent and divergent questions, as cited in Slater (1993). The questions should

- demand recall
- encourage classification and ordering
- encourage the use of data to draw conclusions
- encourage awareness of the limitations of data or of the evaluation of data, and
- encourage awareness of the processes of reasoning used

Issues-Based Geographic Inquiry

To foster active learning and higher-level thinking, GIGI stresses issues-based geographic inquiry. Inquiry generally is the scientific method, and operates like good detective work. Inquiry poses questions and proposes answers about the world, and it tests its answers with real data. To achieve GIGI's goals, students examine specific global issues by pursuing answers to geographic questions (Table 4). Students answer these questions by analyzing and evaluating data using geographic methods and skills. Working as geographers helps lead students to useful knowledge, skills, and perspectives. In a free inquiry situation, students work independently, but with GIGI posing questions and providing data, teachers and students explore the issues together. GIGI materials may be the least teacher-proof geography materials available: they will not work as designed without good teachers guiding students in their use.

Inquiry-based learning should teach students habits of critical and reflective thinking. The issues posed should stimulate multiple and opposing positions, and students should use facts to support different points of view. This context is necessary for developing habits that foster critical perspectives. Interpretation is the key activity. With GIGI, teachers can foster these habits and abilities as they help students interpret data guided by hypotheses, proposi-

tions, arguments, and questions. Teachers should challenge students to raise new questions, question the quality of their data, seek more useful data, articulate relationships they perceive, explain their processes of investigation, and defend their positions and solutions. Unless teachers provide this kind of guidance, GIGI will not meet its goal of teaching responsible citizenship, modern geographic knowledge, and critical and reflective thinking.

Local Examples

GIGI is a world geography, but it demonstrates that issues can work on various geographic levels—personal, local, regional, national, and global. Younger students may often be unable to identify with faraway places, so teachers and students may develop the ability to relate global issues under investigation to examples in their local community. Every community has issues with fundamental geographic dimensions.

If possible, teachers should make every effort to take students into the field so they can see phenomena that relate to their classroom studies. Klein's (1993) field observations during GIGI's national classroom trials convinced the GIGI staff to urge teachers using the materials to make frequent references to their local examples and to encourage their students, whenever possible, to make local field studies related to the issues. Teachers also need to help students find relevance by identifying GIGI issues with real people, especially at the students' grade level, and by making connections to everyday life in as many ways as possible. Teachers eventually will gain familiarity with teaching local examples, especially as they begin to develop field exercises, put a human face on these materials, and adapt the GIGI modules to fit their particular modules. The more the trial teachers worked with the GIGI materials, the more comfortable they became with them.

Fostering Perspectives

The seriousness and complexity of the global issues studied in GIGI can overwhelm students unless teachers foster optimistic and constructive perspectives toward issues. Teachers need to balance the pessimistic connotations of most issues with examples of success and prospects for positive change. Teachers must also help students develop efficacy, an attitude that their actions can have some effect in solving world problems

Table 4: GIGI's Model for Issues-Based Geographic Inquiry

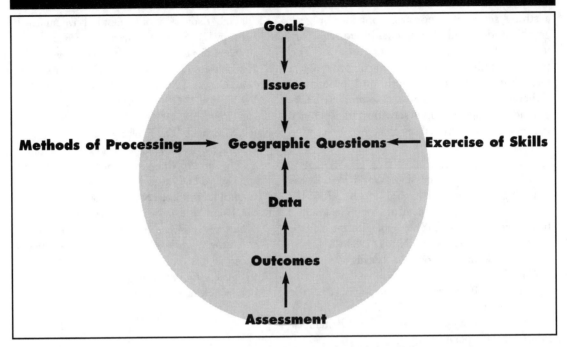

Source: After Frances Slater, *Learning through Geography* (London: Heinemann, 1993).

(Klein 1993). The maxim, "Think globally, act locally" addresses the need to help students organize and take constructive actions that address local variants of the issues they are studying. As student involvement in local projects enriches the educational experience, it can also produce an optimism about their abilities to be a force for change in their community and in their world. GIGI includes lessons and activities focusing on possibilities for positive action.

Fostering certain perspectives, it is hoped, will promote student optimism and constructive behavior. Geography students must learn to respect other people and other lands as well as understand and appreciate unity and natural diversity. They must develop a healthy skepticism toward overly simplified explanations about environmental degradation, human responses to hazards, and serious problems that might result from simple human oversights. Optimistic and constructive perspectives should accompany the development of empathy, tolerance, and open-mindedness. Teachers and materials must avoid sexist and racist language, discourage ethnocentricity, and challenge stereotypes, simple solutions, and basic assumptions.

As with any materials or innovations in education, teacher preparation components at both the pre- and in-service levels are absolutely essential. This preparation must include content, process, and a support system that will be ready to provide assistance when teachers need help. Materials such as those developed by GIGI, AIT, the HSGP and ARGUS (see below) challenge teachers who have had little formal education in geography. Because learning the content of geography depends upon the exercise of higher-level thinking, teachers without such content cannot assist students in speculating, hypothesizing, analyzing, interpreting, and evaluating—all necessary and significant skills and aptitudes for successful issues-oriented teaching and learning.

ARGUS

Activities and Readings in the Geography of the United States (ARGUS) is a new project funded by the National Science Foundation and sponsored by the Association of American Geographers (AAG).[4] ARGUS is not designed as an issues-oriented project, but its activities and twenty-six case studies are replete with issues that have a strong geographical focus. The case studies are regional and topical, and a list of a few indicates the strength of the issues implicit in them: Native Americans, colonies, waves of immigration, Old Dixie, South Florida, suburbia, the Rust

Belt, megalopolis, the Delta and ghetto, Hawaii, and a livable country. ARGUS helps to promote a strong series of conceptual contexts for geographical ideas and phenomena, interdisciplinary uses, and cross-curricular suggestions. The teacher's guide includes an array of pedagogical techniques, flexible in depth and procedure. Other materials include the case studies, background readings, handout activities, transparency masters, and an optional set of slides.

---

[1] Geographic research since World War II has increasingly emphasized applied topics. With the development and refinement of Geographic Information Systems (GIS) technologies, the increase has become exponential. See Natoli (1986, 28-42).

[2] The following material relies heavily on a portion of Hill 1994.

[3] The GIGI Project has been published as the *Britannica Global Geography System* (BGGS) (Chicago: Britannica/Encyclopedia Britannica Educational Corporation, 1994).

[4] Information on and sample materials about ARGUS are available from the AAG, 1710 Sixteenth Street, N. W., Washington, D. C. 20009.

References

Agency for Instructional Technology (AIT). *Global Geography,* a video series. Bloomington, IN: AIT, 1987.

Activities and Readings in the Geography of the United States. Washington, D.C.: Association of American Geographers, 1994.

Cox, M. "Technology Threatens to Shatter the World of College Textbooks," *Wall Street Journal,* June 1, 1993

Dunn, James M. "The Translation of Geography for the Development of Precollegiate Instructional Materials." Ph.D. dissertation, Department of Geography, University of Colorado at Boulder, 1993.

Guide to Programs of Geography in the United States and Canada, 1994-1995/AAG Handbook and Directory of Geographers. Washington, D.C.: Association of American Geographers, 1994.

High School Geography Project. *Geography in an Urban Age.* New York: Macmillan, 1970.

Hill, A. David. "Geography Instructional Materials for Standards-Based Education." *Journal of Geography* 93 (January/February 1994): 14-20.

Joint Committee on Geographic Education, National Council for Geographic Education (NCGE) and Association of American Geographers (AAG) *Guidelines for Geographic Education: Elementary and Secondary School.* Washington, D.C. and Macomb, IL: AAG and NCGE, 1984.

Klein, Phil. "Expressions of Interest in Environmental Issues by U.S. Secondary Geography Students." In *International Research in Geographical and Environmental Education,* 2, no. 2 (1993): 108-112.

National Geography Standards, 1994: Geography for Life. Washington, D.C.: National Geographic Research and Exploration, 1994.

Natoli, Salvatore J. "The Evolving Nature of Geography." In *Social Studies and the Social Sciences: A Fifty-Year Perspective,* edited by Stanley Wronski and Donald H. Bragaw. Washington, D.C.: National Council for the Social Studies, 1986.

Patton, Donald J. et al., eds. *From Geographic Discipline to Inquiring Student: Final Report on the High School Geography Project.* Washington, D.C.: Association of American Geographers, 1970.

Slater, Frances. *Learning through Geography.* London: Heinemann, 1993.

20

ISSUES-CENTERED GLOBAL EDUCATION

by Merry M. Merryfield and Connie S. White

"Education must teach us that all our actions on this planet, physical or social, are irrevocably interlocked."

—Ernest Boyer
Former U.S. Commissioner of Education

"Before you finish eating breakfast this morning, you've depended on more than half the world. This is the way our universe is structured. ...We aren't going to have peace on earth until we recognize this basic fact of the interrelated structure of all reality."

—Martin Luther King, Jr.
U.S. clergyman and civil rights leader

"The salvation of mankind lies only in making everything the concern of all."

—Alexander Solzhenitsyn
Soviet writer and dissident

Remember the first time you saw a photograph of Earth taken from outer space? There it was, a blue, green, and brown planet wrapped in wisps of white and gray. Although you might have looked for your city or country, you found only natural borders, separating water and landforms. For many of us the photograph provided our first global perspective, a new view of our planet as a finite system, as one interconnected world.

If we examine our lives, our community, and our world from a global perspective, issues emerge that are critical to our planet's survival and the quality of life of the earth's peoples. Some of the issues—such as the disposal of nuclear wastes or gene therapy—are as new as the advanced technologies that brought us that photograph of Earth. Others—religious conflict, hunger, questions of human rights—were evident in ancient civilizations and have become global issues as science and technology have accelerated the interconnectedness of the world's peoples. In today's world global issues are a part of the daily lives of American students, teachers, and their communities.

In this chapter we share our conceptualization of issues-centered global education and suggest a framework for infusing a global issues-centered approach into social studies courses. Our ideas come from our experiences as social studies teachers, our study and research of exemplary practice in global education, and our collaboration with other globally oriented teachers in The Ohio State University's Professional Development School Network in Social Studies and Global Education.

What Is Issues-Centered Global Education?

Teachers who teach issues-centered global education generally make a number of distinct decisions that deal with content selection, the process of teaching and learning, and the development of a global perspective. These decisions are interrelated and fit into a holistic framework for issues-centered global education.

Teachers Select Critical Global Issues

Teachers select issues that **1.** challenge and concern citizens today and tomorrow, **2.** affect the lives of persons in many parts of the world, and **3.** cannot be adequately understood or addressed solely in a local or national context (Anderson 1979; Becker 1979; Merryfield 1991). Many of these issues have no immediate solutions, and the questions they raise may not have one "correct" answer. Issues that are significant to the world and of concern to students are often controversial and value-laden. In our research we have found that teachers choose issues that they believe are significant and related to the interests and needs of their students (Merryfield 1993b, 1994). Teachers often find that several issues overlap and must be examined together. We have included in the figure on page 179 many of the global issues relevant to social studies education. In studying issues such as population growth, teachers acknowledge the complex interrelationships among such issues by bringing in content related to environmental impact, implications for human services such as health and education, political agendas of minorities or those who wield power, economic issues such as the generation of jobs, transportation, or housing, and cultural issues such as family planning and religious values.

Teachers Integrate Content across the Disciplines.

The content of issues-centered global education is both discipline-based (mainly from history and the social sciences) and interdisciplinary (integrating appropriate knowledge and skills from other disciplines). Substantive content is the basic building block of issues-centered global education (Merryfield and Remy 1995). Although most of the concepts, factual information, and generalizations are from history, political science, geography, economics, sociology, anthropology, and psychology, at times social studies teachers include content from the sciences, mathematics, literature, music, and art that is essential for understanding complex issues from multiple perspectives (Kniep 1986; Levak, Merryfield, and Wilson 1993).

Teachers Provide a Historical Context.

Issues are examined within a historical context. That is, students understand relevant historical antecedents and how the issue has evolved over time and space. Part of a historical context is an appreciation of the process of globalization (Anderson 1979; Dunn 1988; Kniep 1986). How has an issue that was once only a concern within one culture or region become a global issue that touches the lives of people around the world and can no longer be effectively the burden of a single nation? Every global issue has historical roots that provide important insights and perspectives on its evolution, diffusion, and significance in the world today. Historians such as Ross Dunn (1988), Paul Kennedy (1987, 1993), Kevin Reilly (1989) and

L.S. Stravrianos (1991a, 1991b) consciously make such connections.

Teachers Plan Inquiry and Reflection.

The process of instruction includes in-depth inquiry, open-ended questioning, examination of values, reflective practice, as well as the decision making and controversy that are authentic to citizenship in a democracy (Angell and Avery 1992; Lamy 1990). Issues-centered global education is as much a way of teaching as it is a focus on certain issues. Here, the teacher is a facilitator of inquiry who questions, challenges, and probes—creates experiences for extensive student research and develops authentic assessment and evaluation of student learning. (See Shapiro and Merryfield [1995] for a case study of the development and teaching of such a social studies unit.)

Teachers Build Skills in Perspectives Consciousness.

Students develop skills in perspectives consciousness, the ability to recognize, examine, evaluate, and appreciate multiple perspectives on a particular issue or concern (Case 1993; Hanvey 1975). Issues-centered global education begins with the assumption that people may perceive an issue or event in different ways based upon their beliefs, experiences, and values. Students become adept at putting themselves in other people's shoes, at seeking out and appreciating views that are different from their own. They learn to appreciate the complexity and conflicts that come with the knowledge of multiple perspectives.

Teachers Focus on the Development of a Global Perspective.

Students develop a global perspective—the ability to (1) see the world as an interconnected system, (2) recognize how they are connected, how they affect and are affected by peoples around the world, and (3) appreciate the multiple realities and worldviews as perceived by individuals and cultures as they deal with their interconnected world (Alger and Harf 1986; Anderson 1979; Hanvey 1975). As in perspectives consciousness, students are able to go beyond their own culture or nationality and examine issues globally and through the beliefs and experiences of people different from themselves.

These characteristics are central to instructional decision making in issues-centered global

Figure 1: Global Issues in the Social Studies

Political Issues

peace and security issues, human rights, self-determination, peacekeeping issues, political stability, use of the military, weapons sales, use of space, arms control, military aid, torture, terrorism

Cultural/Social Issues

ethnic conflict, intermarriage, ethnicity, cultural transmission, language policies, religious issues, education and literacy issues, health issues, population issues, global movement of people, refugees, immigration

Development Issues

poverty, sustainable agriculture, capital investment, population, food and hunger, women in development, technology transfer, issues related to dependency

Economic Issues

organization of labor, the global assembly line, non-tariff barriers, free trade, debt issues related to distribution (e.g., of wealth, technology and information, food, resources, weapons), urbanization issues, transportation and communication issues

Environmental Issues

pollution, use of natural resources, land use, extinction of species/biodiversity, disposal of toxic wastes, energy issues, conservation, renewable versus nonrenewable energy, global movement of people, refugees, immigration

interrelationships across issues and problems

---

education. They are complex, yet complementary. Here is an illustration of how they can come together in a world geography course. In their study of the movement of peoples, students raise several issues related to immigration policies, the reasons why people leave their home countries, and the effects that new immigrants have upon their new countries. "Why would anyone leave the country they have grown up in?" "Aren't immigrants taking away jobs from people who have grown up here?" "Aren't most immigrants poor?"

The teacher helps the students frame their questions in such a way that they will compare contemporary immigration in different world areas (Why do people choose to immigrate from Russia, Eritrea, Vietnam, or Mexico?); examine immigration in their own lives and that of their community (How have our families and our community been affected by our own immigration and that of others?); search out the historical background of global immigration (How has global immigration changed in the past 200 years? What are commonalities that many immigrants have shared over time?); and make con-

nections with such issues as human rights and environmental decay (Why are immigrants treated differently by some countries or communities? What are relationships between deforestation and the movement of people?). Taking into consideration particular interests and mandated course content, the students work in small groups to develop profiles of immigration to their community (or city, state, or nation) and to present-day Germany, Hong Kong, Kenya, and Australia. To identify immigration issues, different perspectives, and the concerns of immigrants and other citizens, students use their media center, a local library's on-line data base (e.g., CompuServe), literature about immigrant experiences, and community resource people (e.g., immigrants and people knowledgeable about immigration in other countries). Their profiles include historical time lines, immigration statistics, data from primary sources (e.g., autobiographies, original documents) and secondary sources (i.e., views of historians, sociologists, etc.) that help explain past and current immigration issues from multiple perspectives. After the students present their profiles to the class, the teacher asks probing questions so students examine stereotypes and conventional assumptions about immigrants. Students then draw inferences and redefine issues about immigration globally and within their community.

A culminating activity might be a simulation of a meeting of the European Community to develop a new immigration policy. Taking on different European perspectives, the students use their knowledge on immigration to address the issues facing those countries as thousands of Eastern Europeans and citizens of the former Soviet Union seek to enter their countries. The students' research and reflection results in considerable understanding of immigration worldwide, as well as realization that some issues are very difficult to resolve, there are various legitimate points of view, and the issues are dynamic, changing over time.

Such issues-centered global education must be planned within an overall framework so that the teacher builds a knowledge base, inquiry and perspective-taking skills, and a global perspective over the entire course. In the following section, we suggest such a framework.

An Issues-Centered Global Education Framework

In our experience and research, we have found that teachers approach issues-centered global education with four central objectives and use a variety of strategies to infuse issues-centered global education into conventional social studies. The teachers we work with commonly accept the strategies presented below as good practice.

1. Build a Foundation at the Beginning of the Course.

It is necessary for the teacher to make a conscious effort to establish a common vision of issues-centered global education at the beginning of a course. We cannot assume that students have already developed perspective consciousness, reflected upon their connections with other parts of the world, or engaged in open-ended inquiry. One to three weeks of inquiry and skill-building to develop a global perspective provide a jumping-off point for issues-centered instruction in any social studies course.

Develop perspectives consciousness through examination of conflicting perspectives on historical or contemporary events.

Example: Students are introduced to the concept of perspectives consciousness by first examining different views on an event in their school or community. Then the students are asked to analyze the perspective of a historical account. Without the students knowing it, half are given a firsthand account of Africans meeting Europeans on the Congo River from a European explorer's point of view, and the other half read an African chief's account. As they discuss their analyses in the class, it becomes apparent that something is wrong, that they don't have the same information. Each half then is given the other reading, and the teacher leads a discussion of the implications of multiple viewpoints on the study of history and contemporary events (Merryfield and Timbo 1983).

Develop global perspectives by examining information across local, national, regional, and global data bases.

Example: Students are first asked to brainstorm global problems or challenges that they believe to be today's most critical world issues. With this list on the board, the students are told that the room now represents the total land area of the earth and that they are its total population. Since the current population of the world is approximately five billion, the teacher can calculate the number of people each student represents by dividing the population by the number of students. Providing a global pie chart can help students visualize the U.S. "slice" of a little more than four percent of the world's peoples. As thirty-six percent of the class stands to represent the people in the world suffering from malnutrition, the teacher leads a brief discussion of global issues those people would value and the global consequences of that statistic. Then forty percent of the class stands to represent people who cannot read or write, while two percent (perhaps not even one student) represents those who have a college education.

Students are then grouped as sub-Saharan Africa (eight percent of the class), the Middle East and North Africa (five percent), Europe (ten percent), the former Soviet Union (six percent), North America (six percent), Latin America (eight percent), and Asia (fifty-six percent). Each region is given pretzels or candies to reflect food consumption patterns, gross national product, use of energy, or other indicators of the distribution and consumption of global resources and wealth. In discussion the teacher questions students about global issues that are priorities for the entire planet as well as those for Europeans, Asians, Africans, North Americans, etc. The activity can also focus on the demographics of world religions, ethnic or linguistic diversity, environmental issues or others that are of particular interest to students or relevant to course content. The teacher raises significant questions, such as "What patterns do you see in population and wealth distribution? How do you explain these patterns? How might a farmer in Nigeria or a textile worker in India explain these patterns? Students then reflect on the implications of examining such information and looking at issues from national, regional, multiple, and global perspectives. (The idea for this lesson came from Gary Smith [n.d.]. See other instructional resources on immigration and global distribution at the end of the chapter).

Begin a knowledge base and appreciation of local-global interconnectedness and interdependence.

Example: Several activities teach students about the ways their lives are connected to those of people all over the world. Students can examine a poster from Church World Service, entitled "Before you finish eating breakfast this morning," that depicts where the goods and services found in most American homes originate, along with data on the living conditions and wages of the people who produce those goods. For example, they learn that most baseballs and gloves sold in the United States are made in Haiti, where the infant mortality rate is one in five. People making less than 25 cents an hour assemble radios from Taiwan. Ralph Linton's "100 percent American" (1937) provides a similar historical view, and Robert Woyach's "A Day in the Life of Seymour Someday" (1981) takes us through an entire day of global interconnections. Francis Moore Lappe (1971) provides stimulating and controversial alternatives for how Americans can rethink their roles in the global consumption and distribution of food, agricultural resources, and technologies. Lessons structured around these readings usually awaken interest and raise questions about trade, fairness, dependency, and standards of living. Teacher questioning and debriefing is critical in such lessons if students are to recognize how their personal choices and decisions affect the lives of others around the world. (See Church World

Service listed at the end of the chapter.)

Many instructional materials exist to help students think globally. We recommend *Annual Editions: Global Issues*, *The State of the Earth Atlas* (Seager 1990), World Eagle's maps and monthly updates, Worldwatch Institute's annual *State of the World*, and the World Game. Publications such as *Opposing Viewpoints* and *Taking Sides* provide concise and timely articles on many global issues. All these materials and organizations are referenced at the end of the chapter.

2. Link Issues to Social Studies Content.

How do global issues fit into the already overloaded social studies curriculum? The substantive knowledge of global issues is essential for updating social studies topics for world citizenship. If we look again at the figure on page 179, we can see many relationships between these issues and K–12 social studies. Young children cannot study their community, state, or nation without learning about conflict, cooperation, cultural universals, and diversity. Issues such as the global assembly line, free trade and protectionism, and debt and loans are central to an economics course. U.S. history could not be taught without attention to self-determination, peace and security issues, immigration, or ethnic conflict. A world cultures or geography course can be organized by global issues so that students deal daily with connections across cultures and regions instead of the usual "four-weeks-on-Europe-then-three-weeks-on-Asia" sequence that isolates one world region from another despite their interconnectedness. Alan Backler and Robert Hanvey's (1986) *Global Geography* is an excellent example of a globally oriented geography textbook that connects world regions and cultures.

An issues-centered global approach enriches the social studies by teaching decision making from a global data base instead of a narrower one. We cannot expect adults to deal effectively with global complexity if we do not bring up our children and youth to recognize and take responsibility for their place in the world.

Choose global issues as the knowledge base for teaching social studies concepts and skills.

Example: In world cultures or geography, students can begin studying global issues central to the relationships between humans and the environment, such as agriculture, energy, or biodiversity. We have found that while the issues change somewhat from year to year given world and local events, teachers usually include in their world cultures/geography courses inquiry into population growth, hunger, national boundary disputes, environmental concerns, development issues, trade, and human rights. By focusing on these issues, students learn not only about the five themes of geography (location, place, movement, human-environmental interaction, and region) but also about the implicit interaction of the world's people as they deal with problems common everywhere. Parisi and LaRue (1989) is an excellent source for methods and materials for issues-centered global education.

Organize courses through an issues-centered global approach.

Example: Government and civics courses can be structured around current issues that American citizens face today, such as a unit entitled "Are Minority Rights Protected under Majority Rule?" While students study the structure and function of the U.S. justice system, inquiry is based on issues that are of current interest and concern. It soon becomes obvious to students that all of the "U.S. issues" are connected to events and concerns in the wider world. They learn that American "domestic" decisions, such as changing the prime interest rate or passing a law to regulate acid rain, have an impact on people in other countries. Other countries' decisions—the Iraqi invasion of Kuwait, the economic integration of the European Community, or impoverished Mexicans searching for a better life—continuously affect Americans.

Link social studies content to students' lives through global issues.

Example: Jobs and standards of living, the changing environment, cultural conflicts, and prejudice are issues of vital concern to our nation and to the immediate lives of students and their families. An issues-centered approach can bridge the gap between the global conflicts in the world and real-life concerns and problems in the local community. In each of these areas of concern, students can be encouraged to study and address problems at the local level by thinking globally and acting locally. Through inquiry projects, students can explore significant local issues related, for example, to a controversial development of a new mall on wetlands, the chamber of commerce's wooing of Japanese industry, or hostility over the growing population of Indochinese immigrants in an eastside neighborhood. Part of their research can be finding out how people in other communities have resolved such issues. Some of those communities could be Kyoto, Hong Kong, Berlin, or Gaborone. Putting local issues in a global perspective usually reveals a wealth of new insights and alternatives.

3. Plan Authentic and Personal Experiences.

Issues-centered global education is not simply academic knowledge studied for a test and then forgotten. It is real-life education that flows into one's after-school decisions and personal life. An essential part of global education is firsthand experience with people of different cultures, religions, ideologies, and worldviews. Such experiential education comes from bringing people into the classroom and students into the community through simulations of cross-cultural events and action learning (Wilson 1993a, 1993b).

Provide cross-cultural experiences.

Example: Students may interact with guests from other countries or cultures through a panel on multinational corporations or small group discussions with Chinese students from a local university, for example. As many social studies teachers move toward authentic assessment, international people and experts become consultants to students' research or authentic audiences for their exhibitions. One teacher with whom we work brought in South Africans and new Russian immigrants to work with his students during a research project on international conflict resolution (Shapiro and Merryfield 1995).

One of the most exciting new resources for cross-cultural interaction in schools is electronic communication. At Linden McKinley High School, teachers use computer technology so their students can "talk" with students in various countries through live computer conferencing and electronic mail. Using a split screen, students from Switzerland write about their views of conflicts in Bosnia as students in Columbus, Ohio, ask them questions. Electronic connections create a genuine global village. Teachers who have electronic networks available in their classrooms on a daily basis can have "global" discussions of historical events and contemporary issues. (See information on electronic networks such as PeaceNet, ConflictNet, Econet, and EnviroNet at the end of the chapter.)

Use simulations and role-playing.

Example: Many commercially produced simulations, such as *Starpower*, *The Road Game*, and *Baranga*, teach students about the fundamental conflicts from which global issues arise. In *Starpower* a three-tiered society is created through an unequal apportionment of wealth and power. Students trade and bargain, and the winners of the competition are the participants who accumulate the most points (wealth) by the end of the session. As in real life, some groups have advantages in resources and strategies and always accumulate more wealth. *The Road Game* focuses on the concept of territoriality as teams compete to build roads through each other's land. It helps students recognize how conflicts develop and grow as groups or nations pursue their own goals. *Baranga* is a card game in which students from different "cultures" play an international trading game from their own culture's interpretation of the rules. As conflicts and accusations of cheating occur, students come to appreciate the implications of people interpreting norms of international exchange in different ways.

BaFa BaFa (the high school version) and *RaFa RaFa* (middle school) are simulations in which students are divided into two groups and separated to develop two distinct cultures with different languages, customs, and beliefs. After they practice their culture, the groups send observers and then visitors over to the other group. The new culture seems rather scary, unfriendly, and, at times, bizarre to most visitors; students find that they have a hard time functioning in the other culture. Debriefing usually provides insights into difficulties in entering a new culture. (These simulations are referenced at the end of this chapter under resource organizations: American Forum, Intercultural Press, and Simile II.)

4. Plan Time for Reflection.

Inquiry-oriented learning and the development of a global perspective take time and concerted thought. Sometimes as teachers we rush from activity to presentation to assessment without ensuring that our students are internalizing new ideas, skills, and perspectives. Reflection is as important as research in inquiry-based global education. Teacher questioning in debriefing sessions, journal-keeping, letter-writing, and interviewing are strategies teachers use to help students think about and use new knowledge about their world and their place in it. Inquiry-based reflection

is critical in the development of perspectives consciousness, cross-cultural understanding, and a global perspective (Merryfield 1993a).

Help students think about and connect global issues to problems or concerns in their own lives.

Example: Students often experience intellectual and emotional conflict when, on the one hand, they are disturbed by acts of discrimination against someone of a particular ethnic group or religion in Bosnia or Germany, and yet, on the other hand, they see neighbors or friends treat people "different from themselves" with resentment or discrimination. Open inquiry into prejudice can address this dissonance. Students carry out such an inquiry project by first analyzing newspaper articles about local and national events and issues related to housing, jobs, hate crimes, education, immigration, and ethnic distribution. They work with intergroup attitude questionnaires and surveys, such as Bogardus's (1959) social distance instrument, to understand that negative attitudes exist within their own class. The students reflect in depth as they reconceptualize terms such as racism, prejudice, discrimination, ethnic group, ethnicity, minority group, stereotyping, social stratification, and social distance. They develop case studies that analyze situations representing these concepts.

Then students use their new understandings to examine Robert Coles's (1967) research about the effects of integration on the relationships between self-image and prejudice with children in the South in the 1960s. They observe the children's drawings and discuss Dr. Coles's interviews with the children and their families. This intense reflective study of a global issue of concern to students exemplifies issues-centered global education.

Use reflection to examine societies' assumptions, conventional wisdom, and controversial issues.

Example: Terrorism used to be one of those "it-happens-to-people-over-there" global issues. With the bombing of the World Trade Center and other acts of violence, international terrorism in the United States appears to generate a gut reaction against people of certain religious or ethnic backgrounds. To what extent can this reaction negate any progress that has been made in creating tolerance and reducing prejudice? One way to rebut the popular reaction to terrorism is to have students place terrorism in the contexts of U.S. and world history. Americans and others have used terrorism and other acts of political violence in order to effect change or express frustrations. Activities such as an examination of "one man's terrorist is another man's freedom fighter" force students to think about where their assumptions originate. Other lessons focus on the Sons of Liberty as "terrorists" from the British political point of view. Inquiry leads into multiple perspectives of other "freedom fighters" around the world, as well as the acts of the Ku Klux Klan, the Molly Maguires, the Weathermen, the Black Panthers, and recent "skinhead" and neo-Nazi groups. Students discuss such questions as: When, if ever, are political acts of violence justified? Has the U.S. government ever sanctioned terrorist acts? Was President Reagan's bombing of Libya or President Clinton's bombing of Iraq terrorism?

Reflection is built into the unit from the initial exploration of the meaning of "terrorism" in students' journals and their identification of hypothetical or real examples of terrorist actions or events that illustrate their definitions. Students then work in research groups to examine the Irish Republican Army, the Palestinian Liberation Organization, the Sons of Liberty, the Black Panthers, the Irgun and Stern Gang, Hezbollah, and the Shining Path. Their reports disclose more reflection on why people around the world commit acts of political violence and what can be learned by the consequences of those actions.

Conclusions

Issues-centered global education prepares young people for their adult decision making as citizens in a democracy who are inextricably linked to peoples and issues worldwide. In many ways such study is high interest, motivating, and as stimulating to the teacher as to the students. The processes of inquiry learning and the content of global issues do call for specialized knowledge. Most practicing teachers in today's classrooms did not receive a global education themselves, nor were they taught to teach an issues-centered approach in their preservice teacher education programs. Extensive in-service education and professional development can provide an intermediate step in the preparation of teachers, but ongoing updates and study of global events and historical interpretation are necessary. Issues-centered global educators must be

ready to take advantage of that student question "why is there so much violence in our lives?" as a teachable moment where global perspectives can provide insights into serious issues.

From our perspectives, the rationale for using an issues-centered global perspective approach to teaching social studies content lies not only in pragmatic and philosophic justifications but also in the reality of the classroom. Students must be motivated to learn, and for some students, that motivation must come from teachers' abilities to connect social studies content to their interests and felt needs. To the extent that those students can be challenged by a problem that affects them, the issues-centered approach provides that motivation. Once students see that "their problem" is indeed part of a larger problem that affects people like themselves in other parts of the world, they begin to think globally.

Acknowledgment

This chapter is the product of school-university collaboration in social studies and global education supported by the College of Education, The Ohio State University, and Columbus Public Schools, Columbus, Ohio.

References

Alger, Chadwick F., and James E. Harf. "Global Education: Why? For Whom? About What?" In *Promising Practices in Global Education: A Handbook with Case Studies*, edited by Robert E. Freeman. New York: National Council on Foreign Language and International Studies, 1986.

Anderson, Lee. *Schooling and Citizenship in a Global Age: An Exploration of the Meaning and Significance of Global Education*. Bloomington, Ind.: Social Studies Development Center, 1979.

Angell, Ann V., and Patricia G. Avery. "Examining Global Issues in the Elementary Classroom." *The Social Studies* 83(May/June 1992): 113–17.

Annual Editions: Global Issues. Guilford, Conn.: Dushkin Publishing Group. Published annually. Also available on Africa, China, India and South Asia, Japan and the Pacific Rim, the Third World, and world politics.

Backler, Alan, and Robert Hanvey. *Global Geography*. New York: Teachers College Press, 1986.

Becker, James M., ed. *Schooling for a Global Age*. New York: McGraw Hill, 1979.

Bogardus, Emory S. *Social Distance*. Yellow Springs, Ohio: Antioch Press, 1959.

Case, Roland. "Key Elements of a Global Perspective." *Social Education* 57(October 1993): 318–25.

Coles, Robert. *Children of Crisis*. Boston: Little, Brown and Co., 1967.

Dunn, Ross. *A World History: Links across Time and Place*. Evanston, Ill.: McDougal, Littell and Company, 1988.

Hanvey, Robert G. *An Attainable Global Perspective*. New York: Center for War/Peace Studies, 1975.

Kennedy, Paul. *Preparing for the Twenty-First Century*. New York: Random House, 1993.

____. *The Rise and Fall of the Great Powers*. New York: Random House, 1987.

Kniep, Willard M. "Defining a Global Education by its Content." *Social Education* 50(October 1986): 437–66.

Lamy, Steven L. "Global Education: A Conflict of Images." In *Global Education: From Thought to Action*, edited by Kenneth A. Tye. Alexandria, Va.: Association for Supervision and Curriculum Development, 1990.

Lappe, Francis Moore. *Diet for a Small Planet*. New York: Ballantine Books, 1971.

Levak, Barbara A., Merry M. Merryfield, and Robert C. Wilson. "Global Connections: An Interdisciplinary Approach." *Educational Leadership* 51(September 1993): 73–75.

Ralph Linton. "100 percent American." *The American Mercury*, 50 (1937) pp.427–429.

Merryfield, Merry M. "Science-Technology-Society and Global Perspectives." *Theory into Practice* 30(Autumn 1991): 288–93.

____. "Reflective Practice in Teacher Education in Global Perspectives: Strategies for Teacher Educators." *Theory into Practice* 32(Winter 1993a): 27–32.

____. "Responding to the Gulf War: A Case Study of Teacher Decision-Making." *Social Education* 57(January 1993b): 33–41.

____. "Shaping the Curriculum in Global Education: The Influence of Student Characteristics on Teacher Decision-Making." *Journal of Curriculum and Supervision* 9(Spring 1994): 233–49.

Merryfield, Merry M., and Richard C. Remy, ed. *Teaching about International Conflict and Peace*. Albany, N.Y.: State University of New York Press, 1995.

Merryfield, Merry, and Adama Timbo. *Teaching about Francophone Africa*. Bloomington, Ind.: The African Studies Program, 1983.

Opposing Viewpoints. San Diego, Calif.: Greenhaven Press.

Parisi, Lynn S., and Robert D. LaRue Jr. *Global/International Issues and Problems: A Resource Book for Secondary Schools*. Santa Barbara, Calif.: ABC-CLIO, 1989.

Reilly, Kevin. *The West and the World: A History of Civilization*. New York: Harper and Row, 1989.

Seager, Joni. *The State of the Earth Atlas*. New York: Simon and Schuster, 1990.

Shapiro, Steve, and Merry M. Merryfield. "A Case Study of Unit Planning in the Context of School Reform." In *Teaching about International Conflict and Peace*, edited by Merry M. Merryfield and Richard C. Remy. Albany, N.Y.: State University of New York Press, 1995.

Smith, Gary. *Cultural Sight and Insight: Dealing with Diverse Viewpoints and Values*. New York: American Forum on Global Education, n.d.

Stravrianos, L.S. *The World since 1500: A Global History*. Englewood Cliffs, N.J.: Prentice Hall, 1991a.

____. *The World to 1500: A Global History*. Englewood Cliffs, N.J.: Prentice Hall, 1991b.

Taking Sides. Guilford, Conn.: Dushkin Publishing Group.

Wilson, Angene H. "Conversation Partners: Gaining a Global Perspective through Cross-Cultural Experiences." *Theory into Practice* 32(Winter 1993): 21–26.

____. *The Meaning of International Experience for Schools*. Westport, Conn.: Praeger, 1993.

Woyach, Robert. *Bringing a Global Perspective to World Geography*. Columbus, OH: The Mershon Center, 1983.

____. "A Day in the Life of Seymour Someday." in *World Regions: The Local Connection*. Columbus, OH: The Mershon Center, 1981.

____. *Bringing a Global Perspective to American History*. Columbus, OH: The Mershon Center, 1983.

Resource Organizations

THE AMERICAN FORUM OF GLOBAL EDUCATION
120 Wall Street, Suite 200
New York, NY 10005
(212) 742-8232 Fax (212) 742-8752
A newsletter, ACCESS, *an annual conference on global education, and instructional materials such as* The Road Game *and Smith's* Cultural Sight and Insight: Dealing with Diverse Viewpoints and Values.

AMIDEAST
1100 17th Street, NW
Washington, DC 20036
(202) 785-0022 Fax (202) 822-6563
Videos, instructional materials, student and teacher abroad programs, and conferences.

CENTER FOR FOREIGN POLICY DEVELOPMENT
Brown University
Box 1948
Providence, RI 02912

(401) 863-3155
"Choices in the 21st Century Education Project,"
curriculum development, and teacher education.

CENTER FOR TEACHING INTERNATIONAL RELATIONS
University of Denver
University Park
Denver, CO 80208
(303) 871-3106
Graduate courses, teacher workshops, and instruction-
al materials such as Teaching about Human Rights:
Issues of Justice in a Global Age.

CHURCH WORLD SERVICE
PO Box 968
Elkhart, IN 46515
(219) 264-3102
Video loan service and free materials on global issues.

FOREIGN POLICY ASSOCIATION
729 Seventh Avenue
New York, NY 10019
(212) 764-4050 Fax (212) 302-6123
Scholarly works on foreign policy issues, the annual
Great Decisions *book with the* Teacher Activity
Book, *and teacher in-services.*

INTERCULTURAL PRESS
PO Box 700
Yarmouth, ME 04096
(207) 846-5168 Fax (207) 846-5181
e-mail: intercultural@mcimail.com
Publications on cross-cultural and intercultural
understanding and interaction such as Developing
Intercultural Awareness *and simulations, such as*
Baranga *and* Ecotonos.

MERSHON CENTER
Citizenship Development
   for a Global Age Program (CDGA)
1501 Neil Avenue
The Ohio State University
Columbus, OH 43201
(614) 292-1681 Fax (614) 292-2407
Instructional development such as Bringing a Global
Perspective to American History, Bringing a Global
Perspective to World Geography, World Geography
and National Security, *and* Approaches to World
Studies: A Handbook for Curricular Planners.

PEACE CORPS OF THE UNITED STATES
World Wise Schools Program
1990 K Street, NW

Washington, DC 20526
(202) 606-3970
Program linking Peace Corps volunteers with U.S. schools
(grades 3–12); instructional materials and speakers.

PROJECT ICONS (International Communication and
   Negotiation Simulations)
Department of Government and Political Science
Room 1127E
Tydings Hall
University of Maryland
College Park, MD 20742
(301) 405-4172 Fax (301) 314-9690
Multisite computer-assisted foreign policy simulations
and professional development programs for teachers.

SIMILE II
218 12th Street
PO Box 90
Del Mar, CA 92014
Simulations such as Starpower *and* BaFa BaFa.

THE SOCIAL STUDIES DEVELOPMENT CENTER
2805 E. Tenth Street
Bloomington, IN 47405
(812) 855-3838
Materials on global education such as Lessons from Africa.

SOCIAL SCIENCE EDUCATION CONSORTIUM (SSEC)
3300 Mitchell Lane, Suite 240
Boulder, CO 80301-2272
(303) 492-8154
Teacher in-services, study tours, and instructional
materials such as the Public Issues Series: American
Revolution, Public Issues Series: Immigration,
Global Geography, *and* A Look at Japanese
Culture through the Family.

STANFORD PROGRAM ON INTERNATIONAL AND
   CROSS-CULTURAL EDUCATION (SPICE)
Institute for International Studies
Littlefield Center Room 14C
Stanford University
Stanford, CA 94305-5013
(415) 723-1114 Fax (415) 723-6784
Teacher workshops, summer institutes, study tours,
curriculum development, and other publications.

UNITED NATIONS ASSOCIATION OF THE UNITED
   STATES OF AMERICA
485 Fifth Avenue
New York, NY 10017
(212) 697-3232 Fax (212) 682-9185

Model U.N. program, speakers, publications, and curriculum development. UNA-USA chapters are in many cities across the country.

UNITED STATES INSTITUTE OF PEACE (USIP)
1550 M Street, NW, Suite 700
Washington, DC 20005
(202) 457-1700 Fax (202) 429-6063
National Peace Essay Contest, monthly journal, resource library, grants and fellowships for graduate students and educators, and teacher workshops.

WORLD EAGLE
111 King Street
Littleton, MA 01460-1527
(508) 486-9180 or 1-800-854-8273
Fax (508) 486-9652
Monthly publication, World Eagle *(up-to-date comparative data, graphs, and maps) and series of reproducible atlases,* Global Perspectives Maps *and* Would You Believe? *maps.*

THE WORLD BANK
1818 H Street, NW
Washington, DC 20433
(202) 477-1234
Annual World Development Report, *the* Development Data Book, *and poster kits on population, life expectancy, and GNP per capita.*

WORLD GAME INSTITUTE
University Science Center
3508 Market Street
Philadelphia, PA 19104
(215) 387-0220 Fax (215) 387-3009
Publications, instructional materials, speakers, conferences, and the simulation, "World Game Workshops."

WORLDWATCH INSTITUTE
1776 Massachusetts Avenue, NW
Washington, DC 20036-1904
(202) 452-1999 Fax (202) 296-7365
e-mail wwpub@igc.apc.org
Publications on global environmental issues, such as the annual State of the World.

Electronic Networks

The PeaceNet, ConflictNet, EcoNet, and EnviroNet data bases described below are located at:
INSTITUTE FOR GLOBAL COMMUNICATIONS
18 DE BOOM STREET
SAN FRANCISCO, CA 94107
(415) 442-0220

- **PeaceNet:** Helps the peace, social justice, and human rights communities throughout the world communicate and cooperate more effectively.
- **ConflictNet:** A network of people dedicated to promoting the constructive resolution of conflict. ConflictNet enhances the work of groups and individuals involved in conflict resolution and links users to the worldwide conflict resolution community.
- **EcoNet:** Serves organizations and individuals working for environmental preservation and sustainability. It is a community of persons using the network for information sharing and collaboration in order to enhance the effectiveness of all environmentally oriented programs and activities.
- **EnviroNet:** A free computer network featuring conferences on environmental subjects, daily Greenpeace press releases, and environmental newsletters, as well as real-time e-mail. To gain access and establish an account, set modem to call 1-415-512-9108 (1200 or 2400 baud). For information, call (415) 512-9025.

ENVIRONMENTALISM AND ENVIRONMENTAL ISSUES

by Stephen C. Fleury and Adam Sheldon

Environmental issues are deceptively easy to understand because these struggles metaphorically represent the classic fight between the "good guy" and the "bad guy." But who the good guy is often depends on your vantage point and value system. In other words, unless you understand how social, economic, cultural, and political factors influence people's ideas about what should be done for the environment, your own perspective may remain at an ideological level. What follows in this chapter is an approach for teaching about environmental concerns to liberate rather than crystalize students' thinking.

Curricular materials on social problems often package controversies by presenting students with two or three pre-defined positions. The main intellectual task asked of students is to "take sides," a pedagogical exercise that reinforces their ideological predispositions instead of helping them develop an understanding of the complexity of different perspectives. Probing the value-laden assumptions that underlie various public perspectives about an issue is a significantly more fruitful approach for social studies educators, whose concerns for thoughtful citizenship should be paramount. With such an approach, the dynamics of power in society are more likely to surface—dynamics that otherwise are too easily concealed in the social studies curriculum.

Compared to traditional textbook accounts of how political decisions are made, engaging students in identifying assumptions and posing questions about specific environmental issues provides a more realistic understanding of why some policies are accepted and others are not. Unlike the consensus viewpoint of many textbook accounts, a policy analysis approach helps students clarify why so many people hold so

many different views. The clarification of the value basis of social knowledge should be no minor goal for social studies.

Environmental Issues as Policy Issues

Social issues become policy issues whenever people's beliefs clash over what should be done by those who have the authority to do something. Coplin and O'Leary (1981) have found that policy issues can be successfully clarified by asking *who* is attempting to influence public policy-making, what is the environmental *condition* targeted by the policy, and what is the *proposed* or *contended* policy? They emphasize the importance of being specific when describing each of these components. For example, vague terms such as "big corporations" or "environmentalists" are not very useful for enhancing our understanding of the value conflicts involved in an environmental issue. Instead, we need to know *who* in the industry is speaking? *What* is their personal interest in the outcome? *What* will they personally lose or gain? *Whose views* do their statements reflect: Their own? Official company policy? *How organized* are the people who hold an environmental viewpoint? *What access* do they have to sources of information that are used in making a policy? *To what extent* are the sides aligned according to social class, gender, or race? Responses to these types of questions help when analyzing the implicit value conflicts. These conflicts are often more revealing of the parameters of the policy problem than the so-called hard data that is involved.

Environmental policy issues are even more interesting when we realize that all information, regardless of how "scientific," is value-laden. Scientific information has traditionally been credible with policy-makers because it appears objective and technical. The scientific community, however, increasingly recognizes that the creation and presentation of scientific findings are influenced by human values.[1] The task for educators when analyzing environmental policies—especially social studies educators—is to evaluate the relative merits of technical knowledge within the context of human concerns.

Resources for Studying Environmental Policy Issues

Resources for studying environmental topics abound for social studies teachers. Issue-oriented problems are readily available from newspapers. For example, within a typical three-week period, the *Christian Science Monitor* carried stories about the clear-cutting of virgin woodlands in the Pacific Northwest, the "slash-and-burn" elimination of tropical rain forests for "development" purposes in South America, the difficulties of regulating nuclear energy, the promotion of human genetic engineering, the permitting of hormone injections for greater food production in dairy and beef animals, and the fears of harmful electromagnetic radiation for students and teachers who attend schools adjacent to large power lines.

Here we begin with a newspaper article about an environmental disagreement among some members of the Sierra Club, one of the oldest (and more conservative) organizations concerned with the health of the wilderness. Their disagreement can be used to model a policy-issue analysis for identifying many of the conflicting values often surrounding environmental issues. The identification of conflicting values in this matter will help generate relevant questions about environmentalism that will be useful in the study of other environmental issues.

Issues in the Environmental Movement?

A 26 December 1993 *New York Times* byline reads "Logging Policy Splits Membership of Sierra Club." (p. 20). The leadership of the oldest, largest, and most powerful environmental organization in the United States was embroiled in an internal struggle over environmental goals. The director of the Sierra Club's office in Seattle, who is also the club's "chief forest lobbyist in the Pacific Northwest," sold $10,000 worth of second-growth timber from a ten-acre tract of land he owned in Washington. Critics from chapters

in other states were abhorrent of this sale, claiming, according to the article, that it "shows how far the leadership of the environmental movement has strayed from the ideals of an earlier time."

Explaining that the future of logging lay in the harvest of managed second-growth forests, the director was surprised at the negative press he was receiving. He was not violating any of the Sierra Club's policies. Indeed, the director was not violating the club's logging policy, but the policy itself was a highly contentious item for the membership. In 1990, New York State's 40,000-member Atlantic Chapter proposed the "virtual end to logging in the Northern Rockies." The ensuing debate in the national organization galvanized support of chapters in other states including California, Oregon, Montana, Illinois, and Indiana. The resulting policy change called for the prohibition of logging virgin forests on private or public lands, except for second-growth timber in national forests. Remaining dissatisfied, the leadership of the New York chapter sponsored legislation pending in the national organization to stop "all logging in national forests, period."

The explosive feelings involved in the fight over the Sierra Club's logging policy reveal a couple of significant issues in the study of environmentalism. The first issue is that "environmentalism" includes a range of beliefs and ideas. Many environmentalists are eager to negotiate with the power brokers of society, but others are not. Some believe nature should be preserved in a pristine form. To them, environmental groups should warn and mobilize citizens to do something about environmental dangers. These goals should not be "compromised," regardless of political and economic impairments to society. One club member, Jim Bensman, exemplifies this position:

> Our job is not to facilitate compromise. That is what we pay politicians to do. Our job is to stand up and fight for what we believe is best for the environment.

Others believe, however, that negotiations and compromises are more effective, and that intractable demands are a "turn-off." The head of the Sierra Club in Idaho remarks:

> A hundred years of thoughtful, decent, and pragmatic work in conservation stands

threatened by the rise of ideology, zealotry, and the power of true believers.

A second issue is that environmentalism inescapably includes political and economic issues as well as scientific and cultural ones. Environmentalists are increasingly part of the political mainstream. The *New York Times* article explains that many former environmental group members are in charge of the "very government agencies they have long fought." This change of vantage point, it is alleged, creates dissonance in the way they think about environmentalist ideas. While many environmental policies are successfully lobbied, implementation is problematic. Officials find themselves frequently criticized for disrupting "the lives of ordinary Americans." One official interviewed for the article, a Sierra Club member, poignantly describes the difficulty of supporting certain environmental positions and then facing neighbors whose livelihoods are adversely affected. Accusations of "compromise" and "selling out" notwithstanding, Carl Pope, executive director of the Sierra Club, argues the need for environmentalists to play both inside and outside political circles in order to have influence.

The Identification of Questions to Study

Environmental brouhahas such as the above-mentioned timber sale reveal deep fissures in the American value system. Our economic system produces an enormous appetite for affordable natural resources. Multi-national industries as well as individuals who own small parcels of land are capable of coveting natural resources for private gain, despite the environmental detriments that might be shared by everyone. Environmental conflicts increasingly force us to reconsider definitions of ownership, property rights, and ethics. This leads to questions that arise in the study of almost every environmental issue.

Why are some environmental actions considered thoughtful and pragmatic, and others ideological and zealous? Environmental ideas that complement the prevailing social and economic structure are usually considered pragmatic and thoughtful. The best example is the goal of "sustainable development." The emphasis on educating students about sustainable development has grown since the visibility brought to it

in 1980 by the *Global 2000 Report to the President* and in 1990 by Lester Brown's *State of the World: A Worldwatch Institute Report on Progress toward a Sustainable Society* (Disinger 1990). The question we pose is "Sustainable for what?" And for whom?

One response might be "sustainable for economic development," that is, to continue the transformation of agrarian and small-scale economics into an ever-larger, more interdependent and more cost-efficient production of consumer goods. The idea of development has brought unprecedented wealth, comfort, and lifestyles for many people in the industrialized world. Most people wish to maintain this level of prosperity and, theoretically at least, extend it to others throughout the world. The use of the terms "first world" and "third world" implies an objective evaluation of the state of various economic systems in the world. In reality, these descriptions are laden with implicit values, one of which is the idea that industrial development is both a desired and necessary goal of all people and all nations.

Disinger (1990) suggests that "sustainable development" may seem to be an oxymoron for anyone familiar with the increasing demands that our growing population makes on the world's decreasing resources. Faith that natural resources are inexhaustible or that we can always create a technological solution to problems has eroded among many people in the industrialized world. A growing number of people are concerned about managing our environmental resources in order to preserve our economic values. This environmental position is sometimes called "anthropocentric," as opposed to the "ecocentric" beliefs of deep ecologists.

"Deep ecology" utilizes phrases about the "natural rights" of all living creatures (as well as of nature), about the need to develop an "ecological consciousness," and about "challenging the assumptions" that undergird the worldview of Western society. This language may seem far from the mainstream of social studies education, yet Roderick F. Nash, in *The Rights of Nature* (1989), reminds us that deep ecological principles are based on perhaps the "the single most potent concept" in American political thought— that of liberty:

> Liberalism explains our national origins, delineates our ongoing mission, and

anchors our ethics. Natural rights is a cultural given in America, essentially beyond debate as an idea.

Theodore Rozak (1978) argues that the *"natural environment is the exploited proletariat, the downtrodden nigger of everybody's industrial system. …Nature must also have its natural rights"* (p. 32).

2 **How does environmentalism differ from earlier attempts at conservationism?** Traditional conservationist attempts were anthropocentric—that is, an overriding concern for saving resources was to ensure their availability for use by humans in the future. The additional moral tone of environmentalism distinguishes it from previous conservationist attempts. Placing environmental concerns within the political and moral framework of the United States makes every environmental problem the concern of all citizens. The potential to draw upon the moral outrage of citizens makes ecocentric reasoning a powerful social force in the environmental movement:

> Old-style conservation, recast in ethical terms and plugged into the American liberal tradition, became the new, radical environmentalism. (Nash 1989, 10)

Nash argues that elevating environmental protection to a moral plane is a natural outgrowth of the application and extension of ethics in Western society. Note his description and explanation of the concept of expanding rights (1989, 7) in Figure 1.

One might take issue with Nash's proposition that rights have truly been extended to each of the groups in Figure 1, but his general point is important, because it makes deep ecology understandable as part of the American political tradition.

3 **What is the role of scientific knowledge in environmental disputes?** Deep ecologists align science with the engines of a technocratic society. Because scientific knowledge leads to specialization, it leads to the creation of expertise. The authoritarianism of expertise is rejected by deep ecologists, who correctly perceive that issues of human values are ignored in many policy decisions. The authoritativeness of scientific information is often misused to bolster unques-

Figure 1: The Expanding Concept of Rights

Nature
  Endangered Species Act, 1973
Blacks
  Civil Rights Act, 1957
Laborers
  Fair Labor Standards Act, 1938
Native Americans
  Indian Citizenship Act, 1924
Women
  Nineteenth Amendment, 1920
Slaves
  Emancipation Proclamation, 1863
American Colonists
  Declaration of Independence, 1776
English Barons
  Magna Carta, 1215
Natural Rights

tioned, unbridled technological and economic development.

> The ultimate value judgment upon which technological society rests—progress conceived as the further development and expansion of the artificial environment necessarily at the expense of the natural world—must be looked upon from the ecological perspective as unequivocal regress. (Nash 1989, 48)

But science is somewhat maligned in this scenario, omitting the important role it has played in the development of an ecological consciousness. Grove (1992) writes:

> Arising in a search for utopia, European-based environmentalism first took shape in the mid-18th century. At that time, colonial enterprise began to clash with Romantic idealism and with scientific findings. (p. 42)

Scientists were hired to inventory natural resources during the industrial exploitation of distant islands. As a result of meetings among a growing organization of scientists, various theories about environmental degradation stimulated early conservation policies for these islands. A major breakthrough occurred when French scientists were able to explain local climate changes as the result of the deforestation of these islands (and later to explain the desertification of Africa). The science of ecology has consistently grown to support the idea that everything is interconnected.

4 Should environmental policies proceed incrementally, or do impending environmental dangers require revolutionary changes in the ideas, values, and behaviors of all citizens? Most environmentalists share the belief that resources are ultimately finite and that the earth can absorb only a limited amount of pollutants. They differ, however, in terms of how immediate they perceive the threat and in how drastically they think human activities need to change. Environmentalists who favor sustainable development count on educating and preparing citizens to employ new technologies to solve environmental problems. On the other hand, deep ecologists promote a worldview that calls for living in harmony with nature, recognizing that the world's supplies are finite, increasing recycling, reducing material needs, and limiting resource-consuming technology to necessary human activities.

Relevance to the Social Studies Curriculum

The growth of natural rights, the expansion of ethics, the uses and misuses of scientific knowledge, the economic basis of social policies, and the practice of policy-issue analysis are all enduring topics in the study of environmental issues. These topics also permeate social studies content. Heath's (1988) suggestions of how studies of science and technology can be infused into the social studies curriculum are applicable to environmental issues.

First, teachers can supplement their regular topics with special activities that relate to environmental issues. For example, deep ecology and Nash's (1989) theory of the expansion of ethics and rights can serve as a catalyst for a structured class discussion when students are studying the foundations of the American Constitution or the contemporary status of civil rights. Another approach would be to examine how the selective use of agricultural research since the 1930s lead to the increasing productivity of American farmers, but at a long-term cost to the quality of life in both rural and urban areas by increasing pollu-

tion and forcing the migration of millions of displaced farmers to urban centers.

Environmental issues can also be infused by constructing an environmental unit around a selected social studies topic. For example, students might study the "ecological imperialism" of Europeans. To what degree was the successful global expansion of European cultural, economic, and political influence due to their unintentional transformation of the ecological system? Here one could involve students in studying how microbes, bacteria, and viral strains may have been primarily responsible for the domination of Europeans over the American continents. Such an approach, of course, might help students question whether sacred nationalistic values such as "Manifest Destiny," the "Puritan work ethic," and the "frontier spirit" are really necessary for an enduring sense of democracy.

Another infusion technique is to offer a separate course on the study of environmental issues. The benefit of this approach would be that teachers and students might feel unrestrained by having to "cover" pre-determined content. The problem, of course, is that an issue-centered approach would be symbolically, if not formally, marginalized to one place in the curricular offerings.

The following is an example of a teacher-constructed text and activities for use with students in *examining* the problem of water pollution.

An Issue-Centered Analysis: Water Pollution

The world's freshwater supply has two things in common with other resources on this planet: it is limited, and it is inequitably distributed. When looking at the global map, one is quick to see that water is the major part of the exterior of our planet. This appearance of abundance, however, is deceiving. People may believe that we have an inexhaustible supply of water, but fresh, drinkable water is only a small portion of the earth's total water supply. In fact, if all the earth's water was represented by a gallon jug, the available freshwater would equal just more than a tablespoon! That's less than one-half of 1 percent of the total. Ninety-seven percent of the earth's water is ocean saltwater, another two percent is locked in the polar ice caps and glaciers. More freshwater exists in reserves under the earth's surface, but most of it is too deep to economically tap (National Geographic 1993).

Consider the following excerpt from *World Resources: 1990-91*:

> The quantity of [water] is fast becoming an issue in some areas. Although essentially a renewable resource on a global scale, freshwater is being extracted from some river basins at rates approaching those at which the supply is renewed and from some underground aquifers at rates exceeding natural replacement. Many human activities have high water use rates. As the human population has grown, so have withdrawals of water for agriculture, industry, and municipal use. A new element of uncertainty is potential changes in precipitation and hence in freshwater resources due to changes in climate caused by human *activities*.

Creating a Framework for Studying Water Pollution Issues

In preparing to involve students in examining the water pollution problem described in the above passage, we created a conceptual framework by drawing upon ideas about environmentalism that were discussed earlier in this chapter. Developing this framework provides teachers an opportunity to analyze the content of the above passage, explore what they already know about the topic, and seek other sources, if necessary.

Humans depend on water for survival. Although human uses for water vary, the need for water is constant. The level of this dependency is clear when one realizes that a human can live for a month without food, but will die in less than a week without water. This constant need has created a number of concerns regarding the supply of water on our planet. Issues such as the effect of population on water quality, and questions as to the amount of usable water available will be raised in the adjoining text.

Water tends to attract population centers. Looking at a map of the world's population, one can see that a high percentage of the major population centers are located near large water supplies. Australia's four largest cities—Sydney, Melbourne, Brisbane, and Adelaide—are all situated on its coastline. Lakes and rivers have an equally important effect on inland population centers. Chicago, Pittsburgh, and Cleveland are three of the largest U.S. inland cities, and they are all adjacent to major rivers or lakes.

Water is essentially a renewable resource, but the human rate of extraction is in danger of exceeding its natural replacement rate. Population increases create an exponential increase in water pollution. Doubling the size of the population does not merely double water pollution. In an increasingly industrialized, urbanized society, more water is used personally and commercially.

Environmental policy issues contain opposing or contradictory positions about environmental decisions. Policies are governmental decisions applying to a large number of people. Within any given group, individual experiences give rise to differing points of view. Some points of view are philosophical differences over the relationship between humans, technology, and nature. How a particular view becomes the dominant view in policy decisions is the content of policy analysis.

The sides of an environmental policy issue are often portrayed as "hard" scientific data versus the emotional concerns of citizens. Initiators of proposed policies tend to have arguments that are supported with scientific information. This is a necessary part of the public policy-making process, but one which can be intimidating to non-scientists. Citizen groups usually do not have the power and resources to create an acceptable scientific challenge. Lacking "credible information," oppositional groups are easily cast by the media as weak, emotional, reactive "protesters," or "NIMBYs"—"Not in my backyard"—whose ecological attitudes are shaped by their own self-interests. On an interesting note, self-interest is considered a virtue when teaching classical economics and political theory, but seems to lose this meaning when studying environmental issues.

The public policy analysis model can help develop a clearer understanding of environmental issues. Environmental policy issues are best understood by analyzing the conditions giving rise to the environmental issue, the assumptions of the proposed policies, and the various perspectives of the key players.

In contrast to any scientific-sounding thoughts, angry citizens, irate over the prospect of their children drinking from toxic wells, personify the emotional furor that can accompany water pollution concerns. Equally as emotional, yet somewhat more restrained, are the industrial moguls who quote calculations of long-term economic gain and diminish the negative environmental effects of a given policy. This scenario can be seen in an issue of *National Geographic*, where some Mississippi residents are trying to stop a rayon-making plant from opening:

> There is anger upon this riverfront land. Voices are being raised in the small churches where cardboard fans stir the steamy air of summer, and what was once so easy for a company desiring to locate along the lower Mississippi has become a challenge, even for a giant like Formosa Plastics Corporation. Formosa Plastics planned to build the world's largest rayon-making plant on 1,800 acres of land in the Wallace area. But there were those in the community with this concern for the health of the people and the environment, and one of them is Wilfred Greene. He formed the RAP group, for River Area Planning, which challenged Formosa at every turn until the company abandoned its plans. "We certainly believe there can be something done to help the community economically," Greene said, "but we don't want the chemical plants coming in here to destroy our lives."

This case however, may seem to be an exception, as industry usually wields more economic resources to lobby their position than the residents of a particular area. Hard, "objective" scientific data is usually considered stronger than the emotional "subjective" opposition that citizen groups often utilize as their main weapon. The ability to present a position is often more important than the substance of the position itself. The ability to marshal scientific data in support of a position has political clout. Given this contention, it becomes imperative for individuals to be not only aware of how scientific knowledge relates to power, but to have the skills to analyze this knowledge when necessary. This poses interesting questions for students to pursue:

- What does objective scientific knowledge mean?
- Why should the passion and emotion of citizens lessen the credibility of citizens?

These types of questions allow us to touch upon the value-laden basis of science and to ask who has access to technological information. We can also examine the different methods used to decide an environmental dilemma.

Summary

The questions and activities above demonstrate that teaching about environmental issues

Activity One: Initial Questions

The textual passage above raises a host of questions that can stimulate both classroom discussion and learning activities. One of the most attractive features of analyzing easily available content resources is that activities will emerge from the questions and interests of both the students and the teacher. Every question is a potential activity. As students are engaged by questions related to what they have read, teachers will develop a sense of what the students truly desire to investigate. This enables teachers to find out what the student really wants to learn and also to avoid simply teaching what he or she thinks the students need to know. Standard material such as geography and history are combined with activities that engage the student's preexisting interest. For example:

- What major urban areas are located near water?
- What major urban areas are not located near water?
- How does water help an urban area?

These questions lend themselves directly to a geography activity or unit. Activities could center around population center identification, including demographic data analysis. These lessons could address the concept of human dependency on water. Other questions generated by the students or initiated by the teacher might involve students in analyzing assumptions:

- How much of the Earth's water supply is readily usable?
- What does "readily" usable mean?
- What makes a resource, a resource?

These questions can lead to interdisciplinary lessons about the water cycle or an imagination-based activity dealing with creative inventions that might increase and/or perpetuate the Earth's water supply.

- Why is water inequitably distributed?
- Is there anything that can be done to change this inequity?
- Is it our responsibility to change this inequity?
- Is water free?

These questions involve students in an environmental dilemma, and also encourage them to examine their own system of beliefs as they relate to these environmental issues.

Activity Two: The Application of a Policy Analysis Model

The objectives of this lesson are to have students utilize the policy analysis model to examine water pollution issues, and also to demonstrate presentation skills while pretending to persuade a superfund comptroller to designate money to clean up water pollution in their area.

Students are divided into two groups. Each group is given an article about one area's attempt to clean up a water pollution problem (see "Boston Harbor Clean Up" 1993, "Clean Up Lures People to Charles River" 1993). Each groups' initial task, after reading the article, is to determine the social and economic conditions, the policy players, proposed or actual policies, and critical issues in their article. The next step is to have the groups construct a presentation to convince a government superfund comptroller to allocate funds to clean up their area. The presentations can be delivered to the "comptroller"—the teacher, or maybe a guest speaker on water pollution—who can then evaluate their effectiveness.

Activity Three: Examining Science and Citizenship

An underlying problem in agreeing how to analyze environmental policies is that many students intuitively "turn-off" arguments involving scientific arguments as the final arbiter. Inevitably, some students may feel constrained by the appearance of a purely "logical" method; these may be the same students who become mentally disengaged in a traditional textbook-driven classroom. Their response may not be dissimilar to a large portion of the public who feel disenfranchised by the governing use of mechanisms in society.

Policymakers recognize that how a problem is defined has a great deal of influence on its outcome. Water pollution is an environmental issue that often brings about very strong feelings on all sides. Why does water pollution evoke such strong feelings? Usually the opportunities for jobs and financial needs are pitted against preserving a quality of life. This is a seemingly trite, yet very important question.

can be accomplished with simple and relevant resources. Newspapers and magazines provide a steady supply of current policy debates. Most of these debates can be placed within the context described in the first part of this chapter, namely that the positions of "sustainable development" and "deep ecology" are thoroughly embedded in the political and economic foundations of our American culture. Changes in our cultural ideas about science, ethics, economics, and politics are bound to influence what is meant by "environmentalism," and a close study both of the issue of environmentalism and of various environmental issues in the social studies curriculum will enhance the overall preparation of citizens in our contemporary world.

References

"Boston Harbor Clean Up." *Christian Science Monitor,* March 17, 1993.

"Clean Up Lures People to Charles River." *Christian Science Monitor,* August 9, 1993.

Coplin, W. D. and M. K. O'Leary. *Basic Policy Studies Skills.* Croton-on-Hudson: Policy Studies Associates, 1981.

Devall, B. and G. Sessions. *Deep Ecology: Living as if Nature Mattered.* Layton, Utah: Gibbs Smith, 1985.

Disinger, J. F. "Environmental Education for Sustainable Development?" *Journal of Environmental Education.* (1990)

Grove, R. H. "Origins of Western Environmentalism." *Scientific American,* (July 1992): 42-47.

Heath, P. A. "Science/Technology/Society in the Social Studies." *Clearinghouse for Social Studies/Social Science Education,* Bloomington, IN.

"Logging Policy Splits Membership of Sierra Club." *New York Times,* December 26, 1993.

Nash, F. F. *The Rights of Nature: A History of Environmental Ethics.* Madison: University of Wisconsin Press, 1989.

Rozak, T. *Person/Planet.* Garden City, NY: Doubleday, 1978.

---. *World Resources: A Guide to the Global Environment.* A report by the World Resources Institute in collaboration with the United Nations Environment Programme. New York: Oxford University Press, 1990.

Woyach, R. B. "Ecopolitical Issues and the Secondary Curriculum." *Paper presented at the Annual Convention of the International Studies Association,* Atlanta, GA. ERIC 269313.

---

[1] Thomas Kuhn's *Structure of Scientific Revolutions* (1962) is frequently referred to in discussions about the human value orientation of scientific work.

Below are excerpts of a reply made by Chief Seattle to President Franklin Pierce, who, in 1854, made an offer for a large area of Indian land:

> How can you buy or sell the sky, the warmth of the land? The idea is strange to us. If we do not own the freshness of the air and the sparkle of the water, how can you buy them?... We know that the white man does not understand our ways. One portion of land is the same to him as the next, for he is a stranger who comes in the night and takes from the land whatever he needs. The earth is not his brother, but his enemy, and when he has conquered it, he moves on. He leaves his fathers graves behind, and he does not care. His father's graves and his children's birthright are forgotten. He treats his mother the earth, and his brother, the sky, as things to be bought, plundered, sold like sheep or bright beads. His appetite will devour the earth and leave behind only a desert. ... This we know: the earth does not belong to man; man belongs to the earth. This we know: all things are connected like blood which unites one family. All things are connected.

Lesson: CHIEF SEATTLE'S REPLY
Objectives:
- Students will be able to compare and contrast environmental views of the nineteenth and twentieth centuries.
- Students will identify predictions made by Chief Seattle, and check their accuracy.

Activities:
1. Read Chief Seattle's Reply (see attached text).

2. Each student is asked to make a list of similarities and differences regarding the environmental views of the nineteenth and twentieth centuries. These lists will be shared to determine if the class has identified any consensus items. The student generated lists should lead to some interesting discussion items, such as:
  - How have environmental views changed over the past two centuries? How have they not changed?
  - To what degree could Chief Seattle's claims be justified as "scientific," or do you consider them emotional statements?
  - What do you think Franklin Pierce thought about Chief Seattle's reply?
  - Who uses the environment more effectively, Chief Seattle or Bill Clinton? (This may seem obvious at first, but when one asks what is meant by "effectively," discussion can intensify.)

3. Students will identify two predictions from the reading. The predictions will be analyzed for their accuracy in today's world. For example, in reference to the white man, Chief Seattle states, "His appetite will devour the earth and leave behind only a desert." One could make a case to agree or disagree with this statement, depending on how one interprets it. This exercise can create some very rewarding discussion.

Part Five: Social Sciences

Introduction by Patricia G. Avery

In this section, the authors address issues-centered instruction within traditional social studies subject matter: anthropology, psychology and sociology; civics and government; economics. The authors describe how significant concepts and central issues related to the disciplines can be translated into engaging, powerful classroom teaching and learning. In addition, the authors recommend a range of exemplary resources for the development of issues-based instruction.

The Ligon and Chilcoat chapter describes an issues-centered orientation to the study of anthropology, sociology and psychology. One is struck by the degree to which the concepts in these subject areas—such as culture, prejudice, race, social stratification and deviance—reflect the very issues about which the public expresses grave concern. It is indeed ironic that the behavioral sciences, perhaps best equipped for helping students develop a framework for analyzing personal and public issues, are those courses least often required of high school graduates.

In the classrooms envisioned by Ligon and Chilcoat, controversial social issues are the focal point of instruction. The authors problematize traditional inquiries in the behavioral sciences: "How does a religion influence a part of the culture?" becomes "What role should religion play in forming public policy in a democratic society?" and "How are cultures different?" becomes "How might different cultures live together peacefully?" Using the Sweeney-Parsons Controversial Social Issues Model, Ligon and Chilcoat describe how one issue—intelligence testing—might be addressed in the classroom.

In an approach similar to that of Ligon and Chilcoat, the article by Avery, Sullivan, Smith and Sandell takes traditional questions posed in civics and government courses and reframes them to reflect an issues orientation. The authors use the organizing questions from the National Standards for Civics and Government as a foundation for developing issues-based inquiries. A question from the standards, "What is the relationship of American politics and government to world affairs?" provides the springboard for questions such as "What principles seem to guide U.S. relationships with other countries?" and "What principles should guide those relationships?'

A central theme in the chapter on civics and government is that democracies depend on citizens' abilities to deal with the conflict inherent in politics. Opportunities to experience and understand conflicting perspectives are an essential part of civic education. Avery and her co-authors advocate using structured controversy and cooperative learning to develop students' perspective-taking abilities.

Perspective-taking is also a theme developed by Armento, Rushing and Cook in their chapter on issues-centered economics instruction. The authors suggest that students analyze economic issues according to three major philosophical stances: conservative, liberal and radical. Students can develop a better understanding of the complex dimensions of economics issues by using these conceptual lenses.

Armento, Rushing and Cook present an Issue-Oriented Teaching Model that is grounded in current research on teaching and learning. In a departure from the traditional "principles of economics" orientation of most economic courses, the model focuses on having students develop interdisciplinary perspectives and contextual understandings. Although the model was designed by the authors to address economics issues, it could easily be adapted to other subject areas.

Throughout this section, the authors pose complex questions for exploring issues in the classroom: Do industrialized countries have a "social responsibility" to improve the standard of living of persons and countries with low per capita income? Should the United States trade with countries that have a poor human rights record? How should people with different backgrounds form institutions to support the public good? What are our public responsibilities as citizens in a democracy?

The questions—for which there are no "right" answers—require students to grapple with multiple sources of data, draw concepts and generalizations from many disciplines, analyze conflicting perspectives, and develop their own informed opinions.

As each of the authors notes, in-depth teaching and learning experiences require a special learning environment. Ligon and Chilcoat stress that the controversial issues discussions must take place in a trusting, respectful classroom environment. Avery and her co-authors note that an open classroom climate—one that supports and encourages diverse viewpoints—promotes more democratic attitudes. And finally, Armento et al. describe a "culture of thinking" in the classroom, characterized by curiosity, skepticism, persistence, and contemplation. In short, the adoption of an issues-centered approach cannot be separated from a re-examination of the cognitive and affective dimensions of the classroom. We hope these chapters give readers ideas for developing issues-centered content and environments.

ISSUES-CENTERED APPROACHES TO TEACHING CIVICS AND GOVERNMENT

by Patricia G. Avery, John L. Sullivan, Elizabeth S. Smith, and Stephen Sandell

The major job was getting people to understand that they have something within their power that they could use, and it could only be used if they understood ... how group action could counter violence even when it was perpetrated by the police or, in some instances, the state. My basic sense of it has always been to get people to understand that in the long run they themselves are the only protection they have against violence or injustice. ...People have to be made to understand that they cannot look for salvation anywhere but in themselves. (Lerner 1972, 347)

These are the words of Ella Baker, an activist in the civil rights movement. Baker was a consistent voice in organizing and empowering African Americans from the early 1930s until her death in 1986. She worked tirelessly for the National Association for the Advancement of Colored People (NAACP), the Southern Christian Leadership Conference (SCLC), the Student Non-Violent Coordinating Committee (SNCC), and finally, for the dismantlement of apartheid in South Africa. Baker was frequently the only female in strategy sessions of the African American leadership, and once remarked that she "wasn't one to say yes [just] because [directions] came from the Reverend King" (Cantarow 1980, 84). Although she was a quite vocal and able advocate, she often downplayed her role because she maintained that movements were more effective when associated with ideas and groups rather than a handful of charismatic leaders.

It is doubtful that Baker's voice is heard in most civics and government classes. Her struggles, like those of countless other individuals

committed to social change, do not fit well within the traditional "structures and functions of government" framework.

In this chapter, we briefly examine traditional civics and government instruction, and suggest that it is inadequate for citizens in a multicultural, pluralistic democracy. We argue that issues-centered teaching and learning is particularly appropriate for the civics classroom. Finally, we turn most of our attention to approaches, methods, and materials that support issues-focused civics instruction and provide a central place for the stories of citizen advocates such as Ella Baker.

The Traditional Civics/Government Curriculum

For most students, civics and government classes are associated with diagrams of "How a Bill Becomes Law" and the three branches of government—a reflection of a curriculum that emphasizes the structures and functions of government rather than the skills and processes of politics. In the traditional civics class, democratic values are discussed in the abstract, controversial issues are ignored, conflict is absent, and participation forms the "invisible" part of citizenship education (Stone 1992; Zellman and Sears 1971). Political socialization within schools generally, and civics classes specifically, supports a culture that "marginalizes" the role of conflict and dissent in a democracy (Merelman 1990).

Not surprisingly, most research on political socialization suggests that the traditional formal civics curriculum has a limited impact on students' civic knowledge and attitudes. More than twenty-five years ago, a national survey of young people in grades 10 through 12 concluded that the modest effect of the standard civics course was "so minuscule as to raise serious questions about the utility of investing in government courses in the senior high school, at least as these courses are presently constituted" (Jennings, Langton, and Niemi 1974, 181). Reviews since that time suggest little change in the civics curriculum (Ehman 1980; Ferguson 1991).

A review of eighteen civics and government textbooks by People for the American Way offers a devastating critique of the traditional curriculum:

> What is missing, in a word is controversy. Eighty percent of the civics books and half of the government books minimize conflict and compromise. The dynamic sense of government and politics—the fierce debates, colorful characters, triumphs and tragedies—is lost. Controversies like school prayer and civil rights that have ignited passions at all points along the political spectrum are ignored or barely mentioned. The vitality of political involvement and the essential give and take between people and their elected officials is neglected. (Carroll et al. 1987, i)

Unfortunately, textbooks play a major role in shaping classroom instruction. In the 1988 National Assessment of Student Progress (NAEP), more than 86 percent of the students in the eighth and twelfth grades reported that reading from the textbook was the most common instructional format in their civics class (National Assessment of Student Progress 1990).

Rather than encouraging active political involvement, the traditional civics curriculum succeeds in portraying the political sphere as a complex entity quite removed from students' lives. When participation *is* discussed, it is usually limited to conventional forms of participation, such as voting and letter writing. Young people thus come to view their political role as that of fairly passive bystanders.

The Goals of Civics Instruction

What *should* be the goals of civics and government courses in a multicultural, democratic society? We suggest two primary goals for learning and teaching in the civics classroom. **First, classes should foster the ability to recognize and analyze significant social and political issues, to imagine the short- and long-term consequences of alternative actions, and to evaluate both personal and social costs and benefits of available policy options.** As Guttman (1987) argues most eloquently, deliberation about public issues is critical to the sustenance of democracy. She suggests that the "ability [to reason about politics] is so essential to democratic education that one might question whether civics courses that succeeded in increasing political trust, efficacy, and knowledge but failed to increase the ability of students to reason about politics were indirectly repressive" (p. 107). The public schools can and should provide a forum for developing deliberative skills; the civics classroom is a most appropriate place for fostering reflection on public issues.

The second primary goal is that students become familiar with a repertoire of strategies for meaningful participation in the democratic process. Civics classes or related community service activities should provide opportunities for students to participate in making choices that affect their communities. The traditional conception of political participation focuses on electoral behavior. During the past thirty years, however, students of political socialization have begun to recognize the significance of advocacy, service, and community politics. It is this broader view of political participation that should be reflected in our civics classrooms.

A Rationale for Issues-Centered Civics Instruction

Issues-centered instruction in the social studies is consistent with calls for greater depth and less coverage in our social studies curriculum (Newmann 1990), for teaching for understanding as opposed to knowledge (Perkins and Blythe 1994), for the inclusion of multiple perspectives (Banks and Banks 1989; Tetreault 1989), and for "authentic" learning opportunities and assessment (Newmann and Wehlage 1993). Each of these educational trends supports a sustained examination and analysis of complex public problems.

We believe that an issues-centered approach is *particularly* appropriate for civics instruction. Since politics involves the "authoritative allocation of values" (Easton 1953) and the exercise of power (Dahl 1957), all forms of politics inevitably entail conflict. In fact, a recent textbook about U.S. politics defines politics as "the way people with different values fight over what government should, and should not, do" (Dawson 1987, 19). There are always "winners" and "losers" in the

Table 1: National Standards for Civics and Government Organizing Questions for Grades 5 through 12

I. What are civic life, politics, and government?

A. What is civic life? What is politics? What is government? Why are government and politics necessary? What purposes should government serve?

B. What are the essential characteristics of limited and unlimited government?

C. What are the nature and purposes of constitutions?

D. What are alternative means of organizing constitutional governments?

II. What are the foundations of the American political system?

A. What is the American idea of constitutionalism?

B. What are the distinctive characteristics of American society?

C. What is American political culture?

D. What values and principles are basic to American constitutional democracy?

III. How are the values and principles of American constitutional democracy embodied in the government established by the Constitution?

A. How are power and responsibility distributed, shared, and limited in the government established by the United States Constitution?

B. What does the national government do? (grades 5-8 only)

C. How is the national government organized and what does it do? (grades 9-12 only)

D. How are state and local governments organized and what do they do?

E. What is the place of law in the American constitutional system?

F. How does the American political system provide for choice and opportunities for participation?

G. Who represents you in local, state, and national governments? (grades 5-8 only)

IV. What is the relationship of American politics and government to world affairs?

A. How is the world organized politically?

B. How has the United States influenced other nations and how have they influenced American politics and society?

C. How do the domestic politics and the constitutional principles of the United States affect its relations with the world? (grades 9-12 only)

V. What are the roles of the citizen in the American political system?

A. What is citizenship?

B. What are the rights of citizens?

C. What are the responsibilities of citizens?

D. What civic dispositions or traits of private and public character are important to the preservation and improvement of American constitutional democracy?

E. How can citizens take part in civic life?

Source: Center for Civic Education, *National Standards for Civics and Government* (Calabasas, Calif: Center for Civic Education, 1994). Available from the Center for Civic Education, 5146 Douglas Fir Road, Calabasas, Calif. 91302-1467. Phone: 818-591-9321.

political process, and losers do not often accept defeat without a struggle. Nations, therefore, are democratic not because they ignore conflict or because there is so much consensus that deep conflicts seldom arise, but rather because they have found a way to allow open yet controlled expression of the conflicts that do arise. A large part of their success is that political conflict takes place within a broader consensus on the "rules of the game."

An issues-centered curriculum should enhance students' internalization of this procedural consensus, and at the same time it ought to give them experience with, and an understanding of, political controversy. They should understand that, when conflict takes place among participants who accept the procedural norms that allow for open conflict, it enhances democracy and has the potential to prevent the evolution of permanent "winners" and "losers" in the political process by promoting respect and understanding of different points of view.

An issues-centered civics curriculum should also emphasize how the rules of the game can be changed if they are found wanting. Again, however, some level of consensus must exist on how this is to be done. If there are permanent "losers" in a democratic process, and if the processes of change are thwarted by a permanent and large majority, then such a consensus is unlikely.

In short, then, structuring conflict into an issues-centered curriculum is an essential feature of citizenship education. Students should have experience with reflection about both their political values and their political self-interest. They should also have some practice asserting these values and interests in the face of opposition. Ideally, the curriculum would provide guidelines on how to separate the individual from his or her ideas, and assertive advocacy from aggression or selfish advancement. Learning to "agree to disagree" may be a seldom-learned mode that helps students not only become better citizens but also more effective in their personal relationships.

Approaches, Methods, and Materials for Issues-Centered Civics Instruction

Introducing an Issues-Centered Perspective of Civics and Government

We suggest that an issues-centered civics or government course begin with a careful analysis of several social and political movements in the United States. This is the approach taken by an outstanding text entitled *Civics for Democracy* (Isaac 1992). In this text, students learn about the history of five citizen movements: the civil rights, labor, women's rights, consumer, and environmental movements. Students can see that change often requires the long-term commitment of individuals, such as Thurgood Marshall and Mother Jones, as well as the organized efforts of groups, such as Greenpeace and the United Farm Workers of America. They can become familiar with the wide range of participatory techniques used by citizen movements, including lobbying, boycotting, and demonstrations. Most important, however, ordinary citizens become the focal point of discussion rather than governmental institutions.

Developing an Issues-Centered Civics or Government Course

In this section, we describe how we might develop an issues-centered civics or government course. We use the *National Standards for Civics and Government* (1994) as an organizing framework upon which to pose engaging and often controversial issues (see Table 1). Whenever possible, we try to relate our inquiries to what we believe is one of the most significant concepts in political education—political participation.

❶ THE ROLE OF GOVERNMENT. For example, the first set of questions might lead to an exploration of the role of government in society. How has the role of government changed over time? How have various social groups and organizations viewed the role of government? What purposes should government serve? What purposes should government not serve? Who should decide?

Students might begin an exploration of these questions through traditional literary offerings such as *Lord of the Flies* and *To Kill a Mockingbird*, as well as less well known works such as *Roll of Thunder, Hear My Cry!* and *Summer of My German Soldier*. Literature often provides a "safe context" in which to begin discussion of complex issues (Spurgeon 1991/92). From fiction, students could move on to oral histories (e.g., John Tateishi's *And Justice for All: An Oral History of the Japanese-American Detention Camps*), biographies (e.g., *The Autobiography of Malcolm X*), and nonfiction (e.g., *A Different Mirror: A History of Multicultural America*). Finally, court cases such as *Plessy v. Ferguson* (1896), *Brown v. Topeka Board of Education* (1954), *Miranda v. Arizona* (1966), and *Regents of the University of California v. Allan Bakke* (1978) provide excellent primary source material for examining the role of government. Throughout their inquiry, students should be judging the degree to which government furthers democratic principles and ideals.

❷ CIVIC CULTURE. The second set of organizing questions focus on our civic culture. Students might develop their own description of the civic culture in the United States by examining data such as the following:

- Contributions to environmental, health, youth, and social action groups increased by 25 percent from 1987 to 1991; donations to the arts, education, and religion declined. There were significant increases in donations from one age group—18-to 24-year-olds; contributing was highest among those who had been active in student government or youth groups, had done volunteer work, had wanted to make a change in society, or had witnessed good deeds by someone they admire. (Franklin 1992)

- One in five U.S. high school students say they want to be president of the United States; three-fourths say they want to be president of a company. (Conn and Silverman 1991, 39)
- When asked if they believe in free speech for everyone, about 90 percent of U.S. citizens will say yes. When asked about a more specific situation, such as the Ku Klux Klan appearing on public television or communists marching in their neighborhood, less than 30 percent support the rights of free speech and assembly. (McClosky and Brill 1983)
- Although a majority of women in the United States say they "believe in equal rights for women," only a minority (33 percent) are willing to identify themselves as feminists and, thus, to identify themselves as active participants in the women's movement. (Cowan, Mestlin, and Masek, 1992)
- While most U.S. citizens with formal education beyond high school favor equality between blacks and whites in principle, in practice they appear to be no more likely than other, less well educated citizens to support government policies that promote racial equality. (Jackman 1978 and 1981)
- While the first African American female entered the U.S. Senate in January 1993, voter turnout among African Americans in the 1992 election decreased by 13 percent from the previous presidential election. ("The Voters" 1992)

Based on the preceding data, how might one describe the political culture in the United States? What motivates people to take an active role in political life? What are the obstacles to active participation? What are the short- and long-term consequences of participation and non-participation?

3 POLITICAL POWER. The underlying theme of the third set of questions is political power. In the United States, one of the fundamental principles of our Constitution is the "separation of powers." What is the purpose of the "separation of powers"? What if there were no "separation of powers"? How might the outcome of the Watergate affair or the Iran-contra scandal have been different?

What constitutes an "abuse of power"? Have abuses of power occurred in U.S. history? What mechanisms are designed to prevent the abuse of power? To what degree have they been effective? To explore these questions, students might read excerpts from *It Did Happen Here: Recollections of Political Repression in America* (Schultz and Schultz 1989). The book includes case studies of political repression, ranging from the Palmer Raids to the McCarthy Era to Wounded Knee.

4 INTERNATIONAL ISSUES. The fourth set of questions focuses on the role of the United States in world affairs. What principles seem to guide U.S. relations with other countries? What principles *should* guide those relations? In a structured controversy format, students might explore the role of human rights in shaping U.S. foreign policy. Structured controversy is a powerful method for analyzing a wide range of civic issues; we describe it in some detail here, using the issue of human rights and foreign policy as an example, but encourage interested teachers to read further about this approach.[1]

Structured controversy, an adaptation of cooperative learning, offers participants a format for analyzing complex social and political issues. Table 2 summarizes the basic procedures used in a structured controversy exercise. For example, suppose students were given the following question for value inquiry: Should the United States trade with countries that have poor human rights records? The teacher divides the class into heterogeneous groups of four. Two persons in each group are assigned the pro position, while the other two research the con position. Typically, the teacher suggests readings that will help students develop a given position, and encourages students to explore additional resources. Students outline their position and plan ways to advocate it to the opposing pair. Each pair presents arguments for their position, while the opposing pair listens, takes notes, and asks questions for clarification. The pairs then switch sides and present the opposing side's view. In the final phase, students abandon their "positions" and try to reach a group consensus on the issue based on the merits of the arguments presented.

The question of whether the United States should trade with countries that have poor human rights records is an excellent issue for illustrating the role of controversy and conflict in

Table 2: Sample Structured Controversy Lessons

1. The teachers and/or students select a significant civic issue about which there exists a range of competing, well-articulated views.
   Example: Should the United States trade with countries that have poor human rights records?
2. The teacher groups students into fours, and assigns two students to prepare the "pro" side and two students to prepare the "con" side.
3. The teacher gives students lists of readings to help them organize their positions. For example:
   "Back to Business on China Trade," *New York Times,* May 27, 1994.
   "Clinton's Call: Avoid Isolating China on Trade and Rights," *New York Times,* May 27, 1994.
   J. Donnelly, *Universal Human Rights in Theory and Practice* 20 (Ithaca, N.Y.: Cornell University Press, 1989).
   "Pressures Rise over China's Trade Status," *New York Times,* May 20, 1994.
   A. M. Rosenthal, "License for Torture," *New York Times,* May 20, 1994.
4. Students read the materials, and plan strong, persuasive arguments to present to the "opposing" side. The teacher might give students with little experience in this approach examples of good arguments.

Most Favored Nation Status: Sample Pro Arguments

- The United States will have a greater influence on human rights through regular educational, economic, and cultural contacts with China than by isolating and antagonizing the Chinese government.
- Economic sanctions on China will mean the loss of jobs for U.S. workers.

Most Favored Nation Status: Sample Con Arguments

- Economic sanctions have been an effective tool in promoting human rights in other countries.
- U.S. companies may profit from high tariffs placed on Chinese clothing and textiles.

5. Students on the "pro" side present their position; the opposing pair listens, takes notes, and asks clarifying questions. (The amount of time allotted to presenting positions is predetermined.)
6. Students on the "con" side present their position; the opposing pair listens, takes notes, and asks clarifying questions.
7. Students switch sides, i.e., students on the "pro" side adopt the "con" position and students on the "con" side adopt the "pro" position.
8. Students present their "new" positions to one another.
9. Members of the group drop their positions and try to arrive at a consensus on the issue. Oftentimes, students will develop a third position that reflects elements of both sides.
10. Groups present their consensus statements to the class.

Source: Adapted from D. S. Johnson, R. T. Johnson, and K. A. Smith, *Active Learning: Cooperation in the College Classroom.* Edina, Minn.: Interaction Book Company, 1991.

---

a democracy and the fact that in the political process there are often "winners" and "losers." For example, in the debate over whether to extend Most Favored Nation Status to China, a country that has consistently been found to violate its citizens' human rights—such as the right to voice opposition to the government—there has been considerable conflict over the question of whether the U.S. government should allow free trade with China. One argument in favor of trading with China, despite the country's human rights abuses, is that trade will increase economic, cultural, and educational contacts with China and will thus allow the United States to have a greater influence in that country and a greater role in promoting respect for human rights. It has also been argued that the Chinese government will be unwilling to improve their human rights record if they feel they are being "bullied" into this by the United States through trade policies. Additionally, U.S. corporations, such as American Telephone and Telegraph and Boeing, have found big markets in China, which in turn can mean more jobs for workers in the United States.

Conversely, economic sanctions have proven in other cases to be an effective tool in prompting countries to improve their human rights record (e.g., South Africa). Additionally, the United States has more trade imbalance with China than with any other country. U.S. companies, such as the textile corporations that are unable to compete with cheap labor in China, may stand to gain if high tariffs are placed on Chinese clothing and textiles.

Students could be encouraged to think of other arguments for and against trading with a country that violates human rights abuses—e.g., do trade barriers only punish the citizens while having little effect on the government and officials of the offending country? Additionally, students could read newspaper articles and editorials, government documents outlining the U.S. position over the years on human rights issues, and books that deal more generally with human rights. Students could then debate from the opposing positions of a U.S. corporation that would gain from free trade with China, a U.S. corporation that would be hurt by free trade, and from the positions of a government official and of a human rights advocate.

In the end, students could try to reach a group consensus on the issue, and through the use of procedural rules predetermined by the students, make a final policy decision. An exercise such as this would illustrate for students not only the complexity of politics but also the notion of dealing with conflict and controversy through agreed upon "rules of the game." Students will learn how the rules of the game can benefit one group (e.g., the majority) while disadvantaging another (e.g., the minority), and how checks can be put into the system to protect minority rights and interests.

When compared to conventional debate or individual research projects, structured controversy is more effective in promoting student retention of material, perspective-taking abilities, and critical thinking skills (Johnson, Johnson, and Smith 1991). We suggest that it is an ideal vehicle for exploring complex, multifaceted civic issues, such as the relationship between human rights and foreign policy. It is also consistent with our understanding of the role of conflict and controversy in a democratic society.

5 THE "GOOD CITIZEN." We believe that the fifth set of organizing questions address the most crucial aspect of civic education for young people, and hence it is this area to which we devote most of our attention. The fifth question, "What are the roles of the citizen in the American political system?" encourages students to examine the nature of citizenship in a democratic society. A topic that seems ideally suited to illustrate the issues-centered approach to civics

education is that of "good citizenship." What is citizenship? What are the rights and responsibilities of citizens? How can citizens participate in public life? These kinds of questions are fairly common in most civics curricula. As Schwartz (1984) has shown, however, the prior issue of how we conceptualize and understand concepts such as "political participation" and "citizenship" can predetermine our answers to these former kinds of questions, and can do so in rather non-obvious ways. It may be important, then, to begin by helping students think through (in an active way) how they want to understand the concept of citizenship.

One of the primary goals of civics education in the United States has been to teach students to be "good citizens" in our democracy. While the notion of a "good citizen" is often associated with such behaviors as voting or obeying the law, a basic exercise is to identify, discuss, and debate various understandings of citizenship and the forms of political participation available to and required of a good citizen. Rather than adopt a conventional understanding of citizenship in the United States, a better way to teach about citizenship might be to focus students' attention on the questions "what does good citizenship mean to different people?" and "what do different people think are individuals' rights and responsibilities as citizens?"

Recent political science research offers a variety of conceptualizations of citizenship that can be used to open a debate among students about the role of a good citizen. For example, Conover and Searing (1993) outline two broad conceptualizations of citizenship that have emerged from various political theorists over the centuries: civic republicanism and a contractual version of citizenship. The civic republican perspective mandates a highly active and participatory citizenship rooted in the communal ties that bind individuals together. According to this conceptualization, "citizens ... not only have a right to participate in politics but are also expected to do so, both for their own good and for the good of the community" (p. 4). Conversely, the contractual or "legalistic" perspective outlines a very limited role for the citizen, a role defined more by rights than responsibilities.

In addition to outlining the more theoretical conceptualizations of citizenship, many scholars are interested in identifying the different ways ordinary citizens understand citizenship.

Elizabeth Theiss-Morse (1993), for example, uses a method called Q-analysis in order to discover how individuals conceptualize citizenship. With Q-methodology, individuals evaluate statements (usually developed by the researcher) about a concept according to the degree to which each statement reflects their understanding of a concept, such as "good citizenship."

Four perspectives of citizenship emerged in the statistical analysis. Theiss-Morse labels these the Representative Democracy perspective, the Political Enthusiast perspective, the Pursued Interests perspective and the Indifferent perspective. The Representative Democracy perspective conceptualizes good citizenship as an informed vote based on the belief that political participation and politics are important and that individuals can make a difference in determining policy outcomes. The Political Enthusiast perspective defines good citizenship as participation in a variety of activities—writing letters, protesting, even civil disobedience—that may be more powerful than simply voting in hope of ensuring that individuals' interests are being met by the government. This perspective also encourages citizens to monitor and question the policy decisions of elected officials. The Pursued Interests perspective envisions good citizenship as political participation by those who are informed about politics, and also as active participation in the family and community. It stresses group as opposed to individual political activity. Finally, the Indifferent perspective strictly conceptualizes good citizenship as casting an informed vote.

Theiss-Morse found that an individual's political behavior was highly correlated with his or her conceptualization of citizenship. For example, she finds that "the Political Enthusiasts are most likely to be involved in unconventional activities, while the Indifferent are most likely to shun such activities" (Theiss-Morse 1993, 369). Overall, this research suggests that not only scholars but also ordinary individuals hold a variety of conceptualizations of citizenship. And, these varying conceptualizations of the rights and responsibilities of citizens are likely to affect the varying forms of political behavior people feel obliged to perform as citizens.

This research suggests that one way to enhance citizenship skills is to focus civics instruction around the issue of defining citizenship. Before students can become "good citizens," they need to struggle with the question of

what they think good citizenship entails. Students should be encouraged to question various conceptualizations of citizenship—particularly the most common conceptualization of the passive citizen who votes dutifully—to determine for themselves what they feel are the rights and responsibilities of a good citizen and to consider the consequences and implications of these rights and responsibilities. For example, does a citizen who fails to meet her responsibilities forego some of her rights? One way to encourage them to think more deeply, and perhaps also to act on their thoughts, is to present information about how scholars and other citizens conceptualize "good citizenship."

Orit Ichilov (1990) argues that "as for existing citizenship education, it seems fair to conclude that it directs youngsters to a rather narrow definition of the citizen role" (p. 22). However, it is apparent from the research discussed above that citizenship is a multifarious concept that can be (and has been) understood and manifested in a variety of forms. We believe that by focusing students' attention on the variety of conceptualizations of good citizenship, students can begin to consider more thoughtfully the meaning of citizenship for them and the consequences of that meaning for their lives. The survey presented in Table 3 is comprised of selected statements used by Theiss-Morse (1993), and could be used to stimulate students' thinking about their conceptions of good citizenship.

6 REFLECTIVE DELIBERATION. Underlying the entire set of organizing questions should be a commitment to developing students' skills in reflective deliberation and participation. Throughout any course on civics or government, students should have multiple opportunities to analyze issues of significance to them. The questions shown in Table 4 serve as a guide for analyzing issues ranging from the nutritional value of school cafeteria food to U.S. immigration policy.

Each question embodies fundamental concepts in civics and government. For example, the question "Who seems to have an interest in the issue and its implications?" might prompt a discussion about the role of interest groups in a democracy. The question "Who can do something about the issue?" might encourage students to examine the role and structure of government. Similarly, the question "Is there adequate opportunity for all to demonstrate their beliefs and

Table 3: Survey of Conceptions of Citizenship

Indicate your agreement with the statements below by choosing one of the following responses:

SA = Strongly Agree, A = Agree, D = Disagree, and SD = Strongly Disagree

Given the fact that there's only so much the average person can do...

1. Citizens should let the government know their opinions in several ways: by voting; by writing letters to government officials; and by joining groups that are for or against a government policy. (PE)

2. Citizens should, nevertheless, participate in politics, especially by voting, so they can represent their own political interests. (RD)

3. Citizens should focus their energy on political issues they are really concerned about and then join groups that lobby on these issues. (PI)

4. Most citizens should not waste their time participating because only the wealthy and powerful can influence what the government does anyway. (I)

5. Citizens should still learn about politics by keeping in contact with members of Congress, by voting, by discussing politics, and so on. (RD)

6. Citizens should join political interest groups if they want to have an impact on government decisions. (PI)

7. Citizens should be involved in their local community by joining neighborhood groups and organizations that try to influence local officials about community problems or issues. (PE)

8. Citizens should still regularly participate by voting and discussing politics so government officials have to be responsive to the public. (RD)

9. Citizens should view politics as the making of any important group decisions, which means politics exists everywhere. They should be involved in making all of these decisions. (PE)

10. Citizens should talk about politics often with other citizens to hear different points of view on issues. (PI)

11. Citizens do not need to participate because, ultimately, all of the important decisions are being made by big corporations anyway, not by the government. (I)

Note: These statements reflect a particular conception of citizenship:
PE = Political Enthusiast; RD = Representative Democracy; PI = Pursued Interests; I = Indifferent.
Source: E. Theiss-Morse, "Conceptualizations of Good Citizenship and Political Participation,"
Political Behavior 15 (1993).

---

interests?" lends itself well to an analysis of the role of minority rights within a democratic society. An examination of these concepts *within the context of studying a specific issue* seems to us a more powerful approach than the more traditional presentation of concepts as isolated bits of information. We hope such an approach will help students to develop a deeper understanding of the role of these concepts and issues in a democracy.

Inserting Issues-Centered Content into the Traditional Curriculum

Due to time constraints or district guidelines, many teachers may prefer to adopt a more limited issues-oriented approach. Exemplary materials are available to educators, many of which require only two to three class sessions.

Two resources—*National Issues Forums* (NIF) pamphlets and *Opposing Viewpoints* booklets—offer diverse perspectives on critical social and political issues. The NIF pamphlets, developed by the Kettering Foundation, provide a framework for discussing enduring public issues. More than twenty booklets, including college, adult, and abridged editions, have been developed on topics such as abortion, poverty, the environment, and health care. Each pamphlet describes three or four commonly held positions on a given issue. For example, the pamphlet on criminal violence includes three positions: "Deterrent Strategy: Getting Tougher on Criminals," "Preventive Strategy: Attacking Crime at Its Roots," and "Selective Incapacitation Strategy: Targeting the Violent Few." The costs and benefits of each alternative are presented, as are relevant results from major research studies.

National Issues Forum materials are used by adults in communities across the country. The pamphlets are also quite appropriate for secondary students and have been endorsed by the National Council for the Social Studies as part of the council's Public Issues Program. Whether conducted with adults or secondary students, forums focus on a careful deliberative process, much in the spirit of the classic town hall meeting. At the close of the forum, participants are encouraged to choose a position. Their decisions at this point should reflect a careful consideration of the complexities of the issue.

Similar to the NIF materials, *Opposing Viewpoints* pamphlets encourage students to consider a range of perspectives on important social and political issues. Excerpts from articles written by "experts" or noted voices on a subject are collected and presented for student discussion. The topics of the pamphlets include such diverse issues as racism, the role of the U.S. government, gun control, and numerous other topics. A range of opinions—moderate, radical, minority—are presented on each issue to provide balanced, thoughtful, and convincing arguments on all sides of the debate. The *Opposing Viewpoints* Series can be an effective tool for teaching students how to think critically about issues that are important to their life and role as U.S. and world citizens.

Structuring the Issues-Oriented Civics Class

We believe that an issues-centered civics curriculum will be most effective when it is frequently organized around cooperative learning groups. Cooperative learning groups are an important means by which to teach students values related to being a citizen in a democracy. A cooperative learning situation forces students to learn how to deal effectively with controversy and conflict among individuals within a group setting. Although the concept of cooperation is emphasized, students learn to assert their views within the group, and the reward structure of cooperative learning exercises increases the chances that students will also learn to compromise and cooperate once different views are expressed within the group. This parallels the political process in democracies. As in a democracy, the students must work together in order to resolve their differences and develop solutions to

Table 4: Issues-Centered Discussions of Government and Politics

Understanding the Issue
- What's the issue?
- Have there been similar issues in the past in the United States? Outside the United States?
- Why is it important?
- Who seems to have an interest in the issue and its implications?
- Do interested people/groups define the issue differently?
- Who can do something about the issue?
- Do we need to change laws or consider enforcement, regulation, or issues implementation of present laws?
- Who can or might participate in the discussion?
- What circumstances limit participation of some people or groups?

Identifying Alternatives
- How shall the alternative choices be debated?
- What are our goals in this problem-solving effort?
- Who agrees or disagrees?
- Who influences opinion?
- Is there adequate opportunity for all to demonstrate their beliefs and interests?
- What are the relative values of the costs and benefits we anticipate?

Moving toward Decision and Action
- Who will make the final decision and how?
- How are those people accountable to others they represent?
- How can we influence the final decision?
- Do we feel strongly enough about the issue to take action?
- How will we evaluate the effectiveness of our action?

problems. They learn to handle conflict within a broader framework of consensus, which is necessary in order for individual members of the group—indeed for the group itself—to succeed.

Cooperative learning has also been found to enhance individuals' ability to see the world from another's perspective. Individuals gain "the ability to understand how a situation appears to another person" (Johnson, Johnson, and Smith 1991, 25), which is, in turn, useful for students in their roles as citizens and their willingness and ability to respect the rights and interests of others. This form of empathy and perspective taking is essential to handling serious conflict and disagreement within a broader framework of agreement. Cooperative learning groups are thus particularly well suited for the learning of civics and democratic values.

Regardless of content or grouping strategies, however, civic learning within a closed classroom environment is not likely to promote democratic orientations. A number of studies indicate that classroom climate has a strong impact on students' political values and attitudes (Allman-Snyder, May, and Garcia 1975; Ehman 1977, 1980; Hahn, Tocci, and Angell 1988; Torney, Oppenheim, and Farnen 1975). At the secondary level, young people's perception of a more "open" classroom climate is associated with higher levels of political interest, efficacy, and confidence (see Harwood 1992 for a review of the research). Similarly, issues-centered discussions that encourage the expression of diverse viewpoints tend to promote more democratic attitudes (Ehman 1980; Leming 1985; Torney, Oppenheim, and Farnen 1975). On the other hand, an emphasis on rote memorization and patriotic rituals (e.g., reciting the Pledge of Allegiance) is associated with higher degrees of authoritarianism and less democratic attitudes (Torney, Oppenheim, and Farnen 1975).

In sum, if we are to develop a supportive yet critical democratic citizenry, we must do more than adopt an issues-centered approach. The issues-centered approach, however, may serve as the catalyst for re-examining content, methods, pedagogy, and classroom climate. It is reflection on these issues that may help us find a place for the "Ella Bakers" in our classrooms.

References

Banks, J. A., and C. A. M. Banks, eds. *Multicultural Education: Issues and Perspectives.* Boston: Allyn and Bacon, 1989.

Cantarow, E. *Moving the Mountain: Women Working for Social Change.* Old Westbury, N.Y.: Feminist Press, 1980.

Carroll, J. D., W. D. Broadnex, G. Contreras, T. E. Mann, N. J. Orenstein, and J Steihm. *We the People: A Review of U.S. Government and Civics Textbooks.* Washington, D.C.: People for the American Way, 1987.

Conn, C., and H. Silverman, eds. *What Counts: The Complete Harper's Index.* New York: Henry Holt and Company, 1991.

Conover, P. J., and D. D. Searing. *Citizenship and Political Psychology.* Paper presented at the Annual Political Psychology Conference, University of Illinois at Urbana-Champaign, June 1993.

Cowan, G., M. Mestlin, and J. Masek. "Predictors of Feminist Self-Labeling." *Sex Roles* 27 (1992): 321-330.

Dahl, R. "The Concept of Power." *Behavioral Science* 2 (1957): 201-205.

Dawson, P. *American Government.* Glenview, Ill.: Scott Foresman, 1987.

Easton, D. *The Political System.* New York: Knopf, 1953.

Ehman, L. H. *"Social Studies Instructional Factors Causing Change in High School Students' Sociopolitical Attitudes over a Two Year Period."* Paper presented at the annual meeting of the American Educational Research Association, New York, April 1977.

———. "The American School in the Political Socialization Process." *Review of Educational Research* 50, no. 1 (1980): 99-119.

Ferguson, P. "Impacts on Social and Political Participation." In *Handbook of Research on Social Studies Teaching and Learning,* edited by James P. Shaver. New York: Macmillan, 1991.

Franklin, R. "National Study Finds Surprising Donation Trends." *Minneapolis Star Tribune,* October 27, 1992.

Guttman, A. *Democratic Education.* Princeton, N.J.: Princeton University Press, 1987.

Hahn, C. L., C. Tocci, and A. Angell. *"Five-Nation Study of Civic Attitudes and Controversial Issues Discussions."* Paper presented at the International Conference on the Social Studies, Vancouver, B.C., June 1988.

Harwood, A. M. "Classroom Climate and Civic Education in Secondary Social Studies Research: Antecedents and Findings." *Theory and Research in Social Education* 20, no. 1 (1992): 47-86.

Ichilov, O., ed. *Political Socialization, Citizenship Education and Democracy.* New York: Teachers College Press, 1990.

Issac, K. *Civics for Democracy: A Journey for Teachers and Students.* Washington, D.C.: Essential Books, 1992.

Jackman, M. R. "General and Applied Tolerance: Does Education Increase Commitment to Racial Integration?" *American Journal of Political Science* 22 (1978): 302-324.

———. "Education and Policy Commitment to Racial Integration." *American Journal of Political Science* 25 (1981): 256-269.

Jennings, M.K., K.P. Langton, and R.G. Niemi. "Effects of the High School Civics Curriculum." In *The Political Character of Adolescence,* edited by M. K. Jennings and R. G. Niemi. Princeton, NJ: Princeton University Press, 1974.

Johnson, D. W., and R. Johnson. "Conflict in the Classroom: Controversy and Learning." *Review of Educational Research* 49 (1979): 51-70.

———. "Classroom Conflict: Controversy vs. Debate in Learning Groups." *American Educational Research Journal* 22 (1985): 237-256.

———. *Creative Conflict.* Edina, Minn: Interaction Book Company, 1987.

---. *Cooperation and Competition: Theory and Research.* Edina, Minn.: Interaction Book Company, 1989.

Johnson, D. S., R. T. Johnson, K. A. and Smith. *Active Learning: Cooperation in the College Classroom.* Edina, Minn.: Interaction Book Company, 1991.

Leming, J. S. "Research on Social Studies Curriculum and Instruction: Interventions and Outcomes in the Socio-Moral Domain." In *Review of Research in Social Studies Education,* 1965-1983, edited by W. B. Stanley. Boulder, Colo.: ERIC Clearinghouse for Social Studies/Social Science Education, 1985.

Lerner, G., ed. *Black Women in White America: A Documentary History.* New York: Pantheon Books, 1972.

McClosky, H., and A. Brill. *The Dimensions of Tolerance.* New York: Russell Sage, 1983.

Merelman, R. M. "The Role of Conflict in Children's Political Learning." In *Political Socialization, Citizenship Education, and Democracy,* edited by O. Ichilov. New York: Teachers College Press, 1990.

National Assessment of Educational Progress. *The Civics Report Card.* Washington, D.C.: U.S. Department of Education, 1990.

Newmann, F. M. "Higher Order Thinking in Teaching Social Studies: A Rationale for the Assessment of Classroom Thoughtfulness." *Journal of Curriculum Studies* 22 (1990): 41-56.

Newmann, F.M., and G. G. Wehlage. "Five Standards of Authentic Instruction." *Educational Leadership* 50 (April 1993): 8-12.

Perkins, D., and T. Blythe. "Putting Understanding Up Front." *Educational Leadership* 51, no. 5 (1994): 4-7.

Schultz, B., and R. Schultz. *It Did Happen Here: Recollections of Political Repression in America.* Berkeley: University of California Press, 1989.

Schwartz, J. D. "Participation and Multisubjective Understanding: An Interpretivist Approach to the Study of Political Participation." *Journal of Politics* 46 (1984): 1117-1141.

Spurgeon, C. "Teaching about a Citizenship Issue through Literature." *Citizenship* 2, no. 1 (1991/92): 3-7.

Stone, L. "What Matters for Citizenship Education?" *Theory and Research in Social Education* 20, no. 2 (1992): 207-219.

Tetreault, M. K. "Integrating Content about Women and Gender into the Curriculum." In *Multicultural Education: Issues and Perspectives,* edited by J. A. Banks and C. A. M. Banks. Boston: Allyn and Bacon, 1989.

Theiss-Morse, E. "Conceptualizations of Good Citizenship and Political Participation." *Political Behavior* 15 (1993): 355-380.

Torney, J. V., A. M. Oppenheim, and R. F. Farnen. *Civic Education in Ten Countries: An Empirical Study.*

New York: John Wiley and Sons, 1975.

"The Voters: Gains and Losses in Turnout." *New York Times,* November 8, 1992.

Zellman, G., and D. Sears. "Childhood Origins of Tolerance for Dissent." *Journal of Social Issues* 27 (1971): 109-136.

Table 5: Resources Mentioned in Chapter

Books

Golding, W. *Lord of the Flies.* London: Faber and Faber, 1954.

Greene, B. *Summer of My German Soldier.* New York: Dial Press, 1973.

Malcolm X. *The Autobiography of Malcolm X.* Secaucus, NJ: Castle Books, 1965.

Takaki, R. T. *A Different Mirror: A History of Multicultural America.* Boston: Little, Brown & Company, 1993.

Taylor, M. D. *Roll of Thunder, Hear My Cry.* New York: Dial Press, 1976.

Teaching Materials

National Issues Forum pamphlets. Available from National Issues Forums, 100 Commons Road, Dayton, Ohio 45459-2777. Phone: 800-433-7834.

Opposing Viewpoints Series. Available from Greenhaven Press, Inc., P. O. Box 289009, San Diego, Calif. 92198-9009. Phone: 619-485-7424

Endnotes

[1] Persons interested in using structured controversy in their classrooms can find a more extensive description of the technique in Johnson and Johnson (1979, 1985, 1987).

23 AN APPROACH TO ISSUES-ORIENTED ECONOMIC EDUCATION

by Beverly J. Armento, Francis W. Rushing, and Wayne A. Cook

PART ONE: FRAMING THE APPROACH

What are the economic benefits and costs of dropping out of school? Is there really a trade deficit, and if so, what difference does it make? Are there salary differences between men and women, and if so, why? Should there be? What about salary and employment patterns by gender and ethnicity? What are the causes, and what should "we" do about these patterns? Should farmers around the world be "forced" to operate strictly by the rules of supply and demand? Is every person entitled to health care, and if so, who should pay? Should the minimum wage be raised? What economic and social effects would follow? Who should pay for environmental and safety protection? How should community-owned land be used, by whom, and for what purposes?

These are only a few of the many personal and public policy economic issues of interest to young people who face such problems daily, either in their own lives or in the larger social, political arena. Of course, everyone has an opinion about such questions, but is the opinion informed, thoughtful, and mindful of alternatives, trade-offs, and the short- and longer-term consequences of various policy options? Issues-centered instruction in economics should assist students in developing analytic and reflective ways of thinking about and addressing important economic issues.

This chapter aims to define the nature of economic problems, discuss tools of economic analysis, and present criteria for evaluating solutions to economic issues. We argue that instruction must acknowledge and incorporate ideological differences and multiple interpretations about what is right or wrong when it comes to economic issues. Because some of the ideological perspectives incorporate social, historical, and political dimensions of issues, classroom instruction must be approached in an interdisciplinary manner. Also, since economic issues are often complex, they should be explored in an informed and thoughtful manner. We will propose a plan for organizing instruction around economic issues that facilitates interdisciplinary and informed analysis. Prior to thinking about classroom practice, however, we must consider the nature of economic issues and the implications for instruction.

What is economics?

Economics as a discipline deals with the problem of scarcity. Scarcity occurs when human wants are greater than the resources available to produce goods and services to satisfy those wants. The existence of scarcity forces upon all people the requirement of making choices. A primary objective of the teaching of economics is to prepare students to make rational choices as individuals and as members of society based on objective analysis and the values of the choice makers.

How are economic decisions made?

The primary tools of analysis that have proven to be effective in making economic decisions are fairly simple concepts: opportunity cost, production possibility analysis and trade-offs, and supply and demand analysis. The concept of opportunity cost states that the real cost of obtaining one good or service is the next best alternative good or service that would have been produced with the resources used to produce our first choice. The opportunity cost concept can be applied to any scarce resource. One example is time allocation: should one's time be used to do volunteer work or to go swimming?

Production possibility analysis is most typically used in analyzing macroeconomic choices, since it demonstrates the possibilities between society's choices of producing one basket of goods as opposed to an alternative basket. The classic trade-off is between "guns and butter," or it could be between clean air and less steel production. In actuality, society does not normally make an either/or choice, but some of each when dealing with difficult economic matters. The choices depend not only on the reality of limited resources, but also upon the aggregate preferences or values of society.

Supply and demand analysis also plays an important role in economic decision-making. Supply and demand forces in our market economy generally determine the prices of the factors of production and of the goods and services produced in the economy. The price of a good tells its economic value relative to other goods. As consumers or as producers, we attempt to gain the greatest benefits by allocating our money or our time among the various choices available to us as buyers of goods and sellers of services.

What are objective and normative economics?

If economics only dealt with the theoretical or the abstract—if it only dealt with the tools of analysis—then it would be a fairly straightforward discipline with little controversy associated with it. Of course this is not the case. Economics really has two dimensions: the objective and the normative (subjective). The objective emphasizes "what is" and attempts to explain the process by which choices are made. The normative or subjective dimension deals with "what ought to be." Even in objective economics, there is an assumption that people have developed a set of preferences based upon their own experiences, tastes, and values. What people want will depend on how they feel their economic decisions will satisfy their unique wants (however they may have been derived).

Normative (subjective) economics addresses how people's values influence the future allocation of resources by altering the outcomes of economic decision making or perhaps even by changing the characteristics of the institutions in which economic decisions are made. For instance, as individuals we may refuse to purchase cigarettes, but we and other similar-minded persons may also work for local ordinances against smoking in public (and sometimes private) places. Economic analysis can tell us what should happen to the sales of cigarettes as demand falls, but it does not address whether or not a local ordinance should be put into place to improve individual and public health.

What philosophies (ideologies) guide economic decisions?

The economy of the United States may be described as a private enterprise, market economy. However, economic decisions are made both in the private sector—households and businesses—and in the public sectors—federal, state, and local governments—as well as in the international arena. Although described as a market economy, it is really a mixed system in which resources are allocated outside of markets or are partially directed through the markets. The extent to which the markets are relied upon depends somewhat on the balance within the economy of the "free-market advocates," the "managed-market advocates," and the "radicals." Each group has a philosophical underpinning that guides the position of advocacy that they take. These approaches to economic issues are often closely related to one's political ideology. They define the questions one asks, the data one seeks, and the general parameters one sets for issue analysis.

The free-market advocates (or conservatives) believe that competitive markets allocate resources best and that the individual and the common good is served best when markets are free to function in the absence of outside interference, particularly collective or governmental interference. The free-market advocates believe that the national wealth will be maximized when individuals are allowed to create new products and services and compete in markets for customers. Although they generally recognize that some "public goods" will have to be provided by government, the conservatives believe that these should be limited to just a few, principally those relating to defense, laws and courts, and safety (police and fire). In addition, free-market conservatives generally think that individuals are free and rational and that they make economic choices based on their tastes and preferences. Thus, problems such as unemployment and poverty are often seen as the outcome of individual actions and choices.

The managed-market advocates (or liberals)

go beyond a strictly economic analysis in their examination of issues, looking to social, cultural, historical, and political contexts for clues about causes and solutions to complex problems. Liberals generally feel that markets do not work perfectly and can be improved or made more compatible with society's objectives if governments manage some aspects of market function. For instance, in addition to the public goods described above, the managed-market adherents would contend that the government should be involved in providing for education, workplace legislation, drug and product safety validation, environmental regulations, redistribution of income, and services such as agricultural stations, and subsidies to special groups, such as farmers, married people, dependent children, the elderly, college students, and so forth. In other words, let the markets and their prices guide the system in general, but expect the government to have to intervene to redirect some market outcomes so as to maximize society's general welfare. They believe private property should remain intact, but that the use of and income from property should be subject to redirection by government from the individual or one group to others.

The radical (or critical) advocates think that issues of power, conflict, and exploitation are central to economic analysis. The questions posed by this group take as a premise that "problems" such as discrimination and oppression are normal (i.e., regularly occurring) in society and that for contemporary American society these forces are crucial to the maintenance of the political/economic status quo. The radical economist would have us think of replacing some of the existing institutions with new ones believed to be more harmonious with the values of a more egalitarian and just society. In the world of decision making, conservative, liberal, and radical perspectives are not as clear as the descriptions above might imply. Many free-marketeers relax to some extent to permit government intervention; however, in principle, they attempt to minimize government involvement. In contrast, the managed-market advocates have been willing to suggest that government withdraw from some market activities when the evidence is clear that intervention has not achieved the desired outcomes.

What are the criteria for evaluating economic choices?

Economists generally agree on the set of criteria that should be considered when deciding any economic issue. What they cannot do is determine which is the most important. This is determined by the individual or the group making the decision. The criteria include several factors:

1. **Economic growth.** How will decisions affect the rate of wealth creation? Will the economic pie grow faster or slower, regardless of how it will be sliced?

2. **Economic efficiency.** How is the system organized to make economic decisions? Are the resources used to their fullest to obtain the greatest output for the least inputs?

3. **Income distribution.** Will all parties share in the output of economic activity? Will the shares of outputs be changed by the decisions being made? Who wins and who loses, or do all win?

4. **Economic freedom.** Are individual rights protected? Are some group rights reduced so other group rights are enlarged? Are net freedoms expanded, contracted, or do they remain the same? Are property rights changed? Is freedom of job choice preserved?

5. **Equity.** Is the system fair? Can all people benefit to the extent of their talents and contributions? Does discrimination reduce the "fairness"? Does the market have more or less equity than legislation?

6. **Stability.** Do our decisions make the economy less susceptible to wide fluctuations in income and employment? Can you reasonably anticipate the future?

7. **Economic development.** Does economic growth change our economic structure and economic opportunities? Is development creating not only something different, but something better for people? Do we want more things or a higher quality of life consisting of clean air, short commutes to work, and more "at home time"?

Take health care as a recent case to contrast the two major schools of thinking—conservative and liberal. Under the traditional health care system in the United States, the private sector provides the vast majority of health services delivered. Recently, the coverage and the cost—equity and efficiency—of the system have been brought into question. The free-market advocates predict that if government initiates a comprehensive federal program, costs will rise and individual care will decline, resulting in the aggregate level of care falling. The managed-market group says that the market has left too many Americans outside the health care system and offers a general welfare and equity argument to support legislation on coverage and institutions to deliver health care to the citizens. Some questions one might ask given this situation are: How would you go about recommending the solution to this problem? In the context of alternative philosophies, what solutions do you think would be recommended? What information would you need to address the problem? What kind of economic criteria will you use to assess the potential solutions to the issue? How will the potential solutions affect the people?

We argue that instruction must recognize that there are ideological differences, and it must place the differences within their proper social, historical, and political contexts to be relevant to issue analysis. Economics instruction as it is currently practiced fails to provide students with the tools needed to hear (or understand) the voices of various groups—defined by race, gender, or ideology—whose points of view shape the public discussion of social policy. To remedy this, economic issues should be presented in their complexity, including the reality of multiple interpretations of economic life. To do that, economic issues must be dealt with in an interdisciplinary manner and they should be explored in an informed and analytical manner.

Interdisciplinary Instruction

If classroom economics instruction is to include the full range of ideological perspectives, the curriculum must include questions, data, concepts, and analyses drawn from history and the relevant social sciences. The economic, social, and political world is so complex that economic models alone are restricted in their ability to fully represent reality.

An issues-centered approach would call for a richer, more deeply contextualized focus on "how human beings, in interaction with one another and the environment, provide for their own survival and health" (Nelson 1993, 34), and on the range of problems and concerns that have occurred and continue to occur in that endeavor. A more interdisciplinary approach to teaching economics represents a major break with the mode currently prevailing in the United States.

The dominant approach is uni-disciplinary and often employs choice theory, a popular analytic tool that accentuates "rational" individual behavior and neglects the complex social, historical, and cultural factors that surround and mediate individual choices.

Informed Instruction

Pedagogy as well as content must be informed, balanced, constructed, grounded, and dynamic in order to assist learners as they become more thoughtful (Newmann 1992), analytic, caring, and creative economic decision makers. Some economic issues—such as those dealing with social stratification, unemployment, international trade, taxes, the role of government in allocating and redistributing resources and income, the distribution of wealth, and so on—are so "hot," emotional, and loaded with intensity, and often with dogmatic and pre-determined conclusions, that thoughtful classroom treatment is difficult. Both the content of issues-centered economics instruction and the pedagogy employed are sources of conflict in the classroom. In addition, they are the keys to determining whether learning will be meaningful or aimless.

Issues-centered instruction demands a "culture of thinking" in the classroom: an attitude by teachers and students of curiosity and skepticism; of calmness and contemplation; of informed investigations and logical thinking; of objectivity along with creativity; of role playing and empathy; of persistence in the pursuit of data and alternative perspectives; of doubt and critical thinking; and of questioning, questioning, questioning. Teachers and students must adopt the attitude that other perspectives are valid and reasonable. In addition, all should remain open to their own views changing as they construct new ways of seeing and assessing issues.

Not only should pedagogy be informed by the latest, most relevant insights from theory and research, but issues-centered instruction should be informed by data rather than mere opinion. Students should learn where to find information, how to assess its reliability, authenticity, and validity, and how to interpret data presented in a range of forms.

While it is not the goal of this chapter to develop the research base for issues-centered instruction, we believe there is considerable theoretical and empirical work to guide educators in making wise pedagogical choices. Through the employment of such work, we now propose the following plan for making the transition to a more issues-centered approach to economic instruction.

PART TWO: DEVELOPING THE INSTRUCTIONAL APPROACH

Issues-oriented economics instruction, then, should embody the essential principles developed in part one of this chapter: it should foster an informed and interdisciplinary treatment of issues, and these should be explored from various ideological perspectives. We have developed an issues-oriented teaching model drawing on these principles and on the literature on role taking (Selman 1976), learning (Vygotsky 1978; Wittrock 1986), domain-specific knowledge and knowledge restructuring (Spilich et al. 1979; Voss 1986; Voss et al. 1983; Voss, Tyler, and Yengo 1983; Vosniadou and Brewer 1987), and on problem solving and thoughtfulness (Beck and Carpenter 1986; Newmann 1992). The model blends effective pedagogy with content knowledge to produce an approach that addresses the interpretive and interdisciplinary aspects of economic issues. The model begins with student interest and prior knowledge, and leads them through a purposeful process of inquiry and investigation in which their visual representation and understanding of an issue is reconstructed as they uncover new information and new perspectives.

The model can be applied in elementary, middle, and high school classrooms. Typically, economics is taught as a separate course in high schools. The most prevalent approach is a principles of economics orientation, although courses in personal finance may also be offered. In addition, Advanced Placement economics courses are offered, which are usually highly analytical and conceptual. At the elementary and middle school levels, economic content is generally integrated into the ongoing social studies curriculum, although there are some stand-alone programs, such as Mini-Society, the Stock Market game, and Kinder-economy.

More about the model

STEP 1: Representing and defining the issue and its parameters. Tapping the current knowledge of students, try to identify the broad dimensions of the issue, exploring its causes, con-

The Issues-Oriented Teaching Model: An Outline

Step 1: Representing and defining the issue and its parameters

(This aspect of the model is based on the students' current knowledge and awareness of the issue).

- Identify the issue or the topic for investigation; reframe the issue as questions; represent the issue in alternative ways.
- Identify causes, constraints, sub-issues, and the historical, social, and political factors that influence the central issue.
- Develop a graphic representation to portray the broad dimensions of the issue and to show the way the aspects of the issue relate to one another (causal, chronological, etc.)

Step 2: Linking prior knowledge with new information about the issue

- Brainstorm with students to identify what they know or think they know about any of the questions/categories identified as relevant to this issue.
- Identify what data and sources will be needed in order to address the questions asked.
- Discuss what economic (and other) analytical concepts will be needed to fully understand the issue.
- Conduct data collection and analysis. In addition, at this point in instruction the teacher should design and implement mini-lessons on concepts students will need to understand in order to continue the analysis of the issue.

Step 3: Reconceptualizing/redefining the issue, given new data and ideas

- Ask what new dimensions of the issue are apparent after examining the data and reading alternative opinions?
- Ask if the sub-issues can be redefined and addressed by applying the new factual and conceptual knowledge learned?

Step 4: Developing alternative points of view, with substantiating data

- Ask how conservatives, liberals, and radicals would approach this issue. What criteria would each use to assess the problem? What policy recommendations would persons holding each perspective propose? What are the short-term and long-term consequences of each proposal? What other considerations should be addressed?

Step 5: Stating personal positions, giving supporting rationale and data

- Have students address the questions, What position do I have on this issue, and why? What are the short-term and long-term considerations and consequences of my position? What are the steps and impediments to policy implementation?

texts, and aspects. It is helpful to rephrase questions into as many forms as possible, because this process will uncover aspects of the problem that students may not have initially considered.

For example, suppose students are interested in issues surrounding social stratification and poverty and, therefore, have initially asked *Why are some people (or countries) less well off than others?* As part of the reframing of this issue, students might generate questions such as *Who is poor? What do words like "poor" and "poverty" mean? Why are some people poor? Where do the poor live? What jobs do the poor have? How do poor people get their food, clothing, and shelter?*

What is meant by social class? Who is in what social class (by gender, race, region), and what are the historic trends?

What is the extent of mobility from one socioeconomic class to another? What are the dominant sociological/psychological theories about poverty and social stratification? What percentage of each ethnic, gender, and age group is currently living in poverty? What political issues center on poverty? What percentage of the federal and state budgets go toward poverty-related programs? What are the outcomes of such programs?

How do different countries rank in terms of per capita income and standard of living? What measures indicate general quality of life? Do industrialized countries have a "social responsibility" to improve the standard of living of persons and countries with low per capita income?

Suppose the question raised is *What role(s) should the United States government assume in promoting its interests in international trade?* The brainstorming and representation of the scope of the issue might include such sub-issues and aspects of the issue as *Why do nations trade? What trade agreements does the United States have with other nations? What major trading partners does the United States have, and what is the extent of import/export exchange with each partner? What forms of protectionism, quotas, or other barriers are currently used by the United States and by our trading partners? Should we protect certain industries from international competition? What is our trade deficit, and should we try to reduce it? Should our government have an industrial policy and a national plan for the nation's productivity?*

High school students face many economic issues in their own lives as well as in their formal study of economics. In microeconomics, students might ask *Why are men and women of "com-*parable worth" earning different incomes? Should businesses be concerned with "social responsibility"? Should school attendance be compulsory? Should public education be privatized? Do United States citizens save enough? Who should pay for and receive low-cost housing? Should businesses be able to close profitable factories in a local community to move the business to another country where they would pay lower wages?*

When studying macroeconomics, students might ask *Has the U.S. government become too big? Who should pay for health care, and should everyone be entitled to it? Workfare or welfare? Should the Federal Reserve target zero inflation? Should the government pay reparations to African Americans? Are affirmative action policies equitable? Should any immigrant to the United States be allowed to work at any wage rate? Is the federal budget deficit of any real consequence? Should the rich pay fewer taxes to encourage greater investment? Should the federal government take actions to protect endangered species when it means jobs will be lost?*

When studying international economics, students might ask *Should the world's farmers be protected from the competition of the market? Should countries protect their infant industries? Should the United States have an industrial policy? Should the United States feed the world's poor? How much aid should the United States give to Russia or to Mexico? Should the military-industrial complex be expanded?*

Students' prior understanding of the scope of the issue surfaces during step one, as they attempt to define the parameters, causes, and sub-issues of the problem. Having students organize the content of this brainstorming into a visual representation will enable them to see the major views they currently hold about the issue. Using Post-its, have students write each of their questions, sub-issues, and current information about the issue. The Post-its then can be arranged visually on chart paper to show how the questions and ideas relate to one another. This representation is useful for showing the complexity of many issues, and the graphic can be used as a teaching tool throughout the course of the issue's analysis. As students gather data and identify new aspects of the issue, they can be added to the graphic organizer, which now becomes a dynamic representation of how the students are thinking about the issue.

This same process can be used with students

of all ages, using issues that are developmentally appropriate. Young children are curious and puzzled by economic choices they make or observe in their homes, schools, and communities. Children observe local economic dilemmas as communities decide whether to raise taxes, how to use land for alternative purposes, how to address the needs of homeless persons, or how to use available local resources. Even young children can begin to realize that different people see issues from different perspectives, as they practice the roles of persons attending a town meeting to decide whether to raise property taxes to build new schools. Elementary school students easily learn to portray their representation of a problem visually, and to generate new questions for further investigation. Of course, young students will need more assistance with the procedural and conceptual aspects of an investigation and with skills of data interpretation than older students, but, with expert teacher guidance, they also can apply the five-step, issues-analysis model to their thinking.

Middle school students are actively involved in the economy as consumers, and in many cases as producers and savers, and are conceptually able to understand, at least at a fundamental level, some of the same issues as high school students. Economic issues are dominant in the social studies curriculum at grades six through eight, whether the focus be on the United States or world history, global studies, or regional studies. Economic issues for analysis can also be drawn from current local, national, and world events that are of interest to the students, and the five-step, issues-teaching model can be employed to help students gain a deeper understanding of the dimensions and context of issues: *Should the United States provide economic aid to other countries that are improving their industrial base? Should there be economic incentives for students to get good grades in school? How should a wilderness area in the local community be used, and who should decide its use? How should the state's lottery money be used? Should cigarette producers be allowed to advertise? Should commercial products be sold in schools?* The list of issues that might be of interest to middle school students is endless.

STEP 2: Linking prior knowledge with new information about the issue. Continuing to use the same graphic organizer, students should identify what they know or think they know about the issue and the sub-issues. Misconceptions and errors will surface, and, at this point in the analysis, these should be accepted by the teacher. However, as new information is gathered and processed, students should make corrections and additions to their graphic representation. Discussions of the reliability and accuracy of data sources should be an integral part of any inquiry.

Step two implies a major investigation of the issue, with an identification of data sources and alternative points of view. Research in today's technologically equipped school media centers should enable students to access not only insight-providing data but also editorial commentaries on issues written from various ideological perspectives. In addition, all high school economics classrooms should have copies of books that address important economic issues from different views. These include Feiner's *Race and Gender in the American Economy* (1994) and Schwartz and Bonello's *Taking Sides: Clashing Views on Controversial Economic Issues* (1993).

During this "finding out more" phase of issue analysis, students and teachers should engage in developing the necessary conceptual tools for understanding the data and the issues. For example, on international trade issues, students will need to understand a wide range of ideas, such as quotas, protectionism, NAFTA, trade deficits, comparative and absolute advantage, capital, balance of trade, subsidies, supply and demand, exchange rates, infant industry, dumping, international equilibrium, and so on.

This phase of issue analysis involves a slowing down of dialogue about the issue itself, and a realization on the part of students and teachers that, in order to fully understand it, they must stop and learn underlying concepts and facts. Here, pacing and relating the information to the central issue helps students "remember" why they are doing so much research.

STEP 3: Reconceptualizing the issue, given new data and ideas. After students have conducted a broad investigation of data and perspectives related to the central issue, they should return to their initial conception of the problem, and work to reconceptualize and refine their focus, sharpening their questions, reevaluating sub-issues, and beginning to organize data and views around the related issues. It is useful at this stage of the inquiry to have students develop new graphic representations as a means of comparing their new views with the images they developed initially. Hopefully, the new representation illustrates the students' growth in seeing not only the issue's complexity, but also demonstrates greater accuracy and completeness in identifying sub-issues and information that illuminates the topic.

STEP 4: Developing alternative points of view, with substantiating data. Before launching an in-depth issue analysis, students should consider the nature of differing points of view on economic issues. More mature students can read point-of-view essays by economists from Schwartz and Bonello (1993), for example, and attempt to uncover the essential differences in perspectives. They could then practice identifying these alternative ideological viewpoints in editorials in newspapers and news magazines prior to creating their own policy options based on various perspectives.

Younger students should be able to identify the people who might be interested in the issue being analyzed, and then speculate about how the issue might look from each person's perspective. For example, on the issue of raising property taxes to build new schools, it could be asked *How would the issue look if you were a retired person on a fixed income whose children were grown? What if you were a businessperson wanting to attract new workers to town? What if you were a middle-income home owner with four children in school?* Role-taking gives students the opportunity to see how an issue might look differently depending not only on a person's circumstances—but also on the beliefs and values held by that person.

STEP 5: Stating Personal Positions, Giving Supporting Rationale and Data. Finally, students should have enough information, awareness of alternative perspectives, and conceptual knowledge to make informed judgments about the sub-issues and the major issue under investigation. Students should be able to substantiate these positions, and be able to project the short-term and long-term consequences of their proposed actions and policies. Students can present their views in letters to the editor, essays, editorials, mock economic conferences, video presentations, debates, panel discussions, public hearings, or round table discussions.

In many schools, students are able to connect (via Internet, distance learning) with students in

other communities, even across the globe. Dialogue on environmental issues as well as on critical national issues of privatization, economic growth, unemployment, and international trade are daily matters for many young people (in over a dozen countries) who are part of programs such as the Global Thinking Project, sponsored by Georgia State University. As such programs grow and our capacity to communicate with other people increases, the dimensions of classroom issues-oriented instruction become more exciting and dynamic for teachers and students.

The guiding principles of issues-oriented economics instruction, then, are the same regardless of student age or sophistication level:

- Economics issues are complex and embedded in the social, political, and historical contexts of life. They should be viewed and studied in ways that reflect this richness.
- People have different opinions about how economics issues should be addressed, and these various viewpoints should be considered and evaluated by students as they contemplate their own position.
- Analysis of issues should be informed by reliable and valid data.
- Students learn best when they are interested in an issue and when they are intimately involved in the identification of the problem and in the construction of its dimensions and its "solution."
- Teachers must practice thoughtfulness, balance, objectivity, and issue analysis in their own lives in order to practice the proposed pedagogy in their classrooms.

The role of the social studies classroom is to assist students in informed reflection on important economic matters, to instill dispositions of thoughtfulness and inquiry, rather than impetuousness and dogmatism, and to foster awareness and appreciation for the validity of alternative interpretations of complex issues. To achieve these goals, the social studies and economic teaching communities have much work ahead. Teachers themselves must embody these traits and skills before they can adequately implement issues-oriented economics instruction in any classroom. Teacher education programs must address the development of prospective and mature issues-oriented educators. Additionally, these teachers will need newly conceived instructional materials in order to easily implement such an approach. At present, most economics educators will find themselves developing their own issues-oriented lessons, and will need to identify and gather the available data sources. What is needed is a commitment by all to move toward a more interpretive, interdisciplinary, and informed approach to economic education.

References and Further Readings

Alexander, P. A., D. L. Schallert, and V. C. Hare. "Coming to Terms: How Researchers in Learning and Literacy Talk about Knowledge." *Review of Educational Research* 61, no.3 (1991): 315-343.

Amolt, T., and J. Mattaei. *Race, Gender and Work: A Multicultural Economic History of Women.* Boston: South End Press, 1993.

Armento, B. J. "Changing Conceptions of Research on the Teaching of Social Studies." In *Handbook of Research on Social Studies Teaching and Learning,* edited by J. Shaver. New York: Macmillan, 1991.

—. "Economic Socialization." In *Citizenship for the Twenty-first Century,* edited by W. T. Callahan. Bloomington, Ind.: Foundation for Teaching Economics and Social Studies Development Center, 1990.

Beck, I. L. and P. A. Carpenter. "Cognitive approaches to Understanding Reading." *American Psychologist* 41, no. 10 (1986): 1098-1105.

Feiner, S. F. *Race and Gender in the American Economy: Views from Across the Spectrum.* Englewood Cliffs, N.J.: Prentice Hall, 1994.

Nelson, J. A. "The Study of Choice or the Study of Provisioning? Gender and the Definition of Economics." *Beyond Economic Man: Feminist Theory and Economics,* edited by M. A. Ferber and J. A. Nelson. Chicago: University of Chicago Press, 1993.

Newmann, F. M., ed. *Student Engagement and Achievement in Secondary Schools.* New York: Teachers College Press, 1992.

Schwartz, T. R. and F. J. Bonello, eds. *Taking Sides: Clashing Views on Controversial Economic Issues.* Guilford, Conn.: Dushkin Publishing Group, Inc., 1993.

Selman, R. L. "Social-Cognitive Understanding: A Guide to Educational and Clinical Practice." In *Moral Development and Behavior: Theory, Research, and Social Issues,* edited by T. Lickona. New York: Holt, Rinehart and Winston, 1976.

Spilich, G. J., et al. "Text Processing of Domain-Related Information for Individuals with High and Low Domain Knowledge." *Journal of Verbal Learning and Verbal Behavior* 18 (1979): 275-290.

Tobias, S. "Interest, Prior Knowledge, and Learning." *Review of Educational Research* 64, no. 1 (1994): 37-54.

Vosniadou, S. and W. F. Brewer. "Theories of Knowledge Restructuring in Development." *Review of Educational Research* 57 (1987): 51-67.

Voss, J. "Social Studies." In *Cognition and Instruction,* edited by R. F. Dillon and R. J. Sternberg. Orlando, Fla.: Academic Press, Inc., 1986.

—, et al. "Problem Solving Skill in the Social Sciences." In *The Psychology of Learning and Motivation: Advances in Research Theory,* edited by G. H. Bower. New York: Academic Press, 1983.

—, S. Tyler and L. Yengo. "Individual Differences in the Solving of Social Science Problems." In *Individual Differences in Cognition,* edited by R. Dillon and R. Schmeck. New York: Academic Press, 1983.

Vygotsky, L. S. *Mind in Society: The Development of Higher Psychological Processes.* Cambridge: Harvard University Press, 1978.

Wittrock, M. C. "Students' Thought Processes." In *Handbook of Research on Teaching,* 3rd Edition, edited by M. C. Wittrock. New York: Macmillan, 1986.

TEACHING ISSUES-CENTERED ANTHROPOLOGY, SOCIOLOGY, AND PSYCHOLOGY

by Jerry A. Ligon and George W. Chilcoat

The troubles young people experience today in and out of school are shocking. Youth are worried and troubled by an increasing suicide and homicide rate, drug use among their peers, and disintegration of their families (Ingrassia 1993). Ingrassia (1993) also reported that they worry about their peers stealing from them (68 percent), being attacked (46 percent), or threatened with a gun (24 percent).

How hard is it for students to concentrate on their social studies classes when they have such concerns? To what extent do students today experience what Hunt and Metcalf (1968, 26) called "intrapersonal conflict" and are "uncertain as to what to believe or value"? To the extent that students view the resolution of this uncertainty as being within themselves and their immediate social setting, they are experiencing what Mills (1959) called "troubles." However, students' troubles transcend themselves to the institutions and culture of their society. For students to better understand their troubles, they must examine these societal issues. As social studies educators with a primary purpose "to help young people develop the ability to make informed and reasoned decisions for the public good" (National Council for the Social Studies [NCSS] 1994, vii), we might ask our students: "To what extent are the troubles of U.S. society influenced by:

- the culture of the United States?"
- how individuals learn, perceive, and grow?"
- how people meet their basic needs?"
- how groups and institutions form and change?"
- those who hold power and authority?"
- how power and authority are gained, used, and justified?"

As students grapple with their private lives, they must understand how their individual biography relates to U.S. culture, society, and history. We believe that an issues-centered study of central concepts in anthropology, sociology, and psychology would give students perspective on the problems they face. In this chapter we identify the central concepts for student inquiry in these disciplines, share a model for issues-centered instruction, and suggest resources in teaching these subjects.

Central Concepts of Anthropology, Sociology, and Psychology

No single source contains a listing of the central concepts of each discipline. While the American Psychological Association (1986) is the only organization among the three disciplines to offer an official high school curriculum, lists of suggested sociology units continue to surface (National Commission on Social Studies in the Schools 1989; Gray 1993). Sociologists continue to debate what are the basic concepts of sociology and if they should be standardized—a continuing debate since Emile Durkheim and Max Weber's time (Wallace 1990). Though we do not agree, a faction within the American Sociological Association believes sociology is actually too difficult for precollegiate education (Smith 1981). While evidence suggested that rarely are high school students enrolled in anthropology courses (Erickson 1991), concepts and topics central to anthropology are taught throughout K–12 schooling (Rice 1993).

Issues-Centered Anthropology

Culture—the patterned and learned ways of life and thought that a human society shares—is the concept central to anthropology. Anthropologists attempt to explain why and how the cultures of groups of people are different, "why they have different physical characteristics, speak different languages, use different technologies, and why they think, believe and act" differently (White 1989, 31). Anthropologists also study human biology, archaeology, and linguistics, as well as cultural anthropology (Bodley 1994).

Because anthropologists draw freely from concepts, theories, and methods of all social sciences (Bodley 1994), anthropological concepts are often taught in U.S. elementary and secondary schools within an interdisciplinary framework. Unfortunately, some evidence showed that much of what is taught is "trivial and noninformative" (Rice 1993); the study of culture is more than the study of dance, food, holidays, and history (White 1989). Central concepts and topics in anthropology, in addition to culture, include family, race, ethnicity, evolution, adaptation, and technological change. When students analyze artifacts, original documents, art, and accounts of everyday lives of people, they are modeling the methods of anthropologists (Bodley 1994; White 1989).

We believe strongly that anthropology must become a part of the social studies teacher education curriculum. If the first strand of the social studies discipline's standards (NCSS 1994) is culture and if the position of social studies education professionals is that "social studies programs should include experiences that provide for the study of culture and cultural diversity" (NCSS 1994, 21), then the primary discipline that studies culture should not be overlooked within teacher preparation.

Furthermore, as a discipline that can emphasize "interdisciplinary integration rather than disciplinary exclusiveness" (Rollwagen 1989, 138), anthropology, we believe, is an ideal candidate for issues-centered instruction. Teachers can build lessons, units, and courses around "situations and dilemmas that pose problems, that make us ponder what to do in matters of public policy as well as in private course of action" (Evans 1994, 43). For example, instead of asking "How are cultures different?" an issues-centered lesson might ask "How might different cultures live peacefully together?" This question demands more inquiry because the latter question cannot be answered until students probe the initial question and, in order to arrive at an answer, students must examine the problematic instead of the factual—they eat this and we eat that—

aspects of the cultures under study. A cross-cultural study of religion, taught with an issues-centered approach, shifts the question from "How does religion influence a part of a culture?" to "What role should religion play in forming public policy in a democratic society?" In an issues-centered lesson, the questions for study are open-ended and have no "right" answers but require thoughtfulness and in-depth study of evidence. This shift in focus from studying the factual to studying the problematic admittedly is more controversial, but, in tackling important questions, it interests students.

Issues-Centered Sociology

Sociology is the science of society (Stewart and Glynn 1985) that focuses on two principal aspects of social life: group membership and face-to-face interaction (Henslin 1988). In the classic *Invitation to Sociology*, Peter Berger (1963, 20) wrote that sociologists ask: "What are people doing with each other here?" What are their relationships to each other?" "How are these relationships organized in institutions?" The traditional goal of sociology has been to understand society, but today stronger interest is in practice, where sociologists develop critical perspectives through applying sociology in academic studies, in the workplace (by sociologists and nonsociologists), and in personal use (Basirica 1990; Friedman 1987). An increasing number of sociologists seek improvements in citizenship education and design their own courses with the overriding goal to "promote critical citizenship" (Dressel 1990; Gray 1993).

The central concepts that sociology students may study are numerous. Gray (1989) suggested deviance and social control, family, social stratification, education, and gerontology. "Introduction to Sociology" college texts, which are often adopted for secondary courses, also include: racial and ethnic minorities, demography, collective behavior, human societies and culture, and separate chapters on the institutions of the family, religion, education, political institutions, and the economy. While no precollegiate curriculum recommendations have been released, the American Sociological Association published their own one-semester high school text, *Inquiries in Sociology* (Sociological Resources 1972), which addressed socialization, institutions, social stratification, and change in the social order.

The sociology teacher in an issues-centered

lesson would do well to organize under a question Macdonald (1977, 20) suggested: "How shall we live together?" In issues-centered instruction Berger's questions would be rephrased: "What should people be doing with each other in this situation?" "What should be their relationships with each other?" "How should these relationships be organized in institutions?"

A lesson or unit dealing with racial and ethnic minorities, for example, could ask students at any grade level, "How should we relate to different people?" "How should people with different backgrounds form institutions to support the public good?" "What are our public responsibilities as citizens in a democracy?" None of these questions have definite "right answers." Most will probably be controversial, and all demand reflection, discussion, inquiry. They are also questions, appropriately framed, that should generate a high level of student interest across grade levels.

Issues-Centered Psychology

According to the American Psychological Association (APA) (1986, 12): "Psychology is the science and profession concerned with the behavior of humans and animals." The core areas of study delineated by the APA are the scientific methods of psychology, growth and development, learning, personality, mental health, behavioral disorders, and social psychology.

The teacher of issues-centered psychology would draw from psychologically relevant concepts and topics to teach young people from a more social psychological perspective. The course objectives would include studying the core concepts and theories of psychology; learning the basic skills of psychological research; applying psychological concepts to life; developing critical thinking skills; building reading, writing, and discussion skills; and learning about ethical standards. The key questions in an issues-centered psychology class would be: "What factors influence individual development and identity?" and "How do culture, groups, and institutions influence personal identity?" The teacher using an issues-centered approach could encourage students to reflect upon (Dewey 1933), inquire into (Massialas and Cox 1966), make decisions on (Engle and Ochoa 1988), and dialogue about such controversial topics (Muessig 1975; Sweeney and Parsons 1975) as:

- heredity and environment
- attitude formation and change
- moral development
- racism
- intelligence
- gender issues
- self-esteem
- ethnic and cultural diversity
- minority issues
- substance abuse
- prejudice and discrimination
- sex role development and stereotyping
- tests and measurements of intelligence
- child abuse
- teenage suicide
- interpersonal relations.

All of the topics listed above have implications for how an individual develops a personal identity. Most of the topics—after careful study—could lead to implications for social action. For example, how individuals come to define themselves is influenced by their perception of their intelligence. Definitions of intelligence (IQ vs. multiple intelligences, for example) reflect ways that a culture views intelligence and certainly how schools reward students. Studying intelligence as a controversial issue would allow students to better understand, make decisions, and possibly influence what happens to them in school in the area of testing, ranking, and sorting.

An Issues-Centered Instructional Model

A model of issues-centered education that is readily adaptable to lessons, units, and courses in anthropology, sociology, and psychology is the Sweeney-Parsons Controversial Social Issues Model (1975). It provides teachers with a way to structure classroom lessons and activities to encourage thoughtful examination of decisions and the decision-making process. The teacher follows the model's seven stages, known as phases, assisting the students as they study, examine, analyze, and attempt to resolve the issue at hand.

In selecting an issue for study, the teacher may look to students' interests or timely problems, but it is best to also consider an issue's relevance to the students' lives and whether it concerns the community and/or the larger society. As a result of careful selection, the topic itself and the accompanying investigation activities sustain the students' motivation throughout the study. The lesson used as a sample here is a composite drawn from several social studies teachers and is presented to give readers a fully developed issues-centered lesson. The issue studied in the unit is standardized testing, suitable for study because it is relevant to students'

- "What different kinds of tests have you taken?"
- "What do you think about all of these tests that you and others take?"
- "What do you think about the results of any given test that might determine who you are for the rest of your school or regular life?"

After a lively discussion on each of the five questions, the teacher presents the topic and rationale. These discussions might take up the first day of the lesson.

Phase II: Analysis

The objective of Phase II is to define the issue. It consists of three steps: first, the teacher presents students with selected materials for their reading, looking, and/or listening; second, students engage in a question-and-answer discussion limited to the material's facts, values, and definitions about the issue; and third, upon conclusion of the discussion, the class agrees on a working definition of the issue.

The teacher gives students a copy of "Standardized Testing: A Defense" by K. H. Ashworth (1990). As students read the article, the teacher encourages them to underline information that clarifies the intent of the author or take notes in order to understand the inferences about standardized testing that the article offers. To help the students understand the facts, values, and definitions of the material, the teacher asks students to use their notes to discuss the answers to the following general questions (Sweeney and Parsons 1975, 56):
- What does the material say?
- What is the intention of the material?
- How does the material want you to feel?
- What is occurring in the material?
- What action is happening?

After the discussion, the teacher asks, "What issue appears sufficiently important that we might continue to focus on it through the balance of this unit?"

Phase III: Clarification

Phase III helps students to analyze their own values and belief systems relevant to the issue under study. Students must come to some understanding of how they feel about the issue. This phase allows students to think deeply about their positions and to become acquainted and learn about the positions of others both in and out of the classroom.

lives and the larger community. It also is a contemporary problem that has many facets: e.g., elementary and high school students in many states routinely take standardized tests, and test scores of each school district are often published in the local newspapers for public scrutiny.

Phase I: Selection and Presentation

This first phase is primarily the responsibility of the teacher. The teacher selects a real-life issue, develops a rationale for its study, selects instructional materials, determines the approximate time for the entire lesson, and establishes an open-minded and respectful climate of teacher-student mutual trust. This last area is very important in the entire process of teaching issues. Sweeney and Parsons (1975, 47) explain:

> Perhaps the most important teacher ingredient for the examination of controversial issues, is establishing the emotional climate of the classroom. It is critical that the teacher establish rapport in a class where controversial issues are going to be discussed. There must be mutual confidence that the students can and will supply important information to the discussions. The students must have faith that the teacher can moderate an open and honest discussion of the materials. If the teacher has a bias, the students must be confident that the teacher will show it as a bias.

In the testing lesson, the teacher begins with a series of five questions meant to provoke strong emotional responses:
- "If I use the word *test* or *testing*, what comes to your mind?"
- "How many tests do you think you take in a year?"

The teacher begins this phase by organizing the class into small groups of four students. Students are instructed to discuss their feelings and beliefs about the issue of standardized testing as they understand it. Each group is to take notes on the groups' conversation and report to the whole class. The groups meet for about ten to fifteen minutes, depending on student interest. After a lively discussion, the teacher records the groups' findings on the chalkboard.

The teacher next asks the class what they must do to find answers to any questions that they might have and find outside support for their positions. The students might poll their parents, friends, other students, teachers, and administrators both in their and other high schools. Some might begin a library search of relevant information or expert opinion in such references as *Facts on File* or the *Readers' Guide to Periodicals*. Students then divide up responsibilities and determine a schedule.

Phase IV: Classification and Comparison

In Phase IV the teacher develops activities to help students probe the underlying values in the presented materials, compare those values with their own, support their positions, and determine the influencing sources of their values (personal experience, family, religion, television, etc.). The teacher structures open-minded discussions that analyze different and similar positions and concludes the phase by helping students extract **1.** the basic conflicts inherent in the presented materials, **2.** the students' own values, and **3.** values and conflicts from other sources of information.

In their groups the students discuss the information they collected and then discuss the following questions (Sweeney and Parsons 1975, 61).

GOAL 1: To probe the underlying values in the presented material:
- What are some of the value conflicts which seem to be involved in this issue?
- How many sides are there to this controversial topic?

GOAL 2: To compare student values with those values presented in the materials:
- How do you view the various sides of this issue?
- How did you arrive at your decisions?
- Do you know whether your family would agree with you on your decisions? Why or why not?

- Who do you think influences your decisions? Can you trace some influence to another person? Why do you think it is that person?

GOAL 3: To discuss examples of similar value conflicts:
- What are other examples of the stated value controversy?
- How are they compared or contrasted with our example?
- Have similar questions been raised and resolved in the past? If so, how?

These same questions guide the whole class discussion after the small groups report on their findings. The teacher notes on the chalkboard the value conflicts that emerged from the discussions, such as control of testing results vs. individual self-control; rote memorization vs. multiple intelligences; teaching to tests vs. real-life learning.

Phase V: Reflection

In Phase V students reflect on what they have been thinking and doing concerning the issue and if they have changed their opinions about the issue. The small groups discuss what they believe to be the implications of the values and value conflicts discussed so far in the study. To help the discussion, the teacher asks the students: "What is it we do like about these implications?" "What is it we don't like about these implications?" To elicit student responses, the teacher asks students to personally answer the following questions (Sweeney and Parsons 1975, 64):
- Have my values changed? In what ways? Why?
- Have my values remained as they were? If so, why?
- Have I modified my values? In what ways? Why?
- Having made decisions about the issues involved, what are the implications of the decisions? How do they affect me as an individual?
- What can I do about my decisions?
- If I do act, what are the alternatives of my action?

Phase VI: Application

Phase VI allows students to apply what they have learned and put their values into action. The teacher encourages students to find ways in which to take action based on their decisions and values. Students who do not wish to take part in the implementation of any decision should not be forced to do so. According to Sweeney and

Parsons (1975), the application process is not always an essential aspect of the model.

The teacher asks students, "Assume that you are in a position to solve most of the problems associated with standardized testing as we have discussed them. Based on the alternatives to testing that you have proposed, do you think that some sort of action should be undertaken?" "Do you want to propose some type of action?" "Do you want to carry it out?" After much discussion, students develop possible proposals and carry out their plans.

Phase VII: Evaluation

The last phase, evaluation, is not always a part of the Sweeney and Parsons Controversial Social Issues Model. If evaluation is used, it should emphasize process and students' personal learning during the lessons, not acquisition of specific content. The teacher can use multiple activities to evaluate student learning: ask questions; have written reports; or have a student-initiated activity that is concerned with the student's ability to analyze, take a position, and logically evidence a position.

In this last phase, the teacher asks, "Now that you are somewhat experts in testing and evaluation, should we evaluate our experiences?" "On what should we evaluate?" "And how should we evaluate?" The students, then, design and implement their own evaluation.

We believe that the Sweeney-Parsons Controversial Social Issues Model is an excellent model for teachers to use in developing issues-centered lessons and units dealing with anthropological, sociological, and psychological concepts and topics. The Sweeney-Parsons model capitalizes on student interest and concerns of the community and/or larger society. It offers teachers the flexibility to decide how much time and how much depth might be necessary to study a topic. And, most importantly, it encourages students to thoughtfully examine decisions and the decision-making process as they develop perspectives on the issues they face in everyday life.

Resources in Anthropology, Sociology, and Psychology

Because there are many resources available for teachers who teach concepts from these three disciplines, we have listed on the next page several general resources that offer ideas and other resource materials, some that may help students in developing perspectives about issues.

References

American Psychological Association. *Statement on the Curriculum for the High School Psychology Course.* Washington, D.C.: American Psychological Association, 1986.

Ashworth, K. H. "Standardized Testing: A Defense." *Educational Digest* 56 (1990): 40–42.

Basirica, L. A. "Integrating Sociological Practice into Traditional Sociology Courses." *Teaching Sociology* 18 (January 1990): 57–62.

Berger, P. L. *Invitation to Sociology: A Humanistic Perspective.* New York: Anchor Books, 1963.

Bodley, J. H. *Cultural Anthropology: Tribes, States, and the Global System.* Mountain View, Calif.: Mayfield Publishing, 1994.

Dewey, J. *How We Think.* New York: D. C. Heath, 1933.

Dressel, P. "Films That Put Social Problems in Global Context." *Teaching Sociology* 18 (April 1990): 226–30.

Engle, S. H., and A. S. Ochoa. *Education for Democratic Citizenship: Decision Making in the Social Studies.* New York: Teachers College Press, 1988.

Erickson, P. A., ed. *Interim Report on Precollege Anthropology Committee on Research to the AAA Task Force on Teaching Anthropology in Schools.* Halifax, Nova Scotia: St. Mary's University, 1991.

Evans, R. W. "A Bold Vision for the Future of Social Studies." In *The Future of the Social Studies,* edited by M. R. Nelson. Boulder, Colo.: Social Science Education Consortium, Inc., 1994.

Friedman, N. L. "Expansively 'Doing' Sociology: Thoughts on the Limits and Linkages of Sociological Practice." *ASA Footnotes* 15 (1987): 11.

Gray, P. S. "Sociology." In *Charting a Course: Social Studies for the 21st Century,* a report of the National Commission on Social Studies in the Schools, 71–75. Washington, D. C.: National Commission on Social Studies in the Schools, 1989.

Gray, P. S. "Sociology in the Schools." In *Teaching Social Studies,* edited by V.S. Wilson, J.A. Little, and G.L. Wilson. Westport, Conn.: Greenwood Press, 1993.

Henslin, J. M. *Down to Earth Sociology.* 5th ed. New York: Free Press, 1988.

Hunt, M. P., and L. E. Metcalf. *Teaching High School Social Studies.* New York: Harper and Row, 1968.

Ingrassia, M. "Growing Up Fast and Frightened." *Newsweek,* November 22, 1993, 52–53.

Macdonald, J. B. "Value Bases and Issues for Curriculum." In *Curriculum Theory,* edited by A. Molnar and J. A. Zahorik. Washington, D.C.: Association for Supervision and Curriculum Development, 1977.

- **AnthroNotes, a National Museum of Natural History Bulletin for Teachers** is published three times a year and was originally part of the George Washington University/Smithsonian Institution Anthropology for Teachers Program, funded by the National Science Foundation. Free. Contact: Anthropology Outreach and Public Information Office, Department of Anthropology, NHB 363 MRC 112, Smithsonian Institution, Washington, DC 20560.

- The **Teacher's Resource Packet: Anthropology,** published by the Anthropology Outreach Office of the Smithsonian Institution is also available upon request. It contains information, articles, activities, and resources on anthropology, American Indians, creationism, and local archaeology. Contact at address above.

- The **Guide to Departments of Anthropology,** which describes facilities and programs at over 250 schools and museums in the United States and Canada and a Summer Field School List, is available from the American Anthropological Association, the central professional organization of anthropologists, at 4350 North Fairfax Drive, Suite 640, Arlington, VA 22230, (703)528-1902, ext. 3005.

- **Innovative Techniques,** a resource guide with suggested lessons and activities for teaching sociology, is published by the American Sociological Association. Although it is mainly intended for college level, the high school teacher can adapt the activities and lessons. Send $11.50 for members or $15.50 for nonmembers to the American Sociological Association, 1722 N Street NW, Washington, DC 20036, (202)833-3410.

- **Teaching Sociology** is an excellent American Sociological Association journal for ideas on teaching sociological concepts and topics. Also primarily written for the collegiate level but adaptable.

- **The American Psychological Association Monitor** is the association's monthly high school psychology newsletter, which includes teaching activities and curriculum materials. Careers in Psychology is also available. The APA sends the newsletter free to all its High School Teacher Affiliates. Write the APA, 750 First Street, NE, Washington, DC 20002, (202)336-5500.

- **Teaching of Psychology** is a journal with ideas, lessons, and activities that may be used to improve teaching at all levels.

- **The Opposing Viewpoints Series,** edited by D. L. Bender and B. Leone and published by Greenhaven Press, offers 61 paperbacks dealing with a wide range of controversial topics, many related to anthropology, sociology, and psychology, including abortion, AIDS, death and dying, male/female roles, and racism. Each paperback offers pro and con debates on the specific issue.

- **Rethinking Schools** is a nonprofit, independent newspaper advocating the reform of elementary and secondary public schools with emphasis on urban schools and issues of equity and social justice. It provides editorials, articles of interest, and examples of teaching that would be of interest to teachers employing issues-centered instruction. Contact Rethinking Schools, 1001 E. Keefe Avenue, Milwaukee, WI 53212, (414)964-9646.

Massialas, B. G., and B. C. Cox. *Inquiry in Social Studies.* New York: McGraw-Hill, 1966.

Mills, C. W. *The Sociological Imagination.* Fair Lawn, N.J.: Oxford University Press, 1959.

Muessig, R. H., ed. *Controversial Issues in the Social Studies: A Contemporary Perspective.* Washington, D.C.: National Council for the Social Studies, 1975.

National Commission on Social Studies in the Schools. *Charting a Course: Social Studies for the 21st Century.* Washington, D.C.: National Commission on Social Studies in the Schools, 1989.

National Council for the Social Studies. *The Curriculum Standards for Social Studies.* Washington, D.C.: National Council for the Social Studies, 1994.

Rice, M. J. "Precollege Anthropology/Archaeology." In *Teaching Social Studies,* edited by V. S. Wilson, J. A. Little, and G. L. Wilson. Westport, Conn.: Greenwood Press, 1993.

Rollwagen, J. R. "Anthropology and 'Contemporary Issues': Anthropology, Political Economy, and the General Education Curriculum." *Urban Anthropology* 18 (1989): 135–51.

Sociological Resources for the Social Studies. *Inquiries in Sociology.* Boston: Allyn and Bacon, 1972.

Stewart, E.W., and J. A. Glynn. *Introduction to Sociology.* 4th ed. New York: McGraw-Hill, 1985.

Smith, D. W. " What Went Wrong with the Social Studies Reform Movement." *Indiana Social Studies*

Quarterly 15 (April 1981): 19–24.

Sweeney, J. A. C. , and J. B. Parsons. "Teacher
Preparation and Models for Teaching Controversial
Social Issues." In *Controversial Issues in the Social
Studies: A Contemporary Perspective*, edited by R. H.
Muessig. Washington, D.C.: National Council for
the Social Studies, 1975.

Wallace, W. L. " Standardizing Basic Concepts in
Sociology." *American Sociologist* 21 (Winter 1990):
352–58.

White, J. J. "Anthropology." In *Charting A Course: Social
Studies for the 21st Century*, a report of the National
Commission on Social Studies in the Schools,
31–36. Washington, D.C.: National Council for
the Social Studies, 1989.

Part Seven: An Issues-Centered Curriculum

Introduction by William G. Wraga

If one takes seriously the historic mission of education in the United States to educate enlightened citizens of democracy who act as a check against the powers-that-be, it is difficult to deny the imperative of teaching students how to examine, evaluate, and act upon important public issues. These tasks are, after all, principal competencies of the office of citizen in a democratic republic. Teaching and learning about social issues should, therefore, permeate the public school curriculum. The aim of this section is to offer practical ideas, strategies, and examples of teaching about social issues across the curriculum and throughout the grade levels.

Recognizing that students are faced with social issues on a daily basis, Dorothy Skeel presents a rationale for issues-focused curriculum and instruction on the elementary level, identifies criteria for selecting appropriate issues for children to examine, and recommends specific issues and activities for the primary and upper elementary grades. The issues she recommends relate both to the social studies curriculum and to the local community. Skeel identifies developmentally-appropriate trade books and outlines a sample unit organizing the total curriculum around a particular social issue.

Samuel Totten and Jon Pedersen recognize that not only are students bombarded with social issues in the media as well as the home, school, and community, but also that many students experience social issues first hand. They summarize recent developments in middle level education that point to the need for focusing curriculum and instruction on personal-social issues and offer useful criteria for identifying issues appropriate to middle level students. Totten and Pedersen suggest a variety of ways to incorporate the study of societal issues into all subjects of the curriculum, offering "real life" examples of such practices throughout the chapter. They also suggest the possibilities of examining issues in interdisciplinary units and outline an extensive unit on racism in the United States.

Robert Yager and Martha Lutz briefly build a case for teaching with social issues in science and mathematics on the basis of constructivist learning theory. For these authors, the contexts that students need to construct knowledge meaningfully are found in problematic societal issues to which appropriate science and mathematics subjects are applied. Yager and Lutz indicate that the conditions favorable for knowledge construction are in fact hallmarks of Science-Technology-Society education and review the implications of recent developments in science and mathematics education reform for constructivism and for issues-centered curriculum and instruction. Finally, they describe four examples of issues-centered science and mathematics curriculum and instruction in action.

Acknowledging that adolescents face a myriad of social issues, Ronald Evans and Jerry Brodkey call for a substantive change in the organization of the high school social studies curriculum. After summarizing existing models for issue-focused social studies, namely those developed by Hunt and Metcalf, Oliver and Shaver, Engle and Ochoa, and Stanley and Nelson, they present a new framework that attempts to build upon these previous efforts. Evans and Brodkey propose to organize the curriculum around social realities and related ethical issues. They offer an extensive outline for a high school social studies program that identifies major topics and focus questions for each course. They conclude their chapter by discussing the strengths and weaknesses of their proposal.

William Wraga suggests ways to infuse teaching about societal issues across the secondary curriculum, focusing on those areas not addressed in the other chapters and including cocurricular activities. Wraga explains how the English, fine and performing arts, modern foreign language, physical education and health, and vocational curricula can contribute to developing students' understanding of social issues. He identifies pertinent issues that can be infused into these subject areas, suggests issues-related goals and objectives, presents guidelines for handling controversial issues in the classroom, and describes several interdisciplinary approaches to teaching about issues that combine or transcend the conventional subjects.

The authors in this section regard the reality that students already face pressing social issues and the imperative that the schools prepare students for the office of participatory citizenship as challenges to the K-12 curriculum to embrace teaching and learning about social issues as a means to achieving the greater end of sustaining our fragile democratic republic. It is hoped that together these chapters will serve as a modest resource of useful ideas for the practicing educator who wishes to teach students how to act on societal issues in a thoughtful, responsible fashion. In this way teachers can participate in the historic mission of American education to prepare students for participatory citizenship in a democratic republic.

25 AN ISSUES-CENTERED ELEMENTARY CURRICULUM

by Dorothy J. Skeel

Charlene, a kindergartner, lives in a homeless shelter with her mother and sister. Kenya, a happy African American second grader, hears the epithet "nigger" as his bus pulls away from school. Roscoe, a fourth grader, watches a drug deal go down from the front steps of his home in the projects and wonders if his family will ever be able to live in a better neighborhood. Rachel watches the news each night in her rural home, but does not understand why there is fighting in Bosnia or Rwanda; they do not talk about it in her fifth-grade class. Angela, with her sixth-grade class, takes pictures of the pollution that a chemical company left in a lot around the corner from her school.

Rationale

Elementary school children everyday confront situations like those above and others that are equally difficult for them to understand. The media brings into their homes the stark realities of the problems facing our nation and the world. How do they learn to cope with these problems? More importantly, how do they learn to seek solutions to them? How do they relate the historic events of the past with what is happening in their lives today? How can they become rational, participating members of society?

An issues-centered social studies curriculum offers opportunities for children to develop coping and problem-solving skills and to use the knowledge of the past to understand the present. Issues-centered study leads students to question, to acquire information from different perspectives, to discern fact from fiction, and to develop their reasoning skills. Students confront issues that have plagued society over the centuries, as well as issues that confront their immediate envi-

ronment, the nation, and the world.

Many would question whether elementary school children should study social issues. Parents often do not want their children to raise questions or confront serious matters. Teachers, too, may steer away from controversial issues, especially in the elementary school (Gross 1989). Yet research suggests that "learning activities and materials should be concrete, real, and relevant to the lives of young children" (National Association for the Education of Young Children 1986, 7). Joyce (1970, 255) reminds us, "The natural world of childhood is filled with conflict, aggression, interdependence and warmth. To pretend that their world is bland is false."

Children construct their social knowledge as they attempt to build coherent systems that will allow them to think about and explain their immediate environment and the larger world:

Put another way, children's social judgments are not random responses; rather they are the result of the application of analysis and reason in the social world and are influenced by such factors as peer groups, adults, social and educational environments, experiences, and the institutions to which they are exposed. Social judgments also involve more than the child's "getting along" in the home or school environment. They involve the child's ability to make decisions about such issues as race and ethnicity, citizen concerns of law and justice, and social welfare and economics, many of which make competing claims in a rapidly changing world. (Turiel 1983, as cited in National Council for the Social Studies 1989, 19).

Research tells us that, for our purposes, the early years of life are important, because we are more open to diversity (Stone 1986) and have an interest in and analyze racial and ethnic differences (Semaj 1980). Racial and ethnic prejudices are well established and resistant to change by the time children reach age nine or ten (Joyce 1970). Also by this age, self-concepts are formed, and positive feelings about the self are important in social interactions (Stanley 1985); political socialization is well advanced by the end of elementary school. Additionally, children will have developed a sense of need for consensus and majority rule (Hess and Torney 1967).

Young children develop personal flexibility, creativity, open mindedness, and tolerance of unfamiliar ideas through interaction with their social environment (Joyce 1970; National Association for the Education of Young Children 1986). Issues-focused instruction provides opportunities for children to work with others, learn how to handle conflict, solve problems, develop concern for others, and interact with value issues that they encounter daily in their environment. These experiences will permit children to become reflective citizens who understand their world, who can make rational decisions, and who will be humane, participating members of society.

Developing the Curriculum

How should an issues-centered curriculum for the elementary school be organized? How do teachers decide which issues to pursue? Engle (1989) suggests that teachers should be highly selective and limit study to a relatively small number of topics or episodes (each of which should be examined in depth). The topics should be those that encourage thinking, may be controversial, or are "historical interpretations of the past, or about alternative resolutions to social problems of the present" (ibid., 187). For young children in the early grades, the issues should be more personal, ones that they can understand, and with which they have had experiences. By the third or fourth grade, children can begin to examine more abstract issues.

Selection of the issues to be studied is of crucial importance. Criteria to apply include the following: **1.** Is the issue of real significance? **2.** Is it likely to be or has it been continually recurring? **3.** Will study of the issue help attain the goals of issues-centered education? Will the students become better-informed, thoughtful citizens as a result of the study? **4.** Does the issue require judgment and/or critical thinking? **5.** Are the children sufficiently mature and experienced to thoroughly understand the study?

6. Is it appropriate for the children's developmental level? Each teacher must answer these questions relative to the children in the classroom. However, it should be understood that the study of issues is not an add-on to the curriculum. It is, rather, a different way to look at instruction. It is recognizing that, as a teacher, you are not passing on a set of right answers to children, but that you are assisting them in seeking answers to questions that excite and motivate them, questions that may have many possible answers. Issues are often best stated in the form of questions.

Suggested Issues-Focused Activities

Primary Grades

As an example of issues-focused activities, we will highlight the topic of homes. When kindergarten children are studying about homes, they may ask the questions, Why do people live in different types of homes? Why do some people not have a home to live in? For both questions, there may be several answers. In this situation, instead of giving children pat answers as to why people live in apartments, houseboats, etc., rather provide them the opportunity to think about the different possibilities. The same is true of the homeless situation; there may be various reasons why people are homeless. One of the problems teachers face in having children seek alternative answers is securing information that is understandable to them. Often textbooks present "right" answers, as opposed to giving children the opportunity to arrive at their own conclusions.

Children's literature, both fiction and nonfiction, may serve as useful resources when teaching about issues. As an example, *Houses and Homes,* by Ann Morris, describes various types of houses and homes around the world and the culturally diverse people who live in them; *This Is My House,* by Arthur Dorros, gives full-page illustrations of houses around the world with the text written in the language of the country. A book that asks What does home mean? and answers it multiculturally is *Home: A Collaboration of Thirty Distinguished Authors and Illustrators of Children's Books to Aid the Homeless,* edited by Michael J. Rosen ("Notable Books" 1993). Older children can make use of other resources, including reference books, and can conduct interviews, take field trips, or invite knowledgeable persons to speak to the class.

As children listen to the stories and observe the illustrations about homes, they will begin to examine reasons why people live in the types of homes they do. Questions arise such as Why do some people who live near the water have their houses built on poles? What type of homes do people live in where it is cold most of the year? An activity that might follow would be to pose situations: If you were going to build a home in the mountains, what might it look like? Why? Children can draw pictures of homes; for instance, if they were going to live in the city, what would their home be like? Why? Another activity might be the building of a house out of cardboard boxes. The class can then analyze the issue of people living in cardboard boxes: Why does this happen? What would be some of the problems if you lived in a cardboard box?

Throughout the elementary grades, issues to highlight can be identified within the topics generally included in the curriculum. For instance, as children, (whether in first or second grade) pursue the study of neighborhood or their immediate community, they may focus on the environment. After a walking tour of the playground and several blocks around their school, the issue identified may be the types of pollution present in the neighborhood: Why are they there? Children may identify trash that litters the playground and streets, air pollution from cars, or water pollution, if there is a stream or river nearby. Science may be combined to identify living things in the neighborhood and how they are affected by the pollution.

If litter is one of the problems the children identify, they might collect trash from the playground or a one-block area in the city or a quarter-mile area around the school in a rural or suburban area. The children then separate the trash and categorize it. What are the most common categories of trash? Why do people throw these things away? What can be done to stop it? What is being done to stop it?

Children might do a "waste audit" by checking the amount and kind of waste in their classroom and the school, including the cafeteria. They may examine how much food is wasted, how much paper and paint is thrown away, and if this can be changed (Seefeldt 1993, 191). There are always action plans that children can pursue, including recycling paper, cans, glass, and plastic; developing posters that encourage

people not to litter and reminding them to recycle; learning about laws to fight pollution and writing letters to editors or others to encourage people not to litter.

Environmental issues can be pursued at any age. When studying the westward movement, for example, children can pursue the reason why people moved and what happened to the land and the animals. Sixth graders might look historically at the problems people have had over the centuries in attempting to dispose of their waste. Why has the amount of waste increased? What can be done about it?

As third graders study about their community or communities in other parts of the world, they might pursue the issue of why communities are formed and why they grow up where they do. Interviewing the oldest residents of the community and visiting cemeteries to find out who lived there can provide important information about the community. Were there immigrants from other countries who came there to live? Why did some families remain there for generations while others moved on?

Another issue that may be pursued is housing patterns in the community. Why do people live where they do? Do ethnic and racial groups tend to live only in certain areas? Have social and economic factors caused them to live where they do? Is there prejudice against certain groups in the community? Why? Should attempts be made to alter the old housing patterns? If so, how can they be changed?

Upper Elementary Grades

Research tells us that elementary-age children are already aware of societal attitudes toward different groups of people in regard to housing location, dating and marriage, etc. Children can think critically about these things when they have sufficient experience and active involvement in discussion and inquiry (Ragan and McAulay 1973). As children's thinking abilities develop they are able to deal with more abstract issues. Fourth graders might select a cultural group, either in this country or another country, and determine how the culture has changed. They can then pursue the reasons for the changes. Did the culture change because the environment changed, such as a loss of resources, drought, or famine? Were the changes a result of technology or did other cultural groups cause them to change? Any group of Native

Americans, Aztecs, Mayas, or Incas of Central and South America, or the Irish during the potato famine or any group in a country that was colonized would be used as examples. Current identifiable groups of people that are entering the United States would also be examples.

Fifth graders typically study U.S. history that emphasizes the American Revolution, but do children really understand the concept of revolution and why it occurs? One way to approach this subject is through the issue of when and why revolutions occur. Researching earlier revolutions and modern-day revolutions, children begin to understand that some revolutions are not wars. What are some of the ideas that have been the basis for revolution? How do revolutions start? How is the Industrial Revolution different from the French and American Revolutions? Questioning whether the American Revolution should have been fought will give children a different perspective. How might their lives be different today if it had not occurred?

An issue that is generally connected only to the Civil War is that of slavery. Many children think the only slaves were those brought from Africa. Historically, different groups of people have been slaves or enslavers. Why were people slaves? What were the economic, religious, cultural, and geographical reasons for people becoming slaves? By studying slavery from a comparative perspective, a more valid concept of the term can be realized (Baptiste and Baptiste 1977).

Often, local issues that affect students' lives will become a focus of study. A manufacturing plant closes, leaving many people out of work, affecting the parents of children in the school. What has caused the plant to close? What can be done about it? Are there other jobs available in the community? Do people need new job skills to take advantage of available employment? How can the community help? Another issue that frequently comes up in a community is how to help the increasing number of homeless families. Children need to investigate what services are available for the homeless in the community. Who helps them—public or private organizations? What else can be done? How can the children help out?

Many of the issues above are common to communities across the nation and the rest of the world. After pursuing solutions to the problems in their own communities, children can then expand their study to determine if the same solutions might be workable in other areas of the country or the world.

Integrating Issues Within the Total Curriculum

The following learning activities are intended as examples of what a teacher might do. Teachers may prefer to identify issues related to the units that they currently teach, rather than the issue used here, and other activities can be added depending on the class and the amount of time that will be spent on an issue.

The Example

The study of an issue can encompass the total curriculum, utilizing connections among the subject areas. When we tackle an issue in our everyday world, we do not separate it by subject matter; therefore, it seems reasonable that such an approach in the classroom causes unnecessary schisms. Let us begin with a fifth-grade class that is about to study the American Revolution. Instead of the usual chronological/topical what-were-the-causes approach, we ask the question, "Should the American Revolution have been fought?" As with any other instructional approach, it is important to outline the rationale and objectives for the study.

The Rationale

Students are presented with a situation: Events in history that threatened the American colonists' way of life, such as the imposition of heavy taxes, led them to the decision that it was important to be free from British rule. As a result, we have the Declaration of Independence and the fighting of the American Revolution: Should this have happened? Was the American Revolution necessary?

By pursuing these questions, students view the revolution from several perspectives and become decision makers. After investigating the information available about the events leading up to the war and thereafter, students test several alternatives to war and decide whether they believe it should have happened or could have been avoided. The goal of the study is to foster the skills necessary for democratic citizenship.

The Objectives

In this exercise, students will
• search for information from different perspectives and a variety of sources;

- learn to assess and validate information;
- use skills of critical thinking, problem solving, and decision making;
- become aware of the interrelationships among content areas;
- communicate with members of a group through a variety of means;
- use skills of cooperation in working with the members of a group;
- learn to accept the opinions of others and recognize that opinions will vary.

Integrated Activities

There are any number of possible activities to accompany this study. The following is an outline of some suggestions.

1 Place the Declaration of Independence on a series of transparencies. With the entire class, analyze the document and identify in it the grievances of the colonists. Make a list of the grievances. For example, the British failed to approve laws passed by governors; dissolved houses of representation; kept armies in the colonies during peaceful times; cut off trade with other countries; imposed taxes without colonists' consent; and deprived the colonists of trial by jury.

After the class has identified the grievances, divide them into small groups with each group taking one of the grievances to investigate. Within each group, some students should view the grievances from the perspective of the colonists, while others view it from the perspectives of the Loyalists (those sympathetic to the crown). Each group should identify the event or events that have caused their grievance. Later, after the research is completed, the groups should present their information to the class from both perspectives.

2 Have students read literature that will help them understand what life was like in the colonies at the time of the revolution. Books can be read to the students or they may read them individually or in groups. Some possibilities are the following:

Longfellow, Henry Wadsworth. *Paul Revere's Ride* (Dutton, 1990).

Meltzer, Milton. *The American Revolutionaries: A History in Their Own Words, 1750–1800* (Crowell, 1987); *George Washington and the Birth of Our Nation* (Watts, 1986); *Thomas Jefferson: The Revolutionary Aristocrat* (Watts, 1991).

Roop, Peter, and Connie Roop. *Buttons for General*

Washington (Carolrhoda, 1986).

Smith, Carter, ed. *The Arts and Sciences—A Sourcebook on Colonial America; Daily Life—A Sourcebook on Colonial Life; The Revolutionary War—A Sourcebook on Colonial America* (Millbrook, 1991).

3 Have students take on the role of colonists and write letters to their relatives in Great Britain explaining what is happening in the colonies. Some students should write from the perspective of loyalists.

4 Estimate the distance of the colonies from Great Britain and how long it would take to travel between the two lands. Investigate the number of troops that were brought to the colonies from Great Britain. Find out the number that could be carried in each ship and estimate the number of ships it would take to transport them. Also determine how long it would take to bring supplies for the troops from Great Britain.

5 Investigate the number of troops that were quartered in colonists' homes. Determine what the cost would be to the families to keep the soldiers. Decide whether this was a legitimate grievance. Estimate what the cost would be to quarter troops in people's homes today.

6 After reading *Buttons for General Washington, Paul Revere's Ride,* **and** *Arts and Sciences—A Sourcebook on Colonial America,* **determine the extent of the technology available at that time.** Find out how people communicated within the colonies and with people in Great Britain. Determine how long it would take to get messages from Great Britain to the colonies. Discuss the effect that lags in communication might have on the war. Determine the types of guns and ammunition that both sides had available and whether that could affect the outcome.

7 Develop a time line of the major battles of the Revolutionary War. At the same time, develop a map of Great Britain and the colonies, indicating where battles were fought and what the outcomes were, including the battles at sea.

8 Have students role play. This should be used in seeking solutions to issues or in presenting issues as "real-life" situations, demonstrating how they affect the lives of people. It may also illustrate the complexities of issues and the different value positions people hold. Role playing a discussion between a colonist who is a patriot and one who is a loyalist is one example. Other situations that might be good for role playing would be Cornwallis' surrender to Washington at Yorktown or the signing of the peace treaty in Paris. Murals could be painted as backdrops, providing a more authentic setting for the situation.

9 **Have students draw political cartoons depicting different perspectives of the causes of war, for example, loyalist and patriot positions.**

10 **Using primary sources, such as diaries, letters, and journals, help students understand the feelings and ideas of the people involved in the war.** Abigail Adams' letters to her husband, John Adams, when he was attending the Continental Congress in Philadelphia is a good example. Letters among the delegates at the Constitutional Convention and those who were in Europe, such as Thomas Jefferson, John Adams, and Thomas Paine, tell some of the story of what was happening as the Constitution was being written. Paintings and music from that era could further illustrate what life was like and how people represented it through the arts.

11 **Investigate the forms of government in the colonies before the Declaration of Independence, during the time of the Articles of Confederation, and after the Constitution.** This provides important information to students that will help them make some decisions about the revolution. A data retrieval chart might be used to illustrate the differences among the governments at each of these times and their effect on the colonies and the people.

12 **As a culminating activity, a debate or panel discussion can be held to discuss whether the American Revolution should have been fought.** Alternatives to the war should be discussed. Students should consider what their lives might be like if the war had not been fought. After the debate or discussion, each student should decide whether he or she would have been a patriot or loyalist if he or she had lived at that time. Each should write down his or her decision and give reasons for being a patriot or loyalist.

Summary

This chapter has demonstrated how issues-centered social studies education can be implemented within an elementary curriculum. An example of a historical issue, the American Revolution, illustrates how the total curriculum—including reading and language arts, math, science, the arts, and certainly social studies—can be integrated through such study. One cannot deny the importance of the elementary years in laying the foundation for later and increasingly mature understanding of civic responsibility and the information and skills necessary to make informed rational decisions as a citizen of a democracy. An issues-centered social studies curriculum provides the opportunities to develop those skills and to foster a lifelong habit of active participation for living in a democracy.

References

Baptiste, H. Prentice, and Mira Baptiste. "Developing Multicultural Activities." In *Multicultural Education: Commitments, Issues, and Applications*, edited by Carl A. Grant. Washington, D.C.: Association for Supervision and Curriculum Development, 1977.

Engle, Shirley H. "Proposal for a Typical Issue-Centered Curriculum" *Social Studies* 80 (September/October 1989): 187-189.

Gross, Richard. "Reasons for the Limited Acceptance of the Problems Approach." *Social Studies* 80 (September/October 1989): 185-186.

Hess, R. D., and Judith Torney. *The Development of Political Attitudes in Children.* Chicago: Aldine, 1967.

Joyce, Bruce R. "Social Action for the Primary Schools." *Childhood Education* 46 (February 1970): 254-258.

National Association for the Education of Young Children. "Position Statement on Developmentally Appropriate Practice in Early Childhood Programs Serving Children from Birth through Age 8." *Young Children* (September, 1986): 4-19.

National Council for the Social Studies. "Social Studies for Early Childhood and Elementary School Children Preparing for the 21st Century." *Social Education* 53 (January 1989): 14-23.

"Notable 1992 Children's Trade Books in the Field of Social Studies." *Social Education* 57 (April/May 1993): 197-208.

Ragan, William, and John D. McAulay. *Social Studies for Today's Children.* 2nd edition. New York: Appleton-Crofts, 1973.

Seefeldt, Carol. *Social Studies for the Preschool-Primary*

Child. New York: Merrill, 1993.

Semaj, L. "The Development of Racial Evaluation and
   Preference: A Cognitive Approach." *Journal of Black
   Psychology* 6 (1980): 59-79.

Stanley, William B. *Review of Research in Social Studies
   Education: 1976-1983.* Washington, D. C.: National
   Council for the Social Studies, 1985.

Stone, Lynda. "Intercultural and Multicultural
   Education." In *Elementary School Social Studies:
   Research as a Guide to Practice,* edited by Virginia A.
   Atwood. Washington, D. C.: National Council for
   the Social Studies, 1986.

26 ISSUES-CENTERED CURRICULA AND INSTRUCTION AT THE MIDDLE LEVEL

by Samuel Totten and Jon Pedersen

Whether adults wish to believe it or not, early adolescents are definitely aware of, if not influenced and plagued by, many of the key social issues of our times. How could it be otherwise when the media—radio, television, newspapers, and magazines—flood our homes and schools daily with more and more information about the latest problems and issues facing Americans. Indeed, it is astounding to consider what sitcoms, talk shows, television movies, compact discs, and videos disseminate to our young people. Through such means, they may witness tales of drug abuse, the homeless, racism, discrimination, genocide, child and spouse abuse, gang warfare, degradation of the environment, and poverty. That does not even take into consideration what young adolescents see, hear, and experience in their own homes, schools, and communities.

It is a simple but profound fact that many early adolescents have firsthand knowledge of society's ills and problems. Statistics on the number of early adolescents affected by poverty, violence, homelessness, drug use, and crime open our eyes to the realities:

By the end of October 1992, 4,051 of cases of AIDS were in children less than 13 years of age; 912 cases were in adolescents aged 13–19; and 103,842 cases were in young adults 19–34 years. Because of the 10-year average incubation period for AIDS, many young adults who have AIDS were infected with HIV in their teens.

(Council of Chief State School Officers January 1993, 1)

Between 60 and 75 percent of all adolescents first try alcohol or tobacco products prior to age 15 and as many as 20 to 25 percent already have problems with substance abuse by that age.

(Scales 1991, 28)

At present, one in five young adolescents aged ten to fifteen lives in poverty.

(Hechinger 1992, 30)

About 10,000 adolescents under the age of fifteen annually give birth in the United States.

(Hechinger 1992, 72)

Society can hardly expect young people to become fully engaged, thoughtful, and active citizens if our schools do not prepare them to be informed and skilled in responsibly addressing social issues. The Carnegie Foundation's (Carnegie Council on Adolescent Development 1989, 93) report on middle level education corroborated this point when it asserted that young people should be "encouraged to reflect on the underlying causes of current social problems and to design appropriate action campaigns in response to these conditions."

A key rationale educators have for developing and implementing an issues-centered educational program is to develop "a unitary field, fusing material from the disciplines but organizing it around societal issues or problems" (Evans 1989, 178). At the heart of issues-centered education is the recognition that change and healthy conflict are inherent in a democratic society. The aim of this approach is to develop reflective citizens who are ultimately capable of rationally analyzing, synthesizing, and acting upon issues central to citizenship. Students learn to acknowledge, appreciate, and wrestle with the need to continuously reinterpret, reevaluate, and address societal values, issues, and policies. At the core of the issues-centered instructional process is discussion, problem solving, investigation, and reflection. Finally, inherent in any issues-centered program is the commitment to a learning process in which students examine issues central to their lives.

Middle School Curriculum and Instruction

Surprisingly, while much discussion in the United States has centered on meeting the unique educational needs of early adolescents, discussion about the middle level curriculum has been, at least until very recently, oddly and disturbingly shunted aside or totally ignored. Beane (1990, 5) cogently noted that

> efforts to reform middle level education have made considerable progress in the nearly thirty years of the middle school movement, particularly with regard to developing more widespread awareness of the characteristics of early adolescence and reorganizing institutional features, such as school climate. ... Largely obscured in this search for improved middle level education has been what is probably the most critical question in this or any other kind of authentic school reform: *What should be the curriculum of the middle school?*

Unfortunately, for the most part, the curricular programs in many so-called middle schools today are no different from those found in typical junior highs. That is, they are generally traditional in their approach—"subject centered and largely academic" (Beane 1990, 8). This situation persists despite the fact that over the past forty-five years or so, numerous individuals in both the junior-high (Gruhn and Douglas 1947; Faunce and Bossing 1958; Van Til, Vars, and Lounsbury 1967) and middle level (Moss 1969; Lounsbury and Vars 1978; Arnold, 1985; Vars 1987; Beane 1990) movements have called for at least a portion, if not the total curriculum, to be "problems-based." But, as Beane (1990, 23) pointed out, not only has a problems-based approach largely been ignored but the reality is that "middle school practice continues to be confounded by the deadening effects of low level subject area instruction." Toepfer (1992) agreed and noted that

while the "broad fields," "social problems," and "emerging needs" approaches all have the potential for engaging students in an issues-centered approach, they are the most seldom used approaches in middle level programs today. The two key reasons why the subject-centered approach has held up so long is simple—tradition drives the curriculum and instructional programs of most schools, and public schools are overwhelmingly influenced by the curriculum of postsecondary educational institutions, which have a propensity for approaching curriculum in an almost strictly subject-area fashion.

That said, three recent developments provide hope on the middle level front in garnering middle level educators' commitment to implement a personal and social problems curricular approach. First, the Carnegie Council on Adolescent Development (1989, 15–16) delineated five qualities that it envisions "in the 15-year-old who has been well served in the middle years of schooling." Three are particularly germane to an issues-centered curriculum—the development of **1.** *an intellectually reflective person:* "to analyze problems and issues, examine the component parts, and reintegrate them into either a solution or into a new way of stating the problem or issue"; **2.** *a good citizen:* "accept responsibility for shaping and not simply being shaped by surrounding events. ... a youth who is a doer, not just an observer. ... a feeling of personal responsibility for and connection to the well-being of an interdependent world community"; and **3.** *a caring and ethical individual:* "recognize that there is good and bad and that it is possible and important to tell the difference. ... exhibit the courage to discern the difference as a normal part of daily life and to act on the conclusions reached."

Second, the National Middle School Association (1993) developed a position paper (NMSA 1992) on middle level curriculum, which continues to be germane to a personal- and social-focused curricular approach:

> We strongly support learning experiences which: help young adolescents make sense of themselves and the world around them; address students' own questions and focus upon enduring issues and ideas; and actively engage students in problem-solving and a variety of experiential learning opportunities. ... Further, we advocate learning experiences

which: cultivate initiative and responsibility; involve students in meaningful and useful service activities; and above all, seek to develop good people, fostering caring for others, democratic values, and moral sensitivity.

Third, Beane (1990, 21) has developed a theoretical curriculum framework for the middle level. The goal, in part, is to "integrat[e] information from different subjects within themes that transcend the subjects themselves." More specifically, he argued that "the middle school ought to be a general education school and that its version of general education ought to be of the kind based upon personal and social concerns" (36). He argued that a key dimension

> which a general education must be concerned [with] is the array of larger social issues that face our society and world today and those which are likely to do so in the future. In conceptualizing this dimension we must remember that early adolescents do not live in isolation within that stage of development or apart from larger realities in the world. ... To think that [social] issues are remote from early adolescents is to ... miss the fact that they are real people living out real lives in a very real world. ... These [social issues such as] poverty, homelessness, pollution, and racism are "marginalized" by the typical academic-centered subject area curriculum both in terms of the narrow view of what it presents and by what it leaves out. An adequately framed general education must thus address these issues or risk collapsing under the weight of its own irrelevancy. (38–39)

Selecting Appropriate Social Issues for Study

As for identifying appropriate issues for early adolescents, it is our belief that almost any topic, no matter how serious (AIDS, child abuse, the homeless) or even horrendous (such as the Holocaust) can be addressed in a middle level classroom if done in a sensitive and pedagogically sound manner. In concert with their students, teachers must use professional judgment and discretion, searching for sensitive and accurate information that challenges but does not depress or overwhelm students. Knowing that early ado-

lescents have many and varied needs and interests, educators must develop diverse and versatile curricular and instructional programs. Such an approach reflects the major tenet of middle level education in attending to all aspects of young adolescents' development—cognitive, social, emotional, moral, and physical.

For those working with middle level students, it is a good idea to begin planning issues-centered programs by tapping student curiosity, interests, and experiences. As Berman (1993, 9) observed, it is wise for teachers

> to pay attention to the circumstances of their students' lives and then create the bridge to the larger world. By helping students see the larger context of their lives and enter that context with a sense of confidence and responsibility, they empower and inspire them.

In selecting issues for study, teachers are wise to determine those of the greatest interest to their students and those that may have the greatest influence upon their lives. Issues of local importance often meet these two important criteria (Penick 1985; Pedersen 1992; Harms and Yager 1981; Totten and Pedersen 1993). If a local issue holds interest and has influence, it is likely that students will more readily come to understand that social issues faced by members of their community may also be common across the state, nation, or world. Second, selecting a local issue may help students examine the issue "up close." Third, and possibly most significant, if the students become involved in local community service, the impact of the students' actions will be apparent to them.

A fifth-grade teacher who approached the study of social issues through the personal concerns of his students said:

> I talk to them about the violence in the world and relate that to the violence in their own lives. They are beginning to have strong opinions about these issues by fifth grade. We talk about what could have been done in the situation: What are the possibilities? Who was affected if the situation became violent? What if innocent persons were caught up in this? We often talk about the 'genie' of violence being released from the bottle. Once it's released, you can't

control it. Lots of times situations that occur in school exemplify that quite readily. (Goodman and Kreidler 1993, 81–82)

Involving students in issue selection corresponds with the tenet of middle level education that calls for providing students with ample opportunity "to choose and make decisions" in regard to their studies. Teachers and students could generate a list of possible issues by:

1. gleaning those items that particularly catch students' interest during the daily discussion of current events;
2. conducting a brainstorming session;
3. placing a suggestion box in the classroom in which students submit their ideas;
4. discussing conflicts in the community and/or school for which students want more facts;
5. generating a web from a target word or phrase (e.g., "social issues in our community" or "social issues in which I'm interested" or "social issues that influence young people") to cluster ideas related to interesting issues; and
6. developing a questionnaire and conducting a survey.

Speaking about how a student project on hunger was initiated by her combination fourth- and fifth-grade class in Cambridge, Massachusetts, Susan Hughes reported that it all started with a weekly current events assignment:

> One week in October, the assignment was to bring in a [news item] about something local. One child brought in an article about someone who was homeless in Cambridge. They talked about why people are homeless and who is homeless and what it would be like to be child in a homeless family. I think everybody had probably heard about homelessness, but had never thought about it in Cambridge, right in their own area. Most of the children were devastated by the idea that there might be someone who had lived near them at one point who might be homeless (Reindl 1993, 42)

The children were curious as to what they could do to help address the problem, and from that news clipping, an issue of high interest—hunger—became the focus of a class project. The students chose to study the facets of this issue because they were genuinely interested and concerned about the homelessness problem in their community.

Infusing Social Issues at the Middle Level

Can the study of social issues be incorporated into a school that uses ability grouping? A subject-centered curriculum? A multilingual classroom? A school where student boredom with a staid curriculum has led to outright resistance to learning? The answer to each question is an unequivocal "yes." Indeed, the incorporation of social issues into the extant curriculum can be done in scores of different ways, e.g., within a single subject in or outside of the core curriculum or within a cross-disciplinary or interdisciplinary approach. It can also be done by conducting the study in advisor/advisee classes or within an exploratory curriculum program.

In light of the typical constraints in any public school setting (e.g., time factors and an already packed curriculum), the most opportune place to include an issues-centered course is within the exploratory curriculum. In such programs teachers generally have greater freedom to develop an entire course along such perennial issues as racism, poverty, violence, and individual freedom.

That said, those teachers who are either innovative or working in schools where there is more freedom to be innovative can develop outstanding issues-centered courses within the extant curriculum. An exemplary instance is the one developed by Debbie Bell in northern California (see below).

No matter which approach is used, none precludes incorporating current events, biographies, literature, music, and multicultural strands throughout the study. This not only enriches the curriculum but assists students in making connections between the various disciplines, benefiting students both cognitively and affectively through study that is in depth, not superficial. Such an approach will also more likely meet the needs of students' various learning styles as well as their individual interests.

Take for example Zakiyah Bilal, a seventh-grade English teacher at Solomon Lewenberg Middle School in Mattapan, Massachusetts, who teaches social issues through the study of literature and uses drama and oral history to engage her students. Her students comprise an eclectic group—a mix of African-American, Hispanic American, Asian-American, and

European-American students—yet she makes a special effort to portray the richness of her students' cultures through literature and drama. Speaking of the power of literature, she said:

> Good literature has a way of opening up topics the kids are concerned about. They're children, but they're aware of things. ... There's a lot on kids' minds these days and on mine, too. A student I taught—a sixth grader I remember as the kid who chewed gum—was stabbed to death in a foolish argument. A twelve year old girl was shot to death on a street corner, mistaken for a gang member. ... I don't want to exploit my students' bad experiences, or probe any psychic wounds. But they have the potential to witness another's pain without laughter or mockery, and I want them to learn through literature that the human spirit is resilient, in spite of terrible circumstances and events. I want them to know about the sufferings and eventual triumphs of Jean Valjean and Cosette [characters in Victor Hugo's *Les Miserables*]. About Richard Wright's struggle to become literate in a society where it was a punishable crime for an African American to possess a library card. (Beckwith 1993, 113, 115)

Bilal used drama-oral history methods with Langston Hughes' "Thank you, Ma'am," which allowed her to explore the impact of poverty and repression with her students—many of whom deal with poverty in their own lives. Students read and discussed the literature and acted out folk tales, created alternative endings to stories and poems, shared their own experiences and concerns, and conducted oral histories related to the stories and issues they read.

The incorporation of music is easy to tie to the study of most social issues. Teachers can provide the lyrics of rock artists like Sting, Pearl Jam, Salt-n-Pepa, and others who address social issues in their music. After listening to and discussing why songwriters and singers address such issues, the students could ascertain what the messages are and how accurately the lyrics portray each problem; creating their own socially conscious lyrics and then putting the lyrics to music; performing the songwriters' or their own lyrics; and reading interviews of songwriters and musicians about the social issues on which they base their songs. Similar efforts could be conducted in other fine arts as well.

Another excellent example of the issues-centered approach is Debbie Bell's fifth-grade class at Ohlone School in northern California. She teaches in a self-contained, bilingual classroom where 98 percent of her students are Hispanic, 89 percent are Limited English Proficient, 75 percent meet Chapter 1 requirements, and 90 percent are members of families that qualify for Aid to Families with Dependent Children (AFDC). Bell (1992, 175, 177) shared the impact of her program:

> Through our partnership with university students [from the University of California, Santa Cruz], my fifth graders have challenged the educational status quo. Because of political, economic, linguistic, cultural, and educational "realities"—all social issues—nearly all of my students are (or have been perceived as) at risk of dropping out of school and/or low academic achievement, or at least are very unlikely to go on to higher education, especially above the community college level. Those that do make it into the four-year system are statistically unlikely to graduate. Nonetheless, this partnership has started to redefine my students as "college bound."

Within a partnership between fifth graders and university students who write and exchange letters, share translation duties, read letters aloud to one another, establishing real and lasting relationships, Bell's students examine many of the systemic issues that most teachers shy away from discussing in a school setting, e.g., what it means (and feels like) to be marginalized in a society, the lack of expectations by educators and society at large for certain portions of our society, and the power of knowledge and the abuse of that power by those within the power structure (and how to overcome that abuse).

The middle level curriculum is also rich with possibilities for conducting cross-disciplinary and interdisciplinary studies. A group of seventh-grade students in Basking Ridge, New Jersey, took part in a cross-disciplinary study of the Holocaust, which addressed issues of prejudice, discrimination, and the deprivation of human rights. In this study the social studies teacher taught the basic historical events that led up to and culminated in the Holocaust; the English teacher read portions of Lois Lowry's *Number the Stars* to the students (an account of the Danes' efforts to rescue Jews fleeing the Nazis), and students discussed and wrote about Anne Frank's diary; the math teacher had "students calculate the relationship between the number of Holocaust victims and the current population of New Jersey"; and the science teacher and students examined "the physiological conditions that made it possible for the Danes to desensitize the sense or smell of guard dogs as part of their rescue efforts" (Townsend and Wraga, forthcoming).

Eighth-grade English students in Tacoma, Washington, selected to study about the homeless. They generated focal questions, researched the issue using INFOTRAC (an automated reference system that provides easy and fast computer-aided retrieval of bibliographic references to more than four thousand magazines, journals and newspapers), interacted with guest speakers (including a teacher who had been homeless as well as an advocate for the homeless), read young adult literature whose focus was the homeless, wrote reflective pieces in journals concerning their new insights and feelings in regard to the plight of the homeless, and devised solutions to address the homeless problem.

In Media, Pennsylvania, a seventh-grade middle level teacher and her students conducted an interdisciplinary study of peoples' perceptions and treatment of the physically handicapped, including access and lack of access for such individuals. In doing so, they discussed various disabilities; studied the anatomy of the nervous, muscular, and skeletal systems; conducted simulations where the students were hearing impaired, learning disabled, or physically disabled; interacted with speakers who were disabled; and evaluated the level of access in their school and, when they discovered some buildings did not meet basic requirements, drew up an action plan.

Students of Amy Blanchard, a teacher at Southern Middle School in Louisville, Kentucky, conducted a study of child abuse. Students "interviewed social workers, nurses, and juvenile justice officials, wrote a seven-act play which they performed before an audience, and prepared a booklet for younger students on how to get help" (Lewis 1991, 4).

On a more sophisticated level, the study could involve the use of unifying themes which would result in a study that is more thoroughly inte-grated and interdisciplinary in nature. If, for example, the students focus on AIDS, trends and cycles could be used as one of the unifying themes that tie together all of the disciplines. More specifically, in science the students could study the life cycle of the virus; in social studies, they could track and examine the trends of AIDS infection in the community or state; in health, P.E. or home economics, they could track lifestyle trends (e.g., changes) as the epidemic becomes more worrisome for all members of society; in math, both statistical trends and cycles regarding the AIDS infection rate in a community or state and/or the changes in public opinion as the epidemic becomes more prolonged and widespread could be monitored and studied; and, in literature, students could ascertain and study how the spread and threat of the disease impacts the trends and changes in the type of literature that is produced. This approach, it should be noted, is still far removed from the "general education" model recommended by Beane (1990).

The table on pages 244 and 245 provides an example of an issues-centered unit that covers core curriculum within a U.S. history course through an interdisciplinary study centered around a perennial human issue.

Many subjects, such as art, physical education, health, industrial arts, music and home economics, are often perceived as subjects that do not lend themselves to the study of social issues. The fact is, however, that each of these content areas can address many vitally significant social issues. On a rather simplistic level, for example, substance abuse (including use of steroids), AIDS, and stereotyping could easily and powerfully be tied to the extant curriculum in physical education. Recycling, hazardous substances, pollution, and defective products are all legitimate issues for study in the industrial arts classroom. Home economics lends itself to the study of abuse in families, homelessness, food additives, pesticides, and truth in advertising. Health class promotes healthy life styles and healthy living, and these concerns naturally correspond with such issues as AIDS, substance abuse, water contamination, poverty, and malnutrition. The environment, human rights, civil rights, civil disobedience, and war could all be tied to the art and music curriculums. *Ideally, though, all disciplines, could approach the study according to Beane's (1990) concept of general education.*

Challenges in the Issues-Centered Classroom

One of the major problems in implementing an issues-centered curriculum is the dominance of the subject-centered curriculum and teachers' headlong push to cover everything listed in the curriculum guides, state mandates, and textbooks. This drive for total coverage emits pressure, convincing many teachers that there is no room or time left for the study of social issues. Instead of examining the age-old curriculum question of "what knowledge is of most worth," teachers and administrators take for granted that the subject approach is the best simply because tradition dictates it. However, by using an issue as the context, then integrating the various disciplines into the study, the teacher may "cover" less information but the student will more readily make key connections between major ideas.

Teachers have also faced the challenge of implementing interdisciplinary units effectively. As Beane (1990, 21) stated:

> What interdisciplinary teaching does take place is consistently of a particular kind, namely "simple" correlations of subject areas. For example, many [interdisciplinary] teams undertake thematic units . . . in which various subject areas make subject-specific contributions during some part of the unit. However, the subjects retain their distinct identity in the units and the contributions often depend upon how much time particular teachers want to devote to them in relation to other content they "need" to cover in their subject. . . . [Such teachers end up stopping] short of possibilities for integrating information from different subjects within themes that transcend the subject themselves.

In fact, most middle level teachers only find the time to conduct one or two so-called "interdisciplinary" units a year. By truly working within interdisciplinary teams in which team members design a semester- or yearlong curriculum where the disciplines truly and thoroughly integrate around social issues, teachers are able to move beyond a fragmented approach.

Issues-centered study within heterogeneous group organization presents a challenge because of the wide span of cognitive and moral reasoning abilities that may be represented in a single class, and the vast differences in regard to the students' social and emotional, and physical development. In order to address these problems, different instructional strategies designed for teaching and studying about social issues are recommended with heterogeneous groups, such as Cooperative Controversy (Holubec, Johnson, and Johnson 1992); the Jurisprudential Model for Science, Technology, and Society (Pedersen 1992); the Jigsaw Synthesis (Totten 1995); and Group Investigation (Sharan and Hertz-Lazarowitz 1980; Wheelock 1992).

It is worth noting that the National Association for Gifted Children (1991) argued that providing a homogeneous group for gifted students allows teachers to match instruction to the rapidly developing skills and capabilities for the gifted student. On the other hand, the National Middle School Association is adamantly opposed to rigid ability grouping in educational settings.

Matching Missions

Despite the few challenges of issues-centered education in a middle school setting, the goals of issues-centered education and the tenets of middle school education are compatible. A primary purpose of the study of social issues is to assist students to become reflective, analytical citizens who are capable of participating effectively in a democratic, self-governing society. Middle school educators accept an extremely worthwhile undertaking by preparing young adolescents to ask penetrating questions, to weigh and solve problems, to search out information pertinent to make intelligent, just, and measured decisions, and to add a voice to a shared discussion among all concerned. Through issues-centered education, those who teach early adolescents can capitalize upon youth's deep and abiding concern for the earth, a sense of social justice, and a genuine concern for those who find themselves in unfortunate circumstances.

References

Arnold, John. "A Responsive Curriculum for Early Adolescents." *Middle School Journal* 6 (May 1985): 14–18.

Beane, James A. *A Middle School Curriculum: From Rhetoric to Reality.* Columbus, Ohio: National Middle School Association, 1990.

Beckwith, Barbara. "Literature in the Classroom:

Sample Middle Level Interdisciplinary Unit on U.S. Racism: EIGHTH GRADE U.S. HISTORY

UNIT GOALS

Students will gain:

1. a deeper understanding of racism and its ramifications throughout history in the United States.

2. an appreciation and understanding of key documents, legal structures, and legal options for taking action against racism.

Interdisciplinary Nature of Study

The study draws on and interweaves contributions from such fields as history, political science, English (literature, composition, grammar, speaking, and listening), art, and music.

Identifying Central Issues

Teacher conducts a brainstorming session to ascertain issues of interest that also relate well to students' lives:

- Individual students "argue" their case for inclusion of desired issues.
- Following ample discussion, students vote on the preferred issue of unit study.

UNIT ACTIVITIES

Reflective Practice

Note: *This strand is woven throughout the unit.*

1. Learning logs emphasize reflection, analysis and synthesis of the issue.

2. Class meetings allow students the opportunity to share thoughts and ideas pertaining to the issue.

3. Ongoing discussions with e-mail groups regarding various perspectives on racism.

4. Periodic responses to affective and cognitive questions posed by the teacher.

DAILY ACTIVITIES

Students will:

- brainstorm preconceived ideas of racism.
- share their own experiences in regard to racism:
  1. personally feeling the brunt of it.
  2. behaving in a racist manner.
  3. observing incidents of racism.
- clarify and define the term *racism* after:
  1. webbing or clustering racism as the central theme.
  2. discussing individual webbing.
  3. creating a mind map based on individual webbings as a whole-class activity.
  4. defining racism in small groups, then developing a class definition.

Teacher will:

- share classic examples of racism (e.g., events, incidents, periods) within U.S. history and provide a synopsis of each. Study may focus on any of the following events/periods:
- Civil War
- KKK activity during the 1920s (baiting of Jews, Catholics and Blacks)
- U.S. internment of the Japanese during World War II
- Civil rights movement of the 1950s and 1960s
- Contemporary examples
  1. Skin Heads **3.** Rainbow Coalition
  2. Nation of Islam **4.** Treatment of recent immigrants

Students and teacher will:

- decide on four key areas to examine.
- locate resources (print, audio, video, and conduct searches over the Internet).
- develop e-mail conferences with other classrooms around the United States that are studying parallel issues.
- analyze, synthesize, and discuss key sources of information.

Note: *During the course of unit study, students will examine seminal documents and governmental actions such as the Declaration of Independence, Emancipation Proclamation, the* Brown vs. Board of Education *decision, and the Civil Rights Act.*

Pathways to Social Responsibility." In *Promising Practices in Teaching Social Responsibility,* edited by S. Berman and P. LaFarge, 104-119. New York: State University of New York Press, 1993.

Bell, Debbie. "Public School and University Companeros: Changing Lives." In *Social Issues in the English Classroom,* edited by C. M. Hurlbert and S. Totten, 174-195. Urbana, Ill.: National Council of Teachers of English, 1992.

Berman, Sheldon. "Introduction." In S. Berman and P. Lafarge, eds., *Promising Practices in Teaching Social Responsibility* (Albany, N.Y.: State University of New York, 1993): 9.

Carnegie Council on Adolescent Development. *Turning Points: Preparing American Youth for the 21st Century.*

New York: Carnegie Corporation of New York, 1989.

Council of Chief State School Officers. *Turning Points: State Network News: A Newsletter of Carnegie Corporation of New York Middle Grade School State Policy Initiative* 3 (January 1993): 1-23.

Evans, Ronald W. "A Dream Unrealized: A Brief Look at the History of Issue-Centered Approaches." *The Social Studies* 80, no. 5 (1989):178–84.

Faunce, Roland C., and L. Nelson Bossing. *Developing the Core Curriculum.* 2d. ed. New York: Prentice-Hall, 1958.

Small groups of students will:
- select different mediums and analyze various examples of racism from the periods under study in order to ascertain key similarities and differences during the various periods. They will also examine how the racist incident was addressed or ameliorated through various channels (e.g., social activism, legislative actions, etc.). They will report their findings to the class.

Students will:
- set up a panel discussion on racism. The panel will be comprised of members from NAACP, Rainbow Coalition, local police department, Skin Heads, local member of the clergy, a community college or university history or American studies professor, and other relevant organizations.
- study related literature (short stories; slave narratives; oral histories by freed slaves, interned Japanese during World War II, civil rights leaders, and recent immigrants (especially Hispanics and Asians) and at least one novel (e.g., Ernest Gaines' *The Autobiography of Miss Jane Pittman*).
- study key music, including slave spirituals, gospels, rap, and contemporary rock.
- study art by and about different races that depict incidents of racism and/or solidarity. Students will also develop their own artistic products (including collages, pen and ink drawings, paintings, sculptures, and mobiles) based upon their studies.

CULMINATING SOCIAL ACTION PROJECT

In order to meet the interest of as many students as possible, the teacher and students will brainstorm ideas addressing racism in their school or community. Based on these suggestions, individuals and/or small student groups will design and carry out social action projects. Among the many racism-related projects that might be considered are the following:

1. Writing and acting out a play.
2. Producing and appearing on a public access television show.
3. Initiating and/or becoming a member of an Amnesty International Adoption Group.
4. Developing and conducting a survey on racism for use in the local community and publishing the results.
5. Developing and conducting a panel discussion on racism as a school assembly.
6. Initiating a school-based conflict resolution process and submitting it to the school administration for approval.
7. Developing a community-based lecture series on tolerance in which invited guests give lectures throughout the school year

Goodman, Sara, and William J. Kreidler. "'You Need Lots of Choices': Conflict Resolution in the Elementary Grades." In *Promising Practices in Teaching Social Responsibility*, edited by S. Berman and P. Lafarge. Albany, N.Y.: State University of New York Press, 1993.

Gruhn, William T., and R. Harl Douglas. *The Modern Junior High School*. New York: Ronald, 1947.

Harms, N. C., and R. E. Yager. *What Research Says to the Science Teacher*. Vol. 3. Washington, D.C.: National Science Teachers Association, 1981.

Hechinger, Fred M. *Fateful Choices: Healthy Youth for the 21st Century*. New York: Carnegie Council on Adolescent Development/Carnegie Corporation of New York, 1992.

Holubec, Edythe Johnson, David W. Johnson, and Roger T. Johnson. "Dealing with Conflict: A Structured Cooperative Controversy Procedure." In *Social Issues in the English Classroom*, edited by C. M. Hurlbert and S. Totten. Urbana, Ill.: National Council of Teachers of English, 1992.

Hugo, Victor. *Les Miserables*. Translated by Charles E. Wilbur. New York: The Modern Library, 1931.

Lewis, Anne. "Hewing City Life: Foxfire and Urban Youth." *High Strides: The Bimonthly Report on Urban Middle Grades* 4 (December 1991): 4.

Lounsbury, John H., and Gordon F. Vars. *A Curriculum for the Middle School Years*. New York: Harper and Row, 1978.

Lowry, Lois. *Number the Stars*. Boston: Houghton-Mifflin, 1989.

Moss, Theodore C. *Middle School*. New York: Houghton Mifflin, 1969.

National Association for Gifted Children. *Position Paper: Ability Grouping*. Washington D.C.: NAGC, 1991.

National Middle School Association. *Middle Level Curriculum: A Work in Progress —The Initial Position Paper of National Middle School Association*. Columbus, Ohio: NMSA, 1993.

Pedersen, Jon E. "The Jurisprudential Model of Study for STS Issues." In *The Status of Science-Technology-Society Reform Efforts around the World: International Council of Associations for Science Education Yearbook, 1992*, edited by R. E. Yager. Washington, D.C.: National Science Teachers Association, 1992.

Penick, J. W. *Science, Technology and Society: Resources for*

Science Educators. Columbus, Ohio: SEMAC Information Reference Center, 1985.

Reindl, Sheila. "Bringing Global Awareness into Elementary School Classrooms." In *Promising Practices in Teaching Social Responsibility,* edited by S. Berman and P. LaFarge. Albany, N.Y.: State University of New York Press, 1993.

Scales, Peter C. *A Portrait of Young Adolescents in the 1990s: Implications for Promoting Healthy Growth and Development.* Carrboro, N.C.: Center for Early Adolescence, 1991.

Sharan, S., and R. Hertz-Lazarowitz. "A Group Investigation Method of Cooperative Learning in the Classroom." In *Cooperation in Education,* edited by S. Sharan, P. Hare, C. Webb, and R. Hertz-Lazarowitz. Provo, Utah: Brigham Young University Press, 1980.

Toepfer, Conrad F. Jr. "Middle Level School Curriculum: Defining the Elusive." In *Transforming Middle Level Education: Perspectives and Possibilities,* edited by J. Irvin. Needham Heights, Mass.: Allyn and Bacon, 1992.

Totten, Samuel. "Jigsaw Synthesis: A Method for Incorporating a Study of Social Issues into the Extant Curriculum." In *Cooperative Learning in Secondary Schools,* edited by J. Pedersen and A. Digby, 389–424. New York: Garland Publishing, 1995.

Totten, Samuel, and Jon E. Pedersen. "Taking Action at the Local Level: The Study of Social Issues in the Middle School." *Inquiry in Social Studies: Curriculum, Research, and Instruction—The Journal of the North Carolina Council for the Social Studies* 29 (Spring 1993): 19–33.

Townsend, Regina, and William G. Wraga. "Implementing an Interdisciplinary Unit on the Holocaust." In *Social Issues and Community Service at the Middle Level,* edited by S. Totten and J. Pedersen. Needham Heights, Mass: Allyn and Bacon, forthcoming, 1997.

Van Til, William, Gordon F. Vars, and John H. Lounsbury. *Modern Education for the Junior High School Years.* 2d ed. Indianapolis, Ind.: Bobbs-Merrill, 1967.

Vars, Gordon F. *Interdisciplinary Teaching in the Middle Grades.* Columbus, Ohio: National Middle School Association, 1987.

Wheelock, Anne. *Crossing the Tracks: How "Untracking" Can Save America's Schools.* Boston, Mass.: The Massachusetts Advocacy Center, 1992.

27 TEACHING SOCIETAL ISSUES IN SCHOOL SCIENCE AND MATHEMATICS

by Robert E. Yager and Martha V. Lutz

Traditional science and mathematics classrooms generally lack relevance and use. The National Science Foundation Status Studies provided abundant evidence that 90 percent of all U.S. schools have traditional classrooms (Helgeson, Blosser, and Howe 1977; Stake and Easley 1978; Weiss, 1978). This is true even in most college classrooms and laboratories (AAAS 1990). Students perceive a deep chasm between the classroom's world of explanations and information in the real world. Brumby (1984, 501) offered a succinct diagnosis of the problem, describing how science is presented as "a body of absolute knowledge, most of which is recorded in books, or yet to be discovered by experts." According to Brumby, students see their task as primarily memorization of facts so they can answer their teacher's questions. These students may become highly skilled at rote memorization but without learning to reason. Brumby asked: "When will they begin to use rather than recite their knowledge?" (501).

Issues-centered education provides both relevance and use. It parallels current constructivist learning theory and meets demands for new teaching strategies in science education grounded in such theory. It is also compatible with two vital goals in science education: to assist students in becoming independent learners, and to provide students with opportunities to apply their knowledge to real-world situations. Rather than solving contrived puzzles found in textbooks or lab manuals, students learn about current community and global issues and how scientific and mathematical analysis, problem solving, and research have direct application in their daily lives.

Constructivist theory and its research base provide a critical rationale for issues-centered curriculum. Research from cognitive science has established the importance of constructivism in teaching science and mathematics (Cleminson 1990). This chapter offers science and mathematics teachers a teaching approach that is constructivist, issues-centered, and true to their disciplines.

Constructivist Theory

Constructivism is a theory about how people learn. This explanation developed from observing that individual knowledge is what the mind *constructs*—not what the mind is *taught*. At the heart of constructivism is the need to make connections—between new information coming in and previously learned information already structured in the learner's mind. These connections are most easily made when new information is offered within a context. A familiar, personally relevant context is usually most effective. Constructivism received particular attention after 1985 when cognitive scientists' research was made public (Fosnot 1989; Resnick 1987; Simon and Schifter 1991; von Glasersfeld 1987, 1988). It has emerged as a dominant theme in educational reform.

Constructivism predicts that true learning requires both a context and the active involvement of the learner. It requires learners to take responsibility for their own learning. Because learning and teaching are intrinsically related, effective teachers provide a personally relevant context for students and encourage them to engage in the learning process (Driver and Oldham 1986).

Reinsmith (1993) asserted that, without an appropriate context, no learning can take place. Conventional teaching strategies attempt to create learning only within a textbook's context, and curriculum is too often determined by those who have not set foot in a real classroom for a long time. Although conventional teaching strategies may produce students who appear to have learned the required material, later tests often confirm that the students have not retained much information, and may not have understood it even while they remembered it (Brumby 1984). Constructivist theory predicts such consequences.

Many physicists and physics teachers are concerned by suggestions that schools move to an issues-centered orientation. Will science and mathematics mastery be compromised by issues-centered teaching? When undergraduate physics majors—viewed as the most successful learners in terms of concept mastery, laboratory skills, and motivation—were given real-world problems to investigate, 85 to 90 percent of the time they were not able to solve the problems (Champagne and Klopfer 1984; Mestre and Lochhead 1990). With real-world problems and issues as relevant contexts for learning, students will learn more physics content, understand it better, and retain this understanding longer than if studying physics consists of solving a series of book problems and recalling formulas on exams. If learning is a desirable outcome, then physics proponents need not fear an issues-centered curriculum.

STS: A New Approach to Teaching Science

Science and technology can be learned within the context of human experiences through the teaching approach known as Science/Technology/Society (STS)(National Science Teachers Association [NSTA] 1990–91). This "context of human experiences" means teachers use relevant societal issues in instruction. It is essential in STS to provide a context for all content, which qualifies it as a constructivist teaching strategy. Using a real-world issue provides a context that first engages students in questions, encourages them to search for answers, and finally, extends to testing alternative solutions the students proposed.

The goal of STS is to meet the serious need for an informed U.S. citizenry, capable of making crucial decisions about current problems and issues and taking personal actions as a result of these decisions. STS teachers identify local, regional, national, and international issues, plan individual and group activities around them, and promote actions designed to address or resolve the issues under investigation, emphasizing

responsible decision making in the real world. STS prepares students for current and future citizenship roles.

STS offers science and mathematics teachers a strategy for achieving scientific and technological literacy for all. Analyzing this approach in light of constructivist theory shows how use of issues promotes real learning. Aldridge (1993, 2) described a childhood experience that is a classic, prototypical STS-type investigation: he was "drifting, doing enough to pass but little else." Then a friend's older brother told him about electronics, and his interest was engaged (the initial step in both learning and STS). He learned as much information about electric circuits as he could. He tried to build a circuit but discovered that he needed to learn mathematics, which he had previously "never bothered with" (2). This need stimulated a search for information, another feature of STS. A young Aldridge also discovered that he needed to learn chemistry and physics, and ultimately recognized the need to understand underlying principles, not just repeat descriptive explanations. His initial interest in and experience with electronics provided a sustained motivation and grew into a career in physics.

STS teachers encourage their students to develop their own theories to account for the data they collect in their experiments. Aldridge (1993, 3) believed that all students should have such "science experiences":

> Working one's way through the creation of a theory to account for an entire array of seemingly unrelated scientific principles or laws opens a whole new world of thought. The experience of learning a basic part of science for yourself can be a powerful, long-term source of motivation. The history of science is filled with examples of a small, apparently insignificant learning experience that was sufficient to sustain the person until an exponentially increasing number of such experiences produced major scientific achievements. How many young people have never had even one such experience? These are not privileged experiences open only to the elite few who will become research scientists. They should be open to all students.

STS instruction follows the steps in the construction of knowledge promoted by constructivists. The first step is *filtering incoming stimuli* based on perceived context. (For example, the word set has one meaning for a tennis player, another meaning for an interior decorator, and still another very particular meaning for a mathematician. Knowing the context determines which meaning to use to interpret the word set.) By providing a context, STS focuses the students' attention on relevant stimuli and information.

The second step is *making connections and generating knowledge structures.* This will only happen if the learner is actively involved in the learning process. Without engagement on the part of the learner, no real learning will take place; at best, there will be rote memorization without comprehension, and the information will soon be forgotten. STS satisfies the second condition necessary for construction of knowledge by using real-world issues to engage students.

Finally, the knowledge that an individual constructs must be *tested* against both internal and external information. If the learner perceives consistency, the knowledge will be *subsumed into long-term memory.* STS prescribes that student questions and investigations drive the lessons, so when STS teachers allow students to design and carry out their own tests rather than using prepackaged "experiments" from a text or lab manual, it is consistent with constructivism.

These features of STS (defining a question, designing tests, and engaging in creative thinking based on data) are all basic features of science as defined by Simpson

(1963). STS teachers encourage students to test their ideas (hypotheses), something not done in traditional science classrooms. Students discuss their results, inform others (a feature of basic science), and take action based on the results. These actions may not be science per se, but they illustrate the value of extending science across the curriculum, or even outside the school. Such extensions can engender community support for the science program, provide recognition for students, and generally illuminate the inherent value of science.

STS empowers students with skills, allowing them to become active responsible citizens, responding to issues that influence their lives. STS is structured around issues and problems with local importance and relevance. Many contemporary global problems are rooted in science and technology; radioactive waste, pesticide drift between national borders, and AIDS are just a few examples. Local applications are obvious: what happens to radioactive waste from the local hospital? Do pesticides applied to a lawn or farm field end up on the neighboring lawns or in groundwater? How can individuals reduce their chances of contracting AIDS?

STS advocates propose to make school science a more accurate representation of real science (Yager 1988, 1990). Science content is an emergent property of STS investigations, not a list of prescribed concepts and activities. In STS courses the lists of science concepts and process skills ordinarily used to dictate instruction are

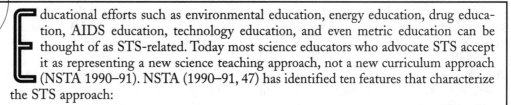

Educational efforts such as environmental education, energy education, drug education, AIDS education, technology education, and even metric education can be thought of as STS-related. Today most science educators who advocate STS accept it as representing a new science teaching approach, not a new curriculum approach (NSTA 1990–91). NSTA (1990–91, 47) has identified ten features that characterize the STS approach:

1. Utilizing issues (with scientific and technical components, and which are interesting and relevant to students) as organizers for the course;

2. Using local resources (human and material) as original sources of scientific or technical information;

3. Involving students in seeking scientific or technical information to solve real-life problems;

4. Extending science learning beyond the class period, the classroom, and the school;

5. Focusing upon the impact of science and technology on each individual student;

6. Viewing science content as relevant to life, not exams;

7. Removing the emphasis on mindlessly mimicking science process skills;

8. Emphasizing career awareness—especially careers related to science and technology;

9. Providing opportunities for students to perform in citizenship roles as they attempt to solve problems and answer questions about the natural world; and

10. Demonstrating that science and technology are major factors which will impact the future.

instead the products of learning: constructed knowledge. If students can use such higher order thinking skills as application, synthesis, and evaluation, learning is evident. Use of skills and knowledge is further evidence of mastery (Yager, Blunck and Ajam 1990).

Examples of Issues-Centered Instruction

Using current problems and issues as curriculum organizers is both motivating and contextualizing for students. In this section of the chapter four authentic narratives about issues-centered science and mathematics instruction illustrate how issues-centered STS courses can be taught. These four examples are not organized around prescribed content areas nor are they focused primarily on scientific or mathematical processes. Instead, each classroom example is organized around a context: an issue of personal relevance to the students.

Analyzing Problems of the Local Airport

Morgan Masters' science students in Chariton, Iowa, made discoveries about their airport when its maintenance funds ran low. These eighth graders were beginning a two-day unit on flight, when a student asked, "Why all this fuss about the airport?" Others questions followed. "Who uses the airport?" "What types of planes land at the airport?" "How much does a pilot's license cost?" None of these questions could be answered by looking in a textbook.

Students searched for answers to their questions. They telephoned airport personnel, city officials, and community business people. The County Extension Offices, the Iowa Department of Transportation, Iowa Civil Air Patrol, and other airports across Iowa gave the students more information. The students set up a network of resources, and each resource contacted led to more ideas, deepening the students' understanding of the issue.

Students surveyed the community to determine what people knew about the airport's financial crisis; the majority of the people were not aware of problems. The students decided to put the airport at the center of the public's attention by planning a "Flight Day." The students took charge of setting up Flight Day activities for this one-day event.

The big day featured hot-air balloonists, stunt pilots, rocket launches, kite-flying contests, and water-balloon launches. Flight Day showcased a variety of community talent and the work of local and state transportation agencies. Students took on various roles—some were system flight analysts (recording flight times and patterns of rockets); others were photographers, video-camera operators, or announcers. The assistant airport manager and a team of students arranged for twenty different pilots and their planes to be available for tours and demonstrations.

Students built community awareness through Flight Day. They followed up with a presentation at the City Council Meeting, voicing their concerns and the concerns of the community. Today repairs have been made to the runways. The airport continues to serve the community's needs. The eighth graders felt that they enlightened the entire community. Flight Day has become a tradition in Chariton, Iowa, continuing to link the school and the community in a special way.[1]

Measuring Crime, Babies, and Grades

In Jennifer Matt's Probability and Statistics class in Cresco, Iowa, students learn on their own by using problems from the "real world." They collect data and then present written and oral reports to people who might be interested in the results. Examples are:

Birth of babies at the Howard County Hospital. Students evaluate data on weight, length, circumference of head, time of birth, length of pregnancy, and other information they select. The students draw conclusions from the data. (Critical features of this experience are that the students select variables for data collection, develop their own hypotheses, and draw conclusions from the data. This is radically different from having the text or teacher tell them what the hypothesis is, what data to collect, and what the "right" answer will be.)

Ambulance calls. Students evaluate data on the time a call is received, length of the run, time to reach the location, time to return to the hospital, and type of call. After the data collection, students are encouraged to speak with the emergency staff with recommendations that have reasoned conclusions drawn from the collected data.

Crime in Cresco. Students evaluate data on the type of crime, when it happened, where it happened, dollar amount involved, etc. Upon evaluation, they look for patterns—e.g., more crime occurs on paydays. (Looking for patterns

Recycling Plastics

What do you do with a garageful of plastic milk jugs? Sixth-grade students at Jefferson School in Charles City, Iowa, certainly know the answer. How many milk jugs does it take to fill a garage or make a recycled picnic table? Charles City students used a donated garage as a recycling center for an entire year, searching for answers to such questions. They used their mathematics and science skills in a way that was meaningful and useful.

It all began one day in science class when someone asked: Doesn't the density of plastic have something to do with whether you can recycle it or not? This question made everyone think. For years sixth graders in science class had explored density, but their teacher, Janet Dunkel, thought exploring this student question would uncover a wealth of understanding connected to an important statewide issue. Dunkel challenges her students on a regular basis to question and devise tests for their questions. For their project students collected plastic containers of all sorts. They contacted engineers and scientists and manufacturers who create plastics, investigating the concept of density in a new way. Students collected, analyzed, and interpreted data. They were not mindlessly memorizing formulas and definitions; they were using them.

Students surveyed the Charles City community to determine personal recycling habits and what people thought of recycling. Apparently, plastic milk jugs were causing the most concern. Charles City did not have a comprehensive recycling plan. The students thought that perhaps they could collect and recycle milk jugs. People began stopping by the elementary school to drop off milk jugs. The students asked if someone could donate "warehouse" space for the jugs. A neighbor donated a vacant garage adjacent to school property.

The Girl Scouts and Boy Scouts heard of the project and offered help by sorting and baling. The local grocery store provided a compactor, and a local trucking firm donated a truck and driver to move the bales of jugs to the recycling center in northeast Iowa. The idea had taken hold, and the project was growing. The students created a proposal for the City Council, asking for the community to assume some responsibility and make recycling part of the overall city plan for waste management. Today Charles City has a comprehensive recycling plan that grew out of the garageful of plastic milk jugs and the concerns of sixth-graders.[3]

in data is a key feature of basic science.) Students recommended the time of day when the police chief should assign more police officers on duty.

Absences and grade-point average. Students collect comparative data on the number of absences in high school and GPA. When they discover a negative correlation, they then must decide if it is significant.

Some students do not like these projects because they do not know what the answer is going to be. Many of Matt's "good" students are good merely because they mimic her steps. It is very difficult for them to think on their own. They really don't want to struggle with learning. They often ask her to "Just tell me how to do it." Other students like the projects because they can see that mathematics is more than working textbook problems.[2]

Beautifying Iowa Roadsides

Clayton County employees won't be spending their time mowing roadsides. Bill Crandall and his biology students have returned areas along highways near Elkader, Iowa, to their natural state. These students are concerned with issues in the real world and have come to view science as a way of thinking and doing.

Students generated questions concerning the best way to manage the roadside near Elkader. Rather than using a text's predetermined and generic ecology questions, the students brainstormed their own ideas and questions, and then defined a specific issue for their attention. For many years, the county's standard operating procedure had been mowing roadside areas on a regular basis. The students viewed roadside areas as places for wildflowers and native grasses to flourish. The students wondered if these areas could be managed in a more efficient and natural way. Students investigated issues of wildlife preservation, effective land management, cost, and beautification of Iowa's highways.

The county gave the students a stretch of highway where they could test their ideas on conservation and integrated roadside management. Many county engineers and officials served as consultants on the project. The students realized that their ideas were working and could perhaps save the county dollars in labor costs and equipment. The students took their data, organizing it into a proposal, and presented it to the county board of supervisors. The students' skills and knowledge in science and mathematics impressed the adult leaders, and the county board approved their plan for change. As a result, the roadsides in this section of eastern Iowa are rich with native grasses and wildflowers.

Since 1990, biology students have monitored changes in roadside areas that have returned to a natural condition. Some of these students have part-time jobs working for the county alongside county engineers. People notice the beautiful Clayton County highways, and other counties are considering this approach to roadside management. The ideas of these high school science students resulted in dramatic changes.[4]

Barriers to Implementing STS as an Issue-Centered Approach

Traditional science and mathematics teachers find the use of social issues to organize their courses a difficult philosophical position. Many prefer to transfer their own knowledge to the students. However, this process (i.e., giving students information that scientists know, and the skills they use) may destroy the chance for a real science experience. The term *passive learning* is an oxymoron. Unfortunately, school administrators and parents are often in favor of maintaining the status quo. They are content to picture teachers as purveyors and students as passive recipients of mathematics and science information. There is clear evidence that such a static view of classrooms, curriculum, and instruction invites failure—students who have not learned how to think.

STS advocates readily accept such "core" ideas as those advanced within Project 2061 (AAAS 1989) or the Scope, Sequence, and Coordination Project (Aldridge 1991). They refrain, however, from identifying a list of concepts as organizers for teaching. They doubt that any set of individuals can determine with complete certainty what all students must know. Instead, STS proponents argue that natural curiosity, a facilitative teacher, discrepant events, current situations and news, and the social structure of schools and classrooms can be used to achieve mastery of all important concepts and processes. Mastery is achieved because students perceive a *need* for information and because they use that information, not because of the efforts of teachers, scientists, or curriculum developers. This does not suggest that teachers should sit idly until students suddenly want to learn. Instead, teachers should determinedly and enthusiastically try to encourage all students to question and become involved.

This encouragement and call to action can provide motivation. If a list of "vital" constructs of science is identified and accepted, STS proponents will work to provide a setting (context) that will assist students in using such constructs in real-world situations. When students internalize learning, it tends to last; it arises from and connects with their experiences in the real world. There is considerable research to indicate that all learners are able to learn more and to retain it longer when the learning takes place in a real-world context (Lochhead and Yager, 1996; Mestre and Lochhead, 1990; Yager, 1993). Surely the real world provides countless problems that need resolution.

Anything that builds upon students' curiosity, encourages students to create explanations, and insists upon explanations being verified and validated, is in reality science. Activity-based science programs have been shown to improve reading readiness skills, stimulate vocabulary development, increase verbal fluency, enhance logical thinking, and strengthen concept formation and communication skills (Pratt, 1981). When such programs are also issues-centered, the advantages are even more pronounced. Using science-related issues across the curriculum is compelling. Science provides real issues, stimulates real curiosity, engenders real tests, allows actual practice with decision making, and provides opportunities for personal actions.

References

Aldridge, B. G. "A Circuitous Route." *Quantum* 3 (July/August 1993): 2–3.

Aldridge, B. G. "Improve Science Education Using 'Basic Science' with Applications." *NSTA Reports!* (May 1991): 8, 32.

American Association for the Advancement of Science. *Science for All Americans: Summary—Project 2061.* Washington, D.C.: AAAS, 1989.

American Association for the Advancement of Science. *The Liberal Art of Science: Agenda for Action, The Report of the Project on Liberal Education and the Sciences.* Washington, D.C.: AAAS, 1990.

Brumby, M. N. "Misconceptions about the Concept of Natural Selection by Medical Biology Students." *Science Education* 68 (1984): 493–503.

Champagne, A. B., and L. E. Klopfer. "Research in Science Education: The Cognitive Psychology Perspective." In *Research within Reach: Science Education,* edited by D. Holdzkom and P. B. Lutz, 171–89. Charleston, W.V.: Research and Development Interpretation Service, Appalachia Educational Laboratory, 1984.

Cleminson, A. "Establishing an Epistemological Base for Science Teaching in the Light of Contemporary Notions of the Nature of Science and of How Children Learn Science." *Journal of Research in Science Teaching* 27 (1990): 429–45.

Driver, R., and V. Oldham. "A Constructivist Approach to Curriculum Development in Science." *Studies in Science Education* 13 (1986): 105–22.

Fosnot, C. T. *Enquiring Teachers, Enquiring Learners: A Constructivist Approach to Learning.* New York, N.Y.: Teachers College Press, 1989.

Helgeson, S. L., P. E. Blosser, and R. W. Howe. *The Status of Pre-College Science, Mathematics, and Social Science Education: 1955–75.* Columbus, Ohio: Center for Science and Mathematics Education, The Ohio State University, 1977.

Lochhead, J., and R. E. Yager. "Is Science Adrift in a Sea of Knowledge? A Theory of Conceptual Drift." In *Science/Technology/Society: Research Implications for Science Education,* edited by R. E. Yager, 25–38). Albany, N.Y.: State University of New York Press, 1996.

Mestre, J. P., and J. Lochhead. *Academic Preparation in Science: Teaching for Transition from High School to College.* New York, N.Y.: College Entrance Examination Board, 1990.

National Research Council. *National Science Education Standards.* Washington, D.C.: National Academy Press, 1996.

National Council of Teachers of Mathematics. *Curriculum and Evaluation Standards for School Mathematics.* Reston, Va.: NCTM, 1989.

National Science Teachers Association. "Science/Technology/Society: A New Effort for Providing Appropriate Science for All." In *NSTA Handbook,* 47–48. Washington, D.C.: NSTA, 1990–91.

Pratt, H. "Science Education in the Elementary School." In *What Research Says to the Science Teacher, Vol. 3,* edited by N. C. Harms and R. E. Yager, 73–93. Washington, D.C.: National Science Teachers Association, 1981.

Reinsmith, William A. "Ten Fundamental Truths about Learning." *The National Teaching and Learning Forum* 2 (1993): 7–8.

Resnick, L. B. "Constructing Knowledge in School." In *Development and Learning: Conflict or Congruence?,* edited by L. S. Liben, 19–50. Hillsdale, N.J.: Erlbaum, 1987.

Simon, M., and D. Schifter. "Toward a Constructivist Perspective: An Intervention Study of Mathematics Teacher Development." *Educational Studies in Mathematics* 22 (1991): 309–31.

Simpson, G. G. "Biology, the Nature of Science." *Science* 139 (1963): 81–88.

Stake, R. E., and J. Easley. *Case Studies in Science Education, Volumes I and II.* Urbana, Ill.: Center for Instructional Research and Curriculum Evaluation, University of Illinois at Urbana-Champaign, 1978.

von Glasersfeld, E. *The Construction of Knowledge.* Seaside, Calif.: The Systems Inquiry Series, Intersystems Publication, 1987.

von Glasersfeld, E. *Cognition, Construction of Knowledge, and Teaching.* Washington, D.C.: National Science Foundation, 1988.

Weiss, I. R. *Report of the 1977 National Survey of Science, Mathematics, and Social Studies Education: Center for Educational Research and Evaluation.* Washington, D.C.: U.S. Government Printing Office, 1978.

Yager, R. E. "A New Focus for School Science: S/T/S." *School Science and Mathematics* 88 (1988): 181–90.

Yager, R. E. "STS: Thinking over the Years: An Overview of the Past Decade." *The Science Teacher* 57 (1990): 52–55.

Yager, R. E. ,ed. *What Research Says to the Science Teacher, Vol. 7. The Science, Technology, Society Movement.* Washington, D.C.: National Science Teachers Association, 1993. commas in original title?

Yager, R. E., S. M. Blunck, and M. Ajam, ed. *The Iowa Assessment Package for Evaluation in Five Domains of Science Education.* 2d ed. Iowa City, Iowa: The University of Iowa, Science Education Center, 1990.

---

[1]Science Teacher: Morgan Masters; Principal: Bernard Stephenson, Chariton Middle School, Chariton, Iowa

[2]Mathematics Teacher: Jennifer Matt; Principal: Charles E. Miller, Crestwood High School, Cresco, Iowa

[3]Science Teacher: Janet Dunkel; Principal: Doug Bergston, Jefferson School, Charles City, Iowa

[4]Science Teacher: Bill Crandall; Principal: Donald Grove, Central Community School District, Elkader, Iowa

28 AN ISSUES-CENTERED CURRICULUM FOR HIGH SCHOOL SOCIAL STUDIES

by Ronald W. Evans and Jerry Brodkey

Adolescents today face real, difficult challenges: teenage pregnancy, drug use, violent communities, racial stereotypes and prejudices, broken homes. Many face the bleak economic realities of escalating college costs, or low-paying jobs for the non-college bound. Their families face the problems of unemployment or declining or stagnant real income. As students walk the streets of our nation's cities they are confronted with homelessness, declining social services, and environmental blight. They will soon face pressing problems of securing health care, finding a job that will allow growth and success, and making decisions about their lives as individuals and as part of a larger community. Unfortunately, the typical social studies curriculum fails to explicitly address these issues, fails to help prepare students for the very real issues and problems they will face in their lives.

For social studies to reach its potential, we believe that the classrooms of the 21st century must be different from the classroom of today. In today's typical high school, the bell rings and thirty to forty students shuffle in. Students sit in rows. A heavy textbook is pulled out of student backpacks, and the lesson begins. Students sit, take notes, complete fill-in-the-blank worksheets, answer questions from the book, study for exams, and are graded on mastery of factual knowledge. Tests are often multiple choice and graded by a machine. Students endure courses in American History, World History, Geography, Government, and Economics. The social studies curriculum, and typical classroom activities, are very similar to what went on in the same space twenty or even fifty years ago (Cuban 1984; Goodlad 1984; Shaver, Davis and Helburn 1979).

Some individual teachers are better at this model than others. In some classrooms, lectures are interesting and discussions are lively: simulation, debate, and role-playing may occur on a regular basis. While these classrooms may be livelier, and students are more involved, the basic pattern remains. Students leave the classroom and leave social studies behind. They enjoy the company of their friends in the halls, and then shuffle off to math, or science, or English, or art. The curriculum, and the school day, are segmented into unrelated packages. Even more damaging is the fact that what is learned is divorced from the rest of their lives.

In the following pages, we develop a proposal for an issues-centered social studies curriculum framework aimed at creating stronger linkages between students' lives and the topics they study in high school social studies. In developing an alternative conceptualization for social studies curricula, we will describe previous models for an issues-centered social studies program and discuss the potential strengths and limitations of each. Following that, we present our own curricular framework, then discuss its potential strengths and anticipate likely criticisms. We have chosen not to include direct discussion of our rationale for an issues-centered approach in this chapter because this is dealt with in depth in another section of the Handbook.

By issues-centered education we mean an approach to education centered around problematic questions, probing questions which have no "right" answer. It is an approach to education that demands thoughtfulness and depth, weighing evidence, values, and consequences. This approach is heavily dependent on reflective discussion using multiple formats, including: socratic seminar, groupwork, role-playing and simulation, student research, and a variety of other formats for large and small group discussion (Evans, Newmann and Saxe 1995). It is an approach that seeks to create a critical dialogue, a problem-posing education in the classroom (Freire 1970).

Content selection should include a mix of emergent and pre-determined curricula and materials. Out of practical necessity teachers must make use of content from history and the social sciences. On each topic considered, a series of lessons or a unit could be developed by using a problem or issue as the starting point and problem resolution as the goal. Given an issues-centered orientation, we believe that consideration of alternative scope and sequence possibilities may help teachers and school districts develop more powerful models for fostering student reflection. Designing a curriculum to facilitate this possibility is a challenge we will examine in the following pages.

Examining Alternative Models

Previous advocates of an issues-centered social studies have developed alternative visions of an issues-centered curriculum. For the most part, these thinkers have conceived of issues education as an approach that would be implemented across the social studies curriculum and infused within discipline-based course offerings, organized chronologically or conceptually. Several other alternatives might be developed and explored. For example, one alternative for the implementation of issues-centered approaches would be to create issues-centered units within discipline-based courses. A second alternative would be to develop courses built around issues and issue areas, a full-blown issues-centered structure. This approach would mean creating an issues-centered alternative to the typical scope and sequence. A third alternative would be to pose an open curriculum in which selection of topics and issues would emerge based on student interests and needs.

Several previous models for an issues-centered curriculum deserve description and comment. Rugg (1939) proposed an entire social studies curriculum centered around what he termed "The American Problem." The curriculum contained strands or themes relevant to major problem-topics and culminated in a two-year course on American Life and Problems. Rugg's tenth grade course is titled, "World Problems and World History" and contains "'Strand' history of two chief concepts: **1.** industrialism; **2.** democracy...

focussed on international problems... 'the World Problem' counterpart of 'The American Problem.'" The two-year capstone course is titled, "The American Problem and Its Historical Background." This is a Problems of Democracy course spread over two years, with the "history of each group of problems directly studied." Though dated, Rugg's framework illustrates a thorough blending of strand history and the in-depth study of problem-topics such as problems of "reconstruction of natural and human resources... economic abundance... labor... farming... housing... social security... democracy and government" (1939, 147). With the exception of the capstone course, however, Rugg's proposed curriculum stopped short of calling for courses titled and devoted to problems and issues.

Hunt and Metcalf (1955 and 1968) proposed a curriculum that would inquire into problematic areas of culture, focusing in particular on "closed areas" of culture as appropriate in a given community. They proposed that "problems, units, projects, blocks of work—call them what you will—should focus on a problematic area of culture," and suggested that such an approach "does not require major disruption of present curriculum patterns. It does require that teachers conceive social-studies courses more broadly. History, for example, will include data from sociology, anthropology, psychology, and the like. But no overhauling of the present pattern of courses seems necessary in order to apply the problem-centered approach recommended here" (1968, 302). Like Rugg, their approach stopped short of recommending a dramatically new course framework. Table 1 provides an overview of their "Problematic Areas of Culture."

Oliver and Shaver (1966) proposed a somewhat similar set of "General Problem Areas" and sample unit topics as a guide for selecting and organizing content for issues-centered education, as illustrated in Table 2. In their analysis of methods of organizing and teaching issues, Oliver and Shaver discuss two different approaches: the historical crisis approach and the problem-topic approach. The first, "the historical crisis approach," focuses on historical periods ripe with multiple issues which are analogous to or may be contrasted with contemporary history, and which may help explain contemporary problems. The second, "the problem-topic approach," begins with selection of a contemporary issue considered important and persistent, then examines relevant

Table 1: Hunt and Metcalf's Problematic Areas of Culture

Power and the Law
- Sovereign Citizen vs. Power Centers
- Law as Protection of the Weak vs. Law as a Weapon of Power
- Courts as Dispensers of Justice vs. Courts as Dispensers of Injustice

Economics
- Government Frugality vs. Government Financing of Needed Projects
- Taxes and Government Spending
- Monopoly and Free Competition
- Free Enterprise and Socialism
- Prosperity and Population Growth

Nationalism, Patriotism, and Foreign Affairs
- War and Peace
- National Honor and Foreign Commitments
- Self-Determination of Nations and Puppet Governments
- Patriotism as Obedience and Patriotism as Critical Inquiry

Social Class
- Rank in a Classless Society
- Earned Success and Fortuitous Success
- Success and Happiness
- Liberal vs. Vocational Education

Religion and Morality
- Religious Belief and Practice
- Science and Religion
- High Pleasures and Low Pleasures
- Democracy and Religion

Race and Minority-Group Relations
- Race and Minority-Group Relations
- Racial Differences and Human Similarity
- Negro Inferiority and Negro Capacity
- Jewish Greed and Jewish Radicalism
- Catholic Conservatism and Catholic Liberalism

Sex, Courtship, and Marriage
- Purity Versus Experience
- Chastity and Peer-Group Status
- The Nice Girl Versus the Good Sport
- Modesty and Sex Appeal
- Career Versus Housewifery

data from a variety of sources, including historical, journalistic, social sciences, etc.

Oliver and Shaver blended these approaches, and chose to site their work in a particular course, United States History, and "allowed chronology to dictate roughly the order of the units." They suggest that "The topic-problem and historical crisis organization of content can thus easily be fitted into a 'conventional' history course. The rationale for our decision was partly convenience: It was more in line with the expectations of children and parents. But it also stemmed from the conviction that a broad chronological framework does give the course additional structure and meaning" (1966, 147). Like both Rugg, and Hunt and Metcalf, Oliver and Shaver developed curriculum strands but stopped short of recommending courses titled by and centered in problem-topics or issues.

In a somewhat similar vein, Engle and Ochoa (1988) developed a "Framework for the Curriculum" in which issues and problems would be selected for their "potential for encouraging thinking, or even controversy, about matters of fact... historical interpretation... or resolution to social problems in the present" (1988, 129). They recommend a modest change from the tradition-al curriculum scope and sequence, and suggest that the subjects of United States history, world history, and geography would remain the primary courses taught, but that their "usual content would be broadened"... and "in some cases combined with content from other disciplines and fields of study"... to be fully relevant to society and its problems. They propose eight suggested curriculum strands, described in Table 3, and, like the scholars discussed above, suggest that these will be helpful in enlivening a standard curriculum and infusing a reflective focus.

One final model for consideration comes from an article which appeared in *Social Education*. In an article titled "Social Education for Social Transformation," Stanley and Nelson develop guidelines for a critical approach to social studies, with broad and general themes for groupings of different grade levels (see Table 4). While their ideas are admirable (if implemented they would lead to a fully issues-centered curriculum), most teachers and administrators prefer more guidance. Unlike the authors of models considered previously, Stanley and Nelson (1986) suggest a major rethinking of scope and sequence. They propose dismantling traditional, discipline-based course titles, and replacing them with social studies work

Table 2: Oliver and Shaver's General Problem Areas

Racial and Ethnic Conflict
- School Desegregation
- Civil Rights for Non-Whites and Ethnic Minorities
- Housing for Non-Whites and Ethnic Minorities
- Job Opportunities for Non-Whites and Ethnic Minorities
- Immigration Policy

Religious and Ideological Conflict
- Rights of the Communist Party in America
- Religion and Public Education
- Control of "Dangerous" or "Immoral" Literature
- Religion and National Security: Oaths, Conscientious Objectors
- Taxation of Religious Property

Security of the Individual
- Crime and Delinquency

Conflict Among Economic Groups
- Organized Labor
- Business Competition and Monopoly
- "Overproduction" of Farm Goods
- Conservation of Natural Resources

Health, Education, and Welfare
- Adequate Medical Care: for the Aged, for the Poor
- Adequate Educational Opportunity
- Old Age Security
- Job and Income Security

Security of the Nation
- Federal Loyalty-Security Programs
- [Foreign Policy][1]

[1]This topic obviously should be the center of a new curriculum, extending our analysis of domestic problems. It might consist of a wide variety of subtopics.

aimed at education for social transformation.

Each of these models has strengths and weaknesses. Each presented innovative approaches that would enhance the intellectual quality of classroom discourse. Only one, that of Stanley and Nelson, offered a description and rationale for an alternative curricular scope and sequence, the others instead suggesting that issues and problems should be a strong part of any curricular framework or scope and sequence. These advocates of issues-centered approaches believed it prudent to offer their models as alternative approaches to teaching traditionally structured courses. This was perhaps a strategic consideration given the expectations of teachers, students, parents, and administrators concerning the curriculum. In each case, the frameworks developed might be viewed in hindsight as emergent models for a more radical departure from the traditional reliance on course structures drawn from the social sciences and history.

Social studies theorists and practitioners owe a great debt to these thinkers. Their work is still the best of social studies theory applied to practice. Yet, we believe that it is time to consider more dramatic departures from typical scope and sequence alternatives.

Developing a Framework for Secondary Social Studies

We believe that the often mediocre state of practice in the field indicates a need to entertain alternative visions and curricular frameworks, and requires that alternative visions be innovative and dynamic. In what follows, we propose a curriculum in which social studies is defined as a unitary field of study that is fully issues-centered, interdisciplinary and extradisciplinary rather than a field that is merely derivative of academic disciplines (Wraga 1993). We believe that we have created a vision that may lead to the kind of border crossing that Henry Giroux espouses, overcoming the boundaries of the traditional disciplines and school subjects and the tension between social issues and academic disciplines as the foundation for the curriculum (Giroux 1992).

Instead of building a curriculum around courses based in the academic disciplines, we believe that a more powerful vision for the future of social studies might be built around certain social realities and the ethical questions and possibilities they raise. This is similar to the problem-topic approach discussed by Oliver and Shaver (1966, 139-140). Imagine a semester-long high school course titled Race and Ethnicity in American Life; another titled Social Class, Stratification and Social Responsibility; another on Gender and Sexuality in Social Life and Culture; another on Ideology, Government, and Economic Life; another titled Power in America; still another, Nationalism, Patriotism, and American Foreign Policy; another on Philosophy

Table 3: Engle and Ochoa's Suggested Curriculum Strands

Environmental Studies

The study of problems that surround human use of the environment. This strand should be organized around a listing of important environmental problems, which should be revised from time to time to bring it into correspondence with current realities and concerns.

Institutional Studies

The study of the origins and the present circumstances of the broad range of social institutions of the United States, including: 1) institutions that express and protect fundamental freedoms, 2) economic institutions, 3) political institutions, 4) global institutions, and 5) the family, religious groups, etc.

Cultural Studies

Why people of different regions, historical backgrounds, nationalities, and ethnic groups grow up differently; How we can live usefully in a world of differing cultures; How people of varying cultures share profound human similarities; and, How we turn cultural differences into assets for social improvement.

Social Problems

One major social problem would be studied for an extended period, in depth, on one occasion each year in each social studies classroom at every grade level with all classes engaged in study at the same time, with principal as leader and involvement of other departments, parents and the community.

Problems in Decision Making

Three groups of questions would guide this study. Epistemological: What is knowledge? What is evidence? Which way of knowing is most dependable? Communications: What are the purposes of the media? How can we judge the dependability of what we read or hear? Values: What do I value most? What do I do when two or more of my values seem to be in conflict?

Internship in Citizenship

A one-year, one-day-a-week internship in some useful social or civic enterprise would be a natural progression from thinking about social problems. Useful volunteer work would be sought with a service, political, or civic organization.

Electives

Electives would focus on nature of the disciplines and methods by which social scientists and historians arrive at dependable knowledge. One-year courses in economics, political science, sociology, anthropology, and journalism. Students would engage in laboratory practice in each discipline, and be expected and encouraged to complete one such elective.

A Democratic School Environment

The school itself must be governed democratically. Never underestimate the willingness of students to particpate in their own governance. Democracy is also exemplified by the respect shown by teachers for intellectual honesty and the intelligence of students to think for themselves.

in Personal and Public Life; another on Media and Social Understanding; another titled Utopian Visions and Competing Ideologies; yet another on Technology, Society and the Environment; another titled Sex, Marriage, and Family Life; and, of course, The School as an Institution.... this incomplete list could go on and on. The main criteria are that the course must have an issue-focus and must not be limited by any of the disciplines sited at the university. A shift to semester-long courses might also help break dependence on massive textbooks and encourage use of multiple sources.

Each of these courses would be extradisciplinary and interdisciplinary by necessity, and each could have strands reflecting what we currently think of as the major sources of knowledge. Each would include cross-national perspectives. Their length may vary; some might be required, others elective. The curriculum might begin with An Introduction to Problems and Issues, and conclude with Philosophy and Life. A course titled Social Research might be included, in which students engage in in-depth research on a community or school issue that is linked to a national or global problem. Most courses could include research components, and time for individual and committee study while consulting with teachers. Perhaps a service learning component could be built in where appropriate. Most importantly, the starting point for each course would be the present manifestations of persistent issues and dilemmas. Students must have first-hand knowledge of the issue, and should be able to study the issue directly both within the school and outside in the community. Each course would be built around the reflective investigation of central questions, problems and issues. Each course would also allow for the kind of in-depth study required for meaningful social education.

It might be helpful to explore the possibilities for a particular course following this approach, and then compare and contrast it with a discipline based course. Let's take American Foreign

Table 4: Stanley and Nelson's Curriculum for Social Transformation

GRADES 7-9	GRADES 10-12
Theme: Testing ideas, refining ethical ideology **Content:**	**Theme: Refining critical thinking proposals for change; social participation** **Content:**
examining criteria • considering ideologies ideas and their sources • political economy of ideas • political geography of ideas • examination of historical examples of ideologies • logic, reasoning, alternative views • ideological dominance and repression • cultural and ideological differences • roots of ideologies • the nature of our culture as compared to others **meanings and messages** media examination • text analysis • historic document study • ways of knowing, different conceptions of truth **discourse development** analysis of language, language theory • concern for ideas of others • justice and equality • improving reading, writing, speaking, listening • discourse, science, and social science **examination of elected social problems** defining significant social issues • developing hypotheses • reconsidering ethical criteria • identifying and evaluating evidence • testing hypotheses • drawing tentative conclusions • proposing potential social improvements • examining contrasting viewpoints • selecting avenues for social participation **taking responsibility for views and actions** **social participation activities**	**reviewing ideas from previous social education work** interdependence • ethics • ideologies • nature, sources and utilization of knowledge • traditional forms of knowledge and their critics • contributions of history and the social sciences **developing and reviewing process skills** ethical reasoning • discourse/discussion responsibilities • conducting research • social criticism • critical thinking: decision making • social participation activities **examining identified significant social issues** local • national • global **considering alternative futures and "relevant utopias" based on ethical justification for social transformation** **proposing ideas for social improvement rooted in justice and equality** **developing interdependent social participation** **active work, over a period of time, in social improvement activities** **evaluating social education**

Policy as an example. In the typical high school today, our nation's role in the world is addressed primarily in courses on United States History. Typically, American foreign policy issues are not explicity addressed, at least not directly, except in the occasional forays into current events. Potentially relevant evidence on the issue is covered as part of the chronological survey of history. In a classroom in which an issues approach is infused, the issue would at least be addressed each time the chronology dictates (Monroe Doctrine, Spanish American War, etc.).

In the alternative vision we have sketched above, our nation's role in the world would receive in-depth treatment through a separate course. The course could begin and end with the question: "What role should the U. S. play in the world?," and would examine alternatives for the future as well as our changing role in the world over time. The course might include units on various aspects of the central issue, e.g., the defense budget, world government, etc. It would also include an in-depth study of key episodes in history and examination of the chronological development of U. S. foreign relations. Specific current problems would be studied, discussed and debated. This approach would, in the end, help to prepare students who are conversant on the issue and knowledgeable about its history. Students would leave the course understanding relevant scholarship and evidence that might help them develop a saner and more sophisticated approach to thinking about foreign policy issues.

An Issues-Centered Framework

In what follows we offer an illustrative scope and sequence, drawing on elements of the works described earlier. Actual courses, possible unit titles and a few of the central issues that might be explored are presented. Throughout, students will be asked to evaluate, critique, and take responsibility for their own education. This framework is only a partial start. It will need considerable further development by interested teachers and curriculum developers who choose to apply this approach. Like any framework, in practical application it would allow students and teachers to pursue "open" topics and issues as desired, or when events or student interests warrant.

Grade 9. Introduction to Problems and Issues (first semester)

This course will introduce students to alternative perspectives on social issues, competing ideologies, and the process of reflection and problem investigation. Students would consider rationales for issues-centered study, the nature of knowledge, meaning and messages, language, and the role of personal, public, and disciplined knowledge in making decisions on matters of interpretation and public policy as well as personal decisions. Students would investigate a select number of issues that are chosen to introduce some of the key issues from the courses that will follow. Students will draw on and consider knowledge from history, the social sciences, and other relevant fields of study as well as community, media, and personal experience. Students will engage in consideration of alternative perspectives, research in field and library, and social participation in the community. In addition, each of these elements will continue to appear and reappear in later courses throughout the curriculum.

Electives: These courses offer greater depth on topics of special interest to students. They may be offered as teaching schedules and student interest permit.

Grades 9-12. One-Semester Courses

All students would be required to enroll in one of these courses each semester for a total of six required semesters. Students may enroll in additional elective courses as schedules permit. Each course would include emergent present-day manifestations of the central issues, study of relevant historical cases and trends from the United States and the world, cross-cultural and global study, and inclusion of relevant art, literature, music, etc. Teachers and students would make judicious selections from a multitude of resource materials.

Race and Ethnicity in American Life

Defining the Issues: Changing Demographics in the U. S. Today

Alternative Perspectives on Racial and Ethnic Conflict

Prejudice and Institutionalized Racism

Racial Patterns in Schools, Housing, and Employment

History of Racial and Ethnic Groups: Chronology and Cases

Immigration: What Should Our Policy Be?

Global Perspectives on Race, Ethnicity and Cultural Diversity

Policy and Personal Responsibility

What impact do race and ethnicity have on our lives? How have attitudes, beliefs and social practices regarding race and ethnicity changed over time? How can we best explain the socioeconomic status of different ethnic groups? What are the origins of race oppression? What should we do about racial oppression?

Social Class, Stratification, and Social Responsibility

Defining the Issues: Social Class in the U. S.

Alternative Perspectives on Social Class

History of Class Conflict in America: Chronology and Cases

Global Perspectives: Class and Caste in World History

Rural Poverty and Urban Blight

The Rich and Super Rich

Middle Class America

Crime and Delinquency: Gangs, Drugs, Prostitution, etc.

Utopian Visions and Competing Ideologies

Schools and Social Class

Social Welfare: AFDC, Social Security, Health Care

Social Policy and Personal Responsibility

How are wealth and income distributed? What determines these patterns? How and why have these patterns changed over time? What role should government play in providing for the general welfare of citizens?

Gender and Sexuality in Social Life and Culture

Defining the Issues: Status of Women and Men

Alternative Perspectives on Gender Oppression

Feminist Thought

Historical Development of Women's Rights: Chronology and Cases

Change in Gender Roles Over Time

Changing Definitions of Manhood

Homosexuality: Gay and Lesbian Rights

The Changing Family

History of Sexuality: Attitudes, Belief, Practices

Dating, Sex, Marriage

Social Policy and Personal Responsibility

What are the origins of gender inequality? How has the role of gender in our lives changed over time? How might we best explain the changing roles of women and men? What role should gender and sexuality play in our lives?

Ideology and Economic Life

Defining the Issues: Conflicting Ideas
    in Economic Life
Alternative Perspectives on Economics:
    Smith, Marx, Keynes, etc.
Government Regulation or Control in
    Economic Life
The Market: Command vs. Free?
Historical Development of the American
    Economy: Chronology and Cases
Industrial Revolution: Blessing or Curse?
Giants of Industry: Industrial Statesmen or Robber
    Barons?
Rise of Labor
Technology and Society:
    Environment vs. Development?
Are Multinational Corporations Beyond Control?
Global Perspectives on Economic Life
Social Policy and Personal Responsibility

How can we best understand the economic aspects of our society and the world? What role should government play in economic life? What is the proper role of government in regulating business? What role should government play in protecting the rights of labor? What role in these matters has government played in different times and cultures?

Power in America

Defining the Issues: What is Power?
Perspectives on Power in America:
    Elitism vs. Pluralism
Historical Development of American Government:
    Chronology and Cases
The Constitution: Protector of Democracy or
    Conservator of Elitism?

Political Institutions: Hierarchies of Control
    vs. Citizen Empowerment
Global Perspectives: Comparing Governmental
    Form and Function
Civil Rights and Civil Liberties
Dissent: Stability vs. Right of Protest
Religious and Ideological Conflict
Power, Words, and Images: Who Controls
    the Media? Who Benefits?
Politics, Power, and Personal Responsibility

Who rules America? Who benefits? How have power relationships changed over time? Is a hierarchical power structure inevitable? How have other cultures handled the question of power? In what ways should we alter or reform the power structure in the United States to gain greater empowerment for the average citizen? When, and under what conditions, should citizens challenge legally constituted authority? By what means?

Nationalism, Patriotism, and American Foreign Policy

Defining the Issues: America's Role in the World
Perspectives on Foreign Policy:
    Missions of Hope or Tragic Imposition
Historical Development of
    American Foreign Policy
American Expansion and Empire
Rise to Globalism: The World Wars
Cold War and Beyond
Nuclear Pasts and Futures
Defining Patriotism: Obedience vs. Critique
The Military: How Much Defense is Necessary?
A Peace Time Draft vs. Voluntary Service
World Government: How Much Power for
    the United Nations?
Policy and Personal Responsibility

What role should the United States play in the world? How and why has the role of the U. S. changed over time? What are the origins of American globalism?

- The Border Mentality: Nationalism and
    International Relations
- Religion and Philosophy in Personal and Public Life
- Media and Social Understanding
- Utopian Visions and Competing Ideologies
- Technology, Society, and the Environment
- Sex, Marriage, and Family Life
- The School as an Institution

- Introduction to the Social Sciences
- Introduction to Social Research

Grade 12. Philosophy and Life (second semester capstone course)

In this course, each student would develop a personal statement of individual and social philosophy, based on the student's own understanding of our society and our world. The course would include a revisiting of issues posed throughout the curriculum, with special focus on philosophical issues including the nature of knowledge, theories of reality, theories of value, and perspectives on social justice. Students will also consider alternative futures and propose ideas for social improvement, engage in community involvement or service learning activities consistent with a personal vision of social justice, consider ethical implications of career alternatives, and other personal choices. Finally, students will be asked to evaluate and critique their own education.

Strengths of the Framework and Potential Problems

While we reiterate our respect for the frameworks discussed earlier and the invaluable contribution their authors have made to the field, we believe that the framework we propose has several advantages over previous proposals. The curriculum builds on student interest in issues affecting their lives. In each course, the relevance of the issues examined will be immediately clear. The focus on a central set of questions in each course will help to create a reflective, engaging environment. In each course, teachers and students will also study relevant strands of historical development, cases and cross-cultural and global aspects of the topic being considered.

Unlike the previous attempts at developing an issues-centered curriculum, we have suggested the establishment of actual courses with issues at center. This is at the heart of our proposal, and is the major distinction between this framework and the earlier proposals we discuss. This choice elevates issues to a more prominent place in the curriculum. If we can achieve this, it will be more likely that books and materials will become reflective and problem-centered in orientation, and that the curriculum will address issues relevant to students' lives. As we indicate above, this framework allows history and social science perspectives to be employed, especially so in courses corresponding to economics and political science, or including aspects of sociology and anthropology. Our proposal also encourages extradisciplinary and interdisciplinary study by siting courses outside any particular discipline.

While we believe that our proposal deserves fair consideration, we recognize that any such proposal will draw a good deal of criticism.

Opposition to issues-centered approaches has long centered around the following main arguments (Evans 1987):

First, critics are likely to charge that the approach lacks content. This charge is patently false. Content for each course may be found in textbooks, and in materials in school and public libraries. If this approach is to be thoroughly implemented, it will mean including more data than the current curriculum typically offers. Of course, current texts aren't organized in an issues-centered fashion. For this approach to take hold, alternative materials will have to be developed; texts, teaching manuals, and discussion guides will have to be created to correspond with this framework. In the meantime, currently available texts and materials can be used effectively, but they will be used only as relevant to the topic and issue under consideration. Until appropriate issues-centered texts and materials are developed, teaching social studies with this framework as a guide would be quite demanding for teachers. Realistically, any department or school district choosing to implement a fully issues-centered curriculum would need sufficient preparation time to locate and create appropriate materials.

Other critics are likely to voice a related complaint that students won't know their history. This depends how history is used in this format. We hope that we have made clear that our framework is heavily historical, that data, cases, strands of chronological development, and consideration of competing interpretations of the past would permeate the curriculum. We believe that this will likely result in a better understanding of historical knowledge gained than in the traditional curriculum.

A related complaint is likely from those who favor a discipline-based approach. They may argue that students won't have a sufficient understanding of disciplined knowledge as a base for intellectual growth and social understanding. Again, we think this depends on how disciplines are used. We view the academic disciplines as helpful but inadequate to the challenge of preparing thoughtful citizens. The focus of our curriculum is on the critical thinking process, part of any intellectual endeavor but beyond the scope of any one discipline or combination of disciplines.

Another likely complaint is that this will lead to a superficial hodge-podge of topics and issues in no logical sequence. We are sensitive to this argument. While there may be no absolutely best logical sequence for social study, we have endeavored to sequence the courses in our proposal from the study of issues and topics close to students lives, to issues they will face as adults, some of which seem further from students' immediate experience. Hence, following the introductory course, we chose to begin the curriculum with issues of race, class, and gender. Each of these areas is immediate to student experience, and later courses explore underlying structures behind these issues in greater depth. Students would have completed in-depth study of race, class, and gender issues by the end of tenth grade. Grade eleven would be primarily devoted to the economic and political issues and institutions that undergird and cut across matters of race, class and gender. By this time in their intellectual development, students should be interested enough in furthering their understanding that these courses will be especially relevant. Each course builds on previous learning, adding greater depth and breadth to student understanding. Finally, in their senior year, students will focus outward, on their relationships with the world and on their own individual relationship with the community.

Another likely complaint, and one with merit, is that legal mandates exist for teaching the U. S. Constitution, U. S. History, and economics, and that in some states, standardized tests require a more traditional curriculum. As we have noted above, each course will contain strong elements of U. S. History. The Constitution and economic content would be infused across courses, but would also be a focus in the 11th grade. We suggest that creative teachers and curriculum developers could build units on these subjects where appropriate.

Conclusion

Given the diversity of ideas and approaches in the field of social studies education, it is impractical to suggest that there is one best scope and sequence. Nevertheless, we believe that our proposal merits consideration and hope that it will inspire discussion and action toward a more engaging curriculum. We recognize the daunting nature of trying to reform school curricula (Cuban 1984; Shaver 1989), yet reformers have had some success over the years. Our proposal must be tempered by a realistic assessment of classroom constancy. It must be amenable to adaptation in a variety of forms and contexts. We recognize the wisdom in continuing to promote an issues-centered focus within present offerings, yet we believe that it is helpful to develop alternatives such as the framework we propose. It is important to continue to offer strong options to the currently dominant interests that would replace social studies with history and geography.

As we noted at the outset, young people today face real and difficult challenges. We believe that teachers and schools ignore those challenges at great peril. The curriculum must, at its very foundation, offer studies relevant to students' lives. Social studies must introduce a rising generation to the challenges and dilemmas faced by all inhabitants of our planet. It must provide them with the knowledge and skills necessary for thoughtful and participatory citizenship so that we might all find better ways to live as part of one family.

References

Cuban, Larry. *How Teachers Taught.* New York: Longman, 1984.

Engle, Shirley H., and Anna S. Ochoa. *Education for Democratic Citizenship: Decision Making in the Social Studies.* New York: Teachers College Press, 1988.

Evans, Ronald W. *Defining the Worthy Society: A History of the Societal-Problems Approach in Social Studies, 1895-1985.* Ed.D diss., Stanford University, 1987.

Freire, Paulo. *Pedagogy of the Oppressed.* New York: Continuum, 1970.

Goodlad, John. *A Place Called School.* New York: McGraw-Hill, 1984.

Giroux, Henry. *Border Crossings: Cultural Workers and the Politics of Education.* New York: Routledge, 1992.

Hunt, Maurice P., and Lawrence E. Metcalf. *Teaching High School Social Studies: Problems in Reflective Thinking and Social Understanding.* New York: Harper and Row, 1955 (2nd edition, 1968).

Oliver, Donald O., and James P. Shaver. *Teaching Public Issues in the High School.* Boston: Houghton Mifflin, 1966.

Rugg, Harold O. "Curriculum Design in the Social Studies: What I Believe…" In *The Future of the Social Studies,* edited by James A. Michener. Curriculum Series no. 1. Washington, D.C.: National Council for the Social Studies, 1939.

Shaver, James P. "Lessons From the Past: The Future of an Issues-Centered Social Studies Curriculum." *The*

Social Studies 80 (September/October 1989): 192-196.

Shaver, James P., O. L. Davis, and Suzanne Helburn. "The Status of Social Studies Education: Impressions from Three NSF Studies." *Social Education* 43 (1979): 150-153.

Stanley, William B. and Jack L. Nelson. "Social Education for Social Transformation." *Social Education* 50 (1986): 528-533.

Wraga, William G. "The Interdisciplinary Imperative for Citizenship Education." *Theory and Research in Social Education* 21 (1993): 201-231.

29 TEACHING SOCIETAL ISSUES ACROSS THE SECONDARY CURRICULUM

by William G. Wraga

ocietal issues are too important to confine to the social studies. Every subject can and should make important contributions to the development of students' understanding of complex issues that they will face as adults. While the previous two chapters offer suggestions for addressing societal issues in the secondary social studies, science, and mathematics curricula, this chapter attempts to orient the reader toward the possibilities for addressing societal issues in other areas of the high school curriculum, namely, English, the fine and performing arts, modern foreign languages, physical education and health, and vocational education. The imperative of interdisciplinary approaches to societal issues and the educative power of the daily operations of the school, including co-curricular activities, will be discussed, as well.

The ability to identify, analyze, and act upon pressing societal issues comprises a requisite competency of democratic citizenship, and as such should be firmly anchored in the local school district's educational philosophy and learning objectives. Local endeavors to identify and develop aims and objectives related to participatory citizenship and the concomitant ability to address societal issues can be informed by notable past efforts to formulate usable educational goals. The Commission on the Reorganization of Secondary Education (1918), the Educational Policies Commission (1938), the Survey Study of Behavioral Outcomes of General Education in High School (French 1957), and Goodlad (1984), a study of schooling, can serve as useful resources in this area. Selected goals from the Educational Policies Commission (1938) are presented in Table 1 as a model of the kinds of learnings issue-focused curriculum and instruction across the subject areas seek to attain,

and against which lessons, units, courses, and programs can be evaluated.

Teaching about Societal Issues in Subject Areas

Each conventional subject in the school curriculum can contribute to students' understanding of social issues, even though not all of them are typically regarded as fertile ground for addressing issues (e.g., Vatter 1994). Insofar as social issues provide a connection between the scholastic treatment of subject matter and the "real world," the study of social issues across the curriculum also can enliven subject areas perceived by students as being divorced from life beyond the school walls. Since curriculum development is most meaningful when teachers and students genuinely collaborate to identify and examine ideas and issues, the examples below should be regarded as possible starting points for examination of social issues and, therefore, also as suggestive rather than exhaustive.

English Language Arts

An effective way to study social issues in the English classroom is to examine the use and abuse of language by public officials and by spokespeople for special interest and lobbying groups (Totten 1992). The National Council of Teachers of English monitors such usage, highlighting its concern by annually presenting its Doublespeak Award to notable efforts to obscure real practice with euphemistic verbiage (Lutz 1989). English classes could maintain their own doublespeak lists and issue their own awards. The current movement to promote so-called politically correct speech could be examined in a similar light, as well. Students also could learn to detect propaganda devices, logical fallacies, and other

Table 1: Representative Curriculum Goals pertaining to Issues-Focused Curriculum and Instruction

1. **Social Justice** The educated citizen is sensitive to the disparities of human circumstance.
2. **Social Activity** The educated citizen acts to correct unsatisfactory conditions.
3. **Critical Judgment** The educated citizen develops defenses against propaganda.
4. **Tolerance** The educated citizen respects honest differences of opinion.
5. **Conservation** The educated citizen has a regard for the nation's resources.
6. **Social Applications of Science** The educated citizen measures scientific advance by its contribution to the general welfare.
7. **World Citizenship** The educated citizen is a cooperative member of the world community.
8. **Political Citizenship** The educated citizen accepts his civic duties.
9. **Devotion to Democracy** The educated citizen acts upon an unswerving loyalty to democratic ideals.
10. **Public Health** The educated person works to improve the health of the community.
11. **Occupational Choice** The educated producer has selected his occupation.
12. **Occupational Appreciation** The educated producer appreciates the social value of his work.
13. **Consumer Protection** The educated consumer takes appropriate measures to safeguard his interests.

Source: Educational Policies Commission, *The Purposes of Education in American Democracy* (Washington, D.C.: National Education Association, 1938), pp. 50, 90, 108.

techniques of persuasion by analyzing a variety of print and non-print texts for such usages (see Lee 1939; Beyer 1987; Paul and Rudinow 1990; Steele 1992).

There is growing emphasis in English education on the idea that since the superordinate purpose of the language arts is to communicate meaning, students best learn the tools of written and verbal communication in the context of purposeful dialogue about matters that are meaningful to them. Additionally, there are signs that English educators are increasingly placing a premium on the social value of communication which moves English curriculum and instruction beyond the mere acquisition of common skills and information and toward treating these areas of competence as vehicles for fostering a common discourse in the name of democracy (Lloyd-Jones and Lunsford 1989; Hlebowitsh, Muller, and Pickett 1991). Together these two developments provide favorable conditions for social issues becoming the focus of student reading, writing, and speaking. A variety of textual materials can be used, both expository and persuasive, including magazine and newspaper articles, news reports, editorials, reference works, and policy books. In this way, social issues become meaningful topics—especially if selected carefully by students—for research and writing assignments that provide the context for developing important language arts competencies and at the same time enable

students to participate effectively in social discourse (see, for example, "Civic Literacy" 1991).

Literature traditionally read in high school English classes is virtually brimming with opportunities for addressing social issues. In American literature, conventional titles such as Paine's *Common Sense,* Thoreau's *Civil Disobedience,* Hawthorne's *The Scarlet Letter,* Stowe's *Uncle Tom's Cabin,* Twain's *Adventures of Huck Finn,* Lewis' *The Jungle,* Hemingway's *A Farewell to Arms,* Steinbeck's *The Grapes of Wrath,* and Miller's *The Crucible* cover a wide range of social and political issues. Titles commonly read in British literature—such as *Julius Caesar, Macbeth,* and almost any work of Dickens—offer similar opportunities. A thematic unit such as "Industrialism in Victorian Literature" or "Evolution in Victorian Literature" could simultaneously introduce students to basic characteristics of the era's literature and to perennial social issues (see Abrams 1968, 1334-1372).

Yet as Tanner (1971, 224) points out, literature selections must transcend traditional reading lists to represent the reality of our polyglot society and to bear relevance and meaning to students of diverse backgrounds. Calls to add to school reading lists literary works written during the twentieth century and by minority authors have come to dominate scholarly discourse on English curriculum, but have made only slight inroads into classroom practice (Gehrke, Knapp, and Sirotnik 1992). Suggestions for diversifying high school reading lists in terms of race, ethnicity, and gender ("Rediscovering America" 1992), the variegated experiences of today's youth ("Adolescent Literature" 1992), and providing a global perspective through literature ("A Global Perspective" 1990) are readily available in the professional literature. Such readings are rich in social issues that can hold special meaning for the groups they represent but also can serve to broaden the perspective of majority students (Hurlbert and Totten 1992).

Fine and Performing Arts

Dewey (1985) contends, "The freeing of the artist in literary presentation … is as much a precondition of the desirable creation of adequate opinion on public matters as is the freeing of social inquiry" (p. 183). He identifies the special role of art in public discourse when he notes, "Artists have always been the real purveyors of news, for it is not the outward happening in itself which is new, but the kindling of it by emotion, perception, and appreciation" (p. 184). The art curriculum can contribute to the development of students' ability and inclination to handle social issues by providing opportunities for them to examine art as a means of expression, as a source of a unique perspective on an issue, and as a reflection of temporal issues.

Painters, for example, have long used their media to comment on social issues of the day. Indeed, entire artistic movements, such as Dada during the post-World War I era and, to a lesser extent, pop art of the 1950s and 1960s, have claimed social commentary as an express purpose. In art classes, individual works can be employed to illustrate the social-political function of artistic expression; across the curriculum, art can be used to raise or represent particular issues under discussion. Famous paintings that deal with political issues include David's *The Death of Socrates* (1787) and *The Death of Marat* (1793), Goya's *The Third of May* (1808), and Picasso's *Guernica* (1937). Similarly, well-known works such as Daumier's *The Third-Class Carriage* (1862) and Munch's *The Scream* (1893) raised issues about the alienation of the individual in modern industrial society more than fifty years before David Riesman coined the term "the lonely crowd."

There is a strong tradition of social commentary in American painting, as well. Notable examples include Copley's *Portrait of Paul Revere*

(c. 1768), characterized by one art historian as "probably the first picture of political protest by an American artist" (Baigell 1974, 60); Innes' *Lackawanna Valley* (1855), an exploration of the relationship between nature, the new technology, and man; Hopper's bleak depiction of individuals who exist in close physical proximity but emotional isolation in works such as *Room in New York* (1932) and *Second-Story Sunlight* (1960); and Wood's satirical representations of American myths and traditional values in works such as the famous *American Gothic* (1930) and *Daughters of Revolution* (1932). Of particular relevance here is the social realism movement during the 1930s, in which artists espoused a wide range of political viewpoints through their painting (see Baigell 1973).

As an artistic medium, photography not only often captures great moments of social and human import, but also can yield insight and perspective on social conditions and problems (Newhall 1978). The work of Jacob Riis around the turn of the century and that of Dorothea Lange and other Depression-era photographers are exemplars in this latter application of the camera's lens. Photographs can be used to raise issues, as sources of information and insights into particular social issues (Lesy 1982), and as subjective statements to be analyzed for inherent biases (Stott 1973). Students can also use the medium themselves to document or comment upon a particular issue under study.

The performing arts also enjoy a long tradition of addressing social issues. From *The Birth of a Nation* to *Do the Right Thing,* for example, films have attempted to comment on issues of race, power, and social structure. Recent films such as *City of Hope, Bob Roberts,* and *Roger and Me,* to cite just a few examples, speak to a range of social issues that could be discussed in relation to cinematic techniques employed by the filmmakers. Similarly, dramatic productions conducted by the school's drama club or visiting professional troupes could be chosen for their potential contribution to student understanding of a perennial or contemporary social issue. To increase the educational impact of the assembly, prior to attending a performance, students could examine the background of the play and related information about the issue(s) it addresses. Following the assembly, students would discuss the implications of the play for the particular issue as well as the role of the performing arts in addressing social issues.

Popular music is a staple of adolescent life and culture, and addresses social issues more often than adults sometimes think. The role of folk music in social protest, for example, is a convenient vehicle for examining societal issues through music. (See the many useful issues of *Folksong in the Classroom.*) Likewise, popular music styles and lyrics can be examined as a reflection of trends and themes representative of particular periods, including the present. Similarly, a consideration of Antheil's *Ballet mécanique* (1925) could serve to open the possibility for students that even formal music attempts to comment on changing social conditions. Furthermore, art students would likely profit from an investigation of issues surrounding government funding of the arts and the First Amendment. Again, these suggestions are offered as examples and clearly do not exhaust the innumerable possibilities for examining social issues through the performing arts.

Modern Foreign Languages

Although during the last half-century the emphasis on the function of modern foreign language education has shifted in both the literature of popular school reform (from cold war preparedness to international economic competition) and the professional literature (from disciplining the mind to appreciation of other cultures to communicative ability), the functions most often promoted commonly include a strong practical *versus* academic bent. The examination of social issues is clearly consistent with and a logical extension of this trend toward the practicality and applicability of foreign language study to social affairs. The modern foreign language curriculum could, for example, provide opportunities for students to investigate issues surrounding the social, political, and economic relationships between the United States and countries and/or regions where the target language is heavily spoken or indigenous. The foreign language program may also be the appropriate place in the school curriculum for students to examine the issue of an official national language in the United States. Although the so-called English First issue is usually the property of bilingual educators in the education field (see Secada and Lightfoot 1993 for a discussion of the politics of the issue), the issue may well be of some interest to students who enjoy an aptitude in language arts.

Physical Education and Health

In developing a case for reconceiving physical education to serve the purpose of "emancipatory education," Bain (1988) raises a number of issues relating to physical education with which she feels physical educators must come to terms, many of which could be examined by students as part of the physical education/health curriculum. The "cult of thinness" in our society, the pervasive influence of sports on our lives, racism and sexism in sports (relating to stereotyping and access, for example), sports-related drug use (i.e., steroids), family planning, sexually transmitted diseases (including HIV/AIDS), and images of alcohol and smoking in the media (including advertising) are among the issues students could consider in the physical education/health education curriculum. Other issues pertinent to these subjects include the salaries of professional athletes, the effects of tobacco use and government subsidy of the tobacco industry, and proposals for a national health plan. As greater attention is devoted to the social variables of health and well-being (e.g., Sagan 1987; Sen 1993), possibilities increase for teaching about social issues in health classes.

Vocational Subjects

The primary purpose of vocational education is usually taken to be that of providing students with marketable job skills. The focus tends to be on fitting students into the existing job market, rather than on providing them with life-long competencies to forge their personal place and ultimately to exert significant influence over their own employment destinies. Concerns about international economic competitiveness have of late focused discussions of vocational education on servicing business-sector needs and nationalistic imperatives more than on enhancing the efficacy of the individual citizen-worker.

Vocational education, however, holds great potential for addressing societal issues. While early writings about vocational guidance placed remarkable emphasis on the personal-social (*versus* political-economic) function of vocational education (see Wraga 1994), in practice the emphasis is usually on developing trade skills at the expense of fostering an understanding of vocations in wider economic, social, and civic contexts. Dewey (1966) is worth quoting at length about the social power of vocational education:

... an education which acknowledges the full intellectual and social meaning of a vocation would include instruction in the historic background of present conditions; training in science to give intelligence and initiative in dealing with material and agencies of production; and study of economics, civics, and politics to bring the future worker into touch with the problems of the day and the various methods proposed for its improvement. (p. 318)

Dewey (1966) emphasizes, "Above all, it would train power of readaptation to changing conditions so that future workers would not become blindly subject to a fate imposed upon them" (p. 319). From this perspective, vocational studies offer substantive opportunities for the reflective examination of social issues that impinge on the nature of work, on opportunities for securing and maintaining fulfilling employment, and on the need to view occupations in the wider socioeconomic context rather than simply as a matter of mastering specific job-related skills.

The recent report of the Department of Labor's Secretary's Commission on Achieving Necessary Skills (1991), which identifies an impressive array of relatively sophisticated competencies that will ostensibly be required of future workers, nevertheless falls into the conventional school of thinking about vocational education. Despite the elaboration of complex skills and caveats such as "We are not calling for a narrow work-focused education" (p. v), the SCANS report discusses its targeted competencies only in the context of solving work-related problems. It omits mention of the skills workers will need, for example, "to protect themselves from on-the-job dangers and from employers who would exploit them or who would discriminate on the basis of race or sex," as Hayes (1991, 253) insightfully indicates. Such skills obviously are those that enable employees to deal with pervasive social issues that impinge directly upon the workplace and upon the lives of workers.

Examination of such issues in vocational education can go a long way toward helping workers to identify and subsequently deal with these issues on the job. Echoing Dewey's call for a broad conception of vocational education, Hayes (1991) notes, "I've read nothing about the SCANS proposals that would help students appreciate the history of the labor movement, the

fight to abolish child labor, or the struggle for minimum wage laws and for workers' rights in general" (p. 253). These are among the numerous social issues highly pertinent to vocational education (which recent proposals for youth apprentice-ship programs seem to neglect, as well). Other issues appropriate for the vocational curriculum include problems created by the application of technology; consumer rights; product safety; right-to-know; and workplace safety. Issues of race, ethnicity, and gender regarding occupational access and salary equity, such as the specific case of women in the military, also provide fruitful opportunities for examining societal issues in vocational classes. Examination of these kinds of issues could even lead to a discussion of the role of government in regulating workplace practices and the trade-offs involved in protecting individual rights and maintaining an effective market. Issues such as these could be examined in almost any vocational course.

In developing a case for integrating social studies and home economics curricula, Gentzler (1991) points to important opportunities for teaching about social issues in home economics courses. Gentzler summarizes the traditional aim of home economics as "helping individuals and families improve the quality of their living" (p. 199) through five areas of study: child and human development; foods and nutrition; clothing and textiles; family and consumer economics; home and family management. Though Gentzler does not raise them in this context, several societal issues are clearly inherent to these areas of study, including issues relating to education, product development, and advertising. The study of the role of advertising in shaping purchasing patterns as well as in manipulating consumers by creating desires (see Ewen 1976), for example, could be a rewarding component of the home economics curriculum.

Gentzler (1991) provocatively calls for collaboration between social studies and home economics departments that would bring to bear an understanding of wider social contexts on traditional home economics topics. Such a unit about world hunger would focus on questions such as "What should be done about hunger in our communities? Are there social structures in place that promote hunger? If so, what steps should be taken to restructure our system to discourage hunger? Is hunger good? Should hunger be resolved?" (p. 199). Gentzler offers similar suggestions for deliberation about social issues surrounding substance abuse.

In summary, myriad opportunities exist for incorporating the examination of social issues into conventional subject areas outside the social studies. Implementation strategies for infusing teaching about social issues into existing courses include the addition of regular lessons, an ongoing independent or group research project, a separate unit of the curriculum, or through co-curricular clubs. Again, insofar as social issues provide a connection between the scholastic treatment of subject matter and students' real-life experiences, the infusion of social issues across the curriculum also can enliven subject areas perceived by students to be divorced from life beyond the school walls.

Interdisciplinary Approaches to Societal Issues

The sheer complexity of many social issues requires crossing conventional disciplinary boundaries to develop a thorough understanding of them, as Gentzler's discussion of home economics-related issues suggests. The school curriculum, therefore, should provide planned experiences through which students learn to integrate and apply knowledge from multiple disciplines in an effort to grasp important social issues.

While numerous terms are used to describe various interdisciplinary curriculum designs, these designs can be organized into three general categories (National Association for Core Curriculum 1992; Vars 1993; Wraga 1993). *Curriculum correlation* involves bringing two or more subjects to bear on a selected topic, issue, or problem in ways that purposefully seek connections between and among the subjects in relation to the topic of study. Correlation is the easiest form of interdisciplinary curriculum to implement since it involves no significant reorganization of the overall school program, with the result that the disciplines (and, therefore, teachers) retain their identities. *Fused curriculum* involves combining the content from two or more subjects into a new course. Fused courses are often team-taught by teachers representing traditional subjects. In such arrangements the disciplines usually remain recognizable although the focus is increasingly on the topic or issue rather than on the subject matter. The *core curriculum* involves focusing on personal-social problems and issues that are meaningful to students, applying subject

knowledge and perspectives as appropriate to the issue at hand without deference to conventional subject divisions. The core curriculum can be either pre-planned by the teacher (structured core) or collaboratively planned by the teacher and students (open core).

What might these theoretical interdisciplinary designs look like in practice? In a correlated issue-focused unit, two or more subjects would schedule a series of lessons devoted to a particular issue to be taught at about the same time, and the teachers would explicitly identify ways in which their respective disciplines illuminate the issue. Using conventional subject matter in English and social studies, for example, issues relating to freedom of speech, public opinion, due process, the dignity of the individual, and the relationship between the individual and the society can be examined through the study of Arthur Miller's *The Crucible* and the time periods in which it was written and about which it was written. Recognizing the work as a 1950s play about the 1690s, students could compare social contexts to consider how Miller used historical drama to illuminate contemporary issues that go to the heart of the American experience. This unit could be extended to include comparative analysis of the film *Dead Poet's Society*—a 1980s film about social conditions in the 1950s—as it deals with issues of individualism and conformity.

Engle and Ochoa (1988) recommend annually devoting a block of time (at least two weeks) to a correlated, school-wide study of a selected social issue. Figure 1 represents possible subject area contributions to an issue-focused unit about acid rain. After determining the problem area to be studied, in this case acid rain, the next step would be to identify specific questions that focus on critical dimensions of the issue. Some of these questions would lead to an informed understanding of many facets of the issue, while others would be open-ended, requiring students to use evidence to take and defend opinions about the issue. Activities would be designed to answer the focus questions, and may resemble those suggested in Figure 1. In addition to subject-related activities, school-wide and community-based activities could foster a wider sense of social responsibility and public-mindedness that transcend the classroom. These activities could include conducting an information campaign or petition drive, holding an assembly featuring guest lecturers and/or student panels about the issue, and devoting a special section of the student newspaper to an examination of the problem area. Such a unit could be correlated among the various subject courses or conducted as a component of a problem-focused or core course.

Examples of curriculum fusion can be found in courses that purposefully blend content from two or more conventional disciplines to address a societal issue. Indeed, the two units just described can be conducted as either correlated or fused curricula. Science-Technology-Society courses and some Problems of Democracy courses fall into this category, as do the courses described by Geller (1973) and Dillingham, Kelly, and Strauss (1975) that integrate subject matter from science and social studies to address issues pertaining to pollution, health care, housing, racism, elitism in the environmental movement, and the ethical use of scientific knowledge. Table 2 suggests learning objectives for an issue-focused unit or course that can also serve as general classroom procedures for formally examining a social issue or problem.

Common Learnings Course Required of All Students

While there certainly are ample opportunities in correlated and fused interdisciplinary curricular organizations for the application of subject knowledge to an examination of societal issues, there is, however, an equally great, if not greater, tendency for such courses to dwell largely, if not solely, on the mastery of pertinent subject knowledge. Ideally then, an interdisciplinary, problem-focused, heterogeneously grouped, full-year core or common learnings course required each year for all students should be an integral, unifying component of every high school curriculum. In this course, students of various backgrounds, abilities, and aspirations would engage in a collaborative effort to tackle common problems and issues. Problem areas could be predetermined by teachers or developed cooperatively by teachers and students. In such a setting, students would have the opportunity to participate in a sustained study of problem areas that would include issues of personal and community health, interpersonal relationships, cultural diversity, racism and prejudice, economic change, global interdependence, the environment, communications and the media, and others. Problem-focused units would correlate with the discipline-centered subjects of the school

curriculum as well as integrate subject knowledge and perspectives as appropriate to the particular problem under study. Again, the unit depicted in Figure 1 could be conducted through a core or common learnings course. Descriptions of secondary core programs can be found in Giles, McCutchen, and Zechiel (1942), Wright (1950), Educational Policies Commission (1952), Tanner and Tanner (1980), and Vars (1993). McDonald and Czerniak (1994) offer a variety of strategies and guidelines for developing interdisciplinary units, and explain the use of planning wheels, webbing, and concept maps.

Societal Issues beyond the Classroom

Teaching and learning about social issues should not be limited to the confines of the classroom. As noted above, students can consider social issues in subject-related clubs or in school assemblies such as dramatic presentations that complement classroom examination of selected issues. In fact, co-curricular activities such as the student government, peer leadership programs, the school newspaper, and the debate society provide numerous opportunities for engaging students in important personal-social issues. Significantly, a positive correlation exists between involvement in school governance and other co-curricular activities and post-graduation involvement in civic and community affairs (Ferguson 1991; Berk 1992). Community service projects obviously offer further opportunities for students to become actively involved in social issues (Nathan and Kielsmeier 1991; Barber 1992). Related directly to the formal curriculum, co-curricular and service activities can make "academic" subjects valuable sources of information about the world beyond the school. In short, the co-curriculum and the daily operations of the school can serve as valuable resources for engaging students in problematic social issues. In 1918 the *Cardinal Principles* report proposed that every high school include among its staff a citizenship director whose job it would be to "foster civic-mindedness through the school paper, debating society, and general school exercises, and give suggestions for directing the thinking of pupils to significant problems of the day" (Commission on the Reorganization of Secondary Education 1918, 28). This recommendation is clearly commensurate with the status the preparation of citizens should hold

Table 2: Sample Learning Objectives for an Issue-Focused Course

Students will learn to do the following:

1. **Identify** local, national, and/or global issues or problems.
2. **Apply** knowledge and concepts from pertinent disciplines to understand these issues.
3. **Explain** the relationships between the disciplines pertinent to the problem/issue.
4. **Assess** the relevance of research information and the credibility of information sources.
5. **Identify** bias in media sources.
6. **Identify** possible solutions to the problems/issues.
7. **Assess** the possible impact of solutions.
8. **Choose** a particular solution and defend it in writing using logic, evidence, personal values, and social ideals.
9. **Generate** the best logical argument against evidence that is in conflict with a chosen solution.
10. **Develop** and **implement** an activity to promote their solution.

Adapted from: E. Wolf, *Foreign and Domestic Policy Practicum Curriculum Guide* (Basking Ridge, N.J.: Bernards Township Public Schools, 1993).

Table 3: Suggested Guidelines for Dealing with Societal Issues

1. Lead students to expect controversy in the classroom.
2. When dealing with an issue, clarify the nature of the issue and agreements and disagreements surrounding it.
3. Ensure student exposure to a best-case, fair hearing of competing points of view.
4. Ensure that sufficient factual information is brought to the discussion to promote the development of informed opinions.
5. Ensure that logic is used as a criterion for evaluating the credibility of arguments.
6. Employ small-group discussions to enable all students the opportunity to participate and to enable the teacher to work individually with more students.
7. Respect students' right not to express their opinions publicly on all issues.
8. Be willing to accept that not all issues can be resolved.
9. Establish closure to all discussions of issues (e.g., deciding when the class will agree to disagree).
10. Occasionally provide opportunities, as appropriate, to revisit previously addressed issues.

Source: Adapted from T. E. Kelly, "Leading Class Discussions of Controversial Issues," *Social Education* (October 1989): 368-370; Social Science Education Consortium, *Science, Technology, Society Training Manual* (Boulder, Colo.: Social Science Education Consortium, 1988).

as an express curricular priority and could go a long way toward actualizing this priority throughout the school program.

Conclusion

Fertile opportunities for engaging students in substantive consideration of social issues exist throughout the secondary curriculum. With relatively slight modifications, virtually any subject area can develop student competency in addressing social issues. Inclusion of social issues in non-social studies subjects may, however, prompt serious rethinking of the purpose and nature of those curriculum areas. Further, however and whatever social issues are infused into the school curriculum, issue-focused instruction requires a sensitivity to the potential volatility of certain issues and should be handled using techniques that ensure fair and balanced treatment of conflicting viewpoints. The guidelines suggested in Table 3 can be useful in any classroom and/or co-curricular treatment of societal issues. Providing structured opportunities for students to reflect systematically on perennial societal

Foreign Languages

Translate news reports from other countries for different perspectives on the issue.

Fine and Performing Arts

- Create and perform a dramatic skit addressing the issue.
- Create a mural addressing the issue

Social Studies

- Map affected areas by regions and nations.
- Evaluate available solutions to the acid rain problem in terms of cost-effectiveness.
- Explain international political and economic implications of the issue.
- Hold a debate on the issue.
- Conduct a petition drive.
- Lobby elected officials.

Vocational Subjects

- Determine the impact of acid rain on the economy and jobs.
- Analyze industrial policies regarding the issue.
- Propose a new industrial policy addressing the problem.
- Invent products or services to help solve the problem.

Mathematics

- Compile and graph statistics on the rate and extent of acreage affected by acid rain.
- Develop mathematical model(s) extrapolating future damage.

Science

- Conduct a lab demonstrating the effects of acid precipitation on plant life.
- Develop a model demonstrating meteorological factors

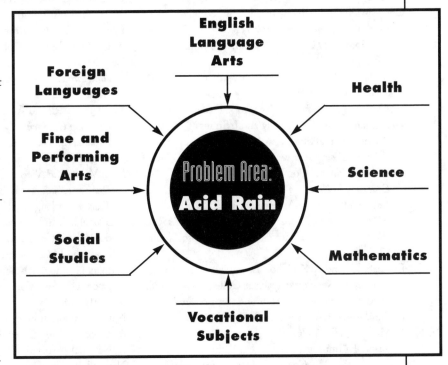

- Explain scientific opinions on the issue.
- Evaluate available solutions to the acid rain problem in terms of its environmental impact.

Health

- Create a poster representing the affect of acid rain on standards of living.

English Language Arts

- Apply reading, writing, and research skills to clarify the issue.
- Access a variety of information sources about the issue.
- Write a letter to the editor of a newspaper expressing a position on the issue.

issues across the curriculum is an important step toward making the secondary school truer to its historic mission of educating enlightened citizens for life in a democratic society.

References

Abrams, M. H., gen ed. *The Norton Anthology of English Literature*. Volume 2. New York: W. W. Norton, 1968.

"Adolescent Literature Comes of Age." *English Journal* 81, no. 4 (April 1992): 35-58.

Baigell, M. *The American Scene: American Painting of the 1930s*. New York: Praeger, 1973.

—. *A History of American Painting*. New York: Praeger, 1974.

Bain, L. L. "Curriculum for Critical Reflection in Physical Education." In *Content of the Curriculum*. 1988 ASCD Yearbook, edited by R. S. Brandt. Alexandria, Va.: Association for Supervision and Curriculum Development, 1988: 133-147.

Barber, B. R. *An Aristocracy of Everyone: The Politics of Education and the Future of America*. New York: Ballantine Books, 1992.

Berk, L. E. "The Extracurriculum." In *Handbook of Research on Curriculum*, edited by P. Jackson. New York: Macmillan, 1992: 1002-1043.

Beyer, B. K. *Practical Strategies for the Teaching of Thinking.* Boston: Allyn and Bacon, 1987.

"Civic Literacy." *English Journal* 80, no. 5 (September 1991): 43-70.

Commission on the Reorganization of Secondary Education. *Cardinal Principles of Secondary Education.* Washington, D.C.: U.S. Government Printing Office, 1918.

Dewey, J. *The Public and Its Problems.* Athens, Ohio: Swallow Press, 1985.

—. *Democracy and Education.* New York: Free Press, 1966.

Dillingham, C. K., C. A. Kelly, and J. Strauss. "Environmental Studies: A Noncosmetic Approach." *American Biology Teacher* 37 no. 2 (1975): 116-117.

Educational Policies Commission. *The Purposes of Education in American Democracy.* Washington, D.C.: National Education Association, 1938.

—. *Education for ALL American Youth-A Further Look.* Washington, D.C.: National Education Association, 1952.

Engle, S. H., and A. S. Ochoa. *Education for Democratic Citizenship.* New York: Teachers College Press, 1988.

Ewen, S. *Captains of Consciousness: Advertising and the Social Roots of the Consumer Culture.* New York: McGraw-Hill, 1976.

Ferguson, P. "Impacts on Social and Political Participation." In *Handbook of Research on Social Studies Teaching and Learning,* edited by J. P. Shaver. New York: Macmillan, 1991: 385-99.

French, W. *Behavioral Goals of General Education in High School.* New York: Russell Sage Foundation, 1957.

Gehrke, N. J., M. S. Knapp, and K. A. Sirotnik. "In Search of the School Curriculum." In *Review of Research in Education,* edited by G. Grant. Washington, D.C.: American Educational Research Association, 1992: 51-110.

Geller, L. R. "Team-taught Course 'Crisis in America' Has Broad Appeal." *American Biology Teacher* 35, no. 2 (1973): 88-90.

Gentzler, Y. S. "Develop Social Responsibility by Having Social Studies and Home Economics Departments Collaborate." *Social Studies* 82, no. 5 (September/October 1991): 198-201.

Giles, H. H., S. P. McCutchen, and A. N. Zechiel. *Exploring the Curriculum.* New York: Harper, 1942.

"A Global Perspective." *English Journal* 79, no. 8 (December 1990): 35-58.

Goodlad, J. I. *A Place Called School.* New York: McGraw-Hill, 1984.

Hayes, L. "Scanning SCANS." *Phi Delta Kappan* (November 1991): 253.

Hlebowitsh, P. S., K. S. Muller, and S. B. Pickett. "The Reemergence of General Education Ideals in Secondary English Education." *Illinois Schools Journal* (Spring 1991): 5-13.

Hurlbert, C. M., and S. Totten. *Social Issues in the English Classroom.* Urbana, Ill.: National Council of Teachers of English, 1992.

Lee, A. M. *The Fine Art of Propaganda.* New York: Harcourt, Brace, 1939.

Lesy, M. *Bearing Witness: A Photographic Chronicle of American Life, 1860-1945.* New York: Pantheon Books, 1982.

Lloyd-Jones, R., and A. A. Lunsford. *The English Coalition Conference: Democracy through Language.* Urbana, Ill.: National Council of Teachers of English, 1989.

Lutz, W. *Beyond Nineteen Eighty-Four: Doublespeak in a Post-Orwellian Age.* Urbana, Ill.: National Council of Teachers of English, 1989.

McDonald, J., and C. Czerniak. "Developing Interdisciplinary Units: Strategies and Examples." *School Science and Mathematics* 94, no. 1 (1994): 5-10.

Nathan, J., and J. Kielsmeier. eds. "Youth Service," (special section). *Phi Delta Kappan* 72, no. 10 (June 1991): 738-773.

National Association for Core Curriculum. *Interdisciplinary Curriculum Terminology.* Kent, Ohio: National Association for the Core Curriculum, 1992.

Newhall, B. *The History of Photography.* New York: Museum of Modern Art, 1978.

Paul, R., and J. Rudinow. "Critical Thinking and Bias." In *Critical Thinking,* edited by A. J. A. Binker. Rohnert Park, Calif: Center for Critical Thinking and Moral Critique, 1990: 170-175.

"Rediscovering America through Literature." *English Journal* 81, no. 5 (September 1992): 17-54.

Sagan, L. A. *The Health of Nations: True Causes of Sickness and Well-Being.* New York: Basic Books, 1987.

Secada, W.G., and T. Lightfoot. "Symbols and the Political Context of Bilingual Education in the United States." In *Bilingual Education: Politics, Practice, and Research,* 92nd Yearbook of the National Society for the Study of Education, edited by M. B. Arias and O. Casanova. Chicago: University of Chicago Press, 1993: 36-64.

Secretary's Commission on Achieving Necessary Skills (SCANS). *What Work Requires of Schools.* Washington, D.C.: U.S. Department of Labor, 1991.

Sen, A. "The Economics of Life and Death." *Scientific American* (May 1993): 40-47.

Steele, J. "TV's Talking Headaches." *Columbia Journalism Review* (July/August 1992): 49-52.

Stott, W. *Documentary Expression and Thirties America.* New York: Oxford University Press, 1973.

Tanner, D. *Secondary Curriculum: Theory and*

Development. New York: Macmillan, 1971.

Tanner, D. and L. Tanner. *Curriculum Development: Theory into Practice.* 2nd Edition. New York: Macmillan, 1980.

Totten, S. "Educating for the Development of Social Consciousness and Social Responsibility." In *Social Issues in the English Classroom,* by C. M. Hurlbert and S. Totten. Urbana, Ill.: National Council of Teachers of English, 1992: 9-55.

Vars, G. F. *Interdisciplinary Teaching: Why and How.* Columbus, Ohio: National Middle School Association, 1993.

Vatter, T. "Civic Mathematics: A Real-Life General Mathematics Course." *Mathematics Teacher* 87, no. 6 (September 1994): 396-401.

Wraga, W. G. "The Interdisciplinary Imperative for Citizenship Education." *Theory and Research in Social Education* 21, no. 3 (Summer 1993): 201-231.

—. *Democracy's High School: The Comprehensive High School and Educational Reform in the United States.* Lanham, Md.: University Press of America, 1994.

Wright, G. S. *Core Curriculum in Public High Schools.* Bulletin 1950, no. 5, U.S. Office of Education. Washington, D.C.: U.S. Government Printing Office, 1950.

Part Eight: Assessment

Introduction by Walter C. Parker

This section of the Handbook is concerned with assessing student learning in an issue-oriented curriculum environment. Its two chapters suggest that the boundaries between assessment work and curriculum work are not well-defined, as once was assumed, but profitably can be blurred to the point at which a discussion of assessment becomes a discussion of curriculum goals, and visa versa.

The theme of these two chapters is that assessments do not merely help educators find out what and how much students have learned; they also serve as the ends for teaching and learning. Whether or not they are ends worth pursuing depends on the kind of thinking, learning, and community life they encourage. Both chapters are based on work that is underway in public schools in the authors' home states of Washington (Parker) and Michigan (Harris).

In the first chapter, several examples of issue-oriented curriculum guidelines are spelled out in terms of performance assessment. I argue that it is important in this kind of curriculum/assessment work to distinguish between *course* and *program* planning, and I identify subject matter—both topics of study and intellectual frameworks for studying these topics—that ought to drive teaching, learning, and assessment at both levels. In the second chapter, David Harris shows how an issue-oriented curriculum target can be clarified *and made more attainable* when assessment criteria are carefully developed. The target of concern for Harris is competent small-group discussion of public issues. This arguably is the central civic competency required of citizens in societies attempting to be democratic (Parker 1996).

"Assessment" is a broad term that includes all the different methods teachers employ to gather information in their classrooms and the many purposes this information can serve. In this introduction, I briefly review these means and ends, address their political dimensions, and then consider assessment as a tool for school reform.

Purposes

Assessment can serve very different masters. One prominent classification scheme identifies three main groups of purposes (Resnick and Resnick 1991). The first is *public accountability and program evaluation*. Assessment of this type permits those in elected and appointed positions to monitor school performance. Here we see especially the phenomenon of standardized testing, with results being used to compare schools and states and even nations. The second class of purposes is the *selection of students for particular schools and programs*. These tests provide information on individuals rather than groups. The Scholastic Aptitude Test (SAT), introduced in 1926, is perhaps the most famous assessment used for this purpose. IQ tests used to select students for special programs and lesser-known tests used for placing students in learning- and behavior-disorder programs are included, too. The third set of purposes is closer to daily classroom life: *instructional management and monitoring*. Here assessment is conducted in order to help students learn and teachers teach. Sample purposes are:

a. developing units of instruction

b. deciding how to teach the rest of a unit

c. judging the depth of student knowledge and the range of their abilities

d. diagnosing student problems

e. motivating students to study

f. providing feedback to students on their progress

g. judging the appropriateness of performance criteria

h. assigning students to small groups for

cooperative work

i. identifying cultural differences so as to provide culturally relevant instruction

j. achieving a cooperative and thoughtful environment.

The two chapters in this section are concerned mainly with this third set of purposes—instructional management and monitoring.

Methods

Assessment methods geared toward instructional management and monitoring can be divided into three approaches: paper and pencil techniques, observations, and interviews.

Paper and pencil techniques are one major way to collect assessment data in the classroom, and these techniques generally take two forms: production and selection (Airasian 1994). Production items require students to construct a response to a question, such as when students write a statement clarifying and supporting a position they have taken on a foreign policy controversy. Selection items require students to choose the best answer from a set of options, as when they choose which group of data best refutes a stated conclusion.

Observation is another approach used to collect assessment data. Teachers have always used observation on an informal basis, and they do so almost continually. For example, they note students' responses to something they say or to a guest speaker's comment. They see a student squint to see the board, race to be in the seat before the bell rings, or walk slowly into the classroom and slump into a desk. Teachers use observation more formally, also, such as when they use criteria to judge students making presentations to classmates or conducting debates. Students may be asked to demonstrate their ability to moderate discussions while another student observes and scores their performance on several criteria the class has been studying.

Interviews are a third, powerful way teachers can gather information (Valencia, McGinley, Pearson 1990). Teachers of writing are increasingly conducting "writing conferences" with their students in which they not only assess a piece of student writing but ask questions to ascertain the thinking behind its production—a student's conception of the writing process, for example, what he or she finds most difficult or easy about it, and whether he or she searched for opposing points of view before taking a position. Similarly, issue-oriented teachers can use the interview to investigate students' conceptions of issues. Doing this sanctions and models conversation about issues above and beyond debate on their particulars. Specifically, teachers can ask students how they conceptualize a particular issue, why they think it became an issue, for whom it is an issue, and whether it is a public or private issue. Also, teachers can ask about historical analogies, and they can move their students toward a multicultural understanding of issues by asking about different perspectives that might be brought to an issue.

These are difficult questions, to be sure. They reflect high standards. Asking these questions indicates that the teacher has a good understanding of the nature of issues; similarly, student responses will indicate their understanding. And that is the point. Interviews allow teachers to apprehend their students' grasp of a task's performance criteria. This is true of any task, whether writing an analysis of a public problem, framing a discussion question, developing a resolution for a debate, or researching value conflicts on an issue. In one-to-one as well as group interviews, teachers can learn what students believe are good performances and why, and they can elicit the meanings students give to the performance criteria that teachers are wanting them to learn.

The Politics of Assessment

Distinctions of this kind among purposes and methods of assessment should help bring some order to our topic, but still it sprawls. Assessment experts themselves belong to an array of camps and sects. Some work directly for the federal government, others for research centers, universities, and regional laboratories, and others for school systems. Some are disgusted with U.S. students' achievement record, others are proud of it, and others believe it is not important. Some are enamored of particular techniques (e.g., "kid watching" and "portfolio assessment"), others are measurement specialists, and others argue over authority issues (e.g., the role of the federal government vis-a-vis states).

The history of assessment practices in the United States and elsewhere reveals that assessment often is not what it appears. While usually assessment is discussed as though it is a politically and culturally neutral activity, assessment in fact has been used for political and cultural purposes. For example, assessment has been used to conserve the status quo by "naturalizing" it; labels are affixed to children as though they signified natural ability rather than differences based on economic and cultural capital (Apple 1992). The disproportionate numbers of African American children labeled "behaviorally disordered" and "learning disabled" is one example, while girls' difficulties with mathematics is another.

Another topic on which the political uses of assessment stand out in sharp relief is *delivery standards* (Porter 1993). Delivery standards—also known as "opportunities to learn" or, simply, "assistance" or "support"—refer to the human and material resources schools offer to students so that they can learn what is expected of them. A truism in education is that students should not be expected to achieve curriculum objectives without assistance. This is why schools do not only provide objectives, but also teachers, curriculum materials, and other resources. It is a well-known fact that these resources are not always forthcoming and certainly not equitably distributed (e.g., Kozol 1991).

At the most general level, the two most powerful forms of support schools can provide to students are (a) high-quality curriculum and instruction that are relevant to the tasks on which students' performances will be assessed, and (b) clear expectations, by which I mean clarification of the tasks at which students are supposed to succeed and the criteria that distinguish successful from mediocre or unsuccessful performances. Both kinds of assistance, in turn, require suitable physical plants, academic and moral climates, relevant materials, and competent, caring faculty. In the words of the New Standards Project, "this means that (students) will be taught a curriculum that will prepare them for the assessments, their teachers will have the preparation to enable them to teach it well, and there will be an equitable distribution of the resources students and their teachers need to succeed" (University of Pittsburgh 1992, 15).

This level of support is a tall order—one that educators generally were unable to meet even before the current movement to raise curriculum standards. This is an important point, because increased assessment activity could *further* threaten students who already are most at risk of school failure. The reason is simple: Increased assessment activity may not be coupled with the necessary support for student learning.

The size of the "at-risk" group could grow in another way, too, by adding to it those students in the middle track of the American secondary school who are now "making it" simply because assessment activity is inconsequential or focused on curriculum standards so low as to require little beyond seat time.

Both assessment *and* the provision of support require a set of curriculum targets that are clearly visible, and such targets generally should be the assessment tasks themselves (Newmann, Secada, and Wehlage 1995). The same thing that makes a curriculum achievable makes student progress assessable and the provision of relevant support possible: clarified targets for teaching and learning.

Assessment and School Reform

What has brought the topic of assessment to the center of educators' attention in recent years? Two developments stand out: renewed claims of school mediocrity in the United States brought on initially in 1983 by a government study, *A Nation at Risk*, and the growing realization that assessment practices were lagging far behind research on thinking and learning. At the intersection of these two forces, assessment reform emerged as a solution to the mediocrity problem. Teacher education was not rising to the task, nor were teacher hiring and retention practices, increased salaries, site-based management, school restructuring, or other promising movements.

The unique promise of assessment as a tool for educational reform is its influence on educators' behavior, which is to say its power to attract and focus teachers' (and students') attention and efforts (Cohen 1987; Smith 1991). This is particularly true of high-stakes assessments that are administered for accountability and selection purposes, but it is also true of more routine classroom assessments as well. The basic notion here is that "you get what you assess" and "you do not get what you do not assess" (Resnick and Resnick 1991, 60). If assessments are geared toward curriculum targets that no one cares much about, then teachers' and students' energies are spent in ways that do not matter. The reverse is also true.

Conclusion

Classrooms are complex social landscapes on which many things are occurring, on many levels, at once. Assessment, therefore, is not a simple matter, and it certainly is no magic bullet. The high hopes put before it are unrealistic. But it is a worthy effort that should bear at least some fruit, not the least of which is exposing the hypocrisy that has allowed educators often to preach one thing while teaching and testing another.

"We have the tests we deserve," Grant Wiggins observed wryly. Students in the United States are "the most tested but least examined in the world" (Wiggins 1993, 3), and the cause is a persistent failure to appreciate the relationship between curriculum and assessment on the one hand, and assessment and learning on the other. We have the tests we deserve, Wiggins continues, "because we are wont to reduce 'assessment' to 'testing' and to see testing as separate from learning—something you do expediently, once, after the teaching is over, to see how students did (usually for other people's benefit, not the performer's)." Just how we got ourselves into this predicament is another matter (see Berlak 1992). Getting out of it is the concern here.

The two chapters that follow try to overcome the disjunctures of curriculum from assessment, and assessment from teaching and learning. They deal with only small parcels of the broad landscape, but they do so in a way that hopefully will suggest lines of reasoning and ways of proceeding that are broadly useful to our readers.

References

Airasian, Peter W. *Classroom Assessment.* 2nd edition. New York: McGraw-Hill, 1994.

Apple, Michael W. "Do the Standards Go Far Enough? Power, Policy, and Practice in Mathematics Education." *Journal of Research in Mathematics Education* 23, no. 5 (1992): 412-431.

Berlak, Harold. "The Need for a New Science of Assessment." In *Toward a New Science of Educational Testing and Assessment,* edited by Harold Berlak, Fred M. Newmann, Elizabeth Adams, et al. Albany: State University of New York Press, 1992.

Cohen, S. Alan. "Instructional Alignment: Searching for a Magic Bullet." *Educational Researcher* 16, no. 8 (1987): 16-20.

Kozol, Jonathan. *Savage Inequalities.* New York: Crown, 1991.

Newmann, Fred M., Walter G. Secada, and Gary G. Wehlage. *A Guide to Authentic Instruction and Assessment: Vision, Standards, and Scoring.* Madison: University of Wisconsin Press, 1995.

Parker, Walter C. "Curriculum for Democracy." In *Democracy, Education, and the Schools,* edited by Roger Soder. San Francisco: Jossey-Bass, 1996.

Porter, Andrew C. "School Delivery Standards." *Educational Researcher* 22, no. 5 (1993): 24-29.

Resnick, Lauren B. and Daniel P. Resnick. "Assessing the Thinking Curriculum: New Tools for Educational Reform." In *Changing Assessments: Alternative Views of Aptitude, Achievement, and Instruction,* edited by Bernard R. Gifford and Mary Catherine O'Conner. Boston: Kluwer Academic Publishers, 1991.

Smith, Mary Lee. "Put to the Test: The Effects of External Testing on Teachers." *Educational Researcher* 20, no. 5 (1991): 8-11.

University of Pittsburgh, Learning Research and Development Center. *The New Standards Project. 1992-1995 : A Proposal.* Pittsburgh: Learning Research and Development Center, 1992.

Valencia, Sheila W., William McGinley, and P. David Pearson. "Assessing Reading and Writing." In *Reading in the Middle School.* 2nd Edition, edited by Gerald Duffy. Newark, NJ: International Reading Association, 1990.

Wiggins, Grant P. *Assessing Student Performance.* San Francisco: Jossey-Bass, 1993.

30 ASSESSING STUDENT LEARNING OF AN ISSUE-ORIENTED CURRICULUM

by Walter C. Parker

Assessment work is 80 percent curriculum work, and curriculum work is 80 percent content selection, more or less. In this chapter on assessment, accordingly, I will spend a good portion of the allotted space on curriculum matters, particularly the problem of deciding which small set of learnings is worth assessing. I will draw on the "authentic" assessment and issue-oriented curriculum literatures as well as my experience as a curriculum planner, teacher, and researcher.

Assessment means finding out what students know and are able to do. While not easy, this is also not terribly difficult. What has to be done generally is the work of imagination and ethnography: Imagining how learners might demonstrate what they have learned, and observing sociocultural life to detect which demonstrations might be most meaningful to the learners themselves, their teachers, and their communities. More difficult is the problem of deciding what knowledge and abilities deserve the concerted effort and persistence of teachers and students (Parker 1991; Shaver 1977). We will turn to this problem first, conducting a search for the essential content—the central understandings and abilities—of an issue-oriented curriculum.

Issue-Oriented Curriculum

Table 1 presents a thought experiment I have used when working with social studies curriculum planning committees in public school districts. I present it early in this chapter for the same reasons that I use it early in curriculum planning work. First, the exercise involves committee members simultaneously in the work of content selection and assessment planning. Second, it encourages them to think beyond their own courses and grade levels to an encompassing unit of analysis—the long-term, cumulative purposes of a K through 12 program of study. It asks a committee to consider, in particular, what products of learning students might be asked to exchange for a high school diploma. The products are to be few in number and collected in a "slim portfolio." If the size of the collection is not limited, choices and rationales become unnecessary and, consequently, the exercise loses power.

This kind of curriculum/assessment work is a "high-stakes" proposition because students' graduation is at stake. Accordingly, controversies abound, and the exercise in Table 1 helps bring them to the surface where they can be discussed. The advantage of *raising* them early, while not trying to *solve* them early,[2] is that the complex problem space of curriculum planning is sketched out in a fairly full and rich way. Furthermore, committee members are actually experiencing issue-oriented discourse, getting a student's-eye view of it. Six issues are central to this planning.

1 CONTENT SELECTION: What subject matters— knowledge and abilities—should students learn across the K through 12 years and be held accountable for having learned? Why these? Stated differently, and realizing that not everything of value can reasonably be taught in school, to which small, important sample of learnings should school time be directed—teachers', students', and administrators'—and based on what rationale?

2 MULTIPLE OBJECTIVES: How important is it to distinguish ability objectives (e.g., weighing alternatives, persuasive reasoning, perspective taking) from knowledge objectives (e.g., the concepts of democracy and pluralism), and to specify both in content selection and assessment work?

Table 1: Planning the Social Studies Graduation Portfolio

Imagine the following:

It's late May and time for the Twin Peaks High School graduation ceremony. The graduates, wearing caps and gowns, file to the podium, where they shake hands with a representative of the school board, receive the diploma, move the tassel from one side of the hat to the other, and descend the stairs. That's it. A few minutes remembered for a lifetime. This year, things are different. The marchers do not approach the podium empty-handed. Instead they carry a slim portfolio containing a collection of their school work. The collection, specified years in advance, has already been judged adequate for the diploma. (Judging occurred during the preceding three months.) The key point in the ceremony is the moment at which the portfolio is exchanged for the diploma—a gesture indicating that the diploma has been *earned*.

What should be some of the contents of the social studies portfolio?

For the present exercise, we are interested only in the social studies portion of the portfolio.

We want to look, therefore, at that portion that will prove to us that *powerful social understandings* and *civic competence* have been demonstrated.

Brainstorm with others a few items that you would want to see there. They should be performances (exhibitions) that prove, more or less, that the desired social understandings and civic competencies have been achieved. They should be worth learning, and most should require students to use their knowledge in challenging ways (e.g., policy analysis and formulation).

Ask someone at your table to monitor the brainstorming session while participating in it. The monitor makes a list of the ideas suggested and keeps the brainstorming moving rather than dwelling on any one suggestion.

NOTE: Be ready to give a progress report in 20 minutes. Try to have 5-10 items on the list by then, and consider it a first draft. Following progress reports, discuss the exercise and some of the issues it raises.

---

3 CONCERTED EFFORT ON CORE CURRICULUM: How much instructional time should converge on a common set of critically important learnings, such as the analysis of public issues, and how much should be left to teachers' own (and often divergent) designs? That is, to what extent should teachers coordinate their efforts, in their different grade levels and courses, on the same subject matter? (I prefer the 60/40 ratio: 60 percent of instructional time is spent on core learnings, 40 percent on learnings of a teacher's own choosing.)

4 ASSESSMENT: How will students, their teachers, and their communities know if, and to what extent, students have learned these things? What are the different kinds of indicators that might represent the desired learning? And, what will be done about students who do not learn them to the degree deemed sufficient?

5 CURRICULUM DIFFERENTIATION: Which students will be expected to learn these things? Which students will not, and why? For example, will the majority of students in a high school study a middle-track American history curriculum that evades rigorous study of great ideas and issues? Will a disproportionate number of work-ing-class students be assigned a less challenging and less interesting curriculum?

6 OPPORTUNITIES TO LEARN: What conditions are necessary and sufficient in schools to support student success on assessment tasks, and what can be done to establish them? A huge gap separates moneyed and poor schools; the development of "world-class standards," consequently, could further disadvantage those students who lack the institutional support needed to reach them.

Whether the activity in Table 1 rouses all these controversies or only a few, it invariably makes clear the intimate connection between assessment work and curriculum planning. This is because the items considered for the portfolio are at once performance assessments and curriculum goals.

Course and Program Planning

Local curriculum planning occurs mainly on two levels: courses and programs. Course planning is common in the United States today and consumes a good portion of the daily professional work of elementary and secondary school teachers. Its object is the set(s) of subject matter and experiences through which a teacher will guide his or her students over an identifiable period of time, such as a year or semester. Elementary school teachers guide their students on several courses at once, usually drawn from the four main fields of study found in schools—social studies, language arts, mathematics, and science.

Whether in elementary or secondary education, course-level curricula often are not connected to broader, long-term goals that would encompass and to some extent shape course-level planning. Courses frequently are ends in themselves—isolated studies that have not been articulated with others toward some planned, cumulative end. This is an old problem, to be sure. A scholar writing in the 1930s about curricula suitable for democracy complained that the conventional school curriculum was utterly without "design," its courses and materials a mere "aggregate of parts serving separate, fixed functions," all "held together in a mechanical way" (Harris 1939, 176).

When, on the other hand, courses are coordinated as a system of studies aimed at integrated outcomes, we have the second level of curriculum development: program planning. Programs differ from one another by their field, scope and sequence, and aims. A program may be as broad in scope and sequence as an entire K through 12 social studies program or smaller, such as a high school social studies or science program, a middle school or elementary school mathematics program, or a primary grades integrated program. What defines a program of study is not the mechanical joining of fragments under one title—e.g., The High School Social Studies Program-but **a.** aims held in common by the several parts, **b.** concerted curriculum and instruction directed toward these common aims, and, **c.** ongoing evaluation and revision of aims, curriculum, and instruction by teachers, curriculum coordinators, and students.

Content Selection

When planning an issue-oriented program or course, content selection is the central task. Advice is plentiful, fortunately; planners do not need to start from scratch. Oliver and Shaver (1974) offer the key principle: subject matter should be derived from a consideration of the demands of citizenship in the modern democratic state. "One cannot discuss the objectives of education without considering the objectives of the society in which education is to operate" (p. 9).

Numerous approaches rest on this principle.

Hunt and Metcalf (1968) concentrated on the study of human conflicts, especially those drawn from "closed" or taboo areas of society—controversial topics on which careful deliberation is socially or politically discouraged. Oliver and Newmann (1967) introduced students to distinctions among several kinds of issues—definitional, empirical, ethical—as well as strategies for moving discussions forward, (e.g., clarifying an issue, stipulating a definition, and drawing an analogy). Newmann (1975) later advocated a "citizen action" approach geared toward exerting influence on public policy. Engle (1960) emphasized decision-making, "which is reflective, speculative, thought provoking, and oriented to the process of reaching conclusions" (p. 303).

Multiple Objectives. Whatever the particular subject-matter angle or emphasis, issue-oriented curriculum visions are united on the requirement of multiple objectives. Recall that the first issue in the list of six above asked not only about essential knowledge—what students should know—but essential abilities—what students should be able to do. These are two types of content objectives to which the issue-oriented tradition gives equal and concurrent attention. There is no agreement on labels for these paired categories. The terms "topics" and "thinking skills," or "content" and "processes" are often used. "Powerful social understandings" (Task Force on Teaching and Learning 1992) and "higher-order thinking," or "HOT," (Newmann 1990a), are precise. In Oliver and Shaver's terms, content selection involves two major decisions: "What topics will one choose as the basis for selecting specific materials of instruction? What intellectual framework will be used to guide the teacher and, in turn, the student in handling these materials?" (1974, 59).

This division is necessary because content selection must occur deliberately on both fronts; yet, the goal for daily teaching and learning must be an effective synthesis of the two. This synthesis could be called "knowledge-in-use" (Sizer 1992) or a "thinking curriculum" (Resnick and Klopfer 1989). It is a necessary synthesis for even the most rudimentary forms of learning (Resnick and Resnick 1991).

As for the first category of objectives—topics—we saw above that the main topical area is public conflict and related policy controversies. Methods and findings from the disciplines are included as well, but they enter the problem space as tools for deliberating conflict and policy rather than as the central objects of study. Oliver and Shaver (1974) identified several problem areas from which controversies might be drawn: racial and ethnic conflict; religious and ideological conflict; security and the individual; conflict among economic groups; health, education, and welfare; and national security. Each problem area has a perennial and cross-cultural quality; each contains potentially many cases across time and space. Careful selection of analogous cases from different historical eras and cultures but within a single problem area should help students understand that publics across time and space have had to deal with many of the same problems. This could make for an extraordinarily rigorous course or program of courses, richly historical and global in scope, and centered squarely on real and persistent problems of democratic citizenship.

The second category of content objectives, the intellectual framework or higher-order thinking (HOT) abilities, is constrained by decisions made in the first category. Needed are HOT abilities with which this particular substantive knowledge is to be formed, elaborated, and refined. Planners have good reason to select a decision-making model, reflective inquiry, or others. Let us for the sake of argument take Oliver and Shaver's (1974) well-developed "jurisprudential framework," which, to one degree or another, includes the others. This framework is less concerned with the skills of formal logic than with *clarification* and *analysis, analogy, weighing alternatives,* and *predicting*—all directed at **a.** problem areas, **b.** selected controversies within problem areas, and **c.** the diverse points of view and value conflicts they entail.

Issue-Oriented Assessment

The most important thing to be said about assessments is that they do not merely help educators find out what and how much students have learned. Rather, assessments set the targets for teaching and learning. When assessments are carefully fitted to curriculum goals—by which I mean that they clarify, specify, and qualify them—the boundaries between assessment and curriculum work are effectively blurred. A discussion of assessment measures becomes a discussion of curriculum goals and visa versa.[3] In this sense, both course- and program-level curricula should "teach to the test," and curriculum planning should begin with "visions of and criteria for success in

those achievements toward which the curriculum will aim" (Newmann and Archbald 1992, 76).

For this to occur, the working notion of assessment needs to change from measures of student learning that are ill-fitted to valued curriculum goals to measures that fit them well. When the fit is poor, teachers rightly complain (and students should as well) that the measure is not a worthy target of teaching or learning.

Performance Assessment

When the fit is good, the targets are meaningful ("authentic") achievements. They are "actual examples of student work that exemplify outcomes specified by content standards" (Simmons and Resnick 1993, 11). Such examples often, but not always, are "performance assessments." That is, they require students to perform[4] on some sort of task[5] that is related meaningfully to a valued curriculum goal.[6] Because the targets are genuine achievements, they require students to become thoughtful judges of their own work. "Theirs is the work of posing questions, making judgments, integrating criticisms, reconsidering problems, and investigating new possibilities" (Zessoules and Gardner 1991, 64). Teachers more likely will be proud to teach to such targets, and students should be able to see the value in working toward them. This is the vision of authentic assessment.

Examples of such targets in other fields can be helpful. Consider, in sports, the gymnastics and figure skating competitions in which athletes are not pitted against one another, but judged on performance criteria known to all. Or consider recitals in music and portfolio exhibitions in the arts. Performance assessments are methods of testing that require students to demonstrate their abilities and knowledge by creating products that display them. The list below (from Office of Technology Assessment 1992, 17) is a continuum of performance formats ranging from constructed-response questions to the more comprehensive "exhibitions" and "portfolios." A constructed-response item can be an efficient and valid means to assess students' knowledge of an important concept relevant to issue-centered study For example, a simple classifying item might have students produce in writing a description of a *perennial public issue* studied in the course, or of *democratic values, citizenship, definitional dispute, analogy, ethical issue,* or *point-of-view.* Whatever the concept, students should not be asked only to produce an example of it, for this gives the teacher too little information. The student also should be asked to produce a statement that explains why it is an example—what attributes does it have that all examples of the concept must have? A classifying task, then, asks both for an example and a supporting argument.

At the other end of the continuum, students might be asked to mount a comprehensive exhibition of the issue-oriented work they have produced over a one-semester senior problems course: a narrated slide show, for example, displaying several public policy forums in which the student has participated, both as moderator and discussant. The third format on this continuum, oral discourse, is featured in the next chapter.

Before proceeding, however, let us look at the full continuum of performance formats. The reader may wish to brainstorm additional examples of each, taking care that each example involves knowledge and/or abilities that are related to issue-oriented social studies as defined above.

- Constructed-response questions require students to produce an answer to a question rather than to select from an array of possible answers (as multiple-choice items do). In constructed-response items, questions may have just one correct answer or may be more open ended, allowing a range of responses. The form can also vary—filling in a blank, writing short answers, drawing an illustration.
- Essays have long been used to assess a student's understanding of a subject by having the student write a description, analysis, explanation, or summary of one or more paragraphs. Essays are used to demonstrate how well a student can use facts in context and structure a coherent discussion.
- Oral discourse was the earliest form of performance assessment. Before paper and pencil, chalk, and slate became affordable, school children rehearsed their lessons, recited their sums, and rendered their poems and prose aloud.
- Exhibitions are designed as comprehensive demonstrations of skills or competence. They often require students to produce a demonstration or live performance in class or before other audiences. Teachers or trained judges score performances against standards of excellence known to all participants ahead of time. Exhibitions require a broad range of competencies, are often interdisciplinary in focus, and require student initiative and creativity.
- Portfolios are usually files or folders that contain collections of a student's work. They furnish a broad portrait of individual performance, assembled over time. As students assemble their portfolios, they must evaluate their own work. (Office of Technology Assessment 1992, 17)

Performance Assessment at the Program Level. At the program level, assessment concentrates on cumulative, long-term targets. Planning committees need to imagine performances that students might exhibit as the combined achievement of an articulated course of study. The case in Table 1 had planners decide the performances that students would collect at the end of the twelfth grade. Issue-oriented performance targets for this graduation portfolio might include those given as samples in Table 2.

The three targets in Table 2 involve the production of coherent and informed civic discourse, both oral and written, which arguably is the most fundamental demand made on citizens in societies organized under democratic ideals (Parker 1996). This list of targets can serve as a one-page curriculum guide for a K through 12 issue-oriented social studies program, and it could double as a specification of performance assessments toward which the resources of the school district should be directed from kindergarten through the twelfth grade. This would be more valuable, in my judgment, than the elaborate K through 12 curriculum matrices that have become conventional in school district curriculum offices, with their long lists of objectives that so often are ignored.

Each target represents a set of integrated, essential learnings. In an experimental high school in Seattle for "at-risk" students, my colleagues and I attempt to accomplish this using a two-column chart. Targets are listed in column one and related learnings are specified in column two. An example is presented in Table 3. Note that the example is aimed at the third graduation portfolio target in Table 2—*discussion competence.* In column one, note that the target is written as a set of general instructions to the student; also note that in the second column both categories of learning—knowledge and abilities—are specified. Column two was added when a parent committee read the target, then wanted to know what the individual learnings were that composed it. This was a helpful prompt, and it caused us to deduce specific learnings from the target, thus specifying them for instruction. The parents

Table 2: Sample Tasks for Graduation Portfolio

1. Issues Identification

Working with three or four other students, you are to develop a list of public controversies (not private) drawn from current news media, then group and label them. Next, identify the two that best exemplify public conflicts that stem from differing interpretations of liberty, equality, justice, and public order/safety. These decisions should be made using group consensus-reaching procedures. Following this work, you will write, relying on "writing-process" procedures, an evaluation of the two issues selected and a narrative description of your group's consensus-reaching process.

2. Policy Analysis

You will be given a list of enduring public issues and asked to develop a conceptual model of one of your choosing. You will need to incorporate in your model at least these things:

a. Diversity. Include an accounting of alternative positions on the matter referenced to the research that you and others have conducted (e.g., library research, surveys and interviews, popular magazines, art). Give evidence that you have included not only centrist positions but marginal views as well, and not only popular but also scholarly opinion.

b. Analogies. Draw two or more historical analogies. Because these are enduring issues, earlier and culturally diverse cases that are somewhat analogous generally can be found. Find two or more, and evaluate the extent to which they parallel the present case.

c. Consequences. Predict the consequences of three or more of the alternatives your research uncovered. Carefully support the predictions you make.

3. Discussion Competence

Collect audio and/or video recordings of your participation in discussions of public controversies. These will be small-group discussions in which public conflicts and policy alternatives are being interpreted and analyzed, and their consequences predicted. Along with the tapes, submit an annotated transcript of a selection of discussion excerpts displaying these and other competencies you identify: stating and identifying issues, using historical and social science knowledge, summarizing points of agreement and disagreement, inviting contributions from others, using strategies to move the discussion forward.

---

were worried, rightly so, that without this specification their children would be expected to perform well on the targeted task without having been adequately instructed on the component knowledge and skills. We have found this two-column format enormously helpful for communicating the school's curriculum and assessment plan in brief and straightforward fashion—both to one another and to our constituencies—the school's curriculum and assessment plan.

Performance Assessment at the Course Level. With a limited number of program-level learning outcomes and performance tasks in place, course planning can proceed in a sharply focused way with the identification of course-level targets. At the course level, it is helpful to expand the chart's design from two to three columns. Performance targets again are listed in column one, related learnings in column two, and the third column lists key curriculum materials. These three columns present, in a concise manner, the course syllabus. This three-column chart may extend over a few pages, because a course typically has a handful of major targets, not just one.

Presented in Tables 4 and 5 are excerpts for two courses. The first of the two is correlated to the third graduation portfolio target sketched in Table 2—*discussion competence*. It is one of several targets for an eleventh-grade American studies course. Note that it requires students to do extensive work with civic discourse. This work must be done across multiple public issues, thereby helping students to construct flexible, case-based understandings. These cases are drawn from more than one historical era. Furthermore, students are expected to write an analysis of their discussion participation. Clearly, this is an ambitious target in most communities, one that would require sustained teaching and learning across a significant period of time. The target takes issues learning deeply into disciplinary knowledge and into the primary practice of democracy—discussion. It is an integrated task, too, requiring students to pull numerous learnings together.

The second of the two excerpts (Table 5) is correlated to the second graduation portfolio target in Table 2—policy analysis—and was designed for a twelfth-grade senior problems course. Note that it is focused on conceptual

Table 3: Program-Level Curriculum Guide

PROGRAM TARGETS	LEARNINGS
3. Discussion competence Collect audio and/or video recordings of your participation in discussions of public controversies. These will be small-group discussions in which public conflicts and policy alternatives are being interpreted and analyzed, and their consequences predicted. Along with the tapes, submit an annotated transcript of a selection of discussion excerpts displaying your competencies as both moderator and discussant, including these and others you identify: clarifying and analyzing issues and alternative courses of action, distinguishing among kinds of issues, listening as well as talking, seeking an array of views, and using strategies to move the discussion forward.	**Essential Knowledge** • Public controversy/conflict • Enduring problem areas versus current events • Ethical, definitional, and empirical issues • Liberty, diversity, order, democracy **Essential Abilities (HOT)** • Reading and writing • Clarifying • Interpreting • Analyzing • Predicting • Moderating • Reasoning dialogically • Listening to and expressing views • Seeking alternative views • Weighing alternatives • Using strategies to move the discussion forward

modeling, which helps students build complex understandings of public issues with an eye toward recommending policy. Study booklets from the National Issues Forum have proven to be a helpful resource; hence they are listed in column three. Each booklet presents three or four viewpoints on a particular issue, such as criminal violence. When students study an issue in this way, working through multiple lenses, reading extensively, and forging shared understandings through discussion, they can build a model of the problem rather than only reacting to it with the first opinion that comes to mind. The performance target in column one assumes that students have studied five policy questions in this way. The target requires students now to *produce* such a study—a briefing booklet—that others, perhaps younger students or even the city council, can use to develop policy.

Conclusion

The main idea of this chapter is that issue-oriented curriculum development and assessment are, at the higher levels of quality, the same thing. The boundaries between assessing student learning and deciding which content is worth teaching and learning are blurred as learning is conceptualized in performance terms. Accordingly, examples of performance assessment are provided, both for programs and individual courses, and these double as curriculum objectives tailored to the goals of issue-oriented education.

Still, we are left with the question: How can a commendable performance be distinguished from one that is mediocre or incompetent? A helpful tool is a scoring rubric. Scoring involves judging levels of quality displayed in targeted performances; a scoring rubric is the set of guidelines scorers use to decide the level of quality in a performance they have observed.

Developing a reliable rubric for a target is challenging work that requires a nuanced understanding of the target (McCollum 1994). Because it can be difficult, developing a rubric can function as a roadblock if it is attempted too soon. That is, it can prevent work on the more fundamental problem of developing ambitious targets for teaching and learning. I have seen this happen so often that I have come to expect it, and I can assure readers that the consequences do not vary: As planning groups become mired in scoring, they back away from the identification of ambitious targets. Because developing good targets for teaching and learning is the chief object of curriculum and assessment work, it is altogether unwise for teachers and curriculum supervisors to get sidetracked by scoring problems. Doing so lets the tail wag the dog.

After valued performance targets have been selected, it becomes necessary to identify gradations (standards/criteria) of performance quality.

Table 4: 11th Grade: American Studies *(excerpt)*

COURSE TARGETS	LEARNINGS	MATERIALS
3. Make audio recordings of your participation in discussions of three public controversies drawn from three major eras of U.S. history. Select the tape with the highest-quality discussion and tape record or write an analysis of (a) the kinds of issues involved, (b) any roadblocks present in the discussion, (c) strategies used to move the discussion forward.	**Essential Knowledge** • Public controversy • Knowledge of the issue selected and types of issues (ethical, definitional, empirical) • Eras of U.S. history • Roadblocks in discussions of public issues **Essential Abilities (HOT)** • Reading and writing • Oral expression • Strategies for moving discussions forward	**A. Discussion** *Taking a Stand* (Oliver & Newmann) **B. Issues** *The Federalist Papers* **and** *Public Issues Series* (Social Science Education Consortium) **or** *Reasoning with Democratic Values* (Lockwood & Harris) **or** *Evaluating Viewpoints* (O'Reilly) **C. Textbook** *The U.S. and Its People* (King, McRae, Zola)

Table 5: 12th Grade: Senior Problems *(excerpt)*

COURSE TARGETS	LEARNINGS	MATERIALS
2. Develop a written and illustrated conceptual model of one of the public issues you examined in this course or a sixth you choose to investigate. Incorporate diverse viewpoints and historical analogies and weigh the consequences of alternative policies.	**Essential Knowledge** • Public controversy • Viewpoints and history on the issue selected **Essential Abilities (HOT)** • Reading and writing • Conceptual modeling • Finding and representing diverse perspectives • Drawing and evaluating historical analogies • Predicting and weighing consequences	**A. Issues** *National Issues Forum* booklets (Kendall-Hunt); news media, libraries; government offices **B. Citizen Action** *Civics for Democracy* (Isaac) **C. Political Theory** *Should We Consent To Be Governed?* (Nathanson)

Doing so has two effects. First, teachers and parents can find out what students know and are able to do in relation to these quality levels. Second, instruction can be fine-tuned; teachers can coach students toward performances at higher levels of quality. The explanation for both effects is this: The gradations needed for scoring are needed also for clarifying the target and, therefore, for fine-tuning instruction.

David Harris's chapter, which follows, demonstrates the point nicely. He presents a field-tested scoring rubric for assessing student performance on a key outcome of issue-oriented education: competent, small-group discussions of public issues. The assessment criteria he provides define the target in a way that will help teachers teach and students learn.[7]

References

Baron, Joan Boykoff. "Performance Assessment: Blurring the Edges Among Assessment, Curriculum, and Instruction." In *Assessment in the Service of Instruction,* edited by Audrey B. Champagne et al. Washington, D.C.: American Association for the Advancement of Science, 1990.

Committee on Social Studies, Commission on the Reorganization of Secondary Education of the National Education Association. *The Social Studies in Secondary Education,* Bureau of Education Bulletin no. 28. Washington, D.C.: U.S. Government Printing Office, 1916.

Engle, Shirley. "Decision Making: The Heart of Social Studies Instruction." *Social Education* 24, no. 7 (1960): 301-306.

Griffin, Alan F. *Alan F. Griffin on Reflective Teaching: A Philosophical Approach to the Subject Matter Preparation of Teachers of History.* Washington, D.C.:

National Council for the Social Studies, 1992 (originally published in 1942).

Harris, Pickens E. "The American School: A Delinquent Institution." In *Democracy and the Curriculum*, edited by Harold Rugg. New York: Appleton-Century, 1939.

Hunt, Maurice P., and Lawrence E. Metcalf. *Teaching High School Social Studies: Problems in Reflective Thinking and Social Understanding.* 2nd Edition. New York: Harper and Row, 1968.

Lockwood, Alan L., and David E. Harris. *Reasoning with Democratic Values: Ethical Problems in United States History.* Volumes 1 and 2 and instructor's manual. New York: Teachers College Press, 1985.

McCollum, Steven L. *Performance Assessment in the Social Studies Classroom.* Joplin, MO: Chalk Dust Press, 1994.

Newmann, Fred M. *Education for Citizen Action.* Berkeley: McCutchan, 1975.

—. "Higher Order Thinking in Teaching Social Studies: A Rationale for the Assessment of Classroom Thoughtfulness." *Journal of Curriculum Studies* 22, no. 1 (1990a): 41-56.

—. "A Test of Higher-Order Thinking in Social Studies: Persuasive Writing on Constitutional Issues Using the NAEP Approach." *Social Education* 54, no. 6 (1990b): 369-373.

Newmann, Fred M., and Doug A. Archbald. "The Nature of Authentic Academic Achievement." In *Toward a New Science of Educational Testing and Assessment,* edited by Harold Berlak et al. Albany: State University of New York Press, 1992.

Office of Technology and Assessment, Congress of the United States. *Testing in American Schools: Asking the Right Questions.* Washington, D.C.: Office of Technology and Assessment, 1992.

Oliver, Donald W. "The Selection of Content in the Social Sciences." *Harvard Educational Review* 27, no. 4 (1957): 271-300.

Oliver, Donald W., and Fred M. Newmann. *Taking a Stand: A Guide to Clear Discussion of Public Issues.* Middletown, Conn.: Xerox Corporation/American Education Publications, 1967.

Oliver, Donald W., and James P. Shaver. *Teaching Public Issues in the High School.* Logan: Utah State University Press, 1974 (originally published in 1966).

Parker, Walter C. *Renewing the Social Studies Curriculum.* Alexandria, Va: Association for Supervision and Curriculum Development, 1991.

—. "Curriculum for Democracy." In *Democracy, Education, and the School,* edited by Roger Soder. Chicago: San Francisco: Jossey-Bass, 1996.

Porter, Andrew C. "School Delivery Standards." *Educational Researcher* 22, no. 5 (1993): 24-29.

Resnick, Lauren B., and Daniel P. Resnick. "Assessing the Thinking Curriculum: New Tools for Educational Reform." In *Changing Assessments: Alternative Views of Aptitude, Achievement, and Instruction,* edited by Bernard R. Gifford and Mary Catherine O'Connor. Boston: Kluwer Academic Publishers, 1991.

Resnick, Lauren B., and Leopold E. Klopfer, eds. *Toward the Thinking Curriculum: Current Cognitive Research.* Alexandria, Va.: Association for Supervision and Curriculum Development, 1989.

Shaver, James P. *Building Rationales for Citizenship Education.* Washington, D.C.: National Council for the Social Studies, 1977.

Simmons, Warren, and Lauren Resnick. "Assessment As the Catalyst of School Reform." *Educational Leadership* 50, no. 5 (1993): 11-15.

Sizer, Theodore R. *Horace's School.* Boston: Houghton Mifflin, 1992.

Task Force on Teaching and Learning, National Council for the Social Studies. *A Vision of Powerful Teaching and Learning in the Social Studies: Building Social Understanding and Civic Efficacy.* Washington, D.C.: National Council for the Social Studies, 1992.

Zessoules, Rieneke, and Howard Gardner. "Authentic Assessment: Beyond the Buzzword and into the Classroom." In *Expanding Student Assessment,* edited by Vito Perrone. Alexandria, Va: Association for Supervision and Curriculum Development, 1991.

---

[1] My thanks to Sheila Valencia, Catherine Taylor, and Ron Evans for comments on earlier drafts of this chapter.

[2] T. W. Roby discusses the rush to pet solutions: "Habits Impeding Deliberation," *Journal of Curriculum Studies* 17, no. 1 (1985): 17-35.

[3] I am grateful to Joan Baron (1990) for conversations on this idea.

[4] The vocabulary of assessment lacks agreement. Tentatively, synonyms for "perform" are construct, create, and demonstrate.

[5] I.e., a project requiring the novel application of knowledge and ability.

[6] I.e., outcome; curriculum standard; objective.

[7] Newmann (1990b) developed another exemplary rubric, this one for assessing persuasive writing/reasoning on issues involving constitutional rights. Harris's and Newmann's rubrics together make a good study of rubric design for issue-oriented outcomes.

31

ASSESSING DISCUSSION OF PUBLIC ISSUES: A SCORING GUIDE

by David Harris

The importance of civic discourse in social studies education has been emphasized in recent scholarship. There is a call to rededicate ourselves to "public talk" as an essential element of the curriculum and to assess the quality of oral discourse produced by students (Barber 1989; Newman, 1992; Parker 1989).

The rationale for oral discourse about public issues is manifold. First, it facilitates the learning of social studies content. The effort to produce coherent language in response to a question of public policy puts knowledge in a meaningful context, making it more likely to be understood and remembered. Second, dialogue among students reinforces the development of social perspectives considered fundamental to democratic citizenship, especially tolerance or taking the role of another. This kind of reciprocal thinking, the persistent effort to anticipate the perspective of another, fosters more than communication; it is the essence of moral sensitivity. Third, intelligent conversation promotes reflection crucial to the preservation of democratic values such as consent of the governed, individual liberty, equality under law and, more recently, national economic prosperity within the world economy. Fourth, when thoughtfully engaged in conversations about public issues, students are building not only substantive knowledge but also higher order thinking abilities. They use complex language to express their ideas. They must speak not in single words or short phrases but in sentences and paragraphs; they share ideas that are not scripted or controlled, as in teacher-led recitation; they must explain themselves, ask questions, and respond directly to comments of previous speakers.

Significant progress has been made recently in assessing students' persuasive writing on civic issues (Newmann 1990), but there has been nothing comparable for oral discourse. If we are destined in schools to get what we assess and not get what we do not assess (Resnick and Resnick 1991), then we are unlikely, for the time being, to produce students who can participate constructively in group discussions of public issues.

This chapter presents a guide for evaluating students' performance in small group discussions of public issues. It integrates the knowledge, skill, and value goals of social studies, is grounded in the theory and practice of teaching public issues (Oliver and Shaver 1966/74), and is designed for convenient use by classroom teachers. Data collected with this tool could be used for improving instruction, for assessing individual student achievement, or as part of larger scale social studies program evaluations. Field testing of the guide has been conducted with social studies students and teachers in middle schools and high schools.

Performance Criteria for a Public Issues Discussion

This scoring guide makes an attempt to identify a set of valid criteria for evaluating the performance of individual students during small group discussion of a public issue. These criteria are derived from the tradition of teaching public issues dating back nearly three decades to the Harvard Social Studies Project, which emphasized classroom discussion of controversial public issues (Oliver and Newmann 1967). The goal of discussion in this tradition is to engage students in substantive conversation that enables each of them to make progress toward constructing a thoughtful position on a question of public policy. Although the emphasis of this guide is on scoring the performance of individu-

BOX A
Assessing Discussion of Public Issues: Performance Criteria

SUBSTANTIVE	PROCEDURAL
• Stating and Identifying Issues • Using Foundational Knowledge • Elaborating Statements with Explanations, Reasons, or Evidence • Stipulating Claims or Definitions • Recognizing Values or Value Conflict • Arguing by Analogy	**Positive (+)** • Inviting Contributions from Others • Acknowledging the Statements of Others • Challenging the Accuracy, Logic, Relevance, or Clarity of Statements • Summarizing Points of Agreement and Disagreement **Negative (–)** • Irrelevant Distracting Statements • Obstructive Interruption • Monopolizing • Personal Attack

als, those scores could be used collectively to assess the performance of groups as well.

An underlying assumption of the scoring scheme presented here is that students have extensive opportunity to practice discussion before being assessed. Practice would consist of both whole-class, teacher-led discussions and discussions among small groups of students. In the context of these discussions, students would learn the assessment criteria and work to improve both their individual and group performance. Teachers would model the kinds of statements implied by the criteria and highlight them when demonstrated by students. Eventually, small-group discussion of a public issue as a learning activity would become indistinguishable from the assessment activity.

The discussion of a public issue has both substantive and procedural dimensions. We want students to know about the issue and to know how to discuss it productively with classmates. A good performance blends the two. The criteria in the scoring guide are therefore divided into two categories. The substantive criteria pertain to students' understanding of the issue, and the procedural criteria pertain to their ability to engage one another in conversation about it. These criteria are listed as Performance Criteria (Box A).

What follows is a brief description of each criterion with an example to illustrate it. The examples are drawn from a hypothetical discussion by high school students of a public policy issue on the national agenda as of this writing:

Should homosexuals be allowed to serve in the armed forces of the United States?

Substantive Criteria

Stating and Identifying Issues. To satisfy this criterion, a student must either state an issue not yet raised in the discussion or identify an issue that has been implied. An issue is a matter of dispute or uncertainty posed as an unresolved question. Public issue discussions revolve around a central policy issue which often entails three subordinate types of issues: ethical, definitional, and factual. If the policy issue has been stated prior to the discussion, repeating it would not satisfy this criterion.

A policy issue is the overarching focus that guides the entire discussion. The main purpose of the discussion is to work collaboratively toward resolution of the policy issue. It is a question about a matter of governance that requires collective decision making in an arena of citizenship and subsequent action to advance the decision. It can be local, regional, national, or international in scope. In our example the policy issue is: Should homosexuals be allowed to serve in the armed services of the United States?

Discussions of public policy issues usually involve subordinate ethical, factual, and definitional issues. Productive dialogue cannot occur if students jump mindlessly from one aspect of an issue to another. In the process of resolving the broader policy issue, it is necessary, deliberately and systematically, to consider other issues embedded within it. An ethical issue poses a question of right or wrong. It asks for a value judgment of what ought to be. A definitional issue poses a question about the meaning of a term. It serves to clarify ambiguity. A factual issue poses a question regarding what is or was. It asks for a claim that can be verified with evidence. The diagram in Box B presents a taxonomy for discussion of public issues:

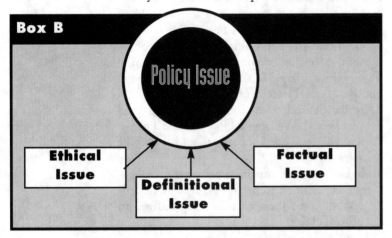

Box B

Policy Issue

Ethical Issue

Definitional Issue

Factual Issue

The three dialogue excerpts below provide examples, respectively, of **1.** an **ethical, 2.** a **definitional,** and **3.** a **factual** issue being stated:

1 Aretha: People really seem to disagree strongly about whether gays should serve in the military.

Bob: There have always been gay soldiers and sailors, but most of them have kept quiet about it.

Cleo: The question is not whether homosexuals have secretly served in the past. That's not an issue. Everyone agrees they have. The question is whether it is fair to exclude someone from military service based on sexual orientation. Do gays have a right to serve their country? **(ethical)**

2 Aretha: Homosexuals might undermine the morale of the fighting force. Their deviant behavior could be upsetting to the majority of those serving.

Bob: What do you mean by deviant behavior? **(definitional issue)** Does deviant mean conduct merely different from what most people do, or does it have to be harmful to others?

3 Aretha: Being near people of the same sex with an amorous attraction to you makes many heterosexuals uncomfortable. If homosexuals

want to join the armed services, they should change their behavior first.

Cleo: Can they? I don't know if it's possible. Is sexual orientation learned or biological? **(factual issue)** I think we have to resolve that question before we can determine what kind of behavior to expect of people

Using Foundational Knowledge. To satisfy this criterion, a student must demonstrate understanding of significant ideas relevant to the issue under discussion. The ideas would be key facts or concepts from pertinent disciplines. The understanding expressed would be deep rather than shallow and free of obvious inaccuracies or misconceptions. Both of the following statements below present an example of using foundational knowledge:

1 Aretha: If the policy toward homosexuals in the military is changed, there will be problems with the Uniform Code of Military Justice, which is a separate set of laws that applies only to those in the armed forces. Several parts of the code would have to be adjusted if the ban is lifted, like who you can live with, or what you can do while on duty or wearing a uniform, or who you can claim as dependents.

2 Bob: Not all groups have the same protection under current federal law. Congress intended the civil rights acts to protect people from discrimination based on race, religion, gender, or national origin, but not on sexual orientation

Elaborating Statements with Explanations, Reasons, or Evidence. To satisfy this criterion, a student would have to make a claim and provide a basis of support for it. The claim might be a position on an issue, or a relevant ethical judgment, or a statement of fact. A position on an issue would be supported with an explanation; an ethical judgment would be supported by reasons; and a factual claim would be verified with evidence. The three dialogue excerpts below provide examples of supporting a claim with **1.** an explanation, **2.** reasons, and **3.** evidence:

1 Aretha: We have been reading and talking about this issue for two days. Is anybody ready to take a stand?

Bob: I think the present policy should continue. Gays should be banned. I have been thinking about what was said about equal rights, and about the good records of homosexuals who have served with distinction. But, for several reasons, I don't think the ban should be lifted. A majority of those currently serving believe the change would lower morale. Many say they will quit the service if gays are allowed. Some prominent military leaders, including General Schwartzkopf, believe that admitting gays will undermine the primary mission of the armed forces—readiness to fight. And there is the point about invading privacy **(explaining a position on the policy issue)**.

2 Aretha: Will the presence of homosexuals violate the privacy rights of heterosexuals?

Bob: Not if men and women live in separate barracks.

Cleo: Separating people by gender would not ensure privacy. People are packed very tightly in army barracks and on naval ships. In the shower or in the sleeping quarters of a submarine there is little privacy. Men or women, even if separated by gender, would still be exposed to the unwelcome glances of gays or lesbians.

Aretha: I think admitting homosexuals would violate the privacy rights of heterosexuals. There is no grouping possible to protect privacy—men with men, women with women, men with women, even gays with gays. When you join the military, you are entitled to a reasonable expectation of privacy. No one should be placed in circumstances where they are the unwilling object of someone's sexual attention **(supporting an ethical judgment with reasons)**.

3 Aretha: If the ban on gays is lifted, there will be more sexual misconduct in the armed forces.

Bob: Do homosexuals commit sexual assaults more than heterosexuals?

Cleo: Not according to a recent Pentagon study cited last month in the federal district court decision from California that we read. The rate of such offenses is higher for heterosexuals than homosexuals in the armed services. Furthermore, look at what the Tailhook scandal suggests about male sailors sexually harassing females. The evidence we have does not support the claim that gays in the military will cause an increase in sexual misconduct **(supporting a factual claim with evidence)**.

Stipulating Claims or Definitions. To satisfy this criterion, a student must stipulate a resolution to an ethical, definitional or factual issue. Stipulation means offering a tentative answer to be accepted at least temporarily in order to move the discussion forward. Stipulations are usually offered when there is no consensus on an issue and the information necessary for resolution is not readily available. To prevent the discussion from getting bogged down and for the sake of argument, a statement can be stipulated to see where it leads. The three dialogue excerpts below present examples, respectively, of stipulating **1.** an ethical claim, **2.** the definition of a term, and **3.** a factual statement:

1 Aretha: Several times equal rights have been mentioned. We keep asking whether heterosexuals and homosexuals should have the same rights.

Bob: Let's assume, for the time being, that people are entitled to be treated equally regardless of sexual orientation **(stipulating an ethical claim)**.

2 Aretha: The President and others have argued that restrictions from the armed forces should be based on conduct. He says it should be what you do, not who you are.

Bob: What is conduct and what is not? Would telling someone you are gay be conduct? Would reading a gay magazine?

Cleo: This is difficult. I have trouble distinguishing between thought, expression, and conduct.

Aretha: Let's say that conduct means expressed behavior. It can be spoken or other kinds of action, but it can't be merely thoughts or feelings. Also, let's agree for our discussion that conduct refers to behavior while on military duty or while off duty but in uniform **(stipulating a definition)**.

3 Aretha: Some people are worried that the military will be overwhelmed by homosexuals, that they will take over and change the culture of the armed forces.

Bob: That fear exaggerates the number of homosexuals in society.

Cleo: How many are there? I keep hearing that 10% of the population is homosexual.

Bob: That figure is based on the Kinsey studies of nearly half a century ago. More recent studies indicate a much lower percentage. *Time* magazine reports that a better estimate is well under 5%. For purposes of our discussion, let's assume that between 2% and 4% of the population is homosexual (**stipulating a fact**).

Cleo: O.K., if we use that figure, how does it affect our thinking about the policy issue?

Recognizing Values or Value Conflict. To satisfy this criterion, a student must identify a core democratic value that has emerged in the discussion or a clash between two or more such values. Core democratic values are concepts that represent the ethical beliefs underlying a democratic society, for example: religious liberty, free expression, equality, fair procedure, property rights, diversity, limited government, or majority rule. These values serve as criteria when citizens make judgments about matters of public concern. Although generally held in common, they are sometimes a source of conflict. The main dispute over policy issues often arises from differences in meaning that people attach to these values or from differences in the priority attached to them. The two dialogue excerpts that follow illustrate, respectively, **1.** recognition of a democratic value, and **2.** identification of a value conflict:

1 Aretha: Our main purpose for having military forces is to defend the country from enemies. The issue of the ban on gays should be decided according to its effect on this mission. What effect does the ban have on the readiness of the armed forces to fight?

Bob: You seem to be saying that the deciding factor should be national security (**recognizing a value**)

2 Aretha: This issue requires us to choose between values.

Bob: Which values?

Cleo: On the one hand we value equality which means all citizens should have an equal opportunity to serve their country. We also believe in privacy as a basic liberty which means people have a right to control information about themselves. These two values seem to clash over the issue of homosexuals in the military. We have to decide which of these values should have priority in this case (**identifying a value conflict**).

Arguing by Analogy. To satisfy this criterion, a student must draw a parallel between the issue under discussion and a similar case. An analogy should be more than a fleeting hint of similarity. The likeness must be rationally elaborated. Analogies are often made to establish or challenge the consistency of an ethical argument. The dialogue excerpt below illustrates this type of analogical reasoning:

Aretha: Maybe gays should be banned from the military for their own protection. If they serve openly, they might become the victims of violent attacks from those who are prejudiced against them.

Bob: That sounds like a "heckler's veto" to me. It gives violent bigots control over public policy. Those who threaten to harm the innocent should should be excluded, not their victims.

Cleo: That reminds me of President Truman's policy of racial integration of the armed forces. There were many prejudiced whites who did not want blacks to serve with them. Some threatened to do them harm. If it's right to ban gays because some dislike their sexual orientation, then it would have been right to segregate blacks because some hated their race (**analogy**).

Procedural Criteria (Positive)

Inviting Contributions from Others. To satisfy this criterion, a student would have to elicit the thinking of a classmate. The purpose of the invitation would be to draw someone else into the discussion and to broaden participation. The invitation validates the worth of everyone's contribution to the discussion. The following dialogue excerpt illustrates such an invitation to participate:

Aretha: We have been discussing this issue for a long time. I am still trying to make up my mind. I'm not sure yet where I stand. I know that Bob supports keeping the current ban and that Cleo thinks it should be lifted. Both of them have presented their reasons, and they know why they disagree. We haven't heard from you yet, Dawn. Do you agree with Bob or Cleo (**invitation**)?

Acknowledging the Statements of Others. To satisfy this criterion, a student must respond to a statement made by another student in a way that builds a consecutive interchange between them. The reply should be responsive to the statement and indicate that the student understood it and thought about it. The following dialogue excerpt illustrates this type of response:

Aretha: If I were homosexual, I wouldn't want to be part of an organization where I wasn't welcome.

Bob: That is your personal attitude, Aretha, but how do you think your feelings about rejection pertain to the policy decision to be made here (**acknowledgement and response**).

Challenging the Accuracy, Logic, Relevance, or Clarity of Statements. To satisfy this criterion, a student must respond to the statement of another student by respectfully suggesting that it is inaccurate, illogical, irrelevant, or unclear. The nature of the challenge should be stated and an invitation to respond to it should be extended. In the example below, the challenge is directed at the logic of a statement:

Aretha: Some people support the ban out of fear of AIDS. Frankly, I am sympathetic. The rate of AIDS among homosexuals is higher than among heterosexuals.

Bob: You have a good point. If gays are excluded, AIDS is less likely to spread in the armed forces.

Cleo: Yes, but it's possible to protect men and women in the service from AIDS without banning homosexuals. Blood testing would do it. We could exclude those who test HIV positive, whatever their sexual orientation. It doesn't follow that the the ban on gays is necessary to prevent the spread of AIDS in the armed forces (**logical challenge**).

Summarizing Points of Agreement and Disagreement. To satisfy this criterion, a student would have to present at least a partial summary of points discussed and their disposition in the discussion so far. The summary clarifies where the discussion has been and sets the stage for it to move forward. The dialogue excerpt below illustrates this type of summary:

Aretha: This can get very confusing. I'm not sure what I believe any more. There are so many issues and there is so much disagreement.

Bob: For some time now we have been grappling with an ethical issue: Is it fair to treat homosexuals differently than heterosexuals? We agreed that it is an issue involving the value of equality. We also agreed that the value of privacy seems to conflict with the value of equality, and that we might have to choose between them to resolve this issue. We also agreed that everyone has an equal right to serve the country. The consensus broke down, however, when Aretha said that national security should take precedence over equal rights because without it there will be no protection of anyone's rights. We have not yet resolved whether or not gays in the military pose a threat to national security (**summary**).

Procedural Criteria (Negative)

Irrelevant Distracting Statements. This criterion would be met if a student made a statement that obviously did not pertain to the issue and tended to derail the discussion. It could be deliberately or inadvertently distracting. The two examples below illustrate such statements:

Aretha: The real problem with the military is the volunteer army. Do you think there should be a draft?

Bob: Could we talk about something that isn't so boring, like where people are partying after the game?

Obstructive Interruption. This criterion is met when a student cuts off what another student has started to say, preventing the statement from being completed and interfering with the progress of the discussion. Only obstructive interruptions that rudely seize the floor for oneself apply here. Some interruptions, made congenially, might be attempts to get a person to be more relevant or brief and would be constructive. An obstructive interruption is readily apparent when it occurs, so no example is provided here to illustrate.

Monopolizing. This criterion is met when one student repeatedly dominates the discussion with the effect of preventing others from contributing. It would not be the result of a single statement but rather a pattern of overpowering others by not yielding the floor. It becomes evident when one student does a conspicuously disproportionate share of the talking. Quieter students consequently withdraw or show reluctance to speak because they have been intimidated by a more vocal student. No example of monopolizing is provided, because it is best detected through direct observation and is difficult to capture in a transcript.

Personal Attack. This criterion is met when a student offensively criticizes another student. This type of personal assault or insult should be

BOX C
Assessing Discussion of Public Issues: Scoring Rubric

The overarching consideration in scoring is the degree to which a student's contribution to the conversation clarifies the policy issue being considered and helps the group make progress toward resolution. Three elements of performance focus the assessment: whether or not the student has a. presented accurate knowledge related to the policy issue, b. employed skills for stating and pursuing related issues, and c. engaged others in constructive dialogue. A student's contribution to the conversation receives one of five scores:

UNSATISFACTORY (1)

The student has failed to express any relevant foundational knowledge and has neither stated nor elaborated on any issues.

MINIMAL (2)

The student has stated a relevant factual, ethical, or definitional issue as a question or has accurately expressed relevant foundational knowledge pertaining to an issue raised by someone else.

ADEQUATE (3)

The student has accurately expressed relevant foundational knowledge pertaining to an issue raised during the discussion and has pursued an issue by making a statement and elaborating the statement with an explanation, reasons, or evidence.

EFFECTIVE (4)

The student has accurately expressed relevant foundational knowledge pertaining to an issue raised during the discussion, pursued an issue with at least one elaborated statement and, in a civil manner, has built upon a statement made by someone else or thoughtfully challenged its accuracy, clarity, relevance, or logic.

EXEMPLARY (5)

The student has accurately expressed relevant foundational knowledge pertaining to an issue raised during the discussion, pursued an issue with an elaborated statement, and has used stipulation, valuing, or analogy to advance the discussion. In addition, the student has engaged others in the discussion by inviting their comments or acknowledging their contributions. Further, the student has built upon a statement made by someone else or thoughtfully challenged its accuracy, clarity, relevance, or logic.

distinguished from a legitimate challenge to someone's argument. The personal attack is abusive and is likely to hurt the feelings of the person targeted. Two examples follow:

1 Aretha: Bob, you said you were worried about government promoting a homosexual lifestyle, that it threatens the stability of family life. That is a stupid idea! There is no such thing as a homosexual lifestyle. They have as many different lifestyles as heterosexuals. I'm sick of your ignorant stereotypes!

2 Bob: Dawn, you hardly say anything, and when you do it doesn't make much sense.

Assessing Students' Performance

The performance of a student can be evaluated while directly observing a small group discussion or afterward if the discussion is recorded. When direct observation is used, a trained scorer silently observes the discussion and records impressions at the close of the discussion. When the discussion is videotaped, a trained scorer records impressions after viewing the videotape. During the videotaping, the teacher need not be present and the discussion need not take place in the regular classroom. Because students can be trained to record videotapes of their discussions, and the teacher can work with the rest of the class while one or more small group discussions are being recorded, the videotape method might prove more practical (and accurate) than direct observation.

Whether the discussion is directly observed or videotaped, the number of students participating should be small enough to provide sufficient opportunity for all members of the group to express their thinking. A group of 5-7 students is recommended, with the discussion lasting approximately 20 minutes. The amount of time might be shorter for elementary students or longer for high school students. Before starting the discussion, students would be presented with the policy issue in the context of a case study. For example, the policy issue of gays in the military could be raised by studying the case of Keith Meinhold, a homosexual naval officer who filed suit in federal court challenging his dismissal from the Navy. The case, which serves as a prompt, could be presented through print, orally, on video, or in some combination of the three media. Students would be given ample time to assimilate the facts of the case and organize their thoughts about the issue it poses before discussion starts. The case might be presented a short time before the scored discussion or, if more

Enter a student's name and then make a check mark (✔) to indicate the student's score.

Student _____

UNSATISFACTORY (1)	MINIMAL (2)	ADEQUATE (3)	EFFECTIVE (4)	EXEMPLARY (5)

Student _____

UNSATISFACTORY (1)	MINIMAL (2)	ADEQUATE (3)	EFFECTIVE (4)	EXEMPLARY (5)

preparation time is appropriate, students might be given one or more days to prepare.

Whether through direct observation or analysis of a videotape, the Scoring Rubric (Box C) is used to determine a rating for the performance of each student as a discussion participant. On the Scoring Sheet (Box D), a rater enters a score for each student using the five-point scale presented in the rubric: **1 = Unsatisfactory, 2 = Minimal, 3 = Adequate, 4 = Effective, and 5 = Exemplary.** The scoring rubric presented is intended for high school students. The standards of performance could be appropriately lowered for younger students while maintaining both the performance criteria and the five-point rating scale.

Training would be required before a rater could use the Scoring Rubric (Box C) with confidence. The training would begin with an introduction to the Performance Criteria (Box A) and their definitions as presented in the preceding section of this scoring guide. After raters are clear about the meaning of each criterion, they are introduced to the Scoring Rubric (Box C).

Once acquainted with the Performance Criteria (Box A) and Scoring Rubric (Box C), raters being trained are ready to view an actual videotape of a student discussion. Two viewings will be necessary at first; one to get oriented to the discussion topic and the students, and a second to attend carefully to the performance of each student. Following the second viewing, raters record a score for each student on the Scoring Sheet (Box D). When determining their ratings, raters should appeal to the descriptors for performances characterized as Unsatisfactory, Minimal, Adequate, Effective, or Exemplary as presented in the Scoring Rubric (Box C). When raters disagree about a rating, they should refer to these descriptors again in an effort to resolve the disagreement.

Reliability. Additional videotapes should be used as needed for raters to reach agreement in their ratings. To help work toward agreement, one or more videotapes, previously rated by experts, could be used to present prototypical performances for the four ratings. As an additional training aid, the generic descriptions for each rating presented in the Scoring Rubric (Box C) could be elaborated to include specific examples of things students might say when discussing a particular policy issue.

Agreement among raters is critical for establishing reliability. Are the ratings consistent among scorers? Is the rating given by one teacher the same as that given by another? The answers to these questions must be "yes" if we are to have confidence that the ratings are reliable. Teachers must be able to report to students, parents, and the public that these ratings are not arbitrary claims based merely on subjective whims. Scores of various teachers should be periodically compared and the degree of agreement should be examined.

There are various ways to establish reliability. One recommended here is to determine the percentage of agreement among raters by simply calculating the percentage of students who receive the same score from various scorers. There would be a minimum of two raters, and an expectation that they would agree at least three-fourths of the time. Beyond this reliability standard of 75% agreement, we might add the requirement that when raters do disagree, most of the time (perhaps 75%), the disagreement is no more than one point on the four-point rating scale. Once these or other standards of reliability have been met, the training of the raters is complete.

Having been trained, raters are ready to evaluate student performance. Individual teachers who have been trained could use the Scoring Sheet (Box D) to assess the performance of their own students. Once a teacher's ratings are established as reliable, it becomes unnecessary to have a second rater for discussions scored by that teacher.

For larger scale program assessments, where small groups are sampled from the classes of several different teachers, possibly from different schools, three raters would be desirable to enhance reliability. Each rater scores each student independently. If all three ratings were the same, the common rating would be entered (for example, ratings of 2, 2, and 2 would be scored as 2). If two ratings were the same and the third rating discrepant by only one point, the discrepant rating would be eliminated (for example, ratings of 1, 1, and 2 would be scored as 1). If there were ratings of three consecutive points, the middle rating would be entered (for example, ratings of 2, 3, and 4 would be scored as 3). The only remaining possibility would be three different ratings separated by more than two points. In that case, the midpoint between the highest and lowest rating would be entered.

Students, teachers, evaluators, and researchers are encouraged to use the authentic assessment tools presented in this guide to promote robust and civil discussion of public issues by young people.

References

Barber, Benjamin R. "Public Talk and Civic Action: Education for Participation in a Strong Democracy. " *Social Education* 53 (October 1989): 355-370.

Newmann, Fred M. " A Test of Higher Order Thinking in Social Studies: Persuasive Writing on Constitutional Issues Using the NAEP Approach." *Social Education* 54 (October 1990): 369-373.

____. "The Assessment of Discourse in Social Studies." In *Toward a New Science of Educational Testing and Assessment*, edited by Harold Berlak et al. Albany, N.Y.: SUNY press, 1992.

Oliver, Donald W., and Fred M. Newmann. *Taking A Stand: A Guide to Clear Discussion of Public Issues.* Middletown, Conn.: Xerox Corporation/American Education Publications, 1967.

Oliver, Donald W., and James P. Shaver. *Teaching Public Issues in the High School.* Logan, Utah: Utah State University Press, 1974 (originally published in 1966).

Parker, Walter C. "Participatory Citizenship: Civics in the Strong Sense." *Social Education* 53 (October 1989): 353-354.

Resnick, Lauren B. and Daniel P. Resnick. "Assessing the Thinking Curriculum: New Tools for Educational Reform." In *Changing Assessments: Alternative Views of Aptitude, Achievement, and Instruction,* edited by Bernard R. Gifford and Mary C. O'Connor. Boston: Kluwer Academic Publishers, 1991.

Part Nine: Teacher Education and Supervision

Introduction by Nancy Fichtman Dana

art Nine of the *Handbook on Teaching Social Issues* focuses on teacher education and supervision. The two chapters in this section explore the initial preparation of issues-centered teachers as well as the supervision of practicing issues-centered teachers.

Chapter 32 explores the question, "How can teacher educators best prepare issues-centered teachers?" by providing an overview of current teacher education practices at institutions of higher education. Three areas are discussed: general education coursework, professional education coursework, and field-based experiences. Through analysis of prospective teacher experiences in these three areas, three recommendations are made for teacher educators: **1.** that they join with arts and science faculty to move large lecture survey courses in the social sciences toward courses that focus on major social problems pursued in depth, **2.** that they augment the pedagogical practices of current social studies methods courses with the discussion of literature and case studies, and **3.** that they make a commitment to locate and develop issues-centered field experiences for prospective teachers.

In contrast to the focus on initial teacher education in Chapter 32, Chapter 33 turns to the development of practicing teachers, exploring the question, "How can supervisors best serve practicing teachers who use issues-centered instruction?" Jerich argues for issues-centered teachers to take charge of their professional growth by conducting self-analysis of their teaching with the aid of the supervisor. This can be accomplished when clinical supervision (characterized by collegiality and equal control of agenda between teacher and supervisor) replaces bureaucratic supervision. Jerich describes the clinical supervision process in depth and offers both teachers and teacher educators a new perspective on professional development.

The reader can explore both key components of teacher education and supervision in this section: initial teacher preparation and continuing teacher education. While the issues surrounding prospective teacher education and practicing teacher education are sufficiently numerous for each to merit its own chapter, the separation is an artificial dichotomy. In addition to examining prospective teacher education and practicing teacher education, it is important to consider the benefits of prospective and practicing teacher collaboration. Hence, after reading the two chapters in this section of the *Handbook,* I invite the reader to ponder the question: "How can we bring together prospective teachers, practicing teachers, and teacher educators to discuss, provide, and continually improve issues-centered instruction for all children?"

This question may be answered through the formation of partnerships. Chapter 32 suggests that partnerships be formed between college of education faculty and arts and science faculty to focus on major social problems. Chapter 33 suggests that the supervisor and practicing teacher become partners in the supervision process. Perhaps what is most needed, however, is the development of a strong, overarching school-university collaborative partnership.

School-university partnerships involve practicing teachers, university faculty, and undergraduate students teaching and researching together to co-develop and examine curricular changes in public schools and teacher education programs. Establishing a school-university collaboration that centers on providing issues-centered instruction at a particular school site may help social studies teacher educators and those involved in the education of social studies teachers implement the recommendations made in this section of the *Handbook.*

AN ISSUES-CENTERED TEACHER EDUCATION

by Nancy Fichtman Dana

Issues-centered education incorporates a teaching approach that emphasizes reflective and critical thinking during the study of issues. The approach does not intend to frame definitive "right answers" but underscores the need for students to become more thoughtful. An issues-centered approach engages students in the critical examination of social practices as they study the social implications of persistent issues. This chapter reports data from a survey of social studies teacher educators concerning how they prepare teachers in the issues-centered approach, and identifies some problems and possibilities inherent in such preparation. It also builds a case for an issues-centered teacher education that underscores the need for teachers to become more reflective about their beliefs regarding social studies teaching and learning. Similar to the goals of issues-centered instruction, an issues-centered teacher education creates opportunities for preservice teachers to engage in critical examination of social practices alongside educational practices and their social implications.

Issues-Centered Teacher Education Programs

To gain insight into the present scope of issues-centered teacher education, I conducted an informal written survey of members of the Issues-Centered Special Interest Group (SIG) of the National Council for the Social Studies. A questionnaire asked each of the 55 SIG members to identify issues-centered courses for elementary, middle, and high school preservice teachers in the following areas: **1.** general education coursework; **2.** social studies course preparation; **3.** specialized methods coursework; **4.** other education coursework; and **5.** field-based experiences. Respondents were also asked:
- In what ways are preservice elementary, middle, and high school teachers engaged with critical examination of social issues and practices throughout their coursework?
- What issues-centered literature (text/readings) do you use/recommend in your course?

Responses to the survey were limited, with information received from only teacher educators at Florida State University, Penn State University, Rutgers University, San Diego State University, Stanford University, University of New Orleans, University of Washington, and University of Wisconsin-Madison. Additionally, one response was from a high school teacher and another was unidentified.

The table on page 300 summarizes information about issues-centered courses required of preservice teachers at the responding universities. Because Stanford did not cite specific course offerings, it is not included. Its fifth-year teacher education program prepares high school teachers. While its program is not issues-centered, many of Stanford's education courses and seminars treat problems and issues.

The table reveals commonalities among various universities' programs and, thus, insights into the preparation of issues-centered teachers. After researching the literature on issues-centered instruction, the structure of universities, and teacher education, I found three general areas, as they relate to the preparation of issues-centered social studies teachers, worthy of discussion: general education coursework, professional education coursework, and field-based experiences.

General Education Coursework

All but two of the surveyed institutions note

Issues-Centered Teacher Education Programming

	GENERAL EDUCATION COURSEWORK	SOCIAL STUDIES COURSE PREPARATION	SPECIALIZED METHODS COURSEWORK	OTHER EDUCATION COURSEWORK	FIELD-BASED EXPERIENCES
FLORIDA STATE UNIVERSITY, TALLAHASSEE	• Schooling in American Society (E)	• Liberal Studies (E)	• Social Studies in the Elementary School (E)	• The Child in the Elementary & Middle School—Multicultural Issues (E)	• Professional Issues Seminar Course (E)
PENN STATE UNIVERSITY, UNIVERSITY PARK	• 50 Plus Credits Many Focus on Issues	• 53 Credits in Social Studies Preparation Work • 6 Credits in Social Studies Methods	• Two Courses Specifically Tied to Issues		• Three Placements Including 15 Week Student Teaching
RUTGERS UNIVERSITY, NEW BRUNSWICK, NEW JERSEY		• Philosophies of History (M, H)	• Methods and Materials in Social Studies (M, H) • Seminars in Social Studies Teaching (M, H)	• Secondary Education in America (M, H)	• Student Teaching (M, H)
SAN DIEGO STATE UNIVERSITY, CALIFORNIA	• Multicultural Education (E, M, H) • Social Context of Education (M, H)	• Social Science Education Methods (M, H) • U.S. History for Teachers (E, M, H)	• Social Science Education Methods (M, H) • Social Foundations of Education (M, H)	• Multicultural Education (E, M, H) • Social Context of Education (M, H) • Introduction to Multicultural Education (E, M, H)	• Field-Based Discussion Seminars (Sometimes)
UNIVERSITY OF NEW ORLEANS, LOUISIANA	• General Introduction to Education (E, M, H) • Critical Issues in Education (E, M, H)	• Global Education (E, M, H)			
UNIVERSITY OF WASHINGTON, SEATTLE					
UNIVERSITY OF WISCONSIN—MADISON			• Social Studies Methods Course (M, H)		• One Student Placed Each Semester in a Public Issues High School Classroom (H)
ANONYMOUS UNIVERSITY	• 20 Credits in Social Science (E, M) • Major in Social Science (H)	• Methods Courses	• Methods Courses	• Two Courses on Issues Related to Multicultural Education • Critical Issues in Education	• Unit Development & Teaching (Sometimes)

some type of issues-centered experience catego-rized as general education coursework. The liter-ature discloses that a majority of general educa-tion courses are introductory or survey courses, are quite large in number, and are delivered in a lecture hall. Common (1993, 9) noted:

> Large classes and lecturing now replace, especially at the undergraduate level, semi-nars and Socratic conversation as the insti-tutions' ideas of best practice. It is difficult to argue that a professor standing at a podi-um with a microphone around her neck and telling a class of six hundred about the caus-es of the American War of Independence is a scholarly act.... Teaching at the university is linked so much to lecturing that building designs incorporate large lecture halls as standard institutional issue.

In order to meet general education require-ments (such as courses in the social sciences) for the purposes of subject-matter preparation, preservice social studies teachers may complete many courses that do not model issues-centered instruction. Griffin (1992, 13–14) wrote:

> The present writer has been unable to find anyone who will say flatly, "The subject-matter preparation of history teachers need not be guided by a conception of what his-tory teachers are supposed to do with sub-ject-matter." That there is at least some pre-sumptive connection seems so obvious that one is somewhat diffident about saying it. Yet the casual fashion in which departments of education "farm out" students to subject-matter specialists, and the absence from educational literature of any but the most perfunctory allusions to how teacher-con-trolled subject matter is supposed to func-tion within the experience of children, forces the conclusions that few institutions have taken the question seriously.

The issues-centered teacher educator must not casually send preservice teachers to other departments for subject-matter preparation. Designers of teacher education programs must look critically at what is occurring in other coursework, and perhaps join together with fac-ulty across the university to help develop issues-centered courses in the social sciences for preser-vice teachers. Engle and Ochoa (1988, 129) wrote of the social studies curriculum, "If survey courses are to exist at all, they must include major social problems pursued in depth." Surely, the same must be true for the social studies teacher education curriculum.

To address this issue, it may be imperative that those committed to creating an issues-cen-tered teacher education program form partner-ships with arts and sciences professors. Mehlinger (1981, 259) discussed the gulf that has existed historically between those who teach courses associated with the academic disciplines and those responsible for courses in professional education:

> The separation between Arts and Science professors and School of Education profes-sors that marks the preservice training of teachers is also rather typical of in-service and continuing education of teachers leading to advanced degrees. The exception occurs when a college or university has received a grant from a private or government founda-tion to conduct a teacher institute. Then, cooperation between Arts and Science and Education professors tends to be the rule rather than the exception. It appears that we cooperate if we are bribed to do so. Without a financial incentive to tear down the institu-tional barriers, we prefer our isolation.

Historically, such partnerships are the result of outside incentives. One such example might be in tenure and promotion criteria. The basis of the success of professors, particularly at large research institutions, for example, is more com-monly based on their research and writing than their teaching. If innovation in teaching were valued as highly as innovation in research, arts and sciences professors and education professors might be more likely to collaborate to develop outstanding teaching models and courses, in particular, the reconceptualization of existing large lecture courses to incorporate the analysis of major social problems.

Professional Education Coursework

As the survey data indicates, of the three coursework categories related to professional education—social studies course preparation, specialized methods coursework, and other education coursework—the issues-centered approach is more dominant in social studies methods coursework. The survey question concerning the critical examination of social issues and practices in methods coursework presented many insights. For discussion's sake, the responses are categorized into prefatory knowledge, engagement and exploration, and teaching.

Prefatory knowledge contains activities that introduce preservice teachers to the notion of issues-centered instruction. Respondents shared such examples as simply defining social issues and viewing various steps and models for developing and dealing with issues in the classroom. These activities build preservice teachers' basic knowledge, and provide readiness for *engagement and exploration*, the category that drew the largest number of activities within the survey. Through such activities as Socratic seminars, debates, panel discussions, simulations, group work, and classroom discussion, preservice teachers examine and explore social issues. Responses that relate to *teaching* inform about preservice teachers' planning and presentation of instruction, such as identifying issues for a particular unit, designing the unit, and developing activities for dealing with identified issues.

Preservice teachers who are exploring issues-centered instruction are advised to read works by the leaders in the field, including Nelson, Carlson, Palonsky, Saxe, Evans, Engle, Shaver, Stanley, Aronowitz, Giroux, Apple, Oliver, Shaver, Hunt, Metcalf, Massialas, Cox, Fenton, Chapin, Gross, Ochoa, Lockwood, Harris, and Zola. To prepare for the study of issues that may emerge from student exploration, issues-centered teacher educators must expand their collection of key readings and literature to assist with classroom issues analysis.

Adler (1991, 79) recommended the use of literature in social studies methods classes to help teacher educators solve the pedagogical problem that faces them, which is:

> finding the stimuli which will open students to asking questions, to taking new perspectives, to examining alternatives. This problem of teacher education is the problem of liberal education generally: how can we emancipate students from mindlessness; how can we free them for the difficult task of making choices.

Adler has required Arthur Miller's drama *The*

Crucible (1953) and Chinua Achebe's novel *Things Fall Apart* (1959) in her social studies methods courses. According to Adler, the issues raised in these novels—individual freedom, law and authority, and social conscience—are relevant to a consideration of citizenship in a democracy (*The Crucible*) and confronting enduring questions about what it means to live in a social world (*Things Fall Apart*). Adler (1991, 81) asserted that such literature:

> can be used to raise questions concerning moral commitment and ethical action. Most social studies textbooks convey seemingly objective facts, with little sense of personal choices or decisions. The personal, emotive, empathetic response to literary works can facilitate the discussion of ethical and political issues as they relate to issues and topics in social studies. Students can thus be shown a perspective on social studies knowledge and curriculum which includes questions of what is right and good, and why. Such questions can be brought to bear, as well, on issues of teaching and schooling.

Teacher educators can help their students further explore issues of teaching and schooling in methods classes through the case-study method, an instructional technique in which the professor presents in narrative form the major ingredients of a problematic teaching situation and preservice teachers engage in problem solving (Kowalski, Weaver, and Henson, 1990). Doyle (1990) and Shulman (1987) were among noted scholars who advocated the infusion of the case study method into preservice teacher education coursework. As teacher educators recognized that teaching is a complex, situation-specific, and dilemma-ridden endeavor, interest in this method resurfaced. According to Wassermann (1993, xiii), "cases are not intended to present the 'unhappy' faces of teaching; they are meant to provide pictures of life in schools, raising issues that beg for enlightened and informed examination." The case-study method is consistent with issues-centered instruction, as teacher educators may use cases to raise issues central to the teaching of social studies, consequently leading preservice teachers in the critical examination of educational practices and their social implications.

Recently published texts contain appropriate

cases, e.g., Shulman and Mesa-Bains (1990), Kowalski, Weaver, and Henson (1990), Wassermann (1993), and Silverman, Welty, and Lyons (1992). "The Case of Joan Martin, Marilyn Coe, and Warren Groves" (Silverman et al. 1992, 60) is such an example; it tells the story of a child named Donald who has been mainstreamed into a regular classroom for social studies instruction. In the text of the case, Donald Garcia is described as:

a 9-year-old, (who) had spent two years in the self-contained LD class. He was an only child, living with his mother and father.... The Committee on Special Education report noted that Donald's mother, whose native language was Spanish, spoke English with some difficulty. Donald understood but did not speak Spanish.

Conflict arises in this case when Donald does poorly on social studies quizzes and the classroom teacher, the special education teacher, and the elementary school principal hold different views regarding the role of mainstreaming and Donald's performance in the regular classroom. Preservice teachers may examine these issues in relation to this case: social studies instruction for special needs students, mainstreaming, assessment of social studies learning, dealing with diversity, and the practice of labeling children. (See Dana and Floyd 1993, 1994 for further discussion of this case within methods instruction.)

Cases provide the context from which issues may emerge as preservice teachers study each problematic situation. Saxe (1994, 111) discussed the use of issues in the teaching of social studies as "something spontaneous; that is, issues can and do emerge when children are studying or discussing or making observations about a particular phenomenon." Saxe differentiated between issues raised by children and issues raised by adults, and teacher educators are wise to keep this difference in mind, remembering that issues they raise may not be fully understood or have value to preservice teachers. During case study discussions, preservice teachers may raise issues they feel are key, which may differ from a specific issue the teacher educator had in mind for exploration and discussion. To ensure the exploration of issues important to preservice teachers, teacher educators may supplement commercially prepared case-study discussion with discussion of

cases written by the preservice teachers themselves, possibly from a field experience coupled with the methods class.

Field-Based Experiences

Field experience is a critical component of the learning-to-teach process. For example, Guyton and McIntyre (1990, 514-34) reported that many teachers—graduates of teacher education programs—remarked that field experiences are the "most beneficial segments of the teacher education program." Even though field-based experiences may be a key component in the education of the issues-centered teacher, the survey data indicated that few field experiences were issues-centered. Two universities did not identify any field-based experience as issues-centered. Of the six remaining institutions, two indicated issues-centered field-based programs were "sometimes" offered, and one institution noted that only one student each semester was placed in an issues-centered classroom.

Issues-centered field experiences may not now be a featured component of preservice issues-centered teacher preparation because teacher educators may not have identified exemplary issues-centered social studies teachers. As institutions confront the logistical difficulties of placing preservice teachers in the field, they may not overtly seek issues-centered teachers as cooperating teachers. Rather, if preservice teachers are placed with issues-centered teachers, it occurs by chance. To maximize the influence of an issues-centered field experience, seeking exemplary issues-centered teachers must become a priority of teacher educators.

Of course, there may be an even simpler explanation for the limited use of issues-centered field experience—a sufficient number of exemplary issues-centered teachers with which to place preservice teachers may not exist. If this is the case, the teacher educator and school personnel can collaborate to focus on issues-centered instruction within the field experience. For example, the practicing/cooperating teacher may identify what topic the preservice teacher should cover during the placement. The preservice teacher, with help from the university supervisor, then identifies issues related to that particular topic and designs and implements lessons and activities for analyzing these issues. In this way preservice teachers are approaching the expected curriculum in a way consistent with issues-centered instruction. An added bonus to this plan is that preservice teachers may help practicing teachers understand and begin to use issues-centered instruction themselves. If interest in issues-centered instruction begins to surface in the cooperating schools, teacher educators can offer to provide in-service programming on issues-centered instruction.

Action Plan for Issues-Centered Teacher Educators

Within this chapter we have explored three components of an issues-centered teacher education—general education coursework, professional education coursework, and field-based experiences. Recommended actions that teacher educators may take to enhance successful preparation of preservice teachers in issues-centered instruction are **1.** joining with arts and sciences faculty to move large lecture survey courses in the social sciences toward courses that focus on major social problems pursued in depth, **2.** augmenting current social studies methods courses' pedagogical practices with the discussion of literature and case studies, and **3.** making a commitment to ensure issues-centered field experiences.

While these actions are central to providing an issues-centered teacher education, a much larger issue looms. Each institution surveyed noted in some way that, although issues-centered coursework was offered, the courses did not exist independently as issues-centered. The courses were issues-centered depending upon *who* was teaching them. Thus, the creation and implementation of an issues-centered teacher education program composed of issues-centered courses, no matter how well planned or envisioned, most likely will not occur until the faculty and instructors for those courses are committed to issues-centered instruction. Issues-centered social studies teacher educators, therefore, have a responsibility to help all educators understand and implement issues-centered instruction, whether it be by sharing course syllabi with colleagues or writing articles about issues-centered instruction for other teacher educators. It is in such actions that the promise of issues-centered teacher education lies.

References

Achebe, C. *Things Fall Apart.* New York: Random House, 1959.

Adler, S. "Forming a Critical Pedagogy in the Social Studies Methods Class: The Use of Imaginative Literature." In *Issues and Practices in Inquiry-Oriented Teacher Education*, edited by B. R. Tabachnich and K. Zeichner, 77–90. London: Farmer Press, 1991.

Christensen, J. C., and L. S. Tafel, ed. "Diversity in Today's Classroom: Teacher Education's Challenge." *Action in Teacher Education* 12, no. 3 (1990): v.

Common, D. L. "Toward the Creation of an Educational Culture and the Restructuring of American Universities." Paper presented at the annual meeting of the American Educational Research Association, Atlanta, Georgia, February 1993.

Dana, N. F., and D. M. Floyd. "Preparing Preservice Teachers for the Multicultural Classroom: A Report on the Case Study Approach." Paper presented at the annual meeting of the Association of Teacher Educators conference, Los Angeles, California, February 1993.

Dana, N. F., and D. M. Floyd. "When Teacher Educators Collaboratively Reflect on Their Practices: A Case Study on Teaching Cases." Paper presented at the annual meeting of the Association of Teacher Educators conference, Atlanta, Georgia, February 1994.

Doyle, W. "Case Methods in the Education of Teachers." *Teacher Education Quarterly* 17, no. 1 (1990): 7–15.

Engle, S., and A. Ochoa. *Education for Democratic Citizenship.* New York: Teachers College Press, 1988.

Grant, C. A., and W. G. Secada. "Preparing Teachers for Diversity." In *Handbook of Research on Teacher Education*, edited by W. R. Houston, 33–40. New York: Macmillan, 1990.

Griffin, A. F. *A Philosophical Approach to the Subject-Matter Preparation of Teachers of History.* 1942. Reprint, Washington, D.C.: National Council for the Social Studies, 1992.

Guyton, E., and D. J. McIntyre. "Student Teaching and School Experiences." In *Handbook of Research on Teacher Education*, edited by W. R. Houston, 514–34. New York: Macmillan, 1990.

Howey, K. R., and N. L. Zimpher. *Profiles of Preservice Teacher Education.* Albany: State University of New York Press, 1989.

Kowalski, T. J., R. A. Weaver, and K. T. Henson. *Case Studies on Teaching.* New York: Longman, 1990.

Mehlinger, H., and O. L. Davis Jr., eds. *The Social Studies. Eightieth Yearbook of the National Society for the Study of Education.* Part II. Chicago, Ill.: University of Chicago Press, 1981.

Miller, A. *The Crucible.* New York: Bantam Books, 1952.

Robards, S. "President's Message." *Action in Teacher Education* 12, no. 3 (1990):

Saxe, D. W. *Social Studies for the Elementary Teacher.* Boston: Allyn-Bacon, 1994.

Shulman, L. S. "Toward a Pedagogy of Cases: A Vision for Teacher Education" Audiocassette recording of speech by author. Reston, Va.: Association of Teacher Educators, 1987.

Shulman, J., and Mesa-Bains, ed. *Teaching Diverse Students: Cases and Commentaries*. San Francisco: Far West Laboratory, 1990.

Silverman, R., W. M. Welty, and S. Lyon. *Case Studies for Teacher Problem Solving*. New York: McGraw-Hill, Inc., 1992.

Wassermann, S. *Getting Down to Cases: Learning to Teach with Case Studies*. New York: Teachers College Press, 1993.

SUPERVISION FOR TEACHER GROWTH IN REFLECTIVE, ISSUES-CENTERED TEACHING PRACTICE

by Kenneth F. Jerich

Reflective teaching encourages the skills needed for students to engage in the evaluation, analysis and discussion of issues. Its principles include identifying a problem, developing hypotheses, testing hypotheses, developing conclusions, applying conclusions to new data, facilitating an open classroom discussion, incorporating empathy and acceptance, and establishing and maintaining rapport with students. To maximize the potential of reflective teaching for issues-centered instruction requires appropriate forms of supervision. Just as reflective teaching can be enhanced by supervision that is designed to promote a thoughtful, well-informed classroom, it can be obstructed by certain kinds of hierarchical and excessively programmatic supervision.

The supervision of teaching practice should be structured to provide opportunities for teachers to reflect upon their teaching, its relationship to learner needs and its contribution to long-term teacher growth. To further these objectives, both teachers and administrators need to address some fundamental questions. These include: What combination of supervisory practice, teacher growth and teacher evaluation is likely to promote significant and meaningful learning in the reflective, issues-centered classroom? To what extent do school leaders view the reflective, issues-centered classroom as central to a school's mission, curriculum and essential learning outcomes? And what does the research on the subject indicate are the best approaches to supervision and evaluation?

Darling-Hammond and Sclan (1992) take a position against bureaucratic supervision, as a means for the development of teachers. According to them, "evaluation is an ongoing set of experiences in which teachers examine their own and each others' work, determine its effective-ness, and explore alternative strategies." (8) Similarly, Gitlin and Price (1992) advocate an empowerment approach that they call "horizontal evaluation." This approach asks teachers to explore their insights on how alternative teaching practices may contribute to the reshaping and improvement of their teaching, and to examine the differences between what they plan for and what really happens in the classroom.

In what ways can supervising a teacher change instructional practice? Grimmett, Rostad and Ford (1992) argue that the ways in which supervisors try to bring about change in instruction can either produce a cataclysmic effect on a teacher's morale or produce a collaborative culture. In the former case, a teacher often feels overwhelmed by high expectations and becomes highly dependent upon and/or resistant to the supervisor. In the latter, a teacher experiences a sense of professional empowerment and the supervisor is seen as an orchestrator enabling the teacher to lead students into "new knowledge, skills, behavior and dispositions." (186). According to Grimmett, Rostad and Ford, teacher development can take place in an environment of collegiality in which a teacher can reflectively transform the classroom experience.

One mode of supervision that is generally recognized in the field to be effective is known as clinical supervision, as formulated by Goldhammer (1969) and Cogan (1973). Sergiovanni and Starratt (1973), and Sergiovanni (1985) suggest that clinical supervision should have a broad conceptual basis. They treat reflection as a central characteristic of successful supervisory practice, a position strongly endorsed by Goldhammer and Cogan (Goldhammer, Anderson and Krajewski 1980). In a setting characterized by this form of supervision, the analysis of instruction incorporates supportive methods that are congruent with how teachers develop and refine their teaching. Holland (1989) suggests that this mode of supervision may be used for evaluative purposes only if it is cast in terms of "formative teacher evaluation." Of course, no implementation of one mode of supervision contrasted to another escapes criticism (Garman, Glickman, Hunter, and Haggerson 1987). *Properly understood and used conceptually, however, clinical supervision provides an avenue for teacher growth, positive reflection on teacher practices, and creativity in the evaluative process.*

McGreal (1983) has also argued that successful teacher evaluation is closely linked to clinical supervision. In the 1993 American Educational Research Association Instructional Supervision Special Interest Group Keynote Address, McGreal argued as well that summative evaluation for teachers should be eliminated and replaced with formative evaluation (1993).

Clinical supervision is more than professional supervision, which incorporates a collegial relationship among professionals, with teachers working together in an open fashion. It is also more than instructional supervision, which is based on a work setting that focuses on improving instruction and curriculum. Clinical supervision embodies both professional supervision and instructional supervision, and is seen as being developmentally based. Characteristics of clinical supervision include collegiality, equal control of agenda between teacher and supervisor, an objective data base for reflective self-analysis about one's teaching, as opposed to the subjective expression of opinions, and strategies for the improvement of instruction that are based on the misinterpretation of data. The phases of clinical supervision (pre-conferencing, data collection of teaching, analysis of data from lesson, post-conferencing) are occasions for interaction between teachers and supervisors aimed at improving instruction.

Clinical supervision includes:
- Identifying the reflective, issues-centered teacher's concerns about instruction.
- Translating the teacher's concerns into observable behaviors.
- Identifying procedures for improving the teacher's instruction.
- Assisting the teacher in setting self-improvement goals for instruction.
- Providing the teacher with feedback, using

objective observational data for instruction.
- Eliciting the teacher's inferences, opinions and feelings about instruction.
- Encouraging the teacher to consider alternative lesson objectives and methods for instruction.[2]

For teachers, beginning or experienced, clinical supervision may be disquieting in the beginning stages of the supervisory process if all that they want the supervisor to do is to directly tell them what the good and bad features were about their teaching. If the supervisor falls victim to this procedure, then the teacher successfully shifts the entire responsibility for the teaching act to the supervisor. Teachers must develop the disposition of taking ownership and conducting self-analysis of their teaching with the aid of the supervisor to realize teacher growth over time. This is especially true for beginning teachers.

Bureaucratic supervision needs to be replaced by clinical supervision, through which the teacher and supervisor work together to establish goals, consider alternatives, and establish mutually decided upon strategies for teacher growth (Jerich 1989). Direct supervision strategies should be replaced with collaborative and non-directive supervisory strategies in which teachers and supervisors interact with each other.[3] I would suggest that for clinical supervision to be considered effective, supervision must *ultimately* help teachers reach the goal of engaging their students in high cognitive student initiated learning—where students freely attach short- and long-term significance and meaningfulness to their learning.

The typical classroom situation at present poses major problems for the reflective teacher (Anrig and Lapointe 1989; Prawat 1993; Raths, Harmin and Simon 1986). The research of Berry and Ginsberg (1990) discovered that all too often classrooms are dominated by prescribed instructional models, strategies, and skills for teaching that emphasize techniques known as "direct instruction." Additionally, Berry and Ginsberg (1990, 169) state:

> The challenge for the future, according to some scholars, is to transform the typical classroom, with a single teacher lecturing to large numbers of students who are required to do seatwork and use "dumbed-down" textbooks, to new classrooms, with teams of

teachers helping students make complex construction of knowledge. In these new classrooms, students would be expected to organize and monitor their own learning and engage in collaborative and situational specific learning activities.[4]

Schmuck and Schmuck (1990), in their analysis of democratic participation in small-town schools, observed more than 50 classes and "soared to heights of delight in some and sank to depths of disappointment in others." (16) They remarked that they saw some classes that were exciting, captivating and quite imaginative. Also, they remarked

> We were disappointed, however, more often than we were delighted. Like other educator writers, we witnessed, in 80% of the classes, what Ned Flanders in 1970 called the rule of two thirds; two thirds of classroom talk is teacher's talk, and two thirds of that is unidirectional lecturing...With our experience we would modify Flanders' means to the rule of three fourths. The classes were typically teacher centered; we saw teachers standing in front lecturing to rows of students, with only occasional student talk as a response to teacher questions (Schmuck and Schmuck, 1990, 17).

Dispositions and Instruction

As a point of departure for the examination of these questions, let us hypothesize, for example, that the use of the Hunter model for lesson planning and instruction to evaluate the reflective, issues-centered teacher (Hunter and Russell, 1981) represents the established instructional and evaluation procedure for a school system. According to this approach, the teacher would begin each class period by announcing the objectives for the lesson. Primarily, a lecture-based teaching approach would be used following the seven basic steps for instruction as outlined by Hunter. According to the expectations established by this school system, the teacher would answer student questions and continue with the lecture/discussion format.

Let us hypothesize also that reflective, issues-centered instruction, for example, the Value-Conflict model of instruction (Hunt and Metcalf, 1968), represents an established format for teaching social studies in a school system. According to this approach, the majority of class time would be spent on discussions, gaming situations, and debates among the students. During the debates, perhaps, the students who held strong beliefs about a certain viewpoint would be asked to defend a different position encouraging them to consider new viewpoints and values that were different from their current beliefs. Students would be engaged in reflective learning geared toward social problem solving. The teacher's role would be to act as a mediator and initiator with the disposition that no teacher judgments or statements would influence the students' attitudes toward a certain answer. A major goal of the teacher, perhaps, would be to develop a student who could look at the various facts presented by a problem and reach some answer by rational thought.

Can a mental picture be created to construct what the reflective, issues-centered teacher and students would have experienced, that is, seeing two different worlds of teaching and learning, if they had witnessed the instructional ebb and flow over time for these two types of classes? Do some teaching approaches work better with certain kinds of content? What kind of classroom microculture would exist in each case? Would student essays derived from non-reflective, issues-centered instruction contain a high level of citation of facts and particulars, but lack an overall sense of reflection, integrative thought, and creativity? Would student essays derived from reflective, issues-centered instruction demonstrate the use of integrative thought and creative expression throughout the essays? To what extent would the two groups of students be able to hypothesize an array of solutions to a problem set forth in the examination? Would there be any substantial difference in the level of reflection and inquiry in the essays between the two groups of students? Would there be any substantial differences in learning outcomes achieved by the two groups of students?

In our hypothetical setting, would the reflective, issues-centered teacher be able to infuse appropriate knowledge bases to structure and execute various teaching repertoires for the class? In contrast, what kind of knowledge bases would the non-reflective, issues-centered teacher use? Could a teacher attribute the use of these types of knowledge bases to the experience of supervisory conferences? More importantly, can a teacher make necessary changes in units of instruction as a result of supervisory input? Can the quality of a supervision program make an "imprint" on a teacher to a degree that it translates into effective teaching and influences the sense students have of a positive learning environment in the classroom?

Strategies for Supervising the Reflective, Issues-Centered Teacher

In view of the above concerns, effective supervisors (instructional leaders) should possess a professional disposition for using clinical supervision to improve teaching, as well as strategies for supervising the reflective, issues-centered teacher for the improvement of instruction (Garman 1990; Murphy 1990; Rallis 1990).

Supervisory Dispositions

As defined by Katz and Raths (1985), the term "disposition" is used "to designate actions and characterize their frequency, for example, asking higher level questions, rewarding approximations, guiding classroom discussions, encouraging students' creativity, and planning worthwhile experiences in the classroom." (303) For example, effective supervisors might have a disposition toward helping teachers to self-analyze their teaching if they make use of this strategy on frequent occasions in several contexts. The context for this disposition might occur during consultation, for example, during a pre-conference or post-conference.

The goals for supervisory treatments ought to include what Darling-Hammond and Sclan (1992) viewed as an ongoing set of experiences where teachers take control of the examination process, and where dispositions are strengthened. What supervisory methods best ensure that the reflective, issues-centered teacher will have a disposition to go on learning after having contact with a supervisor? It is helpful if supervisors regard teachers as clients, not as subordinates. Issues-centered and reflective teaching and supervision should go hand-in-hand.

If Hunter's supervision model is used, for example, the focus of supervision becomes undifferentiated (Garman and Hazi 1988). The frame of reference is exclusively the supervisor's. Negative reinforcement dominates the interactions of the conference. A checklist approach to identify the good and bad things that happen in the classroom dominates the focus of the classroom observation analysis. If this approach is

used to interact with reflective, issues-centered teachers, they may be overwhelmed by the number of suggestions. Reflective, issues-centered teachers, for example, might have the feeling that they can never improve to the degree implied by the criticism and that the conference gives them no grounds for improving. The idea of confirming that teachers either taught extremely well or that they failed represents a form of bureaucratic supervision which has for its purpose a certain kind of quality control. The agenda is determined by the administrator.

In contrast, clinical supervision requires the opposite approach. First, clinical supervision is not seen as using a "Laundry List" of supervisory techniques in which the supervisor points to all the good and bad acts that occurred in the chronological order of a lesson. Clinical supervision is collegial; the reflective, issues-centered teacher and supervisor can work together to establish goals, develop evaluation and consider alternatives. It is based on data rather than opinion or impressions. Data are interpreted in terms of theory or the wisdom of the profession. The teacher takes ownership of problems with open communication.

Second, clinical supervision is more than a "checklist" approach for evaluating instruction followed by supervisors in dealings with teachers. Supervisors should be able to distinguish the difference between using a checklist and working developmentally with teachers to improve teaching. A checklist-style instrument is not well suited to the representation of subtle environmental factors in teaching and learning. It cannot distinguish between who is dominating the conversation or whether the conversation is directed toward the goal of teacher improvement or simply a meandering dialogue with no discernible purpose. If the supervisors are too prescriptive in their dealings with teachers, especially reflective, issues-centered teachers, they may feel intimidated and be resistant to divulging important concerns. Also, little teacher self-analysis takes place if supervisors simply identify crucial issues for teachers and tell them what to do to remedy these concerns.

Third, a reflective, issues-centered teacher's prior dispositions toward supervision for improving teaching may be so strong that they may adversely impact the very nature of the goals for clinical supervision. A major point is that all humans, students and teachers, grow most when they control their own learning. Reflective teachers facilitate this in students, and reflective supervisors facilitate it in teachers. Collaborative effort between educational leaders and the reflective, issues-centered teacher is needed to promote the use of clinical supervision instead of the use of interventionism for the improvement of instruction. Reflective, issues-centered teachers should not be subjected to supervisor experiences that "dumb down" the work of teaching and learning.

Fourth, the mode of supervision plays a direct role in the success of teaching and learning. Instructional leaders must use clinical supervision to guide reflective, issues-centered teachers through the developmental stages for teaching.[5] To be effective, supervisors must be flexible and willing to allow teachers the freedom to set the course of conferences and be prepared to follow any number of these possible courses depending on where reflective, issues-centered teachers wish to go with the discussion. Also, there is a need for clear direction known to both the supervisor and teacher throughout the supervisory process. This is especially important for reflective, issues-centered teachers. Effective supervisors clearly demonstrate the ability to remain nondirective in nature and yet are flexible in providing collaborative opportunities for teachers to reconsider important phases of their teaching that may have been overlooked during the conference.

Any individual who is placed in the position of serving as an instructional supervisor must be able to distinguish the differences between nonclinical and clinical supervision (Sergiovanni 1992; Smyth 1988). Those individuals who are able to identify and incorporate dispositions toward clinical supervision into their roles as supervisors will be better able to conduct clinical-based conferences with the reflective, issues-centered teacher for the improvement of instruction.

Supervisory Strategies

The most important aspects of supervision of the reflective, issues-centered teacher during the pre-conference phases of clinical supervision include
- the atmosphere of the conference
- the specification of teacher concerns
- observing behavior
- drawing up strategies
- goal setting and establishing a timeline

For the post conference phases of clinical supervision, salient features include
- supervisor preparation
- the presentation of data
- teacher self-analysis of data
- relating post-conference conclusions to concerns identified in the pre-conference
- the promotion of continued growth

Pre-Conference Phase

Let us consider five central features of the pre-conference phase of clinical supervision.

Atmosphere of the conference. An open collegial atmosphere between the supervisor and the reflective, issues-centered teacher is essential for the facilitation of maximum teacher growth. There is a delicate balance between supervisor control and teacher control of the pre- and post-conferences. If the supervisor appears "wishy-washy" in the eyes of the reflective, issues-centered teacher, the teacher may question the supervisor's effectiveness and may attempt to guide the discussion away from "dangerous" concerns (that need to be addressed) toward "safer" concerns (that the teacher feels will not jeopardize his/her summative evaluation). There might even be instances where the teacher does not know what the supervisor expects and the conference degenerates into a situation where the teacher rambles on without purpose and the supervisor adopts the role of confidant. If, on the other hand, the supervisor is too "heavy-handed" in his/her dealings with teachers, especially reflective, issues-centered teachers, they may feel intimidated and be reluctant to divulge important concerns. Also, little teacher self-analysis takes place if the supervisor identifies the crucial issues for the teacher and tells him/her what to do to remedy these concerns.

The supervisor might also adopt the posture of the "distant professional" in which he/she says very little and writes a great deal. It is obvious to the reflective, issues-centered teacher that this type of supervisor is uninvolved and does not have a genuine interest in his/her welfare. Other ways in which this type of supervisor can distance himself/herself from the teacher are: **a.** adjusting the furniture in such a way as to place the supervisor behind the desk to leave no doubt as to who is the authority figure and who is not; **b.** positioning his/her seat so that he/she faces away from the teacher (and hence closes himself/herself to a more personal style of interaction); **c.** exhibiting a "closed" body posture thus resulting in further distancing himself/herself from the teacher; and **d.** using a rushed/annoyed tone of voice and frequently uttering short phrases (such as 'uh-huh' or 'O.K.') while the teacher is speaking and thus giving the appearance that the supervisor wishes the teacher to "get on with it" so the conference can end. In addition, a supervisor who is uncomfortable when dealing with teachers or who makes a superficial attempt at congeniality or warmth will do little in the way of convincing the reflective, issues-centered teacher that he/she sincerely cares about his/her growth as a person or professional.[6]

2 The specification of teacher concerns. Specification of concerns by the reflective, issues-centered teacher fosters self-analysis. It also provides the framework for future discussions in the remainder of the pre-conference and the subsequent post-conference. The importance of clearly specifying these concerns cannot be over emphasized. If they are absent in the pre-conference, subsequent discussions lack focus and the supervisor does not know what to look for during the observation phase of the supervisory cycle. These concerns should be possible to deal with in the here-and-now rather than left for consideration in the vague future. It is not appropriate for the supervisor to solicit more than a few concerns during the pre-conference. Since it is impossible to simultaneously give each the attention it deserves, none will be adequately resolved. In addition, addressing more than two or three concerns at once may cause the reflective, issues-centered teacher to feel overwhelmed.

There is often confusion on the part of both teacher and supervisor concerning lesson goals/objectives and teacher concerns. Teachers often simply state their concerns in terms of what aspects of student performance they wish to address rather than focusing on aspects of their own performance in relationship to the significance level of classroom instructional tasks linked to student learning outcomes. Unfortunately, the supervisor all too often accepts only teacher centered concerns, and does not dig deeper to uncover the appropriate student-centered concerns. This unwillingness to "dig" for student concerns based on the significance of the instructional tasks sometimes results in the supervisor being satisfied when a teacher indicates he/she is totally satisfied with his/her performance and cannot come up with any student concerns at all. This smug attitude is a problem in itself and is often not dealt with by strategic questioning by the supervisor. All that is usually necessary in these instances of absent or inappropriate teacher concerns is that the supervisor listen closely to what the teacher is saying and, when necessary, guide the teacher's efforts (by strategic probing and follow-up questions) in directions that are believed to be fruitful. Once the teacher has identified these concerns, the supervisor must mirror them back to the teacher to make sure that both parties have a clear idea of what is being scrutinized.

3 Observable behaviors. If the supervisor does not know what to look for during the observation phase, it is unlikely that he or she will be able to gather the necessary data to address the previously-identified teacher and student concerns. The identification of specific behaviors and dispositions are often missing entirely or mistakenly left to the post-conference (when it is too late).

4 Strategies. The successful identification of appropriate strategies (by the teacher) to deal with the identified concern(s) depends on the success of the previous step in the pre-conference. If the formulation of strategies is left to the post-conference (or neglected entirely), there will be no hypothesis to test during the observation and post-conference phases other than the accuracy of the teacher's assessment of the problem. What is needed is a clearly formulated plan to address teacher concerns before the observation takes place so that the efficacy of the plan can be evaluated during the post-conference. In this way, the reflective, issues-centered teacher not only gets objective observational data from the supervisor as to the validity of his/her concerns, but also sees how his/her efforts to address these concerns (through positive actions) may succeed or fail. Furthermore, if the supervisor (rather than the teacher) takes on the burden of devising possible strategies to address teacher concerns, the teacher will not take ownership of the strategies, and any success or failure will be perceived as due to the efforts of the supervisor and not the teacher. Also, if the teacher devises the plan, the chances are that he/she will be more enthusiastic in its implementation, and the likelihood for success is greater. Too often, when the teacher is unable to devise a strategy, the supervisor steps in with his/her own ideas and shortcircuits the entire process.

5 Goal setting and establishing a timeline. Teacher/supervisor confusion over exactly what constitutes an appropriate goal/timeline is often encountered in this crucial culminating step of the preconference phase. As was the case in the "identification of teacher concerns phase" both parties sometimes do not distinguish between what the students are expected to do (learning outcomes) and what the teacher is expected to do (goals to be used to remedy teacher concerns). Supervisor reactions to stated teacher goals/timelines range from unquestioning acceptance of any and all goals to the overly prescriptive behavior of the supervisor telling the teacher exactly what is to be done and when it must be accomplished. Both extremes are at odds with the spirit of clinical supervision. The "unquestioning acceptance" approach does not provide for the development of teacher self-analysis skills because "Anything is O.K. as long as the teacher came up with it." In addition, it will not allow the teacher to benefit from the supervisor's experience with other teachers in similar situations. The "overly-prescriptive" approach is similarly at odds with teacher self-analysis because (as was the case during the strategy generating phase) the supervisor does all the work and the teacher has no voice in, and hence little ownership of, the decisions being made and the eventual outcome.

Post-conference phase

Let us consider five central features of the post-conference phase of clinical supervision.

1 Supervisor preparation. Although the most effective style of clinical supervision is nondirective in nature, this does not imply a lack of preparation on the part of the supervisor. In order to be effective, the supervisor must not only be flexible and willing to allow the reflective, issues-centered teacher the freedom to set the course of the post-conference, but he/she must also be prepared to follow any number of possible courses depending on where the teacher wishes to go with the discussion. This preparation must include the gathering of objective data, instruments and systems as well as the organization of quantitative and qualitative data to present an impartial picture of what transpired during the lesson being considered. If this data is not available or not presented in a meaningful manner at the appropriate time, the only "fuel" left for the post-conference discussion is opinion and speculation. As stated earlier, there is a need for clear direction (known to both the supervisor

and teacher) throughout the supervisory process. If preparation was lacking in an earlier phase, subsequent stages will suffer because they are built on a weak foundation and lack the necessary focus.

2 The presentation of data. Effective progress toward the resolution of teacher concerns in the post-conference depends not only on the presence of objective data but on the type of data used and when it is introduced. Certain types of data are more appropriate than others when addressing certain teacher concerns. For example, Flanders's Interaction Analysis might still be appropriate for addressing concerns such as the quantity of teacher-talk versus student-talk or how often the teacher follows student responses with praise, but it would not be an appropriate indicator of which students were participating in a discussion or of the cognitive level and appropriateness of the types of questions asked by the reflective, issues-centered teacher. Jadallah's reflective teaching observation instrument is an excellent tool for collecting this type of data.[7] Acheson and Gall (1992) also describe several suitable ways to collect observation data for the classroom. In keeping with the spirit of selfanalysis, the prudent supervisor will introduce appropriate types of quantitative and/or qualitative based data at appropriate times during the post-conference. Presenting the data too early will circumvent efforts by the supervisor to have the teacher express how he/she felt about the lesson. Presenting the data too late will only result in frustration and wasted time because there is nothing (other than opinion and speculation) on which to base the analysis.

3 Teacher self-analysis of data. A common question asked by teachers during the post-conference is: "How did I do?" At this juncture, it is important for the supervisor to reserve comment and redirect the question back to the teacher in a psychoanalyst-like fashion: "How do you think you did?" If the supervisor was to give a positive or negative assessment at this time, the teacher would most likely disregard any objective data that followed and adopt the assessment of the supervisor as his/her own. This is antithetical to the entire process of self-analysis which the supervisor hopes to instill in the reflective, issues-centered teacher. It will not develop the powers of unbiased introspection the reflective, issues-centered teacher will need when he/she finds himself/herself in the field without immediate access to the judgments of a supervisor. The supervisor as facilitator should also resist the temptation to interpret the observational data he/she has gathered when presenting it to the reflective, issues-centered teacher. This is the responsibility of the reflective, issues-centered teacher. For true selfanalysis to occur, the data must not only be objective but must be presented in a value-free manner as well. The data should speak for itself, and any conclusions drawn by the reflective, issues-centered teacher should be solely based on this data and not on how the teacher feels the supervisor has interpreted the data.

4 **Relating post-conference conclusions to concerns identified in the pre-conference.** As was the case during the pre-conference, the success of the current step relies on successful completion of previous steps. Usually problems in this phase are of the "all or nothing" variety. If the supervisor and teacher neglected to identify any concerns during the pre-conference, any conclusions that might be drawn during the post-conference are not anchored to any previously identified needs (or strategies devised to meet these needs) and hence there is no continuity between pre- and post-conferences. Although some might argue that all is not lost if the identification of teacher concerns is left to the post-conference, doing so is akin to closing the barn door after the horse has escaped: It is too late to intervene and devise appropriate strategies (at least for the current cycle), since the observation phase has already been completed. If, on the other hand, too many concerns have been identified during the pre-conference, the reflective, issues-centered teacher will not only be overwhelmed with the amount of data presented, but it will be very difficult for the supervisor to collect and organize such a plethora of information. Since conference time is often limited, it is unrealistic to think that anything but a cursory treatment is possible when trying to analyze more than two or three issues during supervisory consultation.

5 **Continued growth.** When the "long view" of the clinical supervision process is taken, each cycle of pre-conference, observation, and post-conference represents one step in the continuing growth of the reflective, issues-centered teacher rather than an end in itself. It is the responsibility of the supervisor to realize this fact and promote continued growth in the teacher in preparation for the next supervisory cycle as well as later stages of the teacher's professional career. Although it is always more desirable to have the reflective, issues-centered teacher provide ideas for his or her future growth, the supervisor should have a reservoir of such suggestions available in the event the reflective, issues-centered teacher is unable to generate any of his or her own. Too often, the supervisor is either satisfied with the lack of such ideas from the teacher, or is too eager to accept "safe" goals which the teacher knows will not jeopardize his/her perceived status with the supervisor and are easy to accomplish. If the supervisor is an attentive listener and a skilled classroom observer he/she can often use guiding and follow-up questions to assist the reflective, issues-centered teacher in devising long-term goals that are acceptable to both parties and worthy of future discussion.

Concluding Remarks

The most important indicators of success in the clinical supervision process include: **a.** establishing a collegial atmosphere which is conducive to the formation and sustenance of a healthy working relationship between supervisors and reflective, issues-centered teachers throughout the supervisory cycle; **b.** assisting reflective, issues-centered teachers in clearly specifying concerns in an appropriate forum before the classroom observation takes place; and **c.** encouraging self-analysis by reflective, issues-centered teachers of objective observational data as well as assessment of their concerns and appropriate short- and long-term strategies to address these concerns. These goals can be accomplished if the supervisor strikes a delicate balance in the narrow region between the two extremes of no supervisory control, on one hand, and being overly prescriptive on the other, by taking charge without being assertive, and by being open and flexible without allowing the reflective, issues-centered teacher to dominate the process.

The supervisor should maintain a reflective posture to provide opportunities for reflective, issues-centered teachers to discuss their teaching styles without directing prescriptive solutions to concerns about their teaching performance. This "mirror effect" establishes a cooperative atmosphere where reflective, issues-centered teachers can freely express their feelings and concerns about how students can maximize their opportunities for learning in- and outside of the classroom. In clinical supervision, reflective, issues-centered teachers make judgments and evaluations, thus developing their ability to do self-assessment rather than depending upon prescriptive learning provided by the supervisor. Hence, in conjunction with a "mirror effect," the supervisor serves as a facilitator in a guided discovery process that fosters self-analysis by the reflective, issues-centered teacher.

Pre-conferences should be viewed as the opportunity to reinforce the reflective, issues-centered teacher's understandings about teaching models, instructional approaches and student learning. The post-conference plays a critical role in the supervision of the reflective, issues-centered teacher. The post-conference curricular component is inextricably linked to the pre-conference curricular component in clinical supervision. A post-conference is not a simple case of providing feedback. It is much more than that. The clinical post-conference takes on the role of providing a composite picture of the reflective, issues-centered teacher's performance with the goal of further defining or redefining his or her teaching with a view to maximizing student learning. Post-conferences should be viewed as being cumulative episodes that aid reflective, issues-centered teachers to experience where they have been and where they are going in terms of teaching social issues.

References

Acheson, K., and Gall, M. *Techniques in the Clinical Supervision of Teachers: Preservice and Inservice Applications* (3rd ed.). New York: Longman, 1992.

Anrig. G. R., and Lapointe, A. E. "What We Know About What Students Don't Know." *Educational Leadership* 47, no. 3 (1989), 4-10.

Berry, B., and Ginsberg, R. "Effective Schools, Teachers, and Principals: Today's Evidence, Tomorrow's Prospects." In B. Mitchell & L. Cunningham, eds., *Educational Leadership and Changing Contexts of Families, Communities, and Schools. Eighty-ninth Yearbook of the National Society for the Study of Education,* 1990: 155-183.

Blumberg, A. *Supervisors and Teachers: A Private Cold War* (2nd ed.). Berkeley, CA: McCutchan, 1980.

Cogan, M. *Clinical Supervision.* Boston, MA: Houghton Mifflin, 1973.

Darling-Hammond, L. & Sclan, E. "Policy and Supervision," In C. Glickman, ed., *Supervision in Transition,* 1992 Yearbook of the Association for Supervision and

Curriculum Development, 1992: 7-29.

Engle, S. H. and Ochoa, A. *Education for Democratic Citizenship.* New York: Teachers College Press, 1988.

Garman, N. "Theories Embedded in the Events of Clinical Supervision: A Hermeneutic Approach." *Journal of Curriculum and Supervision.* 5, no. 3 (1990): 201-13.

Garman, N. and Hazi, M. "Teachers Ask: Is There Life after Madeline Hunter?" *Phi Delta Kappan.* 69, no. 9 (1988): 669-72.

Garman, N., Glickman, C., Hunter, M., and Haggerson, N. "Conflicting Conceptions of Clinical Supervision and the Enhancement of Professional Growth and Renewal: Point and Counterpoint." *Journal of Curriculum and Supervision.* 2, no. 2 (1987): 152-177.

Gitlin, A., and Price, K. "Teacher Empowerment and the Development of Voice." In C. Glickman, ed., *Supervision in Transition.* 1992 Yearbook of the Association for Supervision and Curriculum Development, 1992: 61-74.

Glickman, C. *Supervision of Instruction: A Development Approach.* Boston: Allyn and Bacon, 1985.

Goldhammer, R., Anderson, R., and Krajewski, R. *Clinical Supervision: Special Methods for the Supervision of Teachers* (2nd ed.). New York: Holt, Rinehart and Winston, 1980.

Goldhammer, R. *Clinical Supervision: Special Methods for the Supervision of Teachers.* New York: Rinehart & Winston, 1969.

Grimmett, P. P., Rostad, P. O., and Ford, B. "The Transformation of Supervision." In C. Glickman, ed., *Supervision in Transition.* 1992 Yearbook of the Association for Supervision and Curriculum Development, 1992: 185-202.

Holland, P. "Implicit Assumptions about the Supervisory Conference: A Review and Analysis of Literature." *Journal of Curriculum and Supervision* 4, no. 4 (1989): 362-79.

Hunt, M., and Metcalf, L. *Teaching High Social Studies* (2nd Ed.) New York: Harper and Row, 1968.

Hunter, M., and Russell, D. "Planning for Effective Instruction: Lesson Design." In *Increasing your Teaching Effectiveness.* Palo Alto, CA: The Learning Institute, 1981.

Jerich, K. F. "Evaluating the Use of Clinical Supervision during pre- and post- Conferences Associated with Microteaching Practice in Teacher Education." *Action in Teacher Education,* 11, no. 4 (1989) 24-32.

Katz, L., and Raths, J. "Dispositions as Goals for Teacher Education." *Teaching and Teacher Education* 1, no. 4 (1985): 301-307.

McGreal, T. "Teacher-directed Evaluation of Teaching:

An Empirical Perspective." Paper presented at the meeting of the American Educational Research Association, Atlanta, GA, April 1993.

McGreal, T. *Successful Teacher Evaluation*. Alexandria, VA: Association for Supervision and Curriculum Development, 1983.

Murphy, J. "Preparing School Administrators for the Twenty-first Century: The Reform Agenda." In B. Mitchell and L. Cunningham, eds., *Educational Leadership and Changing Contexts of Families, Communities, and Schools*. Eighty-ninth Yearbook of the National Society for the Study of Education, 1990: 232-251.

Prawat, R. S. "The Value of Ideas: Problems versus Possibilities in Learning." *Educational Researcher* 22, no. 6 (1993): 5-16.

Rallis, S. F. "Professional Teachers and Restructured Schools: Leadership Challenges." In B. Mitchell and L. Cunningham, eds., *Educational Leadership and Changing Contexts of Families, Communities, and Schools*. Eighty-ninth Yearbook of the National Society for the Study of Education, 1990: 184-209.

Raths, L. E., Harmin, M., and Simon, S. *Values and Teaching: Working with Values in the Classroom*. Columbus: Merrill, 1986.

Schmuck, P., and Schmuck, R. "Democratic Participation in Small-town Schools." *Educational Researcher* 19, no. 8 (1990): 14-20.

Sergiovanni, T. "Landscapes, Mindscapes, and Reflective Practice in Supervision." *Journal of Curriculum and Supervision* 1, no. 1 (1985): 5-17.

Sergiovanni, T. J. "Moral Authority and the Regeneration of Supervision." In C. Glickman, ed., *Supervision in Transition*. 1992 Yearbook of the Association for Supervision and Curriculum Development, 1992: 203-214.

Sergiovanni, T. and Starratt, R. *Emerging Patterns of Supervision: Human Perspectives*. New York: McGraw Hill, 1973.

Smyth, J. (1988). "A 'Critical' Perspective for Clinical Supervision." *Journal of Curriculum and Supervision* 3, no. 2 (1988): 136-56.

[4] Taken from *Devancy and Sykes, "Making the Case for Professionalism."*

[5] See Fuller's work on *The Stages of Teacher Concerns*.

[6] For a more detailed explanation, see Blumberg's *Supervisors and Teachers: A Private Cold War* (1980).

[7] See Engle & Ochoa (1988), *Education for Democratic Citizenship* for a detailed explanation of Jadallah's observation instrument.

---

[1] For a detailed explanation of bureaucratic supervision, see the 1992 Yearbook of the Association for Supervision and Curriculum Development.

[2] See Acheson and Gall, *Techniques in the Clinical Supervision of Teachers* (1992), for complete definitions and descriptions of supervisory strategies.

[3] For a detailed explanation of these supervisory strategies, see Glickman's *Supervision of Instruction: A Developmental Approach* (1985).

Part Ten: Future Oriented, Issues-Centered Education

Introduction by James Barth

Educational reconstructionists, led by George Counts and Theodore Brameld, held that the schools could lead society toward a better future. It was not that the future was pre-determined but rather that helping others to know what the future should be like would contribute to achieving that future. Viewing reconstructionism from the 1990s, some sixty years since George Counts asked: "Dare the schools build a new social order?", there is a sense of naivite about reconstructionists and their Utopian fervor. Who today would suggest that America's schools could lead us toward a better societal life? The faith we once had, not so long ago, in our public schools has faded and in its place is a growing sense of doubt that our schools can even minimally meet the challenges of today, let alone of the future.

Notwithstanding this, many of us continue to pursue curricular reform and new visions for the social studies. It is difficult to imagine anything more relevant to the quality of our lives than an education designed to help us deal with the inevitable conundrums and challenges of a future burdened with a continuing explosion of both knowledge and technology.

In this section devoted to future-oriented social studies education, Wilma Longstreet delves into the alternative futures of social studies in American education. The disintegration of our values and of the concepts that once structured our interactions with each other are discussed in terms of the current social studies program and its inadequacies. Alternative curricula are proposed as ways of increasing the relevance and effectiveness of schooling.

James Barth explores the development of social studies as a world-wide movement. The array of purposes each nation associates with the social studies presents us with a spectrum of alternatives representative, on the one hand, of where the field has been and, on the other, of the field's potential future directions. Most representative of all is the internationalization of the social studies and, by inference, a progressive movement toward international citizenship.

The efforts of Longstreet and Barth are the very embodiment of the hope that many of us still hold for education. While it is true that cynicism and discouragement have become embedded in our educational thinking, it is equally true that cynicism presupposes idealism, and discouragement turns quickly into encouragement with even the faintest hint of success. These two chapters are dedicated to the ideals we hold and the encouragement we feel for the future of social studies education.

34 ALTERNATIVE FUTURES AND THE SOCIAL STUDIES

by Wilma S. Longstreet

Alternative futures are at the heart of issues-centered social studies education. Every time we make a decision about an economic, political, or social issue, we are also making a judgment, consciously or otherwise, about the future course of our society. There are, however, so many issues, so many judgments to be made, so many uncertainties to confront—and so little reflection on our parts about the future and the alternatives it poses for us—that we are hardly cogent in our decision making. We seem to veer mindlessly first in one direction, then in another.

While we continue to study primarily history in the social studies classroom, in the real world of politics we rarely use historical studies to deal logically with current issues of governance or to plan our national futures. We appear to have difficulty in making rational connections (where they do exist) between history, the realities of daily life, and the futures that loom ahead. Memorizing the salient dates of the Civil War or understanding the crucial place of the Monroe Doctrine in our relations with Latin American countries have had limited transfer value for our students and their performances as citizens. There is significant distance between knowing about the events and relationships of our historical roots and engaging in the kind of decision making that is at the heart of any form of democracy—and that ought to be at the heart of the social studies, as Shirley H. Engle (1960) noted decades ago.

The ground-covering way we pursue the study of history has contributed little to the development of decision-making skills among the population. Indeed, judging from our voting record, it may even be a cause of the detachment and apathy that many in our society feel toward the issues of the day and our collective, civic futures. There are, of course, other probable causes for our increasing reluctance to engage civically. We are a people brought up on television and sitcom problems that have clear beginnings, highly stimulating middles, and neat endings. No matter how complex a problem may be, it is usually resolved happily in less than an hour. We are a people that have come to read less, and despite a tremendous increase in the information available to us, we appear bored with it all and unwilling to use it in our decision making. We have, on the whole, come to be apathetic toward, and even angry with, the workings of our democratic republic. Our newspapers continually berate Congress for engaging in extended discussions about the federal budget, social programs, defense, or whatever the current conundrum happens to be, as they and we, their readers, complain about too much talk and too little action. Scorn is heaped on our legislators for being too talkative and apparently unable to bring closure to the nation's problems. Never mind that democracy is about building, often slowly and painfully, compromises that can somehow take most of us and our needs into account. One cannot help but wonder what the newspapers of today would have written about the long discussions that went on during the making of the Constitution and its troubled acceptance by the states. We appear to have taken the position that long, indecisive discussions even about significant, complex issues are indicative of national weakness and failure.

Our reluctance to be engaged by issues creates the conditions for a self-fulfilling prophecy. We do not expect our individual participation to make a difference in the way the future unfolds, therefore, we do not participate, *and we do not make a difference.* The challenge for social studies educators is to turn this situation around by focusing the attention of young people on key, often controversial, issues and by helping them to develop attitudes, skills, and conceptual insights conducive to wise decision making about their civic lives, i.e., about decisions which inevitably affect their individual and collective futures.

This chapter will explore potential curricular revisions of the social studies in terms of an issue-centered, futures orientation. In particular, the following topics will be pursued:

1. the nature of decision making in a democracy and in an era of persistent, continually accelerating change;
2. the adequacy of traditional school subjects (history, the social sciences, and the liberal arts) to serve as the foundation for dealing with current issues and future planning;
3. the role of issues in preparing for the future and the persistence of democracy; and
4. the future-oriented, issues-centered curriculum.

The Nature of Decision Making in a Democracy

In everyday language we allow connotative terms to float unclearly among their various meanings. We often use such terms in our educational jargon. For instance, the term *problem solving* may be used in one discourse to refer to the finding of solutions to mathematical problems and in another discourse to dealing with unpredictable, poorly defined social situations, requiring public relations skills and considerable flexibility. The important point to note here is that this widely used term can represent significantly different skills, attitudes, and conceptual understandings. To say that we want our students to be problem solvers is not by itself sufficient guidance for curricular revision.

The term *decision making* poses similar difficulties. Decision making in the context of a scientific discipline involves deciding about specific parameters, i.e., stipulating the definition of terms, determining the specific methods of investigation, limiting the problem to manageable proportions, and so forth. Decision making within democratic citizenship means trying to understand the complexities and ambiguities that problems typically exhibit as well as learning to make decisions in the face of confusion and uncertainty. It means being able to be tentative and willing to modify decisions as new circum-

stances develop while remaining civically involved and active. There is, in other words, a unique nature to the decision making of citizens involved in the workings of democracy that is somewhat obscured by the wide-ranging connotations associated with the term. Ongoing tentativeness and the continual revision of what ought not to be more than provisional conclusions are essential components to the citizen's decision-making behavior. To be willing to decide despite the ambiguity and seemingly endless debates surrounding a problem, and subsequently to be willing to change one's mind are behaviors that lie at the very core of what it means to participate in a democracy and the planning for its future.

The Adequacy of Traditional Disciplines in Futures Planning

Early in the twentieth century, the sociologist Thomas Jesse Jones proposed redirecting the school study of history toward studies that would contribute directly to the development of good citizens and the betterment of human life (Kliebard 1987; U.S. Bureau of Education 1913). Jones introduced into the school's curriculum the term, "social studies," which continues to be used today. However, as O. L. Davis Jr. (1992, 20) noted, "The social studies never overthrew school history from the curriculum." We have persisted in our pursuit of factually based history as witnessed most recently in the California social studies framework (California Department of Education 1987), which increased the breadth and depth of studies in history, geography, and the social sciences, and in the National Commission on Social Studies in the Schools (1989) report, which recommended three years of in-depth studies in world and U.S. history and geography for high school students. Judging from the report, the Commission considered the study of current problems and issues as having only peripheral importance.

The idea that the experiences of our past, as recounted through history, could contribute to improved decision making in the present has steadily lost validity. Once a reasonable basis existed for expecting the patterns of past experiences to presage current and future patterns. What we induce from history, we induce on the basis of expecting history to, in some way, repeat itself. The fact is we are confronting changes of such magnitude that the inductive uses of history to inform us about present and future behavior are increasingly irrelevant and indefensible. Even Dewey's (Kliebard 1992) conception of school history as a source of perspective and moral guidance for the present is of questionable viability.

The past may have some role in helping us to understand the future, but hardly in the way or to the degree that once was true. In the past, major societal changes in our beliefs, goals, visions, and behaviors were associated with the generational passage of power. The term generation gap has long stood for the differences among generations arising from the propensity of younger people to criticize and evaluate the power brokers of their own day, usually their elders, and from the inevitable "distinctiveness of events" (Bingham 1991), which occurs even when the basic modalities of living have hardly changed. Generation gap is reflective of a passage from the old order to the new order, which, nevertheless, remains quite similar to the old order in most of its structures. In the course of the twentieth century, the generation gap has continued to be a phenomenon of societal life, but its role in cultural upheavals, which have been the central experience of the twentieth century, has diminished considerably. As Alfred North Whitehead (1967) noted in 1929, we can no longer assume "that each generation will live in an environment substantially similar to that of the preceding generation."

We are confronted with more than a cultural gap between generations. Ours is an age dominated by *intragenerational disjunctures.* Significant and quite numerous differences in our way of life arise *within the span of a single generation.* Raging technological revolution has brought us to intragenerational disjuncture, wherein the upbringing of our childhood is largely inoperative for the judgments we must make in our adult lives; and the environments we took for granted as children have been so modified that the assumptions we persist in having about them—assumptions garnered from the experiences of our early years—can mislead and confound the decisions we must take as adults and as citizens (Longstreet and Shane 1993). Persistent, intragenerational disjunctures have fundamentally altered the potentiality of childhood so that childhood no longer offers us a "natural" base from which to view and judge the directions of our lifelong, social existence. We are repeatedly confronted with issues the likes of which have never before challenged humankind and most certainly were not factors in the development of our early belief systems.

This century has witnessed a disintegration not so much of our values but rather of our ability to sustain them. We still acknowledge such basic precepts as doing unto others as we would have them do unto us and honoring our mothers and fathers, but we hardly know how to translate these maxims to apply them to our new realities. For example, if an egg fertilized in vitro (i.e., a "test-tube" egg) were terminated, would that be the equivalent of abortion? What are the ethics involved in having a child for the purpose of transplanting one of its organs to another human being? What does honoring one's father and mother mean to the child who has had several stepfathers and rarely sees his or her biological father?

An Example of Intragenerational Disjuncture

President Harry S Truman probably belonged to the first generation of Americans to have fully experienced intragenerational disjuncture. He was born in 1884 well before automobiles, jet airplanes, motion pictures, radios, air conditioners, and television sets had become culturally ubiquitous and embedded in the very structure of our daily lives; he died in 1972 when all of these and more had become entrenched aspects of our daily lives. There had been little in the first 16 years of young Truman's life and education that in any way prepared him for the drastic changes and traumatic decisions he would face in his lifetime. Truman's most momentous decision, whether to drop an atomic bomb during World War II that would surely kill thousands of Japanese civilians, was taken with precious little understanding, even among the experts of the day, of radiation poisoning and its long-term fallout (McCullough 1992). What could the study of history have told Truman about global villages, nuclear weapons, or artificial intelligence as he grew up in Independence, Missouri, in the 1880s and 1890s when none of these were even glimmers in the historian's firmament?

The public arena is full of talk about how to restore traditional values to society and return our youth to a sense of responsibility. However, restoration of values is really not the question. Clearly, we still share a fundamental core of beliefs about what is right, for otherwise the widespread discomfort about not living up to our values, expressed repeatedly in our mass media, would hardly be a factor in our public discourse. Nor could any form of democracy survive without its members having a shared core of beliefs. It is the pursuit of our values through essentially new and unforeseen circumstances and the often inappropriate match between value(s) and circumstance(s) that results in a sense of continuing frustration. The study of history—as most of us have encountered it in school—does little to contribute to our understanding of issues and circumstances literally unimaginable in the past.

Hardison (1989) has suggested that we are currently experiencing the disappearance of concepts we once took for granted, e.g., nature, reality, and even humanity. Certainly, nature in terms of quarks, lightning speeds, and surrealistic visions of Earth from outer space is a profoundly different experience from the one so idealized by Rousseau in the 1700s and Wordsworth in the 1800s. Increasingly, media control our perceptions of reality, and the distinction between reality and virtual reality is becoming progressively more difficult for us to make.

Our conception of the social studies has become uncomfortably caught between the traditional duties of the cultural conservator involved in transmitting the accumulated wisdom of our past to the young and the growing urgency to prepare them to cope with an uncertain, quite different, highly complex, and not very distant future. Unlike in any other period in human history, the study of the past is of limited relevance and questionable usefulness to today's youth in helping them to prepare for their futures. It provides important data about how problems were solved but not necessarily about how to solve today's problems. The challenge that faces those of us who qualify as "elders" is to transform our knowledge and experience into a curriculum both relevant and useful to a generation whose lives are likely to be profoundly different from our own. They will have to contend not only with the generation gap but with intragenerational disjunctures. In terms of schooling, the challenge is one of transfer, i.e., of having what is studied in school

apply to what is experienced civically outside of school. Judging from the public's low participation in elections and apparent lack of understanding about the workings of a democratic republic (Bennett 1988; Ravitch and Finn 1987), history, as we have traditionally experienced it, is necessary but not sufficient for the task.

From time to time in the twentieth century, the study of the social sciences has been seen as providing us with a different and more adequate filter than that of history. In 1937 Edgar Wesley equated the social sciences with the social studies (Wesley and Wronski 1958). In the 1960s the *New Social Studies*, largely supported by federal grants, undertook to engage social studies students in the social sciences as though they were scientists out in the field (Senesch 1965; Bruner 1974). Though the federally funded projects were well financed and largely run by social science experts, little remains in today's curriculum of those efforts.

Nevertheless, the social sciences provide an important source of theoretical knowledge about our human ways of behaving and our forms of governance (Fraenkel 1973). Their efforts to approach human behavior from a scientific perspective have led to the valuable accumulation of scientifically configured data collected as objectively as possible. As input for civic decision making, objective data is extraordinarily useful. Learning to achieve objective data as scientists would give students an understanding of the desirability of a value-free environment as well as expertise in behaving with objectivity.

There are, however, drawbacks. *Objectivity* means, to quote the *American Heritage Dictionary*, that the data collected is "uninfluenced by emotion, surmise, or personal prejudice." A curriculum centered on achieving skills in objectivity and social scientific methodology is clearly inappropriate for the achievement of objectives related to good citizenship and the subjective valuing that goes with it. Being a good social scientist requires skills that may be only peripherally related to those needed to be a good citizen. The decision making of the social scientist is essentially different from the decision making of a citizen in a democracy. A quarter of a century ago, Shirley H. Engle (1970, 778) made the point that

To make the social sciences the sole basis of citizenship education is to place values and the valuing process outside the pale of social education, since the social sciences are value free.

In terms of the challenges likely to confront youngsters in their not-too-distant future, making value judgments about issues that often have no clear resolution and embody multiple value conflicts must be at the crux of what is studied in the social studies. Like history, the social sciences offer us resources for making decisions, but they help us only indirectly to learn the processes and attitudes of democratic decision making.

Intragenerational disjunctures require us to reconceptualize the purposes of schooling in general and the social studies in particular. The enculturation process that occurs naturally and powerfully in our youngest years, that embeds in us our cultural membership and plants ideas that guide us throughout life, has also come to be the process that most diminishes our ability to evaluate the quality and desirability of change occurring around us. We become encapsulated, i.e., our ability to reason reflectively about the major issues of our times is dominated by "an unconscious 'gut-level' adherence to an interlocking fabric of ideas, ideals, beliefs, values, assumptions, and modes of thought that have been implanted by cultural forces" (Zais 1976, 218). The enculturative processes establish in us a multiplicity of unconscious cultural mind-sets that impede our ability to go beyond the traditional limits of a situation or problem. Enculturation and the subsequent cultural encapsulation of adulthood restrict our ability to think beyond the traditional limits set by the society of our childhood—limits communicated to us by parents who could not possibly have known the numbers and kinds of challenges that we would face as adults. The crisis in values so often sung in newspapers and journals today is largely a crisis between our early enculturation and the array of decisions confronting us, both personal and societal, for which we have almost no preparation. Enculturation allowed to continue its own "natural" course of development directly impedes our ability to deal with the inevitable crises of intragenerational disjunctures, and with the decisions we must make about the direction and nature of our collective futures. The school's curriculum must embody ways of helping young people to confront essentially new issues in terms that help them to move beyond the limits of their own cultural perspectives.

Studying Issues in the Study of Futures

Engle and Ochoa (1988) considered the uses of humanities in social education. As with the social sciences, they found the humanities to be valuable resources for citizenship education but inadequate to the task. The humanities "seek to illuminate the meaning of life" (56), while allowing subjectivity and value judgments to influence their decisions. However, in their view, taken alone, the humanities "are a mixture of the bizarre as well as the substantial" (60). Engle and Ochoa believed that the social sciences and the humanities must be viewed as symbiotic resources that, when taken together, can provide "future citizens with compelling insights into social issues" (56). The study of issues offers a way of linking the many different kinds of insights and understandings acquired from formal structures of knowledge with the numerous, emotion-filled, value-laden civic decisions that repeatedly confront us.

While the social sciences operationalize definitions and converge on specifics, the humanities deal broadly not only with the issues but with the human emotions and subjective reactions that so often complicate the resolution of issues. The humanities can explore new ways of connecting human experience and new approaches to the future. They push at the edges of the possible and help us intuit what we may later discover or invent.

While the traditional social studies program might support the study of future-oriented issues from time to time, it does so at the risk of distorting the study of the disciplines. What is important to understand about a curriculum emphasizing disciplines is that each discipline, whether it be history, or economics, or geography, possesses a structure based on a unique set of concepts, facts, generalizations, and processes that must be learned in their uniqueness (Morrisett 1967; Broek 1965) or else the discipline is not really being studied. In the traditional social studies curriculum, the study of issues could be considered a distracter from the study of disciplines, which, after all, "will be on the test!" In reality, the disciplines serve as distracters interfering with students learning how to engage actively and effectively as citizens of a democracy.

Of course, not all issues are of equal worth in terms of preparation for democratic citizenship.

Studies about the future can be and often have been undertaken in terms of broadly conceived topics without a controversial component. For example, a set of scenarios may be utilized to represent, in a neutral fashion, daily life in the year 2045. The view embedded in this kind of curricular approach is that the future is part of the inevitable cultural drift of society; it is, therefore, in our best interest to understand and prepare for our most likely futures. This seeming neutrality toward the future often leads students to accept the future as though its progression were inevitable rather than a result of the choices made as people and their society traverse a series of controversial issues.

Among the guidelines for issues-centered education put forth by Engle and Ochoa (1988) is that topics or episodes that are not problematic should not be included in the curriculum. This is a crucial curricular position. Learning to deal with hotly contested issues is at the very core of whatever capacity youngsters may develop in directing their own futures as citizens of a democracy.

Furthermore, students must experience active involvement in a wide variety of controversial issues. As John Dewey often noted, no one experience, no one issue can, by itself, be considered of greatest value to education; it is only in terms of what an issue moves toward or into that we can judge its value. To quote Dewey (1938, 87), we need

> to select those things within the range of existing experience that have the promise and potentiality of presenting new problems which by stimulating new ways of observation and judgment will expand the area of further experience.

Dewey believed that if the young rarely encountered controversy in their studies, they would have a fixed and static conception of the ideas involved and would probably not understand how they function in the social milieu. I would further suggest that if the young do not deal with controversial issues of significance for the future directions of society, they are likely to have a conception of the future statically mired in the experiences of their own childhood; they will, in other words, conceive of solutions to the controversies of their futures as though their futures were their past. This is, after all, what we adults are doing today as we increasingly and ineffectually demand a return to traditional values and to the traditional family unit. We are caught in the enculturation of our past.

Future-Oriented, Issues-Centered Curriculum

There are several ways of approaching the development of future-oriented curricula. One, discussed above, involves a neutral overview of likely futures. The future is neither good nor bad, acceptable nor unacceptable, but merely on its way, and we must prepare our young for what it will bring. The RAND Corporation and the Futures Society often issue reports of this ilk. For instance, we might find among their reports that the business office of the future will be in our home, or that distance education will become a significant component of undergraduate instruction, or that virtual reality will be a significant part of on-the-job training. Alvin Toffler's trilogy (1970, 1980, 1990) dealing with the future also makes predictions of this kind. As an example, Toffler (1990) states:

> If large numbers can participate in a mass-appeal game show like *Jeopardy* with a computer tallying their responses, it doesn't take too much imagination to see how similar technology could be adapted to political polling or collective decision-making—and political organizing of a new kind.

It is a matter-of-fact discussion of future directions rooted in our present experience. While Toffler recognizes the social tensions likely to arise, he does not reflect much on how citizens might control and redirect their futures. The future is caught in cultural drift and is going to happen.

The Neutral Approach in Curriculum

In this neutral approach to futures studies, the futures curriculum is typically based on traditional research methodologies linked to scenario activities. The *scenario* itself is used as a tool to explore possible futures in an objective fashion. A range of scenarios involving the major activities of society ensures an adequate scope of study. Issues, when dealt with, are rooted in this milieu of objectivity. A *Delphi technique*, which involves surveying expert opinions, may be employed as a way of deciding upon the most likely of scenarios; discussions might follow along the lines of what must be done to best prepare for the future. Students may engage in *trends analysis*, which investigates, usually in terms of demographics and economics, series of related events and their likely persistence in the future. Students may learn how to conduct *linear projections* involving descriptive data about current circumstances. They may also undertake *cross-impact analyses*, in which they pursue the interrelationships of multiple changes and the impact each would have on the other(s). Another widely used methodology that students may pursue is *environmental scanning*, which involves a continual scanning of systemic, worldwide events in order to ascertain the development of new, possibly unexpected trends.

Certainly a futures unit (or even several units) based on research studies or a combination of scenario and research studies could be inserted into the traditional social studies curriculum. In comparison to other current curricular activities, this would be a somewhat innovative approach. However, little would really change. The objectivity of the scientific disciplines would be exchanged for a value-free albeit topical approach to the study of the future. The kinds of perplexing and often frustrating decisions confronting citizens as well as their need to decide, while remaining tentative and open to other possibilities, would hardly be developed in this neutral approach to the study of the future.

The Controversial Approach in a Futures Curriculum

A controversial approach to futures studies offers greater potential for developing more involved and competent citizens. As Engle and Ochoa (1988, 105) noted, the study of controversial social issues contributes to the "countersocialization" of children, enabling them to face issues in an open and creative fashion.

The circumstances that have led to intragenerational disjuncture require the schools to participate in the enculturative process in a different way and from an essentially new perspective. The schools must see themselves as contributors to the *un*encapsulation of adulthood, i.e., to giving adults greater control over their early cultural development. Instilling a neutral perspective of the future does not correspond to the real circumstances of democratic citizenship in either today's or tomorrow's world. It also does not challenge the values and beliefs acquired in childhood.

The educational conundrum we must face is how to contend with the enculturative process so that schooling can contribute to a coherent society while not embedding traditions in youngster's minds that interfere with their ability to confront their civic problems and participate in the direction of their futures. How do we redirect enculturation from a process that fixes beliefs and closes the mind to one that opens the mind to thoughtfulness about not only the past but the complex issues of the future? Asking the question from another vantage point, how do we enculturate the willingness to reflect upon new ideas and new ways of doing things while maintaining a respect for the great insights of our past? How do we build those inner intellectual, emotional, and attitudinal resources that can help children to see beyond their immediate cultural circumstances? How do we make active participation in the decision-making processes of our democracy a fundamental result of the school's curriculum?

It is clear that a controversial approach to issues, especially those concerning the future directions of society, is a necessary revision to today's social studies curriculum. Children must consider changing what adults of today may be quite satisfied with; and they must deal with issues that adults might prefer to ignore. Children must become "transformative intellectuals" (Giroux and McLaren 1986), i.e., capable of taking an active role in recasting the values and experiences of their heritage into new, albeit still democratic, forms of governance and social life so as to better suit a future we adults can hardly conceive.

The tools of future-oriented studies discussed above as typical components of a neutral approach (the scenario, trends analysis, cross impact analysis, etc.) are equally important to the controversial approach. However, instead of these tools being used to describe the likely faces of tomorrow, they would be employed in helping students to resolve controversial issues. For example, multiple models of the future could be developed for the purpose of comparing and evaluating their likely outcomes. Students could be encouraged to take positions and defend them utilizing scenarios and the research tools.

The Core of the Futures Curriculum

In reconceptualizing the social studies curriculum, regardless of whether we pursue a neutral or controversial approach, we must respond to the question: What knowledge is most useful for helping citizens of a democracy deal with issues and give direction to the future? As educators, we must know that the scope of issues dealt with responds adequately to this question. At least six areas of societal endeavor appear most relevant to our future directions and respond to this key curricular question:

1. communication and information handling
2. uncertainties
3. values development
4. democratic citizenship
5. inquiries; and
6. futures (Longstreet 1979).

Each of the areas holds the potential for helping people to deal more competently with the issues confronting them and with the cultural encapsulation that tends to limit their ability to confront new issues and to develop new value systems.

1 Communication and information handling would involve studying the impact of media on the meaning and understanding that we hold of an issue (McLuhan 1964). It is a subject that would need to be pursued K–12 and beyond. It would help students to examine for each issue how they came to know about the issue, what effects the communication of the issue has had upon their views, and what questions must be pursued if a reasonably broad and fair presentation of the issue is to be achieved. Developing communication literacy is especially important for redirecting the enculturative process from one leading to cultural encapsulation to one building independence of thought. Establishing communication and information handling as a component of the social studies recognizes the need for people to understand and exercise control over the production, uses, and dissemination of information. Video literacy is hardly considered in the current curriculum even though it is widely recognized that our perceptions of the issues are in many ways controlled by the media.

2 Uncertainties would involve issues related to change and the continuing explosion of knowledge and technology. History and great literary works contain many examples of humanity's struggles both against and within uncertainty. An exploration of likely future uncertainties would form a significant base of study. *Evolution, progress* and *democracy* are among the ideas replete

with uncertainty and, as a correlate, with controversy. Ideas such as these form fulcrums around which major issues would be organized. Specific issues under 'progress' might include: Einstein's general theory of relativity and the upheaval that it has brought to our understanding of time and of the nature of the universe; the continuing failure to find adequate storage for nuclear waste and its possible repercussions for our way of life; the hypothetical but not improbable decline in reading and the parallel rise in other means of communicating information. Studying the multiple possibilities in outcomes and repercussions and dealing with the kinds of decisions that might have to be made despite uncertainty would comprise the real content of this subject.

3 Values development would have little to do with the traditional passing on of values from one generation to the next. Rather, it would involve students in the active formation of their own values as individuals and as citizens of a democracy. The process of value formation as a school study is viewed as being analytical, critically evaluative, moving toward generality from a fundamentally subjective base and necessarily controversial.

A series of questions would serve to organize the subject as well as to ensure an in-depth exploration of values. Among these would be: What is useful about having values? Should individually based or societally based values take precedence? Are all values culturally relative or are some values absolute and culture free? How should we go about establishing new values? absolute values? What comprises a good life? What do I most value about my future life?

4 Democratic citizenship would deal with the rise and evolution of U.S. democracy and include comparative studies with other democracies around the world and other forms of governance. In many ways, this would be similar to the ever-present course in civics that most students currently take. Emphasis, however, would be placed on the development of decision-making skills related to the exercise of democratic citizenship. These involve making decisions in the midst of conflicting values, being willing to confront complexity rather than settling for simplistic solutions, working toward long-term goals as well as short-term objectives, making tentative albeit firm judgments while remaining willing to revise judgments in the light of new input, and being knowledgeable about the realities of the political process. This area of study would be closely linked to values development because the content would stress political phenomena, governance structures, and the activities of citizens, all of which are heavily value-oriented. In the last years of high school, the social science disciplines could be offered to students for elective study, a considerable reversal of what usually occurs now when the social studies curriculum offers a problems course or participation in a civic experience in the twelfth grade while concentrating on the disciplines (in particular, history) in the lower grades.

Democratic citizenship would also include active participation in the workings of local and possibly federal government along with studies of significant current issues of governance. As recommended by Engle and Ochoa (1988), a full year, one-day per week citizenship internship directed toward some socially useful enterprise would serve as the culmination of students' active involvement.

5 Inquiries would involve the study of diverse research methodologies ranging from classical scientific inquiry to humanistic modes of inquiry to new, paradigm-breaking forms such as are now developing in the science of Chaos, as these are needed in confronting a variety of controversial issues. It would include, when appropriate, the future-oriented research methodologies discussed above. Both quantitative and qualitative forms of inquiry would be studied from kindergarten through the last grade of high school in an effort to increase students' abilities to deal independently with the significant issues of their times by researching the issues they believe are central to their understanding of what is involved in making a decision.

6 Futures, as a component of the social studies curriculum, would serve as the linking "hub" for the other five components because it would utilize the processes, attitudes, and skills learned in these to develop scenarios of likely futures. Research tools such as environmental scanning and trends analysis would be drawn from the subject of inquiries; analyses pursued in values development and insights into the nature of democracy derived from studies in democratic citizenship would contribute to the quality of judgments made in laying out desirable futures;

uncertainties, of course, would contribute to students' abilities to envision multiple possibilities; and communication and information handling would provide the expressive skills needed in the development of scenarios. With regard to the latter point, scenarios could be presented, utilizing the video camera, the computer, written forms, or a combination of these.

The scenarios would be of several types ranging from linear projections based on quantitative data to more fanciful predictions of an ideal life. In students' earlier years, scenarios would be built around small, concrete experiences subject to improvement or change. For example, a scenario could be developed around ways of improving the neighborhood or the components of an ideal school. Subsequently, more advanced futures studies would become involved in complex plans such as the achievement of a pollution-free urban environment or colonizing other planets in our galaxy.

The radical changes we have been through and those still confronting us require educational activism—i.e., an aggressive effort to fundamentally change how we educate. The various revisions of curriculum discussed here are barely more than a beginning effort. The future and the exploration of civic issues have long been discussed in our educational literature and, for the most part, ignored by the schools. It is time for us to move beyond.

References

Bennett, W. J. "American Education: Making It Work." *The Chronicle of Higher Education* (May 4, 1988): 29–41.

Bingham, M. "A History Based Social Studies Curriculum." Paper presented at the annual conference of the National Council for the Social Studies, Washington D.C., November 1991.

Broek, J. O. M. *Geography: Its Scope and Spirit.* Columbus, Ohio: Charles E. Merrill, 1965.

Bruner, J. S. "Man: A Course of Study." Social Studies Curriculum Project. Cambridge, MA: Educational Services, 1974.

California Department of Education. *History-Social Science Framework.* Sacramento, Calif.: Department of Education, 1987.

Davis, O.L., Jr. "'Your Mother Wears Army Shoes!' The Silly Debate between School History and the Social Studies." In *Citizenship as Social Studies Education.* Bulletin 4. Munster, Ind.: National Council for the

Social Studies Special Interest Group—Foundations of the Social Studies, 1992.

Dewey, J. *Experience and Education.* New York: Teachers College Press, 1938.

Engle, Shirley H. "Decision Making: The Heart of Social Studies Instruction." *Social Education* 24(November 1960): 301–4, 306.

Engle, S. H. "The Future of Social Studies Education and NCSS." *Social Education* 34 (1970): 778–81, 793.

Engle, S. H., and A. S. Ochoa. *Education for Democratic Citizenship: Decision-Making in the Social Studies.* New York: Teachers College Press, 1988.

Fraenkel, Jack R. *Helping Students Think and Value.* Englewood Cliffs, N.J.: Prentice Hall, 1973.

Giroux, H. A., and P. McLaren. "Teacher Education and the Politics of Engagement: The Case for Democratic Schooling." *Harvard Educational Journal* 56(1986): 213–38.

Haas, J. *The Era of the New Social Studies.* Boulder, CO: ERIC Clearinghouse for Social Studies/Social Science Education, 1977.

Hardison, O. B., Jr. *Disappearing through the Skylight: Culture and Technology in the Twentieth Century.* New York: Viking, 1989.

Kliebard, H. M. *The Struggle for the American Curriculum: 1893–1958.* New York: Routledge, 1987.

Kliebard, H.M. *Forging the American Curriculum: Essays in Curriculum History and Theory.* New York: Routledge, 1992.

Longstreet, W. S. "Open Education—A Coming to Terms with Uncertainty." In *Lifelong Learning: A Human Agenda,* edited by N. V. Overly. Alexandria, Va.: Association for Supervision and Curriculum Development, 1979.

Longstreet, W., and H. Shane. *Curriculum for a New Millennium.* Boston: Allyn and Bacon, 1993.

McCullough, David. *Truman.* New York: Simon and Schuster, 1992.

McLuhan, M. *Understanding Media.* New York: Bantam, 1964.

Morrisett, I., ed. *Concepts and Structures in the New Social Science Curricula.* New York: Holt, Rinehart and Winston, 1967.

National Commission on Social Studies in the Schools. *Charting a Course: Social Studies for the 21st Century.* Washington D. C.: National Council for the Social Studies, 1989.

Ravitch, D., and C. Finn. *What Do Our 17 Year-Olds Know?* New York: Harper and Row, 1987.

Senesch, L. *Our Working World.* Chicago: Science Research Associates, 1969.

Toffler, A. *Future Shock.* New York: Random House, 1970.

Toffler, A. *The Third Wave.* Toronto: William Morrow, 1980.

Toffler, A. *Powershift: Knowledge, Wealth, and Violence at the Edge of the 21st Century.* New York: Bantam Books, 1990.

U.S. Department of Education. "Preliminary Statements by Chairmen of Committees of the Commission of the National Education Association on the Reorganization of Secondary Education." Washington, D.C.: U.S. Bureau of Education Bulletin no. 41, 1913.

Wesley, E.B., and S. P. Wronski. *Teaching the Social Studies: Theory and Practice.* Boston: D. C. Heath, 1958.

Whitehead, A. N. *The Aims of Education and Other Essays.* 1929. Reprint, New York: The Free Press, 1967.

Zais, R. S. *Curriculum: Principles and Foundations.* New York: Thomas Y. Crowell Company, 1976.

35 THE ALTERNATIVE FUTURES OF INTERNATIONAL SOCIAL STUDIES

by James L. Barth

Almost forty years ago as a new social studies teacher, I considered my field as only an extension of the American experience and thus exclusively an American creation. International social studies—let alone a concept of alternative futures—was completely unheard of and, for me, several decades in my future. I had no knowledge that countries in Europe, Africa, and Asia were adopting social studies and also struggling with the field's definitions, purposes, aims, and goals. But then why should I have known about the struggle? After all, social studies was just some turn-of-the-century reform of U. S. citizenship education, discussed in theory but not practiced in my school.

Now in the 1990s, social studies as a school subject has become a recognized field worldwide. This, however, is not to say that all countries have adopted social studies as their citizenship education programs, nor have those same countries necessarily chosen the U. S. vision proclaimed by the National Council for the Social Studies (NCSS 1994). The field has become a major international citizenship educational reform movement. If the past forty years are any suggestion, the twenty-first century will witness many alternative futures for citizenship education as the social studies movement continues to gain international momentum. A place to start imagining such futures is by noting future visions of selected countries around the world in light of social studies' past.

Alternative Visions of Social Studies

While purposes attributed to the social studies vary from nation to nation, there does appear to be an underlying, unifying theme captured well by Wesley and Wronski (1973): *"The objec-*

tive of the social studies is to prepare students for intelligent membership in society." It is important to note, however, that Wesley and Wronski's is indeed an American perspective. South Korea's vision of preparing students for "intelligent membership" is different:

> The tendency is one in which the social studies courses give students political knowledge and not the political attitudes of democratic citizens ... the most important purpose of political education in schools has been to maintain the stability of the existing political system. (Chung 1994, 3)

On the other hand, in the West African country of The Gambia, progress, peace, and prosperity are the aims that constitute the basis for their schools' social studies course:

> To implant certain ideals and moral values in the minds of the young has always been among the many reasons for teaching social studies. This is an essential part of education. (Ministry of Education, Youth, Sports, and Culture 1980, 1)

A Nigerian vision would see social studies as:

> the investigation of human activity. It studies man at home, at work, at worship, in politics, at play, in the village, in the nation, everywhere engaged in his busy programme of living. (DuBey 1980, 1)

In addition to intelligent membership, preparation for democracy has been a persistent characteristic of the social studies, as NCSS (1994, vii) declared in its statement of purpose:

The primary purpose of social studies is to help young people develop the ability to make informed and reasoned decisions for the public good as citizens of a culturally diverse, democratic society in an interdependent world.

For many U.S. educators, but not necessarily for Nigerians, Gambians, and South Koreans, "the most important original intent of [social studies] education" is "teaching for democratic life" (Rolheiser and Glickman 1995, 196). Japanese educators may have a slightly different vision that would suggest cultivation of a democratic and peaceful nation but yet:

> The primary objective of social studies is to provide pupils with an understanding of society, and to support their desirable attitudes by establishing a firm foundation for correct moral decisions. (Nagai 1983, 66)

The Tanzanians have a slightly different vision. The aims of social studies are:

> To equip learners with knowledge, skills and attitudes for tackling societal problems. To develop a Tanzanian culture that perpetuates the national heritage, individual freedom, responsibility, tolerance and pays respect to elders. To develop in each citizen an enquiring and open mind clear of bias and prejudice, and a Ujamaa or socialist outlook, particularly the principles of equality and brotherhood which entail a sense of individual and collective responsibility in all areas of activity. (Ministry of Education 1984, 2–3)

In speaking about social studies in Europe, Hooghoff (1994, 5) suggested that:

> citizenship does not imply a narrow, exclusivist Eurocentric perspective ... learning to be a responsible European citizen must involve an appreciation and respect for other cultures and societies. ... A good European citizen is a good world citizen.

Did Wesley and Wronski really get it right? In one sense, yes, but only because "intelligent membership in society" can be interpreted in each country to support desirable attitudes toward its traditions and future goals. Countries do, in fact, have objectives for social studies that express a wide range of differing visions, all of which benefit from intelligent participation in society.

Is There an International Social Studies?

To even think about alternative futures, one must first conceive the variety of different definitions, aims, and purposes that have guided differing visions of social studies. Is there even an international vision of social studies? Must that vision be linked to a promotion of capitalism and democracy? Alternatively, is social studies always linked with some vision of citizenship education as a developed intelligent membership in society? Examining the path social studies took as it transformed from a national to an international field might help to answer these questions. But a thoughtful response to these questions might start with inspecting differing visions of social studies among Americans, Gambians, Nigerians, South Koreans, Japanese, Tanzanians, Europeans, and Zimbabweans. That inspection suggests that social studies is not necessarily linked to a concept of capitalism or democracy but is usually conceived as some form of citizenship education.

The National Council for the Social Studies, an organization founded in 1921 in the United States, provides an international assembly for educators from around the world. The assembly sets forth a guiding vision as a standard on teaching and learning that emphasizes integrated and interdisciplinary curriculum:

> [Social studies] when taught well, is drawn not only from its most ... foundational disciplines but also from the arts and humanities, mathematics and science, current events and students' own interests and experiences. (NCSS 1994, 159)

This vision of integration, of course, has long been established as basic to the development of a social studies program, and is commonly followed throughout countries that have adopted social studies. For example, in Lesotho:

> The integrated approach is a more natural method of learning ... children do not generally think in terms of subjects until they

328

become conditioned to doing so. In any case their natural interests and the personal problems they solve from day to day cut across various subject areas and there is no reason why our methods of teaching should not take this into account ... especially when they are in harmony with the integrated approach which is the basis of Social Studies teaching. (Ministry of Education, Sports and Culture 1981, 2)

The Japanese, on the other hand, adopted an integrated social studies as part of the democratization process required by the Allied occupation forces:

Social Studies became a school subject in 1947 through the enforcement regulations of the School Education Law. ... An integrated social studies curriculum based on the American pattern was introduced in the hope that it would contribute to the democratization of Japan. (Nagai 1983, 61)

Another standard set forth by NCSS's International Assembly involves the development of values:

When taught well, social studies engages students in the difficult process of confronting ethical and value-based dilemmas, and encourages students to speculate, think critically, and make personal and civic decisions based on information from multiple perspectives. (NCSS 1994, 159)

These standards of teaching and learning tend to find support in many social studies syllabi, national curricula, and teacher handbooks in those countries that have adopted social studies. For instance, in Zambia the NCSS vision on teaching and learning would sound like this: "[Social studies] aims at inculcating upon the mind of the learner useful social values such as social interaction, decision making and extrapolation" (Ministry of Education 1983, iv).

Social Studies' Historical Route

It would be fair to say that the social studies movement promoting integration probably began at a most inappropriate time, particularly for those who conceived of organizing scientific inquiry into discrete disciplinary fields. During the late nineteenth and early twentieth centuries, the growth and development of the social science movement into disciplinary fields was in full force; even history for some became a science. Soon after the Civil War, the potential of the social sciences was realized through an emphasis on scientific investigation, with the promise of emerging, discrete academic disciplines. History, not yet assigned to the humanities, along with new fields of economics, psychology, sociology, anthropology, and other branches of science, were to capture the imagination of scholars and university liberal arts faculties with a particular attitude toward knowledge that became the foundation for twentieth-century scholarship.

Today, arguably, there is a trend toward integrating disciplinary fields, especially in the sciences, whereas earlier in the century educators were struggling to identify new fields. At the same time that the social sciences were attempting to identify their own academic boundaries, the social studies attempted a "counterrevolution," structured on integrating the social sciences, history, and, for some, the humanities. The social science and history community did not eagerly receive the idea of social studies as an integrated subject to be taught in schools (Earth 1992, 34). In a modern world where academic reputations are established on research in disciplinary fields, a school subject such as social studies, which calls for a broadly conceived integration of the social sciences and humanities, runs against a popular intellectual trend.

The fragmenting of knowledge into ever smaller bites within discrete disciplines rather than the integration of knowledge, which has occurred during the past hundred years in the United States, has not been lost on the international community. Though social studies as a school subject has substantially spread throughout the world, the notion of an integrated school social studies curriculum could be perceived as being out of step, surely not in harmony with the times. Admittedly, some elementary classrooms feature an integrated social studies (illustrated above by the Japanese and Zambians), but, in most cases, secondary social studies remains true to the twentieth-century preference for separate subjects that derive their content from disciplinary fields. An interesting speculation might be, Will the twentieth-century preference for separate subjects based on disciplinary fields continue, or will the social studies notion of integrated content around significant social-personal problems emerge?

The argument in the United States went beyond integration versus separate subjects. The Progressive Movement championed U.S. reform by favoring a perfected democracy that depended upon an educated citizenry who understood how the political system should work. Education was the way—and social studies was the answer—to how the citizens would learn their responsibilities (Brady 1994, 25).

An earlier social movement called Populism laid a different foundation for the social studies. The Populists imagined a citizenship education that would question the very structure of the political system, believing that, given the political and economic system that existed, democracy would never function for the benefit of the people. So it was that social studies emerged not only as counter to the social science movement but also upon the horns of two movements, Populist and Progressive, both calling for reform, yet in conflict with each other over what changes were needed.

To further complicate the birth of social studies, social scientists who had thoughts about the dissemination of their knowledge conceived social studies as a direct conduit, perhaps a handmaiden. Social studies was conceived as that mechanism by which the citizens would learn about their society—as perceived by the social scientists (Saxe 1991, 2–3). From the social scientists' point of view, schools would feature a social studies that was not integrated but was compartmentalized into discrete social sciences and history. If attitudes of the social scientists were not sufficient to create a stillborn integrated social studies, then factor in the conflict over Populist and Progressive reform. Be sure to include a lack of consensus on definitions, purposes, aims, and goals, and for teaching social studies.

If Americans could not articulate a coherent notion of the field and were thought to be out of step with intellectual twentieth-century trends to create discrete social science fields, then is it little wonder that those outside the United States found the field hard to understand? Notwithstanding arguments against the development of social studies, a vision of the social studies field as an alternative to other forms of citizenship education did, in fact, emerge in many countries by the latter part of the twentieth century.

Social Studies as the Heritage of a Nation

Obviously social studies has survived, though it has not necessarily overcome the problems of perception and application that have plagued the field since its inception. In the United States social studies is clearly intended to reinforce its particular heritage of democracy. But, in fact, the social studies field is the heritage of a nation, as illustrated by how other countries view it. For example, in Sierra Leone social studies is:

structured around the student and spirals out from the family and the local community. Beyond the national level the structure further includes the international community and related issues. (Institute of Education n.d., 1)

Sudan takes the reinforcement of the Islamic faith as the purpose of social studies. The Soviet Union maintained social studies as the way to reinforce communist ideology. Social studies in Japan, in its early phase of development, was perceived as a reinforcement of traditional moral values. Tanzania adopted social studies as one way to promote socialism. South Korean social studies aims at encouraging anticommunism but not necessarily democracy. Germany aims at developing a democratic tradition, yet "a good European citizen is a good world citizen." In short, the field is assigned a purpose in each country. It could be reinforcing democracy, communism, the Islamic faith, precolonial traditions, or the persona of a ruling dictator—as is the case in Malawi and some West African countries—but, in most cases, the attempt is to create a national identity, preserve traditions, and promote social cohesion. In essence, social studies is perceived as nation building. How that nation building is conceived depends upon the country's priorities. Tucker (1981, 318) stated:

Issues that cause social studies to be developmental are: (1) different nations or regions have different reasons for teaching social studies; (2) social studies more than other school subjects influences and is influenced by the social, political and economic values and institutions of society.

There is an American social studies, but then there is also a Spanish social studies, a Russian social studies, a Namibian social studies, a

Nigerian social studies, a South Korean social studies, a German social studies, and as many other differing forms of social studies as there are countries that have adopted the field as their citizenship education.

Organizing an International Social Studies

Though there has been some discussion about creating an international social studies association, as yet most international activities have been sponsored by regional or national social studies organizations. The 1990s brought international social studies conferences, the fourth to be held in Australia in 1997, and the International Association for Children's Social and Economic Education, based in England since 1994. This professional organization encourages global membership. International publications, such as the *International Journal of Social Education* sponsored by the Indiana Council for the Social Studies and Ball State University, are further evidence of the internationalizing of social studies. One could also point to numerous regional organizations such as the National Institute of Curriculum Development (The Netherlands) and the African Social and Environmental Studies Programme (Nairobi, Kenya) and unilateral programs that have encouraged social studies educators to visit other countries—American Fulbright grants and awards, United States Information Agency (USIA) programs, and Japan's Keizai Koho Center fellowships. In fact, countries and corporations sponsor a variety of exchange programs that internationalize the field. Why this interest? What is it about social studies that has attracted international attention?

What Explains the Attraction of Social Studies?

Explaining the widening influence of the social studies movement is complex, but two factors undoubtedly present themselves. One relates to the purpose of social studies and the other relates to the impact of a historical event.

Social Studies in a Rapidly Changing World

Whether "preparing students for intelligent membership in society" (Wesley and Wronski 1973, 42) or "to provide students with the skills and knowledge required to cope with the con-

temporary world" (Becker and Mehlinger 1968, 10), social studies is a simple but attractive thought for many modern countries that face rapid change and also profess a preference for one or more of the following beliefs: freedom of thought, expression of religion, a tolerance and compassion for others, a sense of community, an acceptance of pluralism, and the encouragement of individualism. How can a country that experiences rapid change also effectively profess one or all of these preferences? One response has been to educate students to become thoughtful citizens. For example, in Nigeria:

> social studies ... is expected to inculcate and strengthen in the child basic socializing and humanizing responsibilities through the child's acquisition of fundamental concepts, understandings, values, attitudes and social skills necessary to live in society. (Eheazu 1986, 21)

Nagai (1983, 64) described the Japanese view of citizenship: "In Japan being a good citizen means being a democratic and world-minded citizen with a relevant, deep traditional identity."

Preparation for intelligent membership in society must account for rapid change because the consequences of change affect a citizen's quality of life. For some, change is what social studies is all about—helping citizens control their lives in a rapidly changing world. John Cogan (1994, 338) asked, "What kinds of knowledge and skills are needed to help us cope with and manage change rather than having it direct us?" If change happens very rapidly, as in any highly developed technological society, then change can be dislocating. Rapid change is unsettling and can lead to unhappiness, fractured families, identity crises, unemployment, drug abuse, crime, world wars, economic depression, crises, and chaos. Contemporary Russia, the late Yugoslavia, Iraq, and numerous countries in Africa and the Middle East come to mind. Cogan (1994, 338) summarized the argument: "These are difficult times for the global community. The changes taking place in Russia are a microcosm of those taking place across the planet."

Viewed through a Japanese perspective, change might foster "some undesirable tendencies to anti- or non-social attitudes ... such as a growing concern with self as compared to the group, the company, and the nation" (Nagai,

1983, 63), which in Japan might encourage abandonment of traditional values, discipline, and a moral code of behavior. A social studies unit issued by the African Social Studies Programme, speaking for seventeen African countries, put it this way:

> Changes take place all the time all around us, although they may be small and imperceptible. As many planned changes are associated with progress, people should give proposed changes a chance to succeed ... but when there arises the need to change, such changes must be carefully explained in order to be acceptable to the people. (African Social Studies Programme, 34)

The arguments urge that the study of change ought to be a continuous part of the school curriculum, that the subject matter taught in the curriculum should be selected and integrated in such a way that students identify persistent social problems they must consider carefully throughout their lifetimes. Tamakloe (1988, 61) from Ghana elaborated:

> Social studies requires that knowledge be looked upon as a unit and that all disciplines must contribute to man's understanding. ... Integration enables the pupil, at the early stages of school life, to look at knowledge in a holistic manner. ... Integration facilitates, for the young student, the analysis and description of contemporary problems.

The social sciences, humanities, and other relevant disciplines would provide the content. The curriculum, however, should focus on a country's traditions and skills, those that might help a citizen function effectively in society, thus continuing the process of self-realization and nation building. The philosophy of Liberian social studies education is:

> to be truly Liberian, should flow from the Liberian Cultural Heritage—beliefs, customs, folklores, arts, crafts, and literature ... new needs and priorities. ... Our teachers have therefore to instill these nobler sentiments. (Ministry of Education, R. L. 1979, 3)

The social studies curriculum was not only to emphasize traditions, social problems, skills, and decision-making processes, but was to be developmental. For example, social studies curriculum in the State of Kuwait plays a major role in developing the responsible citizen. The curriculum, grades four through twelve, covers major branches of social studies starting with the community, developing the state of Kuwait, Gulf States, Arab countries, Islamic countries, and the world (Karam 1993, 1). The Department of Curriculum Development and Evaluation (1990, 12) in Botswana cited a practical example of this way of thinking:

> Our Social Studies programme is organized based on the educational theory of learning which we call expanding horizons, or sometimes expanding environments. The theory is that as children grow, their view of the world or environment grows and expands as well. Also their capabilities develop, and in consequence they can do different things at different Standard levels. So, expanding horizons means that children are able to handle more complex and demanding tasks as they grow older and as they proceed through the [social studies] curriculum.

The original notion of a school curriculum founded on a vision of a changing, interdependent, and problem-laden society in crisis required some systematic rational thought process that would be learned in a general education course, i.e., social studies. As change and complexity increase in the life of an individual, social studies, which directly proposes to prepare citizens in a formal school setting for intelligent membership in society, becomes an attractive alternative. Educators who introduced social studies to seventeen African countries at the historic 1968 Mombasa Conference summarized the role of social studies in these words:

> African schools will tend to be used in a deliberate way as instruments of social change. The main functions of the school in this process will be both to facilitate acceptance of change and to foster the notion that individuals have some control over their environment; schools should, therefore, encourage an inquiring attitude to change rather than passive acceptance. (Report of a Conference of Africa Educators, 6–7)

World War II and Social Studies as Nation Building

The second factor influencing the internationalizing of the social studies movement was the Second World War. The social studies movement gathered momentum after the war. Defeated enemy countries, along with recently freed colonial countries, became fertile ground for social studies. The United States, defeated enemies, and ex-colonial countries had at least one thing in common—they were all attempting to form, if not new countries, then at least national identities that would fit their growth and development in the twentieth century (Barth 1994, 11). Obida and Kobiowu (1988, 49) suggested that:

> The introduction of social studies into the Nigerian school curriculum should be understood as part of a general response to the problems of independence, unification and development.

The fact that countries have common interests in establishing unique identities did not mean that there was agreement on what social studies was, or what the curriculum ought to be. It just meant that a concept of social studies as nation building, distinct from other programs of citizenship education, was evolving. Professor Kajuba (1994, 70), past Vice-Chancellor of Makerere University in Uganda, discussed nation building:

> Education, particularly citizenship education, has a big role in the process of nation-building and development. ... It is through this constant search for the "ideal of man" that Social Studies education will contribute most significantly to national integration and nation-building.

The move from colony to independent new country became a significant event. The social studies approach to citizenship education offered an alternative to the colonial model. The United States, along with other excolonial countries, was attempting to imagine educational systems that were supportive of their unique traditions. As colonies, they were required to emulate the education system of their colonizers. Whatever educational system existed from preschool through higher education, it was calculated to create colonial citizens who respected the traditions of their masters and ignored their own. Sir Seretse Khama (1970), Botswana's first president, spoke for all ex-colonial countries and laid a foundation for the introduction of social studies:

> We were made to believe that we had no past to speak of, no history to boast of. The past, so far as we were concerned, was just a blank and nothing more. ... We should write our own history books, to prove that we did have a past; and that it was a past that was just as worth writing and learning about as any other. We must do this for the simple reason that a nation without a past is a lost nation, and a people without a past is a people without a soul.

The social studies approach was flexible enough to offer each new nation the opportunity to abandon colonial traditions, developing its own program for citizenship education. Botswana is an example:

> Botswana Social Studies is different from Social Studies in any other country in the world. Each country that has adopted Social Studies has its own Social Studies curriculum and materials, because each country is somewhat different from, as well as similar to, all other countries. Admittedly this is a bit confusing to some people because they expect, as they do in math and science, the same subject and content being taught in all countries. The content of Botswana's Social Studies conforms to the experience of Botswana's people. That doesn't mean we don't study comparative culture or that we don't recognize our responsibilities as global citizens; but in fact, we do have our own particular program designed to develop our nation, and that is the reason our citizenship education is called Botswana Social Studies. (Department of Curriculum Development and Evaluation 1990, 10)

Preparing Citizens for Nation Building through Social Studies

Citizenship education in many developing countries has evolved through three phases: **1.** traditional society, **2.** colonial period, and **3.** the social studies approach to citizenship education. Senior Inspector of Social Studies, C. M. Mgagula (1988, 2), of the Kingdom of Swaziland, explained citizenship in phase one, traditional society:

> Social Studies is not an entirely new field of study in the Swazi society. As long as Swazis existed, their children have always wanted to learn. The Swazi way of learning was very similar to the [social studies] that we use today. Young people were groomed for adult citizen roles in the Swazi society and those roles enabled them to become useful members of the Swazi society. The local environment and community were used as learning vehicles.

In the first phase, much like most societies throughout the world, the entire educational approach aimed at producing an effective member of society. That society was meant to shape and mold a good citizen who would, in turn, enjoy the best social, economic, and political achievements of that society. In other words, education was a communal achievement where the village raised the child and there was little thought of individual academic achievement. Citizenship training in the traditional society was an integration of all the history, culture, values, and beliefs of the family, community, and ethnic group. Initiation into adult responsibilities was a communal achievement where the good citizen's goal was to fit into the traditional society.

In some traditional societies, during the colonial period the community elders lost the right to instruct and initiate. During the colonial period, phase two, citizenship education became a national, formal education that prepared the "native" for an obligation beyond the family, village, ethnic group, and nation. The obligation was to the colonial empire, because colonial citizenship was not nation building but empire building. Under this citizenship system, the history, government, and economic system of the colonizer was to be honored, as was individual academic achievement. The fact that the content did not reflect the colony was ignored. Mgagula (1988, 12) also explained the second phase, the colonial period:

> In the beginning of the twentieth century missionaries established schools in Swaziland with the express purpose of

enabling the Swazis to read the Bible. With the progress of time, the methods and content of the curriculum tended to alienate the child from the oral and cultural heritage of his society. History and Geography were Eurocentric in that they emphasized heroic deeds of European statesmen and women. Pupils were exposed to concepts which had very little relevance to the needs of the Swazi Nation. Little was drawn from the immediate familiar environment of the child. Also the Swazi pupils knew very little about the pioneers of the Swazi nation. The curriculum in Geography and History was not consistent with Swazi expectations and background.

When independence had been achieved after the Second World War, the social studies approach, the third phase, appeared. In the third phase in many countries, social studies was modeled after the phase-one traditional approach to good citizenship in that local, regional, and national history, culture, and values were integrated and honored as worthy subjects. In brief, the field became internationalized because its integrated social studies curriculum permitted a people to honor their traditions by requiring students in their elementary schools to study their village, their ethnic group, their history as a country, all of which was not examined during the colonial period. The concept of social studies became for many countries the educational reform that freed them finally from foreign colonial traditions that were calculated to deny them their identity. Mgagula (1988, 2) explained why social studies was adopted for citizenship education in phase three:

> When Swaziland regained her independence in 1968, the Swazi nation started to demand radical changes in the entire [citizenship] education system, especially to make the curriculum relevant to the post-independence situation.

There probably is no mystery as to why social studies spread rapidly after World War II, because it evolved at a time when countries were attempting to find an identity, preserve traditions, and respond to new needs and priorities. Social studies evolved from the recommendation of a professional teachers organization at the turn of the century to a world movement eighty years later.

Is an International Vision of Social Studies Possible?

Every country that has adopted social studies is an example of an alternative future because no two programs are exactly alike. Thus, any vision of the field must account for the fact that social studies is likely to continue to be the heritage of a nation. Cogan (1982, 9) may be right—"The world today can best be understood as a singular, albeit complex system." *Is an international vision of social studies possible or desirable?* At present, there is no international vision of social studies, simply because social studies is "country specific." However, that does not preclude that citizenship education programs across countries could not agree on some of the following ideas in their social studies curricula:

- that social studies includes an integrated curriculum and is developmental in the sense that social studies understandings are based upon the mental development of students in the form of expanding environment scope and sequence;
- that the content in the form of concepts and generalizations is derived from the social sciences, humanities, and other appropriate fields, with some notion of nation building and preparing students for intelligent membership in society;
- that the curriculum of social studies is intended to be a country's school citizenship education program. The program is flexible in the sense that definitions, purposes, aims, and goals may be "country specific." However, the content will normally explore a range of citizenship identities, local, regional, national, and international.

The field is not necessarily linked in countries with the study of social problems and issues or with a reflective inquiry thought process. In short, almost all programs attempt to create identity, preserve traditions, and promote social cohesion. *Must a social studies vision be linked to democracy?* In many countries it is, but there are a number of instances where social studies is a citizenship education curriculum in a dictatorship. Also, it is not unusual for new countries that have identified with democracy to adopt social studies and continue to support social studies even though the country may revert to an authoritarian government. The reverse is also true, where a dictatorship has rejected social studies on the grounds that the field is linked to democracy and inquiry.

What might be alternative future visions of international social studies? The field, given its general purpose to develop intelligent citizenship, continues to be, in spite of serious problems of application, a good idea. The same reasoning that would explain the growth of social studies from a modest beginning after the turn of the century to an international movement would justify the thought that social studies will continue to evolve as an international field. As countries become less isolated and more interactive with a world community, the social studies that embraces globalism should prosper. An international social studies organization could well be a consequence of that sense of world community. The NCSS has now laid a foundation for periodic international meetings. Already, inquiries about future international meetings have come from social studies educators in such countries as India, Spain, The Netherlands, West Indies, Canada, Ethiopia, and from countries that have not adopted social studies. In short, the field changes as the interaction between people changes. There are those who would claim that the twenty-first century will differ from the twentieth century because the emphasis will be on integrating knowledge, a new century that places a priority on interpretation and meaning. This is not to suggest that winning new knowledge, the priority of the twentieth century, will not continue to be important, but it is to suggest that what will become a priority will not be the identification of discrete disciplines but problems and issues. In short, the social studies model of integration of the social sciences and humanities focusing on problems and issues will be much closer to how content must be organized for future instruction and less concerned with boundaries between disciplines. As integration becomes a popular theme in the twenty-first century, the social studies, instead of being out of step and harmony with the twentieth century, will not only be in harmony but will take a leadership position as an illustration of a century-old integrated curriculum.

Social studies is likely to be a more attractive field, if not a better idea, in the twenty-first century. The field may very well capture the citizenship education programs of most countries in the world, particularly if the curriculum emphasizes identity, change, problems and issues, global and future concepts, all of which may be in harmony with needs and interests of the new century. A curriculum such as social studies, which was conceived in part to account for change in a society, will become increasingly important as technology and other forces bring about more rapid change. As countries continue to develop and evolve, the internationalizing of social studies will become more significant. Country-specific social studies evolving through an international dialogue is the future of citizenship education.

References

African Social Studies Programme. *Change. African Social Studies Programme*, n.d. (1970s).

Barth. J. L. "The Social Studies: A Reform Movement for Building Nations and Educating Global Citizens." *The International Journal of Social Education* 4, no. 2 (Autumn 1989): 7–21.

Barth, J. L. "Botswana Social Studies Curriculum: Scope and Sequence." *African Social Studies Forum* 3, no. 3 (March 1990): 46–54.

Barth, J. L. "America 2000 Goal 3: A Reactionary Reform of Citizenship Education." In *Citizenship as Social Studies Education*. Bulletin 4. Munster, Ind.: The Foundations of the Social Studies Special Interest Group, National Council for the Social Studies, 1992.

Barth, J. L. "Social Studies Is the Heritage of a Nation." *The Future of the Social Studies*, edited by M. R. Nelson, 11–15. Boulder, Colo.: Social Science Education Consortium, Inc., 1994.

Becker, J. M., and H. D. Mehlinger. "Conceptual Lag and the Study of International Affairs." In *International Dimensions in the Social Studies. 35th Yearbook*, edited by J. M. Becker and H. D. Mehlinger, 1–11. Washington, D.C.: National Council for the Social Studies, 1968.

Brady, H. R. "Is a Democratic Social Studies Possible?" Paper presented at the Third International Social Studies Conference, [National Council for the Social Studies] Nairobi, Kenya, 1994.

Chung, In-Yeop. "Effects of Experimental Curriculum on Political Socialization of Middle School Students in Korea." Ph.D. diss., Purdue University, 1994.

Cogan, J. J. "Global Education: Opening Children's Eyes to the World." *Getting Started in Global Education*, edited by H. T. Collins and S. B. Zakariya, 8–11. Arlington, Va.: National Association

of Elementary School Principals, 1982.

Cogan, J. J. "The Pain of Change." *Social Education* 58, no. 6 (October 1994): 335–38.

Department of Curriculum Development and Evaluation. *Botswana Social Studies Teaching Methods*. Gaborone, Botswana: Macmillan Botswana Publications Ltd., 1990.

DuBey, D. L. *Social Studies Methods for Nigerian Teachers: Learning Activities*. Ibadan, Nigeria: University Press Ltd., 1980.

Eheazu, B. A. "Toward a Social Studies Education Programme for Greater Understanding and Cooperation among Africans: A Sociological View." *African Social Studies Forum* 1, no. 2 (December 1986): 18–27.

Hooghoff, H. "Reform and Renewal in Social Studies: International Perspectives." Paper presented at a symposium of the International Assembly at the annual meeting of the National Council for the Social Studies, Phoenix, Arizona, 17 November 1994.

Institute of Education. "Sierra Leone Teachers Certificate Syllabus in Social Studies." Institute of Education, University of Sierra Leone, n.d.

Kajubi, W. Senteza. "Reflections of a Social Studies Educator on Past and Emerging Perspectives on Constitution Making in Africa." In *ISSC '94: Report on Third International Social Studies Conference*, 63–71. Nairobi, Kenya: 1994.

Kaltsounis, T. "Democracy's Challenge as the Foundation for Social Studies." *Theory and Research in Social Education* 22, no. 2 (Spring 1994): 176–94.

Karam E. M. "Social Studies Curriculum in Kuwait after Liberation of State of Kuwait." Paper delivered at the annual meeting of the National Council for the Social Studies, Nashville, Tennessee, 19–22 November 1993.

Khama, Sir Seretse. Speech delivered at the University of Botswana, Lesotho, and Swaziland, Luyengo Campus, Swaziland, 19 May 1970.

Mgagula, C. M. *The African Social Studies Programme*. Occasional paper. 1988.

Ministry of Education. "Basic Facts about Education in Tanzania." Dar es Salaam, Tanzania: Ministry of Education, 1984.

Ministry of Education. "Zambia Basic Education Social Studies Syllabus." Lusaka, Zambia: Curriculum Development Centre, 1983.

Ministry of Education and Culture. "Zimbabwe Social Studies Syllabus for Primary Schools." Ministry of Education and Culture, Primary Educational Development Unit, 1982.

Ministry of Education, "Liberian Revised National Curriculum." Monrovia, Liberia: Department of

Instruction, Curriculum and Instructional Materials Development Center, 1979.

Ministry of Education, Sports and Culture. Lesotho "Social Studies Syllabus." Maseru, Lesotho: The National Curriculum Development Centre, 1981.

Ministry of Education, Youth, Sports and Culture. "Social Studies: Teacher's Handbook and Syllabus." Banjul, The Gambia: Macmillan Education, 1980.

Nagai, J. "Educating for Responsible Citizenship." *Perspectives on Japan: A Guide for Teachers,* edited by J. J. Cogan and D. O. Schneider, 61–72. NCSS Bulletin 69. Washington, D.C.: National Council for the Social Studies, 1983.

National Council for the Social Studies. *Expectations of Excellence: Curriculum Standards for Social Studies.* NCSS Bulletin 89. Washington, D.C.: National Council for the Social Studies, 1994.

National Council for the Social Studies Task Force on Scope and Sequence. "In Search of a Scope and Sequence for Social Studies." *Social Education* 48, no. 4 (April 1984): 249–62.

Obidi, S. S., and S. V. Kobiowu. "The Origin and Growth of Social Studies in Primary Schools in Nigeria, 1959–1986." *African Social Studies Forum* 2, no. 1 (March 1988): 45–59.

Remy, R. *International Education in a Global Age.* NCSS Bulletin 47. Washington, D.C: National Council for the Social Studies, 1975.

Report of a Conference of African Educators EDC and CREDO on Social Studies. Mombasa, Kenya, 19–30 August 1968.

Rolheiser, C., and C. D. Glickman. "Teaching for a Democratic Life." *The Educational Forum* 59, no. 2 (Winter 1995): 196–206.

Saxe, D. W. *Social Studies in Schools.* Albany, N. Y.: State University of New York Press, 1991.

Tamakloe, E. K. "Research as a Starting Point toward a Rational Teacher Education Programme for Effective Social Studies Teaching in Ghana." *African Social Studies Forum* 2, no. 1 (March 1988): 59–68.

Tucker, J. L., et al. "Teacher Education in Social Studies." *UNESCO Handbook for the Teaching of Social Studies,* edited by H. D. Mehlinger, 298–320. London: Croom Helm, Ltd., 1981.

Wesley, E.B., and S. P. Wronski. *Teaching Secondary Social Studies in a World Society.* 6th ed. Lexington, Mass.: D. C. Heath and Co., 1973.

Part Eleven: Materials and Resources

Introduction by William R. Fernekes

The range of resources for issues-centered education in the social studies is very broad indeed. The resources in this section of the *Handbook* reflect an orientation emphasizing the relationship of issues education to the public good, which is more often than not mediated by the development, implementation and ongoing critique of public policy. Balance was desired in the selection of issues by including policy concerns in the domestic and international/global spheres, as well as those which transcend such divisions (such as Race, Gender and Class, as well as Science, Technology and Society).

Chapter authors were asked to select the 12-15 most outstanding instructional resources available to educators for the design, planning and implementation of issues-centered social studies programs. Criteria for selection of the annotated resources included the following: the annotated resources should **1.** be applicable to a broad cross-section of the student population; **2.** provide actual material for student and teacher use in the classroom; **3.** be readily available in print or accessible from major libraries if out of print; **4.** offer versatile applications in a variety of classroom settings; **5.** contain a multicultural emphasis in content if possible; **6.** embody high quality instructional design; and **7.** have applicability that is not time-bound to the present. In large part, the resources in this section meet all of these criteria, thus representing an excellent starting point for the development of issues-centered social studies curriculum planning and instruction.

Given limitations of space, additional resources minus annotations have been listed at the conclusion of each chapter which warrant further exploration. The resources section contains three divisions. The chapters on domestic economic policy, government policy-making and international affairs and for-eign policy emphasize study of issues where the role of U.S. policy-making is central. The chapters on global development, international human rights and domestic/international children's issues place policy-making within an international dimension, where intergovernmental and international organizations are prominent. The final two chapters on race, gender and class and science, technology and society transcend geopolitical divisions, providing perspectives on issues-centered study that are critical for the understanding of contemporary society and the in-depth study of policy-making in multiple contexts.

General Resources and Materials

Annual Editions. (Discipline-based anthologies of issues-centered controversy, updated every two years). Guilford, CT: Dushkin Publishing Co.

Close Up Foundation. (annual). *Current Issues: Critical Issues Confronting the Nation and the World.* Arlington, VA: Close Up Foundation.

Contemporary World Issues. Series published by ABC-Clio, Santa Barbara, CA.

Kidron, M. and R. Segal. *The New State of the World Atlas* (rev. ed.). New York: Touchstone, 1993.

National Issues Forum in the Classroom. *Issues Handbooks.* (published annually). Dubuque, IA: Kendall-Hunt Publishing Co.

Opposing Viewpoints Series. (Pro-con contemporary and historical issues books and pamphlets). San Diego, CA: Greenhaven Press.

Oliver, D. W., and F. M. Newmann. *Public Issues Series* (rev. ed.). Boulder CO: Social Science Education Consortium.

Public Issues Network Newsletter. (annual). Boulder, CO: Social Science Education Consortium.

Social Issues Resources Series. Available in printed volumes by topic or on CD-ROM. Boca Raton FL: Social Issues Resources Series, Inc.

Taking Sides. (Pro-con books on issues of social controversy). Guilford, CT: Dushkin Publishing Co.

36 THEORY AND PRACTICE OF ISSUES-CENTERED EDUCATION

by William R. Fernekes

Works on the theory and practice of issues-centered education in the social studies proliferated in the period from 1950 to 1975. Characterized by strong emphases on the theory and practice of reflective inquiry, decision-making, and the critical examination of core values, beliefs, institutions and behaviors in U. S. society, a substantial body of literature emerged to reorient social studies education towards the study of social issues and public policy at all levels of schooling (see Hunt and Metcalf, Newmann, Newmann and Oliver, Oliver and Shaver, and Taba, et al). This perspective was prominent in the theory and practice of the "new social studies" from 1960 to 1975, when methods texts, curriculum project publications and many classroom instructional materials focused on issues-centered approaches within existing social studies courses, or as core elements of new curricula. For example, the Harvard Social Studies Project pamphlets in American History employed the jurisprudential approach of Oliver, Shaver and Newmann as their key organizing principle, while textbooks in a variety of subject areas, such as world history, civics and government, and economics utilized issues-centered themes to organize content.

Since the late 1970s, publications on the theory and practice of issues-centered social studies education have been sporadic. Engle and Ochoa's *Education for Democratic Citizenship* is the only work since the mid-to-late 1970s to articulate a comprehensive rationale placing issues study at the center of social studies education, offering a sharp contrast to the neo-conservative orientation articulated by advocates of a history-geography-civics approach to social education such as Diane Ravitch, Chester Finn, William Bennett, and the Bradley Commission on History in the Schools.

Concurrent with the neo-conservative critique of social studies education there emerged a body of literature highlighting critical curriculum theory and its application to schooling practices. A major educational philosopher cited by critical curriculum theorists such as Michael Apple and Henry Giroux is Paolo Freire, whose pedagogical approach to empowering learners is discussed comprehensively in the Shor and Freire volume. The implications of Freire's liberation pedagogy contrast sharply with neo-conservative recommendations for both curriculum and instruction, because Freire's ideas emphasize linkages between the experiences of learners and social issues illustrating inequities in wealth, status and power in late twentieth century capitalism.

An interesting development, virtually simultaneous with the neo-conservative reaction to social studies education and the development of critical curriculum theory, is the renewed interest in issues-centered social studies represented by the National Issues Forum in the Classroom program, the Lockwood and Harris work on ethical issues in U. S. History, and the special issue of *The Social Studies* on Issues-Centered Education. These works blend concise discussions of theory with systematic explanations of instructional practices geared to engaging students in issues-centered learning within the existing social studies curriculum. They harken back to the pathbreaking work of authors from the period 1950-1975, while attempting to show the centrality of issues-centered learning for today's students and teachers.

Resources

Engle, Shirley H. and Anna S. Ochoa. *Education for Democratic Citizenship: Decision Making in the Social Studies.* NY: Teachers College Press, 1988.

Following in the spirit of Hunt and Metcalf, Oliver and Shaver, and Newmann and Oliver, Engle and Ochoa accept Myrdal's "American Creed" as a beginning core for study of essential democratic ideals. They argue citizenship must be focused on cultivating citizens who "have the facility to make intelligent political judgments related to controversial issues in our society" (5). Social studies education's primary purpose is thus to educate citizens through dialogue about the nature of society and the common good, in the process helping children and youth to "acquire the knowledge and intellectual skills needed to keep the discussion open to enable the young citizen to participate in the process of improving the society" (8).

The authors argue that both socializing and countersocializing influences require emphasis in educational settings, with the former being predominant in the early grades (K-5 or 6) and the latter in the higher grades (6 or 7-12).

Countersocialization educates students to improve their rational thought processes with the aim of becoming effective social critics and political problem-solvers. Social studies programs which emphasize socialization (reinforcing existing cultural norms) fail to move beyond their conserving tendencies and thus minimize reforming tendencies. In contrast, Engle and Ochoa argue that the only way everyone in a democracy can be offered their deserved opportunities to develop human potential is through cultivation of critical skepticism about truth claims, refinement of problem-solving skills, and in-depth consideration of issues emphasizing active student decision-making. Democratic habits and attitudes should prevail in the classroom at all grades, but developing critical reasoning processes must take precedence by early adolescence so that independent, reflective reasoning is fostered regularly.

Engle and Ochoa's work provides a very helpful update on the work begun by earlier advocates of reflective thought and issues-centered curricula.

In Chapter 8, a detailed framework for a model curriculum based upon their philosophical premises is offered, while Chapters 9 and 10 contain strategies for curriculum implementation and reflective teaching practices. Very noteworthy is the inclusion in Chapter 11 of concrete suggestions for assessment focused on alternatives to the ubiquitous paper and pencil test. The assessment strategies are consistent with the authors' emphasis on individual and group decision-making, student-centered discussion, and developing divergent thinking processes. The appendix provides a unique teacher evaluation instrument that reorients the supervision process towards the behaviors and attitudes the authors believe are paramount in a reflective educator. Through the questions it poses, this instrument has important potential to refocus teacher evaluation by peers, students or superiors on long-term professional growth and should be carefully examined for possible application in school settings.

Offering a comprehensive justification of social studies as issues-centered education, with a strong focus on reflective decision-making as the core of social studies curriculum and instruction Engle and Ochoa's work effectively blends elements from many earlier works into a coherent program for K-12 classrooms.

Evans, Ronald W., ed. "Defining Issues-Centered Social Studies Education." Special Section in *The Social Studies*, Vol. 83, No. 3 (May/June 1992): 93-119.

Evans has assembled an introductory essay, five articles, and a resource list that updates the status of issues-centered education in social studies. Evans begins the special section with an overview of efforts to define issues-centered education. The articles range from Shaver's discussion of rationales for issues-centered social studies to instructional strategy pieces with specific guidelines for classroom instruction. Among the latter are Oliver, Newmann and Singleton's piece on public issues discussion and Brandhorst's case study illustrating how to infuse issues in the social studies curriculum, employing the Engle and Ochoa reflective thought model with foreign policy concerns. This compendium helps teachers and supervisors examine the historic continuity of issues-centered approaches in the social studies literature, and argues forcefully for their placement at the center of social studies curriculum and instruction. Available from Heldref Publications, 1319 Eighteenth Street, NW, Washington DC 20036-1802. Single copy cost: $7.50.

Hunt, Maurice P. and Lawrence E. Metcalf. *Teaching High School Social Studies: Problems in Reflective Thinking and Social Understanding.* 2d ed. New York: Harper and Row, 1968.

This book is regularly cited in most issues-centered social studies literature that has appeared since its initial publication in 1955. Hunt and Metcalf's advocacy of reflective thought as the core of democratic citizenship is a theme appearing in the work of Oliver and Shaver (1966), and most notably in that of Engle and Ochoa (1988). Building upon Dewey, Hunt and Metcalf argue that the reflective reconstruction of beliefs helps young people clarify and preserve the central ideals of democratic life. Reflective thought is engendered when students are offered opportunities for the critical examination of "closed areas" in civic life, defined as areas where conflicts between core values and beliefs and actual behaviors are illuminated in classroom instruction. Through the study of such closed areas (for example, issues related to gender orientation, race and other controversies in society), students encounter cognitive dissonance, presenting teachers and students with situations where deliberation using a hypothetical reasoning model drawn from the social sciences can contribute potential solutions to social problems.

Part I provides a comprehensive discussion of the philosophical and psychological foundations of reflective teaching, while Parts II and III present detailed examinations of how to teach concepts and generalizations, how to employ value analysis and value clarification strategies, the reflective teaching of history, and the central role of discussion in reflective teaching methodology.

Part IV includes application of reflective thought strategies to "problematic areas of culture" in the social studies, and should be updated based upon societal trends of the past 25 years. Despite its age, this book's discussion of the core elements of reflective thought makes it essential reading for anyone seeking to implement issues-centered education in the social studies.

Lockwood, Allan and David Harris. *Reasoning With Democratic Values: Ethical Decision-Making in United States History.* New York: Teachers College Press, 1985.

This curriculum emphasizes the promotion of social responsibility among students, and includes an instructor's manual and two volumes of case studies drawn from United States History. The curriculum rationale, program goals, and suggested instructional approaches are discussed in the Instructor's Manual, while Volumes I and II contain the historical case studies and accompanying student analysis questions.

Similar to Oliver and Shaver, Newmann and Oliver, and Engle and Ochoa, the authors stress study of core democratic values (life, liberty, property, equality and others) but note that study of core values doesn't preclude conflict or honest debate about the courses of citizen action.

Rational thought is proposed as a prerequisite to taking citizen obligations, rights and responsibilities seriously and to acting responsibly after careful consideration of the ethical dimensions of problems. Relying heavily on Kohlberg's hierarchy of cognitive-moral development, the authors advocate systematic discussion of ethical problems to improve the quality of student reasoning.

Values analysis is the core instructional approach framing each case study, and the authors employ a creative "question and answer" approach in the instructor's manual to justify their choice of values analysis and components of moral education as their preferred instructional approach.

Values clarification is deemed inadequate due to its reliance on ethical relativism, while U.S. History is defended as the context for study of ethical problems given the persistence of ethical dilemmas from the period of colonization to the present and the centrality of value conflict in the development of government policy.

The many strengths of this volume include its systematic approach to instructional activities. Four activities are used with each case study: seeking historical understanding, reviewing facts of the case, analyzing ethical issues, and expressing your reasoning. The authors emphasize that all are integral to the development of improved reasoning. The Instructor's Manual also includes sample lesson designs for teaching specific ethical case studies, with detailed and well-written discussion formats and careful analyses of differing instructional strategies: large and small group discussions, written dialogues, recorded dialogues, and sociodramas.

Teachers employing this curriculum can easily adapt all or part of it within courses in U. S. History, moral education, policy studies, and other subject matter areas (language arts, for example). The suggestions for guiding teacher-led discussions in the Instructor's Manual are helpful, but the sections on grading and evaluation and program evaluation are superficial, lacking effective strategies for evaluating the quality of discussion contributions and student writing.

Massialas, Byron G., Nancy F. Sprague, and Joseph B. Hurst. *Social Issues Through Inquiry: Coping In An Age of*

Crises. Englewood Cliffs, NJ: Prentice-Hall, Inc., 1975.

The authors believe that the schools must undertake the role of creatively examining and reconstructing the culture of the United States. Building upon the work of Hunt and Metcalf, Oliver and Shaver, and advocates of an education that is responsive to patterns of social change (such as Kenneth Boulding), Massialas, Sprague and Hurst believe the goal of citizenship education is to engage students in the continuous examination of societal ideals and belief through active inquiry and effective political participation. They advocate classroom inquiry into social problems that provides support for open-ended discussions and investigations of societal issues, placing the critical examination of values at the center of inquiry. Ultimately, the authors contend that students should emerge from their social studies education with a better understanding of human behavior, values and feelings based upon the discovery, testing and use of valid concepts and generalizations in the humanities and social sciences. Extensive analysis of instructional approaches is included in Chapters 2 through 6, where the teacher role in the inquiry classroom is contrasted with teacher roles in classrooms emphasizing "expository" and "opining" approaches. Many examples drawn from classroom interaction between students and teachers illustrate inquiry strategies, contrasting with strategies emphasizing exposition and opining.

A major strength is the inclusion in Chapters 7 through 10 of assessment strategies for issues-centered instruction, containing the techniques and results from one of the few comprehensive studies of social issues instruction in social studies. Analyses of both teacher behaviors and student attitudes towards social issues instruction are included, along with recommendations for the improvement of inquiry approaches to social issues instruction. The final chapter offers suggestions for the further development of a "social issues through inquiry" orientation to social studies, highlighting needs for improved teacher education (both pre-service and in-service), instructional materials development and more aggressive advocacy of inquiry-based approaches to educational policymakers. This work is a valuable source for teachers and supervisors who want to better implement and assess inquiry approaches to issues-centered education in social studies.

National Issues Forum in the Classroom. *Public Policy Institute Handbook,* 1993. Dayton Ohio: National Issues Forums in the Classroom, 1993.

For ordering information contact: Dr. Jon Rye Kinghorn, National Issues Forums in the Classroom, 100 Commons Road, Dayton OH 45459-2777. Phone: 1-800-433-7834.

This comprehensive handbook for the development of public issues discussion in the schools and citizen deliberation in community forums is employed as a training manual for participants in the summer institutes on the National Issues Forum program co-sponsored by the Kettering Foundation and the National Council for the Social Studies. The handbook is divided into eleven "sessions" (sections) correlated with the summer public issues institute teacher training programs. Session 1 provides a rationale for broad-based citizen participation in deliberation about public issues, drawing upon polling and focus group research concerning why the public in the U. S. has a low rate of participation in political life. This session also contains a concise overview of the forms of deliberation and the skills involved in becoming a more active and knowledgeable member of the public, as well as a precise discussion of the relationship between social studies goals and the knowledge, skills and attitudes promoted in the NIF approach. Session 2 establishes the differing dimensions of political activity, emphasizing that not all political behavior must be adversarial, competitive or "win-lose" in orientation. It includes activities focusing on how students can examine a broader perspective on public issues geared to developing meaningful solutions in the public interest.

Sessions 3, 4, and 6 include hands-on activities for development by students and educators of key components in the NIF approach: large group forums, issue analysis, and small group forums. High quality student handouts are provided, with clear instructions and excellent examples drawn from classroom practice.

Session 7 offers a very incisive summary of how the NIF approach relates to the achievement of citizenship goals in a deliberative democracy. Student objectives are clearly identified and their relationship to developing public deliberation skills and expanding the general knowledge of students is articulated systematically.

Session 8 contains sample lesson activities related to specific issues in the NIF series, while sessions 9 and 10 focus on assessment strategies and how to help students author their own issues book, respectively. The assessment strategies are well-designed and comprehensive, focusing on evaluation of deliberative discussion, writing activities and other forms of "authentic" assessment. The suggestions on how to author an issue book are intriguing and provide a substantial extension activity for students who are well-grounded in the processes of issue analysis and deliberative discussion.

The handbook concludes with an interesting set of handouts consisting of excerpts about the importance of public deliberation in a democracy, with authors ranging from Pericles to Thomas Jefferson and Eleanor Roosevelt. The weak point of the text is session 5, which seeks to have young people gain ownership of the process of learning how to deliberate by "naming and claiming" elements of the approach introduced in sessions one through four. To be convincing, this session requires more concrete examples to demonstrate how this process works in the classroom.

The NIF approach builds upon the earlier efforts in deliberative discussion of public issues introduced by Oliver and Shaver, Newmann and Oliver and others in this chapter. Heavily focused on practical steps to achieve skill in public deliberation, it is a high quality resource for the teacher who wants to implement diverse rationales for issues-centered education. Educators who desire information about the complete NIF classroom program, including the yearly issues books and related audiovisual materials, should contact Kendall/Hunt Publishing Co., 4050 Westmark Drive, P. O. Box 1840, Dubuque Iowa 52004-1840 (Phone: 1-800-228-0810.)

Newmann, Fred J. and Donald W. Oliver. *Clarifying Public Controversy: An Approach to Teaching Social Studies.* Boston: Little, Brown and Company, 1970.

This volume emerged from the Harvard Social Studies Project and related work in the AEP Public Issues Series. Continuing in the tradition of Oliver and Shaver's earlier volume, *Teaching Public Issues in the High School,* Newmann and Oliver strongly advocate supplying students with an analytic scheme and diverse viewpoints that they may use to clarify conflicting value commitments in a democratic society. Closely connected to the detailed study of value conflict are the authors' commitments to helping students develop well-reasoned justifications of their positions that can be defended in public.

At the same time, Newmann and Oliver note that all justifications by students or adults on positions related to issues of public controversy must withstand the tests of rational inquiry, and that public policy disputes, whether they be based upon value conflicts, discord regarding factual claims, or disagreements over definitional issues, must be subject to these rational tests.

Drawing from Gunnar Myrdal's "American Creed," the authors posit the core values in the Creed as sufficiently broad to encompass divergent political, economic and socio-cultural perspectives in the United States. Simultaneously, they view individual human dignity as the foundation value for all others in the Creed, the maintenance of which is the fundamental goal of all democratic societies. By educating students to improve their abilities to engage in rational discussion of public controversy, educators should be able to help students develop a style of public justification for positions reflecting their individuality, rather than simply asking students to copy the teacher's position on a value-based conflict. Use of this "jurisprudential approach" should help people "develop convictions based on firmer grounds than were formerly available" (30) while avoiding indoctrination of students by the authority figure of the classroom teacher. Newmann and Oliver provide excellent examples of discussion processes drawn from their experience with the AEP Public Issues Series.

Classroom excerpts are analyzed in detail and suggestions for leading discussions related to value conflicts, factual disputes and definitional issues are clearly explained. Chapters four through eight provide examples of key value commitments and conflicts from illustrative cases in the Public Issues Series. Few other books dealing with instructional methodology provide such detailed and thoughtful discussions of the problems in teaching about value conflict.

Chapters 9 and 10 address problems faced in implementing the jurisprudential approach and how to teach discussion skills. The section on classroom techniques and evaluating student competence in chapter 9 has excellent ideas for classroom application, again utilizing detailed examples from actual classroom practice. Noteworthy are the clear criteria for establishing rationality of an argument, a core concern of the authors and a central tenet of the jurisprudential approach. While chapter 10 offers useful suggestions for teaching discussion skills, the recommended techniques lack the detail provided in Taba et al. also reviewed in this section.

For anyone seeking to gain a comprehensive understanding of issues-centered education, this volume is a must. Its rationale and discussion of the problems and prospects in the study of public issues remain a central contribution to the field of social studies education.

Oliver, Donald W. and James P. Shaver. *Teaching Public Issues in the High School.* Boston: Houghton Mifflin Company, 1966; Logan: Utah State University Press, 1974.

Originating from work begun in the 1950s at the Harvard Social Studies Project, Oliver and Shaver's volume provides a comprehensive explanation and justification of the jurisprudential rationale for teaching social studies in the schools. Focusing on perennial issues of public policy, jurisprudential teaching requires that teachers and students address ethical, legal, factual and definitional questions about legitimate solutions to public policy issues, both historic and contemporary. Oliver and Shaver view the fundamental purpose of American society as the attempt "to promote the dignity and worth of each individual who lives in the society" (10). This premise connects to the need to defend and promote real human freedom to make choices about competing solutions to ethical dilemmas and public policy options. The authors maintain that in a pluralistic society, **1.** the maintenance of human dignity and individual freedom can therefore only exist when diverse groups recognize that some problems require everyone to address them; **2.** members of all societal subgroups share a set of value commitments and a normative vocabulary that serve as a framework to deal with common problems; and **3.** this normative framework includes procedures for mediation of interpersonal and intergroup conflict.

The curricular content and instructional strategies emphasize the in-depth study of public issues laden with value conflicts. Oliver and Shaver draw upon Gunnar Myrdal's "American Creed" for the identification of core democratic values, and they recognize the need for students to address conflicts between competing values in the creed (i. e., liberty and equality). While retaining commitments to the maintenance of human dignity as a primordinate societal value, students require education in how to resolve value conflicts through rational deliberation.

The book is divided into three parts. Part One contains the intellectual rationale summarized previously, as well as a discussion of alternative approaches to value conflict. Part Two develops a conceptual framework for the teaching of value conflict and how specific analytic concepts can be linked to perennial public issues. Part Three provides very detailed consideration of how to select and organize problem units, discussion methods and problems, assessment of student competence (both with paper and pencil tests and content analysis of discussions), and implications for reform of social studies curriculum and instruction using the jurisprudential approach. A lengthy appendix includes detailed discussion of the research results from the Harvard Social Studies Project work at in a junior high school in suburban Boston, where many of the author's core ideas for curriculum and instruction were implemented, evaluated and modified over a four-year period.

Oliver and Shaver's volume remains the starting point for anyone considering the use of the jurisprudential approach in the social studies. The philosophical rationale is compelling while the analyses of strategies for instruction and assessment, particularly those about discussion, offer many important insights later extended by Newmann and Oliver in *Clarifying Public Controversy* (1970).

Shor, Ira and Paulo Freire. *A Pedagogy for Liberation: Dialogues on Transforming Education.* South Hadley: Bergin and Garvey Publishers, Inc., 1987.

Shor and Freire have created a volume that is unique in design and content. Consisting of edited conversations over a two-year span, the authors address "pedagogy for liberation" as a multifaceted endeavor. "Liberation" pedagogy is teaching that helps students to develop the critical sensibilities to challenge the official curriculum, and by implication the societal status quo that perpetuates inequities of wealth, status and power. For the authors, all inquiry is embedded in political and historical contexts that define the social relations of the classroom.

Teacher-dominated instruction ignoring the lived experiences of students can not be liberatory education. In its place, Shor and Freire view the experiences of the students as essential knowledge open to investigation because student experience has been shaped by the larger historical and social forces of modern capitalism.

Thus, liberatory education seeks to reinvent and reconstruct society as students learn how to critique social experience and "illuminate reality" by linking subject matter content to its economic and social class origins.

The authors advocate careful analysis of student sociocultural backgrounds, which implies detailed study of students' classroom discourse. Liberatory pedagogy requires that teachers understand the language of their students, engaging them in study of problems that establish relationships between core concepts in a subject matter field (social sciences, language arts) and the lived experiences of the students in the class. Teacher authoritarianism is rejected as contradictory in spirit and purpose to working with the students to interpret reality. At the same time, liberatory pedagogues retain justifiable authority in the classroom because they have substantial knowledge and expertise in designing educational experiences which facilitate student critical reflection about society.

Discussion is the preferred core instructional strategy. Freire claims "Dialogue is a moment where humans meet to reflect on their reality as they make and remake it" (98), implying that the teacher and students engage in a journey with a "permanent tension in the relation between authority and liberty" (102). Discussion is directed by the teacher, but the parameters are defined by the interests, experiences and motivation of the students, linked to the concepts introduced and explained by the teacher as the dialogue proceeds.

Most importantly, the authors contend that schooling is only one context among many in the struggle for social transformation. Networks of liberatory pedagogues are necessary to link teachers in schools with educators in unions, social movements, community centers, and other sites. Both authors recognize that substantive social change can't be the sole responsibility of mass public schooling, because the efforts to make education "liberatory" face strong resistance, often embedded in the cultural backgrounds of students and the efforts by conservative policy-makers to limit widespread access to higher education.

This volume's significance rests in its justification of linking all subject matter knowledge to issues that are meaningful to the lived experiences of the students, with the aim of educating students as effective social critics who can take action to transform society. By assisting students to become more effective critics of their own lived experiences, and gradually of their own society, the authors believe the patterns of class conflict and socioeconomic inequality reflected in the selection and organization of knowledge in schools can be altered, and a more just society created. The chapters on methods (4, 6, and 7) lack the detailed analyses offered in other volumes cited in this section, but the strengths of the conversations concerning rationale, student and teacher characteristics, and classroom environment (Chapters 1, 2, 3, and 5) merit serious investigation.

Taba, Hilda, Mary C. Durkin, Jack R. Fraenkel, and Anthony H. McNaughton. *A Teacher's Handbook to Elementary Social Studies: An Inductive Approach.* Reading: Addison-Wesley Publishing Company, 1971.

This volume presents a thorough conceptual structure and philosophical rationale for the organization of the elementary social studies program based upon the work of Hilda Taba. Completed after Taba's death, the book is one of the very few social studies handbooks placing issues at the center of the elementary social studies curriculum.

Core concepts and main and organizing ideas are the basis for the development and organization of knowledge in this program. Employing a spiral structure, the authors divide all instructional objectives into the areas of **1.** thinking, **2.** knowledge, and **3.** attitudes, feelings, and values. Grade level instructional objectives are linked by the periodic reintroduction of key concepts, and main and organizing ideas. Specific facts are subordinate to the key concepts and main and organizing ideas used to structure the spiral from grades one through eight, and depth rather than breadth study characterizes the program. The authors note that by encountering a main and organizing idea at different grade levels, key concepts such as interdependence become "more abstract, more complex and more powerful"(37). Facilitating development of increasing conceptual complexity for the growing child is the use of comparison and contrast in content section. As an example, the interdependence of humans and the physical/social environment is studied by examining diverse cases around the world, ranging across both historical and contemporary time dimensions. In doing so, flexibility of curricular organization is enhanced and reintroduction of the concept at increasing levels of complexity is facilitated.

The greatest strength of this book rests in Chapters 4 through 8, where detailed and well-defined examples of these topics are found: selection and organization of learning activities, teaching strategies and procedures, the key role of questioning, the development of skills and evaluation of student progress. Chapters 5 and 6 contain some of the best discussions of teaching strategies and questioning in the social studies literature. Relevant examples are linked to precise suggestions for the improvement of student reasoning and the development of independent student thought, emphasizing an inductive approach. This volume also includes a thorough discussion of how to evaluate student progress, with usable exercises, procedures and materials that are easily adaptable to a variety of classroom settings.

Although designed for the elementary and middle grades, much of this volume is clearly applicable to any level of social studies education. It is a very useful alternative to the traditional "expanding environments" approach employed in many elementary level social studies programs.

Additional Resources

Berman, Sheldon and Phyllis La Farge, editors. *Promising Practices in Teaching Social Responsibility.* Albany: State University of New York Press, 1993.

Fraenkel, Jack. *Helping Students Think and Value.* Englewood Cliffs: Prentice-Hall, 1973.

Freire, Paolo. *Pedagogy of the Oppressed.* New York: Continuum, 1970.

Hyman, Ronald T. *Improving Discussion Leadership.* New York: Teachers College Press, 1980.

Lee, John. *Teaching Social Studies in the Elementary School.* New York: Free Press, 1974.

Massialas, Byron G. and Fred Cox. *Inquiry in Social Studies.* New York: McGraw-Hill, 1966.

Arbetman, Lee P., Edward T. McMahon, and Edward L. O'Brien. *Street Law. A Course in Practical Law.* Fifth Edition. A Publication of the National Institute for Citizen Education in the Law. West Publishing Company, St. Paul, Minnesota. 1994, 647 pp. $24.96 softcover, $28.96 hardcover.

This is the fifth edition of the popular text first published in 1975. The objective remains the same: to address law in everyday life. Strategies include role playing, mock trials, arbitration hearings, and simulations. The lessons provide knowledge and skills for analyzing, evaluating and resolving legal conflicts. This edition features new text and problems dealing with gangs, guns and substance abuse as well as international law. Designed as the text for a law course, lessons are easily infused into classes examining policy-making or law enforcement. Effective use requires competence in interactive strategies including the skillful use of outside resource persons. **S**

Brady, Sheila, Carolyn Pereira, and Diana Hess. *It's Yours: The Bill of Rights.* Steck-Vaughn, Austin, Texas. 1993, 111 pp. $7.50.

The eight units on U.S. Government and the Bill of Rights in this book include the origins of rights, expression, religion, privacy, equal protection and civic participation. Each lesson integrates a variety of strategies including cooperative learning, role play, simulations and case studies. Designed to meet the needs of students studying English as a Second Language, the simply written text develops higher order thinking skills as students increase English language proficiency. The book would be valuable in U.S. History, Civics or law classes, and for any students with below average reading skills. **I/M S**

Croddy, Marshall, ed. *Streets, the Courts, and the Community.* Constitutional Rights Foundation, Chicago, Illinois. 1992, 63 pp. $17.50.

The ten lessons in this book examine the juvenile justice system, civil and criminal law, and conflict management. The step by step instructor's procedures facilitate effective use of the interactive strategies used to promote interest and participation. The book is designed for at-risk or special needs students, but will be effective when infused into existing courses where the objectives include helping students to understand how criminal and justice systems work. **I/M S**

Croddy, Marshall, and Coral Suter, *Of Codes and Crowns. The Development of Law.* Constitutional Rights Foundation, Los Angeles, CA. 1992, 65 pp. $6.50.

Teachers of World History and World Civilization courses seeking to analyze rules and laws in different regions will find this book valuable. The interdisciplinary approach has students using various methods of investigation, including those from archeology and anthropology. Students examine conflicts and problems of ancient civilizations both in establishing and setting limits on legal authority. Interactive strategies encourage students to reflect on how social and cultural influences pivotal to ancient and diverse settings continue to influence current societies. Many lessons need multiple class sessions, and require attention to time management. **S**

Eyes on the Prize. PBS, available through Social Studies School Service, Culver City, CA., 1987, 60 min. each. Set 1 (1954-65) videocassettes-$119.95 PF150VAP4 or laserdiscs-$129.95 PF150L-AP4; Set 2 (1965-85) videocassettes-$99.95 PF170V-AP4 or laserdiscs-$149.95.

Two sets of 10 videocassettes (or 7 laserdiscs)

cover the struggle for equality and justice during the years 1954-85. Textbook events become real as the news footage and interviews bring powerful personal perspectives to major issues of today. These packages are valuable as supplements for U.S. history and for law courses. **I/M S**

Gallagher, Arlene F. *Living Together Under the Law. An Elementary Education Law Guide.* Prepared by the Law, Youth and Citizenship Program of the New York State Bar Association and the New York State Education Department. New York State Bar Association, Albany, NY. 1988., 162 pp. $8.00.

This is a useful resource for teachers in the elementary school. The book provides lessons and activities in which students analyze their own behavior and that of others while developing tolerance of differences. The ten themes that are examined include: laws are essential; the nature of change; settling disputes; and the relationship between the values and the laws of a society. Each of the themes includes motivational and learning activities. The easy to use case studies, simulations, and conflict resolution activities can be used within existing elementary social studies classes, or integrated with language arts/reading programs. **P/I/M**

Goldman, Roger, Linda Riekes, and Sharon Slane, *Teaching About the Bill of Rights in Elementary and Middle School Classrooms. A Resource Guide for Lawyers, Law Students and Classroom Teachers.* Phi Alpha Delta Public Service Center, Bethesda, MD 1991, 112 pp. $10.00.

Lessons on the Bill of Rights and the Fourteenth Amendment are presented in this book with a focus on rights and responsibilities. Case studies are used by the authors to examine issues relating to sports, gender and discrimination in both school and community settings. Included are useful strategies for effectively using resource persons in designing and presenting lessons, for preparing mock courtroom simulations and for analyzing case studies. The book supplements existing K-8 social studies materials. **P/I/M**

Hiraoka, Leona, and Ken Masugi. *Japanese-American Internment: The Bill of Rights in Crisis,* Portfolio #N61. Jackdaw/Golden Owl Publishing, Amawalk, NY. 1994, 14 documents, timeline and 6 essays. $27.95, with study guide $35.00.

Teachers familiar with Jackdaws will welcome this new portfolio of primary source materials in which the extraordinary challenge to the constitutional system of checks and balances in a threatening and dangerous time is explored. Racism and cultural diversity can be effectively addressed as well as the consequences of prejudice and discrimination. The material is easily infused into U.S. History or World History courses and can be used for case studies, for debates and as the basis of role plays. **S**

Isaac, Katherine. *Civics for Democracy. A Journey for Teachers and Students.* A Project of The Center for Study of Responsive Law and Essential Information. Essential Books, Wash. DC, 1992, 390 pp. $17.50.

One glance at the table of contents quickly reveals why this book is an indispensible resource. The first Section presents profiles of citizen action activities involving students throughout the country. A history of citizen movements is followed by a review of social change brought about by citizen activists in many fields including Civil Rights, Labor, and Women's Rights. Useful for that alone, Isaac's book then provides a focus on the "how to" of citizen action with techniques for individual and group participation. Activities to engage students in using the described strategies and skills are followed by an extensive resource list. **S**

Keller, Clair W. and Denny L. Schillings, eds. *Teaching About the Constitution.* (National Council for the Social Studies Bulletin No. 80) Washington, DC. National Council for the Social Studies, 1987, 122pp. $9.95.

In the five chapters of this book the editors present a list of teaching activities involving an analysis of the Constitution. Interactive strategies are suggested for examining topics that include the consequences of ratification for African Americans and for women. Selected court cases are analyzed. The lessons would be effective and easy to infuse into any study of the Constitution. **S**

Laughlin, Margaret A., H. Michael Hartoonian and Norris M. Sanders, eds. *From Information to Decision Making. New Challenges for Effective Citizenship.* (National Council for the Social Studies Bulletin No. 83). Washington, DC.: National Council for the Social Studies, 1989, 115 pp. $11.95.

The editors have prepared 12 chapters by various authors designed to help teachers to deal effectively with the explosion of information characteristic of current times. Primarily for teachers, the book provides strategies and lessons easy to use in both elementary and secondary classes. Guidelines for integrating the computer, databases and mathematics in problem solving and decision making will be appreciated by teachers seeking to actively engage students in studying issues concerning citizenship. **I/M S**

McMahon, Edward T., and Judith A. Zimmer, National Institute for Citizen Education in the Law, and Terence W. Modglin and Jean F. O'Neil, National Crime Prevention Council. *Teens, Crime and the Community. Education and Action for Safer Schools and Neighborhoods.* West Publishing Company, St. Paul, Minnesota. 1992, 201 pp. $14.96.

This book is a timely resource that confronts students with issues relating to crime and crime prevention. Topics include gang violence, rape, sexual harassment, handgun use, and child and substance abuse. Problem-solving and decision-making activities make use of case studies, role plays, and community resource persons to encourage students to examine facts, statistics and conflicting views. Community projects provide research and service opportunities. The lessons can be infused into U.S. History, Civics, Law or government classes. **I/M S**

We the People. The Constitutional Rights Foundation, Chicago, IL 60605. 1991 Reprinted by Department of Education Grant #S123A00058., 1991, 70 pp. $12.50.

This book includes fifteen lessons that examine law and citizenship. Suggestions for teachers provide clear guidelines for actively involving students in a variety of activities including designing and conducting surveys, peer teaching, examining case studies and simulating court proceedings. Procedures helpful in using controversial materials and topics are provided and include establishing rules for dealing with controversy, identifying the nature of the disagreements, and guidelines for organizing ideas. Topics include lawmaking and special interest groups, regulations and the power of government, juvenile law, and police procedures. The book is designed for infusion into Civics, Law and U.S. History classes. **I/M S**

With Liberty and Justice for All. The Story of the Bill of Rights. The Center for Civic Education, Calabasas, CA 1992, 197 pp. $6.00.

This book presents fifteen lessons that exam-

ine both the historical developments leading to the Bill of Rights and an analysis of the current nature of those rights. Particularly useful are lessons dealing with the expansion of constitutional protections focusing on the experiences of African Americans. First Amendment freedoms and due process of law are well covered. Critical thinking skills are refined through exercises presented throughout each of the lessons. The lessons can be easily integrated into current U.S. History, World History or Civics classes. **I/M S**

Additional resources:

Video cassettes/videodiscs:

ABC News Interactive's Powers of the U.S. Government Videodisc Series. Prentice Hall School Division, Upper Saddle River, NJ. Powers of the President, Powers of Congress, Powers of the Supreme Court. $495 each, $1185 for all three. **I/M S**

Point of View 2.0: An Overview of U.S. History Struggles for Justice Videodisc (Vol.1); *Struggles for Justice* Videodisc (Vol. 2), $195 each. **I/M S**

A Cause for Celebration. Insight Media, NY, NY. 1991, 17 min. $189. Video showing students addressing sexism, racism and classism. **S**

American Voices: 200 Years of Speaking Out. National Archives, available through Social Studies School Service, Culver City, CA. 1989, ZF308V-AP4. 29 min. $65. Primary source materials dealing with petitions to the government. **S**

Kids and Crime. Films for the Humanities and Sciences, Princeton, NJ. 1994, 28 min. $89.95
Donahue "talk show" featuring 15-year-olds talking about their criminal activity. **S**

We the People. Insight Media, NY NY 1992, 23 min. $129.
Video of student perspectives on the stereotyping of Native Americans. **S**

Other books

Harrison, Maureen and Steve Gilbert (Eds.) *Landmark Decisions of the U.S. Supreme Court.* Excellent Books, available from Social Studies School Service, Culver City, CA., 1991, EXB100AP4. $45.50
Set of three books covering background, opinions and legal terms surrounding important cases. **S**
Takaki, Ronald. *A Different Mirror: A History of Multicultural America.* Little, Brown, New York.

1993. 508pp, $27.95.

Examines diverse experiences with American constitutional and legal systems. **S**

The Bill of Rights. More Than Mere Parchment. Law, Youth and Citizenship Program of the New York State Bar Association and the New York State Education Department, New York State Bar Association, Albany, New York. 1991. 136 pp.

Useful information and activities for integrating into any course addressing our fundamental freedoms. **S**

When Justice Is Up to You. Celebrating America's Guarantee of Trial By Jury. Association of Trial Lawyers of America, National Institute for Citizen Action in the Law, and DC Street Law Project. Association of Trial Lawyers of America, Washington, DC. 1992. 104 pp.

Excellent information on juries, historical as well as current, with simulation activities. **S**

Working Together: Lessons in Justice. Law-Related Lessons for Teaching the U.S. Constitution. Constitutional Rights Foundation, Chicago, 1994, 54pp.

Effective and easy-to-infuse lessons focused on the concept of Justice. **I/M S**

Zimmer, Judith A. *We Can Work It Out! Problem Solving through Mediation.* National Institute for Citizen Education in the Law and the National Crime Prevention Council. Social Studies School Service, Culver City, California, 1993. 132 pp. $40.

Indispensable strategies for conflict resolution in the class, the school and beyond. **I/M S**

Computer software:
Creating the U.S. Constitution. Educational Archives. Available through Zenger Media, Culver City, CA. Apple 5.25" disc; IBM 5.25" disc or IBM 3.5" disc, $65.

Useful program for analyzing and designing the Constitution. **I/M S**

Simulations:
Johnson, Cicilia and Ann McMahon. *We the People.* Social Studies School Service, Culver City, CA. $35.

Simulation of the Constitutional Convention. **I/M S**

Police Patrol: A Simulation for the Classroom. Constitutional Rights Foundation, Los Angeles, CA. $17.50.

Excellent activity for use with local police persons. **S**

Primary source materials:
The Constitution. Evolution of a Government. National Archives and SIRS, Inc., Boca Raton, Florida. $40.00

Excellent collection of primary source documents relating the development and interpretation of the Constitution. **I/M S**

INTERNATIONAL RELATIONS/FOREIGN POLICY TEACHING RESOURCES
by Mary E. Soley

After The Cold War: The U.S. Role in Europe's Transition,
A project of the Center for Foreign Policy
Development, Brown University, Box 1948,
Providence, RI, 02912; (401) 863-3155. Copyright
1993, 103 pages, $8.00. Permission is granted to
duplicate for classroom use.

*After the World War: The U.S. Role in Europe's
Transition* is one of ten reproducible curriculum
units developed by the 21st Century Education
Project at Brown University. Major concepts
include: isolationism; internationalism; communism; fascism; containment; the Cold War;
national and regional security; revolution; economic integration; and change. The educational
goal is to "introduce students to the historical
antecedents, current issues, and deeply felt values
that have entered into the national debate on
U.S. policy toward Europe" (page iii).

The unit is divided into student text (three
background readings, descriptions of four U.S.
foreign policy options, and a summary reading on
Europe's uncertain future), a ten-day lesson plan
and student activities, supplementary documents
for the teacher, and suggested readings. The
unit's greatest strengths include well developed
and clearly written readings, the use of a wide
variety of presentation formats (cartoons, quotes,
charts and graphs, pictures and maps), student
activities that promote analysis of differing perspectives and values, and engaging decision-
making activities. It does an excellent job in both
presenting various U.S. foreign policy options
toward Europe and helping students understand
the perspectives and values in each.

The activities rely heavily on students' reading abilities. While the materials are well written,
they are conceptually dense and teachers will
need to make special efforts to clarify major ideas
and define terminology.

High School
Richard K. Betts, editor. *Conflict After the Cold War:
Arguments on Causes of War and Peace.* Macmillan
Publishing Company, 866 Third Avenue, New York,
NY, 10022. Copyright 1994, 519 pages, $29.00.

Conflict After the Cold War is a college text. It
is designed to help students sort out the main
debates about whether war is likely to remain a
major problem in international life. The collection of writing presents contrasting arguments
about the future of the post-Cold War world and
puts them in philosophical and historical context.

A sample of the thirty-nine topics and their
authors includes: "The End of History?" by
Francis Fukuyama; "Perpetual Peace," by
Immanuel Kant; "Liberalism and World Politics"
by Michael Doyle; "The Spread of Nuclear
Weapons: More May Be Better" by Kenneth
Waltz; "Islamic Fundamentalism" by Graham
Fuller; and "America's Changing Strategic
Interest" by Samuel Huntington.

This book provides a overview of the major
ideas needed to teach about war and peace. Its
strengths include the diversity of perspectives
presented and the compilation of both historic
and current essays which influence the development of theory and practice today. The only
drawback is the level of difficulty and sophistication. Still, it is recommended for anyone preparing to teach a course in current world affairs.

Teacher Education, Undergraduate
Adrian Chan and the staff of the Soviet Union and
Eastern Europe Project and the Western Europe
Project. *When Iron Crumbles: Berlin and the Wall.*
Stanford Program on International and Cross-
Cultural Education (SPICE), Stanford University,
Littlefield Center, Room 14, 300 Lasuen St.,
Stanford, CA 94305-5013; (415) 725-1480 or 723-

1114. Copyright 1991, 13 pages, $29.95. Permission is given to educators to reproduce copies of student handouts for classroom use. A twenty-minute video tape is also available at a cost of $19.95.

When Iron Crumbles is only one of the many curriculum units developed by SPICE. In all cases, the compatible relationship between Stanford's scholars and educators makes for exceptionally high-quality instructional materials. The interdisciplinary nature of the publications also adds to their appeal.

Major concepts and themes include: the historical context of World War II, the division of Germany, and the building of the Berlin Wall; the Cold War; conflicts over differing political, social and economic ideologies; and the significance of the fall of the Berlin Wall and German unification. Instructional strategies include activities to develop mapping, writing, and participation skills; learning how to use a variety of primary sources; analysis skills through the use of Germany and the Berlin War as a case study; journal assignments; and a unique teaching strategy entitled "readers' theater." Using role plays, students create and perform scripts that involve important events and multiple voices. Comprehensive instructions are given for using readers' theater, as well as many other instructional strategies. Additional special features include: maps, pictures and cartoons; homework assignments and evaluation techniques; references for student handouts; and a glossary and bibliography. Each of the seven lessons can be integrated separately into the curriculum where appropriate or the unit can be taught in its entirety.

High School and Undergraduate

Charles Chatfield, editor. *Magazine of History,* "Peacemaking in American History." Organization of American Historians, Vol. 8, No. 3, Spring 1994. OAH Magazine of History, 112 N. Bryan Street, Bloomington, IN, 47408-4199; (812) 855-7311. Copyright 1994, 96 pages, $5.00. Permission is granted to duplicate for classroom use.

"Peacemaking in American History" contains five concise well-written essays, a supplement for the 1995 National History Day topic entitled Conflict and Compromise, five lesson plans with student handouts, and information on three different teaching resources. The piece provides a practical, yet intellectually stimulating primer for anyone beginning to teach about peace.

The essays cover such topics as: Alternatives to War in History; Peace as a Reform Movement; The Domestic Side of Foreign Policy; Peace and Women's Issues in U.S. History; and Peace History: The Field and the Sources. Each essay provides major and minor historical concepts, a sample of different perspectives on the events and conditions at the time, and a bibliography of books and other resources to expand one's understanding of the topic.

The lesson plans are titled: Quakers and Indians in Colonial America; Opposition to the Mexican War of 1946; The League of Nations and U.S. World Roles; Nonviolence in the Civil Rights Movement; and Conscientious Objection to the Vietnam War. The essays and lessons are appropriate for middle, high school, and undergraduate courses. While these materials are intended especially for U.S. history teachers, they would make an important contribution to any international relations/U.S. foreign policy course.

The overarching perspective put forth in the publication is the value of teaching about peace and efforts to make peace in American history. The idea of resolving conflicts without resort to violence is a value to study and possibly even promote. On the surface, who could object to teaching about peace? Still, without careful planning and thought, students (and teachers) could be caught in a simplistic debate with the just use of force on the one hand, and the pacifist approach on the other. The issues are extremely complex and should be explored in an open and reflective manner. Teaching about peace is controversial.

Middle and High School, and Undergraduate

James E. Davis and James S. Eckenrod, Instructional Design Associates, and the United States Institute of Peace, developers. *Managing World Conflict: A Resource Unit for High Schools.* United States Institute of Peace, 1550 M Street, NW, Suite 700, Washington, DC, 20005; (202) 429-3844. Copyright 1994, 110 pages, free. Permission is granted to duplicate for classroom use.

Managing World Conflict contains seven lessons (with a total of 74 pages of student handouts) for teaching about the causes of international and intra-state conflict and the approaches to peace. It is designed for use with high school social studies and language arts classes, especially those interested in participating in the

Institute-sponsored National Peace Essay Contest. Selected features of the unit include: a simulation on an international whaling commission conference; activities to diagnose conflicts and explore successful and thus-far failed efforts to make peace; uses of literature for learning about the personal impact of war; writing assignments to promote the development of strong essays; and the examination of political cartoons from around the world to enhance students' abilities to recognize and understand a variety of perspectives. The case studies include: Haiti; Sudan; Former Yugoslavia; Korean Peninsula; Tajikistan; and the Middle East. The Unit also contains a glossary, resource bibliography, resource list, and clear and concise overviews of each lesson.

The greatest strength of the unit is that it focuses in-depth on two major ideas (the causes of conflict and the approaches to peace) in ways that present the complexities of the issues, while at the same time providing practical teaching strategies to help students "unpack" the many components of war and peace. All student activities have built-in assessment tools and a variety of instructional methods are employed. The greatest weakness is time. While lessons can be used separately and infused into existing curriculum where appropriate, the best approach is to teach the entire unit, which could take from approximately 12 to 20 days.

Middle and High School

Jonathan Fore and Heidi Hursh, *Global Studies for the 90s.* Co-published by the Center for Teaching International Relations (CTIR), Graduate School of International Studies, University of Denver, Denver, CO, 80208-0269, (303) 871-3106 and the Social Science Education Consortium, 3300 Mitchell Lane, Suite 240, Boulder, CO, 80301-2272; (303) 492-8154. Distributed by CTIR. Copyright 1993, 149 pages, $26.95. Permission is granted to duplicate for classroom use.

CTIR has developed and published supplemental curriculum materials for preschool through adult groups since 1968. This book emphasizes selected global issues that draw upon history, as well as all the social science disciplines, and provides a context for studying such pressing post-Cold War issues such as democratization, the environment, economic interdependence, and development.

The book contains ten units; each includes 1-3 lessons (an introduction, student objectives, class time needed, materials, and procedures) student handouts, and additional resources. Units could be integrated separately into the curriculum or used sequentially as a global studies course.

The book's greatest strengths include the presentation of significant world issues in ways that middle and high school students can comprehend. The resources for students and activity ideas promote active learning and higher order thinking. Many of them actually sound like fun! There are numerous handouts and, with students working in groups, there are great opportunities for cooperation. Charts, graphs, maps, and timelines are common features.

As is the case when teaching any current issue, teachers need to take the initiative to constantly update the information presented in this book. A wide variety of news sources and perspectives must be sought and the teaching strategies will require modification to one's particular classroom situation. While summarizing activities are included, few specific evaluation criteria or instruments are provided to assess students' work.

High School

Great Decisions 1995 and Great Decisions 1995 Activity Book by the Foreign Policy Association, 729 Seventh Avenue, New York, NY, 10019; (212) 764-4050 or 1-800-628-5754. Copyright Foreign Policy Association. *Great Decisions 1995,* 96 Pages, $11.00. *Great Decisions 1995 Activity Book,* 40 Pages, $11.95. Permission is not granted to duplicate *Great Decisions 1995.* Permission is granted to duplicate the *Great Decisions 1995 Activity Book.*

Available each January, the *Great Decisions* briefing book analyzes eight vital U.S. foreign policy issues. Each 10-12 page article provides background (including historical context), policy options for the U.S., recommended readings, discussion questions, and pictures, charts, graphs, maps, and cartoons. Topics for *Great Decisions 1995* include: Russia and Its Neighbors; Nuclear Proliferation; United Nations at 50; Global Finance; China, Taiwan, Hong Kong; Immigration; and Democratization. A world map is provided.

The strengths of *Great Decisions* are the timeliness and balanced presentation of the topics, as well as the well-written synthesis of the major questions and issues to be discussed. While some parts of the articles may be conceptually dense and therefore difficult for students to understand without additional background, the wide range of global issues and geographic regions covered make for a solid course in current international affairs. Graphs, charts, pictures, political cartoons and quotes can contribute to students' abilities to comprehend the current and complex U.S. foreign policy issues presented. Another strong point is the Activity Book. For each topic, it contains activity instructions (major questions, article summary, activity overviews, objectives, materials, time required, and procedures), student handouts, and glossaries.

High School and Undergraduate

Karen Heller. *U.S. Response - The Making of U.S. Foreign Policy: A Simulation.* Close Up Publishing, 44 Canal Center Plaza, Alexandria, VA, 22314; (1-800-765-3131). Copyright 1990, $21.95 includes the three-day simulation with Teacher's Guide, role cards, team cards and situation cards.

Accommodating up to 30 high school participants, students formulate foreign policy in response to one of six crisis situations (drug trafficking, global pollution, hostage crisis, nuclear disarmament, and territorial aggression). Students role-play in teams the perspectives of U.S. government officials, ambassadors to the U.S. from the countries involved in the situation, and journalists. Instruction emphasizes the abilities to understand multiple perspectives, analyze conflicting facts, values, needs, and objectives, and make decisions. Major concepts include: national interests (security interests, economic interests, and ideological interests); geopolitics; and national resolve.

Given that the simulation is relatively simple and straightforward, its greatest use is as an awareness building activity. While the crisis situations are fictitious, they are fashioned after recognizable events in the past, are interesting, and contain major issues involved in U.S. foreign policy decision-making.

However, these same strengths constitute a weakness. Since a simulation is not reality, and in reality foreign policy is a far more complex and difficult process than depicted here, it is up to the teacher to conduct extensive debriefing. For example, only three types of actors are included in the simulation (U.S. government officials, ambassadors to the U.S. and journalists). In reality, foreign policy decision-making involves many others, such as members of the business community, lobbyists, educators, public interest groups, and bi-lateral, multi-lateral, and international

organizations. This simulation is an excellent introductory activity to a unit on U.S. foreign policy decision-making.

Middle and High School

Mary Lord and Martha L. McCoy, editors. *In Harm's Way: When Should We Risk American Lives in World Conflicts?.* A joint publication of the Study Circle Resource Center and ACCESS: A Security Information Service. Study Circles Resource Center, PO Box 203, Pomfret, CT, 06258; (203) 928-2616. Copyright 1994, 29 pages plus four one-page ACCESS Resource Briefs, $5.00. Permission is granted to duplicate for classroom use.

In Harm's Way is designed primarily for adult discussion groups known as study circles. However, the booklet is of such high quality that it is recommended for use in middle and high school classrooms. The format can be adapted easily. What makes this piece so special is the timeliness and timelessness of the question: When should we risk American lives in world conflicts? This is a central public policy issue that is at the heart of U.S. foreign policy decision making.

The booklet contains four major questions, each with accompanying readings (including different perspectives or positions), discussion questions, and bibliography. Question one focuses on the ethical and value questions that arise when a nation considers military action. It asks, "Are there reasonable grounds for using military force?" The next two questions are: "When should we place American lives in harm's way?" and "Current cases: Are these conflicts our business?" The four case studies presented allow students an opportunity to test the principles and ideas that emerged in the previous sessions against real-life situations. The four cases, (Bosnia, Haiti, Korean Peninsula, and Somalia) are excellent examples because each has a different level of military involvement and risk, and each involves a different set of U.S. goals. An ACCESS Resource Brief is provided for each of the conflicts. Question four asks, "Who is responsible for dealing with conflicts around the globe?" The purpose of this session is to broaden the conversation to include the larger world.

A strength of the booklet and format is that the cases used to "test" students' views can be changed or updated as new international and intra-state conflicts arise. The only drawback to *In Harm's Way* is the absence of student learning objectives, student activities, and assessment tools. However, there are many good decision making models available and most, if not all, could be used with these materials.

Middle and High School

Merry Merryfield and Richard C. Remy, editors.
Teaching About International Conflict and Peace.
Albany: State University of New York Press, 1995.

The initial goal of this project was to develop a practical resource for undergraduate and graduate pre-service social studies methods courses. However, the final product has turned out to be so much more: an extremely valuable resource for any social studies educator who thinks critically about what is important to teach, what values and assumptions these selections represent, and what teaching methods are most compatible.

The book is divided into two major sections: "Linking Content, Methods, and Educational Goals," and "Essays in International Conflict Management and Peace." The first section examines how to connect international conflict and peace content to teaching methodologies and also to the education goals and outcomes identified as the most essential knowledge and skills of a unit. A case study, which provides a model of the process of creating, implementing, and assessing a unit of instruction, demonstrates the step-by-step process of planning and teaching.

The second section includes seven essays on international conflict and peace concepts. They are: Building Peace: A Global Learning Process; The Use and Control of Military Power; Diplomacy, Negotiation, and Peaceful Settlement; Economic Cooperation; Human Rights in International Perspectives, Self-Determination; and Resolving Conflict Over the Global Environment. Also included is a list of resource organizations, chapter glossaries, and a bibliography.

Undergraduate and Graduate Teacher Education

Richard Shultz, Roy Godson and Ted Greenwood, editors. *Security Studies for the 1990s.* Brassey's: a Maxwell Macmillan Publishing Company. Orders to Brassey's Order Dept., Macmillan Publishing Co., 100 Front Street, Box 500, Riverside, NJ, 08075. Copyright 1993. 423 Pages, $50 hardback.

This book was written to "provide instructors and curriculum planners of security studies programs with a model curriculum and model courses that address traditional shortcomings and take account of the dramatic changes in the contemporary international environment" (page 1). Where many scholars, educators, and practitioners in international relations view peace and world order studies as an idealistic approach that seeks to replace conflict in the international system with cooperation, negotiation, and peaceful change, the major conception put forth in this volume is that, even with the end of the Cold War, security studies (national, international, and regional security) will continue to be extremely important.

The book contains twelve chapters, each one on a different aspect of security studies. The format for each chapter is unique, beginning with a twenty to twenty-five page essay on the topic by a leading scholar (examples of the topics include: Causes, Conduct, and Termination of War; The Defense Decision-Making Process; Nuclear Weapons: Doctrine, Proliferation, and Arms Control; Low-Intensity Conflict; Multilateral Collective Security Arrangements; and Environment and Security); there follow a syllabus identifying concepts and readings and one to three discussion pieces carefully critiquing the author's assumptions and decisions on what to include.

The greatest strength of this book is the concise presentation of past and present thinking about the field of security studies. One can acquire a solid overview (and recognize the many different perspectives) simply by reading the twelve essays. While these are very complex topics not generally covered in any depth until the graduate level, resources of this kind can assist teachers in their own understanding of international relations and promote more careful consideration about the development of their own curriculum and the major concepts they will teach.

Undergraduate and Graduate Teacher Education

Daniel C. Thomas and Michael T. Klare, editors, *Peace and World Order Studies: A Curriculum Guide. Five College Program in Peace and World Security Studies.* Fifth Edition published by Westview Press, Inc., 5500 Central Avenue, Boulder, CO, 80301; Copyright Westview Press 1989, 666 Pages, $17.95 paperback.

The fifth edition of the *Peace and World Order Studies Curriculum Guide* presents eleven essays on "perspectives on the curricular agenda" and ninety-three undergraduate course syllabi. Recognizing the dynamic nature of the fields of peace and world order studies, the essays and syllabi for the Guide represent many different perspectives regarding the content to be taught as well as the diverse value orientations that exist. The ninety-three syllabi were selected from over 1,000 submitted for review. The list of authors for the essays, as well as the syllabi, reads like a Who's Who of peace and world order studies (Elise Boulding, Betty Reardon, Chad Alger, Joseph Nye, Anthony Lake, and Gene Sharp are some examples).

Few other resources provide equivalent breadth as well as depth on the current thinking in teaching about these topics. While it would be a rare high school that could devote an entire semester to a course on "social movements and revolution," the Guide provides a much needed tool for one's own professional growth. In addition to the reading lists provided for each of the ninety-three syllabi, the illumination of the concepts in each course is a very useful road map for teachers who require understanding of the larger picture before selecting ideas and simplifying them for student use. The Guide is not suitable for high school students.

The eleven essays include such topics as: differing approaches to peace studies; the research agenda; the evolution of peace studies; pedagogical issues and the interdisciplinary challenge of the field. Selected course syllabi include: introductions to peace and world order studies; global security, arms control, and disarmament; world political economy and economic justice; human rights and social justice; regional conflicts; conflict resolution; ecological balance; women and world order; religious and ethical perspectives; literary and media perspectives; and world order education and teacher training.

39 DOMESTIC ECONOMIC POLICY
by Ronald A. Banaszak

DeKoster, Katie, and Bruno Leone, eds. *Poverty: Opposing Viewpoints.* San Diego: Greenhaven Press, 1994. $17.95 hardcover (order number 066-2), $9.95 paperback (order number 065-4).

Recently revised, this book contains up-to-date comments of experts with differing opinions about the causes of and solutions to poverty, including the benefits and detriments of government policies. The many pro and con statements by experts encourage debate, analysis of arguments and other critical thinking skills which are detailed in a brief teacher guide. This book is useful for any high school course dealing with the issue of poverty, especially government and economics.

Federal Reserve Bank of Kansas City. *Federal Reserve System.* Kansas City, MO: Federal Reserve Bank of Kansas City, 1994. Available free, one per school.

These four videos and print lessons describe the operation of the Federal Reserve System. The third video challenges students to make policy decisions. After students decide, the materials give answers from past and present Federal Reserve leaders. Lesson 10 involves students in a game that deals with distinguishing between facts and myths. This publication is useful primarily for high school economics and government classes.

Kourilsky, Marilyn. *Kindereconomy.* New York: National Council on Economic Education, 1989. $19.95.

This teacher resource manual contains a series of lessons that lead primary level students to understand the working of our economy through reflection on their everyday experiences. These activities do not deal with policy, but do help students experience the economy and the consequences of economic decisions. The lessons are well-described, easily implemented and are based on an experiential learning approach.

Kourilsky, Marilyn. *Mini-Society: Experiencing Real-World Economics in the Elementary School Classroom.* Menlo Park, CA: Addison-Wesley Publishing Company, 1983. $18.00.

This simulation of an economic system in the classroom is an experience-based approach to teaching about economic systems and basic economic concepts. Though it does not deal directly with policy making and is challenging to implement, it is an engaging simulation for middle level students.

National Issues Forum Institute Staff. *The $4 Trillion Debt: Tough Choices about Soaring Federal Deficits.* Dubuque, Iowa: Kendall/Hunt Publishing Company, 1993. Student booklet costs $2.95 and the teacher guide costs $15.00.

After an introductory essay, a pro/con presentation of three policy options causes students to seek public policy that will solve or improve the problem. The intent is to inform students about the topic, but, more importantly, to teach them a deliberative process for dealing with controversial issues. This brief booklet does not overwhelm students and is useful in any high school course dealing with the federal deficit. Additional titles, following the same format, are produced annually and are listed later.

Schug, Mark, ed. *Senior Economist.* New York: National Council on Economic Education. Four issues per year for $16.95.

Each issue of this periodical focuses on a contemporary economic policy issue such as health care reform, free trade with Mexico, or immigrants in the economy. A prominent economist writes a background essay on each topic and three to five complete lesson plans that feature involvement activities and economic reasoning follow. This newsletter is very current and useful for any high school course dealing with contemporary economic issues.

Sid Meier's Railroad Tycoon Hunt Valley, MD: Microprose, 1993. $69.95 (often discounted at computer stores).

This computer game is a powerful interactive simulation involving a number of decisions. The goal is to build a large railroad network. Students manage the railroad for forty or more years and computer generated reports detail the consequences of their decisions. This game is not designed for classroom instruction, but for individual use. There is no teacher guide. Yet it is very intriguing and effective at sparking discussions with middle school and high school students enrolled in U.S. or world history, economics or business courses.

SimCity Orinda, CA: Maxis, 1993. Available at software stores. $39.95 (often available for less)

In this computer simulation, students manage and build a city. They choose to manage one of eight cities and make numerous policy decisions to improve living conditions. This game is a complex multi-tasking piece of software that calculates the results of interaction among many decisions. SimCity can be used in virtually any social studies course from grades 6 through 12, but it was not designed for classroom instruction. No teacher guide is provided, but the computer manual has sections on strategy and urban planning that are content rich.

The Wall Street Journal Classroom Edition Chicopee, MA: Classroom Edition, The Wall Street Journal.

This tabloid-sized newspaper is published monthly, September through May and is available in classroom sets of 30 copies for $150 (nine issues) or $90 (five issues). Also included is a monthly video of news stories on economic events and posters with lesson plans. Articles are taken from the *Wall Street Journal* and have its editorial perspective, but are very timely. The excellent teacher guide provides a variety of activities related to the stories. These include vocabulary, factual recall questions, thought provoking discussion questions, individual projects, cooperative learning activities and writing projects.

The teacher guide also has a matrix displaying the curricular connections of each story to the content of business, economics, English, math, science, government and U.S. history courses. The reading level limits this periodical for use with high school juniors or seniors.

Other Resources

Balancing the Budget. Decisions, Decisions Computer Simulation Series. Watertown, MA: Tom Snyder Productions, Inc., 1991.

Buchholz, Todd G. *New Ideas from Dead Economists.* New York: Plume, 1990.

Cox, Carol G., and Alice M. Rivlin. *Understanding Economic Policy: A Citizen's Handbook.* Washington, D.C.: League of Women Voters of U. S., 1990.

Heilbroner, Robert L. *The Worldly Philosophers: The Lives, Times and Ideas of the Great Economic Thinkers.* New York: Touchstone, 1986.

Leone, Bruce, ed. *Capitalism: Opposing Viewpoints.* San Diego: Greenhaven Press, 1986.

MacNeil/Lehrer Economic Reports. *The Deficit Game: A High School Struggles to Balance the U.S. Budget.* Videocassette, simulation and guide. New York: Cambridge Studios, 1993.

National Issues Forum Institute Staff. *The Poverty Puzzle: What Should Be Done to Help the Poor?* Dubuque, Iowa: Kendall/Hunt Publishing Company, 1993.

The Health Care Cost Explosion: Why It's So Serious, What Should Be Done. Dubuque, Iowa: Kendall/Hunt Publishing Company, 1993.

Prescription for Prosperity: Four Paths to Economic Renewal. Dubuque, Iowa: Kendall/Hunt Publishing Company, 1992.

The Health Care Crisis: Containing Costs, Expanding Coverage. Dubuque, Iowa: Kendall/Hunt Publishing Company, 1992.

Remedies for Racial Inequality: Why Progress Has Stalled, What Should Be Done. Dubuque, Iowa: Kendall/Hunt Publishing Company, 1993.

Health Care for the Elderly: Moral Dilemmas, Mortal Choices. Dubuque, Iowa: Kendall/Hunt Publishing Company, 1993.

Regaining the Competitive Edge: Are We Up to the Job? Dubuque, Iowa: Kendall/Hunt Publishing Company, 1992.

O'Neill, Terry, and Karin Swisher, eds. *Economics in America: Opposing Viewpoints.* San Diego: Greenhaven Press, 1992.

Schumacher, E.F. *Small Is Beautiful: Economics as if People Mattered.* New York: Perennial Library, 1989.

Swartz, Thomas R., and Frank J. Bonello. *Taking Sides: Clashing Views on Controversial Economic Issues.* Guilford, CT: Dushkin Publishing, 1993.

Wekesser, Carol, ed. *Health Care in America: Opposing Viewpoints.* San Diego: Greenhaven Press, 1994.

Wekesser, Carol, and Karen Swisher, eds. *Social Justice: Opposing Viewpoints.* San Diego: Greenhaven Press, 1990.

40 BIBLIOGRAPHY ON SCIENCE, TECHNOLOGY AND SOCIETY

by Samuel Totten and Jon E. Pedersen

Cheek, D.W. (1992). *Thinking Constructively about Science, Technology, and Society Education.* Albany, NY: State University of New York Press. 262pp ($16.95). (Available from State University of New York Press, State University Plaza, Albany, NY 12246.)

This volume synthesizes the major historical and conceptual movements in Science, Technology, and Society (STS) education. The major focus of the volume is on the current thinking and research surrounding STS and the application of these ideas to STS curriculum development in science and social studies classrooms. This resource will be invaluable to educators who are in the incipient stage of developing their own philosophy of using STS concepts and STS curriculum development. This is especially true of Chapter 5, which presents a conceptual framework for STS teaching and a constructivist framework for STS education. It concludes with an extensive and useful bibliography.

Hickman, Faith M., Patrick, John J., and Bybee, Rodger W. (1987). *Science, Technology, Society: A Framework for Curriculum Reform in Secondary School Science and Social Studies.* Boulder, CO: Social Science Education Consortium, Inc.

An excellent resource for teachers in grades 7-12 that provides an overview of the STS theory, a discussion of decision making and cognitive process skills that can be incorporated into STS studies, and a discussion as to how teachers can combine social studies and science in order to fashion an interdisciplinary approach in the classroom.

Hocking, C., Barber, J., and Coonrod, J. (1990). *Acid Rain: Teacher's Guide.* Berkeley, CA: Lawrence Hall of Science GEMS Project. 159pp. (Available from GEMS, Lawrence Hall of Science, University of California at Berkeley, Berkeley, CA 94720.)

Based on the STS model of incorporating science, technology and key societal issues into an integrated study, this booklet delineates how teachers in grades six through ten can implement a unit on the subject of acid rain. In a cogent and detailed fashion, the authors provide an introduction to the unit, discuss the time frame needed to conduct a thorough study, provide explicit directions and discussions of the eight sessions that comprise the unit, suggest ways of extending the unit further, and provide a short but useful annotated resource list. In a helpful section entitled "Behind the Scenes," the authors provide a discussion about acids, bases, buffers, acid rain and the problems it causes, as well as proposed solutions.

Hungerford, H.R., Litherland, R.A., Peyton, R.B., Ramsey, J.M. and Volk, T.L. (1988). *Investigating and Evaluating Environmental Issues and Actions Skill Development Modules.* Champaign, IL: STIPES Publishing Co. 169pp. (Available from STIPES Publishing Co., 10-12 Chester St., Champaign, IL 61820.)

Subtitled "A Curriculum Development Project Developed to Teach Students How to Investigate and Evaluate Science-Related Social Issues," this booklet is comprised of six learning modules on key environmental issues for use with middle level and junior high school students. The titles of the six modules are: "Environmental Problem Solving," "Getting Started on Issue Investigation," "Using Surveys, Questionnaires, and Opinionnaires in Environmental Investigations," "Interpreting Data from Investigations," "Investigating an Environmental Issue," and "Environmental Action Strategies." Each module is comprised of an introduction, objectives, key pieces of information (articles and essays) for the student, learning activities, and worksheets. This is one of the best environmental curriculum programs available.

Lewis, B.A. (1991). *The Kid's Guide to Social Action: How to Solve the Social Problems You Choose — and Turn Creative Thinking into Positive Action.* Minneapolis, MN: Free Spirit Publishing. 184pp ($14.95). (Available from the National Science Teachers Association, 1742 Connecticut Avenue NW, Washington, DC 20009.)

In this book the author discusses the skills necessary to enable students and teachers to take action on science-technology-society issues. Lewis includes examples of projects that have been initiated by students as well as guides and materials for taking social action. The book is comprised of five parts: I. "Life Beyond The Classroom" examines successful projects and provides insights as to how students can create similar projects in their own community; II. "Power Skills" provides the teacher and students with the social action skills needed to accomplish their projects; III. "Initiating Or Changing Laws" examines the process of changing laws or initiating new laws; IV. "Resources" provides the names and addresses of important social action groups, agencies that award money and scholarships to students for social action, and books that provide insights about government, citizenship, the environment and problem solving; and, V. "Tools" provides blackline masters of petitions, proclamations, releases, and resolutions. This book is an excellent resource for teachers in teaching grades 5-12.

Pearson, J. V. (1988). *Science, Technology, Society: Model Lessons For Secondary Science Classes.* Boulder, CO: Social Science Education Consortium, Inc. 216pp. ($17.95). (Available from the Social Science Education Consortium, 855 Broadway, Boulder, CO 80302.)

This resource has four main components. Part one includes an introduction to Science, Technology, Society study and its importance. In part two, Pearson provides matrixes for use in planning the lessons as well as a matrix of the teaching strategies used. Part three provides ten introductory lessons that teachers can use to focus students on STS matters in their classes. Part four outlines twenty-four more sophisticated and complex lessons. This is an excellent resource for secondary (grades 7-12) science and social studies teachers. What is particularly valuable about this resource is that it provides the means for teachers to move from basic lessons to the more advanced.

Ramsey, J.M, Hungerford, H.R., and Volk, T.L. (1980). *A Science-Technology-Society Case Study: Municipal Waste.* Champaign, IL: STIPES Publishing Co. 129pp. (Available from STIPES Publishing Co., 10-12 Chester St., Champaign, IL 61820.)

This volume, which was designed for use by middle and secondary level students, is comprised of three main sections: I. "Teacher Notes," which clearly delineates the four main goals of the unit of study (1. Science Foundations, 2. Issue Awareness, 3. Issue Investigation, and 4. Citizenship Action) and provides direction for the teacher; II. "Student Materials and Activities"; and a glossary. A major portion of Part II is designed so that the teacher can reproduce the handouts (overviews of the issues, key articles, research questions, sample questionnaires and surveys) for student use. The major strength of this resource is that it is structured to assist students to glean a solid base of knowledge, to use that knowledge for in-depth investigation, and then to take action by addressing the issue.

Thier, H.D. (1989) *Chemical Education for Public Understanding* (CEPUP). Berkeley, CA: Lawrence Hall of Science. (Note: This program consists of twelve modules, and each module comes with written support material. Each is approximately 130pp.) (Available from Sargent-Welch Scientific Company, 7300 North Linder Avenue, Skokie, IL 60077.)

Chemical Education for Public Understanding (CEPUP) is a curriculum project developed by the University of California at Berkeley's Lawrence Hall of Science emphasizing the development of students' understanding of chemicals and chemical issues in society. Modules range from $145.00 to $225.00 and include topics such as "Chemical Survey and Solutions and Pollution," "Investigation Ground Water: Toxic Waste: A Teaching Simulation," "Plastics in Our Lives," "Chemicals in Foods: Additives," and "Investigating Hazardous Materials," among others. All are appropriate for grades 6-9. CEPUP is an outstanding curriculum that provides students opportunities to do in-depth investigations on pertinent key environmental and social issues. This curriculum is unique in three major ways: **1.** each module comes complete with all of the equipment and chemicals necessary for the experiments; **2.** the written materials provide accurate and in-depth information, both of which are imperative if students are going to gain a deep understanding of scientific concepts; and **3.** it is interdisciplinary in nature (combining political, social and scientific concepts and issues).

Thirunarayanan, M.O. (Ed.) (1992). *Think and Act. Make an Impact! Handbook of Science, Technology and Society. Volume II. STS in Action in the Classroom.* Tempe, AZ: STS Project-FEE. 323pp. (Available from STS Project-FEE, Arizona State University, College of Education, Tempe, AZ 85287-0911).

This volume is comprised of 33 lessons on an eclectic array of topics, including but not limited to the following: biodiversity, energy, hunger, life science, designing and using satellites, school gardens, earthquake waves, the cost of space exploration, key environmental issues (acid rain, air and water pollution, endangered species, the greenhouse effect, the ozone hole), energy conservation, social action, weather and the water cycle, and wind erosion. While a vast majority of the lessons are geared to the middle level (various combinations of grades 5-8), there are others that are aimed at grades K-6, 3-7, 4-6, 4-8, 6-12, 7-12. A unique quality of this curriculum is that it is informed by the actual experiences of middle level educators who work with early adolescents on a daily basis; the curriculum was exclusively written by middle level educators.

Yager, R.E. (Ed.) (1993). *The Science, Technology, Society Movement.* Washington, D.C.: National Science Teachers Association. 177pp. (Available from NSTA, 1742 Connecticut Ave., NW, Washington, D.C. 20009.)

This monograph, which constitutes volume seven of the NSTA "What Research Says to the Science Teacher" series, is comprised of four main parts and a total of twenty-three essays: Part I. What STS Means; Part II. The Need for STS; Part III. STS in Broader Perspectives; and Part IV. Results of STS. Among the many fascinating essays herein are: "Teacher Strategies Used by Exemplary STS Teachers," "STS in Social Studies — Research and Practice," "Coordination of STS and Community Goals," and "An Issue as an Organizer: A Case Study." This volume not only provides the theory behind and the research-base for STS, but it also provides practical suggestions for the teacher.

Yager, R.E. (Ed.) (1992). International Council of Associations For Science Education: ICASE Yearbook, 1992, *The Status of Science-Technology-Society Reform Efforts Around the World.* Petersfield, UK: International Council of Associations for Science Education 138pp. ($9.95). (Available through Dennis Chisman, International Council of Associations for Science Education Honorary Treasurer, Knapp Hill, South Harting, Petersfield GU31 5LR, UK.)

This yearbook is the effort of the top scholars in Science, Technology, Society (STS) around the world. This volume is particularly strong and useful to teachers in that it provides a comprehensive view of the STS process. More specifically, it provides a definition and rationale for STS, examples of STS initiatives, and an evaluation of STS efforts.

Programs:

National Issues Forums in the Classroom (100 Commons Rd., Dayton, OH 45459-2777). "National Issues Forums in the Classroom seeks to help students discover, through public discussion, their common ground on complex domestic issues. The program's goal is to enhance the quality of civic life by expanding the opportunities for students to discuss and be more informed about specific public issues." The program package includes issue books, a teacher's guide, an implementation guide, and an instructor outline. Among the topics germane to STS that have been addressed by the National Issues Forums are: "The Farm Crisis; Who's in Trouble, How to Respond," "Energy Options: Finding a Solution to the Power Predicament," "Coping with AIDS: The Public Response to the Epidemic," and "The Environment at Risk: Responding to Growing Dangers."

Other Pertinent Resources:

Asimov, Isaac (1991). *Asimov's Chronology of the World: The History of the World from the Big Bang to Modern Times.* New York: HarperCollins.

Bender, David L., and Leone, Bruno (Eds.) *Opposing Viewpoints Series/Juniors.* San Diego, CA: Greenhaven Press.

Among the volumes germane to STS at the middle level in this series are: Pollution, Animal Rights, Endangered Species, The Environment, Forests, Garbage, Nuclear Power, Smoking, and Toxic Wastes.

Goldfarb, Theodore D. (1993). *Taking Sides: Clashing*

Views on Controversial Environmental Issues. Guilford, CT: The Dushkin Publishing Group, Inc.

Laughlin, Margaret A., Hartoonian, H. Michael, and Sanders, Norris M. (Eds.) (1989). *From Information to Decision Making: New Challenges to Effective Citizenship.* Washington, D.C.: National Council for the Social Studies.

Miller, J.D., Suchner, R. W., and Voelker, A. (1985). *Citizenship in an Age of Science.* Elmsford, NY: Pergamon Press.

Newton, David E. (1992). *Science and Social Issues.* Portland, ME: J. Weston Walch.

National Council for the Social Studies (1983). Guidelines for Teaching Science-Related Social Issues. *Social Education,* 47(4), 258-261.

Patrick, J. J., and Remy, R. C. (1984). *Connecting Science, Technology, and Society in the Education of Citizens.* Boulder, CO: ERIC Clearinghouse for Social Studies/Science Education and Social Science Education Consortium.

Toffler, A. (1980). *The Third Wave.* New York: Random House.

ROAD MAPS FOR MULTICULTURALISMS: RESOURCES FOR DIVERSE STUDENT POPULATIONS
by Jane Bernard Powers

Anthologies/Edited Collections

American Eyes, New Asian-American Short Stories for Young Adults edited by Lori M. Carlson. New York: Henry Holt and Company, (1994). ISBN0-8050-3544-3 **J, H, A**

Coming of age, the meaning of home and the meaning of difference are themes in this collection of short stories authored by Asian American writers. "How can a home be safe and secure in a homeland that is dangerous because it rejects you for your difference, or because it invites you to be like everyone else? Is home the place that keeps the ways of another, more ancient homeland, or is it where new replaces old?" These questions are posed by the editor to frame the elusive and changeable significance of home to Asian American young people. (xi) The close-to-the-bone quality of these voices speaking about being American in a country that is so ambivalent about difference makes the collection "an Asian fire."

Bridges and Borders, Diversity in America. The editors of *Time Magazine* New York: Warner Books, 1994. ISBN 0-446-67131-2. **J, H, A**

This is an anthology of critical issues editorialized or featured in *Time* magazines for the past eight decades. "Essays by writers such as Toni Morrison and Barbara Ehrenreich, news stories covering major historical events and feature stories on demographic trends" are part of this multicultured compendium. Articles include, "Hunger Stalks the 'Hogan'" from the 1940's, "The Meaning of Little Rock," from the 1950's, "Marching for Justice" in the 1960's and "Raid at Wounded Knee" are typical of the issues addressed in this valuable resource.

Civics for Democracy, A Journey for Teachers and Students Katherine Isaac Washington D.C.: Essential Books,

1992. ISBN 0-936758-32-5 **H, A**

This issues oriented guide for student citizen action is introduced by Ralph Nader and includes an impressive list of reviewers from a wide range of organizations involved in citizen action including Greenpeace, Citizens Clearing House for Hazardous Waste, Disability Rights Education and Defense Fund and Youth Service America. The text is a well organized road map for student action projects that begins with histories of the civil rights movement labor movement, women rights movements, consumer movement and environmental movement. Student activities, resource organizations and references are included.

Cool Salsa, Bilingual Poems on Growing Up Latino in the United States. Edited by Lori M. Carlson New York: Henry Holt and Company ISBN 0-8050-3135-9 J, **S, A**

Speaking two languages and walking the bridges between two cultures is part of the fabric of growing up Latino in the United States. This collection of poems by first, second and third generation Latinos conveys the vibrancy of Latino presence and heritage along with the pains of "struggling to survive." In two languages, Spanish and English, topics such as dating, finding respect, hot dogs, orange trees and the future are explored and shared in traditional lyrical forms and in street language by this impressive group of poets.

A Different Mirror, A History of Multicultural America Ronald Takaki. Boston: Little, Brown and Company, 1993. ISBN 0-3116-83112-3 **S, A**

Ronald Takaki's book is a history of the interaction of select ethnic groups in American history. It is a very readable sharing of stories that encour-

Keys: E=Elementary, J=Junior High, H=High School
S=Secondary, A=Young Adult

ages the readers "to see ourselves in a different mirror." The Triangle Shirtwaist Fire, Picture Brides, Gold Mountain and El Norte are some of the topics that feature in the narratives of Japanese Americans, Chinese Americans, Chicanas and Chicanos, Native Americans, African Americans, Jewish Americans and Irish Americans. This Revisionist mural of history which includes class and gender issues will be useful for both elementary and secondary teachers who are interested in deepening and reshaping their understanding of American History. The volume includes some pictures and extensive notes.

The Education Feminism Reader. Edited by Lynda Stone with the assistance of Gail Masuchika Boldt. New York: Routledge, (1994) ISBN 0-415-90793-4 **A**

This reader on feminism and education features the theorizing of twenty-two well-known scholars and researchers on the subjects of girls, women, schooling, sources of inequality, ways of knowing and curricula in educational domains. The meaning of difference, separate spheres, critiques of white feminism, moral education, and the connections between multiculturalism and feminism are among the topics included in this dense reader, which is organized in five sections; I, Self and Identity; II, Education and Schooling; III, Knowledge Curriculum and Instructional Arrangements; IV, Teaching and Pedagogy; and V, Diversity and Multiculturalism. Contributors speak from different racial, class, and ethnic perspectives.

Freedom's Children, Young Civil Rights Activists Tell Their Own Stories. Edited by Ellen Levine New York: Avon Books, (1993). ISBN0-380-72114-7 **J, H**

The Civil rights movement of the 1950's and 1960's was an African American drive for freedom that marshalled support from the young people of southern communities. This book tells the stories of thirty young African Americans who were children and teenagers during the human rights struggles of the 1950's and 60's. These young people were drawn into the civil rights movement by virtue of their parents' human rights activism. Many of them were in the initial voter registration drives, protests and school integration efforts. They were the young people who sat in all white restaurants and demanded to be served, who refused to give up their seats at the front of the bus, who integrated

the public schools, and faced violence and death. The book includes a chronology of the civil rights movement, and information on the contributors' current lives.

Hearing us Out, Voices From the Gay and Lesbian Community. Roger Sutton. New York: Little Brown and Company, (1994). **J, H, A**

This book tells the stories of nineteen gay and lesbian youth and adults. The stories that make up the book, based on interviews and edited transcripts by the author, are answers to the question, "what does it mean to be gay?" The author's intent was to address, through personal stories, the serious discrimination and critical health concerns that face gay and lesbian teens today. Humiliation, ostracism, AIDS, the military, gay parenting and an actively hostile adversary in the religious right are among the specific issues facing the population of young people today. "The voices in the book {should} help everyone see the gay and lesbian community as a proud and diverse group of people with their own history, stories and future."

Ordinary Americans, U. S. History Through the Eyes of the Everyday People. Edited by Linda Monk Alexandria, Va: Close Up Publishing, 1994. ISBN 0-932765-47-5 **J, H, A**

This anthology of readings is a collection of 200 first-person accounts of U. S. History featuring the voices of Native Americans, African Americans, Hispanic Americans, Asian Americans and European Americans describing notable and everyday events. For example, the section on "The Plantation South" includes " A Slave Child's View of Plantation Life," by Jacob Stroyer, "A Cruel Mistress," by Angelina Grimke Weld, and "Santa Claus Brought Me These New Clothes" by Harriet Jacobs. Among the other voices in the compendium are those of a former slave, Olaudah Equiano, who describes the passage from Africa to America, Jessie Lopez de la Cruz, who organized her comrades in the fields for the United Farmworkers, and Cheyenne tribeswoman, Kat Bighead. Complete references are included.

The Power in Our Hands, A Curriculum on the History of Work and Workers in the United States. William Bigelow and Norman Diamond. New York: Monthly Review Press, 1988. **S, A**

This is a sixteen-lesson unit on the history of work and organized labor in the United States.

This teacher written curriculum encourages students to reflect on "their own power" and "ability to remake society." (17) The lessons are organized for student participation through role play, simulation and imaginative writing that makes student's "lives become an 'additional text' within the lessons." Union maids, plant closings, racial conflict and cooperation in tenant farming are among the lesson topics included. Student handouts and suggested further reading are included.

Race Identity and Representation in Education. Cameron McCarthy and Warren Crichlow (Eds.) New York: Routledge, 1993. ISBN 0-415-90558 **A**

This recently published collection of articles on multiculturalisms is suggested for teachers who are reaching for theoretical perspectives that clarify race, class, ethnic and gender issues/identities in education institutions and classroom life. One of the centerpieces of the collection is McCarthy's essay entitled, "After the Canon: Knowledge and Ideological Representation in the Multicultural Discourse on Curriculum Reform." His critique and analysis of multicultural education is thorough, incisive and rich in examples of curriculum and student life. Christine Sleeter, Elizabeth Ellsworth, Michael Apple, Cornel West and Fazal Rizvi are among the contributing authors. Notes and an Index are provided.

Tales of Courage, Tales of Dreams: A Multicultural Reader, John Mundahl Menlo Park, CA: Addison Wesley, 1993. ISBN 0-201-53962-4. **J, H, A** (Grades 5-12)

This multicultural reader for students who speak English as a second language tells stories from many cultures including Mexican, Puerto Rico, Native American, Jamaican, Laotian, Lebanese and African American. The reader is divided into eight sections based on themes such as "Tales of Prejudice," "Tales of Courage," "Tales of Triumph," and "Tales of Dreams." Selections include vocabulary study, and the author makes recommendations for use the of the materials with students. The book is indexed.

Teaching in the Multicultural Classroom, Freedom's Plow. Theresa Perry and James W. Fraser (Editors). New York: Routledge, 1993. ISBN 0-415-90700-4. **A**

In the words of the editors, multicultural education is the "fundamental question to be addressed if schools are to be agents of democracy in an increasingly diverse United States. " The

book is divided into four parts that address four major domains; theoretical contexts, voices from teachers, perspectives on the new canon, and power structures in schooling that support multiculturalism writ large.

Unequal Sisters, A Multicultural Reader in U.S. Women's History. Ellen Carol DuBois and Vicki L. Ruiz. New York: Routledge, 1990. ISBN 0-415-90272-X **H, A**

This multicultural reader in women's history provides both teachers and students with an array of narratives or stories that illuminate the differences and connections in women's lives and experiences across time and geographic space. It is centered in the Western United States where there was and is a "confluence of many cultures and races" including Native American, Mexican, Asian, Black, and European-American women. The volume explores issues of relations between groups of women, and the place of family, and politics, in the creation of a tentative narrative of U.S. History. Selected bibliographies of African-American Women, Asian-American Women, Latinas and Native American Women are included in this work.

Books, Individually Authored

Chinese Women of America, A Pictorial History. Judy Yung. Seattle: University of Washington Press, 1986. ISBN 0-295-96358. **J, H, A**

This carefully researched and documented book tells the stories and identifies central issues in the lives of Chinese American women in the United States. The book is organized chronologically into three central periods, 1834-1900, 1900-1945 and 1945-1985. Sexist images of Chinese American women as exotic curios and racist descriptions in popular media are identified in this well organized photographic history. Economic roles and discrimination, social reformers, media images, education and intergenerational tension are among the topics Yung documents.

A Day's Work. Eve Bunting. New York: Clarion Books, 1994 ISBN 0-395-67321-6 **E**

This beautifully illustrated book is about a grandson and his newly immigrated Mexican grandfather who seek work at one of the daily labor pick-up stations in Los Angeles. The context and content of the story address economic opportunity for day laborers, language barriers, and the sustaining value of integrity in work. Contains realistic illustrations.

I Hadn't Meant To Tell You This. Jacqueline Woodson. New York: Delacorte Press, (1994) ISBN 0-385-32031-0 **J, H**

Interracial friendship and class based discrimination are subthemes in this short fictional novel about an adolescent girl who is being sexually abused by her father. The main character, Marie, an African-American, befriends Lena, who is from "the wrong side" of the river in Chauncey, Ohio. Through the evolution of their friendship, Marie discovers that Lena, who lives with her younger sister and her father, has been sexually abused for a number of years. Lena's poignant self-hate, her protectiveness toward her sister and the pains of loss—issues for young women who experience abuse—are sensitively handled in this important book.

An Illustrated History of the Chinese in America. Ruthanne Lum McCunn. San Francisco, CA: Design Enterprises of San Francisco, (1979) P. O. Box 27677, SF CA 94127 Library of Congress Catalog Number, 79-50144. **J, H, A**

Photographs, graphic illustrations, maps and newspaper clippings are among the data sources used to depict the lives of Chinese-Americans in the United States. Chapters in this illustrated history include "Angel Island," the west coast equivalent to Ellis Island, "Exclusion Laws," New Immigration Laws," and the "Anti-Chinese Movement." While the bulk of materials and commentary are oriented to San Francisco, which had the largest population of Chinese-Americans in the United States, there are representations of life in New York, Idaho, Wyoming and other communities. Ethnic discrimination and exclusion are major themes in this work.

My Brother Has AIDS. Deborah Davis. New York: Atheneum Press, (1994) ISBN 0-689-31922-3 **J, H**

This fictionalized account of a young adolescent and her family experiencing the final stages of AIDS with a much loved brother provides a clear eyed and compassionate picture of the emotional and logistic complexities posed by the disease. Lacy's life is profoundly changed by the return of her older brother, who has been in law practice in Colorado. Her father's ambivalence about her brother's sexuality coupled with his guilt and sorrow, the logistic problems and pain associated with a young man's death from AIDS, and the anger that Lacy feels about being helpless and deserted make this a particularly

significant book for a critical issues curriculum.

Night Flying Woman, An Ojibway Narrative. Ignatia Broker. St. Paul: Minnesota Historical Society Press, (1983). ISBN 0-87351-167-0 J and S

As the introduction to this book proclaims, "Night Flying Woman is a story in the tradition of the Ojibway people." (ix) It is also the story of culture contact with strangers which alters the ancient way of life. The tension and alienation from the land experienced by successive generations of Ojibway, known as *Anishinabe* in their own language, is chronicled by an elder and story teller who lived in both urban and reservation communities. Accurate and detailed accounts of the impact of the lumber industry on Ni-bo-wi-se-gwe and her family is a primary focus of this narrative which also celebrates a value system based on conservation of the land and ancient ways.

No Big Deal. Ellen Jaffe McClain. New York: Lodestar Books, 1994 ISBN0-525-67483-7 **J, H**

This fiction book written by a high school teacher from Los Angeles is about a young woman named Janice Green and her social studies teacher, Mr. Podovano, who is gay. When the social studies teacher's sexual identity is made public, he is made the target of homophobia. His car is vandalized, he is harassed at a school dance and Janice's mother threatens to lobby for dismissal. Issues that face gay and lesbian teachers and the conflicts experienced by those who accept and defend difference are the focus of this fictional story of a divided school community.

The Other Side, How Kids Live in a California Latino Neighborhood. Kathleen Krull. New York: Lodestar, (1994). ISBN 0-525-67439-1 **E, J** (Middle School)

This books portrays the lifestyle of three young Mexican Americans who live close to the border between the United States and Mexico in a community called Chula Vista. Bilingualism, language and culture maintenance, and adaptation are among the issues that face first generation Americans such as Cynthia Guzman and Francisco and Pedro Tapia. This book is rich with the photographs of David Hautzig, who documents significant locations in these young peoples' lives. Text includes vocabulary, suggested readings and an index.

This Little Light of Mine, The Life of Fannie Lou Hamer.
Kay Mills. New York: Plume Books, (1993). ISBN 0-452-27052-9 **S, A**

This biography of one of the most courageous and significant freedom fighters in our country's history addresses race, class and gender issues in the context of Hamer's campaign for voting rights. Hamer was an important voice at the 1962 Democratic National Convention where she challenged the credentials committee, saying that if the Mississippi Freedom Democratic Party challengers were not seated, "'I question America." Hamer was a founding member of the National Women's Political Caucus where she voiced her strong opinions on feminism, including, "If white women there think they have problems, 'then they should be black and in Mississippi for a spell.'" (276)

Thousand Pieces of Gold. Ruthanne Lum McCunn.
San Francisco: Design Enterprises of San Francisco, (1981) ISBN 0-932538007-X **J, H, A**

LaLu Nathoy, a young Chinese woman who was "raised in a peasant village ravaged by poverty and drought," sold into slavery by Bandits and shipped to America where she was auctioned off to a saloon owner in Idaho is the subject of this biographical novel by McCunn, a Chinese-American writer. Racism and gender discrimination interract in this story about an exceptional pioneer woman, also known as Polly Bemis, who came to Idaho as a virtual slave in a mining camp, ran her own boarding house, homesteaded twenty acres, and died at eighty on her farm in Idaho, having survived and thrived in a frontier environment.

Who Belongs Here? An American Story. Margy Burns
Knight Gardiner. Maine: Tilbury House, Publishers, (1993) ISBN 0-88448-110-7 **E**

This story is about a young Cambodian boy, Nary, and his family, who flee from "the brutality of Pol Pot and the Khmer Rouge" and come to the U.S. in hopes of creating a better life. For some Americans, Nary is an unwanted alien, a "Gook," who should "Go back home where you belong." This beautifully illustrated book provides a simple and straightforward look at issues of immigration and discrimination that confront young people in schools. The ideas are complex and the language elegantly simple in this award winning book, which is dedicated to the E. S. L. teachers of Maine. An appendix provides vocabulary notes. There is a separate activity guide.

Mixed Media

"Fires in the Mirror" by Anna Deavere Smith produced by Public Television Playhouse, Inc, (1993). Available through PBS Video. ISBN 0-793601001-X 1-80-344-3337 **H, A**

Anna Deavere Smith's one-woman play presents compelling perspectives on urban racial and class conflict. The play, acted out in monologues, presents the views of various players in the Crown Heights, Brooklyn racial turmoil. Smith assumes the personalities of thirty people who were caught up in the demonstrations following the death of an African American child who was killed in an auto accident, and the subsequent slaying of a Hassidic rabbinical student. The play eloquently communicates the intense emotion and complex opinions that attend urban race relations.

"School Colors." (Video) Co-production by Center for
Investigative Reporting and Telesis International for PBS Frontline. Order through CIR, 568 Howard Street, 5th floor, SF CA 94105-3008 For information call 415-543-1200 or 800-733-0015. **H, S**

This video production examines the state of race and ethnic relations at Berkeley High School in Berkeley, California. The controversial video focuses on how integration has worked at Berkeley High School in the last three decades. Faculty relationships with each other and with students, parent involvement, ethnic studies, student home life and ethnic group and intergroup relations are the focus of this video production filmed on site at the school.

"Through Innocent Eyes, Life in Poston Arizona
Internment Camp 1942-1943" (1990) Los Angeles: Keiro Services (P.O. Box 33819, L.A.,CA 90033-0819) ISBN 1-878385-00-3 **E, S**

This audio tape is a collection of poetry and stories written by second generation Japanese-American students (Nisei) confined to internment camps during World War II. The poignant stories and poems are read by third generation (Sansei) and fourth generation students (Yonsei) and are accompanied by a theme song composed for this tape. The tape and accompanying guide are taken from a high school scrapbook project that resurfaced forty-five years after the internment experience. They effectively speak to the importance of carefully drawn context, the power of student voices in framing and communicating about critical social issues, and the force of imagination.

Periodical Publications

Teaching Tolerance. Biannual publication of the Southern Poverty Law Center 400 Washington Avenue. Montgomery, AL 36104. No charge to educators
E, J, H, A

Dream Makers, Dream Breakers: The World of Justice Thurgood Marshall by Carl T. Rowan, and *Skipping Stones: A Multicultural Children's Quarterly* are a small sampling of resources for K-12 classrooms identified and described in this biannual publication. This classroom-oriented publication has a small and impressive advisory board that includes Robert Coles, Mary Hatwood Futrell, Maxine Green, Maya Lin, and Moyra Contreras. Gang violence, homelessness, interracial friendship and case studies of classrooms and teachers are topics explored in the Fall 1993 issue of this extraordinary publication. *Teaching Tolerance* is especially strong in resources for elementary classrooms. It includes phone numbers and addresses.

The Women's History Network News The quarterly newsletter of The Women's History Network, 7738 Bell Road, Windsor,CA 95492s **E, J, H, A**
There is a vast array of resources for critical multicultural teaching featured in this newsletter and in the Network's catalogue. Scholarly books, biographies, exhibits such as "Nuestras Mujeres, Hispanas in New Mexico, 1582-1992," conferences and school based efforts to create curriculum change are regularly featured in this teacher resource. Back issues on special topics are available and resource lists on "Black, Asian, Hispanic, and American Indian Women" are printed in "Women's History Resources" available through the catalog. This resource is particularly strong in book recommendations for elementary classrooms and biographies. The project's commitment to multicultural teaching is evident in the selections.

Ballin, Amy et al. *Trash Conflicts: A Science and Social Studies Curriculum on the Ethics of Disposal.* Educators for Social Responsibility, 23 Garden Street, Cambridge, MA 02138, 1993. 220 pages. $25.00.

The content focus of this book is on solid waste disposal, hazardous waste, and the issue of environmental racism and classism. Curricular applications include U.S. history, civics, geography, and interdisciplinary science and social studies. Although this teacher resource book contains lessons that focus on the student's immediate surroundings, it merits inclusion within this section as immensely helpful regarding basic issues of global sustainability. Students investigate, calculate and role play numerous examples of complex decision-making in which economic, environmental and equity values must be evaluated. The section on "Taking Action" is a textbook example of comprehensive and responsible strategic planning and social action. Background readings and handouts represent multiple perspectives and provide adequate information for informed decision-making. Lessons may be selected and infused or taught together as a semester course. This book's quality would have been enhanced if many of the handouts had been re-typed instead of photocopied.

Recommended Level(s) for Use in Classroom Instruction: I/M

Brown, Jeffrey L., Paula Gotsch et al. *A Sustainable Development Curriculum Framework for World History and Cultures.* Global Learning, Inc., 1018 Stuyvesant Avenue, Union, NJ 07083, 1991. 272 pages. $20.00.

The content focus of this book is the relationship between the environment, economic/social development and equity. Curricular applications include world history/cultures/geography, global studies and international relations.

As noted by a reviewer for the magazine *Green Teacher*, emphasis has been placed on conceptually-oriented teaching as opposed to chronologically-oriented history, and the twelve lessons are effective with students. Twelve infusion methods, e.g., "Replace the course textbook's framework with the Analytical Framework for Sustainable Development," are helpful for teachers planning to integrate global concepts within existing curricula. There is an extensive list of resources, an international collection of children's artwork, and suggestions for student participation beyond the classroom. Some significant resources that were omitted include the *New Internationalist, Signs of Hope,* and the *Red Cross.*

Recommended Level(s) for Use in Classroom Instruction: S,H

Byrnes, Ronald S. *Exploring the Developing World: Life in Africa and Latin America.* Center for Teaching International Relations, University of Denver, Denver, CO 80208-0269, 1993. 137 pages, $26.95.

The content focus of this book is the regions and representative countries of Africa and Latin America, set within a global context. Curricular applications include regional studies, world history, cultures or geography, and global studies. Multiple perspectives and counterstereotyping are fostered. A variety of countries is represented, and important issues are addressed. Varied activities, including role playing, engage students of differing academic abilities. Sufficient information allows substantive treatment of particular topics, such as the role of women in African society or population growth in Mexico City. Lessons have reader-friendly handouts, extension activities and suggestions for evaluation. A lesson on UN Peacekeeping could have

Keys: P=Primary, I=Intermediate, M=Middle, S=Secondary, H=High School

included some conflict resolution substance. The survey of gender roles on p. 55 could use an additional category of "equal," and student handout 3.23 on "Trying Times in Cuba" could use more background information.

Recommended Level(s) for Use in Classroom Instruction: S, H

Crews, Kimberly A. and Patricia Cancellier, eds. *CONNECTIONS: Linking Population and the Environment.* Population Reference Bureau, Inc., 1875 Connecticut Avenue, N.W., Suite 520, Washington, DC 20009-5728, 1991. Teacher's Guide, 80 pages; Student Resource Book 96 pages. Teacher's kit $13 includes both books plus World Population Data Sheet and World Environment Data Sheet; additional Student Resources Books cost $8, but bulk rates are available.

Four introductory and one concluding lesson focus on a world overview of population and environmental concerns, while 8 lessons focus on Africa, 5 on Asia and 4 on Latin America. Curricular applications include area, global, and population studies. The extended newspaper articles in the student book are varied and interesting and represent a unique source of primary source materials written from "Third World" perspectives. Selected print and A/V resources are listed for each section. There is plentiful use of pictures, tables, graphs, maps, quotations and extension activities. The global problems, however, receive so much more detail than do alternative solutions that students may feel problem-solving is futile. It would be helpful if an explicit problem-solving process were applied several times in lessons. Individual lessons would be strengthened if they included more ways that North American students are connected to the specific problem or world region through a local-global connection.

Recommended Level(s) for Use in Classroom Instruction: I/M, S, H

Global Resources: Opposing Viewpoints Series. San Diego, CA: Greenhaven Press, Inc., 1991. 260 pages. $9.95.

The contents of this work focus on the issues of resource scarcity and conservation, the greenhouse effect, population and resource use, rain forests, and sustainable agriculture. Curricular applications include global studies, geography, world and U.S. history. Six chapters organized by a key question, e.g., "Are global resources becoming more scarce?" each contain six essays by major writers or organizations, e.g., Paul Ehrlich and the National Cattlemen's Association, thereby exposing students to excellent primary resources and representative spokespersons on this major issue. Each chapter contains a practical critical thinking activity, such as distinguishing bias from reason. Although the six essays on any particular chapter question will provide a variety of views on that chapter's topic, each viewpoint is paired with its opposite, e.g., the greenhouse effect is real vs. exaggerated. This pairing may have the unintended result of reinforcing students' tendency toward either-or thinking. Three to five perspectives on any one of these issues would help students develop more sophisticated abilities in taking multiple perspectives.

Greenberg, Hazel Sara. *Teaching about Global Issues: Population, Health, Hunger, Culture, Environment.* American Forum for Global Education, 120 Wall Street, Suite 2600, New York, NY 10005. 99 pages, $25.00.

This revision of lessons from earlier publications by this organization contains one lesson each for a global issues overview, population, culture, and economic development, and four each on hunger and on the environment. Curricular applications include area and global studies, and world cultures. A sophisticated level of analysis is applied to the causes of world hunger, and options for social participation are offered. The cultural strengths of the people studied are noted despite their current hardships. Urban life is well represented to counter its omission in most textbooks—especially regarding Africa. Local-global connections with which students can identify are made. The layout is teacher-friendly, but the typeface of student readings is small and uninviting. The lessons on hunger tend to favor the scarcity issue as hunger's major cause instead of addressing the more politically difficult issue of distribution. The concluding activity may raise the ire of Africanists because of the inclusion of the exotic Pygmies. The second-hand descriptions by European writers might have been replaced by first hand sources, such as Ibn Battuta.

Recommended Level(s) for Use in Classroom Instruction: I/M, S

Murphy, Carol E. *What Have You Got to Lose? New World Tropical Rainforests.* SPICE—Stanford

Program on International and Cross-Cultural Education, Littlefield Center, Room 14, 300 Lasuen St., Stanford University, Stanford, CA 94305-5013. 128 pages, 24 slides with script, & a poster. Also available in Spanish. $44.95.

The focus of this work is rainforest, biodiversity, economic development, and prejudice reduction. Curricular applications are interdisciplinary. This is a comprehensive unit, with scientific background and engaging interactive lessons structured to help teachers work with cooperative groups. It contains complex decision-making activities, cultural bias and awareness lessons, examples of students' connections with the rainforest, and an exploration of sophisticated potential solutions to problems raised. Many lessons contain very sophisticated reading levels and concepts that make them appropriate for the upper middle grades and even secondary students, even though the author indicates these materials are for grades 3-8, while the 3-6 week time frame may be a limitation for some.

Recommended Levels for Use in Classroom Instruction: I/M, S

See Me, Share My World: Understanding the Third World through Children's Art. Plan International USA, 155 Plan Way, Warwick RI 02886, 1989. 28 page Teaching Guide, 48 reproducible activity sheets, 8 color children's drawings, 8 B&W photos & training video. $59.

Six themes of daily life—home, food, education, health, work, fun—are explored on a "trip" to 6 countries: Colombia, Honduras, India, Indonesia, Sierra Leone and Thailand. Curricular applications are multidisciplinary: social studies, language arts, art, music, science, health, and physical education. The original children's art from around the world invites elementary students into a counterpart's daily life while the activities focus effectively on comparing similarities and differences and making personal connections. Adequate teacher background is provided for both the art work and its topic as well as the economic development issues addressed. The problem of traditional development terminology is also addressed. The work unit counters the stereotype that poor people are lazy. A unique feature involves the possibility of leasing a large museum-quality display of children's art to tie in with the two week unit. Teachers may want to restructure some of the individualistic learning activities into small group cooperative learning formats.

Recommended Levels for Use in Classroom Instruction: P

Sheldon, Janet E. *IMPACT! How Everything We Do Affects Everything And Everyone:* Environmental Activities With An International Perspective. Environmental Literacy Group, 33770 Woodland Dr., Evergreen, CO 80439, n.d. 133 pages.

Content focus includes toxic waste on land and sea, energy, vegetation, recycling, biodiversity, and human diversity. Curricular applications include science, social studies, and language arts. To avoid scaring young children with the world's woes, these materials emphasize students' making an active contribution to a solution to a problem, and thus to a better world. Teachers do not need extensive background knowledge in science or technology. A broad variety of fun activities will engage young children in active learning. Now that the Asceptic Packaging Council (NYC) is promoting recycling, the lesson on composite food wrappers is somewhat dated.

Recommended Level(s) for Use in Classroom Instruction: P

Snow, Roberta and Richard Golden. *Global Warming Activities for High School Social Studies.* Climate Protection Institute, 5833 Balmoral Drive, Oakland, CA 94619, 1991. 32 pages. $9.85.

The climate change focus includes its relationship to energy, deforestation and recycling wastes. Curricular applications include economics, geography, history, civics, international relations, and global studies. The three-page review of the issue is clear and concise. Engaging activities will motivate students of varying academic abilities to feel they can do something about this global issue. Some of the lessons could be used when studying the industrial revolution in U.S. or world history. The conflict resolution concept of win/win is applied in a game regarding the commons, and clear diagrams of "the problem" are provided for presentation to students. Sample questionnaires would have been useful for the community survey. Insufficient background is provided in the lesson on Chico Mendes' murder in Brazil for students to make decisions on much more than their initial biases.

Recommended Level(s) for Use in Classroom Instruction: I/M, S

Snyder, Sarah. *Teacher's Guide to World Resources: Comprehensive Coursework on the Global Environment.*

World Resources Institute, 1709 New York Avenue, N.W., Washington, DC 20006. 173 pages, $6.95.

Three units focus on the environmental impacts of automobiles, women, equity and sustainable development, and a comparison of India's and China's sustainability issues. Curricular applications include geography, history, and political science, as well as mathematics and science. These units consciously link the related topics of the environment and economic development. Each unit contains enough information to teach one to several classes on the topic, although additional print and audiovisual resources are listed for further extension lessons. The data are current and comprehensive, and significant attention is given to possible solutions to problems. The first two units start with activities involving U.S. or Canadian secondary students and the third unit begins with a brainstorm of what students already know, or think they know, about India and China. Many tables and graphs can be used with students of all reading levels, although many of the student reading materials are at a fairly high level and may be a challenge to some students. At the end of the third unit, brief quotations from individuals or agencies from each country are included so students have access to some non-U.S. perspectives. This unit would have benefited from some literary voices to provide a more human-centered perspective on this highly analytical material.

Recommended Level(s) for Use in Classroom Instruction: S, H

Tooke, Moyra, ed. EDIT #19: EARTH SUMMIT IN REVIEW. Common Heritage Programme, 200 Isabella Street, Suite 300, Ottawa, Ontario, Canada K1S 1V7, 77 pages plus 5 B&W photographs. C$30.

Twenty-four readings on the results of the June 1992 Earth Summit include numerous environmental-development issues. Curricular applications include global studies and international relations. Readings and discussion questions provide primary source materials from the UN system, national governments, and news media. They would be especially useful in a Model UN based on the Earth Summit. Multiple perspectives are provided, especially from Canadian and "Third World" viewpoints. The issue of poverty reduction receives strong emphasis within the context of sustainable development. Positive outcomes within a complex global system are included. Official documents

and summaries, however, lack the human face of human interest stories. The official U.S. positions of the Bush Administration need updating. The teacher may want to create more interactive classroom activities to use with these resources.

Recommended Level(s) for Use in Classroom Instruction: S, H

Wasserman, Pamela and Andrea Doyle. *EARTH Matters: Studies for Our Global Future.* Zero Population Growth, 1400 Sixteenth Street, N.W., Suite 320, Washington, DC 20036. $19.95. 176 pages.

Topics include population dynamics, climate change, air pollution, water resources, deforestation, food and hunger, waste disposal, wildlife endangerment, energy issues, rich and poor, population and economics, the world's women, finding solutions. Curricular applications include social studies, economics, global studies, and interdisciplinary studies. Informative three-page articles on each topic are followed by two to three activities that should engage students, along with extension activities. A good mix of global data and examples facilitates student-generated comparisons. Answers are provided for worksheets. The common thread of population concerns connecting all lessons avoids specific population control strategies. The challenge to the "growth = good" assumption and the raising of ethics within economics are succinct door openers for economics teachers. The "dilemma" cards in the ethics lesson, however, seem too transparent. It would be more teacher-friendly if such items as role cards and student instructions could just be duplicated for student use.

Recommended Level(s) for Use in Classroom Instruction: S

Additional Resources:

The 1994 Information Please Environmental Almanac. Boston: Houghton Mifflin Co., 1994.

Brown, Jeffrey L., Paula Gotsch et al. *Sustaining the Future: Activities for Environmental Education in US History.* Global Learning, Inc., 1018 Stuyvesant Avenue, Union, NJ 07083, 1995.

Brown, Lester R. et al. *State of the World* (Annual). New York: W.W. Norton & Co., 1994.

Brown, Lester R. et al. *Vital Signs 1994: The Trends That Are Shaping Our Future.* New York: W.W. Norton & Co., 1994.

Children and the Environment: The State of the Environment—1990. UNICEF House, 3 United Nations Plaza, New York, NY 10017.

Choices: The Human Development Magazine. United
   Nations Development Programme, One United
   Nations Plaza, New York, NY 10017.

Corson, Walter H. ed. *The Global Ecology Handbook:
   What You Can Do about the Environmental Crisis.*
   Boston: Beacon Press, 1990.

Danant, Jo, ed. *Who's Doing What? A Directory of U.S.
   Organizations & Institutions Educating About
   Development and Other Global Issues.* American
   Forum for Global Education, 120 Wall Street,
   Suite 2600, New York, NY 10005, 1991.

The Environmental Crisis: Opposing Viewpoints Series.
   San Diego, CA: Greenhaven Press, Inc., 1991.

*The Environmental Data Book: A Guide to Statistics on the
   Environment and Development.* Washington, DC:
   The World Bank, 1993.

Great Decisions (Annual Publication). Foreign Policy Association, 729 Seventh Avenue, New York, NY 10019.

Goudie, Andrew. *The Human Impact on the Natural
   Environment.* Cambridge, MA: Blackwell
   Publishers, 1993.

Kennedy, Moorhead & Martha Keys. *Death of a
   Dissident: Simulation.* American Forum for Global
   Education, 120 Wall Street, Suite 2600, New York,
   NY 10005.

Kennedy, Moorhead & Martha Keys. *Fire in the Forest:
   Simulation.* American Forum for Global Education,
   120 Wall Street, Suite 2600, New York, NY 10005.

Lanier-Graham, Susan D. *The Ecology of War:
   Environmental Impacts of Weaponry and Warfare.*
   New York: Walker and Co., 1993.

Luderer, William, ed. *Making Global Connections in the
   Middle School: Lessons on the Environment, Develop-
   ment & Equity.* Global Learning, Inc., 1018
   Stuyvesant Avenue, Union, NJ 07083, 1994.

*Hunger 1992: Second Annual Report on the State of World
   Hunger.* Bread for the World Institute on Hunger &
   Development, 802 Rhode Island Avenue, NE,
   Washington, DC 20018, 1991.

Seager, Joni, ed. *The State of the Earth Atlas.* New York,
   Simon & Schuster Inc., 1990.

Simmons, I.G. *Environmental History: A Concise Introduction.* Cambridge, MA: Blackwell Publishers, 1993.

The State of the World's Children (UNICEF's Annual
   Report). New York: Oxford University Press, 1994.

Third World Resources: A Quarterly Review. Third World
   Resources, 464 19th Street, Oakland, CA 94612-
   2297.

World Game Simulation. World Game Institute, 3508
   Market Street, Philadelphia, PA 19104.

*World Resources 1994-95: A Guide to the Global Environ-
   ment.* New York: Oxford University Press, 1994.

43 TEACHING ABOUT INTERNATIONAL HUMAN RIGHTS: AN ANNOTATED BIBLIOGRAPHY

by Nancy Flowers

There has recently been a burgeoning interest in the field of teaching about international human rights, as teachers recognize that understanding human rights is essential to world citizenship in the twenty-first century.

Amnesty International Human Rights for Children Committee. *Human Rights for Children, A Curriculum for Teaching Human Rights to Children Aged 3-12*. Alameda, CA: Hunter House, Inc., Box 2914, Alameda, CA, 94501-0914, 1992.

Written by a group of Amnesty International educators, this resource book for teachers is structured around ten fundamental principles derived from the 1959 UN Declaration on the Rights of the Child. Each principle is presented with a teaching strategy that interprets it for classroom use and a series of activities that give life and meaning to the strategy. These creative activities include a variety of subject areas (geography, mathematics, language arts, social studies, art, music, and physical education) and are divided into three different developmental levels: the pre-school child, the primary child, and the upper-elementary school child. Following each section is a useful annotated bibliography of additional resources.

Claude, Richard Pierre, ed. *Human Rights Education Handbook*. Philadelphia: University of Pennsylvania Press, 1994.

This collection of essays draws together both theoretical and practical insights on teaching human rights, as well as illuminating case studies of on-going projects in Asia, Africa, Latin America and Central and Western Europe. Although this book defines human rights education very broadly, including training for adults

such as police, military personnel, health professionals and journalists, it also offers many useful ideas and teaching strategies for classroom teachers. Of particular interest are the chapters on professional training for teachers in human rights, which include classroom activities for all grade levels, and on street law for teenagers.

Craig, Ann Armstrong. *The Refugee Experience: Teaching Guide*. New York: Women's Commission for Refugee Women and Children, 122 E. 42nd St., New York, NY 10016, 1994.

This packet, which includes a teaching guide, maps, selected readings, and a video, provides everything a teacher of intermediate or high school needs to teach a unit on refugees. The topics covered include how people become refugees, life in refugee camps, who cares for refugees, repatriation, asylum, and the human rights of refugees. Carefully balanced both politically and geographically, the text focuses on a few specific areas as illustrations of a global crisis: Afghanistan, Cambodia, Mozambique. Activities include the examination of current media, role playing, and community involvement. Also included are a directory of organizations working on behalf of refugees and an annotated bibliography.

Donahue, David and Nancy Flowers. *Uprooted, Refugees and the United States*. Alameda. CA: Hunter House, Inc., Box 2914, Alameda. CA, 94501-0914, 1994.

Most people in the United States cannot distinguish between a refugee and an immigrant. Through classroom activities for many subject areas (U.S. History, government, world history, geography, English, and art), this resource curriculum addresses the history of refugees in the U.S.A., international legal standards and practices, and current refugee issues. The final chapter, "Refugees in Your Community?" leads students to investigate their own towns and encourages community service. The appendices contain useful bibliographies and filmographies, a directory of refugee organizations, and the text of international human rights declarations and conventions.

McQuoid-Mason, David, et al. *Human Rights for All: Education towards a Rights Culture.* St. Paul, MN: West Educational Publishing, 1994.

A joint project between Lawyers for Human Rights (South Africa) and the National Institute for Citizen Education in the Law (USA), this innovative curriculum was initially written to prepare young South Africans for participation in democracy. The text has now been edited for publication in the U.S.A., where the issues it addresses are no less relevant. Students are asked to grapple with hard questions: how to create a new country and determine its bill of rights, how to balance national security against individual liberties, and how to resolve conflicts nonviolently, among others. Unlike many U.S. curriculums, which emphasize civil and political rights, *Human Rights for All* gives equal importance to social and economic rights.

Merkling, Melissa and Patricia M. Mische, eds. "Human Rights," *Breakthrough* 10 (winter/spring 1989). New York: Global Education Associates, 475 Riverside Drive, Suite 1848, New York, NY 10115.

This issue of *Breakthrough*, the publication of Global Education Associates, focuses on human rights and reflects the organization's goal to "advance world peace and security, cooperative economic development, human rights, and ecological sustainability" through education. Individual articles provide a history of human rights, an overview of human rights systems and documents, examination of specific issues such as women's rights and economic rights, and a very original section on human rights and religions, with articles from members of different world faiths. Throughout the text are poetry and quotations from distinguished writers. Back issues of this volume are available.

Reardon, Betty. *Educating for Human Dignity.* Philadelphia: University of Pennsylvania Press, 1994.

Drawing on her many years as a peace educator, Betty Reardon has compiled a sampler of the best lessons for teaching human rights and dignity. Hers is the only book that takes a developmental approach to the subject, with each chapter discussing the social and developmental purposes for teaching human rights at a particular age level; the activities that follow model those suggestions. The authors of the individual lessons provide a rich variety of styles and creative ideas. One chapter offers lists of resource agencies and curriculum materials.

Selby, David. *Human Rights.* Cambridge, England: Cambridge University Press, 1988.

The strength of this text is its examination of different conceptions of human rights and the conflicts that necessarily arise, such as between the right to security and to liberty. Case studies from East Timor, the former Soviet Union, Latin America, Western Europe and North America serve to illustrate these conflicts. Although somewhat dated, the book takes a more global perspective than many U.S. publications, which tend to define rights in terms of the U.S. Bill of Rights. The work of the UN and international human rights groups is also discussed. The book contains illustrations, an index, photographs, and a resource guide.

Shiman, David. *Teaching Human Rights.* Denver: CTIR Publications, University of Denver, 1993.

This collection of classroom activities offers innovative ways of teaching about some familiar themes. Initial lessons introduce students to the Universal Declaration of Human Rights and ask them to compare its provisions with those in the U.S. Bill of Rights and the African Charter on Human and People's Rights. Drawing on examples from Chile, the People's Republic of China, Kenya, South Africa, and the former Soviet Union, the activities encourage students to make cross-cultural comparisons and examine their own society and experiences. Students are continually challenged to think independently and to clarify their views on difficult topics: Are human rights truly universal, or are they subject to cultural relativism? What is the relation between political freedom and the quality of life in a country? *Teaching Human Rights* has broad application across the curriculum, including a collection of poetry, a crossword puzzle, and a range of activities that require research and written expression well suited to many courses.

Starkey, Hugh, ed. *The Challenge of Human Rights Educa-tion*. London: Cassell Educational Limited, 1991.

As one of its major purposes, the Council of Europe strives to "uphold the principles of parliamentary democracy and human rights." Published by the Council, this compilation of essays provides the most comprehensive overview available on teaching human rights. Its approach as well as its authorship, which includes both Canadian and U.S. educators, is international. Most chapters focus on what and how to teach in different levels and institutional settings, as well as on specific issues such as multiculturalism, women's rights, and global studies. Many essays also contain suggestions for classroom activities. Also included is the text of the Council's Recommendations on Teaching and Learning Human Rights and insightful discussion on its implementation.

United Nations. *ABC, Teaching Human Rights: Practical Activities for Primary and Secondary Schools*. New York: United Nations, 1989.

For the teacher just beginning to teach human rights, this booklet provides the ideal starting point. Available in English, French, and Spanish (the official languages of the UN), its activities and teaching strategies are intended to be effective in any cultural setting and to cover the spectrum of rights included in the International Bill of Rights. It offers a rationale for teaching human rights and recommends methodologies that model fundamental concepts such as inclusiveness, equality, and tolerance of differences. Sample activities for elementary age students stress respect for self and others; intermediate and secondary lessons deal with such themes as peace and the right to life, development and the environment, freedoms of conscience and expression, and discrimination based on qualities such as race, gender, or disability.

Whalen, Lucille. *Human Rights: a Reference Handbook*. Santa Barbara, CA: ABC-CLIO, Inc., 1990.

The ideal resource for any course on human rights, this handbook offers a history of human rights in the twentieth century, biographical sketches of human rights heroes, and thoroughly annotated listings of human rights organizations, books, periodicals, and films, as well as electronic information sources such as computer networks and databases. The final section provides the texts of the most significant international human rights declarations and conventions,

excluding, however, the Conventions on the Rights of the Child and the Women's Convention, which were ratified by the UN after the handbook's publication date.

Literature and Personal Narratives

Stories of individuals, from both fiction and the testimony of witnesses, give immediacy, authenticity, and a human face to rights issues.

Argueta, Manlio. *One Day of Life*. New York: Vintage, 1983.

A lyrical first-person novel relating a day of both terror and hope in the life of a Salvadoran peasant during the civil war.

Atwood, Margaret. *The Handmaid's Tale*. New York: Faucett, 1986.

Following a nuclear war, militant Christian fundamentalists control society, including reproduction.

Burgos-Debray, Elisabeth. *I Rigoberta Menchu: An Indian Woman in Guatemala*. New York: Verso, 1990.

Autobiography of the Nobel Peace Prize winner, a Guatemalan Indian who has struggled for her people's rights.

Cheng, Nien. *Life and Death in Shanghai*. New York: Viking Penguin, 1988.

Despite persecution by the Red Guards and long imprisonment, Nien Cheng refused to collaborate with the forces of violent change in her country.

Coetzee, J.M. *Waiting for the Barbarians*. New York: Penguin, 1982.

A modern parable by one of South Africa's finest writers: the commander of a garrison at the edge of "civilization" must weigh his duty against his humanity.

Forché, Carolyn, ed. *Against Forgetting: Twentieth Century Poetry of Witness*. New York: W.W. Norton & Co., 1993.

This splendid anthology serves as a compass of the human tragedies of the century, which are organized by topics such as World War I, the Indo-Pakistani Wars, and African Repression and Apartheid. Containing works from more than one hundred and forty poets from five continents, the collection necessarily unites many cultures through the common experience of suffering.

Solzhenitsyn, Alexander. *One Day in the Life of Ivan Denisovitch*. New York: Penguin, 1977.

Through the experience of a single prisoner in a Soviet gulag, Solzhenitsyn captures both the brutality of the system and the dignity of the individual.

Wiesel, Elie. *Night*. New York: Viking Penguin, 1982.

The memoir of a young boy who survives Auschwitz with his life but not his faith.

CHILDREN'S RIGHTS
by Beverly C. Edmonds

Amnesty International Human Rights for Children Committee. *Human Rights for Children: A Curriculum for Teaching Human Rights to Children Ages 3 - 12.* Alameda, California: Hunter House, 1992, 68pp. (Obtain from Hunter House, Inc., P.O. Box 2914, Alameda, CA 94501-0451 or Amnesty International).

Human Rights for Children takes ten principles asserting the child's right to be protected and provided for from an early United Nations proclamation, the Declaration on the Rights of the Child (1959) and develops activities to explain them to the young child, the primary child and the upper elementary child. For each principle, the authors explain the meaning, offer active teaching strategies (such as drawing, measuring, discussing, visiting, and group awareness exercises), and suggest content areas, materials, activities and children's books to which they relate. The focus is on the child's general development: identity, toleration for others, family and community awareness, providing curriculum for pre-secondary education. The curriculum is imaginative, clearly organized and laid out, and appropriate for the grade levels suggested. In spite of the curriculum's emphasis on active learning, the principles and the activities emphasize others protecting and providing for the child, rather than children exercising rights themselves.

UNICEF-UK and Save the Children. *Teaching About the [United Nations] Convention on the Rights of the Child (CRC).* London: UNICEF, 1993. [Obtain from UNICEF, UNICEF House, 3 United Nations Plaza, New York, New York 10017]. *Teacher's Handbook,* 40 pp.: (with the CRC text); Book 1, 54 pages: The Whole Child (the participation articles); Book 2, 78 pp.: It's Our Right (the provision rights), and book 3: Keep us Safe, 76 pp.: (the protection rights).

A thorough presentation of children's rights, geared for ages 8 - 13. The Teacher's Handbook offers a clear explanation of the CRC and its rights, the history of children's rights and two mind maps explaining how the rights are related. Emphasizing active learning, each booklet offers a variety of stories, activities, worksheets, pictures and cartoon sequences, to engage children in learning about their own rights and to appreciate the rights of all children. The content is multicultural and appeals to children with all levels of skills, facilitating individual country studies and current events investigations as well as an emphasis on global issues. The provision and protection rights are rooted in real-world situations, offering children a variety of action strategies which range from learning about problems to writing letters and publicizing their concerns. A small drawback is that the book is written for schools in the United Kingdom, but the lessons are fully applicable in the USA.

Nurkse, Dennis and Kay Castelle. *In the Spirit of Peace; A Global Introduction to Children's Rights.* New York: Defense for Children International, 1990, 64 pp. [Obtain through Defense for Children International-USA, 30 Irving Place, 9th Floor, New York, New York 1003] The CRC is examined through 23 principles (i.e., freedom from discrimination, refugee children, juvenile justice, rehabilitative care, protection of privacy).

Each topic is a 5-10 paragraph (or cartoon sequence) presentation of a children's rights violation and the background of the country in which it occurred; a map is often included. The authors provide discussion questions and activities for each story, as well as an unofficial summary of articles of the CRC and its full text. Based on the New York Board of Regents' guidelines, the booklet is illustrated by young people and excellent for late middle school and high school world history classes, civics and current events. The activities suggest investigation of the issues, examination of the community and the world, and ways to take action on behalf of children. The content is mature in nature, but presented in such a way that students will appreciate that they have some control over their environment; it celebrates those who stand up for children's rights, and has several examples from the United States.

Children Hungering for Justice. Denver, Colorado: Center for Teaching International Relations, 1992.

Three 20-page curricula are provided on the topics of justice, street children, the right to food, the role of the United Nations and the Convention on the Rights of the Child. The curriculum treats the same themes with increasingly mature activities and discussions for grades K-4, 5-8 and 9-12. There is good teacher background information and grade-appropriate lessons, with charts, diagrams and tables. Underwritten by the Church World Service, the presentations avoid ideology and facilitate teacher-student discussions about what is fair and just for the world's children. Teachers of Geography, World and U.S. history and Current Issues will appreciate these pamphlets, which can be purchased separately. The resource is highly selective of children's rights, but in doing so, it is effective in clarifying issues and possible solutions.

UNICEF, *The State of the World's Children.* New York: Oxford University Press, 1995.

Offering a new edition each year, this summary is the basic source of information (facts and statistics) for high school students or for teachers who want to make up their own units on children's rights. Categories include literacy, poverty, health status, etc. Bill Fernekes and David Shiman have suggested ways to use this resource in a special section on the Rights of the Child for *Social Education* (see below). *The State of the World's Children* is the only place where the most recent information can be obtained inexpensively by U.S. teachers. For use in Geography, World and U.S. History and Current Issues classes.

Edmonds, Beverly C. and William R. Fernekes, eds., "The Rights of the Child," *Social Education.* v. 56, No. 4, April/May, 1992.

This special section of *Social Education* introduces and gives a history of the United Nations Convention on the Rights of the Child to U.S. teachers and provides a rationale for its inclusion in the curriculum. Lesson plans, suggestions for teachers, and information on the state of children's rights teaching around the world are included; the emphasis is on teaching World and U.S. History, Current Issues, and International Relations. The articles by governmental and non-governmental organization representatives about the drafting of the document give an insider's look at the treaty's meaning and potential for ameliorating the condition of children. The international teaching section is the weakest component since the convention had just been adopted by the U.N. when the special section was written. Since 1992, UNICEF and non-governmental organizations have been instrumental in getting the Convention included in national and local curricula.

"The Rights of the Child." New York: UNICEF, 1992.

A strong, high school/ adult-oriented video on the problems which the world's children face, beginning with the problem and ending with UNICEF programs which have alleviated their suffering. Footage from the five major UN world areas is graphic and immediate. The framework for the video is the Convention on the Rights of the Child, but UNICEF has created a fourth "P,""Prevention," which represents its primary UN mandate. Issues of protection and provision are stressed, nearly omitting the child's rights of participation. The video lasts 23 minutes.

"The Universal Declaration of Human Rights,"(U.N. Department of Publications, United Nations, New York 10017)

This video is narrated by young people and concentrates on the rights of children even though the topic is general human rights. It is appropriate for grades 7 and 8 and high school, but once again, does not emphasize participatory rights.

Edmonds, Beverly C. and William R. Fernekes. *Contemporary World Issues: Children's Rights.* Santa Barbara, CA: ABC-Clio, 1996. 300 pages. ISBN 0-87436-764-6. $39.00.

This reference book introduces readers to the history and practice of children's rights in the

United States and internationally in the English-speaking world. It is appropriate for readers in secondary schools and higher education. The book includes a history of children's rights, a chronology of significant events in their emergence, biographies of pathbreakers in children's rights and an extensive collection of documents, statistics and summaries of U.S. Supreme Court decisions chronicling the development of children's rights in the twentieth century. Other chapters include a list of organizations that advocate children's rights and publish materials on the contemporary status of children. An extensive listing of print and nonprint resources is provided, which includes many Internet World Wide Web and Gopher sites on children's rights and related issues.

Afterword

by James P. Shaver

THE PROSPECTS FOR ISSUES-CENTERED EDUCATION

To serve with Shirley Engle as a bookend for a collection of writings on issues-centered education is a special privilege. Shirley was surely among the more articulate and vocal advocates for a social studies curriculum based on the examination of significant social problems. He was without peer in his unflagging passion for changing the curriculum from a predominantly unengaging survey of oversimplified content to one that challenges students to become thoughtful, committed individuals as they mature into their democratic citizenship roles.

In writing the foreword to this handbook, Shirley was, as usual, on the mark in his assessment of the inert, unreflective nature of much of what passes for social studies and in his appraisal of the inappropriateness of such instruction for citizenship education. His call for teaching that addresses the "uncertain and the controversial" in "a continued conversation between students and their mentors while they search together for better ways of doing things" set well the agenda for this handbook, as well as for all of those concerned with citizenship education as an essential obligation of public education.

But what are the prospects for widespread change from textbook coverage to issues-centered instruction? The answer to that question must be framed in the context of another query: What circumstances maintain a social studies curriculum that students too frequently see as irrelevant and uninteresting, and impede teaching that would more effectively enhance students' decision-making power?

Why the Scarcity of Issues-Centered Teaching?

The paucity of issues-centered education is undoubtedly due to a number of factors, discussed in greater detail elsewhere (Evans 1989; Gross 1989; Oliver and Shaver 1966/1974; Shaver 1989; also see Onosko 1991). First and foremost are the demands that issues-centered instruction places on teachers. Although the availability of issues-structured materials makes an issues-centered curriculum more feasible, the heart of such an approach is the teacher's discourse with his or her students. As Oliver and I (1966/1974) noted in regard to one variation of issues-centered education, the jurisprudential approach, the teacher must be

> open to the exploration of ideas, ... able to think in other than categorical terms and to tolerate the conflict of ideas and ideals, ... have a tentative-probabilistic view of knowledge, ... [have] an intelligent, open, inquiring and imaginative mind ... , [value] positively [students'] ways of interpreting reality and approaching the solution of problems ... , [and] be willing to interact freely with his [or her] students, accepting their contributions as valuable and worthwhile to build on. (p. 240)

In addition, an issues-oriented social studies teacher must have an adequately broad base of knowledge in history and the social sciences, a sound understanding of the nature of values and their role in the creation and resolution of political-ethical controversies, and thorough comprehension of the analytic skills that students need to learn to handle the language and factual vaguenesses and disagreements that foster controversy and must be addressed for productive decision-making.

Such a set of teacher characteristics is no small order, and will not result from a directive by someone else—whether a district curriculum coordinator or a university professor in a methods course—to teach from an issues/problem perspective. To what extent such teachers are born or made is not clear. The answer is clouded by the fact that prospective teachers have experienced so little issues-centered instruction in their own K-12 schooling and at the higher-education level. That lack of practicing models on which teachers can pattern issues-centered teaching behavior is to some degree a function of institutional constraints.

Schools are not in general innovative institutions, and teachers who want to use nontraditional patterns of teaching that might induce lively, even heated, classroom discussions often do not find a great deal of support. Principals tend to be concerned with maintaining an orderly school that projects an image of stability to the community; curricula that emphasize controversy and dialectic discourse are troublesome from that perspective. Moreover, in their hesitancy about active student inquiry, principals typically are in accord with the communities their schools serve. Schools are expected to teach knowledge—i.e., facts—not engage children, or even the young adults of high school age, in the discussion of controversial issues, past or present, especially if they might be led to question, or worse, challenge, parental views. Issues-centered teaching focused on contemporary issues is not the only threat. The consideration of issues in not-recent U.S. history might evoke negative community reactions, especially if the discussions stimulate students to reflect on modern issues, such as the extent of present-day personal and societal responsibility for the effects of slavery in early America.

Not only principals, but teachers for the most part reflect the views of the local community, or they would not have been hired in the first place. So, the new teacher eager to initiate issues-centered teaching, or the experienced teacher who might want to do so, may face a nonsupportive, if not antagonistic, peer culture. Other teachers will be worried about textbook coverage; that the requisite chapters are read, discussed, and tested is often considered more important than what the students learned or felt about the content area.

A teacher who doesn't attend to the traditional curriculum may be seen as ineffective, as well as potentially involving his colleagues in community dissatisfaction.

In any event, content coverage is often deemed to be critical, because of the belief that issues should not be discussed without first establishing a solid base of information. From that perspective, issue discussions are not seen as springboards to learning, but as culminating activities. However, the discussions rarely occur, because surveying the prerequisite information base is so compellingly time-consuming, and the assumed need for the superficial coverage of survey courses goes largely unquestioned. The study material, textbooks for the most part, is information focused. Testing emphasizes getting the "correct" answer, stated in the textbook and known by the teacher, to be repeated back by the student, not constructed through the student's problem-centered engagement with the content.

The constraining institutional culture is, of course, usually congruent with the teacher's own educational background. He or she is likely to have had grades awarded for knowing content, not for being reflective about it, except within the *a priori* essay-exam parameters established arbitrarily by a teacher/professor. Teacher education courses, too, tend to focus on how-to-do-it, rather than on analysis leading to decisions about what to do; educational philosophy too often is something to be studied, not something to be done.

In all fairness, however, the best efforts of teacher educators to produce teachers who will engage students in learning to be thoughtful citizens, or in the construction rather than memorization of knowledge, often founder on the community-school culture that prospective teachers so often encounter during practice teaching and as neophyte professionals. They learn from their teaching colleagues not only the expectations in regard to textbook coverage and quiet classrooms, but that content can and should be used for student control (e.g., assigning extra reading or papers to noisy or unprepared students, or threatening an unruly class with a test) and that assignments are often best negotiated with the students so that neither they nor the teacher is inundated with work. Little wonder that Goodlad (1983) found the general emphasis on information recall in social studies that Shirley Engle lamented in his foreword.

What, Then, Are the Prospects?

It is easy to sketch a gloomy picture of schooling when viewed through an issues-centered lens. Although valid in its general dimensions, that portrayal should not be allowed to dictate despondency about efforts to promote or conduct issues-centered education. After reviewing the National Science Foundation's studies of the status of social studies in the late 1970s, I, O.L. Davis, and Suzanne Helburn (1980) concluded that, despite the evidence that pointed to social studies curricula dominated by textbook-based recitation, there were instances of exciting, even brilliant, teaching. Based on her review of the NSF studies, Hazel Hertzberg (1981) concluded that although the basic picture sketched out by me, Davis, and Helburn, was correct, there was evidence of more discussion of controversial issues than we had recognized.

Issues-centered education does happen, as each of us can probably confirm by our experiences as parents or as professional visitors in schools. I think of my son's sociology teacher in a rural, conservative, northern Utah community in the 1970s, who involved his classes in the consideration of issues as controversial as whether abortion should be an option available to women. And, more recently, another son struggled with a world geography class that involved largely the completion of worksheets and map coloring, while the deployment of our troops in Desert Storm went unmentioned, only to move down the hallway the next semester to a teacher who saw world geography as a means to help students understand and reflect about problems such as global conflict, acid rain, and the spread of AIDS.

In short, although there is little hope of widespread systemic change from the traditional, content-centered social studies curriculum to an issues-centered curriculum, that is not reason for total despair. As the NSF studies of curricular status, especially the case studies, made clear, the teacher is the key to what happens in the classroom. Whatever curricular decisions are made or avoided at the national, state, or school district level, the teacher's day-by-day contacts with students determine the curriculum that they actually experience. Individual teachers can and do depart from the conventional curriculum, even within discouraging, restrictive cultural contexts. And there are schools in which issues-centered teaching is supported.

The survey nature of textbooks is often lamented as a major dulling effect on social studies instruction. As noted earlier, however, the teacher's orientation is much more important than the students' reading material. Teachers conscious of the possibilities can have issues-centered discourse in their classes, even with conventional textbooks. Nothing in the material, for example, stops a U.S. history teacher from posing for his or her students the quandary of the incompatibility of the principles of the Declaration of Independence with the contemporaneous institution of slavery, as a sample item in the National Standards for United States History suggests (National Center [1994], p. 75).

If the teacher deems that materials other than the textbook are needed, they can be located or constructed. Most of the materials of the Harvard Project were selected from accessible media, including the information for the case studies we prepared. I have often told teachers who cite the lack of materials as a barrier to issues-centered, especially public-issues, teaching not to be overwhelmed by the task of developing an entire issues-centered curriculum such as that of the Harvard Project (which, as presented in Oliver and Shaver 1966/1974, along with the discussion of selection and arrangement issues, still provides an excellent model for incorporating public issues within a conventional history curriculum). The task becomes manageable if approached a unit at a time. A teacher who develops one new 4- to 6-week unit a year to supplement or supplant the textbook, revising each as it is used, will in five to six years have basically installed a new curriculum.

Fortunately, there is no longer a dearth of issues-centered materials and assistance in the educational literature as was the case in the 1960s and 1970s. Popular magazines, such as *Newsweek* and *The Atlantic Monthly*, have become even more issue oriented in recent years. Perhaps more important, issues-oriented materials can be found in publishers' displays at professional meetings, including the updated Public Issues Series from the Harvard Project, published by the Social Science Education Consortium. Another example, for those interested in issues-centered teaching in U.S. history, is the Ford Foundation-sponsored American Social History Project at the City University of New York. The project staff have been producing materials and propagating teaching to encourage the examination of historical conflicts, especially at the level of common people rather than political and military leaders (Quinn 1993).

Materials developed earlier should not be ignored. For teachers interested in an explication of public-issues-related analytic concepts and skills, and suggestions for teaching them, to supplement the Harvard Project conceptual structure, many educational archives still contain the Analysis of Public Issues Program materials that I and Larkins (1973) developed in cooperation with a team of teachers from Roy High School (Roy, UT). For teachers of history, the Lockwood and Harris (1985a,b) materials for introducing ethical issues in U.S. history will still provide excellent assistance in infiltrating the curriculum, despite some shortcomings that teachers should address (Shaver 1986).

Yet, once again it is crucial to keep in mind that, when all is said and done, materials are not the central consideration. As Oliver and I noted (1966/1974), *"while appropriate materials will be of assistance…, the essence of jurisprudential teaching is the nature of the discourse the teacher chooses to have with his [or her] students,"* (239). Shirley Engle's recounting in the foreword to this book of his experience in Frederick Paxon's History of the West class at the University of Wisconsin in 1936 illustrates the point well: It is the teacher's attitude and orientation, and ability to translate those into teaching behavior, that count.

For that reason, based on the reasonable assumption that teaching behavior is not totally genetically determined or set by early adulthood, teacher educators have a potentially powerful role in shaping the prospects for issues-centered education. They may be able to counter the past experiences of individual prospective and practicing teachers and help them to mitigate the potentially stifling effects of a community-school culture not attuned to controversy as an appropriate or essential instructional focus.

It is tempting to recommend that only those who possess the essential traits for issues-centered teaching noted earlier be admitted to teacher education programs, but such a proposal would be blatantly unrealistic. Similarly, to urge a massive effort by teacher educators to revolutionize the institutional-cultural context of schooling to facilitate, if not encourage, issues-centered instruction would be hopelessly utopian. Both are, nevertheless, actions worth pursuing locally by individuals in positions to encourage and select teacher-education applicants and/or to influence the thinking and attitudes of school administrators, teachers, and parents and other school patrons.

A more modest approach could, however, yield substantial, even if not widespread, effects in both arenas. It is the encouragement of philosophical thinking, that is, the explication and examination of assumptions, their relationships and implications, by prospective and practicing teachers.

A prime proponent of problem-centered teaching, John Dewey (1964b), no mean philosopher himself, regarded educational philosophy as "ultimately the most significant phase of philosophy" (p. 16). And Dewey did not conceive of such philosophy as an esoteric activity carried out by academicians isolated on university campuses. He emphasized that philosophy was not just a subject to be studied prior to becoming a teacher, but an activity in which practicing teachers and administrators should be continuously engaged to "test and develop [ideas] in their actual work so that through the union of theory and practice, the philosophy of education will be a living, growing thing" (p. 16). Otherwise, Dewey cautioned, teaching not based on a "well-thought-out philosophy" is likely to be "conducted blindly, under the control of customs and traditions that have not been examined or in response to immediate social pressures" (p. 17). Dewey's admonition over 50 years ago is an accurate assessment of a major attribute of current education—thoughtlessness that perpetuates textbook recitation and impedes issues-centered teaching.

Dewey's call for the intertwining of work and thought derives from his view of how thinking and, consequently, learning, occur. It would behoove teacher educators, prospective teachers, and practicing teachers interested in issues-centered teaching to read and then return occasionally to Dewey's works, especially *How We Think* (1933) and *Democracy and Education* (1916/1961), and to contemplate their applicability not only to children but to adults.

Dewey was not only issues-centered (if an issue is, as seems logical, considered to be a problem posed correctly), but a constructivist. He emphasized that learning occurs as each individual constructs his or her reality in the process of dealing with problems—quandaries, perplexities, dissonances—that have personal meaning. He noted that if schooling were not so scholastic—focused on "listening, reading, and the reproduction of what is told and read"—but, rather, based on situations like those that interest and engage children in their nonschool lives, we might counter the tendency for children, especially as they move through the grades, to be "so full of questions outside of school ... [but to have a] conspicuous absence of display of curiosity about the subject matter of school lessons" (1916/1961, p. 155). Indeed, rather than having to force students to read textbooks and go to encyclopedias for writing assignments, with problems as the basis for learning, Dewey suggested, there would then be a need for greater student access to reading and other resources.

Dewey's call for active engagement in learning applies to adults as well as children. Problems/issues-centered instruction is needed in teacher education as well as in public education, not only to provide teaching role models but to stimulate critical thought about current practice and the rationale for issues-centered instruction. Lack of student interest in social studies is a concern faced by many prospective and practicing teachers. It is a real problem because of its consequences for teacher well-being. If posed correctly, contemplation of the possible reasons for lack of student interest can result in the productive examination of assumptions about the purposes of schooling and about how people learn, integral elements of a sound rationale from which to teach (e.g., Newmann 1977; Shaver and Berlak 1968).

The engagement of prospective and practicing teachers in rationale-building has implications not only for their willingness and ability to teach from an issues stance within the information-centered school and community climate, but for their professional survival while doing so. Years ago (in 1977, to be exact), I was invited to give a luncheon address to the New Mexico Council for the Social Studies on the topic, "How to Deal with Controversial Issues in the Classroom Without Becoming Controversial in the Community." My emphasis that day came from a deep continuing conviction that I have stated elsewhere (e.g., Shaver 1977; Shaver and Strong 1982), based on my earlier work with Donald Oliver (1966/1974). It is that the most fundamental activity in which a teacher can engage is rationale-building, the continuing development of a sound philosophical founda-

tion for his or her teaching decisions—that is, Dewey's philosophy of education. The philosophizing that goes into the development of a coherent, defensible rationale entails more than examining assumptions about how we learn. Other considerations, especially for issues-centered social studies teachers, include the essence of a democratic society and the implications for the characterization of citizenship, including the role of pluralism, the nature of values, and the consequent roles of both in societal conflict.

To be defensible, issues-centered teaching must be based on more than the assertion that controversy is good for its own sake or that it keeps students interested, as important as the latter is. The ability to articulate a well-founded basis for engaging students in the examination of issues is crucial to garnering support from one's fellow teachers and from administrators, parents, and the community. The importance of a carefully constructed rationale was verified for me personally during the development of the Analysis of Public Issues Program as Larkins and I taught as part of a team with our teacher-collaborators. The occasional inquiries by parents, who certainly were within their rights in questioning the challenges we were providing their progeny, were deflected by a principal who understood well what we were doing and in conversations I had with parents in which we discussed the rationale for our issues-centered curriculum. A carefully justified rationale is essential to teaching about controversy without becoming controversial.

Conclusion

As noted earlier, broad systemic change from the traditional curriculum is not likely. However, the coincidental publication of standards for curricula in social studies and related areas makes this a propitious time for this handbook and for issues-centered education. Curriculum standards from the National Council for the Social Studies (1994) would be expected to evince concern for issues, especially public issues, and they do—in discussing what social studies is and the application of knowledge, skills, and values as citizens (pp. 3-12), as well as in numerous examples of classroom activities to meet the standards. The National Standards for Civics and Government, developed by the Center for Civic Education (1994), also has a strong issues orientation. As is particularly appropriate, the civics-government standards are permeated with a focus on issues that involve disagreements over basic democratic values and principles and, specifically, conflicts over rights (e.g., p. xii).

Not as expected, and therefore even more encouraging, are the sections in the U.S. history and world history standards (National Center [1994], 1994) on "historical issues-analysis and decision-making," including "value-laden issues" in historical and contemporary contexts ([1994], pp. 31-33; 1994, pp. 32-34), and the occasional inclusion of such issues in the examples of student achievement appropriate to the standards. For example, in the standard on racial and gender equity and civil liberties, the question is posed, "Was Eisenhower justified in sending troops to Little Rock, Arkansas?" ([1994], p. 221).

Unfortunately, it is not clear what effects the standards will have. Will, for example, their impacts on textbooks be sufficient to moderate the stultifying content-survey curriculum? The vocal opposition to the history standards from persons such as Lynne Cheney, former head of the National Endowment for the Humanities, who see the U.S. history standards as "the sad and the bad," a too critical and gloomy portrayal of our heritage (Hancock and Biddle 1994), suggests that optimism about widespread effects may be premature.

In the meantime, the prospects for issues-centered education continue to rest with individual teachers. This handbook should be an invaluable source for those who want to understand the justifications for issues-centered education, consider its varying manifestations and its applications in different content areas, learn about the resources available, and be helped to think about the implementation of issues-centered teaching practices. Readers will find the handbook useful as a resource in the development of their own rationales, one to which they will return on occasion in the "continuing reconstruction of experience" (Dewey 1964a, p. 434) that is crucial as the issues-centered teacher confronts the issues that underlie and arise from his or her instructional decisions.

Those reflections and the resultant actions by individual teachers are at the heart of the potential for issues-centered education. In concluding a chapter in another handbook for educators (Shaver 1987), I noted that

the evidence as to the lack of student interest [in social studies] and the extent to which the political knowledge, skill, and attitude goals of citizenship education are not being achieved ... suggests that much of what is being taught is inappropriate. What should be taught and how are critical decisions to be made specifically by individual social studies teachers whose separate choices have a collective impact of major importance to the society (p. 133).

It is in the accumulative power of individual teachers' decisions that the future of issues-centered education lies. This handbook enhances the prospect for optimism about the outcome.

References

Center for Civic Education. *National Standards for Civics and Government.* Calabasas, CA: CCE, August 19, 1994.

Dewey, John. *How we Think: A Restatement of the Relation of Reflective Thinking to the Educative Process.* Boston: D.C. Heath, 1933.

Dewey, John. *Democracy and Education: An Introduction to the Philosophy of Education.* New York: Macmillan, 1961. (Original work published 1916)

Dewey, John. "My Pedagogic Creed." In *John Dewey on Education: Selected Writings,* edited by Reginald D. Archambault. New York: Random House, 1964a. (Original work published 1897)

Dewey, John. "The Relation of Science and Philosophy as a Basis for Education." In *John Dewey on Education: Selected Writings,* edited by Reginald D. Archambault. New York: Random House, 1964b. (Original work published 1938)

Evans, Ronald W. "A Dream Unrealized: A Brief Look at the History of Issues-Centered Approaches." *The Social Studies* 80 (September/October 1989): 178184.

Goodlad, John I. *A Place Called School: Prospects for the Future.* New York: McGrawHill, 1983.

Gross, Richard E. "Reasons for the Limited Acceptance of the Problems Approach." *The Social Studies* 80 (1989): 185186.

Hancock, LynNell and Nina A. Biddle. "Red, White and Blue. Education: Conflict Over a New History Curriculum." *Newsweek* (November 1994): 54.

Hertzberg, Hazel W. *Social Studies Reform: 1880-1980.* Boulder, CO: Social Science Education Consortium, 1981.

Lockwood, Alan L. and David E. Harris. *Reasoning with Democratic Values: Ethical Problems in United States History,* Volume 1: 16071876. New York: Teachers College Press, 1985a

Lockwood, Alan L. and David E. Harris. *Reasoning with Democratic Values: Ethical Problems in United States History,* Volume 2: 1877 to the Present. New York: Teachers College Press, 1985b.

National Center for History in the Schools. *National Standards for United States History: Exploring the American Experience.* Los Angeles: University of California, Los Angeles, [1994].

National Center for History in the Schools. *National Standards for World History: Exploring Paths to the Present.* Los Angeles: University of California, Los Angeles, 1994.

National Council for the Social Studies. *Expectations of Excellence: Curriculum Standards for Social Studies.* Washington, DC: NCSS, 1994.

Newmann, Fred M. "Building a Rationale for Civic Education." In *Building Rationales for Citizenship Education,* edited by James P. Shaver. Washington, DC: National Council for the Social Studies, 1977.

Oliver, Donald W. and James P. Shaver. *Teaching Public Issues in the High School.* Logan, UT: Utah State University Press, 1974. (Original work published 1966)

Onosko, Joseph J. "Barriers to the Promotion of Higher Order Thinking." *Theory and Research in Social Education* 19 (Fall 1991): 341-366.

Quinn, Thomas. "History as Contested Turf: Teaching the Story of America in a New Way." *Ford Foundation Report* 24 (1993): 22-25.

Shaver, James P. "The Task of Rationale-Building for Citizenship Education." In *Building Rationales for Citizenship Education,* edited by James P. Shaver. Washington, DC: National Council for the Social Studies, 1977.

Shaver, James P. Review of *Reasoning with Democratic Values: Ethical Problems in United States History,* Volume 1: 1607-1876; Volume II: 1877 to the Present; Instructor's Manual; by Alan L. Lockwood and David E. Harris. *Moral Education Forum* 11 (1986): 1116.

Shaver, James P. "Implications from Research: What Should be Taught in Social Studies?" In *Educators' Handbook: A Research Perspective,* edited by Virginia RichardsonKoehler. New York: Longman, 1987.

Shaver, James P. "Lessons From the Past: The Future of an Issues-Centered Social Studies Curriculum." *The Social Studies* 80 (September/October 1989): 192-196.

Shaver, James P. and Harold Berlak. *Democracy, Pluralism, and the Social Studies: Readings and Commentary.* Boston: Houghton Mifflin, 1968.

Shaver, James P., O. L. Davis, Jr., and Suzanne W. Helburn. "An Interpretive Report on the Status of Precollege Social Studies Education Based on Three NSF-Funded Studies." In *What are the Needs in Precollege Science, Mathematics, and Social Science Education? Views from the Field,* Washington, DC: National Science Foundation (Publication SE80), 1980.

Shaver, James P. and A. Guy Larkins. *The Analysis of Public Issues Program.* Boston: Houghton Mifflin, 1973.

Shaver, James P. and William Strong. *Facing Value Decisions: Rationale-Building for Teachers.* 2d ed., New York: Teachers College Press, 1982.

Index

Authors cited in bibliographic references in the articles of this book are only included in this index if they are mentioned in the text of the article as well as in a citation. The references to authors and their works that appear in the resource sections that comprise the final part of this book are not included in this index.

C

Campbell, Joseph, 17
Career choices, 46
Carnegie Council on Adolescent Development, 238
Carnegie Foundation, 237
Carretero, M., and Voss, James F., 36
Center for Foreign Policy Development, 185
Center for Teaching International Relations, 186
Central Park East Secondary School, 106-107
Cheney, Lynne, 385
Cherryholmes, Cleo H., 75, 155
Chief Seattle, 196
Children's Defense Fund, 102
Church World Service, 181, 186
Cisneros, Sandra, 107
Citizenship (see also Democracy)
    constitutional principles, 32-33, 60
    definition, 6
    democratic principles, 6, 9-11, 27-28, 35, 52-53, 143, 145-146, 149, 164
    education, 52-53, 66, 202, 205-206, 317-325, 330
    multiculturalism (see also Multiculturalism), 121
    participatory, 27, 30
    preparation, 6, 10, 317-325
    proactive, 9
    procedural ideals, 59
    public debate, 59-65
    reflective decision-making abilities, 9, 46, 50
    role, 9
    skills, 59
Civics and Government (see also Nationalism)
    citizenship
        behavior, 206
        civic republicanism, 205
        conceptions, 207
        contractual, 205
        defining, 206
        education, 202, 205-206
        perspectives, 206
    conflict and controversy, 200-201, 322
    conventional, 199-200, 207
    goals, 200
    human rights and trade, 203-205
    issues-centered
        cooperative learning, 208-209
        inserting into conventional curriculum, 207
        lesson plan, 208
        rationale, 200
        topics
            citizenship, 205-206
            civic culture, 202-203
            international issues, 203-204

            political power, 203
            reflective deliberation, 206-207
            role of government, 202
    national standards, 201
    Q-analysis, 206
    textbooks, 200
Clarity, 77
Clark, K.B., and Clark, M.P., 102
Classroom
    climate, 11, 26, 31-32, 34-37, 63-65, 82
    community, 52
    criticism, 78
    discussion
        agenda, 64
        background knowledge, 83
        concluding discussion, 86-87
        controversy, 83
        definition, 81
        disequilibration, 82
        disrespectful behavior, 82
        environment, 34
        format styles
            council, 85
            fishbowl, 85
            debate, 85
            mock trial, 86
            panel discussion, 85
            Quaker, 85
            role playing debate, 85
            role playing for social values, 85-86
            simulation, 86
            Socratic, 85
            variations, 86
        higher-level thinking, 84
        large-group, 85
        moderating, 82
        perennial puzzlers, 83
        reflection, 65
        roadblocks, 65
        rules, 82
        sensitivity, 64
        skills, 64
        small-group, 85
        social issues, 81-82
        stating the issue, 64
        student reaction to questions, 84
        subsequent courses of action, 87
        teacher's role (see Teachers' Roles)
        topics, 82
        transitions, 64-65
        wait time, 84
    inquiry-based, 67-68, 73, 174
Clinton, Bill, 76, 143, 184, 196

Contributors

Rodney F. Allen is Professor of Social Studies Education at Florida State University, Tallahassee.

Beverly J. Armento is Research Professor and Chair of the Middle/Secondary Education and Instructional Technology Department at Georgia State University.

Patricia G. Avery is Associate Professor of Curriculum and Instruction at the University of Minnesota.

James L. Barth is Professor of Social Studies Education in the Department of Curriculum and Instruction at Purdue University.

Ronald A. Banaszak is Director of Youth Education Programs at the American Bar Association, Chicago.

Jerry Brodkey teaches at Menlo-Atherton High School, California.

Jeffrey L. Brown is Executive Director of Global Learning, Inc.

Cleo Cherryholmes is Professor of Political Science at Michigan State University, East Lansing, Michigan.

George Chilcoat is Associate Professor of Elementary Education at Brigham Young University.

Wayne A. Cook is a high school teacher of economics and social studies in Fulton County, Georgia.

James K. Daly is an Associate Professor in the College of Education and Human Resources, Seton Hall University, South Orange, New Jersey.

Nancy Fichtman Dana is Assistant Professor of Education at Pennsylvania State University, University Park, Pennsylvania.

Beverly C. Edmonds is an advisor to Amnesty International Children's Action Network.

Shirley Engle was a public school teacher, professor and national leader of social studies for more than forty years. He inspired two generations of social studies teachers to bring issues into American classrooms.

Ronald W. Evans is an Associate Professor in the School of Teacher Education at San Diego State University.

Patrick Ferguson is Professor and Head of the Department of Secondary Education at Arkansas Tech, Russellville, Arkansas.

William R. Fernekes is Supervisor of Social Studies at Hunterdon Central Regional High School, Flemington, New Jersey.

Stephen C. Fleury is Associate Dean in the School of Education at the State University of New York at Oswego.

Nancy Flowers is Curriculum Coordinator for Amnesty International USA.

Stuart Foster is Assistant Professor of Social Science Education at the University of Georgia, Athens.

Jesus Garcia is Professor of Social Studies Education at the University of Illinois at Urbana-Champaign, Champaign, Illinois.

James R. Giese is Executive Director of the Social Science Educational Consortium, Boulder, CO

Richard E. Gross is Professor Emeritus of Education at Stanford University.

Carole L. Hahn is Professor of Social Studies Education at Emory University.

David Harris is Social Studies Education Consultant with Oakland Schools, Waterford, Michigan.

Hilda Hernandez is Associate Professor of Curriculum and Instruction at California State University, Chico.

A. David Hill is Professor of Geography at the University of Colorado. He was the head of the Geography Inquiry into Global Issues project supported by the National Science Foundation.

Kenneth F. Jerich is Associate Professor of Curriculum and Instruction in the College of Education at Illinois State University, Normal, Illinois.

Gloria Ladson-Billings is Associate Professor of Curriculum and Instruction at the University of Wisconsin-Madison.

Jerry Ligon is a Professor in the Department of Interdisciplinary Studies, National-Louis University, St. Louis, Missouri.

Wilma Longstreet is Professor of Curriculum and Instruction at the University of New Orleans.

Martha V. Lutz is a Research Associate at the Science Education Center of the University of Iowa.

Byron G. Massialas is Professor of Social Science Education at Florida State University, Tallahassee.

Merry Merryfield is Associate Professor of Social Studies Education at Ohio State University, Columbus, Ohio.

Devon Metzger is Professor of Education at California State University, Chico.

Salvatore J. Natoli was Director of Publications at National Council for the Social Studies prior to his retirement in 1993.

Jack L. Nelson is Professor of Education at Rutgers University.

Fred M. Newmann is Professor of Curriculum and Instruction at the University of Wisconsin at Madison.

Anna S. Ochoa-Becker is Professor of Education at Indiana University, Bloomington.

Joseph J. Onosko is Associate Professor of Education at the University of New Hampshire.

Walter C. Parker is an Associate Professor in the College of Education at the University of Washington, Seattle.

Jeff Passe is an Associate Professor in the Department of Curriculum and Instruction at the University of North Carolina at Charlotte.

Jon Pedersen is Associate Professor of Curriculum and Instruction at the University of Arkansas, Fayetteville.

Jane Bernard Powers is Associate Professor of Elementary Education at San Francisco State University.

Sharon L. Pugh is Associate Professor of Language Education in the School of Education, Indiana University, Bloomington.

Francis W. Rushing is Professor and Chair of the Economics Department and Director of the Center for Economic Education at Georgia State University, Atlanta.

Stephen Sandell is Director of the Humphrey Forum at the University of Minnesota.

David Warren Saxe is Associate Professor of Education at Pennsylvania State University, University Park, Pennsylvania.

James P. Shaver is Dean of the School of Graduate Studies and Professor of Secondary Education at Utah State University.

Adam Sheldon is a teacher at T. Aaron Levy Middle School, Syracuse, and a doctoral candidate at Syracuse University.

Laurel R. Singleton is Associate Director of the Social Science Educational Consortium, Boulder, Colorado.

Dorothy Skeel is Professor of Social Studies Education at Vanderbilt University.

Elizabeth S. Smith is a graduate assistant in the Department of Political Science, University of Minnesota.

Mary Soley is Deputy Director of ACCESS, an international affairs information service in Washington, DC.

John L. Sullivan is a Professor of Political Science at the University of Minnesota.

JoAnn Cutler Sweeney is Chair of the Department of Curriculum and Instruction in the College of Education at the University of Texas at Austin.

Lee Swenson is Social Studies Department Chair at Aragon High School, San Mateo, California.

Josiah Tlou is Associate Professor of Curriculum and Instruction at Virginia Institute of Technology, Blacksburg, Virginia..

Samuel Totten is Professor of Curriculum and Instruction at the University of Arkansas, Fayetteville.

Connie S. White teaches social studies, global history and government at Linden McKinley High School, Columbus, Ohio.

William G. Wraga is Assistant Professor in the Department of Educational Leadership at the University of Georgia, Athens.

Robert Yager is Professor of Science Education at the University of Iowa.